David
1990

MEDIEVAL
&
RENAISSANCE
DRAMA
IN ENGLAND

Editorial Board

JOHN F. ANDREWS
G. E. BENTLEY — *Princeton University*
DAVID M. BEVINGTON — *University of Chicago*
ANN JENNALIE COOK — *International Shakespeare Association*
JONATHAN DOLLIMORE — *University of Sussex*
CHARLES R. FORKER — *Indiana University*
BARRY GAINES — *University of New Mexico*
O. B. HARDISON, JR. — *Georgetown University*
CYRUS H. HOY — *University of Rochester*
STANLEY J. KAHRL — *Ohio State University*
ALVIN B. KERNAN — *Princeton University*
WILLIAM B. LONG — *AMS Press, Inc.*
BARBARA MOWAT — *Folger Shakespeare Library*
JEANNE ADDISON ROBERTS — *American University*

MEDIEVAL

RENAISSANCE DRAMA IN ENGLAND

An Annual Gathering of Research, Criticism, and Reviews

IV

EDITOR
Leeds Barroll

ASSOCIATE EDITOR
Paul Werstine

AMS PRESS
New York

Medieval and Renaissance Drama in England welcomes essays on the English drama before 1642. There is no limitation on length other than appropriateness to the task at hand. Footnote references should conform to the style found in this journal; articles should be accompanied by return postage. Articles may be sent to the Editor, Department of English, University of Maryland, Baltimore County, Catonsville, Maryland 21228 USA.

Copyright © 1989 by AMS Press, Inc.
All rights reserved

ISSN 0731-3403
Set ISBN 0-404-62300-X
Volume IV ISBN 0-404-62304-2
Library of Congress Catalogue Card Number: 83-45280

All AMS books are printed on acid-free paper that meets the guidelines for performance and durability of the Committee on Production Guidelines for Book Longevity of the Council on Library Resources.

Manufactured in the United States of America

Contents

Foreword	ix
Notes on Contributors	xi
The Cornish Mermaid: The Fine Thread of Androgyny in the *Ordinalia* GILLISANN HAROIAN	1
"A little more than kin, and less than kind": Incest, Intimacy, Narcissism, and Identity in Elizabethan and Stuart Drama CHARLES R. FORKER	13
Building Stories: Greg, Fleay, and the Plot of *2 Seven Deadly Sins* SCOTT MCMILLIN	53
Evidence for the Assignment of Plays to the Repertory of Shakespeare's Company ROSLYN L. KNUTSON	63
Antonio's Revenge: The Tyrant, the Stoic, and the Passionate Man KAREN ROBERTSON	91
The Tragedy of Bussy D'Ambois and the Creation of Heroism JAMES N. KRASNER	107
Responses to Tyranny in John Fletcher's Plays ROBERT Y. TURNER	123
Bonduca's Two Ignoble Armies and *The Two Noble Kinsmen* ANDREW HICKMAN	143
Competition for the King's Men?: Alleyn's Blackfriars Venture S. P. CERASANO	173
Lady Mary Wroth Describes a "Boy Actress" MICHAEL SHAPIRO	187
Alienation and Illusion: The Play-Within-the-Play on the Caroline Stage CHARLOTTE SPIVACK	195

REVIEWS

Anne Barton. *Ben Jonson, Dramatist* MICHAEL WARREN	213

Catherine Belsey. *The Subject of Tragedy: Identity & Difference in Renaissance Drama* 217
    PAUL GAUDET

Gordon Braden. *Renaissance Tragedy and the Senecan Tradition: Anger's Privilege* 223
    MARION TROUSDALE

Michael D. Bristol. *Carnival and Theater: Plebeian Culture and the Structure of Authority in Renaissance England* 228
    THOMAS CARTELLI

Walter Cohen. *Drama of a Nation: Public Theater in Renaissance England and Spain* 231
    JONATHAN DOLLIMORE

Audrey Douglas and Peter Greenfield, eds. *Cumberland, Westmoreland, Gloucestershire*, Records of Early English Drama 237
    CLIFFORD DAVIDSON

Malcolm Evans. *Signifying Nothing: Truth's True Contents in Shakespeare's Text* 240
    CHARLES H. FREY

Patrick Grant. *Literature and the Discovery of Method in the English Renaissance* 243
    SUZANNE GOSSETT

Michael Hattaway. *Elizabethan Popular Theatre: Plays in Performance* 247
    WILLIAM B. LONG

Michael Hattaway, ed. *The New Inn* by Ben Jonson, The Revels Plays 252
    EJNER J. JENSEN

Homo, Memento Finis: The Iconography of Just Judgment in Medieval Art and Drama, Early Drama, Art and Music Monograph Series 256
    PETER W. TRAVIS

Ritchie D. Kendall. *The Drama of Dissent: The Radical Poetics of Nonconformity, 1380–1590* 258
    ARTHUR F. KINNEY

Arthur F. Kinney. *Humanist Poetics: Thought, Rhetoric, and Fiction in Sixteenth-Century England* 263
    PHILIP ROLLINSON

William Kupersmith. *Roman Satirists in Seventeenth-Century England* 264
    KATHARINE EISAMAN MAUS

Contents

Clifford Leech. *Christopher Marlowe: Poet for the Stage*, edited by Anne Lancashire
    R. A. FOAKES   266

Theodore B. Leinwand. *The City Staged: Jacobean Comedy, 1603–1613*
    CAROL LEVENTEN   268

Peter Lindenbaum. *Changing Landscapes: Anti-Pastoral Sentiment in the English Renaissance*
    THEODORE B. LEINWAND   273

David Lindley, ed. *The Court Masque*, The Revels Plays Companion Library
    CATHERINE M. SHAW   275

Giuseppe Mazzotta. *The World at Play in Boccaccio's "Decameron"*
    MICHAEL D. BRISTOL   278

Patricia Parker and David Quint, eds. *Literary Theory/Renaissance Texts*
    PETER ERICKSON   282

Gail Kern Paster. *The Idea of the City in the Age of Shakespeare*
    NANCY ELIZABETH HODGE   289

Martha Tuck Rozett. *The Doctrine of Election and the Emergence of Elizabethan Tragedy*
    LOIS POTTER   294

G. B. Shand, with Raymond C. Shady, ed. *Play-Texts in Old Spelling: Papers from the Glendon Conference*
    PHILIP R. RIDER   297

Simon Shepherd. *Marlowe and the Politics of Elizabethan Theatre*
    HARRY KEYISHIAN   303

Peter W. Travis. *Dramatic Design in the Chester Cycle*
    J.A.B. SOMERSET   310

John Wasson, ed. *Devon*, Records of Early English Drama
    WILLIAM TYDEMAN   314

Linda Woodbridge. *Women and the English Renaissance: Literature and the Nature of Womankind, 1540–1620*
    ELIZABETH H. HAGEMAN   318

Sheldon P. Zitner, ed. *The Knight of the Burning Pestle*, by Francis Beaumont, The Revels Plays
    MICHAEL HATTAWAY   322

CORRESPONDENCE

from JONATHAN DOLLIMORE	327
from J. R. MULRYNE	329
Index	335
Contents of Volumes I, II, and III	349

Foreword

THIS fourth volume of *MaRDiE* is issued with our thanks to those who have been so encouraging in their reception of its predecessors. We also continue to welcome contributions from scholars in all areas of the world, and we note that papers are not restricted to any specific length. We particularly invite the work of scholars concerned with medieval drama, just as we continue to welcome proposals for reviews or review-articles. For although reviews are ordinarily invitational, proposals will be given most serious consideration.

—LEEDS BARROLL
Editor

Notes on Contributors

MICHAEL D. BRISTOL is Professor of English at McGill University and the author of *Carnival and Theatre: Plebian Culture and the Structure of Authority in Renaissance England*. He has recently completed a book-length study of Shakespeare as an ideological institution in the United States that will be published in 1989.

THOMAS CARTELLI is Associate Professor of English and Chair of the Humanities Division at Muhlenberg College.

S. P. CERASANO, Associate Professor of English at Colgate University, is a theater historian at work on a biography of Edward Alleyn.

CLIFFORD DAVIDSON is Professor of English, co-editor of *Comparative Drama*, and Executive Editor of the Early Drama, Art, and Music project at the Medieval Institute at Western Michigan University. He has published extensively on Medieval and Renaissance drama and art; his most recent book is *The Guild Chapel Wall Paintings at Stratford-upon-Avon* (1988).

JONATHAN DOLLIMORE, Lecturer in the School of English and American Studies at Sussex University, is author of *Radical Tragedy* and co-editor of *Political Shakespeare*. Currently he is writing a study of sexuality, transgression, and sub-cultures.

PETER ERICKSON is the author of *Patriarchal Structures in Shakespeare's Drama* and co-editor of *Shakespeare's "Rough Magic": Renaissance Essays in Honor of C. L. Barber*. His essay on *The Merry Wives of Windsor* appeared recently in *Shakespeare Reproduced: The Text in History and Ideology*, edited by Jean E. Howard and Marion F. O'Connor; a new essay, "Adrienne Rich's Re-Vision of the Shakespearean Tradition," is forthcoming in *Women's (Re)Visions of Shakespeare*, edited by Marianne Novy.

R. A. FOAKES is Professor of English at the University of California, Los Angeles. His recent publications include editions of *A Midsummer Night's Dream* and *Troilus and Cressida*, as well as S. T. Coleridge's *Lectures 1808–1819: On Literature*.

CHARLES R. FORKER, Professor of English at Indiana University, has recently published *Skull Beneath the Skin: The Achievement of John Webster* and is currently at work on a collection of essays to be entitled *Fancy's Images: Symbolic Contexts, Settings, and Perspectives in Shakespeare and His Fellow Dramatists*. He is editing Marlowe's *Edward II* for the Revels Plays.

CHARLES H. FREY, Professor of English at the University of Washington, is author of *Shakespeare's Vast Romance: A Study of "The Winter's Tale"* and *Experiencing Shakespeare: Essays on Text, Classroom, and Performance*. He is editor of the forthcoming collection of essays entitled *Shakespeare, Fletcher, and "The Two Noble Kinsmen."*

PAUL GAUDET is Associate Professor of English at the University of Western Ontario. Author of several articles on Shakespearean drama, he is currently involved in a study of *Troilus and Cressida* and Shakespeare's turn-of-the-century plays.

SUZANNE GOSSETT is Professor of English at Loyola University in Chicago. Her most recent work includes "A New History for Ralegh's *Notes on the Navy*" in *Modern Philology* and "'Man-Made, Begone!' Women in Masques" in *English Literary Renaissance*.

ELIZABETH H. HAGEMAN, Professor of English at the University of New Hampshire, is currently working with eight other scholars on an edition of Richard Hyrde's 1529 translation of Juan Luis Vives' *Instruction of a Christian Woman*.

GILLISANN HAROIAN is an Instructor of English at Baruch College of The City University of New York and an editor of *Ararat*, a literary quarterly based in New York City. She is currently at work on a book-length manuscript on the use of goddess imagery in the modern novel.

MICHAEL HATTAWAY is Professor of English Literature at the University of Sheffield. He is the author of *Elizabethan Popular Theatre* and *Hamlet, The Critic's Debate* and co-editor of the *Cambridge Companion to Elizabethan and Stuart Drama*. He is currently editing *1-3 Henry VI* for the *New Cambridge Shakespeare*.

ANDREW HICKMAN studied at McMaster University, Ontario and at Corpus Christi College, Oxford where he completed a doctoral thesis on the plays and collaborations of John Fletcher. He now lives in Scotland where he is a full-time civil servant and a part-time tutor for the Open University.

NANCY ELIZABETH HODGE is Executive Secretary of the Shakespeare Association of America and Lecturer in English at Vanderbilt University. She is working on a book about gender relations, status, and social mobility in *The Merchant of Venice*.

EJNER J. JENSEN is Professor of English Language and Literature at the University of Michigan. He is author of the recent *Ben Jonson's Comedies on the Modern Stage* and has written widely on Renaissance drama and satire.

HARRY KEYISHIAN is Professor of English at the Madison, New Jersey, campus of Fairleigh Dickinson University and Director of Fairleigh Dickinson University Press. He is currently at work on a study of the revenge motif in Shakespeare.

ARTHUR F. KINNEY is Thomas W. Copeland Professor of Literary History at the University of Massachusetts, Amherst. He is Founding Editor of *English Literary Renaissance* and editor of the Renaissance titles in the Twayne English Authors Series. His *Continental Humanist Poetics*, a companion to *Humanist Poetics: Thought, Rhetoric, and Fiction in Sixteenth-Century England*, has just been published. Also recently published are *John Skelton: Priest as Poet* (1987) and *Renaissance Historicism* and *Sidney in Retrospect* (collections from *English Literary Renaissance*, both in 1988). He is presently at work on a full-length book on *Macbeth*.

Notes on Contributors

JAMES N. KRASNER, a graduate student at the University of Pennsylvania, is completing his dissertation on visual perception and illusion in post-Darwinian nature writing.

ROSLYN L. KNUTSON is Associate Professor of English at the University of Arkansas at Little Rock. She has published articles on various aspects of commerce among the Elizabethan playing companies and is presently at work on the repertory of Shakespeare's company.

THEODORE B. LEINWAND is the author of *The City Staged: Jacobean Comedy, 1603-13*. Sections from his work-in-progress on popular culture and Shakespearean drama have appeared in *Renaissance Papers* and *Shakespeare Studies*.

CAROL LEVENTEN is Assistant Professor of English at Adrian College. She is working on a book about women in Jacobean city comedy.

WILLIAM B. LONG, who has taught English Renaissance drama at Washington University in St. Louis and at The City College of New York and is currently senior editor at AMS Press, has been writing about the workings of Elizabethan and Jacobean acting companies in their theaters for some years.

KATHARINE EISAMAN MAUS is the author of *Ben Jonson and the Roman Frame of Mind* and of a number of articles on Renaissance and Restoration literature.

SCOTT MCMILLIN, Professor of English at Cornell University, is the author of *The Elizabethan Theatre and "The Book of Sir Thomas More."* He is currently writing a book about the Queen's Men, 1583-1600.

LOIS POTTER is Senior Lecturer in English at the University of Leicester. She is one of the General Editors of the Revels History of Drama in English, has published on Shakespeare, Milton, and Civil War literature generally, and is presently editing *The Two Noble Kinsmen* for the Arden Shakespeare.

PHILIP R. RIDER is Publications Editor at the Computing Information Center, Northern Illinois University, and is one of the editors of *Analytical and Enumerative Bibliography*. He has contributed to *Papers of the Bibliographical Society of America* and *Research Opportunities in Renaissance Drama*, among other journals, and is at present compiling a chronological index to the revised *Short Title Catalogue*.

KAREN ROBERTSON is Assistant Professor of English at Vassar College. She is now working with Carole Levin on a collection of essays on sexuality in Renaissance drama.

PHILIP B. ROLLINSON is Associate Professor of English at the University of South Carolina. He has written *Classical Theories of Allegory and Christian Culture*, as well as many articles on Old English Literature, Spenser, and Milton.

MICHAEL SHAPIRO is Associate Professor of English at the University of Illinois at Urbana. He is the author of *Children of the Revels: the Boy Companies of Shakespeare's Time and Their Plays*, as well as numerous essays, reviews, and notes on Shakespeare and other Renaissance dramatists. He is currently completing a book on Shakespeare's heroines in male disguises.

CATHERINE M. SHAW of McGill University has published numerous essays on Shakespeare and other Renaissance dramatists. She is the author of books on the masque in Renaissance drama and on Richard Brome and has edited *The Old Law* by Middleton and Rowley and *The Obstinate Lady* by Aston Cokayne. At present she is working on a stage history of *Richard II*.

J.A.B. SOMERSET is Associate Professor of the Department of English at the University Western Ontario. He is editor of *Four Tudor Interludes* and *A Play of Love* and author of many articles on Medieval and Renaissance drama. He is editing the Shropshire and Staffordshire dramatic records for Records of Early English Drama and is preparing *The Stratford Festival Story*, a computer-based catalogue-index to the Stratford, Ontario, Shakespearean Festival.

CHARLOTTE SPIVACK is Professor of English at the University of Massachusetts, Amherst. Author of *George Chapman* and *The Comedy of Evil on Shakespeare's Stage* and co-author of *Early English Drama*, she has also published numerous articles on Shakespeare and other Renaissance dramatists. She is a member of the Editorial Board of *English Literary Renaissance* and currently is working on a book about female roles on the Stuart stage.

MARION TROUSDALE is Professor of English at the University of Maryland at College Park and author of *Shakespeare and the Rhetoricians*. Her essays on Renaissance drama have appeared in *Shakespeare Quarterly*, *English Literary Renaissance*, *ELH*, and *Renaissance Drama*.

PETER W. TRAVIS, Professor of English at Dartmouth College, is the author of *Dramatic Design in the Chester Cycle* (1982). He is presently writing a book on the poetics of Chaucer's parodic styles.

ROBERT Y. TURNER, Professor of English at the University of Pennsylvania, is the author of *Shakespeare's Apprenticeship* as well as articles on Shakespeare and other Renaissance dramatists, especially those who wrote tragicomedies.

WILLIAM TYDEMAN is Professor of English at the University College of North Wales, Bangor. Among his publications are *The Theatre in the Middle Ages* and *English Medieval Theatre 1400–1500*; he has edited *Four Tudor Comedies* and is currently engaged on an edition of *Gorboduc* and *The Spanish Tragedie*.

MICHAEL WARREN, Professor of English Literature at the University of California, Santa Cruz, is co-editor of *The Division of the Kingdoms* and author of several articles on English Renaissance drama.

The Cornish Mermaid: The Fine Thread of Androgyny in the *Ordinalia*

GILLISANN HAROIAN

Critics have long puzzled over the First Doctor's defense of Christ's divinity in the Cornish *Ordinalia*:

> He might well be
> Half man and half God.
> Human is half the mermaid,
> Woman from the head to the heart;
> So is the Jesus.
> ("Passion," ll. 1740–1744)[1]

Robert Longsworth, for example, admits being confounded by this passage.[2] He notes that the doctor's "curious use by analogy of the mermaid . . . is an unusual if not unique example of its kind."[3] He calls attention to the popularity of mermaid emblems in Cornish churches but explains that they function as negative symbols, of diabolical temptations through lust, and he ends by remarking that this makes "all the more remarkable [the] function [of the mermaid analogy] in the *Ordinalia*."[4]

A close study of the Cycle, however, reveals that the mermaid analogy is explicable within the context of the *Ordinalia*. I will argue that the Cornish Christ is, first, an androgynous figure; furthermore, this androgyny is an important clue to Christ's dualistic nature; it expands into an emblem of the author's continual emphasis on both Christ's humanity, as a son of Mary, and his divinity, as a son of God. This conception renders the Cycle remarkably different from most others.

I begin with the mermaid emblems that are both abundant and used positively in Cornish churches; those churches were built by and for fishermen and their families, to whom the superstitions of mer-folk were especially familiar.[5] Indeed, the Cornish have nearly twice as many legends about individual mermaids as the next closest locale, the Hebrides;[6] The most involved and popular of these legends deals with the Mermaid of Zennor. In a note, unrelated to such lore, Harris mentions that the author of the Cornish Cycle presumably resided at the former Collegiate Church of the Blessed Virgin Mary and Saint Thomas of Canterbury at Glasney. Nearby was the Church of Saint Senara at Zennor, possessing the most fabulous carvings of mermaids. Later, a Bishop Bronescombe appropriated this Church to Glasney College in 1270.[7]

Only one critic, Jenner, was so struck by the First Doctor's use of the mermaid analogy as "remarkable" that he researched and made the connection with local lore, deciding that "it was not for nothing that a mermaid is found carved on bench-ends and over doors of Cornish churches."[8] In a revised version, Jenner added: "It evidently symbolized the two natures of Christ . . . [though] the councils of Ephesus and Chalcedon might have found some fault with the advocate's way of expressing what is known in theology as the Hypostatic Union"; he therefore concluded that the scene, though founded on Luke 23:7-12, was rendered original by the addition of the doctors' argument.[9] However, Jenner stopped short of considering the analogy and its implications in the context of the whole work.

To appreciate the force of the mermaid legends and carvings to the medieval Cornish playwright and his audience, consider a brief episode that showed the mermaid's continuing impact in Cornwall five hundred years later: a traveller met a local gardener who explained that the mermaid had a "spiritual significance" to him and his fellows and cited the *Ordinalia* as illustration.[10] Thus, both for its intended audience and its author, the emblem had a much deeper significance than critics have yet noted.

The Christian Art Index at Princeton University confirms the singularity of this use of the mermaid as symbol of Christ. While there are many listings for mermaids in art, those references are scattered, with no concentration such as that evident in Cornwall, and by far the majority are associated with the diabolic. An example of the traditional bias against the mermaid is best shown by one marble statuette, in the Louvre, of the Mother Mary holding the Christ Child while she treads on a mermaid. This negative association has even led some critics to misread the Cornish passage on the mermaid.

As Mikhail Bakhtin has noted, "Differences in plot follow from differences in value."[11] Therefore the exceptional use of the mermaid—and female saints—in the *Ordinalia* should be examined through the special meanings that these held for the original culture that produced them. For instance, the region's special legacy of Celtic river goddesses has led to many claims by Cornish families of merman or mermaid ancestry.[12] If the mermaid is inextricably woven into the fabric of Cornish life, it is no coincidence that she would be woven into the fabric of the *Ordinalia*, even if elsewhere the mermaid had negative associations in the prevailing Christian symbology. The Cornish playwright obviously culled his symbol from local lore and made a daring inversion of his Church's bias toward the mermaid. He wove her symbolism into his play, in the process revealing much about the dualistic nature of his Christ.

In the *Ordinalia*, the author meant what he said: his Christ is womanly from the head to the heart (though some translations have erred in this crucial aspect).[13] The mermaid symbol of this nature is given at a crucial point—the trial of Christ. It is reinforced throughout the play: before Christ is born, he is prefigured through a woman, Saint Maximilla; after he dies, Christ is represented by a woman, Saint Veronica; while he is alive, Christ's crucial actions are sometimes echoed by those of the reformed Mary Magdalene. Also, the tradition of the shrewish *uxor* is generally absent from the *Ordinalia*. Contrary to other *Corpus Christi* authors, who drew out and colored boldly the anti-woman threads of the Christian tapestry, the Cornish author from the start sought to mute these tones and stitch creative, attractive patterns for many of his women, never losing sight of the fact that Christ was a Son of Mary as well as of God. This renders the Cornish Cycle less absolutist in its portrait of women than the other Cycles.

To begin charting this unique role given to women throughout, we note that the author first repeats that prelapsarian Adam's helpmate was his equal, not his inferior:[14]

> Forthwith from one of thy ribs,
> I make to thee an equal
>   ("Beginning," ll. 100–101)
>
> Do thou give a name to her,
> To take her for thy equal.
>   (103–104)

Eve is created, Adam names her, and she thanks God for "creating me like to thee" (109); thus the Cornish God is demonstrated as embracing the feminine, as well as masculine, elements.

When Adam and Eve fall and are exiled from the Garden, the Cornish Adam blames his wife, in accordance with convention. God, in turn, attributes the fall of man to Eve, but he also takes particular care to warn Adam:

> Nor must thou allege
> That thou art punished
>   because of thy wife.
>   (321–322)

The Cornish playwright's concern with the role of women is attested further by the act of naming. As is generally true in the Scriptures, naming is the exclusive province of Adam, who names Eve and his heirs. When Eve gives birth to her third son in the *Ordinalia*, she must turn to Adam for bestowal of their son's name, Seth. However, the Cornish playwright, unlike any other *Corpus Christi* author, gives the right of first proclaiming the name of Christ over to a woman. Christ, who will redeem both men and women, is first named by the apocryphal Maximilla. This scene, unique to the *Ordinalia*, indicates the playwright's concern with the shaping power of women in his drama of the Redemption.

In fact, the bishop, who is present in the temple when Maximilla calls out Christ's name, is enraged by this act:

> What vengeance to thee, O fool's head,
> Where has thou heard God called Christ

> By a man in this world born?
> I have the law of Moses,
> And in all that same
> His name is not written.
>   (2641-2646)

The Cornish word for man, *den* (2643), may or may not be an impersonal pronoun. Yet, clearly, the bishop is incensed by Maximilla's gender, especially her sexuality. The names that he calls her—"jade girl" (2649) to "witch" (2668)—are directed at her womanhood. The executioners reinforce this pattern by calling Maximilla a "strumpet" (2705, 2728, 2753), "jade" (2736, 2741, 2746) and "daughter of evil" (2736). While the men may initially be incensed at Maximilla's act of naming a new god, they soon generalize and impugn her as a female. The boundary between the specific act and general vituperation is thus thoroughly blurred.

The bishop wonders about the best way to punish Maximilla and asks a nearby knave for "counsel like a man" (2672) on the subject. The bishop decides to take the knave's recommended course of physical violence. In this scene, machismo shows its strongly negative aspects in the *Ordinalia*, while the earthly Christ emerges as possessing the traditionally feminine traits of sweetness, pacifism, and so forth.

The bishop subsequently curses Maximilla for not being "obedient" (2763) to him, and it is clear that Maximilla should not be so to this man. With this argument between Maximilla and the bishop, and the later scene between Veronica and the Emperor, the Cornish playwright demonstrates that even the strongest man on earth should listen to the most modest Christian woman, who emerges as a repeated type of wise and gentle, but extremely firm, grace by the end of the *Ordinalia*.

Maximilla refuses to bow: "I will not recant, foolish bishop" (2655). She refers to the three-branched tree, from which the cross shall come, as a "good type" of the three persons in the Trinity (2659). Her reference demonstrates the playwright's awareness of typology in this scene, as throughout the play; consequently, when Maximilla herself is beaten and martyred by four executioners, as the Cornish Christ will be buffeted and martyred by four, the Cornish playwright has fashioned her into a non-traditional but definite type of Christ, and he has set her on footing just as sure as that of the established male types of Abel, Noah, and others.

This conclusion is supported by a comparison of this scene with its source, which is well documented to be the anonymous thirteenth-century Latin *Legende*.[15] In that work, Maximilla sits on the wood, her clothes catch fire, she cries to Christ as Lord and God, and she is stoned by the Jews for blaspheming, thus becoming the first martyr for Christ.[16] The two elements that the Cornish playwright uniquely stressed—the sexual curses and the four torturers—show how consciously he was reinforcing her womanhood and her status as a type of Christ.

In further recognition of the feminine in Christ, the Cornish playwright post-figures him in Saint Veronica. The extensive use of Veronica, like that of Maximilla, is also peculiar to the *Ordinalia*.[17] Compared to the other Cycles, an unusual proportion of Part Three ("Resurrection") of the *Ordinalia* revolves around females, and the Cornish playwright also creates unusual, complex, and extensive scenes with the Magdalene.

In Harris's translation, Veronica says of Christ, "I am one of his followers" (p. 223). This sentence should have read, "I *am* one of his women" (compare Norris, "Resurrection," l. 1667). The Cornish word used here, *vynynes,* is in fact the plural of *woman.*[18] Here we have yet another example of textual bias in the Harris translation, undercutting what is a persistent view of the playwright, the recognition that women are not only the heralds but also strong resonators of the Incarnation.

Veronica proceeds to cure the Emperor Tiberius in Christ's name. The Emperor then has the wisdom to reverse the prevailing order and take counsel only from this woman. She instructs him to remove Christ's cloak from Pilate and advises him through to the end, telling him to place Pilate's body in an iron box and throw it first in the river, then into the ocean. She clearly speaks for heaven and Christ, and Tiberius exclaims,

> O Veronica, on my faith,
> A counsel good and perfect
> To me thou hast given.
> ("Resurrection," ll. 2141–2143)

After his conversion, he praises Christ as both the "Son of God" and the "Son of Mary" (2200). From this point on, Christ is referred to as much as "the Son of Mary" as "of God," and sometimes more so, as when Tiberius says,

> My blessing on thee, Veronica,
> And the blessing of the Son of Mary,
> My dear Lord.
> (2237–2239)

The link between the Virgin Mary and Christ is carefully developed in the *Ordinalia.* In certain, select scenes Christ is clearly made Mary's "Son on earth" ("Passion," l. 2948); the Mother is used continually to reinforce Christ's link to humanity. A comparison of these scenes to those where emphasis is laid on Christ as "Son of God" clarifies the Virgin's role. In Part One ("Beginning") of the *Ordinalia,* Christ is foreshadowed in certain visions but not referred to with any great frequency. In Part Two ("Passion"), from the moment he comes onstage to his Crucifixion, Christ's identity is subject to severe question. He is named as the "Son of God," some twenty-five to thirty times,[19] but rarely as the "Son of Mary." However, his relationship with God the Father is often questioned. The references begin with Satan's scorn, "If thou be the Son of God above" (60), and continue with Caiaphas, "If thou art the Son of high God" (1324); with Herod, "If thou art Son of the God of grace" (1769); with Annas, "If thou be Son of the great God" (2867); with the Executioners, "If thou be Son of God" (2865); and with Jesmas, "If thou be Christ,

Son of dear God" (2891). The truth begins to emerge only as the enemy comes to recognize it. At the height of his folly, Beelzebub declares, "He is Christ, the Son of God named" (1951). Meanwhile Mary, like the namer Maximilla, has been one of the strongest to affirm Christ's identity in the midst of these men's doubts: "He is Son of God in every way" (2935). Even some of Christ's disciples, such as Judas and Peter, have denied him. When Peter does so, it is the gentle Portress who declares,

> He ought not to deny him,
> For he is of Galilee,
> And his man, always brought up with him.
> (1280–1282)

What does Peter immediately reply? "Woman, don't talk folly!" (1283).

The switch to more frequent references to Christ as the "Son of Mary," some twenty-five to thirty,[20] comes with the Via Dolorosa scene. Some obvious reasons readily occur: Christ's Crucifixion is made possible by his semi-mortal origins; his subsequent Resurrection irrevocably establishes his identity to even the most foolish disbelievers in the play; last, these scenes are the most pathetic, establishing him as the medieval Man of Sorrows, where the emphasis is frequently on bereaved motherhood.[21]

Upon close inspection, this balance between Christ as "Son of God" and "Son of Mary" reveals Mary's function to be similar to that of the mermaid. The mermaid is a creature of eternal youth who belongs both to this world and to another, as Christ does, and Mary alone provides the link between earth and heaven: through her, the Christian hero bridges the mortal and the immortal, as most heroes do. Consider the lines

> The Son of God will rise
> When he will;
> For Jesus Son of Mary,
> He made heaven and this world,
> ("Resurrection," 942–945)

or

> That he is son of Mary,
> And God likewise.
> (933–934)

Thus, in the final section, "Son of Mary" and "Son of God" come to be used in conjunction to illustrate the Hypostatic Union. The Cornish want manifestly to touch their divinity, to feel his humanity. Accordingly, Mary asks to touch her son and receives his body into her hands ("Passion," l. 3165). None of the critics has recognized this aspect of the Cornish Mary's dramatic role.

Interestingly, adjectives applied to Mary are constantly reflected in the Cornish Christ. He is continually named "sweet," "pure," "tender," and "sorrowful," all associated with Mary, and somewhat with the other women—but rarely with men—in the play. These stereotyped but pleasing female traits of purity and sweetness, in the midst of so much sadness, count in making this Savior a mermaid indeed. Similar details concerning the importance of females occur throughout the play.[22]

Lastly, certain actions of Mary Magdalene particularly affirm Christ's divinity. After Christ appears to her in the garden and she informs the apostles, Magdalene has a crucial confrontation with Thomas. This scene is another one unique to the Cornish Cycle. The Magdalene is absent in the doubting Thomas scenes of the York N-town, Chester, and Wakefield pageants, although she does have a brief scene with Peter and Paul in the Wakefield cycle.

In the *Ordinalia*, Thomas attacks Magdalene principally because she is a woman. In response to his shout, "Silence, and speak not, thou woman!" ("Resurrection," l. 917), Magdalene, with all the force of a Maximilla, asserts the truth of the Resurrection of the "Son of Mary" (923). The hostile Thomas persists, "Peace, chattering woman, say no more" (1067), and Magdalene replies with firm rectitude, "Thomas, thou art very stupid" (1105). She continues, undaunted and outspoken, to advise Thomas to have faith, and she criticizes him for having a hard heart. Philip, in turn, speaks of Christ as the "head of man and woman" (1396), the typical idiom of the Cornish playwright, and Judah similarly pronounces, "To him we unlocked, / Men and women" (1445–1446).

Here, once more, a woman has transmitted the word of Christ in the *Ordinalia*. The critical consensus concerning the Cornish Magdalene has glossed over the importance of her role. Harris, for example, notes only briefly that Thomas rejects Magdalene's argument because she is a former sinner and a woman.[23] Longsworth also notes that Thomas rejects "the *girl's* credibility" (italics mine).[24] This identification alone is sufficient to indicate an insensitivity to the Cornish dramatist's very real concern over the role of the Magdalene, who is, after all, a full-grown woman, reformed adulteress, and disciple of Christ. Furthermore, although Longsworth sees that the Magdalene episode "repeatedly affirms Jesus [as] indeed the Son of God,"[25] he, and others, have failed to make the palpable association of the roles of Maximilla, Magdalene, and Veronica as significant and unique manifestations of the role of women in Christian salvation history as espoused by the Cornish playwright. In my mind, that disposition is carried over to and perhaps highlighted by the reference to Christ as mermaid.

Yet another scene gives emphasis to Magdalene's role. When, washing Christ's feet, she is reproached by Judas, Christ comes to her defense and reproaches him in turn: "To wash my feet thou hast not offered" ("Passion," l. 518). The Cornish playwright has written the scene to emphasize Magdalene's motives for the deed. Christ proclaims that she performed it "through love" (549), and this shall raise her spiritually above the others. The scene also precedes closely and prefigures Christ's washing of the apostles' feet, during which he bids them to wash each other's after he is gone (875–879).

It is, then, through the roles of women, that female love, service, sweetness, counsel, and purity are interwoven throughout the Cornish depiction of Christ. The mermaid analogy reinforces this pattern. In fact, at points in the *Ordinalia*, Christ is womanly not only from the head to the heart, but also from the head to the foot: he is anointed in the head by the Virgin Mary, in the heart by Mary Mother of James, and in the feet by Mary Magdalene ("Passion," action between ll. 3201 and 3202).

The importance of this clear pattern of women in the *Ordinalia* is heightened when one recalls that scholarship has shown patterned sequencing to be crucial to the thematic unity of the medieval cycles.[26] Examining this sequencing of the genre in the *Ordinalia* reveals how central female figures are. Consider Maximilla's position. Hers is the final major episode in the Holy Rood legend, the most powerful unifying factor in the play.[27] While documenting this critical factor, Bakere notes that Maximilla's proclamation of Christ as God is climactic as it completes the legend of the Holy Rood and thus the preparation for the Passion itself; Bakere then proceeds to detail how the closely unified theme and structure rely on this and two other factors: (1) the direct historical narrative from the Fall to Redemption, and (2) the use of major historical figures as types of Christ.[28] Bakere, in exploring these three, devotes a chapter to detailing the Christ types in scenes such as the Abraham and Isaac, and others—except Maximilla's, where her criticism, like all others' of the *Ordinalia*, stops. I would like to stress that not only is Maximilla a type of Christ, but also because she is one at *the* climactic moment of the play, she is therefore, arguably, one of the most powerful within the play.

When Christ praises Magdalene for washing his feet, he also praises her gentle kiss and reproaches Judas: "Never a kiss to me didst thou give"("Passion," l. 522). The kiss Christ finally receives in the Garden from Judas is hard and deceitful, not the soft, pure kiss of Magdalene, which comforts us, in our sorrows. This gentleness is, in the end, the very thing that the medieval Man of Sorrows encompassed.

Here lies one final device that androgyny provides in the *Ordinalia*. The feminine Christ is the one who nurses us in the midst of our earthly woes. Upon his ascension to heaven, Christ's nature must be transformed radically, and so he sheds his mortality, the humanity of his Mother, and becomes the powerful King of Kings. He is no longer Mary's son on earth, but God's son in the Kingdom. But the Cornish playwright never quite lets us forget that as much as woman might be considered the weaker partner in Christianity, she is always an equal heir to grace (1 Peter 3:7). When the Cornish Christ breaks open the gates of Hell, Eve cries out, "Blessed be the time / That he was born of woman" ("Resurrection," ll. 152–153). Adam echoes this sympathy somewhat by identifying Christ's companions, Enoch and Elijah, as "Creatures from the bosom of woman" (191). The emphasis upon a woman—this time Eve—is, once more, peculiar to the Cornish Cycle. In the Chester Cycle, an all-male chorus greets Christ in this scene, and the playwrights of the other

Cycles merely bestow on Eve a brief greeting that makes no mention of Christ's link with the feminine.

As Bakhtin points out, the hero is an extremely complex literary formation who "is constructed at the point where the major structural lines of the work intersect."[29] If we are culturally blind to one of those lines, as critics have been in the *Ordinalia*, our view of the hero must be incomplete. Only by exploring as fully as possible all themes can we arrive at a thorough evaluation of any work's characters, be they male, female, or androgynous.

NOTES

1. Of the two available editions, there were many reasons why Edwin Norris's two-volume *The Ancient Cornish Drama* (1859; rpt. New York: Benjamin Blom, 1968) was chosen over Markham Harris's, *The Cornish Ordinalia: A Medieval Dramatic Trilogy* (Washington, D.C.: Catholic University of America Press, 1969). The first is that Norris prints the Cornish text opposite his translation; thus the reader can deal directly with the original.

    The very thing that Norris (and Harris, p. xxv) considered a fault in his translation ends up, often, to be an advantage. Norris specifies repeatedly that he undertook the task solely "to preserve from obscurity and possible destruction the most considerable relic of the language" (I, vi). Consequently, the literal Norris loses some of the plays' energy and poetry, but he also loses some of the personal biases and nuances that Harris imposes on the text (see Notes 13 and 14). Harris, aiming for more readability, fluidity, naturalness, and idiomatic vigor (p. xxvii), achieves noteworthy results, but at times he does so at the expense of introducing quite subjective interpretations.

    The additional material with each text varies with intent. Because Norris's sole purpose was linguistic, he carefully noted at the bottom of pages any renderings that he considered doubtful, to alert the reader. Harris did not, though he provided a good Introduction to the play that highlights important information about the manuscript's author, date, region, sources, analogues, amphitheaters, and staging.

    This comparison of editions is made solely to note that, for the purposes of this paper, which demanded a close reading of the language, Norris's edition was better suited. However, both editions used together provide the fullest view of the play.

2. See Robert Longsworth, *The Cornish Ordinalia: Religion and Dramaturgy* (Cambridge, Mass.: Harvard University Press, 1967), p. 95.

3. Longsworth, p. 95.

4. Longsworth, p. 162.

5. For a discussion of mermaids in lore and history, see Gwen Benwell and Arthur Waugh, *Sea Enchantress: The Tale of the Mermaid and Her Kin* (New York: Citadel Press, 1965), p. 128.

6. Benwell, p. 178.

7. Harris, pp. ix, 260.

8. Henry Jenner, "The Cornish Drama," *Celtic Review*, IV (1907–08), 48.

9. Henry Jenner's manuscript entitled "The Sources of the Cornish Drama" in the County Museum of Truro, Cornwall, p. 93.

10. Benwell, p. 133.

11. M. M. Bakhtin and P. N. Medvedev, *The Formal Method in Literary Scholarship* (Cambridge, Mass.: Harvard University Press, 1985), p. 17.
12. Benwell, p. 145.
13. Herein lies a crucial error in Harris's translation. According to R. Morton Nance, *A Cornish-English Dictionary* (Marazion: Worden, 1955), p. viii, the Cornish *colon*, in which the *c* is sometimes mutated as *g*, denotes *heart* in the feminine but *belly* in the masculine (p. 11). The linguist Norris established the gender from "Beginning," l. 1758:

    gans nader ythof guanheys   By an adder I am stung,
    hag ol warbarth vynymmeys   And altogether poisoned
    afyne trois the'n golon .   From foot to the heart.

    Norris remained consistent in his translation of the term and provided a note on the word's etymology and use in the cycle (II, 342). Unlike Norris, Harris wrote off the mermaid analogy as "serio-comic" (p. 260) and translated the word as *belly* (p. 132), with no rationale but his subjective assumptions.
14. Harris also rendered a dubious translation of Cornish *parow* ("Beginning," l. 100) and *par* (104), whose first meaning, according to Nance, is "equal" or "match" (p. 72). Harris translated the words as "fellow" and "mate" (pp. 4, 5), which render connotations quite different from the meaning of the Cornish text. Since the passage in question involves God's creation of Eve, the point is of some importance to the author's apparent conception of female roles in the cycle.
15. See Jane A. Bakere, *The Cornish Ordinalia: A Critical Study* (Cardiff: University of Wales Press, 1980), p. 87.
16. See Esther Casier Quinn, *The Quest of Seth for the Oil of Life* (Chicago, Ill.: University of Chicago Press, 1962), p. 107.
17. Harris, p. xii.
18. The error of translating "women" as "follower" becomes more flagrant when one remembers that Cornish was a language with gender, as noted by R. Morton Nance, *An English-Cornish Dictionary* (London: Haycock Printers, Ltd., 1965), p. vii. Nance's dictionary lists as feminine *benen*, or woman, and *benenes*, women (p. 197). The words for *follower* are completely different—*holyer, sewyer, dyskybel* . . . (p. 69)—and they are generally masculine.

    Vynynes, in the sense of *women*, is a variant of *benenes*. The sounds *b*, *v*, and *m* were mutations of the same sound, as were *y* and *ee* (Nance, *Cornish*, p. viii). Thus, the Cornish manuscript varies: *benenes* for *women* in "Resurrection," l. 697; but *venen* for *woman* in l. 15; *vynyn* for *women* in l. 851; *venyn* for *woman* in "Beginning," l. 251; *vynynes* for *women* in "Resurrection," l. 1667; or, *morvoron* for *mermaid* in "Passion," l. 1741, and *vorvoran* for *mermaid* in l. 2403. Norris is very careful in his translation of the many distinctive words for females in Cornish: *voran* (variation of *moran*) as *girl*, for example ("Resurrection," l. 1044). Having set out to do a literal translation to preserve the language, Norris seems more heedful of the intricacies of Cornish.
19. The following are references to Christ as "Son of God" from his initial appearance in Part Two ("Passion") to the Via Dolorosa scene (1. 2590): ll. 60, 99, 153, 160, 278, 288, 326, 404, 425, 747, 962, 1033, 1043, 1097, 1127, 1324, 1328, 1379, 1383, 1460, 1486, 1491, 1577, 1651, 1667, 1694, 1721, 1769, 1911, 1951, 2173–2174, 2461.
20. The following are references to Christ as "Son of Mary" from the Via Dolorosa (1. 2590) scene: "Passion," ll. 2591 (immediate), 2595, 2604, 2933, 2943, 2948, 2952, 3100, 3169, 3181, 3188; "Resurrection," ll. 23, 428, 436, 442, 447, 455, 463, 472, 479, 495, 630, 864, 934 (with God), 944 (with God), 1199–1200, 1212, 1323, 2200 (with God), 2238, 2413, 2428.

(Of course, during the period when Christ's nature as the "Son of God" is being emphasized, there are also references to Christ as "Son of Mary," and there is ample reminder that Christ is "Son of God" during the sections stressing Christ as "Son of Mary"; the shift is one of predominance during certain scenes.

21. Martin Stevens, "The Theatre of the World: A Study in Medieval Dramatic Form," *Chaucer Review*, 7 (1973), 234-249.
22. Some examples of the details on females are as follows. In Part One ("Beginning"), Christ's blessing is given to "Men and women likewise" (11. 2836-2837); Abel must have the blessing of his mother as well as his father before his sacrifice (455-456); God promises the oil of mercy clearly to Adam *and* Eve (329-330); in the first vision of Christ, which is Seth's, the cherub clearly repeats that the child shall redeem both Seth's mother and his father (811-814). In Part Two ("Passion"), blessings from the Father are again clearly bestowed on a man and his wife (684-685); another reference repeats that through the Crucifixion all people, "male and female," will be redeemed (767-768). In Part Three ("Resurrection"), Mary Mother of James speaks to the Virgin Mary of "All the blessings of women" (817-818); Christ is labeled "head of man and woman" (1396); and repeated again is the fact that with his blood Christ redeemed "Man and woman" (2431-2432). There are more references. The point is simply that the audience receives continual reminders that women are blessed with men as heirs to grace.
23. Harris, p. xv.
24. Longsworth, p. 90.
25. Longsworth, p. 94.
26. Stevens, p. 248.
27. Bakere, pp. 86-87.
28. Bakere, pp. 86-87.
29. Bakhtin, p. 22.

"A Little More Than Kin, and Less Than Kind": Incest, Intimacy, Narcissism, and Identity in Elizabethan and Stuart Drama

CHARLES R. FORKER

I

After Shakespeare makes Hamlet bemoan the "most wicked speed" with which his mother and uncle have hastened to "incestuous sheets"(*Hamlet*, I.ii.156–157),[1] the hero sustains the shock of learning from the ghost that "the royal bed of Denmark," now "A couch for luxury and damned incest" (I.v.83–84), shelters not only a fratricide but also a probable adulteress. In this sequence the dramatist was raising a sensational subject guaranteed simultaneously to horrify and attract sophisticated thinkers and ignorant groundlings alike. That Renaissance culture was fascinated by forbidden forms of sexuality—especially desire within the confines of the family—is attested by the popularity of the subject in the poetry, prose fiction, and drama of the period. Spenser, for instance, touched upon it in *The Faerie Queene* (III.vii.47, 48; III.xi.3, 4), allegorizing the most extreme form of unchastity imaginable in the twin giants Ollyphant and Argante, monsters incestuously conceived by a Titaness in union with her own son, who reduplicated the incest of their conception by uniting with each other while still in the womb. More centrally, Milton adapted St. James's homily on the unholy triad of lust, sin, and death (James 1:15) in a similarly double incest: in *Paradise Lost* (II, 761–767) Satan fathers Death upon Sin (his own daughter); then Death rapes the figure who has become both his mother and his sister.

Arthurian romance also made much of incest. In Malory's redaction of the legend, for instance, King Arthur begets his bastard son Mordred upon his sister Morgause; then Mordred compounds the incestuous circumstances of his birth by seeking to commit adultery with Guenevera, his stepmother—a notorious example of the "bold bawdrye" of which Ascham so disapproved in *The Scholemaster* (1570).[2] Since Arthur expires from a wound inflicted by Mordred, incest might well be thought to condition the events leading to his death. Thomas Hughes's Senecan tragedy, *The Misfortunes of Arthur* (1588), incorporated the tradition of fatal incest and transmitted it to the stage. Continental writers of fiction who treated incest include such well-known names as Marguerite of Navarre, Basile, Bandello, Cinthio, and Montemayor, many of whose tales readily found their way into English.[3] Greene's *Pandosto* (Shakespeare's source for *The Winter's Tale*) and the story of Apollonius of Tyre (which lies behind *Pericles*) are both typical of romance in their inclusion of the incest motif.

Reviewing my somewhat desultory reading of Renaissance plays, I count no fewer than thirty-eight dramatists who made various uses of the incest theme—mostly in plots but occasionally also in imagery—in some sixty comedies, tragedies, tragicomedies, moralities, histories, romances, and pastorals. The range of genres is no less impressive than the widespread authorship. Shakespeare himself produced six plays in which incest figures directly or by implication—*Richard III* (a history), *Hamlet* and *Lear* (tragedies), *The Comedy of Errors* (a Plautine farce), *Measure for Measure* (a dark comedy), and *Pericles* (a romance) [4]; and *All's Well That Ends Well* and *Henry VIII*, for reasons that will become apparent later, might be added to the Shakespearean list, although neither play actually mentions incest or specifically underlines any sexual impropriety in connection with it. But the roster extends also to dramas by Phillip, Gascoigne, Preston, Lyly, Lodge, Greene, Peele, Hughes, Chettle, Haughton, Jonson, Marston, Chapman, Dekker, Mason, Barnes, Webster, Beaumont and Fletcher, Middleton, Tourneur, Ford, Massinger, Shirley, Wilson, and Brome. Seven of the *Tenne Tragedies* of Seneca, collected by Thomas Newton in 1581 and translated by himself, Jasper Heywood, and others, involve incest directly or as background; and even courtly and academic amateurs such as Margaret Cavendish, Walter Montague, Samuel Harding, Joseph Rutter, Lodowick Carlell, Thomas Randolph, and Sir John Suckling wrote plays that turn on incest.[5] It is therefore possible to deny unequivocally a recent statement by Denis Gauer, a writer on Ford, that "incest has seldom been treated by literature or drama,"[6] and to suggest that Marlowe alone among the playwrights of the first rank avoided the topic as a subject for dramatization—perhaps because homosexuality, an alternative form of sexual nonconformity, engaged his attention more urgently.

Renaissance concern with the theatrical possibilities of incest is hardly surprising. Freud in *Civilization and Its Discontents* held that the almost universal prohibition in Western culture against coition with close relatives amounted to "perhaps the most drastic mutilation which man's erotic life has in all time experienced."[7] According to Freud and his school, social order has always required us to resist our primary instinctual passion for the parent of the opposite sex, repressing or diverting it to more acceptable objects; nevertheless, the depth and pervasiveness of the resulting neuroses continue to prove, as Freud demonstrates, how formidable and difficult the process of transference or sublimation inevitably becomes. Anthropology, the handmaiden of psychology, has likewise tended to insist on the centrality of the incest taboo for the construction and development of civilization.[8] One can say, then, that Elizabethan drama, like the art of other periods, simply represents a particularly imaginative attempt to take account of socio-psychological tensions inherent in the human situation—the more so, perhaps, because drama as a genre especially thrives on such conflicts. I would suggest, however, that special environmental factors more proximate than the Oedipal archetype account for the particular proliferation of incest stories and figures of speech on the Elizabethan stage. The most important of these intellectual and sociological pressures may be attributed to the humanistic literary tradition, the emotional climate within the family, and recent dynastic history (with its related theological debates concerning marriage, divorce, and remarriage).

II

Steeped as they were in classical mythology and history, the Elizabethans were constantly being reminded in their reading of incestuous situations and relationships. Plato, in *The Republic*, had notably relaxed traditional restrictions against incest for the purpose of breeding intellectual strength through eugenics, even going so far as to propose that "the law [of the ideal city] will allow brothers and sisters to cohabit if the lot so falls out and the Delphic oracle approves." Tacitus and Suetonius had gossiped about the lurid incests of the Roman emperors—of Claudius's marriage to his niece Agrippina, of Nero's dalliance with his mother (that same Agrippina who, as a younger woman, had attracted his stepfather), of Caligula's copulation with two different sisters, and of Domitian's seduction of his niece. Cicero in his *Pro Caelio* had hinted at the sexual liason between the notorious Clodia (Catullus's "Lesbia") and her brother Publius Clodius, while Quintus Cicero, Asconius, and Plutarch (in works that Jonson would use as the basis for a passage in his second Roman tragedy) recounted how Catiline had debauched both his sister and his daughter. Classical drama, both Greek and Roman, was replete with incest, Sophocles, Euripides, Aristophanes, Seneca, Plautus, Terence, and Menander all being cases in point. Seneca was especially fertile ground, for the English translations mentioned above include dramatizations of the stories of Thyestes, Hippolytus, Oedipus, Agamemnon, and Octavia, all of which turn to some extent on incestuous affairs. Thyestes deflowered both his sister-in-law, Aerope, and his daughter, Pelopeia; Hippolytus was seduced by his mother Phaedra; Oedipus slept unwittingly with his mother Jocasta (Gascoigne and Kinwelmersh adapted the Euripidean version of the same myth in their drama, *Jocasta*); Agamemnon's wife Clytemnestra took Aegisthus (the offspring of Thyestes' incestuous union with Pelopeia) as her lover; and Octavia, daughter of the emperor Claudius, married Nero, her uncle.

Juvenal made seduction inside the family circle one of his targets in *Satire I*, while in *Satire II* he alluded pointedly to the emperor Domitian's incest with his niece Julia, to be imitated by Marston, who invoked the same scandal to spice up *The Scourge of Villanie* (1598). Herodotus related the barbaric and incestuous monstrosities of Cambyses, King of Persia, in an account that indirectly became the source for Thomas Preston's early Elizabethan shocker. And the promiscuous life of Cleopatra, who successively married two of her brothers in accordance with the incestuous tradition of the house of Ptolemy, obviously riveted the Renaissance imagination; Dio

Cassius (in a passage that Shakespeare may have known) mentioned how Julius Caesar, when the Queen of Egypt was his mistress, settled both her and her brother-husband in his house at Rome "so that he . . . derived an ill repute on account of both of them." The mythographers Parthenius and Hyginus both recounted the familiar tale of how Harpalyce was ravished by her father Clymenus, who was later horribly punished (like Thyestes) by having his son, the product of the incest, served up to him in a meal. And Fulgentius moralized the lusts of Semiramis, legendary Queen of Assyria, who "flamed with desire for her own son" Ninus, consuming "her dignity as a mother" to become "his bride," the horrors of which story the Italian playwright, Muzio Manfredi, dramatized on the stage in 1593.[9]

But the poet whom everyone read was of course Ovid, who, in his *Heroides* (XI), drew upon the myth of the children of Aeolus. In this legend five pairs of brothers and sisters, apparently not realizing the forbidden nature of their attraction, coupled with each other after the example of their youngest siblings, Macareus and Canace. As a consequence, Canace was forced to commit suicide while the parallel incests, perhaps because the participants enjoyed divine status, went unpunished.[10] The *Metamorphoses* (both in the original and in Golding's famous translation) provided an even more accessible collection of incest myths. Here one could read of Nyctimene's defiling of her father's bed (II.742–745), of Menephron's rape of his mother (VII.492–494), of Byblis's ungovernable lust for her twin brother Caune (she pursued him relentlessly until frustration turned her into a weeping fountain [IX.542–786]), of Myrrha's passion for her father, King Cinyras, from whose union Adonis sprang forth (X.327–588), and of Phaedra's perverse attraction to her stepson Hippolytus and its fatal consequences (XV.550–613).[11]

At one point in Ovid's extraordinarily popular poem Byblis bewails the fate of mortals, who, unlike the gods, are denied the pleasure of incestuous cohabitation. She envies Saturn and Ops, Oceanus and Tethys, Jupiter and Juno, and the children of Aeolus, all of whom (in Golding's words) "matched with theyr [brothers and] susters" without reproach and therefore "are farre in better case than wee" (IX.590–591). A little later Ovid makes Myrrha extend her envy to "dame nature" because that lady embraces within the pale of her sexual tolerance all earthly creatures *except* human beings: how can incest infringe the "bondes of godlynesse" when even beasts enjoy a privilege proscribed to mankind?

> The Hecfer thinkes no shame
> Too beare her father on her backe: The
> Horse beestrydes the same
> Of whom he is the syre: The Gote dooth
> bucke the Kid that hee
> Himself begate: and birdes doo tread the self
> same birdes wee see
> Of whom they hatched were before. In
> happye cace they are
> That may doo so without offence. But mans

>   malicious care
> Hath made a brydle for it self, and spyghtfull
>   lawes restreyne
> The things that nature setteth free.
>   (X. 360–367)

In these passages Ovid visualizes the plight of human sexuality as essentially tragic: humankind is compelled by its very nature to forgo desires that both deities and animals may indulge without restraint but that men and women, uniquely, can pursue only at the cost of their certain destruction.

Incestuous lovers on the Jacobean and Caroline stage sometimes complain in just such Ovidian terms, seeking to justify forbidden longings against the tyranny of the moral law. Thus Arbasces in Beaumont and Fletcher's *A King and No King* can condemn himself for bestial appetite in lusting for his supposed sister Panthea yet wish that he could live uninhibited by the scruples inherent to his humanity:

>   Accursed man,
> Thou bought'st thy reason at too dear a rate,
> For thou hast all thy actions bounded in
> With curious rules when every beast is free.
> What is there that acknowledges a kindred
> But wretched man? Whoever saw the bull
> Fearfully leave the heifer that he lik'd
> Because they had one dam?
>   (IV.iv.131–138)[12]

Giovanni in Ford's *'Tis Pity She's a Whore* tries to rationalize his incestuous desire for Annabella in the opposite way by identifying her, in a perverted kind of Platonism, with deity:

>   Must I not praise
> That beauty which, if framed anew, the gods
> Would make a god of if they had it there,
> And kneel to it, as I do kneel to them?
>   (I.i.20–23)[13]

(This line of reasoning is not far removed from that of King Rasni in Greene and Lodge's *A Looking Glass for London and England* [1590], who tries to justify his marriage to a sister Remilia by citing the incest of Jupiter and Juno as a precedent [I.i.87–91].) Ford's confused young man, however, also tries to rationalize his obsession on grounds of the natural affinity between *human* siblings:

> Say that we had one father, say one womb
> (Curse to my joys!) gave both us life and birth;
> Are we not therefore each to other bound
> So much the more by nature? by the links

> Of blood, of reason? nay, if you will have 't,
> Even of religion, to be ever one,
> One soul, one flesh, one love, one heart, one *all*?
> (I.i.28–34)

And again: "Nearness in birth or blood doth but persuade / A nearer nearness of affection" (I.ii.239–240).

Giovanni's argument from nature is deliberate and quasi-logical, unlike the attitude of Aeolus' sons and daughters who, failing to understand "that incest among humans was displeasing to the gods," as Robert Graves phrases it, "innocently paired off . . . as husbands and wives." But the naïve lovers of Montemayor's incest story in *Diana* take a line similar to that of Ford's ardent youth by suggesting that their supposed kinship actually accounts for the erotic attraction that they feel toward each other:

> But tel me now (I pray thee) what certaintie hast thou, that we are brother and sister? No other (saide she) then of the great love I beare thee. . . . And if we were not brother and sister (saide I) wouldest thou then love me so much as thou dost? . . . I understand thee not said she, but (me thinkes) (being brother and sister) it binds us to love one another naturally.[14]

Classical literature and myth, together with their later redactions, then, provided ample precedent for the ambivalent attitude toward incest in the drama of Shakespeare's age—precedents that not only reinforced the Judeo-Christian horror of sexual relationships within the family but that also offered sympathy for persons who violated, or wished to violate, the taboo.

In a sizable number of Renaissance plays, usually comic or tragicomic, the plot turns on the amorous attraction of supposed brothers and sisters who cannot marry until the fact that they are congenitally unrelated emerges surprisingly at the denouement; or, alternatively, on the obverse of this pattern—that is, on love affairs between apparently unrelated persons whose incestuous marriages are prevented almost at the steps of the altar by a revelation of their true parentage. In the latter situation, theatrical sleight of hand typically permits the threatened incests to be converted into nuptial realignments that satisfy the requirements of social respectability and romantic fulfillment at the same time.[15] The dramas of averted incest include titles as diverse as Lyly's *Mother Bombie*, Beaumont and Fletcher's *A King and No King*, Middleton's *No Wit, No Help Like a Woman's*, Shirley's *The Coronation* and *The Court Secret*, Randolph's *The Jealous Lovers*, and Carlell's *The Deserving Favorite*. Plays that involve the incest-mistaken identity nexus more tangentially or obliquely are Jonson's *The Case Is Altered*, Fletcher's *Women Pleased*, Massinger's *The Guardian*, and Shirley's *The Opportunity*. An interesting reversal of the pattern of incest avoidance appears in Shirley's *The Gentleman of Venice*, a comedy in which the hidden kinship of two lovers (they are first cousins only) actually makes an otherwise unacceptable marriage possible; for when the noble-spirited and gently-spoken hero of this play (a gardener named Giovanni) turns out to be the Duke's son (by reason of babies secretly exchanged in their cradles), he now qualifies for the hand of a royal lady. Giovanni's instinctive drift toward a blood relation, despite her initial spurning of him as a mere commoner, only proves that heredity is a better guide to the discovery of a fitting spouse than humility, however crucial the latter may in fact have been. What we may call a permissible incest—that is, marriage that threatens but never actually violates the carefully drawn boundaries of illicit consanguinity—becomes meritorious in Shirley's play and validates the time-honored aristocratic and romantic principle that blood will tell.

III

The wide appeal of plots that connect the threat or magnetic pull of incest with confusions of identity would seem to reflect a deep insecurity in upper-class families of the period about genetic origin and lineage. Sons and daughters of more prominent families were often farmed out to wet nurses in their infancy and thereby deprived as children of parental nurture and affection. The literary cliché, anciently derived from romance tradition, of the midwife or wet nurse who substitutes her own child or that of a confidante for that of her master (usually out of political or economic motives) must have raised in the minds of some playgoers the specter of illegitimacy, if it did not stimulate fantasies of being elevated suddenly to wealth and noble rank.

Lawrence Stone in his revealing study of the emotional and sexual climate of the family in Renaissance England describes a number of conditions that support the hypothesis that links the desire for closer intimacy with uneasiness about identity. Although respect for patriarchal authority was strongly enforced, little in Elizabethan upper-class houses sustained close affectional ties within the nucleus. Personal relationships between husbands and wives, between parents and children, and between siblings of the same sex tended to be cool if not strife-ridden and acrimonious. The number of bastard children who figure in Elizabethan and Stuart plays is partly a reflection of the numerous adulteries that constantly disrupted family harmony, particularly at the upper and lower ends of the social spectrum. Church canons forbidding the divorce of unhappily wedded partners undoubtedly encouraged sexual infidelity, and indeed the discovery of incest or arguments about too close a genealogical affinity could be among the few valid excuses for dissolving a marriage. Blood or family ties, then, were likely to be regarded as having immense political and social importance, even as their emotional implications might either threaten or subversively excite. As Stone puts it, "marriage meant not so much intimate association with an individual as entry into a new world of the spouse's relatives, uncles, nephews and distant cousins. . . . Kinship was an institution whose purpose was the mutual economic, social and psychological advancement of the group. . . ."[16]

The emotional or psychological gratification of individuals enjoyed very low priority and was not considered to be a rational objective of marriage.

Primogeniture tended to stir up animosities between the heir to an estate and his younger brothers, whose prospects for a secure future would be uncertain at best, unless, of course, the heir should meet with some untimely (and perhaps secretly desired) misfortune. Rivalry among marriageable daughters over which of them should be auctioned off first to a rich or influential spouse, and with how generous a dowry, could be as intense as that between brothers. Shakespeare gives us some sense of the all too common malaise between siblings in *The Taming of the Shrew*, *As You Like It*, and *King Lear*, whereas Webster's two great tragedies raise hostility between brothers and between brothers and sisters to the level of criminal pathology.

George Wilkins's *The Miseries of Enforced Marriage* (1607), a play based to some extent on historical persons, presents a veritable anthology of strained family situations—a young man compelled by his autocratic guardian to desert his true love and marry a girl for whom he has no feeling, a sister whose chief motive for marriage is the desire to relieve the poverty of her brothers, a son who is glad to learn of his father's death, and the intense jealousy of deprived younger brothers, directed against an elder spendthrift one. Heywood and Rowley's domestic drama, *Fortune by Land and Sea* (ca. 1607–09) also reflects a significant demystification of the family. Here Philip Harding is reduced to menial status in his own household by a tyrannical father (who intends to disinherit him) for presuming, for romantic reasons, to marry a girl of no means, while two hateful younger sons, spoiled, irresponsible, and grasping, despise their older brother and are finally punished for their arrogance by being made to depend upon him totally, once he has come into the family estate. In a more satiric vein, city comedies by Jonson (such as *Volpone* and *Epicoene*) and by Middleton (such as *The Family of Love*, *A Trick to Catch the Old One*, and *A Chaste Maid in Cheapside*) also depict family life as characterized by suspicion, jealousy, greed, fragmentation, and sexual infidelity. Given the predictable tensions between siblings of the same sex and between offspring and parents who often forced them into marital alliances for nakedly unromantic purposes, it is hardly unlikely that many children grew up with the simultaneous fear of, and unsatisfied need for, greater intimacy with their closest kin.

Since so many of the incestuous or would-be incestuous relationships in Elizabethan drama concern involvements between brothers and sisters, it is interesting to notice in Stone's analysis the relative absence of reasons to assume coolness or affectional distance between sons and daughters of the same household. It is probably more than mere coincidence, for instance, that the affection of the two brother-and-sister pairs in *Fortune by Land and Sea* (Susan Forrest and young Forrest, Anne Harding and her brother, a merchant) is as warm as any in the play—a play, as has been pointed out, that makes a maltreated elder son the brunt of ill feeling from both his father and his younger brothers. Indeed, as Stone suggests, "the brother-sister relationship" in the sixteenth and seventeenth centuries, simply because it would be comparatively untainted by marital and economic pressures, may often have been "the closest in the family."[17] If this was true, the social context may throw light upon the darkly troubled love-hatred of characters like Vittoria and Flamineo in *The White Devil* or of Duke Ferdinand and the title figure of *The Duchess of Malfi* with its strong infusion of fraternal sadomasochism and undertow of carnal attraction. Frank Whigham even goes so far as to interpret Ferdinand's incestuous impulse toward his sister, because it is coupled with his contempt for the baseness of her alliance to a mere servant, as a radical sexualization of the threatened aristocrat's fear of the contamination of his class; in this reading, a smotheringly close attraction to a sister becomes a symbol of the need to insist upon endogamy within a rigidly defined elite—"a *social posture*, of hysterical compensation—a desperate expression of the desire to evade degrading association with inferiors."[18]

As for the numerous dramatic plots that feature lovers who do not know that they are brother and sister, it is tempting to regard these as symbolic expressions of an unconscious desire for closer emotional affinity within families that tend to deny or deprecate such intimacies. Such plays usually awaken their lovers to a fresh or heightened sense of identity through a happy ending that discloses their true parentage, while releasing them to marry in a way that unites the satisfactions of intimacy with economic, political, and class approval—that is, with the values of a limited exogamy on which family stability and social enhancement are taken to depend. Such plays, in other words, may be interpreted as gratifying their audiences through a kind of psycho-sociological wish-fulfillment by means of the manipulations of a theatrical technique that capitalizes on both predicatability and surprise.

Dramatists sometimes complicate our responses to the more tragic examples of incestuous involvement on the stage by silhouetting the forbidden attraction against a backdrop of worldliness, vulgarity, cynicism, or brutality. In *Women Beware Women*, for instance, Middleton forces us to assess Isabella's involvement in a sexual liason with Hippolito (her uncle) by contrasting it with the most repellent of alternatives—forced marriage to the rich but imbecilic Ward, whom the reluctant bride "loathe[s] . . . more than beauty can hate death / Or age, her spiteful neighbour" (II.i.84-85).[19] Isabella must be trotted out for inspection by her repulsive and witless bridegroom like a brood mare at Smithfield Market to have her "good parts" (III.iii.5)—her hair, her eyes, her nose, her teeth, her breasts, her voice, her bum, her posture—put on public display for the consideration of the prospective wife-shopper. This degrading commercial ritual makes the competing union between uncle and niece almost desirable by comparison, and, in fact, Middleton uses the contrast to dramatize a pattern of emotional displacement that tends to equate incest with the only psycho-sexual fulfillment available to lovers in the play.

Guardiano, uncle to the Ward and cynical promoter of the unsuitable marriage, describes Isabella's close companionship with Hippolito before he pushes his idiot nephew in her direction:

> *Guardiano.* take one mark more:
> Thou shalt ne'er find her hand out of her uncle's,

>   Or else his out of hers, if she be near him.
>   The love of kindred never yet stuck closer
>   Than theirs to one another; he that weds her
>   Marries her uncle's heart too.
>   *Ward.*   Say you so, sir,
>   Then I'll be asked i' th' church to both of them.
>   (III.iii.14–20)

And, in fact, Isabella's father—a man who thinks of his daughter as a mere breeding machine—has commented already on the special intimacy between his brother and her:

>   Look out her uncle, and y' are sure of her.
>   Those two are ne'er asunder; they've been heard
>   In argument [*i.e.*, conversation] at midnight, moonshine nights
>   Are noondays with them: they walk out their sleeps,
>   Or rather at those hours appear like those
>   That walk in 'em, for so they did to me.
>   Look you, I told you truth; they're like a chain:
>   Draw but one link, all follows.
>   (I.ii.62–69)

To which Guardiano responds with ironic blindness: "Oh affinity . . . / 'Tis work clean wrought, for there's no lust, but love in 't, / And that abundantly . . ." (I.ii.69-72).

In her distress at being paired off lovelessly with a mental defective, Isabella, naturally enough, turns to Hippolito, her "best friend" (I.ii.186), who loves her "dearlier than an uncle can," "As a man loves his wife" (I.ii.211–217). Hippolito, for all the "black lust" (IV.ii.66) of his incestuous behavior and, later, his murderous mission against Leantio (the antihero of the coördinate plot), at least possesses intelligence; and when the retarded Ward wants a demonstration of Isabella's dancing (Middleton gives the dancing distinctly sexual overtones), it is symbolically her uncle rather than the oafish fiancé who takes her as partner on the floor. Afterwards, when the Ward himself attempts to dance with his would-be wife, the stage direction tells us that "*he ridiculously imitates Hippolito*" (III.iii.227). The sexual displacement is dramatized in terms of a social ritual at once comic and sinister.

But Middleton complicates responses still further, as Dodson has argued,[20] by suggesting that Livia, the sophisticated, amoral worldling of the tragedy, diverts her potentially incestuous affinity for her brother by subconsciously displacing it upon her niece. Early in the play she speaks to Hippolito in language of suspiciously unique ardor:

> *Livia.* My best and dearest brother, I could dwell here;
>   There is not such another seat on earth
>   Where all good parts better express themselves.
> *Hippolito.* You'll make me blush anon.
> *Livia.*   . . . thou art all a feast,
>   And she that has thee a most happy guest.
>   Prithee cheer up thy niece with special counsel.
>   (I.ii.144–151)

The quasi-erotic attraction of sister to brother expresses itself as a smoothing of the way for his seduction of his more youthful and naïve female relation, a girl whom they both call niece.

Glossing over Hippolito's moral scruples as of no true importance compared to the gratification of his physical desire, Livia relieves his "fearful" and guilty "grief" (II.i.20) by arranging to cover the incest with the lie (to Isabella) that the younger woman is not in fact related to him at all:

>   'tis but a hazarding
> Of grace and virtue, and I can bring forth
> As pleasant fruits as sensuality wishes
> In all her teeming longings. This I can do.
> . . .
> You are not the first, brother, has attempted
> Things more forbidden than this seems to be.
>   (II.i.29–47)

Then, having dealt with her half-acknowledged desire for her brother by rechanneling it into a sexual union of uncle and niece, Livia supplies her own carnal needs by taking on as a surrogate the virile young bourgeois, Leantio, whose adulterous wife Bianca has just displaced him by allowing herself, through naïve entrapment, to become the mistress of a duke. *Women Beware Women*, as its title subtly implies, articulates a tangle of sexual and emotional substitutions in which incest becomes a significant factor in the symbolism. The tragedy explores kinship in its biological, moral, social, and psycho-sexual dimensions, making brilliant dramatic capital out of their elaborate, subtle, and ironic cross-relations.

The figure of the coarse and brutal husband with whom a more refined woman is forced to cohabit appears in two of Ford's major plays. In both cases incest becomes part of the contrastive structure. In *'Tis Pity She's a Whore* the neurotic, sensitive, and intellectually gifted student Giovanni is set off, in his hothouse obsession for his sister Annabella, against a trio of suitors, each of them less attractive than he—Grimaldi (the cowardly cutthroat who ambushes rivals in the dark), Bergetto (a parcel of stupidity cut from the same cloth as Middleton's Ward), and Soranzo (the hypocritical philanderer whom Annabella actually marries to conceal the shame of her brother's having made her pregnant). Ford portrays Soranzo as a more acceptable spouse for Annabella than his two rivals, but after Soranzo discovers that his wife is with child, he becomes a jealous monster of the most rebarbative sort, physically abusing her onstage as a "notable harlot," raging at her "hot itch and plurisy of lust" (IV.iii.4–8), and threatening (in an ironic prolepsis of Giovanni's incestuous sacrifice) to "rip up [her] heart" so that he may discover the identity of "the prodigious lecher" who has supplanted him and "Tear" him "joint by joint" (IV.iii.53–55) with his teeth. Ultimately, of course, Giovanni exceeds even Soranzo's monstrosity when, having turned madman, he ritually murders his sister to preserve the perverted exclusiveness of their special and (to him) inviolable love; but until the tragic climax, Ford treats the incestuous relationship with considerable sympathy—not as a bestial abomination but as a tragic but humanly comprehensible error, in comparison with which arranged and affectionless marriages are crude, destructive, and even barbaric.

The Broken Heart, at one point, also dramatizes the same contrast between a sensitive brother-sister intimacy and the "torture" and "barbarous thraldom" (I.i.49–54)[21] of the lady's marriage to an insanely jealous, superannuated dotard. Bassanes, the suspicious old man who keeps his beautiful wife under lock and key, has virtually "buried" Penthea in her own "bride-bed" (II.ii.38). Ironically, it is the brother Ithocles who has unnaturally condemned his sister to this living hell, but, in a private reunion with her that underscores the mysterious emotional affinity of long-separated twins, the brother repents his former cruelty and shares with Penthea the secret of his own love for the Princess Calantha, which he dares not communicate even to his closest friend or to the lady herself.

Ford's dialogue verges on the erotic, mingling Ithocles' "languishing affections" (III.ii.53), that is, his remorse for his wrecking of Penthea's love life, his joy at being reunited with her, and his need to relieve a bottled-up desire for Calantha by confessing it to the sole confidante who may serve immediately as a surrogate object of devotion and, later on, as an intercessor or proxy wooer:

> *Ithocles.* Sit nearer, sister, to me; nearer yet.
> We had one father, in one womb took life,
> Were brought up twins together, yet have lived
> At distance like two strangers. I could wish
> That the first pillow whereon I was cradled
> Had proved to me a grave.
> *Penthea.*   You had been happy.
> Then had you never known that sin of life
> Which blots all following glories with a vengeance,
> For forfeiting the last will of the dead,
> From whom you had you being.
> *Ithocles.*   Sad Penthea,
> Thou canst not be too cruel. My rash spleen
> Hath with a violent hand plucked from thy bosom
> A lover-blest heart, to grind it into dust;
> For which mine's now a-breaking.
> . . .
> *Penthea.*   Pray kill me.

> Rid me from living with a jealous husband.
> Then we will join in friendship, be again
> Brother and sister.
>   (III.ii.33–67)

It is scarcely astonishing that the brutish Bassanes, excluded from this exquisite, quasi-amorous closeness, breaks in upon it with a drawn dagger, wildly accusing his wife of "bed-sports" and the "swine-security of bestial incest" (III.ii.135–150). Bassanes' rage is almost comic in its violence—a stage illustration of what Burton describes in *The Anatomy of Melancholy* under the category of postnuptial love melancholia. Prominent among the symptoms of such husbandly jealousy is the "suspecting not strangers only, but brothers and sisters, father and mother, nearest and dearest friends."[22] Soranzo in *'Tis Pity* and Bassanes in *The Broken Heart* both approach the status of Burtonian caricature in their most irrational moments; hence, in context, they make intimacies between brother and sister, whether overtly incestuous or not, seem comparatively refined and idealistic. In any case Ford's Annabella and Penthea, as well as Middleton's Isabella—each one a victim of enforced marriage—are all complex women and suffer the indignity of being paired with gross, stupid, or unfeeling men who treat them as mere goods and chattels. Such women remind us of Penelope Devereux, the "Stella" of Sidney's sonnets, who was married off in youth to the intellectually limited Baron Rich (an unattractive peer whose vast wealth made a pun of his name). This unhappy match proved so unpalatable that the couple soon separated; and it is an index of the degree to which respectable society must have sympathized with her plight that Lady Rich was permitted to live in open adultery with Charles Blount, Lord Mountjoy, whose several children she bore. It is also relevant to note that throughout her marital difficulties she remained especially close to her brother, the Earl of Essex, at whose house in the Strand she was often resident. Lady Rich's admirer, Sir Philip Sidney, as his dedication of the *Arcadia* shows, was himself particularly fond of his sister Mary; the gossip-mongering John Aubrey in his *Brief Lives* even passes on the report of certain "old Gentlemen" that "there was so great love between" them that "they lay together, and it was thought the first Philip Earle of Pembroke was begot by him, but he inherited not the witt of either brother or sister."[23]

IV

If the domestic and marital climate of Renaissance England made for ambivalent attitudes toward incest, both stimulating and repressing it by turns, the political and theological debates of the period only confused matters further. Indeed we may speculate whether psychic conflicts that surfaced or half-surfaced within the home would not inevitably be mirrored, in some manifestation or other, at the more public levels of church and state. With the Reformation came considerable relaxation of the medieval canons prohibiting marriage between distant cousins and between persons related ecclesiastically such as godparents and godchildren. In 1563 Matthew Parker, Elizabeth's Archbishop of Canterbury, issued a table reducing to thirty the relationships (counting the male and female equivalents together) that fell within the proscribed degrees of kindred and affinity. By 1603 these had become canonical in ecclesiastical law, and modern reprints of the Anglican Prayer Book of 1662, still in official use in England, often append a table of twenty-five prohibited relationships along with the Thirty-nine Articles. It was not until 1907 that Parliament repealed the old law prohibiting marriage between brothers and sisters-in-law, and indeed the history of proscribed degrees in matrimony is forbiddingly labyrinthine. Not surprisingly, there was much disagreement and uncertainty in the sixteenth century on the subject as well as conflict on certain points between ecclesiastical and civil law.[24]

In any event, conservative views continued to engage more liberal ones throughout the Tudor and early Stuart reigns. Marriages within the same family for purposes of dynastic expansion and aggrandizement were frequently sought and solemnized, usually requiring a papal or archiepiscopal dispensation. Richard III in Shakespeare's play attempts unsuccessfully to marry his niece, Elizabeth of York, with a view to legitimating his tenure of the crown and coöpting possible opposition.[25] The marriage that takes place instead between Elizabeth and Henry Tudor is portrayed as uniting at long last the white rose with the red. The symbolic, propagandistic, and political desirability of such a union is obvious in the play, but Shakespeare makes little of the actual degrees of kindred and affinity between the new King and Queen (they descended in different branches from a common ancestor—Catherine Swynford, third wife of John of Gaunt) and ignores the historical fact that special permission from the Pope was required to legalize their nuptials.[26]

In *Hamlet* the hasty marriage between Hamlet's uncle and his mother obviously disgusts the young Prince of Denmark, shaking his faith in human nature to its core; yet what Hamlet and his father's ghost choose to regard as the blackest of sexual transgressions seems to occasion no great objection in Denmark generally. Hamlet's sardonic comment on his unwelcome sonship to the usurper of his father's throne, "A little more than kin, and less than kind" (I.ii.65), encapsulates a complex irony, for although the speaker puns bitterly on "kind," implying that the new marriage shows his uncle to have acted both cruelly and against nature, he unintentionally points up the isolated state of his own indignation. And one effect of the remark, as Sir Thomas Hanmer noted in the eighteenth century, is simply to call attention, through the use of a proverb, to a relationship "so confused and blended that it was hard to define."[27] Horatio, Hamlet's ally, expresses no open disapproval, and even the couple themselves feel minimal guilt. Of course the King and Queen must put as good a face as possible on their marriage in public, but, privately also, they are remarkably untroubled by bad conscience. Claudius in his agonized prayer soliloquy is almost wholly concerned with the murder of his brother, not incest, and Hamlet has to work very hard to bring his mother to a sense of sexual sin; even then, we cannot be sure that her conversion is permanent.[28] One reason for the apparently wide acceptance of the new marriage may be territorial, for Claudius refers to Gertrude in his opening speech as "Th' imperial jointress to this warlike state" (I.ii.9). That is to say, the title may imply not only that the Queen holds authority coextensively with her husband but that she has also brought a valuable jointure to the Danish throne—probably lands or a strategically important estate that would make the kingdom politically, economically, or militarily stronger.

But, of course, royal or noble marriages might be contracted for precisely the opposite reason—that is, because the parties were *not* blood relations. One of the most convincing explanations that anthropology has yet advanced for an insistence on exogamy is not the fear of genetic malformations (as some still suppose) but rather the strongly felt imperative to strengthen the tribe through family ties to a political and economic power base beyond itself. The pattern survives in Shakespeare. When Henry V marries Katherine of Valois at the end of the second tetralogy, he symbolically strengthens England by absorbing what has now become a foreign culture and hostile territory into the national blood stream. Katherine asks, "Is it possible dat I sould love de ennemie of France?" And Henry responds, "I love France so well that I will not part with a village of it. I will have it all mine. And, Kate, when France is mine and I am yours, then yours is France and you are mine" (*Henry V*, V.ii.170–177). The annexation of France by a Plantagenet king who quarters his arms with the *fleur de lys*, yet speaks but a few syllables of broken French, neatly culminates in a dynastic marriage to a partner who is paradoxically both native and foreign—in a kind of geopolitical incest in which England weds her closest European sibling and historic enemy at a single stroke.

Incest, then, whether literal or symbolic, might be regarded as relatively beneficial or repugnant depending on particular circumstances. At all events, among the upper classes, intrafamilial intercourse and marriage often seem to have been officially deplored but covertly tolerated or at least lightly punished.[29] At the peasant level, crowded rural dwellings probably made it difficult to prevent, despite the strenuous prohibitions of the church; but the argument against incest was economic as well as moral: if sexual attachment to close relations was dangerous to the soul, it was also injurious to the social fabric by concentrating too much wealth within a single family instead of spreading and diffusing it via the institution of exogamous wedlock. Dramatists and literary artists, if they were historically cognizant in a deliberate way, tended, of course, to look to the aristocracy for precedents and examples.

Elizabethans familiar with their recent past could hardly be unaware of how centrally the question of incest had dominated the reign of Henry VIII. Elizabeth's father, like Shakespeare's Claudius, had married his brother's widow when he came to the throne, and the usual papal dispensation had been obtained to allow the impediment of affinity to be set aside. But the threat of incest here was less shocking than in *Hamlet* because Catherine of Aragon (unlike Gertrude) had never consummated her marriage to Prince Arthur (Henry's older brother) and consequently (again unlike Gertrude) was childless.[30] Levirate marriage (the union of a brother's widow with her brother-in-law for the purpose of having children and thus preventing the extinction of a family) had ancient biblical sanction. Historians have often assumed that Henry's later "scruples" about the incestuous nature of his first marriage derived cynically from political necessity—his need to produce a male heir—and that this, in turn, impelled him to reject Catherine for Anne Boleyn, a spouse who seemed to promise greater fertility. The psychoanalytic historian, J. C. Flügel, has argued, however, that a simultaneous fear of, and attraction to, incestuous situations, whether symbolic or actual, tended to dominate Henry's sexual and marital life from start to finish.

Flügel points out that Henry's parents (Henry VII and Elizabeth of York) were technically incestuous, as noted already, and circumvented the impediment of kindred and affinity only through a papal exemption; that Henry VIII created a second symbolic incest after his marriage to Catherine by entering upon an affair with Mary Boleyn, the elder sister of the woman who was to become his second queen; that when the King executed Anne for treasonable adultery, the charges included the allegation that she had slept with her brother, Lord Rochford; that Henry's third marriage to Jane Seymour (the mother of Edward VI) involved still another breach of the affinity principle—affinity in the third degree—thus requiring a dispensation from Archbishop Cranmer; that Henry had approached Jane through her brother, Sir Edward Seymour, who acted as a co-participant in the courting process; that after Jane's death, Henry considered but rejected a marriage to Mary of Guise, who was already affianced to Henry's nephew, James V of Scotland; that Catherine Howard, Henry's fifth queen, was a first cousin of Anne Boleyn and therefore, technically, a relative; that Henry, in order to marry his sixth wife, had forced Catherine Parr to break off an engagement to his own brother-in-law, Sir Thomas Seymour, and so forth. In Flügel's analysis, Henry VIII's deep sexual conflicts—his unconscious wish to be opposed by, and to overcome, a sexual rival, his impulse toward, and horror of, incest, his irrational desire for a lover at once sexually experienced and chaste—were all interconnected and sprang, very likely, from the same source—a deeply imbedded Oedipal pattern of jealousy for the father and sexual attraction to the mother.[31]

Renaissance dramatists could hardly have known the more intimate details of a king's love life, let alone have rationalized them according to the Freudian categories of Flügel, although a play such as *The Duchess of Malfi*, with its dark mixture of sexual attraction and sadistic jealousy in Ferdinand, suggests a pattern not wholly foreign to what Flügel describes in Henry VIII. But playwrights would certainly know that Henry's several marriages had been notorious for the sexual and moral controversies they had unleashed and for the political and dynastic consequences, both good and bad, that had flowed from them. Perhaps they reasoned that, but for Henry's scruples about incest, Gloriana would never have ruled England at all. Or, if they were inclined to defend the incestuous necessities of nuptial politics within the royal family, they might nevertheless thrill to sensational crimes of incest emanating from a depraved country like Italy. Barnabe Barnes, for instance, in *The Devil's*

Charter (1607), had dramatized the most lurid scandals of the Borgias, including Pope Alexander VI's copulation with Lucrezia (his own daughter) and her lustful affair with her brother Cesare (a cardinal turned soldier). Among Alexander's motives, of course, as the sources make clear, was family pride (one thinks again of Webster's Ferdinand) and the consolidation of power (as in the case of Richard III's marital strategies). The infamous history of Count Cenci, who had seduced his daughter Beatrice and then had been murdered at her behest, also fed the appetite for sensational horror, as did the story of Niccolo III, Marquess of Ferrara, who executed his wife and son on the same day for engaging in a secret love affair. This story, as already explained (see note 3 [B] below), probably influenced *The Revenger's Tragedy*. Alessandro de Medici, another notorious lecher, attempted to seduce the aunt (or, in some versions, the sister) of his cousin Lorenzino, who then had him stabbed to death in the bedchamber where the assignation was to have taken place; a version of these well-known incidents was put on the stage by Shirley in *The Traitor* (1631), although Shirley circumvented the incest by removing the blood relationship between the lady and the seducer. Although Dante's *Divine Comedy* would have to wait until the eighteenth century for an English translation, many Renaissance readers and poets would know of the famous incestuous affair (evoked with consummate pathos in Canto V of *The Inferno*) between Francesca da Rimini and Paolo, the handsome brother of her physically deformed husband Gianciotto, son of Malatesta da Verrucchio. Here again forced marriage had cut athwart sexual romance with tragic consequences, for the ugly brother, surprising the illicit lovers at a moment of indiscretion, stabbed them both to death in 1285. Closer to home was the scandal of Anne Lake, Lady Roos, who, quarreling with her husband, slandered the Countess of Exeter by charging her with "adulterie, incest, murther, poison and such like peccadillos"; at the trial in 1619 Lady Roos was exposed as a liar, and later, according to a report by John Chamberlain, accused (in the confession of an accomplice to her libel) of having herself had incestuous relations with her brother, Sir Arthur Lake.[32]

Henry VIII's "great matter," his attempt to secure from Rome an annulment of his marriage to Catherine of Aragon, stimulated a great deal of theological discussion not only in England but on the continent. Learned churchmen were enlisted by all parties to the debate, and scholarship was ransacked for precedents.[33] The issue was thorny because scriptural exegetes could point to open contradictions and discrepancies in the Bible. The proof text on which Henry founded his case was Leviticus, which in two different places explicitly forbids marriage to a sister-in-law: "if a man shall take his brother's wife, it is an unclean thing: he hath uncovered his brother's nakedness; they shall be childless" (Leviticus 20:21; see also 18:16). The reasoning here apparently is that, since man and wife are one flesh, copulation with one's sister-in-law is tantamount to copulating with one's brother. But Catherine's supporters and defenders cited Deuteronomy 25:5, a passage that specifically enjoins a husband's brother to marry his widow, *if* there have been no children (as was of course the case with Prince Arthur and Catherine).[34] It goes without saying that the church, on both Levitican and Pauline authority (see Leviticus 18:6–30 and 1 Corinthians 5:1–5), had anciently condemned more direct forms of incest—those involving consanguinity rather than mere affinity. This they associated with witches and demons as so self-evidently repugnant to the word of God that no intellectual or theological argument need be advanced against it. Incest prohibition, in effect, became the unequivocal answer to which it was unthinkable even to frame the question. In the Second Book of Samuel (13), for instance, Amnon's rape of his half-sister Tamar (daughter of King David) and the revenge taken by Absalom (a third of David's children) offered a classic example of what tragic results might flow from incestuous passion. Peele, indeed, had given this "kindlesse love" (l. 295) and "heinous lust" (l. 376) dramatic expression in *David and Bethsabe* (1587).[35] King Herod's marriage (after a divorce) to Herodias, the wife of his half-brother Philip, presented another tragic instance of incest (see Matthew 14:3–12; Mark 6:17–29; Luke 3:19–20), for John the Baptist's rebuke of the immoral union had been a putative cause of his decapitation, as the official book of *Homilies* suggests.[36]

Still, for the curious or thoughtful, biblical riddles and problems remained. The children of Adam and Eve obviously had no choice but to commit incest in order to propagate the human race, and, in a sense, Eve was the daughter (or sister) of Adam, having come from his rib. In Genesis 19, the daughters of Lot had tricked their father through drunkenness into engendering Moab and Benammi, the progenitors of two important tribes (the Moabites and Ammonites).[37] And Sarah was the half-sister of her husband, the revered Abraham. Closer to Henry VIII's situation was the case of Judah's three sons (Er, Onan, and Shelah) in Genesis 38, each of whom in succession married, or was to marry, Tamar in what would seem to be at least a partial vindication of the Deuteronomic text; but the matter was further complicated by the fact that Tamar went on to conceive twins by Judah himself, her father-in-law. Also, according to some interpreters of the early church, the half-brothers Heli and Jacob married the same woman in turn—a woman who became the mother of St. Joseph (see Matthew 1:16; Luke 3:23).[38] In the Book of Ruth the title figure, a widow, took to husband Boaz, a kinsman of her deceased spouse Mahlon (Ruth 4:10–13). And, in addition, there was the puzzle in Luke's gospel of Christ's being questioned by the Sadducees as to which of seven brothers who married the same woman in succession would be acknowledged in heaven as her true husband (Luke 20:27–36).

By and large, the exegetical arguments for the validity of Henry's marriage to Catherine were weightier than those against (Shakespeare in *Henry VIII* scrupulously avoids taking clear sides in the debate, making the King refer cloudily to "many maz'd considerings" [II.iv.183]), but, as Roland Frye shows, the cultural revulsion against all incests in principle persisted nevertheless, and the monarch's guilty feelings and dynastic needs had the effect of agitating the ecclesiastical waters turbidly. Suffice it to say, then, that the dramatists and writers of the period were composing in an intellectual, cultural, and political milieu that not only raised the subject of incest to unusual prominence but that also nurtured contrary and discrepant attitudes towards it. Whether the imagined experience of incestuous attraction excited or repelled them—and often it seems to have done both—literary practitioners found the topic a useful vehicle for exploring themes and ideas central to the moral and psychological concerns of their art.

V

One of Marguerite of Navarre's tales from the *Heptameron*, englished as early as 1597, illustrates the special potency of incest as a fictional motif—a potency that would extend perhaps even more saliently to the drama. And, given the moralistic tendency of most sixteenth-century fiction, we are astonished to read at the conclusion, apropos of the incestuous lovers: "Never was there such love between husband and wife, never were a husband and wife so close. For she was his daughter, his sister, his wife. And he was her father, brother and husband. They endured for ever in this great love" (p. 321).[39] Marguerite's Novella Thirty tells of a youthful widow whose devotion to her dead husband and concern for her small son cause her to become a religious recluse. She vows never to remarry and cannot even attend a wedding or hear a church organ without suffering pangs of conscience. Her motive for this rigidity of life is to avoid any situation that might lead to sexual temptation and hence to sin. When her son reaches adolescence, he becomes sexually interested in his mother's maidservant, who then complains to her mistress about the boy's improper advances. The mother, who distrusts the report of her son's carnal behavior, decides to test it by having the maidservant arrange a tryst with the lad and then substituting herself in the bed. Intending to punish the boy if he should show any sign of lust, the mother, to her surprise, becomes sexually aroused herself. As the narrator phrases it,

> so fragile was her nature, that her anger turned to pleasure, a pleasure so abominable, that she forgot she was a mother. Even as the dammed-up torrent flows more impetuously than the freely flowing stream, so it was with this poor lady whose pride and honour had lain in the restraints she had imposed upon her own body. No sooner had she set foot on the first rung down the ladder of her chastity, than she found herself suddenly swept away to the bottom.
>
> (p. 318)

Without her son's ever realizing that he has slept with his own mother, she conceives a child by him, for which sin her conscience torments her to the end of her days. The didactic emphasis of this ironic incest falls on the mother's spiritual pride and, by implication, on the unnatural ferocity with which she has repressed healthy and normal instincts: to quote Marguerite, "instead of humbling herself and recognizing how impossible it is for our flesh to do otherwise than sin unless we have God's help, she tried . . . through her own prudence, to avoid future evil" (p. 318).

Fearing further intimacy with her son, the mother sends him away next morning for military training without even saying goodbye, then conceals her pregnancy by visiting a "bastard brother" (p. 319) who lives far away—the only person in whom she feels she can confide. When the child (a daughter) is born, the midwife is told that the mother is the bastard brother's wife, so that a second symbolic incest is employed to clothe the first in the garb of respectability. The guilty mother hides the shameful evidence of coitus with her son by masquerading as the wife of a man who is actually her half-brother. After giving birth, the mother returns home to live more austerely than ever, disciplining herself by fasts and other devotional rigors, while the baby girl is farmed out to a wet nurse by her supposed father, the bastard brother. At the age of puberty, the girl is sent to be reared at court so that her true identity may continue to be hidden, and so that, having no estate of her own, she may be suitably married off to a gentleman of aristocratic station. Meanwhile the son, now grown to manhood, wishes to visit his mother, from whom he has long been absent. She however, still fearing the temptation to incest, imposes the condition that he first be married. The son therefore travels to court where he meets, and unwittingly weds, the girl who is also his sister and daughter. He now intends to bring home the happy bride to meet the woman who has just become her mother-in-law as well as her mother and symbolic grandmother. By satisfying his mother's demand that he marry—a demand intended to forestall incest—the son has in fact embraced the very disaster that his mother had sought so sedulously to avoid.

The marriage of the son-father to his daughter-sister, both parties being ignorant of their consanguinity, completes a mounting progression of three incests in the tale—an escalation of familial entanglements with comic possibilities; but Marguerite's story divides itself neatly between comedy and tragedy by the double nature of its ending. The mother, when she perceives what horror she has wrought, almost dies in guilty despair, but is finally driven to make her confession to a papal legate, who, after consulting "several doctors of theology" (p. 321), enjoins her to reveal nothing to her children but to do secret penance for the rest of her life. The father-brother-husband and his daughter-sister-wife are "very much in love" (p. 321) and live out their days in connubial felicity, while the mother-grandmother-mother-in-law suffers agonies of remorse, withdrawing to weep at the slightest expression of affection between the married pair. Awareness becomes the index of sin. The children are innocent because they committed incest without knowing it, whereas the mother knew what she did in sleeping with her son, and so must endure perpetual grief for the extraordinary consequences. The story accommodates a dual perspective on incestuous love affairs, identifying them with suffering and a kind of spiritual death at the conscious level, yet depicting them also as potentially happy and fulfilling at the deeper stratum of the subconscious.

Marguerite's tale contains in embryo a surprising number of the motifs and ideas that Renaissance dramatists, even if they did not know her narrative, would develop variously in both comic and tragic directions. We may therefore use it as a kind of window through which to view at a distance, as it were, some of the more prominent landmarks of the diverse plays that make up the theatrical skyline of forbidden love.

The bed trick, of course, was hardly to be limited to plots involving physical incest, as Shakespeare's *All's Well That Ends Well* and *Measure for Measure* and Middleton's *The Changeling* remind us; but all three of these plays toy with the ironic intersection of moral and sexual identity in the dark, a theme of which the erotic substitution in Marguerite's tale might seem to be a fitting emblem. Nor should we forget that disturbing, unnatural, or monstrous conjunction as a concept enters these plays in metaphorical and symbolic ways. Thus when the Countess in *All's Well* portrays herself as a surrogate "mother" (I.iii.135) to Helena, her adopted "daughter" (I.iii.150) tries to evade the association, recognizing that her love for Bertram would then amount to incest of a kind: "the Count Rossillion cannot be my brother" (I.iii.152). Against this background the physical union of Bertram and Helena, during which the Count fails to recognize his cohabitant, seems somehow tainted—a troubling compound of the illicit with the chaste and permissible. Also when Claudio in the second Shakespearean comedy begs his sister to save his life at the price of her chastity, Isabella indignantly suggests that the substitution of a sister's maidenhead for a brother's head would be "a kind of incest" (III.i.138). In Middleton's tragedy, too, the horrible coitus between Beatrice and De Flores becomes figuratively consanguineous since his physical ugliness is conceived as a projection or extension of her moral squalor; when she refers to herself in the final scene as the infected "blood" that has been purged from her father for his "better health" (V.iii.150–151),[40] the metaphor also appears to include her carnal partner who holds her wounded body in his arms.

Intimacies between brother and sister, whether physical or other, occur twice in Marguerite's tale—first, between the guardian and the parent, and second, between the children. It would be pointless to list the numerous Elizabethan and Stuart plays in which incest between siblings, whether contemplated or indulged, serves as a means of arousing prurience or horror or becomes the focus of dramatic suspense; Webster's *Duchess of Malfi*, Beaumont and Fletcher's *A King and No King*, Ford's *'Tis Pity She's a Whore*, and Brome's *The Lovesick Court* spring to mind. But it is worth emphasizing that Marguerite treats brother-sister relationships with special attention and sympathy, whether they are sexual or not (the royal authoress herself was famously close to her brother, Francis I), even as the great majority of the playwrights do. The appearance of the bastard brother is also notable, reminding us of sexual noncompliance in a related key. The incestuous liason in *The Revenger's Tragedy* is motivated partly by the resentment of an illegitimate son for his father. Innovatively, however, Tourneur(?) makes this incest between a bastard son and an adulterous stepmother not merely another illustration of courtly depravity but also an agency of vengeance. The lascivious Duke not only dies kissing the poisoned skull of a woman he had tried in vain to seduce but must bear the additional humiliation, as he dies, of watching himself incestuously cuckolded by the illegitimate issue of his own lechery.

The figure of the midwife is linked in Marguerite, as in many of the comedies and tragicomedies, with the falsification of parentage; and additionally, in the French tale, we have the use of the wet nurse and the separation of children from their parent and from each other so that they become unrecognizable when they meet as adults. In the *Heptameron* also, Marguerite makes it clear that choice of a marriage partner is anything but free. The incestuous union between the brother and sister comes about only because the mother of the tale insists on her son's taking a mate before he returns home and because the sister's mentor (the Queen of Navarre), knowing that her charge's suitor is rich, handsome, and of noble birth, in effect instructs her to marry him. As we have seen already, enforced marriage on the stage is typically a form of emotional imprisonment from which incest offers a kind of desperate or illusory escape, whereas in Marguerite, the elders ironically drive the lovers—and drive them happily—into each other's arms.

Still another characteristic of Marguerite's tale that gets reflected obliquely in certain stage dramatizations of incest is the mixture of respect for, and skepticism of, ecclesiastical authority. The female protagonist of Marguerite's narrative unwittingly courts carnal knowledge of her son by imposing upon herself and, by implication, upon him, an exaggerated and unnatural asceticism stemming from misdirected piety; a commentator in the frame story remarks that the heroine of the tale was probably "one of those foolish, vainglorious women who had had her head filled with nonsense by the Franciscans" (p. 322). Nonetheless, it is the papal legate, on the expert advice of theological scholars, who renders the nicely balanced judgment at the end—namely that she has sinned mortally, while her children are adjudged to have done nothing wrong. In this bifocal attitude toward the clergy (the Franciscan order, the legate of the Pope, the doctors of theology) Marguerite adumbrates that commingling of sympathy for incestuous lovers with a genuine revulsion against incest itself that makes plays like Ford's *'Tis Pity* so subtly complex and problematic.

By her stress on the overlapping of roles (a young man who is father, brother, and husband to the same girl, a woman who is at once that same girl's grandmother, mother, and mother-in-law), Marguerite touches upon problems of psychic identity infinitely deeper and more disturbing than those implied by the changeling device and the misidentifications that issue from it. It is true that the son of the story never recognizes his blood kinship to either of his sexual partners; but, apart from our titillation at his ignorance of the truth, the story fascinates us because of its frightening erasure of the definitional boundary lines that traditionally separate members of the same family and thereby confer a kind of security upon them. Plots that dissolve or merge these comforting distinctions of role threaten us with confusion and uncertainty, terrify us with the possibility of absorption into a trackless wilderness of liminality. For a few (Ford's student Giovanni may be a case in point) such an experience might qualify as a harrowingly pleasurable adventure, a Faustian assault upon the unknown; but for most, it equates with death, a crossing to that bourn from which no traveler returns.

One can recognize this matrix of fear, challenge, and the mergence of roles in a play like *Pericles* where Antiochus attempts to maintain his incestuous relationship to his daughter by posing a riddle for prospective suitors to guess—at the risk of their lives, of course, should they fail:

> I am no viper, yet I feed
> On mother's flesh, which did me breed.
> I sought a husband, in which labor
> I found that kindness in a father.
> He's father, son, and husband mild;
> I mother, wife, and yet his child.
> How they may be, and yet in two,
> As you will live, resolve it you.
>   (I.i.65–72)

The solution, of course, is that the daughter feeds on her mother's flesh because she sleeps with her father, who was once married to, and was so one flesh with, her mother. Antiochus is now both father and husband to his daughter-wife, and, in addition—by the same kind of crazy logic that made the woman of Marguerite's story at once a mother and grandmother to the same girl—Antiochus is his own son-in-law because he functions as his daughter's spouse. Conversely, the daughter plays the role of her own mother-in-law by virtue of serving as her father's wife.

At the rhetorical level such superimpositions of role function as elaborate puns, double entendres, or exercises in metaphysical wit, but, considered psychologically, they point toward chaos and death. They also suggest an overloading of the emotional circuits, the burdening of a single relationship with different but highly charged kinds of intensity—in the case of Antiochus, with the paternal and the husbandly, in the case of Marguerite's young man, with the paternal, the brotherly, and the husbandly (although he remains unaware of the first two). This surplus of propinquity, of course, constitutes one of the standard objections to incest. Montaigne, in his essay, "Of Moderation," cites St. Thomas Aquinas as an authority for asserting that genital love within the "forbidden degrees" will necessarily be "immoderate": in the words of Florio's translation, "if the wedlocke, or husband-like affection be sound and perfect, as it ought to be, and also surcharged with that a man oweth to alliance and kindred, there is no doubt, but that surcrease may easily transport a husband beyond the bounds of reason."[41] Criminal madness, extending even to murder, is precisely the result of the incestuous attraction that we observe in Webster's Ferdinand and Ford's Giovanni.

The symbolism of role-confusion and the frustrations and agonies that it can generate reaches a dizzying, even potentially absurd, complexity in Brome's *The Lovesick Court,* where the threat of incest gets entangled with the conflict, familiar from romance tradition, between the competing claims of love and friendship. Through a notably vermiculate plot, the dramatist manages to explore a number of issues implicit in the problem of incest, only a few of which would occur to a reader who considered Marguerite's narrative in isolation. But Brome's play is worth discussing in some detail if only because it shows, as the tale from the *Heptameron* does more simply, how incest can become the emblem for a whole congeries of role and identity puzzles basic to close emotional relationship. Early on, Brome telegraphs a clue that his play is to introduce the theme of incest by making the Delphic oracle announce in riddling fashion that a solution to the central amorous-dynastic conundrum "Requires an *OEdipus* to construe it" (I.ii);[42] but the shadow of illicit sexuality emerges gradually, and we come to recognize its significance only at the denouement.

The Lovesick Court presents supposed twin brothers, Philocles and Philargus, who contend for the hand of the Princess Eudina (and hence for the crown of Thessaly), rather as Palamon and Arcite contend for Emilia in *The Two Noble Kinsmen*. The two young noblemen, believing that they are brothers, love each other as much as they love Eudina (at one point they invoke the myth of Castor and Pollux), while she, in turn, loves both of them with a devotion that will admit of no priority:

> O, ye Gods!
> Why made ye them two persons, and assign'd
> To both but one inseparable mind?
> Or, Why was I mark'd out to be that one,
> That loves and must embrace, or two, or none;
> O my perplexity.
> (I.ii; pp. 105–106)

Although the three figures are shown to waver under pressure, divided loyalty traps each in an emotional impasse. From the lady's point of view, the twin suitors represent the bifurcation of a single identity—one soul, as it were, occupying distinct bodies; and she must either complete herself psychologically by uniting with both or forgo romantic fulfillment altogether. (Shakespeare approaches the same idea in *Twelfth Night*—though with the important difference of separating the siblings by gender—when he makes Sebastian, a kind of duplicate of Cesario-Viola, so easily replace his twin in the affections of Olivia, who may now wed a male version of the same identity that she has cherished from the beginning.)

Like Eudina, Philocles and Philargus also confront crises of self-completion; they must wrestle with the paradox of sacrificing their identities in the very process of realizing them, caught up, as they are, in the toils of emotional attachment and distancing. As Philocles puts it,

> I must proceed to gain *Eudinas* love
> From my *Philargus* or I loose my self.
> And gaining it, I must forgo *Philargus*,
> And equally be lost.
> (II.i; p. 110)

Maneuvered through deception into a duel over the lady, each combatant seeks to die unselfishly at the hands of the other; later, when Philocles abandons Eudina in favor of his rival, having lost in a drawing of lots, he prays that "she may lively find / She has my love in [Philargus's]" and "that in [him] / She has us both" (V.i; p. 156).

As early as the end of Act Two, it becomes clear that Brome has fashioned an equilateral triangle, each point of which is so tensely, reciprocally, and hopelessly drawn to the other two that the full satisfaction of everyone's desire would require the mergence of all three persons into a single being—the assimilation of their separate personalities into a kind of androgynous trinity in which individuality would be blurred or even obliterated. Such a state, of course, would be equivalent to death, so that it is not suprising that in the course of the action each of the lovers wishes to die, while Philargus actually appears at one point to do so. Eudina exclaims that "Love's number's one" (II.i; p. 115), and the brothers are "each / *Wedded* [italics mine] to others friendship," each "More studious for the other then himself" (II.i; p. 118). Philargus verbalizes the fatal interdependency of the triad: if Eudina should be driven to suicide by the nature of her impossible choice, both he and his twin would also "fall by necessary consequence" (III.iii; p. 129). A little later she remarks that "One friendship, yet, must marry us all three" (III.iii; p. 130).

As in Marguerite's tale, family and romantic relationships tend to fuse. But in Brome, three distinct kinds of emotional involvement are in operation—erotic love, twinship (the closest kind of blood brotherhood), and passionate friendship, each emotion overlapping the others so that a painful and chaotic stasis results. Eudina wishes to "die . . . Rather than live in this confusion" but proposes weakly and fatalistically that all three participants "continue thus with Maiden love, / With modest freedom, unsuspected joyes, / *As we had all been formed in one womb* [italics mine], / Till Heaven determine of us" (II.i; p. 118). Brome's figure of prenatal togetherness in a context of unfulfilled sexual desire is revealing; for in this drama incest not only enters the plot at two crucial points but also symbolizes, almost generically, the "lovesickness" of the title—that is, it stands for the problem of undifferentiated feeling and for the psychological overheating that results from the confounding and intermingling of intensities (heterosexual romance, biological fraternity, and male bonding) that society wisely controls by individuating and keeping apart. Of course the metaphorical retreat into the womb also implies immaturity, as though the adolescent lovers of this murkey three-way relationship had yet to achieve adult personhood; indeed the boys' uncle, exasperated by the refusal of his nephews to compete strenuously enough for the Princess, regards their sticky idealism as infantile: "I could even swadle 'em both for a brace of Babyes" (V.i; p. 153). Such symbolism also relieves the dramatist, it will be noted, from having to individualize his youthful characters in any but the most rudimentary and functional way, for the shifts and changes of the plot obviously require that the young men be interchangeable.

Brome breaks up his impossible triangle in the conventionally predictable way—that is, as in *Twelfth Night,* by introducing a fourth term so that it may be converted into a parallelogram. But the route to a happy resolution is unusually—one might almost say parodically—labyrinthine, since it involves not only the apparent death and resurrection of one of the principals but the prurience of two potentially incestuous love affairs as well.[43] Placilla, who is assumed until the end of the play to be a sister of the twin youths, tries to suppress an erotic attraction to Philocles, her feelings being rendered more painful by the fact that her "brother," the object of her guilty desire, charges her (with a kiss!)—as his other self—to woo Eudina in his behalf; thus, like Viola wooing Olivia for Orsino in Shakespeare's comedy, Placilla is compelled ironically not only to hide her love but also, frustratingly, to work against it.

The second potential incest involves Philocles and Eudina, who are about to marry at the play's end after poison seems to have eliminated the rival candidacy of Philargus; for just as the King is about to join the couple in matrimony, the long-hidden secret that they are really brother and sister and that the two boys are *not* after all twin brothers comes suddenly to light to surprise, titillate, and further perplex the audience. (Brome, like Marguerite, employs the time-honored device of a midwife, Garrula, although in this case the character possesses the secret knowledge of the children's true origin and so becomes a knowing, rather than an unwitting, party to the deception.) When it finally transpires that Philargus is no corpse (as was thought) but only drugged, his revival makes possible a double union. Placilla can now marry Philocles (the man she had guiltily regarded as her brother), and Eudina, who actually *is* the sister of Philocles, can marry Philargus, the symbolic, if nonbiological, twin of the man she had been on the point of espousing.

As in Marguerite, incest thus functions as at once problem and solution, although somewhat more cloudily than in the *Heptameron*. Actual brothers and sisters cannot finally be united, however much their sensual desire may generate theatrical suspense. As one speaker warns when the King is unwittingly about to marry his daughter to his son, "You will sooner joyn / The Wolfe and Lamb, Falcon and Dove together" (V.iii; p. 166). But Brome can nullify Placilla's guilt and satisfy her longing at the same time by making her beloved turn out to have different blood in his veins; and he can also overcome Eudina's inability to choose between two equally dear aspirants for her hand by revealing, at the last minute, that one is ineligible (by reason of being a blood brother); thus his "twin" may step handily into the role of husband (by reason of *not* being a kinsman) with no sacrifice of romantic excitement.

The technical flaw in this overly schematic solution is the final arbitrariness of the Placilla-Philocles union, which is patched up hurriedly in the last few moments of the drama. Brome's emphasis falls on the marriage of Eudina and Philargus and on the succession to the throne of Philocles (now revealed to be the dying King's heir) as a compensation of sorts for being denied his princess. Placilla's romantic wishes are at last gratified, as required by the artificial neatness of the ending, but we are given no indication that Philocles regards his supposed former sister as a happy substitute for Eudina or as an appropriate future queen. He appears merely to accept her with a shrug and a mythological allusion, casting her "as *Juno* to [his] *Jupiter*, / Sister and Wife" (V.iii; p. 169).

The significant feature of this somewhat diffuse but psychologically suggestive play is its delight in showing not only the complete irrationality of emotional attachment, but also how closely and dangerously illicit forms of sexual desire can tread upon the heels of the licit. Here, too, Brome shares common ground with Marguerite. Consanguinity, assumed in the relationship between Placilla and Philocles until the last moment, serves as the frailest of barriers, even though the actual kinship between him and Eudina, revealed with mysterious suddenness, snatches lovers back from the edge of a tragic abyss because the play must end comically. Accidents of birth become fortunate or unfortunate technicalities as fate decrees; but the implied lesson, as in the *Heptameron*, is that passion is all but irresistible and that, unchecked by such knowledge, would easily override restraints or taboos that claim their authority only from religion and the culture. The play suggests also, through the mechanisms of plot rather than through any richness of characterization, that at some deep stratum of the psyche all attractions between people, whether they be brothers, sisters, lovers, or friends, are somehow unitary in nature; and that within this frighteningly undifferentiated nexus of magnetisms—sexual and nonsexual, romantic and fraternal, incestuous and nonincestuous—lies the possibility of annihilation as well as an opportunity to discover the uniqueness of the self. Brome, of course, is not up to *dramatizing* such self-discovery; it remains implicit merely as a proposition of the plotting. And the pattern of substitutions is equally intriguing, as we observe Placilla having to woo Eudina for Philocles, see Philocles end up with Placilla for his wife instead of Eudina, watch Eudina marry Philargus in lieu of Philocles, hear Philocles hand over Eudina to his "brother" as an extension of himself, and so on. Such actions suggest a disturbing fluidity or instability at the heart of personality and portend a world in which the vital demarcations in social, sexual, and family relations are at best only provisional. The theme of incest obviously plays its part in the evocation of this concept in both the *Heptameron* and Brome's tragicomedy.

Finally, Marguerite's tale suggests, although only distantly, the notion of incest as a buried metaphor for narcissism. The lady substitutes herself in her maid's bed out of the felt need to impose her own specialized attitudes upon an adolescent boy—to expose, punish, and repress natural biological impulses in the developing lad that would separate him morally, psychologically, and physically from herself, that would force her to acknowledge his independence. Subconsciously, at least, she wishes to regard her son as a duplicate of herself, a kind of mirror image or reflexive extension of her own commitment to chastity. The egotism that underlies this foolish attempt is already explicit in the tale; the narrator refers to her "root of pride" (p. 319), and a listener in the frame observes aphoristically that "He is a wise man . . . who recognizes no enemy but himself, and who distrusts his own will and counsel, however good and holy they may appear to be" (p. 321). Moreover, the fact of the son's unconscious gravitation to his own sister for a bride, when he might have chosen from all the eligible ladies of Navarre, again invites the concept of a self-enclosed or dangerously circular eroticism.

Pausanias in his *Description of Greece* (IX, 31) connects the myth of Narcissus to brother-sister love. This late classical work mentions an alternative version of the famous story, one in which "Narcissus fell in love with his [twin] sister, and when the girl died, would go to the spring, knowing that it was his reflection that he saw, but in spite of this knowledge finding some relief for his love in imagining that he saw, not his own reflection, but the likeness of his sister."[44] A similar suggestion shows up in Montemayor's *Diana* where the love affair between Abyndaraez and Xarifa, who suppose they are brother and sister, ripens near a "cristalline fountaine" in which the young man sees the image of his beloved "so lively represented, as if it had beene she her selfe": "I still beheld her . . . goodly counterfaite truely translated into verie hart. Then said I softly to my selfe. O, if I were now drowned in this fountaine, where with pride I behold my sweete Lady, how more fortunate should I die then *Narcissus*?"[45] As I have suggested elsewhere, Webster gives us a twisted and frightening version of the symbolic union of self with twin sister in the tense scene of *The Duchess of Malfi* where the heroine, combing out her hair as she looks into her mirror, suddenly catches the reflection of her brother's incestuously menacing presence.[46] Here disease superimposes itself upon health, the image of brother upon sister, in a symbolic fusion of incest and narcissism, for of course it is an aspect of self that Ferdinand both loves and wishes to destroy in his twin.

Twinship, indeed (as we have already observed in Brome's *Lovesick Court*), is a not infrequent component of incest plots. In addition to Webster's *Duchess* (which involves physical twinship between the title character and Ferdinand, as well as symbolic twinship between the cruel brothers), we might instance Fletcher's *Monsieur Thomas* (a comedy) and Ford's *The Broken Heart* (a tragedy). The idea of incest as narcissistic twinship was of course already implicit in Plato's *Symposium*. In this dialogue Aristophanes accounts for both homo- and heterosexual attraction by his humorous myth of how Zeus, displeased with the overweening pride and complacency of mortals, split them down the middle, causing each half (with its independent set of genitalia) to seek reunion with its complement. Hence incest impinges upon the fascinating idea of the Doppelgänger, of the brother or sister as pursuing shadow or alter ego (often a symbolization of guilt) or, alternatively, as a projection of the ideal self (a way of imagining self-completion or union with one's own perfected essence). Although the symbolism of incest tends, of course, to be negative in Renaissance consciousness (as the link with narcissism would imply), the idea of union between an identity that is at once the same as, and yet other than, the self is not without its attractions. The narcissistic model of incest most often connotes an egocentric self limited to whatever authority the unique experience of that self can assert; hence it represents a psycho-sexual turning back upon the known, the safe, and the emotionally underdeveloped. But contrariwise, it may also point toward wholeness, spiritual enlargement, and even androgyny (as in Aristophanes' union of male and female halves that, in junction, reconstitute their original totality as a single being dynamically richer and more kinetic than the sum of its separated parts).

Milton suggests something like this in his conception of Adam and Eve, who were originally one until God, through the agency of Adam's rib, separated the female from the male body by endowing the woman with physical, psychological, and spiritual independence; the poet thereby envisioned our first parents as the prototypical incestuous couple. Adam and Eve are one flesh in the sense that they are husband and wife, but they are one flesh also—brother and sister or perhaps father and daughter—by virtue of their originally common blood stream. In *Paradise Lost* the prelapsarian sexuality of earth's first lovers, far from suggesting a solipsism, projects a relational structure in which, according to a recent commentator, "each partner enriches the life of the other because imagination and feeling, reason and desire, the life of spirit and the life of the senses, are not categorically isolated according to gender . . . identity is not other than community . . . [and] the distributions of domestic power are conditioned by the greater power of unselfish love."[47] In other words, when Adam calls Eve "Best image of my self and dearer half" (V.95), he expresses a sexual ideal, at least symbolically incestuous, that represents the precise opposite of the detestable incest of Sin and Death in the same poem. To quote once more from the essay mentioned above, Milton explores "the movement from self-absorbed primary narcissism to a recognition of the self as an image of an other": to "become an image of an other is to give that other visible, palpable, significant presence in the world, to provide symbolic form to the other's self. Eve thus stands in the same identifying relation to Adam as the Son stands in relation to the Father."[48] Although it is probably impossible to cite a close analogue to Milton's myth of "incestuous" and mutual self-completion as an ideal in the largely secular drama of the Renaissance, the author of *Paradise Lost* may serve to remind us that automatic or merely reflex condemnations of incest on the stage are likely to oversimplify and therefore short-circuit issues that cry out for more sophisticated analysis.

We may now consider two well-known dramas on the theme of incest that approach the problem of narcissism from different directions—Beaumont and Fletcher's *A King and No King* and Ford's *'Tis Pity She's a Whore*. In the tragicomedy, the militaristic King Arbasces is characterized as a compound of opposites, "vainglorious and humble," "angry and patient," "merry and dull," "joyful and sorrowful" (I.i.84-85). Nevertheless, arrogance and self-absorption dominate his character in the early acts, and when he praises the sister from whom he has been separated since childhood, he conceives her as a female version of his ideal self: "Nature did her wrong / To print continual conquest on her cheeks / And make no man worthy for her to take / But me that am too near her . . ." (I.i.167-170). Later when he is smitten irresistibly by love for her, and she for him, he tries irrationally to deny her independent existence, to expunge the forbidden lust he feels by annulling her symbolically into a nonpresence, by reconstituting her as a kind of psychological ghost of his interior being: "She is no kin to me nor shall she be; / If she were any, I create her none, / And which of you can question this? (III.i.165-167). Thus, from his own troubled perspective, Panthea incarnates the image of the warfare between reason and passion, between the angel and the beast, that rages in Arbasces' breast. Simultaneously she represents to him "blessedness / Eternal" (III.i.138-139) and "damnation" (III.i.189); she is "fair and wise / And virtuous" (III.i.190-191)—a female mirror of his brightest ideals—but also "a disease," "an ungodly sickness" (III.i.193-195), who gives back a shadow of the loathsome temptation and guilty desire that gather so threateningly in the darker recesses of his incipient depravity.

The only way to penetrate this psychic and moral impasse is of course to reveal that Arbasces is, in actuality, neither the king nor the brother that he thought himself to be. A familiar device of plotting does service in a somewhat unexpected way, for a sudden and dramatic metamorphosis of genetic identity allows Beaumont and Fletcher to close the apparently unbridgeable divide between moral idealism and carnal desire. A new genealogical self makes possible a new psychological self, so that passion and reason can be reconciled in a healthy Christian marriage. Arbasces' discovery that Panthea is not after all his sister allows him to break out of the narcissistic and solipsistic box in which he had been confined and to acknowledge his beloved's otherness. Marriage can now fulfill its proper psychological function as the institution that traditionally sanctifies and confirms the individuality of lovers while at the same time making them one flesh.

Ford's Giovanni, perhaps even more than Arbasces, is the narcissist *par excellence*, for in his auto-intoxication with his sister Annabella, he sees a kind of perfection that would remove her from external reality and set her up as a private, arbitrary icon of his own subjective fashioning. Not content to share his sister with the world, he demands, as a perceptive critic puts it, "a unity more complete, more self-sufficient than human life permits."[49] In the face of all social and religious pressures to the contrary—indeed partly *because* of these pressures—Giovanni is swept along in his self-isolating passion to contract a secret incestuous union with Annabella that he equates with the sacred and ecstatic. R. J. Kaufmann points out, with particular reference to this tragedy, that "Ford's [romantic] characters are all self-defining and nonpolitical. They do not so much defy society as deny its relevance to their lives."[50] It is in this context that Giovanni reacts to his sister's lapse into repentance and conventional morality as a betrayal of their mutual dedication to a higher truth; and, like Othello, he must kill the thing he loves to preserve forever the perverse mystical absolute of which he has made her the human embodiment. When his projection of self insists on a will and mind of its own, he must destroy it to prevent the implied violation of psychic oneness. Thus Giovanni's evisceration of Annabella's heart—an abhorrent literalization of Petrarchan imagery—becomes a religious sacrifice to his narcissistic conception of purity.

VI

The happy and unhappy resolutions of the two plays by Beaumont and Fletcher and by Ford may be taken to illustrate alternative paradigms of the incest problem in Renaissance drama. In *A King and No King* the collaborating dramatists validate the impulse toward incest mechanically, by expediently removing the impediment of consanguinity at the eleventh hour (as Brome does for Philocles and Placilla in *The Lovesick Court*). But this somewhat facile maneuver, which becomes a cliché of incest plots, may be interpreted to imply that the taboo itself stimulates the imagination to creative displacements and substitutions—strategies, so to say, that make it possible to heal the breach between the erotic and spiritual drives indigenous to our nature. Robert Stein, a disciple of Jung, not only regards the propension to incest as a fundamental of human love but also sees in it a symbolic expression of man's need to reconcile his passional with his intellectual and spiritual requirements, his body with his soul.[51] Looked at in this way, Arbasces, by legitimately marrying Panthea after he has incestuously lusted for her, frees the static and deadening opposition between the instinctual and rational components of his personality and unifies them fluidly in a fertile and generative interchange. He breaks free of the enchaining divisions that had kept his physical and idealizing natures asunder and overcomes his narcissism by granting Panthea an independent identity complementary to, and co-equal with, his own—an identity endowed with its own creative potential.

'Tis Pity She's a Whore dramatizes a more tragic model of incest. As Giovanni becomes ever more obsessively narcissistic in his passion for Annabella, he moves increasingly toward a terrifying obliteration of identity—first hers and finally his own. The bloody heart impaled on his dagger is "A heart," as he tells us so grotesquely, "in which is mine entombed" (V.vi.27). This play suggests that if love isolates itself too completely from objective reality, it feeds on and ultimately consumes itself. Its perverse and rarefied specialness platonizes or abstracts itself out of existence. What may look from inside the temple of narcissism like religious mystery and sacrificial rite is seen by the sane who live outside as madness, depravity, monstrous egotism, unnatural lust, and sanguinary dismemberment. The savage mutilation of Annabella's body becomes an emblem of psychic violation and the disintegration of integrity.

These contrasting images of incest portray the paradoxical interrelatedness of separation and union, not only within the psyche but also in erotic alliances between people. They point respectively toward order and toward chaos, toward life and toward death. The abiding mystery of incest has always lain somehow in our instinctive perception of its simultaneous strangeness and familiarity, in its power to repel and to attract, in its intimations of a numinous oneness and in its threat of annihilation. It is therefore small wonder that the great playwrights of the Renaissance saw in it the stuff of drama. At its most probing and exploratory, it became a way of vitalizing in the theater that perennial paradox to which Shakespeare gave such lyrical expression in "The Phoenix and the Turtle":

>   Property was thus appalled,
>   That the self was not the same;
>   Single nature's double name
>   Neither two nor one was called.
>
>   Reason, in itself confounded,
>   Saw division grow together,
>   To themselves yet either neither,
>   Simple were so well compounded,
>
>   That it cried, "How true a twain
>   Seemeth this concordant one!"
>   (ll. 37-46)

Incest, as the image of the phoenix suggests, could contain the double, even mutual, possibilities of self-immolation and self-renewal. Sixteenth- and seveteenth-century drama, a drama of which erotic passion is so significant a component, could scarcely fail to take account of concerns as close to the human heart as these.

NOTES

1. The text of Shakespeare quoted throughout is David Bevington, ed., *The Complete Works of Shakespeare* (Glenview, Ill.: Scott, Foresman, 1980).

2. William Aldis Wright, ed., *Roger Ascham: English Works* (Cambridge: Cambridge University Press, 1904), p. 231.

3. (A) Giovanni Battista Basile's *Pentameron* (III.2; trans. Benedetto Croce, ed. N. M. Penzer [New York: Dutton, 1932], I. 232-240) includes the tale of "The Girl with the Maimed Hands" in which a brother's proposal of marriage to his own sister causes her to cut off her hands, which she sends to him as a gift.

   (B) Bandello's large collection of novelle contains two incest stories (I.44; II.35); see the translation by John Payne in *The Novels of Matteo Bandello . . . Now First Done into English Prose and Verse* (London: Villon Society, 1890), II, 242-252; V, 4. The first narrative (which may be a source for the relationship of the Duchess and the Duke's bastard son in *The Revenger's Tragedy*: see L. G. Salingar, "*The Revenger's Tragedy*: Some Possible Sources," *Modern Language Review*, 60 [1965], 5-9) recounts how a teen-age count and his young stepmother, a marchioness, were discovered in bed together by the father-husband and beheaded; the second is a retelling from Marguerite's *Heptameron* of a young man who unwittingly sleeps with his mother and marries his daughter (I discuss Marguerite's version of the tale later in this essay).

   (C) Cinthio's *Hecatommithi*, famous for the stories on which *Othello* and *Measure for Measure* are partly based, relates the unhappy love affair of Oronte, a commoner, and Princess Orbecche, whose mother and brother were executed for the crime of incest by her father, King Sulmone. Cinthio used the same story (II, 2) for his widely influential Senecan tragedy, *Orbecche* (1541)—a story, in either its dramatic or narrative version, that could have influenced Webster's *Duchess of Malfi* (see *Hecatommithi ouero Cento Novelle di Gio. Battista Giraldi Cinthio* [Venice: Deuchino & Pulciani, 1608], pp. 187-199; also Gunnar Boklund, "*The Duchess of Malfi*": *Sources, Themes, Characters* [Cambridge, Mass., Harvard University Press, 1962], pp. 28-31). P. R. Horne discusses the incest motif in both the play and the novella (see *The Tragedies of Giambattista Cinthio Giraldi* [London: Oxford University Press, 1962], pp. 51–52, 58–59).

(D) Book Four of Jorge de Montemayor's popular romance *Diana* (translated by Bartholomew Yong) contains the interpolated tale of the noble Moor Abdynaraez and his beloved Xarifa, who are reared together as brother and sister, fall in love, and only later discover that they are not blood relatives (see Judith M. Kennedy, ed., *A Critical Edition of Yong's Translation of George of Montemayor's "Diana" and Gil Polo's "Enamoured Diana"* [Oxford: Clarendon Press, 1968], pp. 166–184).

4. Richard III attempts to marry his own niece, Elizabeth of York (*Richard III*, IV.iv.297–298); Hamlet's uncle marries Gertrude, his own sister-in-law; Lear in his madness rails against an imaginary hypocrite, "thou simular of virtue / That art incestuous!" (*King Lear*, III.ii.54–55), apparently with the unnaturalness of his own daughters in mind; Adriana mistakes her brother-in-law, Antipholus of Syracuse, for her own husband and tries to treat him as her mate (*The Comedy of Errors*, II.ii); Isabella speaks of Angelo's attempt to barter her brother's life for her virginity as "a kind of incest" (*Measure for Measure*, III.i.138); and Antiochus sleeps with his daughter (*Pericles*, I.i.126–132). Mark Taylor discusses father-daughter relationships in *Shakespeare's Darker Purpose: A Question of Incest* (New York: AMS Press, 1982), discovering repressed incestuous desire almost everywhere; the preponderance of his "inferences" (p. xi) regarding the unconscious motivation of men toward their female children seems to me unduly strained and fanciful; see Joseph Candido's judicious review, in *Shakespeare Studies*, 20 (1988), 323–332.

5. Lois E. Bueler lists forty-two Renaissance plays that involve the incest motif, categorizing them according to whether the incest is actual or imagined only, and whether it is witting or unwitting (see "The Structural Uses of Incest in English Renaissance Drama," *Renaissance Drama*, ed. Leonard Barkan, New Series, 15, [1984], 115–145). Including cases of symbolic and metaphorical incest as well as elements of plot, we may expand Bueler's roster of plays to embrace the following dramas: Gascoigne's *Jocasta* (1566), Hughes's *The Misfortunes of Arthur* (1588), Peele's *Edward I* (1591), Jonson's *The Case Is Altered* (1597), Marston's *The Malcontent* (1604), Chapman's *The Tragedy of Charles, Duke of Byron* (1608), Beaumont and Fletcher's *Cupid's Revenge* (1608), Jonson's *Catiline* (1611), Fletcher's *Monsieur Thomas* (1615), Massinger's *The Bondman* (1623), Shirley's *The Opportunity* (1634), Ford's *The Fancies Chaste and Noble* (1635), Shirley's *The Coronation* (1635), *The Gentleman of Venice* (1639), and *The Court Secret* (1642). The dates given here and throughout are those of Alfred Harbage in *Annals of English Drama, 975-1700*, revised by S. Schoenbaum (London: Methuen, 1964).

6. Denis Gauer, "*Heart and Blood*: Nature and Culture in *'Tis Pity She's a Whore*," *Cahiers Elisabethains*, 31 (April 1987), 45.

7. Sigmund Freud, *Civilization and Its Discontents*, trans. James Strachey (New York: Norton, 1961), p. 51.

8. David F. Aberle and his colleagues conveniently summarize the leading anthropological theories on the origins and importance of the incest taboo; see "The Incest Taboo and the Mating Patterns of Animals" in Paul Bohannan and John Middleton, eds., *Marriage, Family and Residence* (Garden City, N. Y.: Natural History Press, 1968), pp. 5–11. The most widely promulgated of these theories tend to account for the nearly universal prohibition of incest in terms either of order *within* the family or of stability and social advantage *between* families in the larger social order. The incest taboo, for instance, is said to regulate the erotic impulses of the developing child, forcing him to direct these impulses outside the nuclear family and so learn social maturity and responsibility; or, it is held, the

taboo outlaws sexual competition within the home with a view to preventing familial disruption, internal chaos, and self-destruction. A third hypothesis asserts that the collective good of a broader social organism (the securing of internal peace, economic benefits, and reciprocal assistance; the making of common cause, defensively or offensively, against an enemy group) necessitates the barrier against incest. Even the widely discredited view that inbreeding necessarily threatens the genetic health of the family has lately been garnering fresh support, although such a view, whatever its scientific validity, would be largely irrelevant to the analysis of pre-Darwinian cultures.

Probably the most influential theory of incest for students of literature has been that of Claude Lévi-Strauss, who argued in *The Elementary Structures of Kinship* (trans. James Harle Bell, John Richard von Sturmer, and Rodney Needham [Boston: Beacon Press, 1969]) that the taboo arises from the need to control the exchange of women in society with something like equality and to prevent their monopolization by a selfish few. Lévi-Strauss's principle of sexual reciprocity thus explains the need for exogamy, although often within a limited collectivity: "neither fraternity nor paternity can be put forward as claims to a wife, but . . . the sole validity of these claims lies in the fact that all men are in equal competition for all women, their respective relationships being defined in terms of the group, and not the family" (p. 42). To quote Lévi-Strauss's summation of the "rule of reciprocity," "The woman whom one does not take, and whom one may not take, is, for that very reason, offered up" (p. 51). Lévi-Strauss's formulation has been faulted on the ground that it does not properly distinguish between sexual relations and marriage (see, for instance, Francis Korn, *Elementary Structures Reconsidered: Lévi-Strauss on Kinship* [London: Tavistock Publications, 1973], pp. 13–16); but Renaissance plays, particularly those with comic endings, usually make as little practical distinction between the two as the French anthropologist.

René Girard brings us full circle by attempting to fuse the insights of Freud with those of cultural anthropology. Girard, beginning with an analysis of Freud's *Totem and Taboo*, relates both murder and incest to the traditions of ritual violence and the scapegoat or surrogate victim in primitive religion. As societies cure their tendency to internal violence by choosing for ritual sacrifice a victim from outside the group who nevertheless represents the group symbolically, so they cure their desire for sexual conquest within the family by substituting an outside partner for the insider forbidden them: "The problem is always the same: violence is both the disease (inside) and the cure (outside). Violence, like sexual desire, must be forbidden wherever its presence is incompatible with communal existence" ("*Totem and Taboo* and the Incest Prohibition," in René Girard, *Violence and the Sacred*, trans. Patrick Gregory [Baltimore, Md.: Johns Hopkins University Press, 1977], p. 220).

9. (A) For Plato's views on incest, see *Plato: The Republic* (V), trans. Paul Shorey (London: William Heinemann, 1930), I, 459–469; the quotation appears on pp. 467–469.

(B) For Nero, see Tacitus, *Annals* (XIII.13; XIV.2), trans. John Jackson (London: William Heinemann, 1937), IV, 21, 109; also Suetonius, *The Lives of the Caesars* (VI.28), trans. J. C. Rolfe (London: William Heinemann, 1914), II, 133.

(C) For Caligula, Claudius, and Domitian, see Suetonius, *The Lives of the Caesars* (IV.24; V.26; VIII.22), trans. Rolfe, I, 441; II, 55, 383.

(D) For Clodia and her brother, see Cicero, *Pro Caelio* (XIII.32; XIV.35; XV.36) in *Cicero: The Speeches*, trans. R. Gardner (London: William Heinemann, 1965), II, 445, 449, 451.

(E) For Catiline, see Quintus Cicero, *Commentariolum Petitionis* (9), trans. Mary Isobel Henderson, in *Cicero: Letters to His Friends* (London: William Heinemann, 1979), IV, 756–757; Asconius' commentary on Cicero's oration *In Toga Candida* (82), in A. C. Clark, ed., *Q. Asconii Pediani Orationum Ciceronis Quinque Ennarratio* (Oxford:

Clarendon Press, 1907), pp. 91–92; and Plutarch's *Life of Cicero* (X), in *The Lives of the Noble Grecians and Romanes*, trans. Sir Thomas North (London: Nonesuch Press, 1930), IV, 203.

(F) For Seneca, see Thomas Newton, ed., *Seneca, His Tenne Tragedies*, with an introduction by T. S. Eliot (1927; rpt. Bloomington Ind.: Indiana University Press, [1966]). *Jocasta* by George Gascoigne and Francis Kinwelmersh has been edited by John W. Cunliffe in *Early English Classical Tragedies* (Oxford: Clarendon Press, 1912), pp. 65–159.

(G) For Juvenal's references to incest, see *Satire I* (ll. 75–78) and *Satire II* (ll. 29–33) in *Juvenal and Persius*, trans. G. G. Ramsay (London: William Heinemann, 1918), pp. 9, 18–21. For the imitation by Marston, see *The Scourge of Villanie (Satyre I*, ll. 13, 32–40) in Arnold Davenport, ed., *The Poems of John Marston* (Liverpool: Liverpool University Press, 1961), pp. 103–104, 268, 271; in *Satyre II* (ll. 21–25), Marston, following Chapman's *Hero and Leander* (V.5–10), also alludes to the incest of Phoebus and Aurora, who were brother and sister (ed. Davenport, pp. 106, 180).

(H) Preston's immediate source for *Cambyses* was Richard Taverner's *Second Booke of the Garden of Wysedome* (London, 1539), which, in turn, derived from Herodotus (see Robert Carl Johnson, ed., *A Critical Edition of Thomas Preston's "Cambises"* [Salzburg: Institut für Englische Sprache und Literatur, 1975], pp. 6–11, 192); the Greek historian treats Cambyses' incestuous marriage in III.31–32 (see *Herodotus*, trans. A. D. Godley [London: William Heinemann, 1938], II, 41–43.

(I) The quotation from Dio Cassius is from *Dio's Roman History* (XLIII.27), trans. Earnest Cary (London: William Heinemann, 1916), IV, 261.

(J) For the Harpalyce-Clymenus incest, see G. A. Hirschig, ed., *Parthenii Erotica* (13), in *Erotici Scriptores* (Paris: Firmin Didot, 1856), p. 12; also H. J. Rose, ed., *Hygini Fabulae* (Lugduni Batavorum: A. W. Sijthoff, [1934]), p. 143.

(K) The quotation from Fulgentius appears in *On the Ages of the World and of Man* (3) in Leslie George Whitbread, trans., *Fulgentius the Mythographer* (Columbus, Ohio: Ohio State University Press, 1971), p. 194; P. R. Horne discusses Manfredi's *Semiramis* briefly in *The Tragedies of Giambattista Cinthio Giraldi* (London: Oxford University Press, 1962), p. 154.

10. Versions of the story differ; see Robert Graves, *The Greek Myths* (New York: George Braziller, 1955), I, 160–161. Ovid confines himself to the tragic incest of Macareus and Canace.

11. Citations of the *Metamorphoses* are taken throughout from Arthur Golding's translation, ed. W. H. D. Rouse (New York: W. W. Norton, 1966).

12. Robert K. Turner, Jr., ed., *A King and No King*, Regents Renaissance Drama (Lincoln, Nebr.: University of Nebraska Press, 1963), p. 102. I cite this text throughout. Similar Ovidian reasoning, as Bueler points out, occurs in Tourneur (*The Atheist's Tragedy*, IV.iii.124–130), in Brome (*The Lovesick Court*, III.iii), and in Suckling (*Aglaura*, II.iii.5–18).

13. Derek Roper, ed., *'Tis Pity She's a Whore*, The Revels Plays (London: Methuen, 1975), p. 8. I cite this text throughout.

14. Graves, *The Greek Myths*, I, 160; Kennedy, ed., *Montemayor's "Diana,"* p. 169. See notes 3 (D) and 10 above.

15. Bueler notices the importance of the incest motif as a convenient device for complicating and resolving plots in Renaissance plays as well as for defining moral character. The plots that involve unwitting incest frequently allow courtly dramatists to demonstrate that aristocratic honor and idealistic love cannot finally conflict with each other, since the

doctrine that "true love . . . results from the urge to seek honor" ("The Structural Uses of Incest," p. 125) is written, as it were, into the code of cavalier values. Bueler regards the efficient switching of partners, in denouements to which unwittingly incestuous courtships have been the prelude, as bearing out Lévi-Strauss's account of the incest taboo with its correlative principle of reciprocity or exchange of women as necessary to the sexual economy of a healthy society (see note 8 above).

16. Lawrence Stone, *The Family, Sex and Marriage in England, 1500–1800* (London: Weidenfeld and Nicolson, 1977), p. 86. See also Natalie Zemon Davis, "Ghosts, Kin, and Progeny: Some Features of Family Life in Early Modern France," *Daedalus*, 106 (1977), 87–114; Davis discusses incest in relation to marriage customs and family indentity (pp. 102–105). In addition to her essay, I am indebted to Professor Davis for a provocative private conversation in which some of the ideas contained in this paper germinated.

17. Stone, *The Family, Sex and Marriage*, p. 115. In corroboration of Stone, David Bergeron points to the close personal affection between Prince Henry and Princess Elizabeth at James I's court, whereas the king himself tended to be jealous of his oldest son's popularity. Charles (Henry's younger brother), being more studious and less athletic than the heir to the throne, was also more distant toward him; see Bergeron, *Shakespeare's Romances and the Royal Family* (Lawrence, Kan.: University of Kansas Press, 1985), pp. 58, 62.

18. Whigham, "Sexual and Social Mobility in *The Duchess of Malfi*," *PMLA*, 100 (1985), 169.

19. J. R. Mulryne, ed., *Women Beware Women*, The Revels Plays (London: Methuen, 1975), p. 39; all further citations of the play are from this edition.

20. Daniel Dodson, "Middleton's Livia," *Philological Quarterly*, 27 (1948), 378–380.

21. T. J. B. Spencer, ed., *The Broken Heart*, The Revels Plays (Manchester: Manchester University Press, 1980), p. 76. All further citations are from this edition.

22. Robert Burton, *The Anatomy of Melancholy*, ed. Holbrook Jackson (London: Dent, 1964), III, 281.

23. Oliver Lawson Dick, ed., *Aubrey's Brief Lives* (London: Secker & Warburg, 1968), p. 139. I owe this, as well as several additional references, to George Robin Schore, "'Incest? Tush!': Jacobean Incest Tragedy and Jacobean England," Diss. State University of New York at Stony Brook, 1982, p. 43.

24. See Richard Burn, *The Ecclesiastical Law* (London: Sweet, Stevens, and Norton, 1842), II, 439–451; also W. K. Lowther Clarke and Charles Harris, *Liturgy and Worship: A Companion to the Prayer Books of the Anglican Communion* (London: S. P. C. K., 1932), pp. 470–471.

25. Richard outrageously proposes the marriage to his sister-in-law, Queen Elizabeth: "If I have kill'd the issue of your womb, / To quicken your increase, I will beget / Mine issue of your blood upon your daughter," to which the queen responds that God, not to mention "the law, my honor, and her love," expressly "forbids" such alliances between close kindred (*Richard III*, IV.iv.296–298, 341–346). Richard's earlier marriage to Lady Anne Nevill also involved a family relationship, for Richard's father, the Duke of York, and Anne's grandfather, the Earl of Salisbury, were brothers-in-law. Richard and Anne were thus cousins by marriage. See Charles Ross, *The Wars of the Roses: A Concise History* (London: Thames and Hudson, 1976), Table II.

26. For the family relationship of Henry VII and Elizabeth of York, see Ross, *The Wars of the Roses*, Tables I and II; also Charles Ross, *Edward IV* (Berkeley, Calif.: University of California Press, 1974), Tables I, II, and III. For the degrees of relationship and the papal dispensation, see J. A. Twemlow, *Calendar of Entries in the Papal Registers Relating to*

Great Britain and Ireland: Papal Letters 1484–1492, XIV (London: Her Majesty's Stationery Office, 1960), 1–2, 14–27; also William Campbell, ed., *Materials for a History of the Reign of Henry VII* (London: Her Majesty's Stationery Office, 1873; rpt. Kraus, 1965), I, 392–398; also S. B. Chrimes, *Henry VII* (Berkeley, Calif.: University of California Press, 1972), pp. 330–331. It is a pleasure to acknowledge the assistance of Professor Kenneth G. Madison of Iowa State University with the historical background of Henry VII's marriage.

27. See Horace Howard Furness, ed., *A New Variorum Edition of Shakespeare: Hamlet* (Philadelphia: J. B. Lippincott, 1877), I, 33. Hanmer was uncertain about the proverb, but it is no longer in doubt; see Morris Palmer Tilley, *A Dictionary of the Proverbs in England in the Sixteenth and Seventeenth Centuries* (Ann Arbor: University of Michigan Press, 1950; rpt. New York: AMS Press, 1985), K38.

28. One sign of how heavily the obsession with incest weighs upon Hamlet is his allusion to Nero as he approaches the interview with his mother in her closet: "Let not ever / The soul of Nero enter this firm bosom. / Let me be cruel, not unnatural; / I will speak daggers to her, but use none" (III.ii.392–395). The conscious reference, of course, is to Nero's murder of his mother Agrippina; but the Roman emperor's incest with her was almost equally notorious. It is just possible, too, that the choice of Claudius as the name for Hamlet's uncle, a strangely Roman name for a Danish usurper, was influenced by the memory of the emperor Claudius, who (as noted previously) had married Nero's mother incestuously; see note 9 (B) above. The best treatment of the moral and theological implications of incest in the play is that of Jason P. Rosenblatt in "Aspects of the Incest Problem in *Hamlet*," *Shakespeare Quarterly*, 29 (1978), 349–364.

29. Toleration, of course, was by no means universal. Roland Mushat Frye cites several cases of incest between brothers and sisters-in-law for which public penance in church and "a sizable fine" were the penalty; see *The Renaissance Hamlet: Issues and Responses in 1600* (Princeton, N. J.: Princeton University Press, 1984), pp. 80–81. By the reign of Charles I, some of the laxity that had characterized the morality of his father's court was disappearing. In 1631, for instance, the second Earl of Castlehaven was executed for a whole catalogue of sexual deviations that included, in addition to wife-rape, sodomy, voyeurism, and sadism, the attempt, at least, to debauch his own daughter-in-law when she was but twelve years old as well as commanding a servant to copulate with her; see T. B. Howell, ed., *A Complete Collection of State Trials* (London: Longman, Hurst, Rees, Orme, and Brown, 1816), III, 401–418. In addition, Stuart P. Sherman suggests that the plot of Ford's *'Tis Pity* may glance at the case of Sir Giles Allington, who was found guilty of having married his half-sister, the procurer of the license being fined £2000; see Sherman, ed., *"'Tis Pity She's a Whore" and "The Broken Heart"* (Boston: Heath, 1915), p. xxxvi.

30. Rosenblatt, in the essay cited above, discusses this contrast.

31. J. C. Flügel, "On the Character and Married Life of Henry VIII," *International Journal of Psycho-Analysis*, 1 (1920), 24–55; rpt. in Bruce Mazlish, ed., *Psychoanalysis and History* (Englewood Cliffs, N. J.: Prentice-Hall, 1963), pp. 124–149.

32. For the case of Alessandro de Medici, see Henry Edward Napier, *Florentine History* (London: Edward Moxon, 1847), V, 1–64; also John Stewart Carter, ed., *The Traitor*, Regents Renaissance Drama (Lincoln, Nebr.: University of Nebraska Press, 1965), pp. ix–x. For Lady Roos, see N. E. McClure, ed., *The Letters of John Chamberlain* (Philadelphia: American Philosophical Society, 1939), II, 144–145, 217–218.

33. The classic treatment of the debate appears in J. J. Scarisbrick, "The Canon Law of Divorce," in *Henry VIII* (Berkeley, Calif.: University of California Press, 1968), pp. 163–197.

34. "If brethren dwell together, and one of them die, and have no child, the wife of the dead shall not marry without unto a stranger: her husband's brother shall go in unto her, and take her to him to wife, and perform the duty of an husband's brother unto her.
   And it shall be, that the firstborn which she beareth shall succeed in the name of his brother which is dead, that his name be not put out of Israel."

35. Charles T. Prouty, gen. ed., *The Dramatic Works of George Peele* (New Haven, Conn.: Yale University Press, 1970), III, 202, 204.

36. "If whoredome had not beene sinne, Surely Saint *Iohn* Baptist would neuer haue rebuked king *Herod* for taking his brothers wife, but he told him plainely, that it was not lawfull. . . . he would rather suffer death . . . then to suffer whoredome to be unrebuked, euen in a king. . . . truly *Iohn* had beene more then twise mad, if hee would haue had the displeasure of a king . . . and lost his head for a trifle"; see Mary Ellen Rickey and Thomas B. Stroup, eds., *Certaine Sermons or Homilies* (Gainesville, Fla.: Scholars Facsimiles Reprints, 1968), p. 80.

37. Continuation of the race or the founding of a new dynasty might perhaps, as in Lot's case, be thought to mitigate or even excuse incest; yet Tourneur in *The Atheist's Tragedy* made D'Amville, the atheist of the title, attempt to seduce his daughter-in-law with a similar motive. Clearly Tourneur used the incestuous impulse of his villain as simply another facet of the character's unambiguous depravity.

38. See Henry Snyder Gehman, ed., *The New Westminster Dictionary of the Bible* (Philadelphia: Westminster Press, 1970), pp. 321–322.

39. The first English text of this narrative appeared by an anonymous translator in *The Queene of Nauarres Tales, Containing, Verie pleasant Discourses of fortunate Louers. . . .* (London: V[alentine] S[ims], 1597). I quote throughout from the modern translation by P. A. Chilton: *Marguerite de Navarre: The Heptameron* (Harmondsworth: Penguin Books, 1984).

40. N. W. Bawcutt, ed., *The Changeling*, The Revels Plays (London: Methuen, 1958), p. 108.

41. *Montaigne's Essayes*, trans. John Florio, I, 29; see the edition by L. C. Harmer (London: Dent, 1965), I, 211.

42. *The Dramatic Works of Richard Brome Containing Fifteen Comedies Now First Collected in Three Volumes* (London: John Pearson, 1873; rpt. New York: AMS Press, 1966), II, 102. This edition prints each play with separate pagination but without line numbers; all further citations of *The Lovesick Court* are given parenthetically in the text by act and scene, followed by the page number for this play within volume II.

43. Bueler would have us read the entire play as a late parody of the fantastic plotting and unbelievable romanticism—of the clichés, in other words—that increasingly characterized so much cavalier drama in the Caroline period. Although there is much absurdity in *The Lovesick Court*, Brome seems to build a recognition of this factor into his subplot in which the servants, Varillus and Tersulus (in their rivalry over Doris, a waiting-woman), act out a deliberately comic, below-stairs version of the contest between Philocles and Philargus. If the principals themselves were meant to be taken as a joke, the satire of the underplot would, in a sense, be deprived of its function. This is not to deny that, at specific moments, the high-born romantic lovers invite mockery in the extremity of their plight, but such irreverence is intermittent rather than sustained.

44. W. H. S. Jones, trans., *Pausanias's Description of Greece* (London: William Heinemann, 1935), IV, 311.

45. Kennedy, ed., *Diana* (IV), pp. 169–170.

46. See my *Skull Beneath the Skin: The Achievement of John Webster* (Carbondale, Ill.: Southern Illinois University Press, 1986), pp. 310–311, 328. I have restated this idea in somewhat altered form in "'Three Fair Medals Cast in One Figure': *Discordia Concors* as a Principle of Characterization in *The Duchess of Malfi*," *Iowa State Journal of Research*, 61 (1987), 373–381.
47. William Shullenberger, "Wrestling with the Angel: *Paradise Lost* and Feminist Criticism," *Milton Quarterly*, 20 (1986), 78.
48. *Ibid.*, pp. 79–80.
49. Roper, ed., *'Tis Pity She's a Whore*, p. xlv.
50. R. J. Kaufmann, "Ford's Tragic Perspective," *Texas Studies in Literature and Language*, 1 (1960), 534.
51. Robert Stein, *Incest and Human Love: The Betrayal of the Soul in Psychotherapy*, second ed. (Dallas: Spring Publications, 1984).

Building Stories: Greg, Fleay, and the Plot of *2 Seven Deadly Sins*[1]

SCOTT McMILLIN

The manuscript Plot of *2 Seven Deadly Sins* offers major evidence for the history of the Elizabethan acting companies in the 1590s, in part because it joins other extant Plots in showing the patterns of doubling by which relatively small troupes of players put on relatively large plays, and in part because it stands out as the largest collection of actors' names among Elizabethan backstage documents. Twenty actors are named, in various degrees of abbreviation, giving us nearly the complete acting personnel of some Elizabethan company at some point in its career. The company is not named, nor is the Plot dated, but those used to working with the bits and pieces of data from which the history of the Elizabethan theater must be written know that twenty actors' names in one document is a bonanza. All accounts of the London theater scene in the late sixteenth century must make use of the *Sins* Plot.

For over fifty years there has been a settled opinion about the provenance of this Plot. My purpose is to examine the reasoning by which the opinion was allowed to settle, for a half-century of scholarship based on what was originally a series of hypotheses runs the risk of turning the series of hypotheses into fact, and that raises the possibility that we are pretending to knowledge that we do not actually have.

First, however, I would like to perform an experiment. The clearest evidence in this case consists of the twenty actors' names. The experiment is to see what generalizations can be derived from the data of these names, without resorting to hypotheses that depend on other names. The distinction between *generalization* and *hypothesis* is important to the account that follows. A generalization describes the distribution of data, and a good one ought to be evident to all. A hypothesis is an explanation of things that need explaining—things that have implications of congruence but need the narrative assistance of a hypothesis to explain them. The names of the actors on the *Sins* Plot are data. They are fit for generalization if they can be trusted. They appear in a document written by one who appears to have known more about the Elizabethan theater than we know. He worked there ("he" will be recognized as an hypothesis) and was a witness to events that we cannot behold. Having given no sign of being wrong or misleading in what he wrote, he deserves our credence. Let us see if a generalization can be made about the data that he wrote.

I will list the actors' names as they appear on the Plot and will place beside each name a summary of other data: the early connections with London acting companies that can be established for the same names from other documents. The information from other documents is drawn from Nungezer's *Dictionary of Elizabethan Actors* (New Haven: Yale University Press, 1929).

Of the twenty names in the Plot, twelve bear complete surnames.

Plot	Company Connections from Other Documents	
Mr. Brian	Strange's 1593	Chamberlain's 1596
Mr. Phillipps	Strange's 1593	Chamberlain's 1598
Mr. Pope	Strange's 1593	Chamberlain's 1597
R. Burbadg		Chamberlain's 1595
W. Sly		Chamberlain's 1598
R. Cowly	Strange's 1593	Chamberlain's 1601
John Duke		Chamberlain's 1598
		Worcester's 1602
Ro. Pallant		Worcester's 1602
John Sincler		King's 1604
Tho. Goodale	Berkeley's 1581	
John Holland	unknown	
T. Belt	unknown	

Seven of these twelve actors belonged to the Chamberlain's men in the later 1590s or just after the turn of the century. An eighth first appears in the King's men of 1604, the continuation of the Chamberlain's men. The other four do not give us a pattern of distribution. There is no reason to say that they were *not* with the Chamberlain's men before 1602 (when Pallant and Duke show up in Worcester's men), but in fact there is no documentary evidence about their company connections at that time. Strange's men, with whom four of the eventual Chamberlain's men are known to have toured in 1593, are also an important possibility. If one were dealing with hypotheses, one might argue (as has certainly been done) that Strange's men were a forerunner company to the Chamberlain's men, so that the majority of data would be distributed to one company instead of two. For the sake of the experiment, however, the clearest generalizations from the actors' names alone is that the Plot had some connection with the Chamberlain's men in 1594–1602 or, secondarily, with Strange's men before 1594.

The other eight names in the Plot do not have surnames, but Greg was willing to make the conjectural identifications shown here:

Plot	Greg	Company Connection
Harry	?Henry Condell	Chamberlain's 1598
Kit	?Chris. Beeston	Chamberlain's 1598
Vincent	?Thomas Vincent	Chamberlain's (Bookkeeper)
Saunder	?Alexander Cooke	King's 1603
Nick	?Nicholas Tooley	King's 1605
Ro.Go.	?Robert Gough	King's 1619
Ned	unknown	
Will	unknown	

Nothing can be based upon these conjectures, of course, but it may be noticed that the conjectures do not point toward any company beside the Chamberlain's/King's men. There is nothing here to undercut the primary generalization that the names on the Plot coincide frequently with names documented for the Chamberlain's men in the later 1590s or the secondary generalization that some coincidence of names can be found with Strange's men of before 1594.

That is not to say that the Plot orginated with the Chamberlain's men or with Strange's men. Other generalizations would have to be considered, and hypothetical possibilities would have to be explored. How many of the Chamberlain's men documented from the later 1590s (Shakespeare, for example) do not appear on the Plot? How many of Strange's men documented from around 1593 do not appear? What evidence do we have of a relationship between the two companies? The generalizations about the Chamberlain's men and Strange's men are only starting points, but they strike me as good ones. There is a pattern of distribution to the data of the actors' names, and the generalizations ought to be taken as an advantage.

In the settled opinion about the provenance of the Plot, the actors' names are not taken as an advantage. They are taken as a problem to be solved. They are the recalcitrant evidence that a hypothesis cannot explain, and thus they become the occasion for introducing a second hypothesis. When this happens to data, the data-brokers of the profession should take notice.

Greg and Chambers, between whom the settled opinion was transacted, assumed that the *Sins* Plot had to date from before May 1591.[2] They disagreed on exactly where it originated, but their contest over the fine points is not at issue here. By assuming a date before May 1591, Greg and Chambers implicity denied the primary generalization derived from the actors' names alone, for the Chamberlain's men were not formed until 1594. That does not mean Greg and Chambers were wrong. It only means that they did not follow the lines of our experiment and isolate the documentary evidence of the actors' names. They had other things to think about, and those other things produced an explanation that has been regarded as plausible for half a century. Let us see what those other things were.

The fullest statement of the settled opinion comes from Greg, in his *Dramatic Documents from the Elizabethan Playhouses* of 1931: the Plot is there said to represent a revival of the second part of Richard Tarlton's *Seven Deadly Sins*, performed not by the Queen's men (with whom Tarlton wrote and acted) but by either the Admiral's men or Lord Strange's men, or perhaps by the two companies acting together, between September 1588 and the spring of 1591 at one of the playhouses owned by James Burbage.

Now it is obvious that some names beyond those of the actors listed on the Plot have entered into the settled opinion. How did Richard Tarlton and James Burbage become associated with a document that names only the son of one and the other not at all? Moreover, the settled opinion gives firm dates for the Plot: between September 1588 and the spring of 1591. Our generalization on the evidence of actor's names looks timid by comparison. "The later 1590s"—the generalization cannot even name the years precisely, while Greg gives the month and the season, and is nearly certain of the playhouse. How was he able to do this?

He was able to do this because he based his reasoning on hypotheses concerning the title of the Plot, the ownership of the Plot, and the family relationships of one actor who *is* named in the Plot, Richard Burbage. These hypotheses depend on one another—that is, the second is called into existence to tie up a loose end left hanging from the first, and the third arises as an opportunity that the second makes available for the seizing. Let me number the hypotheses and then discuss them in order.

1. The Plot of *2 Seven Deadly Sins* represents a play known to have been written by Richard Tarlton on the same subject.
2. Edward Alleyn owned the Plot.
3. Richard Burbage was loyal to his father.

We begin with Tarlton and Hypothesis 1. Tarlton is known to have written a play on the Seven Deadly Sins—both Gabriel Harvey and Thomas Nashe said so. If nothing stood in the way of connecting Tarlton's play with the Plot of *2 Seven Deadly Sins*, we would have a reasonable documentary basis for identifying the two. But something does stand in the way: Tarlton is not named on the Plot, and none of the twenty actors who are named can be connected with the company that Tarlton acted with, the Queen's men. This is where the actor's names become recalcitrant. They stand in the way of one hypothesis and thus become the problematic ground for calling another hypothesis into play. How could Tarlton's play have turned into a document naming actors from another company?

Greg solved this problem by saying that since some other plays from the Queen's men are known to have passed to companies headed by Edward Alleyn in about 1589–92, it may be imagined that Tarlton's *Sins* play followed a similar route. The Plot, that is to say, represents a later version of Tarlton's play, which had been transferred from the Queen's men to another company, this second company being headed by Alleyn (for reasons to be discussed) and consisting of the actors who are named on the Plot. The evidence for plays transferred from the Queen's men to Alleyn's companies, as Greg presents it, consists of "*Friar Bacon* and perhaps *Orlando Furioso*" (*Dramatic Documents: Commentary*, p. 109). He used "perhaps" for *Orlando* because the example does not fit his needs. The author of *Orlando* (Greene) was accused of selling the play first to the Queen's men, then, when the Queen's were in the country, to the Admiral's men. If this is to be believed, it is more obviously a case of fraud than of the transfer from one company to another that Greg takes it for. The *Friar Bacon* example is also weak. It depends on assuming that there was only one "Friar Bacon" play, the one published with the Queen's men named on the title page, which would have to be the "Friar Bacon" listed in the repertory of Strange's men in 1592. In fact, however, there are two "Friar Bacon" plays, and by 1931 Greg knew that there were two. The second is a manuscript play that had only recently come to light, but Greg describes it in another section of *Dramatic Documents*. It now passes under title of *John of Bordeaux*, but Friar Bacon is its hero, and it assigns a speech to John Holland, who cannot be found among the Queen's men. It is likely that this "Friar Bacon" is the one listed for Strange's men, obviating the need to hypothesize a transfer from the Queen's men.

Nevertheless, the main point is not to wonder about the soundness of Greg's generalization but to notice the network of hypotheses he is weaving. The presence of actors' names is now being explained by a hypothetical transfer of Tarlton's play to a second company.

Why did Greg insist that the second company had to be headed by Edward Alleyn? Alleyn is not named on the Plot. The answer is that the Plot is preserved at Dulwich College, founded by Alleyn. Since many of the theatrical documents at Dulwich were in fact owned by Alleyn, Greg assumed that the *Sins* Plot was owned by Alleyn too (the absence of Alleyn's name among the actors he explained by noting that two leading roles have no actor assigned, so perhaps Alleyn lurks there). So Hypothesis 2 is not only that the Plot was transferred to the named actors but that the named actors included an unnamed Alleyn, who was the final owner of the document.[3]

Thus Hypotheses 1 and 2 reach from Richard Tarlton to Edward Alleyn. We have yet to find James Burbage in all of this. He emerges from the intersection of Hypothesis 2 and Hypothesis 3. Richard Burbage *is* named on the Plot. When could he have acted in a company involving Edward Alleyn? One immediately available possibility is June 1594, when according to Henslowe's *Diary* the Admiral's men (with Alleyn) and the newly-constituted Chamberlain's men (presumably with Burbage and most of the fully named actors on the Plot) acted together. There are difficulties with this possibility, but my point is that Greg and Chambers never considered it, so certain were they of Hypothesis 3, the loyalty of Richard Burbage to his father. This is the hypothesis that dates the Plot prior to May 1591. The Admiral's men had been acting at James Burbage's Theatre for some time around 1590–91, but a row between the company and their landlord broke out in May 1591 and probably brought the association to an end.[4] Greg and Chambers thought it self-evident that Richard Burbage, who seems to have been acting with the company at his father's theater, would not have deserted his father and followed the company after the row. Fathers and sons do not split up under pressure—that is the generalization underlying Hypothesis 3, that the Plot must be dated prior to May 1591.

This generalization depends on experience of the world, but I ask my readers in judging it not only to review their first hand knowledge of father-son relationships, but also to imagine being the son of James Burbage, a father whose temperament was reported more than once to be short on patience, long on rage. Some time before his argument with the Admiral's men, James Burbage had been accused of fraud by the heirs of his partner who said he was pocketing more than his share of the playhouse profits. In the brawl that broke out, young Richard is reported to have applied a broomstick to his father's foes, tweaked a nose, and uttered large oaths, but I am not sure that our imaginations should stop with that image of father-son unity. When a while later James Burbage withheld some money due the Admiral's men, roared an insult about their patron, and antagonized at least one member of the company to the point of testifying against him, he was disrupting relations with one of the leading companies in London. A talented teen-age actor might be disappointed in a father who disrupts relations with one of the leading companies in London. Richard had been getting some roles with the Admiral's men, the company headed by the most famous actor of the day, the company with whom a career could readily be built. If the Admiral's men left Burbage's Theatre at that point and moved across the river to the newest playhouse in London (that is what Greg and Chambers assume), can we be certain that Richard hung back with his father? I am, of course, saying more than I know about Richard's ambitions, but Greg and Chambers were assuming more than they knew about his family devotion. On neither view should theater history be built, and I shall build nothing on the possibility that Richard Burbage went with the Admiral's men, so long as we doubt whatever is built on the possibility that he did not.

Greg kept a notebook of "wise saws" on his desk. One of them, from Henry Bradley, reads: "A hypothesis ought to be a one-storied building only."[5] In arguing that the *Sins* Plot represents a play originally written by Tarlton and transferred to Alleyn's company at about the time that Richard Burbage was proving loyal to his father, Greg was building higher than one storey. The building does not look secure to me. It does not look as well-founded as the generalization that can be derived from the actors' names alone, although it does accomplish one thing the generalization cannot accomplish: it does *tell* a story. If the resulting structure seems flimsy, one knows this is untypical of Greg. He was usually a one-storey scholar, and the question I would pursue from the example before us is not how often did Greg build houses of cards (hardly ever), but why did he build this one? One cannot suppose that it was a hasty gesture, a casual mistake, an accident. He (and Chambers) worked on the question of the *Sins* Plot for twenty-five years before announcing the settled opinion. They were attracted by storey-building in this case, engaged by it, and I would like to think for a moment longer about why they were so engaged.

The answer must involve the theater historian whom Greg and Chambers had reason to correct most often, F. G. Fleay. Hypothesis 1 orginated with Fleay. It was he who said that Tarlton must have written the play represented by the *Sins* Plot, and his evidence was not restricted to the comments by Harvey and Nashe about Tarlton's play on the subject. Fleay was driving at something else, something that has to be recognized as a form of economy, I think, and it seems to have been the economy of the reasoning which made Greg and Chambers accept—always—Fleay's basic postulate.[6]

Fleay's basic postulate was that Tarlton's play on the Seven Deadly Sins, mentioned by Harvey and Nashe, lies behind the titles "Five Plays in One" and "Three Plays in One" listed for the Queen's men on the Court schedule for 1585. There is nothing to indicate that the Court plays were about the Deadly Sins or were written by Tarlton. There is nothing to indicate that Tarlton wrote a two-part play or that he wrote anything called "Three Plays in One" or "Five Plays in One." There is only the arithmetical ingenuity of getting Five Plays and Three Plays to equal Seven Deadly Sins. This Fleay accomplished by imagining that Tarlton's supposed two-part play had an induction of some length, which joined to seven playlets about the sins would make eight units in all, divided into five and three for the Court performances.

The intriguing part of Fleay's hypothesis is that he had a trace of evidence for the induction that gives eight units. Off to the side of his Tarlton speculation, unrelated but waiting to be used, was the Plot of *2 Seven Deadly Sins*, which has an induction. Moreover, it gives a playlet to each of its sins. The structure of an induction followed by playlets is there to be seen on a theatrical document about the Seven Sins. Thus the economy of getting seven into eight (this is capitalist economy) seems to have a documentary basis. Readers of Fleay will know what is about to happen. Because the Plot is called upon as evidence for the arithmetic, it is deemed to have some historical connection with Tarlton's play. The historical position of the evidence is established by the historian's *use* of the evidence.

Why did Greg not reject this notion out of hand? The answer may have to do with the further refinement that Fleay gave to his argument, for it is here that the economy becomes dazzling. The induction represented on the Plot, as the shrewd reader will have noticed, introduces the *second* part of a two-part play, whereas Fleay's hypothesis requires an induction to the *first* part. Moreover, the induction of the Plot is followed by only three Sins-playlets, making the arithmetic of "Five Plays" and "Three Plays" difficult: this should be "Four Plays in One." Fleay finessed these difficulties by a glance at Henslowe's *Diary*, which indeed lists a production of something called "Four Plays in One" for Strange's men in March 1592. No matter that Strange's men are different from the Queen's men who played "Five Plays" and "Three Plays" at Court. No matter that seven years separate the Court performances from Henslowe's or that Henlowe's record shows no sign of referring to the second part of a two-part play. The numbers were too elegant to be resisted, and Fleay swept them into equation by announcing that the Plot was drawn up in 1592 for a revival of Tarlton's old "Three Plays in One," which became "Four Plays" by *borrowing* the induction from the old "Five Plays." Thus Fleay was able to connect an item in Henslowe's *Diary* of 1592, two Court records for a different company in 1585, allusions to Tarlton's playwrighting in Gabriel Harvey and Thomas Nashe, and a theatrical Plot naming many actors who were Shakespeare's fellows.

It will be seen that the arithmetical economy of Fleay's hypothesis is the sign of a more ambitious economy, the economy by which one apparent hypothesis explains widely separated items of documentary fact. Historians always find this economy attractive: "Four Facts in One" is even better than "Four Plays in One." Anyone who writes Elizabethan theater history today has learned to resist such grand moves toward narrative economy, and our mentors are Greg and Chambers more than anyone else, but in his early work Greg accepted this particular bundling as "one of Fleay's most brilliant contributions to dramatic history,"[7] and he and Chambers relied on it for a quarter of a century.

Finally Greg discovered a flaw. In his *Dramatic Documents* of 1931 he studied the induction on the Plot and discovered that it is fully integrated with the playlets that follow. It is not detachable. It shows no sign of having been borrowed from a predecessor play. It shows signs only of belonging where it is (pp. 111–112).

At this point Greg was in position to doubt Fleay's entire hypothesis and recognize that the Plot may be unrelated to the Five-plus-Three Court performances of 1585, unrelated to Tarlton's play on the deadly sins, and unrelated to the Queen's men. This could have been the moment for looking at the evidence of the actors' names on the plot. Instead Greg denied one part of Fleay's hypothesis and preserved another, although both parts depend on what was now known to be mistake. Greg used Fleay's mistake about the induction to deny the connection between the Plot and Henslowe's "Four Plays in One," but preserved the connection between the Plot and the Five-plus-Three court performances of 1585, which happens to depend on the same mistake about the induction. It is only the presumption of a single induction that allows one to think of eight units for seven sins, and when Greg discovered that *2 Seven Deadly Sins* had its own induction, he could have noticed that the arithmetic simply does not work the way that Fleay wanted it to—there is no longer a sign of something to turn seven into eight. Seven into *nine* could be produced from the assumption there was an induction for Part 1 as well as for Part 2, but not seven into eight. Yet Greg continued to follow Fleay in assuming that the Plot had to be related to the Court plays and that they had to be authored by Tarlton.

What led Greg to make this mistake? The economy of the arithmetic is charming enough, but the stronger attraction, I imagine, is the enlarged economy that the arithmetic produces: the economy of storytelling. Fleay linked the greatest names of the Elizabethan theater—Tarlton, Alleyn, Burbage, Shakespeare's fellow actors—into one story, generating a unity out of varied bits of data, and this drive for narrative economy has its attractions. Economy was, I suspect, a more complex interest for Greg than for most of us; but I am sure it is at least a simple interest for everyone. In refusing to discredit the linked hypotheses of Fleay's argument—and in using them to create linked hypotheses of his own—Greg was resorting to a need that all of us can discover in our work. This paper has not hesitated to become hypothetical in the interests of outlining a story about Greg and Fleay, and the reader who wants it to be a better story is wishing for stronger doses of hypothesis.

There is something else about Hypotheses 1, 2, and 3. Each is founded on an appealing figure of authority. Hypothesis 1 has Tarlton the author, Hypothesis 2 has Alleyn the owner, and Hypothesis 3 had James Burbage the father whose son would not leave him. Thus the economy of story-building in this case connects the author, the owner, and the father in an enterprise that bears some relationship between Greg and the authority-figure whom he laid to rest, Fleay. One does not simply eliminate a father in these affairs; one incorporates something of the father as well, and in preserving one element of Fleay's hypothesis, Greg did not show that the *Sins* of the father are visited on the son so much as he repeated the bias of his father's mind even as he defaced that father's work. Fleay's theater history curves toward authorship. He was one of the first to study the data of the less-distinguished, the actors, but his thinking was organized by the category of playwright. This bias for authorship goes back to *his* spiritual father, and the grandfather of us all, Malone, who mutilated the documents of the owner-actor Alleyn by cutting out the signatures of the authors for his own collection. The task of destroying and preserving the father in one gesture never ends.

Let us return to the data. Twenty actors, whose names are given at least in part, acted with one another in the second part of a two-part play, author unknown, on the Seven Deadly Sins. The most obvious company with whom these names come together according to other documentary data is the Chamberlain's men in the later 1590s. Another strong possibility is Strange's men of about 1593. These are generalizations about the data, and they do not tell a story. The story would depend on hypothetical reasoning that will not be undertaken here. When it is undertaken, I urge that it be grounded on data and the generalizations that can be derived from them. The data will normally concern figures of no pre-established authority—twenty actors in the present case, grocers and huswifes and wig-makers in other cases that theater historians can name. Beginning with an authorial hypothesis about Tarlton, Greg had to deal with the actors' names as a problem to be overcome when in fact they are the groundwork for a one-storey building.

I will touch, in closing, on a *datum* about Strange's men. It is documented in Henslowe's *Diary* that Strange's men played something called "Henry VI" in 1592–93. It happens that the Plot of *2 Seven Deadly Sins* represents a play about Henry VI: the imprisoned King is visited by the poet Lydgate, who is kind enough to put on playlets about Envy, Lechery, and Sloth for the edification of his highness. Theater historians have tended to assume that the "Henry VI" put on by Strange's men in 1592–93 is Shakespeare's *1 Henry VI*. I am inclined to think so too, but I am struck by how easily the possibility has been ignored that Strange's "Henry VI" relates instead to the Henry VI play outlined on the Plot. The Greg-Chambers dating of the Plot as prior to May 1591 has prevented us from seeing this possibility, but I suspect that the bias in favor of authorship is operating here too. To find "Tarlton" the author of the play represented on the Plot may be what caused Greg to hold on to part of Fleay's hypothesis even when he had turned up reason to discredit it entirely, and if "Tarlton" attracts the Plot to his name, think how strongly "Shakespeare" attracts Strange's "Henry VI," which might belong to nothing more august or canonized than the Plot, this handwritten and torn piece of backstage paper.

Like Lydgate before his King, I seek to broaden the lesson: beware of the many-storied building, to be sure, but beware also of the desire for an Author—for the building will often be erected for him.

NOTES

1. This paper originated in the 1987 theater-history seminar of the Shakespeare Association of America, chaired by S. P. Cerasano.

2. W. W. Greg, *Dramatic Documents from the Elizabethan Playhouses: Stage Plots: Actors' Parts: Prompt Books*, 2 vols. (Oxford: Clarendon Press, 1931), I, 17–18, 111–113. E. K. Chambers, *The Elizabethan Stage*, 4 vols. (Oxford: Clarendon Press, 1923), II, 125, 307; III, 497. Chambers, *William Shakespeare: A Study of Facts and Problems*, 2 vols. (Oxford: Clarendon Press, 1930), I, 51. An earlier essay of mine accepted Greg's dating: "The Plots of *The Dead Man's Fortune* and *2 Seven Deadly Sins*: Inferences for Theatre Historians," *Studies in Bibliography*, 26 (1973), 235–243.

3. Even this assumption may have an underlying problem. That a manuscript belongs to Dulwich does not prove that it came from Alleyn. William Cartwright left a sizable collection of pictures and books to the College upon his death in 1687, and although the book collection was traded for theological tracts and was never catalogued, it apparently did include manuscripts. The manuscript play called *The Wizard*, now in the British Library, carries a modern notation that it was once in Cartwright's collection. Thus it is slightly possible that the *Sins* Plot came from Cartwright. Cartwright was an actor (as was his father) and a bookseller. He could have picked up theatrical documents from various companies at various times. It should also be noted that when the Plot first came to light it was not at Dulwich but was being put up for auction at Sotheby's in 1825 as part of James Boswell the younger's library. It was claimed as the property of Dulwich at that time and was turned over to the College. Its location before 1825 is not easily determined. Greg thought it was removed from Dulwich by Steevens or Malone sometime after 1780. None of the other three Plots in the Boswell sale was claimed by Dulwich, and *2 Seven Deadly Sins* is the only Plot now in the College collection.

4. The evidence presented in C. W. Wallace, *The First London Theatre* (Lincoln, Nebraska; University of Nebraska, 1913) is summarized in Chambers, *Elizabethan Stage*, II, 391–393.

5. F. P. Wilson, *Shakespearian and Other Studies* (Oxford: Clarendon Press, 1969), p. 247.

6. F. G. Fleay, *Chronicle History of the London Stage: 1559–1642* (London: Reeves and Turner, 1890), p. 83.

7. *Henslowe Papers* (London: A. H. Bullen, 1907), p. 129.

Evidence for the Assignment of Plays to the Repertory of Shakespeare's Company

ROSLYN L. KNUTSON

Throughout the seventeenth and eighteenth centuries, the primary interest of theater historians in quartos of anonymous Elizabethan dramas was in authorship: who *wrote* all of those bad plays? Could Shakespeare have done so, in whole or in part? In the late nineteenth century, when commercial features of the drama became apparent by way of Henslowe's *Diary*, interest shifted to the companies: who *played* all of those bad plays? Could Shakespeare's company have owned some of them? Around the turn of the century, F. G. Fleay, W. W. Greg, and E. K. Chambers tackled the problem of assigning plays to company owners. The task was a double one, for they had to work out what constitutes evidence for the attribution of a play to a company's repertory as well as to compile the playlists. When the data existed, they built cases for play assignments on such records as the title-pages of quartos and the accounts of the Offices of the Chamber and Revels. When the data did not exist, they fell back on conjectural relationships between plays and companies such as authorship and the migration of texts from one company to another.

Repertory lists are useful research tools. They enable us to analyze the features of a given play—its artistic and theatrical properties as well as its commercial value—in the context of the offerings at its own and other playhouses. Unfortunately, the lists that Fleay, Greg, and Chambers compiled may not be as accurate as we have thought. Over the last fifty years, scholars have turned up much new information on the playhouse world in Shakespeare's time, including company affiliations of players, business practices held in common by playhouse entrepreneurs, provenance of texts printed by stationers, and composition of the audience. One effect of this research has been to remind us that the success of a given company was dependent first upon the commercial appeal of the assortment of plays that it offered to the public year after year.

It is therefore a good time to reevaluate the evidence and strategies of argument that we have used to assign plays to company repertories. The cases for four works with putative or possible claims to ownership by the Chamberlain's men will serve as illustrations of the evidence available and the arguments associated with that evidence. I begin with the relatively straightforward claim of *Thomas Lord Cromwell*, the evidence for which is information in the Stationers' Register and on the title-pages of its quartos. I continue with the more problematic claims of *Edward III* and *Edward II*, the cases for which raise the issues of authorship and the migration of playbooks (respectively). I conclude with the case for *The Tartarian Cripple, Emperor of Constantinople*, a fanciful claim in that the work may not even be a play. Yet I choose to consider it such here in order to direct attention to types of entries in the Stationers' Register that may hold clues to lost plays and company owners. In the discussions that follow, I am more interested in demonstrating the persuasiveness of certain kinds of evidence than in establishing the presence of one or more of these works in the repertory of Shakespeare's company.

Thomas Lord Cromwell

Thomas Lord Cromwell was registered at Stationers' Hall on 11 August 1602. William Cotton, a London bookseller, entered the copy; along with the title, he provided the company provenance of the play: "as yt was lately Acted by the Lord Chamberleyn his servant[es]."[1] In the same year, William Jones (also a London bookseller) published the play with an advertisement on the title-page that repeated the company attribution entered in the Stationers' Register: "As it hath beene sundrie times pub*likely Acted by the Right Hono*rable the Lord Chamberlaine *his Seruants.*"[2] On 16 December 1611, John Browne, Sr. (bookseller) acquired the text, and Thomas Snodham printed it in 1613 with a revised title-page that advertised the company by its current name, "the Kings Maiesties Seruants." There is no other evidence that the play belonged to Shakespeare's company. Its assignment to the repertory therefore depends entirely on the accuracy of the information in these stationers' records.

For over two hundred years theater historians have been taught to be skeptical of the claims in title-page advertisements. Ever since the editors of Shakespeare took to heart the apparent warning in the address to readers of the 1623 Folio by John Heminges and Henry Condell about "stolne, and surreptitious copies," we have feared that the stationers who traded in plays were guilty of underhanded business practices. Because some quartos are shortened and garbled texts, we have guessed that the stationers obtained these plays dishonestly, either by stealing a copy themselves or bribing a player to do so. Because some quartos were not entered in the Stationers' Register, we have surmised that the stationers intentionally circumvented the established procedures of their trade in order to produce a black-market text. Because some title-page claims of revisions and authorship appear to be erroneous, we have assumed that stationers tried to increase their sales by false advertising.

The title-page of *Thomas Lord Cromwell* (Q1602) is one of those we have been invited to question, for, in addition to claiming ownership of the play for the Chamberlain's men, the title-page attributes authorship to "W. S." In 1656, Edward Archer published a catalogue in which he attributed forty-eight plays to Shakespeare.[3] The ascription of two of the quartos, *Thomas Lord Cromwell* and *The Puritan*, apparently derives from their title-page advertisements of "W. S." In 1664, after having published the Folio collection of Shakespeare's works the year before,

Philip Chetwinde brought out a second issue into which he added not only *Thomas Lord Cromwell* and *The Puritan* but also *Locrine*, which is also advertised in quarto as by "*VV. S.*"[4] Edmond Malone excluded these titles from the chronology of Shakespeare's plays in 1790 (he had included them in 1778), and most theater historians have not taken the ascriptions seriously since. But some have taken the title-page attributions of these texts to "W. S." seriously enough to suspect that other information on the title-pages may be tainted. Leo Kirschbaum, for example, believes that we may "legitimately doubt Jones' attribution [of *Thomas Lord Cromwell*] to Chamberlain's" because Jones was trying "to cheat the buyer" of the quarto by advertising Shakespeare as its dramatist.[5]

However, the number of advertisements that are corroborated in discrete records of theatrical activity argues that the information about company affiliation on title-pages is, for the most part, reliable. One such record is Henslowe's *Diary*, the book of accounts and memoranda kept by Philip Henslowe, landlord of the Rose playhouse, 1592–1603. In entries for the Admiral's men, Henslowe recorded payments for all ten of the plays that were to come into print between 1598 and 1604 with title-pages naming the company patron by the Lord Admiral's title, the Earl of Nottingham. The plays and the dates of their initial appearances in Henslowe's records are as follows: *Doctor Faustus* (30 September 1594), *The Blind Beggar of Alexandria* (12 February 1596), *The Comedy of Humors* [*Humorous Day's Mirth*] (11 May 1597), *The Downfall of Robert Earl of Huntingdon* (15 February 1598), *The Death of Robert Earl of Huntingdon* (8 March 1598), *Two Angry Women of Abingdon* (31 January 1599), *The Gentle Craft* [*The Shoemakers' Holiday*] (15 July 1599), *1 Sir John Oldcastle* (16 October 1599), *Old Fortunatus* (30 November 1599), and *Patient Grissil* (26 December 1599).[6]

Further, Henslowe's *Diary* corroborates the title-page claims of three plays owned by companies other than the Admiral's men. In April 1595 Cuthbert Burby registered *George a Greene* at Stationers' Hall; when he published the text in 1599, he advertised it on its title-page as the stage property of the Earl of Sussex's men. Henslowe's records for Sussex's men, 1593–94, show that the company offered "gorge a grene" or "the piner of Wiackefelld" five times (*HD*, 20). The first quarto of *Titus Andronicus* in 1594 names three companies on its title-page; Henslowe recorded the play in the repertory of one of these, Sussex's men, in 1594 (*HD*, 21).[7] The title-page of the second quarto of 1600 adds the Chamberlain's men to the list of company owners; Henslowe recorded the play in the repertory that the Admiral's and Chamberlain's men offered together at Newington (*HD*, 21).[8] In 1594 Richard Jones acquired and registered a copy of *A Knack to Know a Knave* (7 January); he published the text later that year. Both the entry in the Register and the title-page of the quarto assign the play to Edward Alleyn and his company (with Kempe's "applauded merriments") (*BEPD*, I, 10; no. 115). A touring license issued by the Privy Council in May 1593 confirms the fellowship of Alleyn and Kempe by naming both as members of Strange's men.[9] Henslowe's *Diary* establishes that *A Knack to*

Know a Knave was owned by Strange's men in 1592–93 (*HD*, 19–20 ["ne," 10 June]).

Between 1597 and 1654, thirty-nine plays were published with title-pages that advertise them as the Chamberlain's men's or as the King's men's. Henslowe's *Diary* (as we have seen) confirms the advertisement of *Titus Andronicus*. Other documents and theatrical allusions corroborate twenty-five more of the title-page claims. Records of performances given at Court confirm twelve of the advertisements: those for *Othello*, *The Merry Wives of Windsor*, *Henry V*, *Every Man in his Humor*, *Every Man out of his Humor*, and *The Merchant of Venice* (Revels Accounts, 1604–05);[10] *A King and No King* (Revels Accounts, 1611–12 [*WS*, II, 342]); and *Much Ado About Nothing*, *The Merry Devil of Edmonton*, *The Maid's Tragedy*, *The Alchemist*, and *Philaster* (Chamber Accounts, 1612–13).[11] We depend upon an allusion in John Marston's "Satire X" in *The Scourge of Villainy* (1598) for corroboration of the *Romeo and Juliet* attribution; the allusion links a performance of the play to the Curtain playhouse, where we assume Shakespeare's company frequently performed around 1596–97.[12]

Another dozen title-page claims are supported by independent identification of the plays with members of the companies indicated on the title-pages. For example, in the quarto of John Marston's *The Malcontent* that advertises the play as the King's men's, there is a new Induction in which five of the company players appear in their own names as characters (Dick Burbage, for one).[13] The title-page of *Two Noble Kinsmen* seems accurate because the name of a company player is in the stage directions (Curtis Greville). That of *Richard II* is confirmed by the testimony of Augustine Phillips, a member of the company, concerning a command performance of the play at the Globe on 7 February 1601 (*WS*, II, 325). In the 1616 edition of Ben Jonson's works, cast lists of the King's men published with the texts identify *Sejanus*, *Volpone*, and *Catiline* as company property; these lists corroborate the company affiliation advertised on the title-page that was given each play specifically for the edition. John Heminges and Henry Condell serve as witnesses to the reliability of quarto title-page advertisements of the plays by Shakespeare that were later published again in the Folio edition in 1623. The Folio edition did not supply a title-page and cast list for each play, as did the 1616 edition of Jonson's works, but Heminges and Condell did call Shakespeare their "Friend, & Fellow" in the dedicatory letter. Thus they imply that the texts they collected had been performed by the company in which they and Shakespeare had worked, the Chamberlain's–King's men. Because Heminges and Condell chose the following plays for the First Folio, more quarto title-page advertisements (although not otherwise corroborated) appear to be confirmed: *Richard III*, *2 Henry IV*, *A Midsummer Night's Dream*, *Troilus and Cressida*, *King Lear*, and *Hamlet*.[14]

Ten plays including *Thomas Lord Cromwell* do not appear in records of the acting company's business; therefore, we do not have support for their company affiliation outside of the stationers' records. But it is a good sign that in each case the quarto advertising company ownership was the first edition, that the maiden run had occurred only a few years before publication, and that the company named on the title-page was in business at the time both of the debut and of the appearance of the quarto.[15]

One source of error in title-page attributions of plays to companies is the stationers' inclination to repeat information from a previous title-page. For example, the second and third quartos of *The Taming of A Shrew* (1596, 1607) and the second quarto of *The True Tragedy of Richard Duke of York* (1600) repeat the attribution to Pembroke's men from the title-pages of the first quartos, although that group of players had disbanded in 1593. Another source of error is the confusion of an old text with a similar play. In the case of *The Famous Victories of Henry V*, the first quarto (1598) advertises the plays as the Queen's men's, apparently accurately (due to Tarlton's association with two roles). A second quarto appeared in 1617 with a new title-page naming the King's men. Perhaps the text had changed owners, but it seems more likely that the stationer confused it with a similar play in the King's repertory and revised the title-page accordingly. Still another source of possible error is a long delay in publication. *Alphonsus Emperor of Germany* was apparently written in the mid-1590s,[16] but it was not printed at that time. When it was finally published about sixty years later (1654), its title-page named the King's men and referred to a performance that they had given eighteen years before (1636). Because several documents indicate the presence of a play called "Alphonso" in the King's repertory, 1630–36, G. E. Bentley accepts the title-page claim, but his enthusiasm for the attribution is dampened by the gaps of time between the composition of the play, the performance cited on the title-page, and the publication of the text.[17]

Evaluation: Fragmentary though it is, the evidence from various documents with theatrical information—Henslowe's *Diary*, the Chamber and Revels Accounts, and miscellaneous references in official papers and literature—corroborates the attributions of company ownership on the title-pages of play-quartos, attributions sometimes repeated from entries for the plays in the Stationers' Register. In a few cases, title-pages supply obsolete information or indicate a confusion of a text with one of a similar title. However, the title-page of Q1602 of *Thomas Lord Cromwell* does not appear to be such a case. From the claim in the Register that the play "was lately Acted," we may infer that a stationer acquired it while the memory of its stage run was fresh in the minds of potential customers. Both the registrant (Cotton) and the publisher (Jones) had the same understanding about which company owned the text. When the first quarto appeared (1602), the Chamberlain's men were in business in London as they had been when the play was on stage. When the second quarto was published (1613), the Chamberlain's men—now the King's men—were still in business in London. The second quarto has a new title-page that substitutes the name of the King's men. This revision implies that *Thomas Lord Cromwell* continued to be identified with the company with which it had begun its stage life, the Chamberlain's-King's men.

Edward III

The identification of *Edward III* with the Chamberlain's repertory does not stem from the entry in the Stationers' Register on 1 December 1595 or from the title-pages of Q1596 or Q1599;[18] rather, it stems from the attribution of the play to Shakespeare. In 1656 Richard Rogers and William Ley printed a catalogue of plays in conjunction with a text of *The Careless Shepherdess*; among the twenty-three titles assigned to Shakespeare, Rogers and Ley listed *Edward III*. The catalogues of Edward Archer in 1656 and Francis Kirkman in 1661 (revised in 1671) did not continue the Shakespearean ascription, and Philip Chetwinde did not select *Edward III* to be one of the plays canonized in the second issue of the Third Folio in 1664. In 1760, however, Edward Capell resurrected the assignment when he printed the play in *Prolusions; or, Select Pieces of Ancient Poetry*.[19]

In 1879 J. P. Collier made the connection between authorship by Shakespeare and ownership by the Chamberlain's men, asserting that *Edward III* was "the earliest historical play Shakespeare ever wrote, and in which Richard Burbage had performed . . . ; and it must have been represented in 1594 or 1595."[20] Collier's real interest in this subject was the kinship that he thought he had discovered between Richard Burbage and Cuthbert Burby (whom he mistook for Cuthbert Burbage). In an edition of *Edward III* (1874), Collier asserted that Burby, "a bookseller of repute," was Richard's brother, and so, Collier implied, Burby regularly received authoritative texts from Richard's hands.[21] F. G. Fleay ascribed *Edward III* to Marlowe, but he nonetheless declared that the Chamberlain's men acquired the text in 1594.[22] Chambers did not assign the play to the Chamberlain's men in *The Elizabethan Stage*, but in *William Shakespeare* he commented that it is one of four plays outside the First Folio "which can be seriously thought of as, in whole or in part, the work of Shakespeare" (I, 532). On no more evidence than Capell and Collier cited (which is none), the bonds between *Edward III* and Shakespeare, and consequently between *Edward III* and the Chamberlain's men, tightened. Thus R. B. Sharpe's observation in 1935 that it "is usually accepted as a Chamberlain's play" represents the tradition of its company affiliation accurately.[23]

Obviously, identity of the dramatist of *Edward III* matters to compilers of Shakespeare's canon, but does it matter to compilers of the Chamberlain's repertory? It does, if the Chamberlain's–King's men owned all of Shakespeare's playbooks as historians of company repertories have generally assumed. There is considerable evidence to support this assumption for plays in the canon but not for the plays in the Apocrypha.

Let us consider first the evidence that indicates the company affiliation of the plays that Shakespeare is thought to have written after he joined the Chamberlain's men in the early summer of 1594 or shortly thereafter. According to the chronology of E. K. Chambers in *William Shakespeare* (which is somewhat obsolete but adequate for my purposes here [*WS*, I, 270–271]), twenty-six of the thirty-six plays eventually printed in the Folio edition of 1623 began their stage lives between 1595 and 1613.

Nineteen of these are identifiable as the property of the Chamberlain's or King's men by some kind of documentary evidence. Eleven appeared in print with the company named on the title-pages of one or more editions: *Richard II, Henry V, 2 Henry IV, Much Ado About Nothing, A Midsummer Night's Dream, The Merchant of Venice, The Merry Wives of Windsor, Hamlet, King Lear, Troilus and Cressida*, and *Othello*. Records of performances at Court establish the company provenance of another five plays: *Measure for Measure, The Tempest, The Winter's Tale, Julius Caesar*, and *1 Henry IV*.[24] Simon Forman, the notorious astrologer and forecaster of his own death day, provides credentials for two plays, one and probably both of which he saw at the Globe: *Macbeth* and *Cymbeline* (*WS*, II, 337–339). Several letters describe the fire at the Globe on 29 June 1613 and allude to a performance of *Henry VIII*. The one from Thomas Lorkin to Sir Thomas Puckering on 30 June 1613 connects the play to the company: "while Burbage's company were acting at the Globe the play of Henry VIII" (*ES*, II, 419).

According to Chambers's chronology, ten of the plays in the First Folio may have been written before 1595. The evidence suggests that Shakespeare's company had acquired six of these plays by 1605 (at the latest). Title-pages referring to the Chamberlain's men establish the affiliation for three: *Richard III, Romeo and Juliet* ("the L. of *Hunsdon's*"), and *Titus Andronicus*. Henslowe's *Diary*, in an entry for the Admiral's and Chamberlain's men at Newington, further documents *Titus Andronicus* and adds one more: *The Taming of the Shrew*.[25] The Revels Account of 1604–05 names two of Shakespeare's plays that, according to Chambers, antedate 1595: *The Comedy of Errors* and *Love's Labor's Lost* (*WS*, II, 331).

Collectively, therefore, the evidence from stationers' records, accounts of performances at Court, theatrical records, and references to performances in miscellaneous contemporary literature indicates that twenty-five of the thirty-six plays in the 1623 Folio were staged by Shakespeare's company. The eleven plays without evidence of their affiliation—the three-part *Henry VI, Two Gentlemen of Verona, King John, As You Like It, Twelfth Night, All's Well That Ends Well, Antony and Cleopatra, Timon of Athens*, and *Coriolanus*—appear in the Folio in "good" texts. This fact implies that Heminges and Condell had ready access to copies of the plays, most reasonably because the plays were in the company's inventory. It seems, therefore, that if Shakespeare wrote *Edward III*—whether before or after he joined the company in 1594—the Chamberlain's–King's men were most likely to have acquired it.

But what if Shakespeare did not write the play? Is the ascription to him nonetheless valuable as evidence that his company owned it? In fact, only nine of the twenty plays dubiously ascribed to Shakespeare on title-pages and in the catalogues of 1656 and 1661 can be placed in the Chamberlain's–King's men's repertory on documentary evidence. Of those plays published before 1656, four have title-pages naming the King's men as well as Shakespeare: *The London Prodigal* (Q1605), *A Yorkshire Tragedy* (Q1608), *Pericles* (Q1609), and *Two Noble Kinsmen* (with John Fletcher, Q1634). The other two plays printed with title-pages alleging Shakespearean authorship apparently did not belong to his company. The quartos of *1 Sir John Oldcastle* (Q1600, Q1600[1619]) advertise the plays as the Admiral's men's. The quartos of *The Troublesome Reign of King John* (Q1591, Q1611, Q1622) name the Queen's men. For both plays, the ascription to Shakespeare was added to a second (and much later) edition. Most drama historians have rejected the possibility that the company acquired these plays in the belief that the belated ascriptions arise either out of a confusion of these texts with Shakespeare's plays or from fraudulent advertising.[26]

The catalogues published in 1656 and 1661 repeat the ascriptions to Shakespeare in title-page advertisements; they also add new ones. Richard Rogers and William Ley, who originate the ascription of *Edward III*, give Shakespeare *Edward II* and *Edward IV* as well. But there is no documentary evidence to link either one with the Chamberlain's men. The early title-pages of *Edward II* advertise it as the stage property of Pembroke's men; the quartos of the two-part *Edward IV* advertise Derby's men. A second catalogue, published by Edward Archer in 1656, makes ten new attributions to Shakespeare. Most theater historians believe that five of these books were the property of the Chamberlain's–King's men: *Thomas Lord Cromwell*, *The Merry Devil*, *Mucedorus*, and *The Roman Actor*, on the basis of title-page advertisements of the company; and *Chances*, on the basis of a bill from the King's players for performances at Court in 1630–31.[27] For the other five (*The Arraignment of Paris*, *Hoffman*, a two-part *Hieronimo*, *The Puritan*, and *A Trick to Catch the Old One*) there is no evidence to support an assignment to Shakespeare's company.[28] In 1661 Francis Kirkman published a catalogue in which he made one new attribution to Shakespeare (with William Rowley): *The Birth of Merlin*. Kirkman subsequently published the play with a title-page advertising it as Shakespeare's and Rowley's, but he did not specify a company (Q1662). There are no records of the stage history of the play.[29] This evidence indicates that the dubious ascription of a play to Shakespeare is not a reliable clue to the play's owners. We therefore cannot justify using Shakespeare's alleged authorship of *Edward III* as evidence in the assignment of the play to the repertory of the Chamberlain's men.

However, before closing the case of *Edward III*, we should take note of several circumstances of the theatrical enterprise in the 1590s that may be more germane to the company affiliation of the play than the identity of its dramatist (if he was not Shakespeare). One is that the registration of *Edward III* at Stationers' Hall (December 1595) and its initial publication (1596) locate the play in a period when the theatrical business was booming. Henslowe's entries for 1594–96 show that the Admiral's men acquired perhaps as many as fifty-six plays (half new, half old) between May 1594 and July 1596. Henslowe's profits were high, and the calendar of performances was continuous and full. A second reason is the size of yearly repertories. The playlists for each of the companies in Henslowe's *Diary* suggest a battery of thirty to nearly forty plays, depending on the number of weeks of playing per year. In the forty-nine weeks of 1594–95, the Admiral's men put about thirty-seven plays on stage, about twenty of which appear to have been new. The other London companies with a growing business would have had a comparable number of plays in production, unless they operated by radically different repertory practices. The market for dramatists was therefore excellent.

If we can determine when *Edward III* was on stage, we may be able to narrow the search for its owners by determining which companies were buying texts for London performances at this time. Let us assume for the moment that it was in production some months before Burby obtained a copy. The language of the title-page advertisement—"*As it hath bin sundrie times plaied about the Citie of London*" (*BEPD*, I, no. 140)—implies not only that it had been performed fairly recently but also (by the use of the past tense) that it was no longer being offered. We thus arrive at a period of years from the reopening of the playhouses in the spring of 1594 to the publication of the play in 1596 when it is most likely to have been in the active repertory of a company in London. Let us further assume that its publication in 1599 comes near the end of a period when its publisher expected it to have a market with buyers of play-quartos. We thus expand the time from the years of 1594–96 to those of 1594–1600 when the stationers' interest in the text implies that *Edward III* was popular enough to warrant its printing.

What companies were in business in London during this time? The Admiral's men were, playing briefly at the Newington playhouse (June 1594) but mostly at the Rose (beginning 14 May 1594). Due to the careful bookkeeping of Philip Henslowe, however, we may be reasonably sure that the Admiral's men did not acquire *Edward III*. Henslowe recorded the company's performances on a daily basis into the fall of 1597; thereafter he entered payments for most of the new plays that they bought as well as for the old ones that they revived. He did not enter *Edward III* (or a similar title) for the Admiral's men through March 1603. Sussex's men had been in London at the Rose at Eastertide 1594, sharing a run with the Queen's men. *Edward III* was not in their repertory then, and since Sussex's men disappear from theatrical records from 8 April 1594 until 1602–03 (*ES*, II, 96), they seem to have been out of business for more than a year before Burby obtained a copy of the text. At the other end of the time frame were the companies at the Boar's Head playhouse, 1598–1600. After the first year of operation (in which an unidentified company played there), Derby's men leased the stage in 1599–1600. We know only a few of the plays that they may have performed, none of which is similar to *Edward III*, and it seems unlikely that they would have obtained the text as late as 1599.[30]

Three companies, however, are good candidates as owners. After the Eastertide run at the Rose with Sussex's men, the Queen's men stayed in business. On 8 May 1593[1594], Henslowe recorded a loan to his nephew Francis "for his share to the Quenes players when they brocke & went into the contrey to playe" (*HD*, 7). On 1 June 1595 he recorded a second loan to Francis for a half-share "wth the company wch he dothe play wth all" (*HD*, 9). William Ingram reads these entries as signs that the Queen's men left London for a provincial tour around May 1594 and returned around June 1595, just as Francis Langley's new Swan playhouse on the Bankside became ready for occupancy.[31] We do not know the titles of their offerings, but several plays advertised as the Queen's men's were published in the late 1590s (for example, *The*

Old Wives Tale, 1595; *The Famous Victories of Henry V*, 1598; *Clyomon and Clamydes*, 1599). In February of 1597 a company of Pembroke's men came into the Swan, where they played until late July. A contingent of the players moved over to the Rose in October and very soon became Admiral's men (*HD*, 60). In 1600 another group of Pembroke's men appeared briefly at the Rose. In the plays that Henslowe recorded for each company, however, there is no *Edward III* and no play of a similar title.[32] The third company was the Chamberlain's men. Starting in June 1594 until they settled into the Globe in the late summer of 1599, they performed at several locations: the Newington playhouse, the Cross Keys, the Theatre, the Curtain, and perhaps the Swan. Yet for this company, as for the others, the partial repertory list gives no hint of *Edward III*.

The body of scholarship on *Edward III* has not confirmed that it was new in 1594–95. On the contrary, according to Karl P. Wentersdorf, it was composed around 1589–90.[33] If he is right, we must find some kind of evidence that it had value as a revival piece in 1594 or later in order to justify its placement in the repertory of any company in the mid-to late 1590s. Usually the evidence of a play's revival is in such records as Henslowe's *Diary*, accounts of performances at Court, the private correspondence of courtiers, allusions in the published literature, and various personal papers (for example, diaries). *Edward III* is not mentioned in any of these kinds of documents. An alternative is to discover signs of revision in the text. On this basis, Richard Thornberry argues for a new production of *Mucedorus* sometime between April of 1604 and the publication of Q1606, for which run the company altered the play's epilogue to refer to James I instead of Elizabeth.[34] There is not even this kind of evidence for *Edward III*; the texts of Q1596 and Q1599 have only the most minor of linguistic and orthographic differences.

In 1594 many plays that had been on stage a few years before (when the London playhouses were closed) had a commercial value comparable to that of new plays. We infer this value from the records in Henslowe's *Diary*. In 1594–95, revivals brought Henslowe (and by implication, the Admiral's men) excellent receipts. Of the fifteen plays that the company revived through February 1595, five brought Henslowe more than 60s. on opening day (*Mahomet*, 65s.; *1 Tamburlaine*, 71s.; *Doctor Faustus*, 72s.; *The Siege of London*, 63s.; *Long Meg of Westminster*, 69s.). Six averaged more than a 30s. return to Henslowe per performance (the aforementioned, plus *2 Tamburlaine*). Nine remained profitable enough to be continued into the fall of 1595. Two, *Doctor Faustus* and *The French Doctor*, were still on stage in the fall of 1596; a third, *Long Meg of Westminster*, was in revival. Furthermore, many of these old plays did not exhaust their audiences with one revival. *The Massacre at Paris* was returned to the stage in November 1601 (*HD*, 183). *The Jew of Malta* and *Doctor Faustus* were given not only second (*HD*, 34, 60) but third revivals (*HD*, 170, 206). *The French Doctor* and one or both of the *Tamar Cham* plays (revived in 1595–96) were back in production in 1601–03 (*HD*, 187, 178, 205).

The only evidence that *Edward III* might likewise have been a profitable commodity for some company is the fact that Cuthbert Burby published it soon after he registered it and that he published it again three years later. We may reasonably assume that Burby expected Londoners to buy the play, but we have nothing tangible to indicate why he might have thought so. It is tempting to conjecture that his hopes were raised by a recent and successful run of the play at a local playhouse.

In order to support such a guess, however, we must find instances in which the printing of a play coincided with or followed within a year or two of its stage run. In fact, there are not many. Out of all the plays (new and old) that the Admiral's men presented from May 1594 to March 1603, very few were printed at all. Those that were registered and/or printed, however, appeared in quarto during or shortly after their runs. Examples are the run of *A Knack to Know an Honest Man* from October 1594 to November 1596 and its registration on 26 November 1595 and publication in 1596; the run of *The Blind Beggar of Alexandria* from February 1596 to April 1597 and its publication in 1598 (registration in August); and the run of *The Comedy of Humors* [*Humorous Day's Mirth*] from May to sometime after October 1597 and its publication (without registration) in 1599. In addition, a few of the plays that stationers obtained in 1599–1600 had had recent runs: for example, *Two Angry Women of Abington* (*ca.* January 1599), *Old Fortunatus* (*ca.* November 1599), *1 Sir John Oldcastle* (*ca.* November 1599), and *Patient Grissil* (*ca.* December 1599; entered in Stationers' Register 28 March 1600 [Q1603]). There is also an instance of coordination between an apparent revival of *The Spanish Tragedy* in 1601–02 (when the Admiral's men paid Ben Jonson for additions to the text [*HD*, 182, 203]) and the publication of a version of the play (with additions) in 1602.

The stage and printing histories of the plays by Christopher Marlowe owned by the Admiral's men after 1594 exemplify the checkered response of stationers to the successful run of a play at a local playhouse. On the one hand are the instances in which stationers seem to have been aware of the play's currency. For example, Richard Jones produced a quarto of the two-part *Tamburlaine* in 1590 and 1593, presumably in the wake of the plays' initial popularity on stage around 1587–89. He produced a third quarto in 1597, at some distance after the revival at the Rose in 1594–95. Edward White produced a quarto of *The Massacre at Paris* in 1594; because it advertises the play on its title-page as having been staged by the Admiral's men, the quarto appears to capitalize on the revival of the play at the Rose in June 1594. Thomas Bushell obtained the rights to *Doctor Faustus* on 7 January 1601 and published a quarto in 1604; the Admiral's men apparently revived the play in 1602–03, at which time they bought additions from Birde and Rowley. On the other hand, the stationer who owned the text before 1601 did not publish an edition in conjunction with the Admiral's revival, 1594–97. White did not reissue *The Massacre at Paris* when it was revived in 1601. Nicholas Ling and Thomas Millington did not produce a quarto of *The Jew of Malta* when the Admiral's men revived it in June 1594, January 1596, and May 1601, even though the stationers had owned the text since 17 May 1594.

The body of data we have on stage runs and the publication of texts is obviously fragmentary. If a play was not given at the Rose between 1592 and 1603, it is probable that we know nothing specific about the dates of its performances. Unless copies have survived, we cannot be certain that we know every year in which that play was published. We can document *some* instances in which quartos were printed soon after a stage run, and these instances are enough to suggest that stationers did on occasion look to the commercial market created by a play's recent success on the stage.

Further, when quartos were published for no apparent reason, we may guess that some of these publications followed a revival or even a maiden run. For example, Edward White registered and published *Arden of Feversham* in 1592, at about the time the play was new; he reprinted the play in 1599. What was his interest at that time in a seven year-old text about a forty-eight year-old murder? *A Looking Glass for London and England* brought Henslowe very modest receipts in the spring of 1592; Thomas Creede printed the play in 1598. What led him to think in 1598 that it had enough commercial value to warrant a new edition, and why did Thomas Pavier buy the play in 1600 and have Creede print it again in 1602? What led Cuthbert Burby to publish *George a Greene* in 1599 when he had owned the text since April 1595? And, finally, what led him to print *Edward III* in 1596 and again in 1599 if it had not been performed as recently as 1594–95? We may learn that Burby had no knowledge of or interest in activity at the playhouses, but until we do, the coincidences of stage runs and editions of Admiral's plays (including those by Marlowe), plus these inexplicable publications of old texts, keep open the possibility that the editions of *Edward III* are a sign that after June 1594 the play was in the active repertory of one of the London companies.

Evaluation: Although a few theater historians have been sufficiently convinced of Shakespeare's hand in *Edward III* to enter it among the properties of the Chamberlain's men (where it has become entrenched), there is no evidence from the Stationers' Register, title-page advertisements, or other Elizabethan documents to support the claim. If Shakespeare did write the text, however, the possibility is strong that the Chamberlain's men acquired a copy. Yet on the evidence that we now have, we cannot establish Shakespeare's authorship beyond a reasonable doubt. Therefore we cannot assign *Edward III* to the Chamberlain's men on the basis that the company acquired all of Shakespeare's plays. Nevertheless, if the play had a stage life after the playhouses reopened in 1594, there is a chance that the Chamberlain's men acquired it. Unlike Pembroke's men, who were in London for less than six months of 1597, and unlike the Queen's men, who appear to have been in the city only for part of 1595–96, the Chamberlain's men were at one of the London playhouses from 1594 to 1599, apparently as regularly as the Admiral's men were at the Rose. Perhaps in the data scholars are currently publishing about the business of the companies in the 1590s, the affiliations of players, and the responsiveness of stationers to playhouse activity, some information on the stage history of *Edward III* will turn up. We may then be able to determine its company affiliation on documentary evidence and put the issue of authorship aside.

Edward II

Marlowe scholarship is singularly incurious about the stage history of *Edward II*. It would seem that the title-pages of its quartos say all on the whereabouts of the play that needs to be said. The edition in 1594, which was preceded on 6 July 1593 by a registration at Stationers' Hall, advertises the play on its title-page as having been "sundrie times publiquely acted *in the honourable citie of London, by the* right honourable the Earle of *Pembrooke his seruants. Written by* Chri. Marlow *Gent.*" (*BEPD*, I, no. 129). William Jones, who had registered the copy and published the 1594 quarto, put out another edition in 1598. It too named Pembroke's men. On 16 December 1611, Jones sold the rights to Roger Barnes, who published a text in 1612 with the same company attribution as Q1594 and Q1598. Barnes sold the copyright to Henry Bell on 17 April 1617, but Bell waited until 1622 to issue an edition. The first run of the title-page repeated the company claim from the earlier quartos, but at some point in the printing, the formula "the late Queenes *Maiesties Seruants at the* Red Bull" was substituted for the reference to Pembroke's men.

The companies to which these title-pages assign *Edward II* are, first, the company of Pembroke's men that turns up in provincial records and the Chamber Accounts in 1592–93. Edward Alleyn asked for news of these players in the summer of 1593; and answering in a letter dated 28 September 1593, his father-in-law, Philip Henslowe, said that "they are all at home and hauffe ben t⟨his⟩ v or sixe weackes for they cane not saue ther carges ⟨w⟩ᵗʰ trauell as I heare & weare fayne to pane the⟨r⟩ parell for ther carge" (*HD*, 280). Second, Q1598 is roughly contemporary with the return of a company of Pembroke's men to the London scene. An organization by that name leased the Swan playhouse early in 1597 and performed there until the Privy Council suspended playing on 28 July. A number of the players moved to the Rose in October and joined the Admiral's men. In 1612 when the third quarto of the play was published, the London companies surviving past 1603 had acquired royal patrons. Fleay supposes that members of Pembroke's men had already joined Worcester's men, who became Queen Anne's company in 1604.[35] It is Queen Anne's men to which the later version of the 1622 title-page refers; the company played at the Red Bull from about 1607 to 1617 (*ES*, II, 446–448).

However, the argument that *Edward II* passed from one organization of Pembroke's men to another until it came into the hands of Queen Anne's men runs counter to the story that theater historians usually tell about the companies coming out of the provinces in 1593–94. We have assumed that when these troupes went out of business, they sold their apparel and playbooks, and their players began looking elsewhere for employment. Evidence for this corporate disintegration and dispersal of property comes from various sources. One is Henslowe's letter to Alleyn that Pembroke's men had to pawn their apparel to pay the debts that they had accumulated on tour. Another is the flood of playbooks that stationers registered in 1593–94. Pembroke's men, for example, appear to have sold not only *Edward II*

(S.R. [that is, entered in the Stationers' Register] 6 July 1593) but also Part One of *The Contention of York and Lancaster* (S.R. 12 March 1594), *The Taming of A Shrew* (S.R. 2 May 1594), and Part Two of *The Contention*, or *The True Tragedy of Richard Duke of York* (Q1595). Sussex's men sold *Titus Andronicus* (S.R. 6 February 1594) and *George a Greene* (S.R. 1 April 1595). The Queen's men sold *Friar Bacon and Friar Bungay* (S.R. 14 May 1594), *The Famous Victories of Henry the V* (S.R. 14 May 1594), *The True Tragedy of Richard III* (S.R. 19 June 1594), and *1 Selimus* (Q1594).

A third sign that the troupes dissolved their sharers' agreements and sold their gear is that both their players and playbooks turn up in later companies. One beneficiary of the collapse of Strange's men was the company of Admiral's men that leased the Rose on 14 May 1594, played briefly with the Chamberlain's men at the Newington playhouse, and then settled in at the Rose, beginning 15 June 1594. The Admiral's men obtained at least two players from the members of Strange's men on tour in the summer of 1593 (Alleyn and Downton) and at least three playbooks from the repertory that Henslowe listed for Strange's men in 1592–93: *The Massacre at Paris*, which the Admiral's men revived in June 1594; the two parts of *Tamar Cham*, which they revived in May and June of 1596; and *The Spanish Tragedy*, which they revived in January 1597. They acquired two plays from the stock most recently performed by Sussex's men with the Queen's men at the Rose in April 1594. One, *The Ranger's Comedy*, appears to have been brought to the offerings by the Queen's men; the second, *The Jew of Malta*, had been performed by every company leasing the Rose since 1592. The Admiral's men revived both plays in June of 1594. In the fall the company returned both parts of *Tamburlaine* to the stage; the title-pages of the quartos in 1590 and 1593 identify the previous owners of the texts as an earlier version of the Admiral's men.

The Chamberlain's men acquired players and books out of the same pool. The touring license for Strange's men in 1593 names five men who appear either as payees for the Chamberlain's men in the Chamber Accounts of 1594–97 or in the cast list printed with *Every Man in His Humor* in 1616: Will Kempe, Thomas Pope, John Heminges, Augustine Phillips, and George Bryan. A play that has been conjecturally identified as Shakespeare's *Henry VI* is in Henslowe's playlists for Strange's men ("ne," 3 March 1592).[36] We cannot document a performance of Shakespeare's *Henry VI* by the Chamberlain's men, but it is reasonable to assume that they acquired it, for it was the company's property when Heminges and Condell prepared the 1623 Folio. Henslowe's entries for Sussex's men, 1593–94, include *Titus Andronicus*, and the playtext appears to have traveled both to a stationer (S.R. 6 February 1594) and to the Chamberlain's men straight from Sussex's inventory.

Other information and theories on the Chamberlain's acquisitions point to Pembroke's men. One connection is the migration of *Titus Andronicus*, *The Taming of the Shrew*, and *3 Henry VI*. Because *Titus Andronicus* and "bad" versions of the other two plays (*The Taming of A Shrew*, *The True Tragedy of Richard Duke of York*) were published as Pembroke's texts, some theater historians assume the company originally owned the "good" texts, which passed to the Chamberlain's men.

Henslowe's *Diary* appears to document performances of the first two plays by the Chamberlain's men in 1594, and although there is no similar record for the third, its availability to Heminges and Condell in 1623 indicates its ownership by the company. In another connection, we find the names of several actors preserved in the texts of various Pembroke's plays. In two of these (*The Taming of A Shrew, 3 Henry VI*), either the name of Will Sly or John Sincler appears. Both men later became Chamberlain's men.[37] Greg adds a third connection; he believes that *Hamlet* and *Hester and Ahasuerus* may have come from Pembroke's with the Chamberlain's other two plays in the Newington run.[38] A fourth connection is Shakespeare. Since *2 Henry VI, Richard III, Two Gentlemen of Verona, Romeo and Juliet*, and other of Shakespeare's plays allegedly written before 1594 cannot be found in repertories of Strange's, Sussex's, or the Queen's men, some theater historians have guessed that Pembroke's company owned the playbooks.[39]

Yet not even Fleay conjectures that Shakespeare's company acquired *Edward II* from Pembroke's men along with the other texts. We are asked to believe, then, that Marlowe's play languished in the provinces before and after 1597 or (worse yet) that it was not played at all until Queen Anne's men acquired a text. Either fate was a dreadful waste of commercial property. The genre of the play would in itself have guaranteed an audience. In the mid-1590s, the vogue for tragical histories using the English chronicles was on the rise. This play, in addition, treated that subject matter sensationally. It exposed the "evil" of a weak king who neglected the administration of his kingdom to frolic with his baseborn lover. It raised sensitive issues in politics and marriage by dramatizing the treason of Mortimer and the adultery of Queen Isabella. In the character of Lightborn, it featured a businesslike and ruthless executioner without precedent in earlier drama. In the horrific impalement of Edward, it staged a conclusion without equal in the drama yet to come.

Any company in 1594 would have known that a play by Christopher Marlowe could draw an audience. In the late 1580s when *Tamburlaine* was brought to the stage by the Admiral's men, it was instantly popular. That popularity created a sequel, *2 Tamburlaine*, and the plays went through two editions in three years' time. When both texts were acquired and revived by the Admiral's company of 1594, they were still popular enough to bring in receipts to Henslowe that were comparable to the best of the company's new offerings. *The Jew of Malta* had been played successfully by three different companies at the Rose (and it was old even then) before the Admiral's men acquired it in 1594. It was to bring Henslowe slightly lower receipts at the Admiral's revival, but the company continued to rotate the play into production (1596, 1601). *The Massacre at Paris* had brought Henslowe his second highest receipts of Strange's 1592–93 run (74s.), exceeded only by the play given on 3 March 1592 (76s.8d. [*Henry VI*]). The Admiral's men revived *The Massacre at Paris* twice, in 1594 and again in 1601. They also acquired *Doctor Faustus* from one of the companies breaking apart in 1594. Although it had been in production in 1594–97 for so long that its receipts dropped down to 5s., the Admiral's men felt *Doctor Faustus* worth the investment of 40s. for additions in November 1602.

Obviously, had *Edward II* been for sale in 1594, the buyer would have acquired a commodity of considerable value.

Evaluation: The title-page advertisements of *Edward II* appear to indicate that the play remained with a company of Pembroke's men until the Queen Anne's men acquired a copy of it a dozen years later. However, Pembroke's players ran into debt in 1593. Along with pawning theatrical gear, one of their remedies when they returned to London was to sell a "good" copy of *Edward II* to William Jones. The company may have kept a copy too, but the title is not among those that Greg attributes to Pembroke's men from Henslowe's records in the fall of 1597.[40] The dramatic ingredients of the play, plus the reputation of Marlowe's successes, suggest a ready market with a London company. Plays *did* migrate from defunct companies to surviving ones in 1594. There was a track between Pembroke's men and the Chamberlain's men along which some Shakespearean texts traveled.[41] Even though there is no evidence to document a stage life for *Edward II*, its printing in 1594, 1598, 1612, and 1622 hints of an extended popularity. It is plausible to deduce that the popularity resulted at least in part from its presence among the offerings of a London company in the mid-1590s. From 1594 to 1603, that company seems not to have been the Admiral's men, whose plays on the Edward subject matter were *The Spencers* (1599) and *Mortimer* (1602). Appealing as it may be to imagine that it was the Chamberlain's men who had *Edward II* with which to counter the Admiral's five Marlowe plays and who might have performed it while introducing *Richard II*, Shakespeare's own study of failed kingship, there is no evidence on which to argue for the attribution.

The Tartarian Cripple

On 14 August 1600, Cuthbert Burby and Walter Burre entered *Every Man in his Humor* in the Stationers' Register. On the same day, following the entry for Jonson's play, there is the registration by Burby of a work called "The famous Tragicall history, of ye Tartarian Crippell Empo^r of Constantinople" (*BEPD*, I, 16; II, no. Θ25). It is not clear from the language of the entry that *The Tartarian Cripple* was a playbook.[42] If it was, though, the context of its registration may identify the company that owned the text. The owners of *Every Man in his Humor* were the Chamberlain's men, and Burre advertised the play as theirs when he published it in quarto in 1601; the Revels Account for 1604–05 records that it was one of ten plays that the King's men performed at Court over Christmastide; and, in the 1616 folio, the play carries a cast list of Chamberlain's players as well as a new title-page naming the company ("the then Lord CHAMBERLAIN his Servants" [*BEPD*, I, no. 176]). The proximity of the two entries suggests that *The Tartarian Cripple* may also have been obtained from the Chamberlain's men.

However, to assume as much merely from the fact that *The Tartarian Cripple* was entered on the same day by the same stationer as *Every Man In* is to ask far more of stationers' records than they have ordinarily been trusted to yield. It may be, though, that the myths we have inherited about the ethics of stationers have blinded us to legitimate information on theatrical business in their records. As we have seen in the case of *Thomas Lord Cromwell*, these myths have made us unduly skeptical about the reliability of advertisements of company ownership of plays in the Stationers' Register and on title-pages. The research of Peter Blayney exposes as myth the belief that plays printed without registration were either pirated or published illegally from the viewpoint of stationers' regulations. Blayney also argues that the "staying entries" are not signs that the companies hired stationers as agents to supervise the flow of their playbooks onto the market; rather, these entries put the registration "on hold" until proper authority (from the Bishops or the Wardens) could be secured.[43]

Another myth is that companies did not want a stationer to obtain one of their successful offerings because they feared that another company would then get a copy of it and mount a rival production. However, there is no evidence that the companies competed in this way. More than a dozen of Shakespeare's plays reached print during a period of intense competition among the London companies (1594–1603), and nothing in theatrical records suggests any of the London-based organizations bought and staged one of these plays.[44] In the most famous and public case of stolen playbooks, that of *The Malcontent*, the King's players comment in the new Induction on an exchange of plays that resulted in their acquiring *The Malcontent* from the boys' company at Blackfriars. They do not imply that the boys' company "found" the *Jeronimo* text at a bookstall or that they themselves might retaliate by purchasing the Blackfriars play in quarto. What companies did instead of buying printed texts was to imitate the offerings of other companies with new texts of their own, as in the clusters of plays on such popular topics as the Wars of the Roses, Richard III, and Henry V. The case of *The Malcontent* seems to be one in which the boys' company violated the decorum of competition by duplicating not the subject matter of Hieronimo's tragedy but the very text itself, for which offense the King's men returned "one for another."

Yet another myth is that companies did not want stationers to print plays because playgoers who could read might prefer to buy quartos rather than attend performances. There are no statistics to mark the patterns of attendance at all of the playhouses, of course, but there are signs that the appearance of a quarto did not ruin the audience for a play. Both parts of *Tamburlaine* were in print before the Admiral's men mounted a revival in 1594–95, yet the play had excellent receipts to Henslowe. *The Spanish Tragedy* was in print before the Admiral's men revived it in 1597, yet it also brought in receipts to Henslowe with a better average than half of the company's new plays. The first part of *Sir John Oldcastle* was in print before Worcester's men acquired the text from Admiral's men and mounted a revival. Had the company expected it to be a commercial risk, they might not have invested 50s. in additions (*HD*, 213, 216) and close to £15.10s. for new apparel (*HD*, 214). Several editions of *Richard II*, *Richard III*, and *1 Henry IV* came out after each was first retired from the stage. We have rationalized the appearance of such quartos by explaining that companies did not mind so much having a play published when its stage run was concluded; however, companies knew that they would bring many of their old books back into production. If quartos had been a serious threat to company profits, the Chamberlain's men might have guarded these premium offerings more closely.

In fact, there were some circumstances when the companies seem to have been willing to trade with stationers. One was during the period of transition from the 1593–94 companies to those of 1594. Twenty playbooks reached print in 1594 alone, more than a dozen of which had recently been in the repertory of a company that would not survive the transition. Another is in 1600. Fourteen plays were printed that year, and another fourteen were registered at Stationers' Hall (not including *The Tartarian Cripple*). Various explanations have been offered, none thoroughly satisfactory. From the viewpoint of the companies, though, it is fair to say that 1599–1600 was a period of vigorous competition. At the Boar's Head Inn in 1598, a new playhouse had opened, which was successful enough that first year to justify renovations and expansions of the galleries. The Chamberlain's men built a new and reportedly fancy playhouse in 1599. The Admiral's men built one in 1600. The boys' troupes were back in business by 1600. Worcester's men did well enough at the Boar's Head in 1600–01 and at the Rose in 1602–03 to survive the playhouse closures of 1603–04 and emerge in 1604 as Queen Anne's men. Presumably, the company remaining at the Boar's Head, Derby's men, would have survived as well if their leader, Robert Browne, had not died of plague in 1603. It is conceivable, therefore, that the companies were selling texts to stationers as a way of advertising the quality of offerings at their respective houses. Twelve of the fourteen quartos new in 1600 carried references on their title-pages to the companies that owned the plays.

With the mythology of play companies' commerce with stationers thus under siege, we are justified in looking again at entries in the Stationers' Register to see what information they may yield on the subject. There are, in fact, several mass entries from which we may infer that all of the plays being registered came from the inventory of the same company. One is an entry on a fly leaf of Register C, itself undated but containing two dated items:

> my lord chamberlens mens Plaies Entred viz̃
> 27 may. 1600 To m^r Rob̃t[es]. A morall of
> cloth breches & velvet hose/.
> 29. May. To him. Allarum to London/.
> (*BEPD*, I, 15)

Whatever the purpose of the list, its language makes clear that both plays came from the repertory of the Chamberlain's men, as indeed the separate entry of *Cloth Breeches and Velvet Hose* on 27 May 1600 specifies.

A second mass entry of interest is the so-called "staying entry" of 4 August [1600]. It contains the titles of four plays, none of which had been registered previously. Three of these plays—*Henry V*, *Every Man in his Humor*, and *Much Ado About Nothing*—were subsequently published in quartos with title-pages advertising them as the Chamberlain's men's. They also appear attributed to the company in one of the records of Court performances: *Henry V* and *Every Man in his Humor*, Revels Account of 1604–05; *Much Ado About Nothing*, Chamber Account of 1612–13. Without question, the three were Chamberlain's property. What of the company affiliation of the fourth play, *As You Like It?* We have its presence in the First Folio to indicate the Chamberlain's men, but we may also reasonably infer that it belonged to the company from its registration with other Chamberlain's plays.

A third mass entry with implications of company ownership occurs in the Register on 14 May 1594. Adam Islip registered five titles separately, one after another, each with its own notation of the 6d. fee. At a later time, Islip's name was canceled and that of Edward White was inserted. The five titles are "the Historye of ffryer Bacon and ffryer Boungaye," "The moste famous Chronicle historye of Leire kinge of England and his Three Daughters," "the famous historye of Iohn of Gaunte sonne to Kynge Edward the Third wth his Conquest of Spaine and marriage of his Twoo daughters to the King[es] of Castile and Portugale," "the booke of David and Bethsaba," and "a pastorall plesant Comedie of Robin Hood and little Iohn" (*BEPD*, I, 10–11). It is certain that four of these titles were plays and that two of the plays had belonged to the Queen's men. The question that the entry raises is whether the coincidence of the mass registration implies that the fifth title was also a play and that the three titles unidentified with a company also belonged to the Queen's men.

We know that *Friar Bacon and Friar Bungay*, *King Leir*, and *David and Bethsabe* were plays because quartos survive. The language of the entry for *Robin Hood and Little John* ("a pastorall plesant Comedie") identifies it as a play. Until Greg noticed the mass entry, however, no one had argued seriously that the fifth title in the mass entry was a play.[45] For Greg, "the company it [*John of Gaunt*] keeps . . . [leaves] little doubt of its dramatic character" (*BEPD*, II, Θ12). *Friar Bacon and Friar Bungay* and *King Leir* belonged to the Queen's men; both appear in the combined repertory of Sussex's and the Queen's men at Eastertide 1594 (*HD*, 21), but neither appears in the repertory of Sussex's men alone. White published *Friar Bacon* in 1594 with a title-page advertising it as the Queen's company's. There is no evidence to identify the owners of the other plays. Their sole association with a company is their presence in the entry of 14 May 1594 with two properties from the holdings of the Queen's men.

Of course, some mass entries contain titles of plays and chapbooks mixed together, and the plays come from different companies. On 14 August 1600, for example, Thomas Pavier entered six titles in the register: "The historye of Henrye the vth wth the battell of Agencourt," "The Spanishe Tragedie," "An Interlude Called Edward longe shank[es]," "The fyrste pte of the gentill Crafte," "An Interlude of Iack strawe," and "The lookinge glas for London" (*BEPD*, I, 16). Read in the most obvious way, the entry contains one Shakespeare play from the repertory of the Chamberlain's men, one Kyd play from the repertory of Admiral's men, one Peele play perhaps from Queen's, one anonymous play from a repertory unknown (*Jack Straw*), one Lodge and Nashe play from the repertory of Strange's men (*HD*, 16–17), and one chapbook (*The Gentle Craft*). A significant difference between the Pavier and White registrations, however, is that Pavier bought the titles from stationers. The entry states specifically that the copies were "thing[es] formerlye printed & sett over to the sayd Thoms Pavyer" (*BEPD*, I, 16).

In addition to mass entries, the Stationers' Register contains instances in which two plays were entered together or in sequence. The format of the entries implies that the titles were bought from the same source. On 23 August 1600, Andrew Wise and William Asply registered *Much Ado About Nothing* and *2 Henry IV*. It is clear that the plays were entered together: the stationers' names appear once, the phrase "Twoo book[es]" and the attribution to Shakespeare refer to both plays, and the registration fee is entered as one sum ("xij^d" [*BEPD*, I, 16]). On 19 June 1594, John Danter registered two plays, "Godfrey of Bulloigne wth the Conquest of Ierusalem" and "the lyfe and deathe of Heliogabilus" (*BEPD*, I, 12). These entries are connected by the phrase "an other enterlude" and by the rendering of the fee in one sum, but they are separated by the repetition of Danter's name at the start of the second entry. On 14 May 1594, Thomas Creede entered "The famous victories of henrye the ffyft" and "Iames the ffourthe slayne at fflodden" (*BEPD*, I, 10). Like the Danter entries, these two are connected by a verbal reference ("by the like warrant"), but they are separated both by the repetition of Creede's name and the discrete entries of the 6d. fee.

From the advertisements on the title-pages of their quartos, we know that *Much Ado About Nothing* and *2 Henry IV* belonged to the Chamberlain's men. It may be that the titles in the other pairs of registrations came from the same companies. If so, we may be able to identify the affiliation of one play from that of the other. In the case of *James IV* and *The Famous Victories of Henry V*, Thomas Creede printed one play in 1598 with a title-page advertising it as the Queen's men's (*The Famous Victories of Henry V*). He printed the other (*James IV*) in the same year with a title-page identifying only its author (Greene), not its company. Perhaps the entry in the Stationers' Register offers a piece of evidence that the play's owners were also the Queen's men.[46] In the cases of *Godfrey of Bulloigne with the Conquest of Jerusalem* and *Heliogabalus*, we do not know the company affiliation of either text. It is possible, though, that the *Godfrey* play was owned by Strange's men in 1592 and later by the Admiral's men. The argument for such an attribution is as follows: Danter's *Godfrey* could be the *Jerusalem* in Henslowe's lists for Strange's men in the spring of 1592 (*HD*, 17; Greg, *BEPD*, II, no. Θ15). It may also be the *Godfrey of Bulloigne* that the Admiral's men revived on 26 July 1594 (not marked "ne") and for which they bought a second part ("ne," 19 July). From which company did Danter acquire *his* text (if, indeed, his is one of these)? Since he registered his play on 19 June 1594, he apparently acquired it at about the time the Admiral's men acquired theirs. Perhaps Strange's men sold one copy of their *Jerusalem* to Danter and one to the Admiral's men. And (to stretch the coincidence even more) while Strange's men were selling Danter one playbook, perhaps they offered him another—*Heliogabalus*—that they had not had in production when they were at the Rose (and in Henslowe's records) in the spring of 1592.

The entries of *The Tartarian Cripple* and *Every Man in his Humor* are similar to the pairings cited above in several ways. Like the Danter and Creede entries, they repeat the name of the stationer. Like the Creede entry, each specifies the 6d. fee. However, the format is also different: Burre was not a party to the second registration, the entry for *The Tartarian Cripple* fails to include a phrase that looks back to the previous entry, and the *Cripple* entry cites a different warden as the authority for registration of the copy. The question here, then, is not only about the company provenance of *The Tartarian Cripple* but also about the nature of its text. Is its registration just after that of *Every Man in his Humor* mere coincidence, or does it indicate that a play from the Chamberlain's repertory is being registered?

If it should be that *The Tartarian Cripple* was a play (whoever its company owners), a fascinating stage history has been lost with it. That history involves the principle of competition by which companies exploited the successful narrative materials in their own repertory and those of other companies with duplicate plays, sequels, and spin-offs. In the years between 1594 and 1603, the Admiral's and Chamberlain's men drew on similar topics regularly. For example, in November 1595, the Admiral's men introduced a play called *Henry V*; in 1596, the Chamberlain's men introduced *1 Henry IV*, which they followed with two sequels and a spin-off (*The Merry Wives of Windsor*). The Admiral's men also acquired a two-part spin-off (the *Sir John Oldcastle* plays). Also in 1596, the Admiral's men revived *The Jew of Malta*; the Chamberlain's men had *The Merchant of Venice* by the fall. Sometime before 1597, the Chamberlain's men staged *Richard III*; years later (1602), the Admiral's men put money down on Ben Jonson's *Richard Crookback*. In 1597 the Admiral's men brought out *The Comedy of Humors*, which the Chamberlain's men followed with Jonson's two "humors" plays. In 1599 the Admiral's men bought *Troilus and Cressida*; Shakespeare's play by the same title was on stage about 1602. Around 1600–02, the Chamberlain's men put on *Thomas Lord Cromwell*; in the summer of 1601, the Admiral's men were paying for one part of *Wolsey*, with a second part to follow.

If *The Tartarian Cripple* was on stage sometime in the year or two before Burby acquired a copy, it followed revivals of well-known plays on the matter of Tamburlaine. Henslowe's *Diary* shows that the Admiral's men revived *1* and *2 Tamburlaine* in 1594 and played both into the fall of 1595 (12, 13 November). Six months later (May, June 1596), they revived two old plays from Strange's repertory: *1* and *2 Tamar Cham*, which Greg identifies as stories of Temuchin, more familiarly known as Jenghis Khan.[47] According to Henslowe's *Diary*, they bought one or both of these from Alleyn on 2 October 1602 for a revival. We do not know whether the Admiral's men revived Marlowe's pair in the years after 1597, but Tamburlaine's "cotte with coper lace" and "breches of crymson vellvet" were in the inventory that Henslowe made in 1598 (*HD*, 321-322). New and separated issues of the plays came out in 1605 (Part Two) and 1606 (Part One). The title of *The Tartarian Cripple* seems to identify the main character as Tamburlaine himself.[48] It also indicates one piece of pseudohistory that the narrative treated: Tamburlaine's march westward to Angora, where he defeated Bajezeth and thus enabled the Christian city of Constantinople to break free of Turkish control.[49] Of special interest to Shakespeareans in this conjectural stage history of ersatz Tamburlaines, no doubt, is that the Chamberlain's men probably had *2 Henry IV* in production sometime in 1598. One of the play's finest comic moments is Ancient Pistol's mock-Tamburlainian rant about hollow pampered jades. Clearly, Shakespeare makes the joke at the expense of Marlowe's *Tamburlaine,* played by the Admiral's men, but the joke doubles back on the Chamberlain's men if they also had or were to have a Tamburlaine play on stage.

Evaluation: The only evidence that *The Tartarian Cripple* was a play is its registration at Stationers' Hall in an entry that follows immediately after one for *Every Man in his Humor.* Both entries were made by Cuthbert Burby. The coincidence of *The Tartarian Cripple* entry with the entry of a play owned and recently performed by the Chamberlain's men invites the conjecture that Burby had also acquired *The Tartarian Cripple* from that company. But even if the *Cripple* did not share the stage with plays by Shakespeare, the fact remains that the Stationers' Register has incidences of mass and sequential entries in which the plays being registered belonged to the same company. In cases such as *As You Like It, Much Ado About Nothing,* and *2 Henry IV,* there is reliable evidence of company affiliation in other records. However, for those titles for which there are no other data on ownership, as in the cases of *David and Bethsabe, Robin Hood and Little John,* and *James IV,* or no other data on their very existence, as in the case of *The Tartarian Cripple,* the entries in the Stationers' Register provide a context where we may find some clue to the identity and provenance of works.

Describing the search for information on Shakespeare's theatrical career, Edmond Malone recommends that "[e]very circumstance . . . should be sifted and examined with our utmost industry and care; every hint, however slight, must be seized and investigated, and every allusion, however dark or mysterious, must, if possible, be unfolded and explained."[50] Sifting hints, many of the theater historians who assign plays to company owners have thought that Shakespeare's authorship guarantees that a work was owned by the Chamberlain's–King's men. It does. Alleged authorship, however, is not in itself evidence of the play's company affiliation. We have also thought that the migration of playbooks from the troupes that toured the provinces in 1592–94 to new companies in 1594 means that the Chamberlain's men acquired secondhand texts in the early years of their corporate life. It does. However, the fact of playbook migration does not identify the texts that survived or the companies that obtained them. A more fruitful line of research for the company affiliations of texts allegedly by Shakespeare and possibly on stage after June 1594 is the commercial market for quartos in the second half of the 1590s. The publication of these plays could be the initial clue in a chain of evidence that leads to a company in business in London.

The history of scholarship on stationers and their contacts with the playhouse world has caused us to distrust the information on company owners that these men provided in the Stationers' Register and on the title-pages of the quartos they produced. Yet that information appears to be good, especially for the relatively current plays of current companies. The discovery that title-pages carry accurate information on company owners encourages us to look at entries such as mass and sequential registrations in the Stationers' Register more closely. With the judicious examination of circumstances and investigation of hints, we may find that these stationers' records hold not only the names of lost plays but also the identity of the companies that brought the plays to the stage.

NOTES

1. W. W. Greg, *A Bibliography of the English Printed Drama to the Restoration*, 4 vols. (London: Bibliographical Society, 1939–59), I, 18. Throughout the essay, I quote Greg's transcriptions of the Stationers' Register, hereafter referred to as *BEPD* and cited in the text; I alter the plural ending "e" to "es" (in brackets) and alter "f" to "s".

2. *BEPD*, I, no. 189. Throughout the essay, I quote title-page information from Greg's transcriptions, hereafter cited in the text by the number that Greg assigns to each play; I omit hyphens that occur at line breaks.

3. *BEPD*, III, 1330–1338. Throughout the essay, I cite the play catalogues as reprinted in *BEPD*.

4. Chetwinde seems to have made the association of *Locrine* on his own. Neither Rogers and Ley in 1656, Archer in 1656, nor Francis Kirkman in 1661 ascribed *Locrine* to Shakespeare. In the second edition of his catalogue in 1671, however, Kirkman picked up the attribution (*BEPD*, III, 1354).

5. *Shakespeare and the Stationers* (Columbus: Ohio State University Press, 1955), p. 179. As many theater historians have observed, "W. S." need not be Shakespeare at all. Baldwin Maxwell discusses alternative identifications of the initials in *Studies in the Shakespeare Apocrypha* (1956; rpt. New York: Greenwood, 1969), pp. 9–13.

6. Throughout the essay, I use the text of Henslowe's *Diary* edited by R. A. Foakes and R. T. Rickert (Cambridge: Cambridge University Press, 1961), hereafter cited as *HD*. I provide page references only when the date of the entry is inadequate documentation.

7. We have no reason to disbelieve that *Titus Andronicus* was associated with Derby's and Pembroke's men, as the title-page of Q1594 also claims. The issue is how that association took place. One popular view is that the playbook migrated from Derby's to Pembroke's to Sussex's men. Paul E. Bennett offers an alternative: that Sussex's men included players from the other two organizations who were still identified with their former patrons ("The Word 'Goths' in 'A Knack to Know a Knave,'" *Notes and Queries*, 200 [1955], 462–463). An appeal of Bennett's suggestion is that it makes the case of *Titus Andronicus* analogous to that of *A Knack to Know a Knave* in the amount of specific and accurate information that traveled with its playbook to stationers and was subsequently used as advertising.

8. Greg reasons that *Titus Andronicus* belonged to the Chamberlain's men because the title did not turn up in the diary for the Admiral's men from 15 June onward (Henslowe's *Diary*, 2 vols. [London: A. H. Bullen, 1904, 1908], II, 85).

9. J. R. Dasent, ed., *Acts of the Privy Council of England*, 32 vols. (London, 1890–1907), XXIV, 212.

10. *William Shakespeare: A Study of Facts and Problems*, 2 vols. (Oxford: Clarendon Press, 1930), II, 331–332. Subsequent citations from this work (hereafter referred as *WS*) occur in the text. The advertisement for *Every Man out of his Humor* is not in its 1600 quarto but on its title-page in the 1616 folio.

11. *Collections*, Volume VI, Malone Society Reprints (Oxford: The Malone Society, 1961), pp. 55–56. The advertisement for *The Alchemist* is not in its 1612 quarto but on its title-page in the 1616 folio.

12. E. K. Chambers, *The Elizabethan Stage*, 4 vols. (Oxford: Clarendon Press, 1923), II, 196. Subsequent citations from this work (hereafter cited as *ES*) occur in the text.

13. For the employment records of the players, see Edwin Nungezer, *A Dictionary of Actors* (1929; rpt. New York: AMS Press, 1981). All of the information in this essay on the biography and company affiliations of players is taken from Nungezer, unless otherwise noted.

14. It is the first quarto of *Hamlet* (Q1603) published by Nicholas Ling and John Trundell that carries an advertisement of the King's men (an entry for *Hamlet* in the Stationers' Register on 26 February 1602 by James Roberts lists it as belonging to the Chamberlain's men). One text that we believe the company performed, the second quarto (Q1604–05), does not. If the registration of and the advertisement in Q1603 refer to that specific text and not to the play more nearly represented by Q1604–05, *Hamlet* may not belong in a list of plays with corroborated title-page advertisements of company. Two additional plays in this list have entries in the Stationers' Register that name the Chamberlain's or King's men: *Troilus and Cressida* (7 February 1603) and *King Lear* (26 November 1607). Where claims of the Chamberlain's or King's men occur in the Stationers' Register, these claims are repeated subsequently on title-pages except in the instance of one play: on 8 February 1605, Thomas Pavier registered *The Fair Maid of Bristow* at Stationers' Hall, and the entry says that the play had been "played at Hampton Court by his ma[t][es] players" (*BEPD*, I, 20); the title-page in 1605 repeats the site of the performance, but not the name of the company.

15. The others are *A Warning for Fair Women, A Larum for London, Satiromastix, The London Prodigal, The Miseries of Enforced Marriage, The Revenger's Tragedy, The Devil's Charter, A Yorkshire Tragedy,* and *Pericles* (I would add *Mucedorus* except that it is the third quarto, not the first, that carries the advertisement of Shakespeare's company; all the same, the specific details of the advertisement [the Shrovetide performance, reference to the Globe] leave little doubt that the attribution is correct). The date of stage runs is, of course, a controversial issue on which there is almost no evidence unless the play turns up in Henslowe's *Diary*. For most plays, the dates of composition are determined by allusions, which are then interpreted by various scholars, often variously. The stage run is presumed to follow closely on the composition. There are some differences of opinion on the dates of composition and stage histories of the above-listed plays, but for only one—*A Warning for Fair Women*—does the received opinion date the composition of the play as much as ten years before its publication. In a recent edition, Charles Dale Cannon says that "most of the critics believe *A Warning* dates from 1588–1590" (*A Warning for Fair Women: A Critical Edition* [Mouton: The Hague, 1975], p. 44). He also says that these critics do not provide substantive evidence for the date. In my opinion, many of the guesses on dates are

based on the belief that the play in question is bad and (further) that bad plays must be old. Curiously, F. G. Fleay, who so often guesses incorrectly, trusts the title-page claim that *A Warning for Fair Women* had been "lately . . . acted" (*BEPD*, no. 155), and he assigns the play to 1598-99 (*A Biographical Chronicle of the English Drama, 1559-1642*, 2 vols. [1891: rpt. New York: Burt Franklin, 1969], II, 54).

16. F. T. Bowers, "The Date and Composition of *Alphonsus, Emperor of Germany*," *Harvard Studies and Notes in Philology and Literature*, 15 (1933), 165-90.

17. *The Jacobean and Caroline Stage*, 7 vols. (Oxford: Clarendon Press, 1941-68), V, 1287-88.

18. Cuthbert Burby entered *Edward III* and published both quartos. It may seem that he would have advertised the Chamberlain's men on the title-page if they had owned the play and he had known that. However, his text of *A Knack to Know an Honest Man* (1596) does not advertise the Admiral's men, though the play had been on the stage at the Rose since 22 October 1594 and was in production until 3 November 1596. Even very well-known plays came into print without an advertisement of company. Andrew Wise published *1 Henry IV* several times at the height of its popularity and of the controversy over the Oldcastle name (1598, 1599), but he never advertised the Chamberlain's men, although he had published or was to publish four other texts carrying their name.

19. Capell argues that the style of the play is similar to Shakespeare's and that "no known writer" was capable of writing so well; he readily admits the absence of "any external evidence" for the attribution ([London, 1760], pp. ix-x).

20. *The History of English Dramatic Poetry to the Time of Shakespeare; and Annals of the Stage to the Restoration*, 2nd ed., 3 vols. (London: G. Bell, 1879), I, v.

21. *King Edward the Third; a Historical Play* (London: T. Richard, 1874), p. ii.

22. *A Biographical Chronicle of the English Drama, 1559-1642*, II, 62. Fleay attributed Shakespeare's additions to a revival *ca.* 1594 (II, 214).

23. *The Real War of the Theaters* (Boston: Heath, 1935), p. 101.

24. For *Measure for Measure*, see *WS*, II, 331. For *The Tempest* and *The Winter's Tale*, see *WS*, II, 341-342. For *Julius Caesar* ("Caesars Tragedye") and *1 Henry IV* ("The Hotspurr"), see *Collections*, VI, 56.

25. H. J. Oliver discusses the identification of Henslowe's title as Shakespeare's play in an edition of *The Taming of the Shrew* (Oxford: Clarendon Press, 1984), pp. 30-32.

26. Henslowe's *Diary* documents the history of *1 Sir John Oldcastle* with the Admiral's and Worcester's companies (*HD*, 126, 213). There is no record of the stage life of *The Troublesome Reign of King John*.

27. Bentley, I, 28.

28. *The Arraignment of Paris* belonged to the Children of the Chapel, according to its title-page in 1584; we know of no stage runs after that date. The title-page of *Hoffman* (Q1631) advertises a performance at the Phoenix. The King's men gave performances there in 1630-31 (Bentley, I, 27-28), but there is no record of their having offered *Hoffman*. The title-pages of the *The Puritan* (Q1607) and *A Trick to Catch the Old One* (Q1608) advertise the Children of Paul's. Greg considers the two-part *Hieronimo* a ghost title ("Authorship Attributions in the Early Playlists, 1656-1671," *Edinburgh Bibliographical Society Transactions*, 2 [1946], 313).

29. Rowley was a King's man in the last year of his life, 1625-26. In *William Shakespeare and "The Birth of Merlin,"* Mark Dominik defends the collaboration of Shakespeare with Rowley, but he does not insist on an attribution of the play to the King's repertory (New York: Philosophical Library, 1985).

30. Herbert Berry lists the plays probably staged at the Boar's Head (*The Boar's Head Playhouse* [Washington, D. C.: Folger Books, 1986], pp. 124–127).

31. *A London Life in the Brazen Age* (Cambridge, Mass.: Harvard University Press, 1978), pp. 116–120. Ingram finds evidence that in 1595 Francis Henslowe took up lodgings in the tenements Langley built in the vicinity of the Swan.

32. Greg assigns *Hardicanute, Bourbon, Branholt, Alice Pierce, Black Joan, Stark Flattery*, and *Dido and Aeneas* to Pembroke's men in 1597 (*Henslowe's Diary*, II, 186–190). Henslowe recorded two titles for the company in 1600: *Like Unto Like* and *Roderick* (*HD*, 164).

33. Wentersdorf rests much of his argument on allusions in the play to the battle of the Armada in 1588; since he believes that Shakespeare is the author of the play, it is much to the benefit of his position to establish an early date ("The Date of *Edward III*," *Shakespeare Quarterly*, 16 [1965], 227–231). MacD. Jackson argues by way of inter-play borrowings that *Edward III* was once in repertory with Pembroke's plays, 1592-93 ("'Edward III', Shakespeare, and Pembroke's Men," *Notes and Queries*, 210 [1965], 329–331).

34. "A Seventeenth-Century Revival of *Mucedorus* in London Before 1610," *Shakespeare Quarterly*, 28 (1977), 362–364.

35. *A Chronicle History of the London Stage* (1890; rpt. New York: Burt Franklin, 1964), p. 139. Chambers thinks it is "just possible" that Pembroke's men moved over to Worcester's company (*ES*, II, 134).

36. In "The Date of *2, 3 Henry VI*," Hanspeter Born argues persuasively that the play Strange's men performed starting on 3 March 1592 was the play eventually published in the First Folio as *1 Henry VI* (*Shakespeare Quarterly*, 25 [1974], 324–326).

37. Scott McMillin discusses other connections between Pembroke's and the Lord Chamberlain's men in "Casting for Pembroke's Men: the *Henry VI* Quartos and *The Taming of A Shrew*," *Shakespeare Quarterly*, 23 (1972), 157. Karl P. Wentersdorf is the most recent scholar to argue that Shakespeare and Burbage were players for Pembroke's; but he has no new data on the subject ("The Origin and Personel of the Pembroke Company," *Theatre Research International*, 5 [1979–80], 64–66).

38. *Henslowe's Diary*, II, 163 (headnote to Section V).

39. On the evidence of inter-play borrowings, A. S. Cairncross argues for the location of *Richard III* and *Romeo and Juliet* in Pembroke's repertory ("Pembroke's Men and Some Shakespearian Conspiracies," *Shakespeare Quarterly*, 11 [1960], 335–349).

40. See note 32. None of Pembroke's titles is a play that we can identify as of 1592-93 vintage, except possibly *Aeneas and Dido*. Marlowe and Nashe wrote a *Dido* that was performed by the Children of the Queen's Chapel according to its title-page (Q1594). We have no record of its stage history.

41. There were also tracks out of the Chamberlain's men. Sometime between 1599 and 1602, three players transferred from that company to Worcester's men. One of these was Christopher Beeston, who became manager of Worcester's in 1612. Perhaps the business instincts manifest in 1612 had earlier prompted him to acquire an old playbook or two and take them to his new fellows as he evidently took apparel (*HD*, 215, 219). Some players routinely obtained both plays and playing gear, most notably Edward Alleyn, who sold both to the Admiral's men, 1598-1602. If Beeston were such a one, we must assume that he did so with the company's approval, for he seems to have left the Chamberlain's men on good terms. At least, when his former master and fellow player, Augustine Phillips, died in 1605, Phillips left Beeston 30s. in gold.

42. The wording of the title, "famous Tragicall history," is similar to the formulas used for playbooks in the Stationers' Register, as in the "famouse tragedie of the Riche Iewe of Malta" (17 May 1594) and the "Tragecall historie of Kinge Leir and his Three Daughters" (8 May 1605). Yet it is not as definitive as are the entries, "Two Plaies or thinges. thone called the maid[es] metamorphosis thother.gyve a man luck & throwe him into the Sea" (24 July 1600) and "an Enterlude called the Malecontent Tragiecomedia" (15 July 1604). Nevertheless, something about *The Tartarian Cripple* caught the eye of Chambers, who includes it in a section of lost plays although he concedes that it is "not necessarily a play" (*ES*, IV, 403).

43. These issues are discussed in a paper that Blayney delivered at the Folger Shakespeare Library in May, 1987.

44. Charles J. Sisson has published records from the Star Chamber that show a provincial company with printed texts of *King Lear* and *Pericles* in 1609-10. The players were Lord Cholmeley's, and the occasion of their performances was Candlemas, at Gowthwaite Hall, Nidderdale ("Shakespeare Quartos As Prompt-Copies," *Review of English Studies*, 18 [1942], 135–140).

45. Chambers, for example, thinks it more likely "the chap-book source" of the play that Hathway and Rankins sold to the Admiral's men in 1601 (*ES*, IV, 401).

46. In "Thomas Creede and the Repertory of the Queen's Men 1583–1592," G. M. Pinciss suggests that Creede himself is a clue. Pinciss shows that a good number of plays with title-pages advertising them as the Queen's men's were printed at Creede's shop (*Modern Philology*, 67 [1970], 321-330).

47. *Dramatic Documents from the Elizabethan Playhouses: Stage Plots: Actors' Parts: Prompt Books*, 2 vols. (Oxford: Clarendon Press, 1931), I, 161–162.

48. Presumably, Tamburlaine was the only lame conqueror from the Tartars famous enough to attract the interest of Elizabethan Englishmen. Because the titles of plays on similar subject matter did often echo one another, as in the *Henry V* plays, we might expect the author of *The Tartarian Cripple* to name the hero explicitly. However, there was a precedent for allusive titles: for example, *Richard III* and *Richard Crookback*; *The Jew of Malta* and *The Merchant of Venice* ("otherwise called," according to its entry in the Stationers' Register, "the Iewe of Venyce" [*BEPD*, I, 13]); and *Friar Bacon and Friar Bungay* and *John a Kent and John a Cumber*. Some titles echoed just a word from the titles of their models: for example, *The Taming of the Shrew* and *The Tamer Tam'd*. There are also instances in which the title of a play did not advertise the subject matter that it shared with an earlier drama: *The Four Prentices* makes no allusion in its title to the previously staged two-part *Godfrey of Bulloigne*; *Look About you* makes no allusion to its prominent character, Robin Hood. The plays that we know as *John of Bordeaux* and *Woodstock* may have been known by titles indicating their relation to the matters of Friar Bacon and Richard II, but they may not have.

49. The historical Tamerlane, of course, was never emperor of Constantinople. However, according to Michael Prawdin, Tamerlane's defeat of the Turks earned him as much adulation from the city as if he had been: "[t]he victory of Angora was celebrated by the Byzantines as if it had been their own. The Emperor sent gifts to Tamerlane, and recognized his supremacy. Tamerlane's renown as the saviour of Christendom spread throughout Europe" (*The Mongol Empire: Its Rise and Legacy*, trans. Eden and Cedar Paul [London: Allen & Unwin, 1940], p. 496).

50. *The Plays and Poems of William Shakespeare*, ed. James Boswell, 21 vols. (London, 1821: rpt. New York: AMS Press, 1967), II, 167.

Antonio's Revenge: The Tyrant, the Stoic, and the Passionate Man

KAREN ROBERTSON

In a sepulcher, lit by flickering tapers, just after midnight, the revenger meets the pretty little Julio, son of his enemy, Piero. The innocent and loving child, prattling of his fondness for his "brother," embraces Antonio. And Antonio, in the central revenge action of Marston's *Antonio's Revenge* (1599–1601), stabs the child to death.[1] This murder has received strong critical condemnation, yet such judgment fails to recognize the context—social and literary—in which such an action can be seen as heroic. In this paper I will show how the extreme vengeance taken by Antonio can be sited within the imaginative boundaries of Marston's Elizabethan contemporaries.

This play has rightly been seen as heavily influenced by Senecan models, yet it is more than an imitation. The killing of Julio is a dramatization of a topos of literary Senecanism—the idea of necessary excess in vengeance—that has contemporary English significance. Antonio's exceeding of Piero through the murder of the latter's heir was an idea already accepted by large numbers of Englishmen when, in 1584, they joined the Bond of Association and swore to take vengeance on an heir in punishment for the sins of the parent. Such public commitment to the principles of the blood feud demonstrates the vitality of the revenge ethic in the period. When, with the killing of Julio, Marston chose to dramatize the Senecan topos of excess, he was pushing to an extreme in a fiction an idea already sworn to in principle by some members of his audience.

The play recounts the reeruption of the blood feud between two ducal families, that of Piero Sforza, Duke of Venice, and Andrugio, lately of Genoa. Piero secretly poisons his enemy, Andrugio, and, in a plot to break the engagement between his own daughter, Mellida, and Antonio, murders Feliche, son of the Stoic, Pandulpho. The tyrant triumphs, checked only by the imperturbability of the Stoic, until the midpoint of the play. Antonio's sacrifice of Julio is the single action that makes the tyrant grieve.

Marston embeds his examination of contemporary concerns about the blood feud and tyrannicide within the fashionable context of literary Senecanism. The play offers a clear exploration of the dual poles of the Senecan tradition: Stoic commitment to restraint and Senecan excess in vengeance. Marston places his hero between two literary types: Piero, a Senecan tyrant, and Pandulpho, a Stoic exemplar. Although Marston allows the Stoic a temporary individual triumph over the tyrant, the play demonstrates that Stoic restraint cannot halt the progression of tyranny. The cleansing of the state is effected only through Antonio's engagement in right passion, a ritual purification through the blood of Julio that is condoned by the entire onstage audience at the end of the play. The Senecan model affirms the potential benefit of contemporary vengeance. Antonio's tragedy lies not in the method of vengeance chosen, but in the frailty of his loving bond with Mellida. The projects of the sons cede to the rigidity of the patriarchal conflicts.

Modern critical condemnation of the murder of Julio is expressed in unusually emotional language. "Antonio has butchered an innocent child in cold blood,"[2] "the sensitive, poetic young lover has become a remorseless, bloodthirsty murderer,"[3] or "Antonio, in contrast [to Julio] is an inhuman monster."[4] Fredson Bowers, who sees Julio's murder as "gratuitous" and "outrageous," explains, "By every English tenet, Antonio is a cruel and bloodthirsty villain who has overstepped the bounds of revenge."[5]

The finale, when Antonio is hailed by all and invited to rule Venice (an offer he declines, choosing to enter a monastery), proves particularly troubling to these critics. Bowers deprecates this moral lapse and lays the blame on the influence of Seneca:

> But such delay, and for such reasons, particularly when united with the outrageous murder of Julio, should have stamped Antonio as a villain who must suffer death at the end. That Marston continued to treat Antonio as a guiltless hero, must be laid to the obvious influence which the morality of Seneca exercised on the play.[6]

Geoffrey Aggeler makes a useful distinction between the morality of Seneca's moral essays and his tragedies. Then, assuming that Marston must adhere to the Stoic standard of the essays, he uses that as the standard by which to condemn Antonio: "For Marston, then, as for Seneca and Epictetus, commitment to blood vengeance involves a surrender of reason to passion and a consequent total destruction of moral restraint."[7] Charles and Elaine Hallett's archetypal analysis of revenge motifs operates from the presumption that revenge is an act of madness and then proceeds to explore the psychology of that madness.[8] While they touch on the motif of excess in vengeance, they operate from an unexamined assumption of the superiority of reason over passion, both for Renaissance audiences and contemporary readers, and they see Antonio's assertion of identity between Piero and Julio as simply mad.[9] I find the ahistoricism of this archetypal analysis unconvincing because rooted in unexamined assumptions about revenge and unexamined assumptions about the author.[10]

Gordon Braden's complicated understanding of Renaissance notions of Senecanism offers a more helpful guide to the play. Braden explores Stoicism as a philosophy of the will,[11] a philosophy of particular importance to the patrician class of Rome subject to imperial domination and, by extension, to the Renaissance aristocracy under pressure from centralization of monarchical power. Braden's analysis allows us to see the tyrant, the Stoic, and the passionate man as three examples of Senecan will.

Braden's discussion of the play, however, is brief, and he comments on the play only as a version of *Thyestes*.[12]

The extent of critical condemnation of *Antonio's Revenge* marks the dangers of the importation of external moral standards to a drama.[13] While none goes so far as Eleanor Prosser, who uses homiletic and governmental injunctions against revenge to establish the damnation of the protagonist revenger, all but Braden are secure in their condemnation of Antonio's revenge. Bowers, confident that he knows what English tenets are, has created a playwright who does not recognize that his hero is actually a villain. It is true that those in Marston's original audience who demanded that their fictions adhere to legal or homiletic dogma might have reacted with the horror displayed by these modern critics. Yet for those who, in 1584–1585, had signed the Bond of Association or engaged in the debate over the Bond, this revenge play may have offered an intriguing investigation of the morally ambiguous actions to which they or their acquaintances had subscribed. I examine the Bond of Association to demonstrate the range of action deemed appropriate by a considerable number of gentlemen, those, in Ann Jennalie Cook's view, most likely to form members of the theater audience.[14]

The Bond closely resembles the code of revenge to which Antonio adheres.[15] In joining the Bond of Association, Englishmen signified their readiness to pursue to the death the assassin of Elizabeth I, the claimant to the throne on whose behalf such action was performed, and that claimant's heirs. The oath, devised by Burghley, was aimed at constraining attempts on Elizabeth's life by removing any possible advantage to her possible successor, Mary Queen of Scots. When English subjects participated in the Bond, they indicated that assassination of an illegitimate ruler and that ruler's heir were not actions outside their moral constructs. *Antonio's Revenge* presents on stage an action previously conceptualized by the signatories of the Bond.

The language of the Bond, drawn up after the assassination of William of Orange and during heightened fears for the Queen's safety, is extreme. Vengeance is to be pursued "as well by force of armes, as by all other meanes of revenge." (Bowers' view of English tenets is challenged in that phrase.) The signatories of the Bond were to pursue to the death any by whom or for whom an assassination was even attempted. The Bond promised the "utter extirpation" not simply of the claimant to the throne, but also of that claimant's heir, even if that individual had not assented to the plot.[16]

Englishmen eagerly joined the Bond of Association. A letter from Derby to Leicester attests to its popularity:

> He found all the gentlemen of Lancashire most ready and willing to join the "Association for the defence of Her Majesty's person." He himself most reverently upon his knees, bare headed in the church, took his oath first, ministered unto him by the Bishop of Chester; and so to the rest, six at a time. The gentlemen of Cheshire, with the same zeal and cheerfulness joined the association,[17] not one by word or countenance seeming malcontent.[18]

The Earl of Huntingdon records an even greater enthusiasm in the North, with the number of seals so cumbersome that transportation of the bonds was a problem:

> Since I received the copy of the instrument of association for the preservation of Her Majesty's person, I made divers gentlemen of this country acquainted therewith, and it was so made known in all this shire that above 300 gentlemen have earnestly desired to be admitted into that honourable society, and have sealed, subscribed and sworn to perform its contents. The city of York and divers . . . gentlemen in the commission of the peace that did not come to me at York, having sealed, subscribed, and sworn thereto among themselves . . . and admitted such of the meaner sort of gentlemen, and of the principal freeholders and clothiers about them as sued to be accepted into that society; so that, especially about Halifax, Wakefield, and Bradford, 5,300 of that sort have sealed, subscribed, and sworn thereto, besides the said gentlemen and corporations, and others have and will in other places do the like.
>
> I thought to have sent up the instruments I already have, but as it will be too cumbersome to do so by the post, there being 7,500 seals at the least, I retain them until I hear from you.[19]

Huntingdon's letter demonstrates the numbers and class of potential revengers committed to private vengeance, by any means, against Elizabeth's successor and that successor's heir, should the queen be assassinated.

Antonio's decision to murder the son of the tyrant dramatizes a dilemma conceptualized, though not enacted, in Elizabethan society. Such verbal constructs of violent revenge, as in the Bond and on the stage, may have served as substitutes for violent action. Lawrence Stone documents a decreasing number of assaults between members of the aristocracy in the period 1580–1639. Tudor centralization of justice may have, for a time, channeled violence in action into violence enacted.[20]

Parliamentary discussion of the Bond of Association grants further insight into the ethical dilemmas that engaged the Elizabethans. In debate, a number of signatories of the Bond expressed their distress that failure to pass the Bond into law placed them in the morally ambiguous position of being sworn to an oath not ratified as law of the land.[21] Ethical distress was voiced over the moral dilemma of an oath that was not legally sanctioned; there was less discussion over the ethical propriety of private vengeance. Despite protests, not all provisions of the Bond were passed into law. Signatories of the Bond, Privy Councilors, members of Parliament, lords of the Church, as well as the "meaner sort," found themselves religiously enjoined to an action that would not have legal sanction. Parliamentary failure to ratify all provisions of the Bond presented each signatory with a dilemma. Each man, in a matter of vengeance against an illegitimate ruler, would be forced to devise right action for himself. Antonio's choice of any means of vengeance against the tyrant offers one possible model for action. The play, with its serious examination of possibilities of resistance to tyranny, offers to the audience the example of a hero who finds a way, through right passion, to execute justice on a monstrous tyrant. While Piero is clearly a Senecan tyrant, his two major opponents also illustrate two poles of Senecan response. In the first two acts, Pandulpho offers the conventional posture of the Stoic philosopher. In the final three acts, Antonio, through his submission to passion, confronts and finally defeats the tyrant. Only through Antonio's action of revenge, when he takes on the furor of the Herculean hero,[22] is the expansion of tyranny checked.

The delineation of the revenger as hero is not without ambiguity, for Marston deliberately compares Antonio with Piero. Yet those critics who see Antonio as having simply changed places, physically and morally, with the tyrant neglect the monstrosity of Piero's actions. While both claim the name "revenger," Piero is significantly distinguished from Antonio by the former's reasons for action. Piero's is a self-identification that springs from a defeat in love. For that defeat, years later, Piero secretly poisons his former rival, Andrugio, and murders Feliche in an assault on Antonio's happiness. That Piero has calumniated his innocent daughter matters not. The disastrous repercussions to the state of a villain-ruler are limned in Piero's advancement of a fool, Balurdo, and in the trial scene in Act Four. Piero as criminal, prosecutor, and judge blocks all legal forms of redress in the state. To act at all, Antonio, like the Englishmen who participated in the Bond of Association, must act beyond the law. But for these Englishmen, the monstrosity of an assault on Elizabeth overrode ordinary sanctions against murder, or even against secret vengeance. Those plotting against Elizabeth were to be pursued by "all other meanes." Vengeance could be justified if the cause were great.

The dramatic attention granted to Pandulpho exposes the inadequacy of the conventional Stoic response in the face of the expansion of tyranny. Pandulpho, like Antonio, has lost a male blood-relative: the former mourns his son; the latter, his father. Stoic fortitude and consolation are central issues in the first two acts as Pandulpho attempts to teach Antonio the appropriate Stoic behavior before misfortune. In the second act, Pandulpho has a temporary triumph over the tyrant but is banished, and the power of the tyrant remains unchecked by Pandulpho's display of personal fortitude. Act Three offers us the example of a different challenge to tyranny when Antonio first learns of his father's murder, swears vengeance, and commits himself to action.

The transformation of Antonio from grieving child to agent of vengeance is carefully developed over the three soliloquies of III.i. The first soliloquy makes emphatic Antonio's isolation. At the opening of the scene, his mother Maria has seemed to accept Piero's suit. Separated both from Mellida and from his seemingly treacherous mother, Antonio can claim only the filial connection, one that pulls him toward the tomb:

> Tomb, I'll not be long
> E'er I creep in thee, and with bloodless lips
> Kiss my cold father's cheek.
> (III.i.13–15)

The image of the kiss evokes an ordinary world of filial and parental affection turned upside down, for it is the child who wakes and the parent who sleeps. The disruption of familial love is intensified by the child's need to kiss a corpse, the properties of which seem already to have begun to seize the child whose lips are "bloodless." The son insists on the centrality of the bond between father and son, with his repetitions of the word *son*: "view thy son," "a cursed son," and "thy son most wretched," (III.i.19, 23, 25).

At this moment of grief and isolation, Antonio is confronted by the ghost of his father, who demands from Antonio the filial duty of revenge:

> Antonio, revenge!
> I was empoison'd by Piero's hand;
> Revenge my blood! Take spirit, gentle boy.
> Revenge my blood!
>
> (III.i.34–37)

A curious grammatical ambiguity in the ghost's imperative makes "my blood" both direct object and appositive. This ambiguity emphasizes the identity between the blood of father and son. Andrugio's blood runs in Antonio's veins; so the injury to one is an injury to the other. The ghost's erroneous report that Piero's suit to Maria has been successful—"Thy mother yields consent / To be his wife and give his blood a son" (III.i.39–40)—strips Antonio of his other living relative. The patriarchal bond is absolute. Even the tyrant yields to the desire for continuity of his blood line through the son. Andrugio demands vengeance from an agent scarcely differentiated from his own vitality:

> Thou vigor of my youth, juice of my love,
> Seize on revenge, grasp the stern-bended front
> Of frowning vengeance with impeised clutch.
> Alarum Nemesis, rouse up thy blood,
> Invent some stratagem of vengeance
> Which, but to think on, may like lightning glide
> With horror through thy breast.
>
> (III.i.44–50)

The spirit calls on the living emanation of his vigor, juice, blood. Antonio's development from child to man is to be marked by vengeance.

The ghost has instructed his son to grasp the forehead of vengeance. The novel conflation of the emblem of opportunity with that of vengeance parallels an image used earlier by Piero. Over the grave of Andrugio, he exulted:

> I have but newly twone my arm in the curl'd locks
> Of snaky vengeance. Pale, beetle-brow'd hate

But newly bustles up.

(II.i.7–9)

The verbal echo makes a significant comparison between the two revengers, as does a subsequent visual parallel. As Piero entered, "*his arms bare, smear'd in blood, a poniard in one hand, bloody, and a torch in the other*" (I.i.0 SD), so Antonio enters his mother's bedchamber, "*his arms bloody, a torch and a poniard*" (III.ii.75 SD). These parallels make clear the horrifying dangers of vengeance; the revenger courts transformation into the monstrous. Yet participation in blood vengeance may be marked by grave and honorable purpose. We must note the verbal distinction between Antonio's vengeance and Piero's. For Antonio the task of vengeance is stern and weighty, "stern-bended front" and "impeised clutch." For Piero, vengeance "bustles." The distinction between stern duty and merely energetic bustling may mark the distinction between a hero and a villain. It is Richard III who bustles in the world.

The most provocative of the ghost's lines is the final Latin tag: "*Scelera non ulcisceris, nisi vincis*" (III.i.51). This line from Seneca's *Thyestes* [23] conveys the notion of excess crucial to an understanding of the kinds of revenge taken in this and other revenge tragedies. The topos expresses the outrage that forms the emotional core of revenge and that competes with the Scriptural *lex talionis*. Unlike the evenhanded Mosaic code, the Senecan *sententia* reflects the feeling that a simply equivalent blow fails to punish the initiation of hostility. Recompense to the injured party can be achieved only by an extra measure of punishment, the exceeding in vengeance. That extra measure forms an element in determining the kind of revenge that will provide satisfaction.[24] This Senecan notion of excess certainly presents dangers within a society. If each revenge must exceed the previous one, not only the continuation but also the escalation of the blood feud is guaranteed. To those responsible for social order such an idea must be troubling. It was Elizabeth herself who recognized the potential for chaotic blood feuds in the Bond of Association and insisted that the provision for the execution of the heirs of a claimant be withdrawn from the Parliamentary bill.[25] At this moment in the play, however, audience judgment of this motif of excess may remain suspended as they watch the unfolding of vengeance.

The ghost lays the heavy charge on his son and departs. In the ensuing action, members of the court, awakened from sleep, run before Antonio. Roused from sleep come those central to his revenge: mother, tyrant, and tyrant's heir. Maternal intervention in the process of vengeance is inconsequential. Maria, who finds her son chanting lines in Latin, can believe only that her child is mad. In *Antonio and Mellida*, the use of a different tongue marked the separation of the lovers from others. Antonio's use of Latin here, the language in which his father charged him with his filial duty, marks Antonio's allegiance to the patriarchal bond.

The parting with his mother precedes a soliloquy of utter disillusionment with humanity. So despairing is Antonio that he proposes that, should the Pythagorean theory of transmigration be correct, spirits should choose to inhabit the bodies of beasts rather than those of men. The speech is remarkable not only because its view of mankind is so bleak but also because, for the first time, Antonio is shaken from his customary subjectivity. The child is moving toward an adult perspective on the world. Instead of his earlier laments so filled with the words *I, me, mine*,[26] this speech describes the general condition of humanity and represents it as devilish:

> Still striving to be more than man, he proves
> More than a devil; devilish suspect,
> Devilish cruelty, all hell-strain'd juice
> Is poured to his veins, making him drunk
> With fuming surquedries, contempt of heaven,
> Untam'd arrogance, lust, state, pride, murder.
> (III.i.119–124)

This little anatomy of mankind is a portrait of a species that has taken on the face of Piero. The tyrant, successfully having turned all to Stygian darkness as he planned in his opening soliloquy, governs a monstrous humanity.[27] At this moment of maximum despair, Antonio commits himself to murder. "Ay, I will murder" (III.i.128) leaves open the question whether Antonio has become part of the devilish humanity that he condemns. Despite his resolution, Antonio cedes the opportunity for immmediate gratification of vengeance. When Piero appears, "Antonio *offers to come near and stab*; Piero *presently withdraws*" (III.i.138 SD). The relinquishment of immediate gratification is explained as an insufficient punishment for Piero's evil, for a speedy death would not grant to the tyrant adequate insight into the evil that he has inflicted. Antonio defines a fitting vengeance as one that will force Piero to suffer in ways comparable to the suffering of his victims. When the tyrant is sated with sorrow, then vengeance will be achieved: "I'll force him feed on life / Till he shall loathe it. This shall be the close / Of vengeance' strain" (III.i.140–142).

This notion of surfeit is an appropriate image for the initiation of the countermovement of the play. Piero has been repeatedly associated with images of feeding, particularly of excess—vomiting, belching, bursting. Piero opens the play promising to feed his vengeance: "This morn my vengeance shall be amply fed" (I.i.110) and says he has sucked the blood of his victims: "I have been nurs'd in blood, and still have suck'd / The steam of reeking gore" (II.i.19–20). Pandulpho makes the tyrant's hunger clear in claiming that the breast of the wise man is "not pierc'd by savage tooth / Of foaming malice" (II.i.83–84) and even more so in calling Piero "thou rifted jawn" (II.i.136). Piero is a gaping abyss, a maw that must be crammed with death. Excess leads to extrusion. Piero, coaching Strotzo for a false confession, describes his role: "thy honest stomach that could not digest / The crudities of murder; but, surcharg'd, / Vomited'st them up in Christian piety" (II.ii.205–207). When Antonio promises to glut Piero's voracious stomach with life until life itself is loathsome, perhaps neither he nor the audience foresees precisely what he means. Yet he is searching for a method that will make manifest the unnatural appetite of the tyrant.

Julio, the instrument of Antonio's revenge, has been pulled to the graveyard by the same prescience that distinguishes Antonio: according to Forobosco, the child cries "that bugbears and spirits haunted him" (III.i.138). Again, like Antonio, Julio is abandoned by his father in that dark place. Julio, apprehending his connection with Antonio, approaches him fearlessly and names him "brother."

At Julio's mention of his father, Antonio is startled into a fierce and joyful recognition that heaven has provided an instrument for his revenge:

> Thy father! Gracious, O bounteous heaven!
> I do adore thy justice: *venit in nostras manus*
> *Tandem vindicta, venit et tota quidem.*
> (III.i.150–152)

Antonio attributes the fortuitous arrival of the child to the intervention of providence. Delighted with the happy concord of midnight, a graveyard, and Piero's blood—"time, place, and blood"—he holds the means to his revenge in his arms and feels like a god (III.i.157). From bleak despair, he moves to a fierce joy at his own potential for action and triumph over human corruption:

> Methinks I pace upon the front of Jove,
> And kick corruption with a scornful heel,
> Griping this flesh, disdain mortality.
> (III.i.161–163)

Yet contemplation of the joy of action leads to an immediate dilemma, the dilemma central to the blood feud. Assertion of the equivalence of blood between father and son eradicates the differences between father and son. Confronting Julio, Antonio explicates the difficulty of killing only Piero's blood:

> O that I knew which joint, which side, which limb,
> Were father all, and had no mother in't
> That I might rip it, vein by vein, and carve revenge
> In bleeding rases!
> (III.i.164–167)

Antonio's dilemma is that of the revenger who would take revenge on both the illegitimate ruler who injures and his heirs. The equivalency of the blood of father and son, claimed earlier by Andrugio's ghost with the words "revenge my blood," is here confronted by Antonio. Julio's blood is Piero's and therefore the child must suffer for his father's crimes. That fluid which contains the mother, because inextricably mixed with that of the father, cannot be spared. The tragedy in part lies in the unavailability of maternal intervention in the patriarchal succession from father to son. This notion of the culpability of the child for the sins of the father, rooted in

Judeo-Christian tradition and sanctioned by the codes of the blood feud, is the crux of the revenger's dilemma. Antonio decides to resolve the difficulty of distinguishing the seat of guilt, separating guilt from innocence, by action: "But since 'tis mix'd together, / Have at adventure, pell-mell, no reverse!" (III.i.168).

The terrible dilemmas of revenge are made most extreme in this scene with the pathos of Julio's pleas for his life and invocation of his sister. The name of Mellida makes even more powerful the horrors of the blood feud. Antonio must kill his bride's young brother or betray his own father. Antonio, at first swayed to pity by Mellida's name, then responds to the imperative of his father's ghost: "Revenge!" (III.i.174). The patriarchal link is dominant, as Antonio explains to Julio:

> It is not thee I hate, not thee I kill.
> Thy father's blood that flows within thy veins
> Is it I loathe, is that revenge must suck.
> (III.i.178–180)

The child's body contains the guilty blood of his father; the child's soul is loved:

> I love thy soul, and were thy heart lapp'd up
> In any flesh but in Piero's blood
> I would thus kiss it.
> (III.i.181–183)

Antonio's adoption of the word *pell-mell* signifies his recognition of the inevitable dangers and confusions of action and the potential disorder implicit therein.[28] Antonio kisses the boy as he stabs him; he weeps as the child's wounds weep. In the place of Finkelpearl's psychopath, let us see a son compelled by iron duty. The repetition of Piero's name and the appearance of Andrugio's ghost remind us that the two sons suffer for the sins of the fathers. Julio accepts his sacrificial role: "So you will love me, do even what you will" (III.i.186). Any participant in the ceremony of the mass is forced to confront the notion that love can be expressed through sacrifice, a parallel that Marston makes explicit later in the scene.

This scene, with its dramatization of the terrible nature of vengeance and of hereditary culpability, presents an extreme version of the revenge code. The task demanded by the father of his son leads to a violent conflict of loyalties and of loves. Rather than simplify the tragedy of blood by moral condemnation and a demand that drama mete out precise punishments for easily defined sins, we might instead recognize that tragedy springs from our recognition of the terrible choices offered us in the world. Antonio, presented through the first two acts as a sympathetic hero, is forced to make a choice between his father's dead spirit and the son of his enemy. The innocent child dies as a sacrifice to a code which claims that injury is not repaid unless it is exceeded. The emotion aroused by Antonio's dilemma is more powerful when he retains our respect. Summoned to act by his father's ghost and his own heart, Antonio can lapse into his customary response—which is to wail at his sufferings–or he can move to end them.

Philip Edwards, in his analysis of the twentieth-century critical tradition of dismay at Hamlet's submission to violence, attempts to right the imbalance that diminishes the tragic effect of the play. He uses René Girard's study, *Violence and the Sacred*, as a ground for the proposal that violence is one method of approaching the sacred.[29] Edwards then quotes Tyndale to remind us of the difficulty of satisfying the demands of a deity whose instructions can be known only obscurely. That quotation is pertinent to the duties demanded of Antonio: "To steal, rob, and murder, are no holy works before worldly people; but unto them that have their trust in God they are holy, when God commandeth them."[30] Correct discrimination of God's demands are exactly at issue in the play. Antonio attributes the appearance of Julio to providential intervention.[31] Marston, whose literary career preceded his ordination and installation as vicar of Christchurch, Hampshire, offers in this play a representation of sacrificial violence that may approach the sacred.

The careful construction of sympathy for Antonio prior to this scene and the delineation of Piero's monstrosity prepare the audience to witness Antonio's participation in violence. Marston sets the play in one of the Italian city-states of English imagination, at a deliberate distance from contemporary London, so that the hero's entrance into the violence of Senecan excess can be viewed sympathetically. Such response, however, is not overtly directed until the final scene, so that Marston can exploit to the fullest the possible range of audience reaction. In choosing to emphasize verbal and physical parallels between Piero and Antonio, Marston creates extreme ambiguity about the revenger. Some horrified by the sacrifice of an innocent, may condemn the agent of such a revenge. Others may feel Antonio's tragic conflict and be moved to pity the revenger. Others may approve the revenge. All may feel awe in witnessing his submission to sacred violence. The double image of the revenger, one hellish, the other perhaps the instrument of providence, presents a fascinating problem in discrimination. For an Elizabethan audience, some of whom had been participants in a vow of public vengeance against the heir of a claimant to the throne, Antonio's act must have had particular resonance.

Marston pushes the scene to a further extreme as Antonio sprinkles his father's tomb with blood. This ritual action may seem a Black Mass or a version of the true mass, in which the son sacrifices himself for the world and for the father. Both Julio and Antonio can be seen as victims of a feud they did not begin. Julio, the innocent, gives his blood for his father's sins, while Antonio, also innocent, must abandon passivity and act as his father demands.[32] His duty is hellish and his bloody hands lifted to heaven cry out "like insatiate hell": "More! / My heart hath thirsting dropsies after gore" (III.i.212–213).

This line makes clear the dangers that Antonio courts by his submission to blood. Once blood is tasted, his appetite may become as insatiable as the tyrant's. Engagement in passion places him in further ambiguous connection to Piero, for the tyrant has demonstrated an easy ability to feign passion in order to deceive others.

Piero's false confession in Act One, his instructions to himself when he hears the news of Andrugio's death, "Fut, weep, act, feign," allied with the intriguing stage direction, "*Give seeming passion*" (I.ii.241), and his instructions to Strotzo, "Do it with rare passion, and present thy guilt / As if 'twere wrung out with thy conscience' gripe" (II.ii.181–182) both call for mere shows of passion. The theatrical taint associated with passion is made clear in Antonio's rhetorical disclaimer to Mellida that his emotions owe nothing to the bombast of the tragedian: "Madam, / I will not swell like a tragedian / In forced passion of affected strains" (II.ii.104–106). Yet acknowledgment of deception by passion does not eliminate the possibility that right passion can be appropriately expressed.

The correctness of Antonio's engagement in action and passion is confirmed in the small scene in which Pandulpho and the fool Balurdo join the band of revengers. Pandulpho's renunciation of his pose of Stoic indifference is extremely important. When he explains, "I spake more than a god" (IV.ii.74), he is repudiating the arrogance of the Stoic stance of superiority to all mortal suffering. Pandulpho abandons a reason that has made him less than human and submits to Antonio's earlier argument that lack of feeling removes a man from the world: "Patience is slave to fools, a chain that's fix'd / Only to posts and senseless log-like dolts" (I.ii.271–272). The movement of the Stoic into a world of feeling—"Man will break out, despite philosophy" (IV.ii.69)—signals his return to humanity. A similar transformation enables the fool, Balurdo, to feel. In prison Balurdo has moved from senselessness to apprehension of suffering; he has felt cold, hunger, and the need for a clean shirt. His list of necessities, the simplest requirements of man, signal his entry into a world of human feeling: "Nay, and you talk of revenge, my stomach's up, for I am most tyrannically hungry" (V.ii.68–69). This oddity of the inclusion of Balurdo in the band of revengers signals the importance that Marston places on feeling as a sign of humanity. In presenting the man of passion as the hero, and paralleling with a fool the Stoic whose exercise of reason makes him unfeeling, Marston is overturning a commonplace of the period about the relative merits of reason and passion. Passion, in the case of Balurdo, transforms the insentient fool, one without reason, into a human. Passion becomes the spring for the action that is necessary if evil is to be resisted. Stoicism provides a dangerous rationale for passivity before the depredations of a tyrant. Piero's imperial ambition, his desire to "pop out the light of bright religion" (IV.i.267), and his willingness to murder any who might resist him are not thwarted by Stoic fortitude. Antonio's passion offers a method for opposing overweening evil.

Even more astonishing confirmation of the value of passion than Antonio's transformation of the insentient Balurdo is the transformation of Piero himself. In the final scene, Piero, bound and tongueless, is reduced to the dog of Antonio's epithet, "Behold, black dog!" (V.iii.71). Yet at this moment of degradation, Piero weeps. His tears, which requite the revengers for their own tears, signal Piero's entrance into human feeling. Presented with the limbs of Julio, Piero *"seems to condole his son"* (V.iii.80 SD). At last he endures the pain he has inflicted on others. The lesson is explained by the living victims of Piero's tyranny, Pandulpho, Antonio, and Maria. Piero must suffer as they have suffered and endure the painful rupture of the bonds that make a family:

> PANDULPHO. Was he thy flesh, thy son, thy dearest son?
> ANTONIO. So was Andrugio my dearest father.
> PANDULPHO. So was Feliche my dearest son.
>
> *Enter* Maria.
>
> MARIA. So was Andrugio my dearest husband.
> (V.iii.81–84)

To exact punishment for loss, the revengers must banish "pity, piety, remorse": "grim fire-ey'd rage / Possess us wholly" (V.iii.89, 90–91).

The revenge is terrible, pitiless, and remorseless, as Piero is forced to live in the state that he has created. The revengers enter into rage to accomplish the task that Piero himself has named godlike: "You know how godlike 'tis to root out sin" (II.i.107). The revengers take on heroic dimensions and enter a realm of fiery rage to purge corruption from the state. In exacting the penalty of vengeance and exceeding their enemy, remorselessly they force one whom they regard as the devil (V.iii.138) to feel and then to die. After that achievement, they retreat from society.

The revenger risks damnation when he takes on the tasks of a god. He steps beyond the limits that restrain ordinary men—"graves and ghosts / Fright me no more" (III.i.128–129). When Piero invited the Stoic to take on a god's task in the rooting out of sin, inadvertently, he spoke only the truth. The task of the revengers in cleansing the state of corruption is at least the action of a demigod, as Antonio is praised for his Herculean effort. Any lingering doubt about the ghost's assertion that vengeance is heavenly—"'Heaven's just; for I shall see / The scourge of murder and impiety'" (V.i.24–25)—is banished by the onstage acclamation of Antonio by the remaining courtiers of Venice. The extraordinary nature of his action is emphasized in their reference to Hercules: "Thou art another Hercules to us / In ridding huge pollution from our state" (V.iii.129–130). Behind Hercules lies the shadow of one even greater to Elizabethan audiences. Antonio, rejecting the phrase "poor orphan," characterizes himself as "standing triumphant over Belzebub" (V.iii.138). Antonio, in cleansing the hellish Venetian state, takes on the lineaments of Christ.

The play extends its subject from the emotional and political complications of the blood feud to the religious. Antonio, though offered a ducal crown, chooses to retreat from the world into a monastery, an acknowledgment that after participation in godlike rage, a return to ordinary society is not possible. The image of the monastery suggests the double nature of revenge. A man enters a monastery to atone for his sins in the world, and yet the monastery elevates the man, for the monastery partakes of the divine.

In the act of revenge, the revenger steps outside the conventions of daily morality. The revenger of blood who kills his enemy commits an act of murder that is, according to the ethical constructs of the society, not ordinarily condoned. Marston, in *Antonio's Revenge*, presses against the limits of the possibly acceptable revenge when he creates a hero who kills a child and then forces the father to feed on the flesh of his son. These acts alone are enough to mark Antonio, for many modern critics, as tainted and corrupt. The play itself courts that possibility by stressing the similarities between Antonio and Piero, when true revenger reflects false. Even though the revenger hero risks damnation, true justice is achieved when the tyrant is forced to weep. Punishment for the sins of the father has been graphically visited on the body of the son, and it is the sight of that suffering body which finally ensures that the tyrant comprehends the suffering he has inflicted on others. *Antonio's Revenge*, while using popular Elizabethan notions of Senecanism, offers oblique commentary on contemporary issues of tyrannicide and vengeance pertinent to that audience. Through revenge the hero has found a suitable method to cleanse the state of its polluting leader. Right passion has achieved what cool reason could not.

NOTES

1. All quotations from the play are taken from the edition by G. K. Hunter, *Antonio's Revenge* (Lincoln, Neb.: University of Nebraska Press, 1965).
2. Robert Ornstein, *The Moral Vision of Jacobean Tragedy* (Madison, Wis.: University of Wisconsin Press, 1965, p. 155.
3. Philip Finkelpearl, *John Marston of the Middle Temple* (Cambridge, Mass.: Harvard University Press, 1969), p. 153.
4. Eleanor Prosser, *Hamlet and Revenge*, 2nd ed. (Stanford, Calif.: Stanford University Press, 1971), p. 60.
5. Fredson Bowers, *Elizabethan Revenge Tragedy 1587–1642* (Princeton, N. J.: Princeton University Press, 1940), pp. 123, 124.
6. Bowers, p. 124.
7. Geoffrey Aggeler, "Stoicism and Revenge in Marston," *English Studies*, 51 (1970), 508.
8. Charles and Elaine Hallett, *The Revenger's Madness: A Study of Revenge Tragedy Motifs* (Lincoln, Neb.: University of Nebraska Press, 1980).
9. Halletts, pp. 170–171.
10. For example, "His [Marston's] empathy with the revenger is so great that there is almost no separation between character and author: he can follow Antonio into the very depths of the madness" (p. 176).
11. Gordon Braden, *Renaissance Tragedy and the Senecan Tradition* (New Haven, Conn.: Yale University Press, 1985), p. 20.
12. Braden, p. 173.

13. Richard Levin's admonitions in *New Readings vs. Old Plays* (Chicago, Ill.: University of Chicago Press, 1979) are pertinent.
14. Ann Jennalie Cook, *The Privileged Playgoers of Shakespeare's London, 1576–1642* (Princeton, N. J.: Princeton University Press, 1981).
15. I shall refer to the document as the Bond of Association, although it was also called the Instrument for the Queen's Safety.
16. Bond in Francis Hargrave, *A Complete Collection of State Trials*, 4th ed. (London: T. Wright, 1776), I, 143. *Calendar of State Papers Domestic, 1581–90* (hereafter *CSP Domestic*), ed. Robert Lemon (London, 1865) lists the following originals of the Bond: one signed at Hampton Court by the Privy Council; one for the clergy "signed by the Archbishops of Canterbury and York, nine Bishops of the province of Canterbury, Dean Goodman, Dean Nowell, and a great many other of the clergy present" and one signed by "dignified Clergy of the province of Canterbury." Instruments from twelve counties are collected: Cornwall, Devon, Dorset, Hertford, Somerset, Kent, York, Cardigan, Flint, Monmouth, Pembroke, Carnarvon, and the town of Ludlow and the city of Worcester (signed "by above two hundred persons"). October 1584, pp. 210–212.
17. *CSP Domestic 1581–90*, 6 November 1584.
18. The last detail is included in J. A. Froude, *Reign of Elizabeth, Part IV*, Volume XII in *History of England from the Fall of Wolsey to the Defeat of the Spanish Armada* (1826–70; rpt. New York: AMS Press, 1969), p. 46.
19. *CSP Domestic Elizabeth James I, Addenda, 1580–1625*, ed. M.A.E. Green (London, 1872), p. 130.
20. Lawrence Stone, *The Crisis of the Aristocracy 1558–1641* (Oxford: Clarendon Press, 1965). Appendix XV, "Recorded acts of violence and duels involving peers between 1580 and 1639" records a slow decline in the probability of a peer being involved in a duel or an act of unregulated violence. Through the period examined, the probability of an aristocrat being so involved drops from 63% between 1580–1599, to 40% between 1600–1619, to 22% between 1620–1639. For a discussion of Tudor centralization of justice and attitudes toward revenge, see Ronald Broude, "Revenge and Revenge Tragedy in Renaissance England," *Renaissance Quarterly*, 28 (1975), 38–58 and "Four Forms of Vengeance in *Titus Andronicus*," *Journal of English and Germanic Philology*, 78 (1979), 494–507.
21. For further discussion of Parliamentary debate over the Bond, see J. E. Neale's lively discussion in *Elizabeth I and Her Parliaments 1584–1601*, 2 vols. (New York: St. Martin's, 1958) II, 34, to which I am greatly indebted. John Sibly in a brief article mentions the significance of the Bond for a number of revenge plays: "The Duty of Revenge in Tudor and Stuart Drama" *Review of English Literature*, N.S. 8 (1967), 46–54. For further discussion of the Bond, see also my "Rigorous Justice: The Imperative of Blood Revenge in Three Tragedies, 1599–1611," Diss. Columbia University 1980, pp. 39–55.
22. See Eugene Waith, *The Herculean Hero* (London: Chatto, 1962) and Braden.
23. Translated by John Cunliffe as "Injuries are not revenged except where they are exceeded," quoted by Hunter.
24. This requirement that the initial assault be reciprocated with an assault that exceeds the first has a suggestive connection to the question of reciprocity and excess in gift-giving in tribal societies. See Marcel Mauss, *The Gift: Forms and Functions of Exchange in Archaic Societies*, trans. Ian Cunison (New York: Norton, 1967).
25. Neale, II, 52.
26. For example, "My woes more weighty than my soul can bear" (I.ii.293) and "Let none out-woe me; mine's Herculean woe" (II.ii.134).

27. "Will I not turn a glorious bridal morn / Unto a Stygian night?" (I.i.89–90).
28. The use of the word *pell-mell* makes prominent a further link between Piero and Antonio: "Pell mell! confusion and black murder guides / The organs of my spirit" (II.ii.222–223) were Piero's words in the soliloquy immediately preceding this scene. The verbal echo again draws the tyrant and the hero closely together in an ambiguous pairing. *Pell-mell* is repeated later in the play in association with the word *vengeance*: When the band of revengers swear and link arms, Antonio instructs, "Let's think a plot; then pell-mell vengeance!" (IV.ii.118). The word is repeated once more at the final moment of revenge; stabbing Piero, Antonio calls, "Now, pell-mell! Thus the hand of heaven chokes / The throat of murder. This for my father's blood!" (V.iii.108–109).
29. René Girard, *Violence and the Sacred*, trans. Patrick Gregory (Baltimore, Md.: Johns Hopkins University Press, 1977).
30. William Tyndale, *Doctrinal Treatises*, Parker Society (1848), p. 407, quoted in Philip Edwards, "Tragic Balance in 'Hamlet'," *Shakespeare Survey*, 36 (1983), 43–52.
31. While Antonio may be criticized for blurring the distinction between the demands of God and those of the father, such elision is common in patriarchal discourse. George Geckle, in "*Antonio's Revenge*: 'Never more woe in lesser plot was found'," *Comparative Drama*, 6 (1972–73), 323–335, removes all responsibility from Antonio by displacing the cruelty of the revenge onto Andrugio's ghost. This argument, though strong, by attempting to shift the responsibility for the hero's submission to violence, simplifies audience response.
32. Girard's comments on the kind of person chosen for sacrifice are pertinent here. As a child, Julio has not yet been fully integrated into the society. Antonio, a ruler's son, about to marry, is on the verge of integration into the society, but he too remains the chosen outsider, one who must perform an act of sacrificial violence that finally enables restoration of the community destroyed by Piero's appetite. Girard, pp. 12–13.

The Tragedy of Bussy D'Ambois and the Creation of Heroism

JAMES N. KRASNER

Bussy D'Ambois has frequently been referred to as a hero of epic proportions. The relationship between Chapman's understanding of the epic hero and his portrayal of Bussy, a tragic hero in a degenerate time, has already been insightfully examined by Richard Ide in his book *Possessed with Greatness*.[1] But Ide neglects to discuss Chapman's view of the relationship between artist and hero that so thoroughly informs *The Tragedy of Bussy D'Ambois*. The major conflict in the play is not between two different visions of the hero but between two different visions of the hero-making artist. Both Bussy and Monsieur attempt to transform a man into a legend with words, but while Monsieur is more politically adept, Bussy's superior poetic craftsmanship assures him the artistic victory. Bussy becomes a hero for his words rather than his deeds, and political heroism is shown to be insignificant when compared with artistic creation. *The Tragedy of Bussy D'Ambois* was published in 1607, at a time when Chapman was redefining his notion of heroism. His two translations of Homer's *Iliad*, published in 1598 and 1611 respectively, also demonstrate a shift of emphasis from the hero to the artist. In this essay I will demonstrate the ways in which the conflict between the artist as political myth-maker and the artist as aesthetic creator is played out both in Chapman's translations and in *The Tragedy of Bussy D'Ambois*.

In 1598 Chapman published the *Seaven Bookes of the Iliades of Homer*, which contained translations of Books One, Two, Seven, Eight, Nine, Ten, and Eleven. Later that year he published a segment of Book Eighteen under the title *Achilles' Shield*. Between the publication of these translations and his final, definitive version of 1611, many revisions were made and Books One and Two were entirely rewritten. The differences between the Achilles portrayed in the first edition of 1598 and the final one of 1611 are striking, as are the differences between the various introductory notes to the two editions. Invariably the earlier edition emphasizes the unconquerable spirit of the main character, while the second version, hosting a somewhat diminished hero, points up the artistic stature of the poet.

It has often been theorized that Chapman lost faith in a heroic ideal with the fall of his personal hero, the Earl of Essex. Ide states,

> Since 1598, however, apparently owing to Essex's tragic blunder and subsequent execution as well as to Chapman's careful review of the second half of *The Iliad* there has occurred a significant change in Chapman's conception of both Essex and

Achilles. . . . [T]he moral ambiguity of Bussy's behavior confirms that Chapman is no longer able to extol "ancient virtue" without qualification. In this respect, Bussy D'Ambois documents Chapman's painful reassessment of Essex and the Achillean heroism that the translator of the *Iliads* had celebrated in 1598 with partisan naivete.[1]

Such a reassessment of Achillean heroism is apparent when one compares the "Preface" to the 1598 version, addressed to "The Most Honored now living Instance of the Achilleian vertues eternized by divine Homere, the Earle of Essexe," and the dedication "To the High Borne Prince of Men Henrie," in the 1611 version. The Preface is a plea for financial support in which Chapman insists upon the importance of "so firme an Eternizer as Homer" (Preface. 59) to any great man, be he an Achilles or an Essex.[2] Chapman is both appealing to his would-be patron's vanity and social position and exalting his own role as the "Eternizer" of the great. In a long and tenuously reasoned argument, Chapman answers the question, "what place with the greatest doth an eternizer merit?" (P. 76–77). Since the "adamantine foote" of eternity "treades uppon scepters, riches, sences, sensualities and all the safron-guilded pomp of ignorant braveries" (P. 73–74) and can only be conquered by "knowledge," the "eternizer's" place should certainly be a high one. Homerical writing is the "true Heire of true knowledge" and therefore must "inherite his father's dignitie" (P. 86–88). In other words, Essex deserves a biographer as much as Achilles did. "Helpe then, renown'de Achilles, to preferre and defend your grave and blamelesse Prophet of Phoebus," (P. 88–89) cries the hero-worshipping, would-be eternizer, encouraging the hero to "stirre your divine temper from perseverance in godlike pursute of Eternitie" (P. 66–67). The Preface is an attempt to make clear to the Earl his potential for greatness, a greatness that can be fully realized only with the help of a poetic "eternizer."

In the dedication of the 1611 *Iliads*, "To the High Borne Prince of Men, Henrie Thrice Royall Inheritor to the United Kingdoms of Great Brittaine, &c.," however, the actual hero is obscured by the shadow of the poet. The role of the poet is not only grander and more sweeping than in the 1598 Preface, but it has also significantly changed from "eternizer" to "creator." Poetry is capable of a great deal more than preserving the memory of great men. It is capable of raising "Humanitie to her height" (Dedication. 39), and shining through "all the pompe of kingdomes," it "graceth all his gracers" (D. 46–47). Poetry creates the metaphors through which "Learning . . . In earth present his [God's] fierie Majestie" (D. 78–79). Justice and Truth are best set forth by poetry rather than "untruss't Prose" (this dedication, unlike that of 1598, is written in verse), for

>   as in a spring
> The plyant water, mov'd with any thing
> Let fall into it, puts her motion out
> In perfect circles, that move round about
> The gentle fountaine, one another raising;

> So Truth and Poesie worke, so Poesie, blazing
> All subjects falne in her exhaustlesse fount,
> Works most exactly, makes a true account
> Of all things to her high discharges given,
> Till all be circular and round as heaven.
>   (D. 114–123)

Such a grandiose designation of power and worth to things poetic is necessary here partly because Chapman is caught in the usual Renaissance dilemma of justifying "Poet's faining" (D. 61). It is all right that poets tell stories (write lies) because their work is typically true and therefore working in the cause of the Truth. Chapman needed no such justification in the 1598 dedication. Nowhere in the earlier text does he mention the possibility that *The Iliades* might not be true. Achilles, like Essex, is a great historical figure; Homer has merely glorified his already heroic lineaments. Chapman "affectionatelie consecrates" to Essex an *Iliades* in which Homer "(with his owne soule) hath eternizde Armies of Kings and Princes" (P. 54–55), but to Prince Henry Chapman offers the chance to "learne these [heroic] rights . . . And let you see one Godlike man create / All sorts of worthiest men" (D. 14, 18–19). That the poet is "Godlike" there can be little doubt. "Seas, earth and heaven he did in verse comprise, / Out-sung the Muses and did equalise / Their king Apollo" (D. 41–42)—Homer would hardly have made such a claim for himself. Thus, the somewhat sycophantic if necessary "eternizer" of great men, has become the prime mover of culture and the creator of typical greatness that lives eternally.

The actual text of the two *Iliads*, shows a similar diminution of the hero and glorification of the poet between the 1598 and 1611 versions. John Channing Briggs, in his article "Chapman's *Seaven Bookes of the Iliades*: Mirror for Essex,"[3] successfully demonstrates that many corrections have political overtones, but he does not discuss the concomitant change in Achilles' character that results. Ide, on the other hand, notes the distinctions in character, describing the early Achilles as exemplified by "over-ruling Wisedome," and the latter by "'Predominant Perturbation,' heroic passion, heroic spirit,"[4] but Ide denies a clear diminution in the nobility, emotional intensity and physical aggressiveness of the 1611 hero. The Achilles of 1598 is "divine" (I. 122) and capable of "violent fury" (I. 215) and deep devotion to Briseis (I. 360–369), whereas the 1611 Achilles is merely "God-like" (I. 119), prone to "anger" (I. 208), and more concerned with loss of face than loss of his mistress (I. 351–355). The contrast is pointed up by the interpolated farewell to Briseis in lines 360–364 of the 1598 version.

> Shee wept and lookt upon her love; he sigh't and did refuse.
> O how his wisdome with his power did mightilie contend—
> His love incouraging his power and spirite, that durst descend
> As far as Hercules for her, yet wisedome all subdude.

As Briggs points out, this tender moment, cut from whole cloth by Chapman, is meant "to focus on the power of Achilles' passionate anguish, and then to praise the hero for subduing that passion with an even more powerful fortitude guided by wisedome."[5] It is such "passionate anguish" barely restrained from breaking out into violence that is the hallmark of the 1598 Achilles. Ide argues that "inward fortitude" is more characteristic of the 1598 Achilles but offers no convincing examples.[6] If this Achilles is more often commended for containing his wrath, it is only because his wrath itself is so much more powerful. He is a man capable of great love and great hatred, willing to "descend / As far as Hercules" to regain his heart's desire. Deprived of Briseis, he "melts anger in laments / Upon the shore of th'aged deepe; viewing the purple seas / And lifting his broade hands to heaven, he did with utterance ease / His manlie bosome" (I. 366–369). By way of contrast, no claim is made that the 1611 Achilles will dive down to hell, and he weeps not for sorrow but "for anger" (I. 352). Rather than a "manlie" "utterance," this is a "sad plea / Made to his mother" (I. 354–355) with "wet eyes." Despite Chapman's vigorous attempts to defend these tears in the "Commentarius," the childishness of the 1611 Achilles cannot help but impress the reader, particularly when it is compared to the manly stature of his 1598 progenitor.

With the diminution of the hero's stature, one finds a concomitant increase in the power and importance of the artist. This is nowhere so apparent as in Chapman's partial translation of Book Eighteen, published in the same year as the *Seaven Bookes* under the title of *Achilles Shield*. As a scholar and artist, Chapman could not have overlooked the significance of this passage as a symbol of his own endeavors. The Vulcan of 1598 is more the blacksmith than his 1611 counterpart. Chapman's conception of poet as creator who "infuseth" his "spirit" "into the scope of his worke" (P. 54) did not come to its full realization until after the fall of Essex. This first Vulcan forges a shield in which "many thinges with speciall grace / And passing arteficiall pompe were graven" (*Achilles Shield*. 156–157), but in the 1611 version, the second Vulcan's authority and wisdom—"his hand did shew / (Directed with a knowing mind)"—engender a creation that has "a rare varietie" (XVIII. 435) and a seeming life of its own. In the first version, we are led to admire the technical skill of an artificer who can so exactly imitate nature, while in the second we witness the creation of a whole new world.

> 1598:
> In it was earthe's greene globe, the sea and heaven,
> Th'unwearied Sunne, the Moone exactly round
> And all the starres with which the skie is crownd,
> The Pleiades, the Hyads and the force
> Of great Orion, and the Beare, whose course
> Turnes her about his Sphere observing him
> Surnam'de the Chariot, and doth never swimme
> Upon the unmeasur'de Ocean's marble face

Of all the flames that heaven's blew vayle enchace.
(AS. 158–166)

1611:
For in it he presented earth, in it, the sea and skie,
In it, the never wearied Sunne, the Moone exactly round
And all those starres with which the browes of ample heaven are
                                                                            crownd—
Orion, all the Pleiades, and those seven Atlas got,
The close-beamed Hyades, the Beare, surnam'd the Chariot,
That turnes about heaven's axletree, holds ope a constant eye
Upon Orion; and, of all the Cressets in the skie,
His golden forehead never bowes to th'Ocean Emperie.
(XVIII. 436–443)

Although the changes in the second version are minor, they are important in that they contain more specific references to the artist and depict an infusion of personality into nature through the increased use of personification. The reader is twice reminded of the artist's presence: first by the active voice in line 436 and again by the reference to Atlas' begetting of the Pleiades in line 439. The cosmos is portrayed not as a list of names, as in the 1598 version, but as a human form whose "browes" are "crownd" with stars, who "holds ope a constant eye" upon Orion, and whose "golden forehead never bowes." The heavenly bodies become parts of a human figure rather than figures on a map, and we are reminded that they are the production of an individual. Vulcan's nature is not simply an imitation of an actual world; it is an artifact created and enlivened by a distinct personality.

The difference between line 293 of the 1598 version and line 538 of the 1611 version reveals the important distinction between the two conceptions of the artist. In the first case Daedalus is said to "dresse" the labyrinth—in the second he has "made" it. The artist of the 1598 version dresses up nature, much in the same way that the poet of the *Seaven Bookes* "eternizes" or popularizes the hero. In the 1611 version, however, the artist makes, or "creates," a world of his own, circumscribed by his own spirit and infused with his own soul. In *The Tragedy of Bussy D'Ambois* we witness a struggle between these two conceptions of the artist, resulting not only in the diminution of the hero and the enhancement of the artist but also in the representation of the hero as artist and of artistic creation as heroism.

II

The presence of the eternizer becomes apparent when Monsieur steps on stage in the first scene of the play. In Monsieur, Chapman offers us a character who views the political operation of artistry much as did the Chapman who wrote the Preface of 1598. Monsieur explains that he has come to see Bussy because "'Tis fit I get resolved spirits about me" (I.i.44)[7] so that "In his rise therefore shall my bounties shine" (I.i.51). Monsieur intends to advance Bussy that he himself may gleam with reflected glory. Such is the stated or unstated ulterior motive of all eternizers, to serve as (in Chapman's words to Essex) a "grave and blameless prophet of Phoebus." The fact that Monsieur is Bussy's superior in rank makes Monsieur's enternizing role all the more calculated and despicable, but no less deferential. Monsieur attempts to appeal to Bussy's desire for historical notoriety, listing the names of past heroes and emphasizing that if they had remained in an obscured retreat they "had been still unnam'd" (I.i.72). This is exactly the same technique used by Chapman in the Preface to Essex. By raising the hero to notoriety, the eternizer will himself become notable:

> for as the light
> Not only serves to shew, but render us
> Mutually profitable: so our lives
> In acts exemplary, not only win
> Ourselves good Names, but doth to others give
> Matter for virtuous Deeds, by which we live.
> (I.i.76–81)

But Bussy is not properly dressed to gain such a name, and it is the dresser's role "T'enchase in all shew, thy long smother'd spirit" (I.i.112). Bussy will be set in gold, like the soldiers on Achilles' shield. This gold will be an "outward gloss" to "Attract Court eyes," (I.i.109–110) to himself as well as to his faithful eternizer.

Monsieur, the eternizer, because of his understanding of artistry as a process of "dressing" or gilding the real world, adopts rhetorical techniques which are primarily concerned with renaming. He will take an exceptional but mortal man and rename him as an eternal hero, just as Chapman proposed that he would do for Essex. Consequently, word-substitution, simple comparison, and the compilation of verbal heaps comprise Monsieur's entire rhetorical arsenal. When he pleads with Henry for Bussy's life in II.i, Monsieur jumbles his litigious vocabulary in order to redefine Bussy's murder of Barrisor as a heroic deed. "Manly slaughter / Should never bear th'account of wilful murder," (II.i.150–151) he states, and proceeds to explain that gentlemen should not be answerable to law. When Henry objects that the law cannot be so easily renamed, Monsieur counters with more dubious equivalences, setting "a murder'd fame," against "a murder'd man" (II.i.171–172). Describing Bussy's opponent he uses the words "murderous," "slain," "die," "murder'd," and "wilful murder," all in lines 168–173; "But my friend," he says of Bussy "only saved his fame's dear life, / Which is above life," and proceeds to phrase his defense with a vocabulary containing "preserves," "uprightness," "worthy," and "survive" (ll. 174–179). Similarly, in wooing Tamyra in II.ii, Monsieur alludes to the shifting nature of language:

> Honor, what's that? your second maidenhead:
> And what is that? a word: the word is gone.

> The thing remains . . .
> A husband and a friend all wise wives have . . .
> . . . my honour? husband?
> Dames maritorious ne'er were meritorious.
> (II.ii.60–62, 69, 83–84)

Such Falstaffian rhetoric betrays both Monsieur's self-serving association with language and the limitations of the eternizer's rhetoric. Because of Monsieur's essential cynicism, the seduction is impressive as neither logic nor romance. He is encouraging Tamyra to surrender her honor because it can be renamed as anything and is therefore ultimately worthless. Monsieur's rhetoric cuts both ways; he can with equal ease gild a weed or blast a lily, but he can do so only through a relatively arbitrary process of rhetorical similitude. He juggles and puns, but he offers no legitimate arguments or truly convincing observations.

Monsieur's poetic skill is as intense, and as narrow, as his rhetorical skill. His addiction to the extended simile is another form of renaming without truly addressing the object of discussion. Tamyra's honor is a word, and when "the word is gone, / The thing remains; the rose is pluck'd, the stalk / Abides" (II.ii.61–63). The words and looks of a king "Are like the flashes and the bolts of Jove, / His deeds inimitable, like the sea / That shuts still as it opes, and leaves no tracts, / Nor prints of precedent for poor men's facts" (I.i. 37–40). Such comparisons are ornamental, but rather commonplace. Monsieur uses conceit and simile effectively, but they invariably take the form of bejeweled equivalence. Just as the 1598 Vulcan fashions a shield that is an ornamental imitation of nature, so Monsieur uses simile to embellish but not to investigate or enliven.

Bussy, on the other hand, follows the lead of the 1611 Vulcan, transforming metaphors into multi-faceted conceits that seem to take on a life of their own. Unlike the eternizer, who seeks only to coat the world in gold, the creator brings that golden world to life. Bussy's major poetic techniques involve the complex networking of metaphors and the use of conceits that flow across the border from poetry into actuality. In the first scene, Bussy adopts and enlivens Monsieur's rhetoric in almost every line:

> *Mons.* Up man, the sun shines on thee.
> *Buss.*   Let it shine.
> I am not mote to play in't, as great men are.
> (I.i.55–56)

> *Mons.*   Leave the troubled streams,
> And live as thrivers do at the well-head.
> *Buss.* At the well-head? Alas what should I do
> With that enchanted glass? See devils there?
> Or (like a strumpet) learn to set my looks
> In an eternal brake.
> (I.i.82–87)

> *Mons.*   The rude Scythians
> Painted blind Fortune's powerful hands with wings,
> To shew her gifts come swift and suddenly,
> Which if her Favourite be not swift to take,
> He loses them for ever. Then be rul'd;
> Stay but a while here and I'll send to thee.
> *Buss.* What will he send? some crowns? It is to sow them
> Upon my spirit, and make them spring a Crown
> Worth millions of the seed-crowns he will send.
>   (I.i.113–121)

Bussy continually uses Monsieur's figures as springboards for his own more interesting and involved conceits. Where Monsieur deals in simple equivalences in which one metaphor names one idea (he uses light and gleaming imagery in his discussion of fame throughout the first scene but never takes advantage of the wealth of other possible meanings for these provocative images), Bussy multiplies Monsieur's seed images into burgeoning and entangled poetic passages.

Just as the poet described by Chapman in the 1611 dedication can comprise "Seas, earth and heaven" in his verse, so Bussy seems to speak things into being. At points he seems visionary, describing his hand as "stuck full of laurel" when he makes peace with Guise (III.ii.124), or toying with the uncomprehending Monsieur:

> *Mons.* How now, what leap'est thou at?
> *Buss.*   O royal object!
> *Mons.* Thou dream'st awake; object in th'empty air?
> *Buss.* Worthy the head of Titan, worth his chair.
> *Mons.* Pray thee what mean'st thou?
> *Buss.*   See you not a Crown
> Empale the forehead of the great King Monsieur?
> *Mons.* Oh, fie upon thee.
>   (III.ii.303–308)

Bussy is not simply teasing here, he is demonstrating the limitations of Monsieur's imagination. To Monsieur, the rhetorician and dresser of language, words are words and reality is reality, the first being tools to manipulate the second. But to Bussy, words are capable of becoming reality. The fact that an actual crown may not be visible is of little importance, for by describing the crown he calls into being an image of Monsieur's ambition that is vivid enough to make Monsieur curse him.

Bussy is capable of bringing images of people as well as objects to life. In III.ii, he creates a rogues' gallery of corrupt civic leaders, all of whom are engaged in dynamic, burlesque activity. The "Great Man" is portrayed "rising from a clapdish," "Piling a stack of billets," and confessing "like a huge unlading Argosy" (III.ii.28, 32, 38). The clergyman sings like a lark and tunnels like a mole, surrounds himself with gourmet fare, and vents "their Quintessence as men read Hebrew" (III.ii.46). The lawyer has, like an infernal alchemist, succeeded in transforming the law into a harpy and blood into gold. Such brilliant descriptions seem to demonstrate Chapman's claim in the 1611 Dedication that poetry shines through "all the pompe of kingedomes," making "a true account" of social ills. More important, however, is the fact that Bussy, like the "Godlike" 1611 poet, is capable of creating "all sorts" of "men." Bussy's ability to conceive of and imagistically enliven individual personalities far outstrips Monsieur's, and it is this difference that is most crucial in distinguishing the creator from the eternizer. The eternizer can praise or blame, but it takes a creator to bring a character to life.

The contrast between the poetic techniques of Bussy and Monsieur is most obvious in III.ii when they describe one another. Monsieur's description is a tour de force of name calling. He uses his old tricks of comparison, renaming, and piling words upon each other to present Bussy as the embodiment of every known bestial vice. The resultant protean characterization is less an accurate description of Bussy's personality, as Dollimore would have us believe,[8] than it is a demonstration of Monsieur's rhetorical and poetic idiosyncrasies raised to their height. Because Monsieur is skilled at simple comparison, he renames Bussy in every line. Bussy is like "a wild horse or tiger" (III.ii.337) his valor is a "ravenous wolf" (III.ii.339), he is "more ridiculous and vainglorious / Than any mountebank; and impudent / Than any painted bawd" (III.ii.359-361), and altogether "more absurd / Childish and villainous than that hackster, whore, / Slave, cut-throat, tinker's bitch, compar'd before: / And in those humours wouldst envy, betray, / Slander, blaspheme, change each hour a religion; / Do anything, but killing of the King" (III.ii.351-356). Monsieur's rhetoric bristles with slanderous epithets, dissipating ultimately into a mockery of Bussy's "toad-pool" (III.ii.365) complexion.

According to Ide, this speech represents the "Shakespearean point of view." "Except for the contextual specification of 'but killing of the King,' Seneca might have said much of the same about the bloody primitives."[9] Seneca might have indeed, but Seneca would have been making a general description of a group, not a specific characterization of one man. Certainly this is rhetorically powerful. Such a congeries of libels has rarely been assembled in the English language. But ultimately the speech is no more than that—a collection of epithets, a bundle of comparisons and names. The Bussy described by Monsieur is not recognizable as the Bussy on the stage, except in the intensity of his "Cannibal valour" (III.ii.339). No consistently imaginable feature or dazzling poetic image emerges from the text, and this is where the limitation of Monsieur's use of language shows. Since Monsieur is capable of renaming and simple comparison alone, he can increase the intensity of his condemnation only volumetrically. If Monsieur were capable of maintaining and embroidering the intricacies of an extended metaphor, he could create a Bussy who embodies the ills Monsieur describes, rather than a plaster figure laden with dissociated epithets. Monsieur's speech may succeed as malediction, but it fails as poetic characterization.

In Bussy's description of Monsieur, however, we are presented with a cunningly and insightfully engraved portrait of a living character. Rather than attempting to diminish his opponent by comparing him to the savage and uncivilized, as does Monsieur, Bussy manipulates metaphors that emphasize Monsieur's corrupt social skills and political power. Monsieur is portrayed as a static Machiavel, "the very Prince / Of all intelligencers" (III.ii.387–388), manipulating the state with his sticky, finely woven web. All the imagistic action of the piece flows from Monsieur's body. His "voice / Is like an eastern wind, that where it flies, / Knits nets of caterpillars, with which you catch / The prime of all the fruits the Kingdom yields" (III.ii.388–391). His head is as "curs'd fount" (III.ii.392) of vices; his tongue is "so scandalous, 'twill cut / A perfect Crystal" (III.ii.395–396); his breath "will / Kill to that wall a spider" (III.ii.396–397). Monsieur's description of Bussy's felonies are indirect. The hearer is made to imagine another malefactor committing the crime, whether it be a tiger, a tinker's wife, a mountebank, or an Ajax, then to associate that malefactor with Bussy. Bussy, on the other hand, creates dramatic situations in which Monsieur himself is a character. We see him killing a spider with his breath, jesting with God, kissing horror and speaking caterpillars into being. Furthermore, whereas Monsieur at no point mentions himself, Bussy creates two scenarios for himself, in the beninning and at the end of the speech. In line 37 Bussy's silhouette swaggers across the text as he challenges "any friend" of Monsieur's and lays "This poor stillado here, 'gainst all the stars, / Ay, and 'gainst all your treacheries, which are more: / That you did never good, but to do ill" (III.ii.378–380).

In some senses Bussy's rhetorical technique is unfair. He creates a nearly three-dimensional image of Monsieur, which seems to live and move by itself. Rather than simply allowing this image to overwhelm Monsieur's jumbled images, thereby winning the flyting match, he, the fleshly Bussy, means to take on his verbal creation. It is not a verbal sword by which Bussy will swear and challenge, but his actual rapier, "This poor stillado here." The "you" addressed in the challenge is indistinguishable from the "you" who, a few lines later, is "the very / Prince of intelligencers." Thus Bussy conflates his verbal creation with the actual man standing beside him, causing them, at least for the duration of the speech, to become one. Against such strategies Monsieur's bundles of epithets is powerless.

Such sophistication with levels of voicing shows that Bussy's creations are weighted toward the dramatic. Like the 1611 Vulcan's, the hallmark of the creator's work is embodiment rather than ornament. Chapman is celebrating the superiority of the dramatic creator over the courtly or political eternizer. The worst Monsieur can do is to compare Bussy to a mountebank, just as the best the poet of 1598 could do was to compare Essex to Achilles. Chapman's later conception of the poet, represented by Bussy, is capable of creating any number of Achilleses (or Parises) who are, seemingly, ready to leap from the page and engage their creator in single combat.

It is surprising, however, that although Bussy is the most artful creator of characters on the stage, his own character remains rather foggy. Much of his poetic prowess is expended in the creation of dramatically imagistic moments that, like the "hawking" passage, set static, idealized images of himself against dynamic and detailed, if corrupt, images of his enemies. The characterizations of the clergyman and the lawyer are not as incisive or artful as the description of Monsieur, but they do succeed in creating substantial figures for Bussy to "hawk at." The only character lacking is Bussy himself. That he is a righteous and valiant "eagle" we unserand, but what of his personality? Similarly, in IV.i., Bussy fancies himself as embodied vengeance:

> Were I the man ye wrong'd so and provok'd:
> (Though ne'er so much beneath you) like a box-tree
> I would (out of the toughness of my root)
> Ram hardness in my lowness, and like death
> Mounted on earthquakes, I would trot through all
> Honours and horrors: through foul and fair,
> And from your whole strength toss you into air.
> (IV.i.84–90)

For all its blood and thunder, this passage is not a character description. Bussy threatens his foes with hyperbolic images of an abstract strength rather than with heroic elements of a strong character. He does not, as in the portrait of Monsieur, or even of the clergyman, weave motivations, idiosyncrasies, or essential social nature into the images. The valiant hawk, and the vengeance trotting "like death / Mounted on earthqakes," may be grand, but they are also faceless.

Bussy's patrons are equally incapable of delineating his personality. Henry attempts to characterize him with the glowing tag of "Man in his native noblesse" (III.ii.91), but by associating him with an entire golden age full of individuals, Henry's description only emphasizes Bussy's inchoate identity. From Henry we learn that Bussy has "spirit and state," "nerves," and "genius" (III.ii.97, 106–07), but these are the stock and trade of political encomium. As when Monsieur compares Bussy to the sea (I.ii.138–146) or to "the most royal beast of chase" (III.ii.152–157), the comparisons serve to expand, rather than encapsulate, Bussy's nature by associating him with a generic range of individuals or with vastness itself. The only consistently clear note in Henry's speech is the oft-repeated name "D'Ambois." It seems that Bussy, like Tennyson's Ulysses, has "become a name," without first having been a man. Bussy insists on defining himself by contrast with vibrantly created corruption, while Henry and Monsieur, trapped in the sweeping generalities and exalted platitudes of court language, are incapable of creating any kind of insightful portrait.

How is it that Bussy, through his verbal dynamism, is capable of creating everything but himself? This question can best be answered with reference to Bussy's lauded "epic" heroism. Ide has demonstrated that the true tragedy of *The Tragedy of Bussy D'Ambois* is that the "assertion of heroic spirit in the active life alienates Bussy from society's standards of acceptable behavior."[10] Epic heroes do not fit into the social structure of Bussy's world. Neither, as the flatness of Bussy's character demonstrates, do they fit into its artistic conventions. The epic hero is faceless in an age when individuality is an issue and pure types seem out of place. Glorious epithets do not stick to Bussy; they invariably seem like ersatz courtly eulogy or hearkenings to an inapplicable past. It is enough for Homer to describe Achilles as "the swift-foote God-like sonne / Of Thetis" (1.119), but we want something more psychologically precise than "the fiery D'Ambois," or "Great D'Ambois." The inapplicability of the Homeric voice is illustrated in Nuntius' self-consciously Homeric description of the duel. Nuntius announces his diction the moment that he "comes forward" to address the audience.

> What Atlas, or Olympus lifts his head
> So far past covert, that with air enough
> My words may be inform'd? And from his height
> I may been seen, and heard through all the world?
> A tale so worthy, and so fraught with wonder
> Sticks in my jaws, and labours with event.
> (II.i.25–30)

The conventional invocation to the Muse seems fraught with uncertainty. The mountains of inspiration are hidden in "covert," and the tale seems almost too difficult to tell. Are these merely the formulaic disclaimers of the epic poet or indications of the limitation set on epic style by modern subject matter? At first glance, the description of the duel seems a charming nugget of Homericism set in the midst of the play. When compared to its parallels in *The Iliads*, however, it emerges as a stark representation of a distinctly non-Homeric world. Chapman's Achilles glitters "like day," "Like fire-light, or the light of heaven shot from the rising Sun" (22.117–118). Bussy too is a fire, but not the divine, enduring fire of the sun. He is "like lighted paper . . . at once both fire and ashes" (II.i.72–73) or "like a pointed Comet" (II.i.82) in a darkened sky. Bussy can claim no diffused pantheistic association with the divine in nature, for his spirit does not partake of the enduring sunlight, but brilliant, mutable flame. Barrisor falls like "an Oak / Long shook with tempests, and his lofty top / Bent to his root, which being at length made loose . . . / Storm-like he fell, and hid the fear-cold Earth" (II.i.94–96, 101). Homer's heroes fall like felled trees, victims of the woodsman's axe (13.168) or Jove's thunderbolt (14.345), they do not topple wearily, corrupted by weather and age. The Unicorn simile is of particular interest, for it demonstrates the difference between Bussy's soldiership and that of Homer's heroes. Orsilichus and Crethon are described as "two young Lions . . . / Bred on the tops of some steepe hill," who "rush out and prey on shepe, / Steeres, Oxen" (5.551–554). Similarly, the Greeks and Trojans "Like wolves on one another rusht" (4.501). But Bussy is described not as a natural, if violent, creature obeying instinct, but as a fantastical beast malevolently, almost sadistically, crushing his foe by "Nail[ing] him with his rich antler to the earth" (II.i.123). We understand that Bussy is valorous, glorious and fiery, perhaps even a bit vicious, but it is also made unavoidably clear that such labels are not in themselves enough to define a character. The epic voice, like the epic eternizer, is a thing of the past.

In the failure of Nuntius' speech to capture a concise picture of Bussy's character, we see the failure of a Homeric imitator to celebrate a great Renaissance man. The Chapman who called Essex "Most true Achilles" must have come to realize that such comparisons can only undermine themselves through anachronism. Ide has demonstrated the problems with such historical analogies. But Ide has not addressed the fact that Bussy does succeed as a stage presence and that he does so on a characterizational shoestring. Monsieur, the Eternizer, is no more successful in destroying Bussy's greatness than he is effective in creating it. Monsieur uses verbal ornamentation to elevate Bussy, then to destroy him, but Monsieur is incapable of diminishing Bussy's splendor as a stage presence. The reason is simple enough. Bussy is the most memorable character because he is given the best lines. His motivations are foggy, his actions frequently inconsistent or directed by others, but when all is said and done, Bussy can really talk. From the first moment of the play he is the most powerful poet on the stage. Moreover the he is a dramatic poet, a dramatic creator, more than he is a dramatic character. It is as though Chapman has stepped into his own play in the position that had things been different, Essex should have occupied. The artist has replaced the hero. In *The Tragedy of Bussy D'Ambois*, then, the artistic creation of character, rather than its historical enactment, is the favored form of heroism. And it is the artist rather than the warrior whom Bussy imitates in his dying moments.

Homer:
In it, the never wearied Sunne, the Moone exactly round
And all those starres with which the browes of ample heaven are crownd—
Orion, all the Pleiades, and those seven Atlas got,
The close-beam'd Hyades, the Beare, surnam'd the Chariot,
That turnes about heaven's axletree, holds ope a constant eye
Upon Orion; and, of all the Cressets in the skie,
His golden forehead never bowes to th'Ocean Emperie.
(18.436–443)

Bussy:
            O my fame,
Live in despite of murder; take thy wings
And haste thee where the gray-ey'd Morn perfines
Her rosy chariot with Sabean spices;
Fly, where the Evening from th'Iberian vales
Takes on her swarthy shoulders Hecate
Crown'd with a grove of oaks; fly where men feel
The burning axletree, and those that suffer
Beneth the chariot of the Snowy Bear.
(V.iii.145–153)

Bussy asks that his fame live on, but it is his words that will live to create that fame. The worthiest epic hero is not Achilles but Vulcan.

The Tragedy of Bussy D'Ambois enacts a personal and artistic struggle for Chapman. In Bussy and Monsieur, Chapman has created two characters with two contrasting poetic styles. The eternizer, the vision of the artist apparent in the 1598 *Iliades*, struggles against Chapman's later understanding of the artist as creator, celebrated in the 1611 version. But the very existence of a number of dramatic characters determines that the later conception of the artist will prevail. It is his ability to offer examples of poetic style contrasting along characterizational lines that demonstrates Chapman's power as a dramatic creator. In a dramatic medium, the eternizer, the dresser of lifeless forms, is powerless, and the creator becomes "Godlike," fashioning a world of dazzling vitality and "rare varietie," and, by the end of the play, making "even death to live." As a final gesture before dying, Bussy presents a distinct emblem of the creative technique. He offers his sword to Montsurry with the words,

> Take it, and only give it motion,
> And it shall find the way to victory
> By his own brightness, and th'inherent valour
> My fight hath still'd into't, with charms of spirit.
> (V.iii.162–165)

This sword then, is like one of Vulcan's tripods, "To whose feete little wheeles of gold he put, to go withall / And enter his rich dining roome—alone, their motion free, / And backe againe go out alone, miraculous to see" (18. 333–335). Rather than an implement of war, the sword has become an emblem of Bussy's creative power—beaten, as it were, into a pen. The sword is imbued with Bussy's personality, just as the shield made by Vulcan is imbued with his, and just as the *Tragedy of Bussy D'Ambois* is imbued with Chapman's. To be a true hero, the great man must first be a great artist.

NOTES

1. Richard S. Ide, *Possessed with Greatness: The Heroic Tragedies of Chapman and Shakespeare* (Chapel Hill: University of North Carolina Press, 1980), p. 75.

2. *Chapman's Homer*, ed. Allardyce Nicoll, I (Princeton, N.J.: Princeton University Press, 1956). All further notes to Chapman's Homer or the prefatory matter to his translations are from this edition.

3. John Channing Briggs, "Chapman's *Seaven Bookes of the Iliades*: Mirror for Essex," *Studies in English Literature 1500–1900*, 21 (1981), 59–73.

4. Ide, p. 77.

5. Briggs, p. 70.

6. Ide, p. 77.

7. George Chapman, *Bussy D'Ambois*, ed. Nicholas Brooke, The Revels Plays (Cambridge, Mass: Harvard University Press, 1964). All references are to this edition.

8. Jonathan Dollimore, *Radical Tragedy: Religion, Ideology and Power in the Drama of Shakespeare and his Contemporaries* (Brighton: John Spiers, 1984). In Dollimore's chapter entitled "Bussy D'Ambois: A Hero At Court," Dollimore contends that Bussy's conception of self is completely constructed for him by Monsieur and the King.
9. Ide, p. 87.
10. *Ibid.*, p. 75.

Responses to Tyranny in John Fletcher's Plays

ROBERT Y. TURNER

A surprisingly large number of dramas in the Beaumont and Fletcher canon depicts an absolute ruler attempting to exert his will over his vulnerable subjects. Since the figure of the tyrant appears in plays from the outset to the end of Fletcher's career, no matter who the collaborator, it is reasonable to assume that Fletcher had a personal fascination with the tyrant, or—to be more precise—with the problems of subjects living under such a ruler. In the earlier stages of Fletcher's career, when he worked with Beaumont, the tyrant appears mainly in tragedies: *Cupid's Revenge* (ca. 1607–12), *The Maid's Tragedy* (ca. 1608–11), and *Valentinian* (written alone, 1610–14).[1] After Beaumont's withdrawal from the theater, the tyrant disappears from most of Fletcher's tragedies except for *Rollo, Duke of Normandy* (a collaboration with Massinger and probably Chapman and Jonson, 1616–24) and *The Double Marriage* (1619–23, with Massinger) and resurfaces in such tragicomedies as *The Loyal Subject* (1617), *The Humorous Lieutenant* (1619?), *A Wife for a Month* (1624), all by Fletcher alone, and the *The Custom of the Country* (1619–23, with Massinger). Two other plays include a character who is not strictly a tyrant but who exercises so relentless a force over others that the plays can be mentioned with this group: *The Tragedy of Thierry and Theodoret* (1607–17, with Massinger and probably Beaumont) and a tragicomedy, *The Prophetess* (with Massinger, 1622).

Despite the shift from tragedy to tragicomedy, Fletcher's thinking about tyranny changed little during his career. Most of the characters and their predicaments that appear and reappear until 1625 are set in his imagination by two early plays, *Cupid's Revenge* and *The Maid's Tragedy*. Whatever personal compulsion he may have felt about the situation of an absolute monarch attempting to exert his will over helpless subjects, he must have found that it touched a responsive chord in his audience, for he rang changes on it year after year. Since it is a commonplace in studies of Beaumont and Fletcher that they were attuned to their times, taste-makers for Jacobean audiences, it seems more than likely that the political climate of James I's rule fostered the playwrights' interest in the difficulties of living under a ruler who claims absolute power. The possibility strengthens when one looks for a comparable number of tyrants in dramas during the last ten years or so of Elizabeth's reign. In that time, plays about political figures dramatized the Wars of the Roses, the deposition of Richard II, the assassinations of King John and of Julius Caesar, all of which focus on struggles of competing claims for authority. Sackville and Norton's commentary about the purposes of the much earlier *Gorboduc* helps us understand the Elizabethans' apprehensions about an orderly succession of power in the rule of an unmarried monarch. Once James I, the father of three children, ascended the throne in 1603, the problem of royal succession disappeared, but by 1607 or 1608, it appears that another anxiety emerged and was exploited by Fletcher's plays, that of living under an implacable and inescapable monarch.

The extravagance of James I's claims for his authority, combined with his unresponsive, if not disdainful, behavior in public ceremonies, I suggest, provoked some disquieting fantasies of tyranny in his subjects, fantasies to which Fletcher's plays gave a local habitation. The King envisioned himself as "schoolmaster of the realm" and seldom neglected the chance to state his beliefs about the royal prerogative. Before he became King of England, he published not only a book on demonology but also two works on rulership that articulated the position he was never to change. The *Basilikon Doron*, a kingly gift of advice to his son, Prince Henry, first appeared in Scotland in 1599 and went through a number of editions in England. Less familiar because it was issued anonymously in 1598 and again in 1603, but later identified by inclusion in James's *Works* of 1616, *The Trew Law of Free Monarchies* contains graphic statements about his view of power.

> And as ye see it manifest, that the King is ouer-Lord of the whole land: so is he Master ouer euery person that inhabiteth the same, hauing power ouer the life and death of euery one of them: For although a iust Prince will not take the life of any of his subiects without a cleare law; yet the same lawes whereby he taketh them, are made by himselfe, or his predecessours; and so the power flowes alwaies from him selfe.
>
> (p. 63)[2]

This is a fair example of the way that James argues, removing all checks from himself except that of God and allowing no ground for opposition. Not content to defend himself and all just rulers, he presses his case to include Nebuchadnezzar and Nero. Even tyrants remain divine deputies, instruments of God's punishments, visited upon wicked subjects, and deserve unquestioning obedience. The subjects' only recourse is amendment of their own lives and prayer that God relieve them of their heavy curse (McIlwain, p. 67). Although this argument can be found in the *Homily Against Rebellion and Willful Disobedience*, the impact intensifies when the ruler himself enunciates it.[3]

What characterizes James's prose, for all its self-serving emphasis, is a lively imagination. The *Demonology* testifies to a strain of wild fancy that can be sensed also in the way in which he argues for unquestioning obedience from his subjects. To press his point, James postulates worst-case scenarios not unlike the plays by Fletcher and his collaborators. A strident passage from *The Trew Law* could serve as the source for one of their plots:

> Can any pretence of wickednes or rigor on his [the father's] part be a iust excuse for his children to put hand unto him? And although wee see by the course of nature, that loue vseth to descend more then to ascend, in case it were trew, that the father hated and wronged the children neuer so much, will any man, endued with the least sponke of reason, thinke it lawfull for them to meet him with the line? Yea, suppose the father were furiously following his sonnes with a drawen sword, is it lawfull for them to turne and strike again, or make any resistance but by flight?
> (McIlwain, p. 65)

This hypothetical situation, set out with James's gift for a sharp turn of phrase, could focus a subject's attention mightily. What James fails to do is to imagine the confrontation from the viewpoint of the children—or his subjects. Beaumont and Fletcher do just that in *Cupid's Revenge*, as if to follow through James's narrative to its bitter conclusion. Leucippus, the son, finds himself oppressed by his father, the old Duke, who suspects him to be a political rival. The high-minded and innocent young Prince refuses to raise a hand against his father and despite intense provocation remains the very embodiment of passive obedience of the sort that James would claim from his subjects for Nero or Nebuchadnezzar. Controlled throughout by the divine power of Cupid, the play dramatizes at excruciating length what absolute and unanswerable power, unchecked by scruple, can feel like.

James did take special care to add a clause about a ruler's moral responsibility, but his assertion that he was answerable to God (and to none other) probably struck him as greater justification that it did his subjects. Given the reality of power in England, the role of the Commons in granting revenues to the king and the established judicial system based on common law, there were sufficient checks on the monarch, even if we discount James's personal character, to forestall a tyrannical exercise of power. If nothing else, James's notorious love of the chase and his negligence in matters of state would in some measure allay anxieties about any campaign for total domination. Even so, the King was obtuse about the impact of his behavior and exhibited a tactlessness that evoked disquiet in his subjects. Testimonies abound as to Elizabeth's responsiveness in public to displays of affection from her subjects, a high standard against which to measure James's responses to Londoners' enthusiastic welcome upon his first entrance to the city.[4] He felt ill at ease in public and neglected to encourage the devotion of the populace. When on 21 March 1609 (1610), he addressed both Houses of Parliament to reassure them, among other things, that he disapproved of Dr. John Cowell's *The Interpreter* (1607), a law dictionary extolling civil law over common law, James lectured them nevertheless on the nature of his unanswerable power to any but God Himself. Elizabeth, by contrast, focused her speeches on thanking Parliament for its support and avoided insistence upon her prerogative.[5] Whatever the realities of power, James's behavior, so different from what his subjects had grown to expect from their ruler, could be seen as sufficient to generate apprehensions in playwrights and populace.

In James's speech proclaiming his dedication to the practice of common law against Dr. Cowell's dictionary, he located the difference "betwixt a rightfull King and an usurping Tyrant" in the power of conscience over will: "the proude and ambitious Tyrant doeth thinke his Kingdome and people are onely ordeined for satisfaction of his desires and vnreasonable appetites" (McIlwain, p. 278). This distinction is commonplace and would hardly warrant notice if the crucial attribute were not the unpredictable will. What determines whether the will follows common law or private appetite? The will's instability becomes apparent when James elaborates upon the rightful exercise of unanswerable power of God, king, and father:

> Kings are iustly called Gods, for that they exercise a manner or resemblance of Diuine power vpon earth: For if you wil consider the Attributes to God, you shall see how they agree in the person of a King. God hath power to create, or destroy, make, or vnmake *at his pleasure*, to giue life, or send death, to iudge all, and to be iudged not acomptable to none. . . . Now a Father may dispose of his Inheritance to his children, *at his pleasure*, yea, euen disinherite the eldest vpon iust occasions, and preferre the youngest, *according to his liking*; make them beggers, or rich *at his pleasure*; restraine, or banish out of his presence, as hee finds them giue cause of offence, or restore them in fauour againe with the penitent sinner: So may the King deale with his Subiects.
> (McIlwain, pp. 307–308; italics mine)

In this passage James uses *pleasure* four times (if "liking" is included) to a single mention of "iust occasions" in discussing the motives of power. Dr. Cowell's *Interpreter*, in fact, raises a version of this issue about motives by its definitions of *subsidy, king, parliament,* and *prerogative.* Cowell provoked such an outcry that James disclaimed approval of *The Interpreter* even though it agrees with many of his own statements about kingship. At issue, of course, is the necessity of checks upon the ruler's will. Whether he chooses to follow principles of right reason or of appetite lies in the will, as Iago says. The Parliamentary opposition insisted on shifting the locus of power to a source of law beyond the ruler's will, but James saw the crux of the issue differently, stressing the importance of law itself, not its source. In this regard, it is worth observing how he redefined the tyrant in his 1610 speech to Parliament: "A king gouerning in a setled Kingdome, leaues to be a King, and degenerates into a Tyrant, as soone as he leaues off to rule according to his Lawes" (McIlwain, p. 309). Yet this formulation evades the issue that James's subjects wished to resolve, the status of "his" laws and protection against a ruler's unpredictable will. What renders the will pliable to the solicitations of desire or firm in its dedication to law? To ask such a question is to demand yet another notion to explain what the "will" itself explains. The obscurity, if not mystery, surrounding the faculty of will can account in part for the complex uses of the term in the Elizabethan and Jacobean periods. Ulysses in *Troilus and Cressida* assimilates the will to appetite (I.iii.119–124); Troilus affirms it as the bedrock of integrity (II.ii.62–69).[6] The will, which could be seen as the source either of fickleness or constancy, fascinated Fletcher as the very stuff of drama from the outset of his career, a fascination that he adapted readily to the depiction of tyrants.

A "clash of wills" best describes the way that Fletcher's plays dramatize the exercise of the tyrant's power over his subjects. Unlike Shakespeare, Fletcher had little interest in tracing the careers of ambitious characters like Richard III or Macbeth, who murder characters in their ascent to illusory triumphs. Instead Fletcher's tyrants are firmly in power when his plays begin. Unlike even Jonson's Tiberius in *Sejanus* (1603), Fletcher's tyrants express their disregard for restraints by invading the bedroom. His thinking about this connection between ruler and subject does not expand to all sections of the state, as is the case in *Macbeth* or *Sejanus*. Instead the tyrant moves quickly from state affairs to a desired female, so that political issues merge with personal desire. The most intense version of this experience appears in the relatively early play, *The Maid's Tragedy* (ca. 1608–11), where Amintor discovers on his wedding night that his marriage has been manipulated for the convenience of the King. Fletcher reworks this predicament some fifteen years later in *A Wife for a Month* (1624) in what may well have been the last of his plays written without a collaborator: King Frederick, jealous of Valerio, sentences the latter's marriage to last but one month and end with his death. The King adds in secret to the newly wedded husband that if the groom should sleep with his bride or tell her of this prohibition, she will lose her life too. In *The Custom of the Country* (1619–23), which Fletcher wrote with Massinger, the governor enjoys the custom of either preempting the husband on the wedding night or ransoming the bride's maidenhead. These bizarre episodes taken in isolation would confirm the received opinion of Fletcher as a seeker after piquant situations to titillate a jaded audience. They become less startling when placed with other Jacobean dramatizations of the tyrant's power, including Duke Ferdinand's intrusion into the Duchess of Malfi's bedroom or Duke Brachiano's disruption of Vittoria Corombona's marriage in *The White Devil*, or the tyrant's disinterring the dead body of his loved one in *The Second Maiden's Tragedy*.[7] Fletcher found in Lucrece a model more to his taste than the poor young woman like Jane Shore or like Bianca in Middleton's *Women Beware Women* (ca. 1620–27), succumbing to temptations of riches and position.[8] Fletcher returned repeatedly to the spirited heroine, fiercely dedicated to honor, proclaiming her integrity in the face of her ruler's overwhelming power. The struggle of wills, his to satisfy his lusts, hers to preserve her virtue, captures the essentials of Fletcher's thinking about tyrants, the limits of their power, and the nobility of subjects. His plays exploit the anxieties aroused by James's insistence on his power and placate them by the depiction of heroic subjects, whose dedication to honor even the most loyal Cavalier would find compelling.

I

The genre best adapted to render the conventional tyrant was tragedy, according to Sir Philip Sidney and George Puttenham, who wrote in the generation preceding Beaumont and Fletcher. In the *Apology for Poetry* Sidney said that tragedy makes "kings fear to be tyrants, and tyrants manifest their tyrannical humors," and in *The Art of English Poesie*, Puttenham said that in tragedies, the "infamous life [of tyrants] and tyrannies were layed open to all the world, their wickedness reproched, their follies and extreme insolencies derided."[9] Yet Fletcher's tyrants behave in ways that fit either tragedy or tragicomedy. The traditional features of the tyrant, such as the cultivation of fear rather than love in subjects, neglect of the responsibilities of government, generosity to sycophants, suspicions and sleeplessness, may get an obligatory nod insofar as they serve to dramatize the tyrant's effort to please his will at any cost.[10] But the characteristic act for satisfying himself is to separate husband from wife, parent from child, friend from friend, only to find that his actions bring no satisfaction. Ruler and subject gravitate toward the restricted, even domestic, space, with little sense of the commonwealth behind the walls. This intimacy imparts a special Fletcherian claustrophobia to the tyrant's rule, only to reduce something of his grandeur. More important, the intimacy elevates the subject, whose sexual attractiveness compels the tyrant to behave in ways that, in the tragedies, destroy him. The victim takes his or her place at center stage, where appropriately Fletcher and his collaborators invest their fullest creative attention; we find in their plays a variety of oppressed subjects, but their tyrants appear very much alike, at times almost faceless. In *The Maid's Tragedy* the only speaking character without a name is the King. This imbalance of attention creates opportunities for praising the victimized subjects and thereby comforting the audience in the shadow of threats, if not destruction, from the tyrant.

Beaumont and Fletcher may have stumbled onto their formula for the tyrant plays with what was one of their first collaborations, *Cupid's Revenge* (*ca.* 1607–12). Cupid signifies not only the concupiscent passions but also the irascible that release themselves in revenge. Power is indeed doing what satisfies the will. Cupid's will is assimilated to appetite, and appetite wills what it wishes without the restraint of will. This god becomes a chilling and vivid embodiment of the absolute monarch doing exactly as he pleases to his subject. But Leucippus, the pious son of Cupid's mortal surrogate, the old Duke, embodies another aspect of the will. Leucippus refuses to lift an arm against his father's misguided antagonism. As a docile subject, Leucippus defends his passivity with words that could be lifted from James's claim for unquestioning submission or from the *Homily Against Rebellion and Willful Disobedience*. His loyalty, maintained under the utmost difficulties, discloses a heroic exercise of will that provides some measure of comfort for an audience experiencing unrelieved and unanswerable power, both divine and parental. One might recall here that James defended the royal prerogative not only by appeal to divine sanction but by likening it to parental claims upon children.

Whether Fletcher wrote *The Faithful Shepherdess* (1608–09) before or after his collaboration with Beaumont on *Cupid's Revenge*, this pastoral tragicomedy testifies to his early interest in the mysteries of the will. The play dramatizes the will's connection with sexual appetite in a variety of characters, ranging from the totally abstemious to the indiscriminately lascivious. The audience ranges in its responses from laughter at the weak-willed Cloe to admiration for the firm-willed Amoret, unwaveringly faithful despite the brutal treatment of her loved one, Perigot. We find in *Cupid's Revenge* a similar range of characters, from the lascivious widow Bacha, who generates scorn rather than laughter, to Leucippus, whose loyalty to his father despite the latter's irrational antagonism generates amazement, if not admiration. Both plays depict a diversity of characters that stimulates us to wonder at the mystery of the will, but the plays probe no further into that mystery, remaining content to display a spectacle of diversity for our contemplation. This attitude toward the will carries over to the other tragedy about tyranny that Fletcher wrote with Beaumont, *The Maid's Tragedy*, as well as to *Valentinian*, written alone, and to *Rollo, Duke of Normandy* and *The Double Marriage*, both written with Massinger. When Fletcher turned to tragicomedy in dramatizing the confrontation of tyrant and subject, whether writing alone or with Massinger, he maintained the same outlook toward the will. But the fact that he wrote without collaboration three of these four plays that end happily, and wrote them in the mature years of his career, suggests a personal inclination toward reassuring the audience (*The Loyal Subject, The Humorous Lieutenant, A Wife for a Month*, all by Fletcher alone). Generally speaking, Fletcher and his collaborators were ready to exploit anxieties about an unrestrained ruler, but for the most part they chose to alleviate those anxieties by casting the victim in an admirable light, defiant if not triumphant over the tyrant's threats.

In both genres it was the "big scene" that absorbed Fletcher's attention.[11] The give-and-take between ruler determined to have his will and subject equally adamant in preserving integrity constitutes the purest Fletcherian moment in these plays. The encounter at its most typical occurs in *Valentinian*, written with no collaborators, where the ruler tricks Lucina, wife of Maximus, to come alone to court. Like Lucrece, Lucina resists the emperor with all the moral arguments at her command: "Ye are too neere the nature of the Gods, / To wrong the weakest of all creatures: Women" (II.vi.33–34).[12] Her comment reverberates beyond the confines of the stage to recall James's notion of the ruler. Likewise, Valentinian's counterargument resembles the terms of the debate about Dr. Cowell's *Interpreter*:

> Know I am far above the faults I doe,
> And those I doe I am able to forgive too.
> (III.i.119–120)

> Justice shall never heare ye, I am justice.
> (III.i.34)

Valentinian discovers that in satisfying his will he fails to calculate the force of will in his victim, the crucial supplement that Fletcher's tragedy adds to James's argument from the ruler's viewpoint. Unlike Shakespeare's *The Rape of Lucrece*, *Valentinian* includes a dialogue between tyrant and victim after the rape, when Lucina discloses how the value of her honor overrides her ruler's demand for her acquiescence and patience: "Your only vertue now is patience" (III.i.30). Valentinian's insulated view of his prerogative has not taken the measure of her fierce sense of integrity, which is a matter of life or death. That revelation and Valentinian's acknowledgment of it, manipulated for maximum dramatic intensity, form the climax of their struggle.

Lucina knows that she must kill herself to maintain her integrity, and her husband Maximus assents, though sadly, to her resolution. Aecius, both loyal supporter of Emperor Valentinian and friend of Maximus, tries to argue for a practical course of action: remain alive and help Valentinian repent: "Death only eases you; this, the whole Empire" (III.i.219). For Maximus and Lucina, honor resides as well in the eyes of the world as in the dedicated will. The stain of rape, says Maximus, cannot be contained:

> Nor staies it [the stain] there, but that our names must find it,
> Even those to come; and when they read, she livd,
> Must they not aske how often she was ravishd,
> And make a doubt she lov'd that more then Wedlock?
> Therefore she must not live.
>   (III.i.241–245)

It takes an ultimate act of will, suicide, to validate Lucina's integrity. Maximus and Lucina see themselves as much a part of history as Valentinian does, and so the imperatives of honor constitute their counter—and Fletcher's—to the tyrant's unrestricted prerogative, an argument that places limits on the subjects' passive obedience. Lucina loses the contest of force, but not of wills. Death for her, as a martyr to her integrity, is hardly a defeat and assures the audience of the limits of the ruler's power.

This paradox of victory in defeat emerges more obviously in the comparable "big scene" of *The Double Marriage*. The "libidinous tyrant" Ferrand puts Juliana on the rack in hope of extracting information about her rebellious husband Virolet. She exults in her refusal to talk: "My life is thine, / But in the death [, the] victory shall be mine."[13] By this time in Fletcher's career, 1619–23, the big confrontation has become somewhat perfunctory. Juliana glories so readily in her suffering that it comes as little surprise when the tyrant admits defeat: "Unloose her, I am conquer'd" (p. 335). Earlier versions of the big scene are more heartfelt. In *Cupid's Revenge*, Act Three, scene two, Queen Bacha holds the position of power and tries to seduce her stepson, Leucippus, first by temptation and then by threats to his life. He maintains his integrity, one of the few moments of assurance in a bleak play, for behind Bacha's power lies Cupid's. The god can arrange events to destroy Leucippus' life but not to alter Leucippus' will.

Here in the recesses of the psyche lies the ultimate comfort that Fletcher and his collaborators hold out to their audience, once they have aroused anxieties about tyranny. Defiance is one way that they dramatize the power of will; unpredictability is another. The arrangement of events in *The Maid's Tragedy* reveals the importance of being unable to predict how characters will behave. Amintor, the most victimized subject, should be the character most ready to defy his king, since Amintor discovers on his wedding night that his wife is the King's mistress, who married Amintor only to avoid suspicions about her royal liaison. Yet it is the honor of another character, Melantius, brother of the mistress, that compels him to convert his sister to murder the King. Amintor remains firm in his loyalty to the King and spokesman for passive obedience despite his humiliation. The peculiar reversal must be understood as something more than an oddity for entertainment. To predict is to control. The King indeed tells Amintor that he counted upon Amintor's loyalty in choosing him for the marriage. To underline the significance of predictability, Beaumont and Fletcher include a scene where the King faces the problem of predicting Melantius' loyalty, aroused by the accusations of Calianax (IV.ii). The subject's unpredicted action proves to be simultaneously a grand dramatic gesture, a *coup de théâtre*, and a viable political comment. This coincidence of political conviction and lively drama must have clicked for Fletcher because he continued throughout his career to build scenes upon the unpredictable will of the defiant subject.

All the tragicomedies that include tyrants appeared in the latter part of Fletcher's career, a fact that suggests this genre to be more appropriate than tragedy to render his mature reflections on the experience of living under a ruler who claims absolute power.[14] What we find instead is disappointing, for the tragicomedies rework the patterns set in the tragedies. The tyrant, of course, is not killed but either converted or removed, so that his subjects emerge from any encounters triumphant. If these later plays disclose the essential Fletcher, we find a playwright unable to conceive of the tyrant not locked in a conflict of wills with a defiant subject. The tyrant's will must relent, for the subject's will remains inviolable, and as such, a comfort to the audience.

The Loyal Subject (1617) neatly reverses the tragic pattern. Here the tyrant is young and unmarried, taken finally into the warm embrace of the loyal subject's family and married to the eldest daughter. The tyrant satisfies his will not by breaking a happy marriage, but in a happy marriage. Before his conversion, he mistreats the loyal old subject, Archas, father of the good family as well as general of the army. The young ruler exercises his will against the worthy old general first with neglect, then with insults, and finally with torture. But old Archas never deviates from his loyalty despite the unprovoked, wilful antagonism of his young Duke, and this strength of will converts the ruler, who embraces old Archas, rejects his evil advisor, and accepts Archas' daughter, significantly named Honora, in marriage. *The Humorous Lieutenant* (1619?) reworks the rivalry between an old king and his son that first appeared in *Cupid's Revenge*. Unlike the wicked Bacha in the earlier play, the heroine Celia is young, spirited, virtuous, remaining fully committed to the son and defending her honor in the obligatory confrontation with the old King, Antigonus:

>   *Antigonus.*   Say I should force ye?
>   I have it in my will.
>
>   *Celia.*   Your will's a poore one;
>   And though it be a Kings will, a despised one,
>   Weaker then Infants leggs, your will's in swadling clouts:
>   A thousand waies my will has found to checke ye;
>   A thousand doores to scape ye: I dare die sir.[15]

Celia need not imitate Lucrece because the old King submits to her nobility, acknowledges the limits of his power, and allows his son to marry her.

A Wife for a Month (1624), probably the last drama Fletcher wrote by himself, rings a variation upon *The Maid's Tragedy*. The tyrant disrupts the wedding night by sentencing Valerio, the bridegroom, to die one month after marriage and then tells him in secret that he must neither sleep with his bride Evanthe nor disclose this prohibition to her or she will lose her life. This situation gives rise to a titillating dialogue between the expectant bride and her evasive groom, reminiscent of the eager Amintor and the reluctant Evadne. A sequence of big scenes, interviews dramatizing a fierce contest of wills, also recalls *The Maid's Tragedy*. First, King Frederick tempts Valerio by offering to spare his life and bestow riches, provided Valerio give up his wife to the King's pleasure for a brief time, an arrangement to be kept secret from the world. Next Evanthe suffers a similar temptation from the bawd Cassandra. Both refuse. In a subsequent scene Evanthe wavers momentarily when King Frederick slanders Valerio, accusing her husband of cowardice for refusing to sleep with her in order to save his own life. Time and again Fletcher hits the note of "will" in rendering these confrontations. At the outset the evil advisor Sorano tells King Frederick, "I had thought you had been absolute, the great King . . . Your will and your commands unbounded also" (p. 3).[16] When Frederick insists upon having his way with Evanthe, he proclaims, "'Tis my will," and she retorts, "'Tis a most wicked one" (p. 6). Thus they fulfill the pattern that Fletcher's audience must have come to expect. Yet the play deviates from the formula to achieve a happy ending, perhaps because the threats of the tyrant are too dark for a conversion to be acceptable.[17] Frederick is removed from power by an elder brother, the rightful heir, who has been kept in the wings throughout the play, too "feeble" to assume rulership. By this device Fletcher manages to remove the tyrant without overt defiance of James's doctrine of passive obedience.

One could account for the recycling of the familiar in a slightly different key by saying that Fletcher lacked invention, that his imagination flowed in well-cut grooves, or that as an indefatigible professional he met the demand for new plays with an economy of marginal variation. Yet the overall variety in his canon suggests not so much a poverty of imagination as a conviction at work. Did he feel that in the final analysis the relation between an absolute monarch and his subjects allowed for no other possibility than the subject's triumph? In a contest of wills, the ruler, not the subjects, must finally give way, either to die or to change in some fashion satisfactory to his subjects. This outcome raises a problem about the responses to Fletcher's plays by the Master of the Revels and by the royalist supporters of the King, if not by James himself.

II

Franco Moretti recently linked the death of kings in English tragedy from the time of *Gorboduc* with the regicide of Charles I: "Having deconsecrated the king, it thus made it possible to decapitate him."[18] However that may be, Moretti's contention restores a sense of the inflammatory potentiality of killing kings on stage. Retaliation against a tyrant holds obvious assurances for an audience, but it happens to be an act proscribed by James's defense of the royal prerogative. Yet the tyrants in Fletcher's tragedies are killed by their subjects, and the very repetition of this fictional deed can be seen to make tyrannicide familiar to the imagination. If Fletcher's plays about tyrants "mystify" the will, his tragedies "demystify" the audacious deed. In this regard, the question arises about Fletcher's political attitude, especially in the light of the critical tradition marked by Coleridge's famous judgment on the "hollow extravagance of their [Beaumont and Fletcher's] ultra-royalism." Philip J. Finkelpearl has, to my mind, put this opinion to rest in a searching essay on both Beaumont and Fletcher's connections with members of the Parliamentary opposition to James and his royalist supporters.[19] Yet Margo Heinemann says in her study of oppositionist drama that reflected the values of the Parliamentary Puritans in the Jacobean and Caroline period, "Fletcher, not Shakespeare, Jonson or Middleton, was the Cavaliers' favourite dramatist."[20] In this connection G. E. Bentley's finding is pertinent: the plays in the Beaumont and Fletcher canon were performed more frequently at court than plays by any other dramatists between 1616 and 1642.[21] Both positions are, I believe, correct, for Fletcher and his collaborators managed to present the tyrant in ways that evaded censorship and appealed to the privileged theatergoers, whether royalist or oppositionist.

As sons of gentry, both Fletcher and Beaumont were close enough to the courts of law, Houses of Parliament, and the royal court to be alert to the concerns of the privileged, who were the most likely to see and hear their monarch or read his works. Ann Jennalie Cook's study of the finances and social status of playgoers supports the contention that the Jacobean audience would bring to the theater an interest in matters of state.[22] In fact, early in James's reign a cluster of plays reveals a topical interest in the new ruler by their depiction of a monarch who improves his ability to govern by taking on a disguise to go among his subjects: Middleton's *The Phoenix* (1603–04), Marston's *The Malcontent* (1603–04) and *The Fawn* (1606), and

Measure for Measure (1604). Broadly speaking, the hopeful attitude in these plays reflects an outlook of the audience for their new King. It is hardly stretching plausibility to see in the number of tyrants that begin to appear on stage about the time of *Cupid's Revenge* (*ca.* 1607–12) a reflection of discouragement consequent upon a growing acquaintance with James's behavior and an exploitation of anxieties about being trapped under a bad monarch. John Day's *The Isle of Gulls* (1606) was probably the first play to mount a thinly disguised satire on James's fondness for hunting, boasting, and devotion to favorites, although *Eastward Ho!* (1605) contained incidental comic allusions to the selling of knighthoods.[23] Day was called before the Star Chamber to defend himself, and he stressed the fact that his play derived from Sidney's *Arcadia*. The trouble faced by Day and the actors, probably imprisoned for a time, served to warn and perhaps even to tempt other playwrights. Beaumont and Fletcher heeded Day's experience, for they avoided obvious topical allusions and hedged their criticism sufficiently to have it both ways—pusillanimous, no doubt, but also delightfully ingenious.

The sensitivity of the playwrights to their own boldness can be discerned in the care they took to include a spokesperson for passive obedience, a character who talks as if has studied James's speeches and the *Homily Against Rebellion and Willful Disobedience*. The very presence of such commentary ironically signifies topical relevance of the plays and works against the theatricality of the stories and foreign setting that disclaim relevance. Amintor, the abused husband in *The Maid's Tragedy*, gives voice to the royalist position; Aecius, friend of Maximus the victimized husband in *Valentinian*, supports the Emperor despite the immorality of his actions. In *Rollo* Aubrey tries to restrain the enemies of Rollo, prays for his reform, and upon discovering that he himself has been condemned to death by Rollo, volunteers to kill himself to obey his ruler. In *Cupid's Revenge* Leucippus is the earliest of these high-minded characters and sets the pattern. Even though he has the support of the citizens, who recognize in him their hope for a judicious ruler and free him from prison, he refuses to take a step against the misguided old Duke, his father. Leucippus' sensible cousin Ismenus pleads with him in the name of "reason" to move at least against the wicked Duchess, but Leucippus replies, "Well, pardon *Ismenus*, for I know / My courses are most just; nor will I staine em / With one bad action" (IV.v.30–32).[24] His passivity, pushed to an extreme by outrageous provocations, appears more to provoke frustration in the audience than generate admiration for his loyalty, and that response may well fit Beaumont and Fletcher's agenda. The playwrights take care always to pair the spokesperson for passive obedience with a plain speaker of common sense, ready to oppose the ruler who disregards the moral—if not legal—claims of his subjects. As Ismenus urges Leucippus to take up the sword in *Cupid's Revenge*, so Melantius opposes Amintor's passivity in *The Maid's Tragedy*, Maximus against Aecius in *Valentinian*, Edith against Aubrey in *Rollo*, and the Duke of Sessa against Virolet in *The Double Marriage* (the last pair fit the pattern less precisely than the others).

As clear as these contrasts between characters are, Fletcher and his collaborators take precautions to complicate the audience's sympathies. In *Cupid's Revenge* the audience may find exasperating Leucippus' refusal to act, but it cannot give wholehearted endorsement to Ismenus, who urges swift and direct action. Ismenus can take the measure of the wicked Bacha, but he goes too far in urging the death of her daughter Urania, whom the audience knows to be innocent, disapproving of her mother, and in love with Leucippus. The spokesperson for common sense lacks the moral sensitivity of his reluctant friend, who warrants a measure of admiration for his moral integrity. The way the playwrights hedge their dramatizations of all the pairs of characters enables them to have it both ways. A sympathetic attitude toward the royalist supporter would relieve the privileged Jacobean playgoer of the discomforts entailed in approving the death of a ruler. Audience response could be critical without the taint of being subversive.

Balanced against the sympathetic royalist is the fate of the tyrant's assassin, which weighs on the side of criticism. Dramatic logic would seem to demand that the killer of the tyrant be killed, just as the revenger in a revenge tragedy usually also must die. Certainly the outcome for the assassin is central to signify the moral attitude of the tragedy, as Lysippus interprets the death of the King in the concluding lines of *The Maid's Tragedy*: "Unlookt for suddaine deaths from God are sent, / But curst is he that is their instrument"(V.iii.294–295).[25] Yet neither this tragedy nor the others of the group quite conform to this dictum. Although the assassin never enjoys an unqualified triumph, neither does he experience unqualified defeat. The playwrights arrange events so that the playgoers can interpret the outcome in several ways.

In *The Maid's Tragedy*, for instance, Beaumont and Fletcher complicate the motive and identity of the "instrument." Melantius acts as the tyrant's primary opponent by making all the arrangements for his death; yet it is Evadne, his sister and mistress to the King, who actually commits the tyrannicide. She dies, but not from regret over the murder, an act that she interprets as redeeming her honor. Instead she dies in grief over her husband Amintor's rejection. Melantius remains alive at the conclusion, saddened not because he has brought about the King's death, but because Melantius' friend Amintor has died. Amintor kills himself in grief, not because of the King's death, but because Amintor inadvertently killed Aspatia. By crossing a fatal love story with the killing of the tyrant, Beaumont and Fletcher deflect whatever pious comments might be evoked by the tyrannicide. Without Lysippus' final couplet, the audience would most likely focus on the lives wasted by the tyrant's self-centered deeds.

Similar tactics hedge the practical proponents for tyrannicide in the other tragedies. In *Cupid's Revenge* Ismenus is saved from acting against the wicked Queen because her own intrigues rebound against her, and she destroys herself in despair. In *Rollo, Duke of Normandy* Edith plans to kill Rollo to avenge her father's death, but after she lures him to a rendezvous, another character, Hammond, intervenes unexpectedly to do the actual killing and then kills himself, so that Edith like Melantius remains alive. Fletcher and his collaborators allow the sympathetic Edith to want the death of the tyrant without having to pay the price. Having it both ways here borders on sentimentality. *The Double Marriage* ends like *Macbeth*, where the tyrant is removed from the throne by open battle; the citizens of Naples support the Duke of Sessa's attack on their ruler and allow the Duke to go free at the conclusion without punishment or a hint of sorrow. The most subtle arrangement for the assassin—and the one that has caused the most critical commentary—occurs in *Valentinian*. To avenge his wife's death after she is defiled by Valentinian, Maximus mounts a complicated intrigue against the Emperor. At the moment of success, Maximus delivers a lengthy soliloquy in which he considers suicide to join his dead wife and his friend Aecius, sacrificed in Maximus' plot to kill the tyrant. The play could have ended, unhistorically, to be sure, with such a deed, but midpoint in the soliloquy Maximus reverses himself and with a sudden, new motive of ambition decides to become emperor himself.[26] The plot cranks up again, he succeeds in his plan, only to be poisoned at the moment of triumph. The audience is left to ponder whether Maximus' death arises from tyrannicide or from ambition. One can postulate a connection between the two, but events of the play leave the matter uncertain. To moralize his tyrannicide, Maximus could have recalled his intrigue and regretted it as he died, but he remains silent. Again, Fletcher manages to provide for two outlooks; the instrument of tyrannicide does die, but his death need not be construed as a judgment on tyrannicide.

To account for these deaths of tyrants, who at many points echo James I's absolutist claims, one seems driven to postulate inattentive Claudiuses at court and a sleepy Master of the Revels. Dale Randall's study of Ben Jonson's subtle criticism of Buckingham and his family, the very actors and audience of *The Gypsies Metamorphosed* (3 and 5 August 1621), depends upon both thickheaded courtiers and King as well as sharp-witted observers to savor the irony.[27] Yet Sir George Buc's sensitivity to contemporary political events just two years earlier, when he censored Fletcher and Massinger's manuscript *Sir John van Olden Barnavelt* (1619) gives us some conflicting evidence.[28] Perhaps the history of *Believe as You List*, which preserves the interplay between Sir Henry Herbert's objections and Massinger's corrections, provides the clearest picture about censorship and tolerance of political criticism.[29] The Master of the Revels objected to the original version of 1630 about the deposition of Sebastian, King of Portugal, by Philip II of Spain, a topical analogue to the exiled Frederick of Bohemia, husband of James's daughter Elizabeth and a sympathetic cause for English Protestants. Massinger changed only the setting and times to Rome, saving himself trouble by choosing new names for his characters that were metrically equivalent to the old ones. The analogy to Frederick remained, encoded for those who wished to interpret it. We find here a tacit agreement between playwright and censor, the one not to be stridently obvious, the other not to be too suspicious. Annabel Patterson has given us the most thorough discussion of this *modus vivendi*; the English Renaissance writer understood "how he could encode his opinions so that nobody would be *required* to make an example of him."[30] The tragedies of Fletcher and his collaborators that depict tyrannicide reveal their understanding of this unwritten agreement.

III

The impression of Fletcher that gradually emerges from this cluster of plays about tyrants is one of an accomplished Jacobean professional, ready to exploit fears implicit in the political climate. Yet the notion that, as a committed entertainer, he was eager to comfort his audience, once he aroused their anxieties, needs to be qualified by considering three plays: *Cupid's Revenge, The Tragedy of Thierry and Theodoret* (ca. 1607–17), written with Massinger and probably with Beaumont, and *The Prophetess* (1622), written with Massinger. *Cupid's Revenge* once again sets the direction for later developments.[31] Cupid exercises his divine will to bring about an unrelieved sequence of deaths: Princess Hidaspes; her dwarf Zoylus; Timantus, a venal courtier; Urania, daughter to Queen Bacha; the wicked Bacha herself; the old Duke, and Leucippus, the Prince. This unrelieved experience of power strikes a twentieth-century reader, I venture to say, as oppressive to the point of monotony, and we can only surmise that Fletcher and his audience at their particular Jacobean moment were fascinated by what they feared—a hostile, unappeasable force invading their private lives, even to the very heart of their being. It is this aspect of Cupid's power that makes it especially claustrophobic. Not only are his victims unable to mount a counterattack, but some of them also suffer a conquest of will. Although Leucippus manages to maintain his integrity against Cupid's power, Princess Hidaspes and the old Duke succumb to uncharacteristic passions and undergo a change of identity. In none of the three plays is the figure who exercises unlimited power a ruler of state. This dissociation from political issues may have released Fletcher and his collaborators to devise worst-case scenarios in response to the specter of absolute power.

In *Thierry and Theodoret*, a tragedy, and *The Prophetess*, a tragicomedy, Cupid's counterparts are women. Brunhalt, the mother of Thierry and Theodoret, uses her position as dowager queen to destroy both sons in gratifying her lust and ambition. Although the Princes become aware of their mother's behavior, they remain incapable of taking sufficient countermeasures because of her parental claim, not unlike the old Duke's claim in *Cupid's Revenge* or James's claim as father of his subjects, and the sons fall victim to Brunhalt's intrigues. *The Prophetess* differs because the figure of unanswerable authority, Delphia, enacts her relentless power justifiably, but even the clear warrant for her actions cannot alter their oppressive effect. As the title character, she helps direct Diocles to become emperor of Rome when he agrees to marry her niece. After he gains the throne, he refuses to fulfil his obligation and then confronts a series of setbacks predicted by Delphia. Although Delphia enjoys neither divinity nor royal birth, she is so attuned to supernatural forces, described variously as "fate," "fortune," and "destiny" in the play, that her opponents remain defenseless against her. Like Cupid, she appears able to manipulate the passions of Diocles' nephew Maximinian and his betrothed, the Princess Aurelia, to disrupt Diocles' triumph and bring him to submission and repentance. No matter how right her claims are, no matter how agreeable the outcome (Diocles steps down from the throne to retire with Delphia's niece as his wife), the spectacle of irresistible power remains distasteful.

All three dramas, two tragedies and a tragicomedy, create a peculiar sense of a claustrophobic world that no doubt evoked responses appropriate to Jacobean sensibilities. The plays appear to issue from the same outlook as the tyrant plays, from a mind stimulated by the monarch's talk of absolute power, but in these instances the plays are designed less to protest that notion of power than to evoke an acknowledgment of it. To face the worst fantasies can in itself be a release, an acknowledgment of what otherwise one would evade. Worst-case scenarios create a distinctive appeal by their very effort to be the "worst." These three dramas, then, constitute an addendum to Fletcher's plays about tyrants, testifying to his full imaginative engagement with the threats of unopposable power.

NOTES

1. The dating of these plays is taken from Alfred Harbage, *Annals of English Drama 975-1700*, rev. ed. S. Schoenbaum (Philadelphia, Pa.: University of Pennsylvania Press, 1964). Attributions are taken from Cyrus Hoy, "The Shares of Fletcher and His Collaborators in the Beaumont and Fletcher Canon," *Studies in Bibliography*, 8-15 (1956-1962).

2. All references to James I's political writings are taken from the edition by Charles Howard McIlwain, *The Political Works of James I* (Cambridge, Mass.: Harvard University Press, 1918; rpt. 1965).

3. John Chamberlain wrote to Sir Ralph Winwood at the Hague, 24 May 1610, about James's speech of 21 March before both Houses of Parliament: "I heare yt bred generally much discomfort; to see our monarchial power and regall prerogative strained so high and made so transcendent every way, that yf the practise shold follow the positions, we are not like to leave to our successors that freedome we receved from our forefathers" (Robert Ashton, ed., *James I By His Contemporaries, An Account of His Career and Character as Seen by Some of His Contemporaries* [London: Hutchinson, 1969], p. 70).

4. Sir John Oglander reported the King as saying, when told that his subjects came out of love to see him, "God's wounds! I will pull down my breeches and they shall also see my arse" (quoted in David H. Willson, *King James VI and I* [London: Jonathan Cape, 1956], p. 165). The Venetian Ambassador assessed James's character in a report of 1607: "He does not caress the people nor make them that good cheer the late Queen did, whereby she won their loves: for the English adore their Sovereigns, and if the King passed through the same street a hundred times a day the people would still run to see him; they like their King to show pleasure at their devotion, as the late Queen knew well how to do; but this King manifests no taste for them but rather contempt and dislike. The result is he is despised and almost hated. In fact his Majesty is more inclined to live retired with eight or ten of his favourites than openly, as is the custom of the country and the desire of the people" (*James I By His Contemporaries*, p. 10).

5. For instance, in Queen Elizabeth's "golden speech" to Parliament, 30 November 1601, she says, "And though God has raised me high, yet this I count the glory of my crown, that I have reigned with your loves. This makes me that I do not so much rejoice that God hath made me to be a queen as to be a queen over so thankful a people" (George P. Rice, Jr., ed., *The Public Speaking of Queen Elizabeth* [New York: Columbia University Press, 1951], p. 106).

6. Line references are to the edition by Kenneth Palmer, *Troilus and Cressida*, The New Arden Shakespeare (London and New York: Methuen, 1982).

7. James I invaded the bedroom of his daughter Elizabeth and Frederick on the morning after their marriage to question the new groom on his experience, an odd variation on the extreme experience that Fletcher used several times to dramatize the tyrant. Robert Ashton comments on this: "The salacious pruriency which impelled him [James] to visit the newly-weds in bed and question them in detail about the events of their wedding night—a practice which the King indulged on other similar occasions—shews him in one of his least attractive lights" (*James I By His Contemporaries*, pp. 87-88). See also Jonathan Goldberg, *James I and the Politics of Literature* (Baltimore and London: Johns Hopkins University Press), pp. 85-112.

8. Ian Donaldson discusses the connection between sex and politics in *The Rapes of Lucretia, A Myth and Its Transformations* (Oxford: Clarendon Press, 1982), pp. 103-142.

9. Sir Philip Sidney, *An Apology for Poetry*, ed. Forrest G. Robinson (Indianapolis and New York: Bobbs-Merrill Co., 1970), p. 45. George Puttenham, *The Arte of English Poesie*, Kent State English Reprints (Kent, Ohio: Kent State University Press, 1970), p. 49. See also Herbert Lindenberger's definition of a "tyrant play," *Historical Drama, The Relation of Literature and Reality* (Chicago, Ill.: University of Chicago Press, 1975), p. 40.

10. W. A. Armstrong discusses the tradition of the Renaissance characterization of the tyrant in "The Influence of Seneca and Machiavelli on the Elizabethan Tyrant," *Review of English Studies*, 24 (1948), 19-35. For the tradition of political thought, see Oscar Jaszi and John D. Lewis, *Against the Tyrant, The Tradition and Theory of Tyrannicide* (Glencoe, Ill.: The Free Press, 1957), especially pp. 75-79.

11. My notion of the "big scene" depends upon John Reibetanz's discussion in *The "Lear" World: A Study of "King Lear" in Its Dramatic Context* (Toronto and Buffalo, N. Y.: University of Toronto Press, 1977), pp. 36ff.

12. Quotations are from the edition by Robert K. Turner, Jr., in *The Dramatic Works in the Beaumont and Fletcher Canon*, IV (Cambridge: Cambridge University Press, 1979).

13. Quotations are from the edition by A. R. Waller, *The Works of Francis Beaumont and John Fletcher*, VI (Cambridge: Cambridge University Press, 1908), 334.

14. An argument can be made for including *A King and No King* (1611), written with Beaumont. Through much of the play Arbaces is tempted to act the tyrant and impose his will upon Panthea, but unlike Fletcher's tyrants, Arbaces struggles with his conscience; moreover, his potential victim is responsive to his love. On balance, given these differences and the reversal at the end of the play, I exclude this tragicomedy from the group. In Act Four of *Philaster* (ca. 1608-10), written with Beaumont, the King finds his daughter Arethusa missing and commands that she be found. When he realizes that his subjects cannot fulfill his wish, he rails about the limits of his power and evokes comparisons with James's godlike claims: "Alas, what are we Kings? / Why doe you gods place us above the rest, / To be serv'd, flatter'd, and ador'd, till we / Beleeve we hold within our hands your thunder? / And when we come to try the power we have, / There's not a leafe shakes at our threatenings" (IV.iv.46-51). This absurd belief in absolute power hardly conforms with the contours of the King's shrewd character elsewhere in the play. As a gratuitous

moment of hyperbole, it could have been inserted as a knowing wink at the audience. But like *A King and No King*, *Philaster* exhibits insufficient evidence to warrant inclusion among the tragicomedies about tyrants. The quotation from *Philaster* is taken from the edition by Robert K. Turner, Jr., in *The Dramatic Works in the Beaumont and Fletcher Canon*, I (Cambridge: Cambridge University Press, 1966).

15. Quotations are from the edition by Cyrus Hoy in *The Dramatic Works in the Works Beaumont and Fletcher Canon*, V (Cambridge: Cambridge University Press, 1982). Clifford Leech classifies this play among Fletcher's comedies and judges it to have "some claim to be considered as the best of Fletcher's work" (*The John Fletcher Plays* (Cambridge, Mass.: Harvard University Press, 1962), p. 49.

16. Page references are to the edition by A. R. Waller, *The Works of Francis Beaumont and John Fletcher*, IV (Cambridge: Cambridge University Press, 1907).

17. For instance, Valerio says, "Methinks 'tis impossible / There should be such a Devil in a Kings shape, / Such a malignant Fiend" (p. 47).

18. Franco Moretti, "A Huge Eclipse, Form and Deconsecration of Sovereignty," *Genre*, 15 (1982), 8.

19. Philip J. Finkelpearl, "The Role of the Court in the Development of Jacobean Drama," *Criticism*, 24 (1982), 138-158. The quotation from Coleridge can be found in *Shakespearean Criticism*, ed. Thomas M. Raysor (London and New York: E. P. Dutton, 1960), I, 133; see also I, 122.

20. Margot Heinemann, *Puritanism and Theatre, Thomas Middleton and Opposition Drama under the Early Stuarts* (Cambridge: Cambridge University Press, 1980), p. 237.

21. G. E. Bentley, *The Profession of Dramatist in Shakespeare's Time* (Princeton, N. J.: Princeton University Press, 1971), p. 210. See also the list of performances at court in Bentley's *The Jacobean and Caroline Stage*, 7 vols. (Oxford: Clarendon Press, 1941-68), I, 108-135, and E. K. Chambers, *The Elizabethan Stage*, 4 vols. (Oxford: Clarendon Press, 1923), III, 224-225.

22. Ann Jennalie Cook, *The Privileged Playgoers of Shakespeare's London, 1576-1642* (Princeton, N. J.: Princeton University Press, 1981). Martin Butler questions her conclusions in *Theatre and Crisis 1632-1642* (Cambridge: Cambridge University Press, 1984), pp. 293-306.

23. See Margot Heinemann's discussion, *Puritanism and Theatre*, pp. 44-45, and E. K. Chambers, *The Elizabethan Stage*, I, 326; III, 286.

24. Quotations are from the edition by Fredson Bowers in *The Dramatic Works in the Beaumont and Fletcher Canon*, II (Cambridge: Cambridge University Press, 1970).

25. The quotation is from the edition by Robert K. Turner, Jr., in *The Dramatic Works in the Beaumont and Fletcher Canon*, II.

26. Marco Mincoff discusses this odd juncture as an example of Maximus' "deterioration of . . . character once he succumbs to the temptation of disloyalty," ("Fletcher's Early Tragedies," *Renaissance Drama*, 7 [1964], 73). Clifford Leech accounts for the difficulty by characterizing the tragedy as "a study of how suffering and loss, for Maximus does suffer in Lucina's loss, can corrupt" (*The John Fletcher Plays*, p. 128).

27. *Jonson's Gypsies Unmasked, Background and Theme of "The Gypsies Metamorphos'd"* (Durham, N. C.: Duke University Press, 1975).

28. See T. H. Howard-Hill's Introduction to the edition, *Sir John van Olden Barnavelt*, Malone Society Reprints (London: The Malone Society, 1979).

29. See C. J. Sisson's Introduction to his edition of *Believe as You List*, Malone Society Reprints (London: The Malone Society, 1929). See also Margot Heinemann, *Puritanism*

and Theatre, pp. 218–219. Annabel Patterson discusses Massinger's critical drama in *Censorship and Interpretation, The Conditions of Writing and Reading in Early Modern England* (Madison, Wis.: University of Wisconsin Press, 1984), pp. 79–91, esp. p. 86.

30. *Censorship and Interpretation*, p. 11. In a more restricted survey, Philip J. Finkelpearl finds that James I displayed "an intermittent predilection for tolerance [of free speech] and even compassion," ("'The Comedians' Liberty': Censorship of the Jacobean State Reconsidered," *English Literary Renaissance*, 16 [1986], 133.

31. John Astington's careful assessment of the evidence about the play's reception makes a strong case that *Cupid's Revenge* rather than *Philaster* established Beaumont and Fletcher's reputation as major playwrights. "The Popularity of *Cupid's Revenge*," *Studies in English Literature*, 19 (1979), 215–227.

Bonduca's Two Ignoble Armies and *The Two Noble Kinsmen*

ANDREW HICKMAN

This paper suggests that Fletcher's *Bonduca* and Shakespeare and Fletcher's *The Two Noble Kinsmen* [1] share a similar theme: they are both dramas of choice that set up an antithetical structure in order to express the problematic nature of discrimination. In making this suggestion, the paper also claims for *Bonduca* a complexity not normally credited to it or to Fletcher. The apparent preference for the Romans and the idealization of honor in the play are unobtrusively but firmly displaced as Fletcher probes beneath superficial impressions and rigorously explores the audience's discriminatory powers.

The likelihood of some relationship between *Bonduca* and *The Two Noble Kinsmen* increases almost as soon as the suggestion is made. Fletcher, of course, provides an important common element, and both plays seem to date from the same period. *The Two Noble Kinsmen* was performed in 1613, probably in the second half of that year,[2] while *Bonduca* is with less precision dated 1611–14.[3] Evidence for a date of *Bonduca* more closely approximating that of *The Two Noble Kinsmen* is suggested by the play's apparent topical references. William Appleton's hesitant suggestion that "Fletcher intended Caratach as a portrait of Raleigh" creates more problems than it solves, but his previous suggestion that the elegy for the young Hengo is "an appropriate tribute to young prince Henry," who died in November 1612, is more persuasive.[4] Henry, like Hengo, represented "the hopes of *Britain*," and was a "Royall graft" (V.iii.160–161)[5] untimely cut down. To maintain that a possible topical allusion determines a play's date is a circular argument, but it is interesting that both *Bonduca* and *The Two Noble Kinsmen* are held to allude to Henry's death. *The Two Noble Kinsmen* has been elaborately linked by Glynne Wickham with events surrounding Prince Henry's death and the subsequent marriage of his sister Elizabeth to the Palsgrave. Wickham's argument, which is startling and stimulating in its association of Palamon with the Palsgrave, Arcite with Henry, Emilia with Elizabeth, Theseus with James, Hippolyta with Anne, and even Pirithous with Carr, does not always fit snugly, but then, as Wickham frustratingly points out, Shakespeare was far too skilled to have made the "veils of correspondences . . . so transparent as to allow of only one interpretation."[6]

The plays disclose further, less contentious relationships. *Bonduca* reveals rich veins of imagery, and at least one of its images has a counterpart in *The Two Noble*

Kinsmen. In *Bonduca* Caratach compares the speedy running of the cowardly Britons to wind in a cornfield:

> the light shadows,
> That in a thought scur ore the fields of Corn,
> Halted on crutches to 'em.
> (I.i.93–95)

In *The Two Noble Kinsmen*, Arcite describes his athletic prowess and is drawn to a similar image:

> Well I could have wrestled,
> The best men called it excellent; and run
> Swifter than wind upon a field of corn,
> Curling the wealthy ears, never flew.
> (II.ii.76–79)[7]

The same comparison is applied to the same action in order to stress superior speed, and it is not surprising that commentators on the authorship of the play generally agree in giving this scene to Fletcher. In broader terms, each play, as Clifford Leech observes, possesses scenes suggestive of the other:

> *The Two Noble Kinsmen* has . . . some relationship with Fletcher's *Bonduca*, where the doubtful response of the gods to the Britons' sacrifice before the battle resembles the riddling signs offered by Mars, Venus and Diana in the last act of this play.[8]

Although the heavenly signs in *The Two Noble Kinsmen* (V.i) are the more spectacular, while the episode in *Bonduca* (III.i) makes more use of music and procession, the similar shape of the two scenes cannot be missed. Both present a sequence of kneeling supplicants who, in an atmosphere of solemn ritual, seek the support of gods; but the gods respond ambiguously.

These scenes of invocation are central since not only do they represent the clearest relationship between the two plays but also they figure crucially in the plays' shared concern with discrimination. It seems to me that the characters' appeals to the gods to show favor encourage the audience to consider its own allegiances. The ritual action of the masque-like temple scenes affords opportunity for reflection in which the audience is invited to choose with the gods whether the supplicants deserve support. In both plays the invitation to exert discrimination is pressed upon the audience by the dual, antithetical structure in which two warring armies, in the case of *Bonduca*, and two rival knights, in the case of *The Two Noble Kinsmen*, create opposing centers of interest. Both plays establish contrasts that encourage the audience to exert discriminatory powers, but in the end both plays suggest with slightly different emphasis the difficulty of discrimination. In *The Two Noble Kinsmen* the audience is left with a recognition that choice is difficult, since man's power to choose is limited; instead we must accept "that which is" and cease to dispute with the gods, our controllers, who "are above our question" (V.iv.135–137). *Bonduca*'s concerns are more humanistic—since men shape that which is—and even less straightforward, since the problem of choice is not so openly explored as in *The Two Noble Kinsmen*. Indeed there seems to be nothing problematic about discrimination at first; the contrasts between Britain and Rome seem weighted in favor of Rome, and it is only gradually that this impression is seen to be a distortion. In *Bonduca* discrimination is difficult since apparent contrasts turn, upon closer inspection, into parallels.

I should like to try to demonstrate these contentions by taking first the play that would seem more likely to contain complexities. *The Two Noble Kinsmen* exploits many ways of revealing man's uncertain and limited ability to make choices: chosen actions, like the intention of Theseus to marry and the intention of Palamon and Arcite to desert Thebes, are put off, the one temporarily, the other permanently; chosen ways of life are abruptly altered by the imposition of imprisonment or banishment upon Palamon and Arcite and of marriage upon Emilia; and, above all, love overpowers rational discrimination and renders Palamon, Arcite, and the Gaoler's Daughter bound without choice in destructive obsessions. The difficulty of putting preferences into effect is accentuated by the crucial difficulty of arriving at a preference. The hinge of the play—but not, significantly, of its source, Chaucer's *The Knight's Tale*, in which Emily is not offered the choice—is the charge laid upon Emilia to choose between her rival lovers and her inability to make the needful discrimination. Such a charge, it seems to me, is also laid upon the play's spectators, who are required not only to choose whether to favor Palamon or Arcite but also to discriminate amongst the various contrasted values that the play presents. *The Two Noble Kinsmen* is a great either/or play, in which many comparisons are offered but few are resolved; contrasts remain contrasted. The play constantly demands discrimination of us, but the audience, like Emilia, is in an impossible position and cannot choose.

One of the methods by which the audience is reminded of its obligation to choose is to confront it with contrasts. At the beginning life and death are symbolically contrasted, and throughout the play there is much tonal contrast between fighting, sport, and ritual, which is itself contrasted in the courtly ritual surrounding Theseus and the knights and in the rustic morris of the countryfolk. The play also contrasts characters and concepts: the noble Theseus is implicitly compared with the tyrant Creon (compare I.ii.81–83), and Theseus himself is moved to contrast past joys and present griefs (I.i.59–70). These contrasts, however, might be called "closed" since, although they are significant in themselves and suggest, for example, the relationship of joy and sadness, the relative merit of the values being contrasted is not disputed either by the rest of the play or by the experiences of the audience. Closed contrasts are not open to dispute and variety of interpretation but serve to direct interpretation.

Other contrasts in the play, however, are open to dispute and interpretation; the audience is required to establish the relative merits of the contrasted values and, in doing so, to discriminate and choose. Such a process occurs, for example, when the apparently indisputable closed contrast made by Palamon and Arcite between the joys of liberty and the sorrows of captivity (II.i.55–109) is turned into an open contrast by Arcite's consoling philosophy, quickly taken up by Palamon, in which they contend that captivity is not distressing since it is a means of preservation from the world's evils (II.i.109–164). Interpretation of this now-open contrast depends upon myriad, fluid factors involving staging, characterization, and our own emotions. Is the visual image of captivity so powerful, and is the verbal image of the joys of the lost world so poignant, that they linger to discredit the consolation? Do Palamon and Arcite speak sincerely or are they tentatively clutching at philosophical straws? Are they caught up in a current of uplifting consolation or stranded on the rock of tedious imprisonment where they can only talk (compare II.i.165–171)? My aim is not to justify any one interpretation of this scene but simply to demonstrate that by means of the open contrast in which values are disputed, interpretation becomes both imperative and problematic. The audience is invited to enter the debate, to choose between the relative values of liberty and captivity. In a more genuinely balanced example, when Arcite is banished and Palamon sent to closer confinement, the audience is invited to evaluate the kinsmen's contrasting and, in the case of Arcite, surprising arguments that the other is the better off (II.i.304–315; II.ii.1–23). The contrasting arguments open an implied debate, which carries on in the audience, about whose situation is the more favorable.

The difficulty of choosing between the values of these contrasts is slight in comparison with the play's central open contrast of love and friendship, which is exemplified by the love rivalry of the two friends Palamon and Arcite but never debated by them. Instead the contrast is given prominence by the discussion of Hippolyta and Emilia about the male friendship of Theseus and Pirithous, which provokes Hippolyta to wonder whom Theseus loves best (I.iii.44–47). Emilia's suggestion that Theseus loves his bride best perhaps betrays more tact than conviction since, as her account of her girlhood friend Flavina illustrates, she sets greater store by friendship (I.iii.47–82). Emilia's assertions that "true love 'tween maid and maid may be / More than in sex dividual" and that she will not love any "that's called man" (I.iii.81–82; 85) are tested by later events, through the course of which she comes to reveal some affection for Palamon and Arcite (compare IV.ii.1–54). Her earlier celebration of friendship has, however, the greater potency, as is confirmed later when she confesses to Diana to be "maiden-hearted" (V.i.151). Similarly, the triumph of love represented by Palamon's union with Emilia is a hollow victory since it is won at the expense of the friendship of Palamon and Arcite, a friendship that has seemed more precious and more sincerely affectionate (compare III.vi.1–106) than their seemingly obsessional and faintly ludicrous love for Emilia. The debate between love and friendship established by Hippolyta and Emilia reechoes in the various analogues and comparisons offered by the play. The Gaoler's

Daughter who, like Palamon and Arcite, loves on sight and with little apparent hope of furthering her love, emphasizes by her madness the obsessional and destructive nature of love that is also evident in Palamon and Arcite. Although her love is vigorously discriminatory and sexual, in contrast to Emilia's less appealing inability to choose between her lovers and to her relative lack of desire, the Gaoler's Daughter, nevertheless, is tricked in her madness into accepting the substitution of the Wooer for Palamon, an action that anticipates Emilia's acceptance of the substitution of Palamon for the dying Arcite. Love finally exerts no choice. But in fact the bedtrick played upon the Daughter enhances the value of love in the play since the Wooer, who faithfully suffers the Daughter's scorn and madness and who without jealousy effects her cure, exhibits in his domestic love a quiet nobility and real affection that are missing in the more extravagant tones of Palamon and Arcite. Love is also enhanced by Theseus' awed evaluation of marriage (I.i.170–174) and by the mutual respect shown by Hippolyta and Theseus, whose friendship for Pirithous is never predatory, and which provokes a debate on love and friendship that has already been decided in Hippolyta's mind (I.iii.94–96).

Both the open debate about love and friendship and also the commentary upon it established by analogues and comparisons invite the audience to enter the debate and to weigh the contrasted values. Philip Edwards accepts the invitation and describes the contrast in terms of that between innocence and experience:

> We are given, clearly enough, a life in two stages: youth, in which the passion of spontaneous friendship is dominant, and the riper age in which there is a dominant sexual passion, leading to marriage where it can. The movement from one stage to the next, the unavoidable process of growth, is a movement away from innocence, away from joy.[9]

But while the description is suggestive of Emilia's situation, it fits less well the joyful, mature love of Theseus and Hippolyta. Palamon and Arcite do not seem to have progressed from friendship to sexual love since they had both enjoyed love affairs during friendship. Their earlier experience and the present experience of Theseus and Pirithous suggest that love and friendship may be compatible, joyful, and valuable; at other times, as events prove, love can destroy friendship. Whatever one's interpretation, there can be little doubt that *The Two Noble Kinsmen* continually requires the audience to discriminate by presenting us with unresolved, open contrasts of relative values between which we are impelled to make choices. In an important sense our inability to resolve the contrasted values is a reinforcement of the major message of the play: man does not choose.

The frustrated requirement of the audience to choose is mirrored by invitations to choose, to show favor, in the action of the play. When the Theseus of Shakespeare and Fletcher departs from the source to charge Emilia to choose between Palamon and Arcite (III.vi.285), he echoes the implied charge laid upon the audience for most of the play. Emilia cannot choose at this stage nor at a later stage when, desiring to end the strife through election, she can bring herself only to the realization that choice is impossible (IV.ii.1–54). Her discussion of the two knights proves itself to be an ever-open contrast, but it is made up of two apparently closed and contradictory contrasts in which the recognition of the absolute superiority of Arcite (IV.ii.6–30) is succeeded by the recognition of the absolute superiority of Palamon (IV.ii.31–45). The structure is similar to the opening of the earlier contrast between liberty and captivity in which the superiority of liberty is succeeded by the superiority of captivity, and both structures, it seems to me, are intentionally provocative. Emilia's apparent and surprising choice of Arcite and then her apparent choice of Palamon provoke the audience to enter the debate and to react with her to the desire to choose and to the unfairness of favoring either knight in such strongly absolute terms:

>   Palamon
> Is but his foil; to him, a mere dull shadow.
>
>   Palamon, thou art alone
> And only beautiful.
>   (IV.ii.25–26; 37–38)

This is not to say that Palamon and Arcite are as indistinguishable as, in Kenneth Muir's comparison, Tweedledum and Tweedledee.[10] On the contrary, John P. Cutts points out each knight's distinctive color scheme, which is not found in Chaucer and which distinguishes Arcite, associated with black and swarthiness, from Palamon, associated with red and white,[11] while Richard Proudfoot draws attention to Palamon's initiation of the quarrel and that "in every encounter between them in Acts II and III it is Palamon who takes the offensive while Arcite refuses to admit that his grievance is just and maintains an irritating calm in face of his accusations."[12] Arcite is the stronger willed and he leads Palamon to share his views on, for example, leaving Thebes (I.ii.1–83) and the consolations of captivity (II.i.122–151). The characterization of Palamon as the lover and of Arcite as the soldier is established by the end of the second act when Palamon is loved by the Gaoler's Daughter (II.iii) and Arcite has demonstrated his physical prowess before Theseus, who has not seen "Since Hercules, a man of tougher sinews" (II.iv.2). The existence of these distinguishing features, and of others acknowledged in Emilia's discussion (IV.ii.1–54), validates the desire of both Emilia and the audience to choose between the knights—for if they were identical then choice would be immaterial—and frustrates that desire since none of the distinguishing features denotes clear superiority. Their contrast is a fair one, but it remains open.

In order to sustain the tension for as long as possible between the desire and the inability to choose, it is not until the last act that there emerges some apparent basis for clear distinction, which offers to help resolve the open contrast. The last act dramatizes the request for favor in the appeals of Arcite, Palamon, and Emilia to the gods,[13] and it is the knights' choice of deity as well as the quality of their invocations that offer the audience scope for judgment. Their combat of words in a sense replaces their physical combat that takes place off-stage. The knights' appeals to the gods for support encourage the audience to consider who does best and who deserves our favor; the invocations are offered to the theater audience as well as to the heavenly audience for judgment.

How, then, does the audience respond to the knights' speeches? The differences that they present—Arcite's is short, pithy, and less rhetorical, more "soldierly" perhaps, than Palamon's ornate, lover's magniloquence—seem intended to encourage discrimination, but both have flaws that prevent the audience from choosing confidently between them. Arcite's speech is flawed by his faith in the ability of force to nurture love, and his faith produces disturbing juxtapositions:

> You know my prize
> Must be dragged out of blood; force and great feat
> Must put my garland on me, where she sticks,
> The queen of flowers.
> (V.i.42–45)

There seems to be a ghastly suggestion in these lines that Emilia, the queen of flowers, is stuck to the victor's garland by blood, which in the succeeding image fills the camp like a brimful cistern. Later in the speech the repellent, though perhaps just, medicinal metaphors confirm the massive destructive force of war (V.i.64–66). Mars is acknowledged by Arcite to be the destroyer of men, of cities, and, most tellingly, of "teeming Ceres' foison" (V.i.53). The harm done to Ceres, the goddess who in the wedding masque of *The Tempest* blesses Ferdinand and Miranda with *"Earth's increase, foison plenty"* (IV.i.110),[14] implies that there should be no fruition for the "Youngest follower of . . . [Mars'] drum" with the queen of flowers (V.i.57).

But if Arcite's alliance with blood and destruction suggests that—as a lover—he invokes the wrong god, Palamon's invocation suggests he addresses the correct god wrongly. Following his initial catalogue of Venus' impressive power over such significant subjects as Mars and Diana (V.i.80, 92), Palamon's speech develops into a satirical attack. Palamon is obsessed with the distorting power of love to make aged lovers ridiculous and to create hideous unions. The man of seventy who with his hoarse throat abuses "young lays of love" (V.i.89), gives way to the terrifying eighty years-old cripple "who / A lass of fourteen brided" (V.i.108–109), and Palamon later proceeds to increase the age limit of lovers to ninety (V.i.130). The lingering impression of the speech is not one of the revitalizing power of love "To put life into dust" (V.i.110) or of its ability to make loving unions from unlikely materials, but one of love's perversity. Love is responsible for no beauty or tenderness; instead love disturbs the dust of death—and perhaps dries the dew of youth—in order to play a macabre joke:

>   I knew a man
>   Of eighty winters—this I told them—who
>   A lass of fourteen brided. 'Twas thy power
>   To put life into dust; the agèd cramp
>   Had screwed his square foot round,
>   The gout had knit his fingers into knots,
>   Torturing convulsions from his globy eyes
>   Had almost drawn their spheres, that what was life
>   In him seemed torture. This anatomy
>   Had by his young fair fere a boy, and I
>   Believed it was his, for she swore it was,
>   And who would not believe her?
>   (V.i.107–118)

M. C. Bradbrook considers that this speech "leads a monster into Venus' pageant, almost a death's head, to the bridal"[15] and that the metaphoric intrusion of near-death in marriage anticipates the widowed bride Emilia and echoes the opening scene in which the bereaved queens interrupt Theseus' wedding. The complexities of Palamon's speech invite interpretation, and perhaps Kenneth Muir is correct to imagine a Palamon of "disillusioned temperament" who has found Venus' yoke heavier than lead and more stinging than nettles (compare V.i.96–97).[16] What then of Palamon's appeal near the end to the "most soft sweet goddess" (V.i.126), an appeal that blatantly contradicts the descriptions in the preceding lines? Is this to be taken as Palamon's intentional irony, his desperate last appeal, or his lack of awareness?

The riddle cannot be readily interpreted, and it is connected to the problem of response that is concentrated in the last three lines of the anecdote quoted above. If Palamon had finished his story with the statement, "This anatomy / Had by his young fair fere a boy," then any doubts about the child's paternity would reflect only the perversity of the doubter's imagination. As soon as Palamon makes paternity a matter of belief, however, the audience is licensed to consider whether the young mother's claim is credible. To go on to ask "who would not believe her?" implies resistance to belief, and Palamon's statement of personal belief suggests his is a minority opinion. It is important to try to decide whether Palamon casts this slur upon the girl's character accidentally or intentionally. The lines confront the audience with two interpretative choices, neither of which does credit to Palamon, since he becomes either pathetically naïve or hypocritical. It should be remembered that Palamon's anecdote is apparently intended to rebut the slanders of the "large confessors" against women, "this I told them" (V.i.105, 108). Such men, it seems to me, would gleefully reinterpret Palamon's profession of sincere belief. If Palamon does speak sincerely, then we have to see him as foolishly naïve, and this is an interpretation that perhaps tallies with his self-righteous repudiation of worldly behavior (V.i.98–107) and with his apparent ignorance of the unlovely nature of his "most soft sweet goddess." On the other hand, if we choose to feel that Palamon is speaking ironically in order deliberately to encourage ambiguity about the child's paternity, then qualities come into focus that are equally unappealing. If Palamon wishes to be ambiguous in order to cast a slur upon the girl's character, then he is perpetrating the crime of which he is proclaiming his innocence:

> I have never been foul-mouthed against thy law;
> Ne'er revealed secret, for I knew none; would not,
> Had I kenned all that were; I never practised
> Upon man's wife, nor would the libels read
> Of liberal wits; I never at great feasts
> Sought to betray a beauty, but have blushed
> At simpering sirs that did; I have been harsh
> To large confessors, and have hotly asked them
> If they had mothers—I had one, a woman,
> And women 'twere they wronged.
> (V.i.98–107)

The suggestion that these lines are not to be taken at face value is perhaps contained in the bathos of Palamon's hot threat and in the blatant appeal for an emotional response to his pious reference to his mother, "a woman." In addition, his record is not as unblemished as he pretends to maintain. We have already witnessed his willingness to discuss with Arcite the "wenches / We have known in our days" (III.iii.28–29), and Palamon belies his profession that he does not love him "that tells close offices / The foulest way" (V.i.122–123) when he suggestively reminds Arcite of the lord steward's daughter:

> *Palamon.* She met him in an arbour.
> What did she there, coz? Play o'th'virginals?
> *Arcite.* Something she did, sir.
> *Palamon.* Made her groan a month for't—
> Or two, or three, or ten.
> (III.iii.33–36)

Arcite's response is to remind Palamon of the latter's conquest of the marshal's sister (III.iii.36–42), and perhaps the reminder hurts Palamon's pride in the chasteness of his love, since he immediately returns to the serious issue of their quarrel.[17] He certainly seems proud of his chastity in the invocation in which the abundance of first person pronouns—fourteen in lines 98–126—witnesses the drift of the speech away from a celebration of Venus to a celebration of Palamon. Indeed, his self-love seems more immediate than his love for Emilia, whom Palamon, unlike Arcite, does not mention. In addition, the delight with which he recounts the perversity of love and his sophisticated punning—"the agèd cramp / Had screwed his square foot round" (V.i.110–111)—make it appear unlikely that Palamon would be naïve about love unintentionally.

In conclusion, then, Palamon is at best a fool, at worst a knave. We want to decide which description is the more accurate, but we cannot. In performance an actor would probably have to go some way to make the choice for us, but this does not affect the point that an interpretative choice must be made or that we are then required to decide how Palamon's uncertain flaws weigh against the unsuitability of Arcite's reliance on Mars. Like Palamon and Arcite we look to the gods for help, since they may be able to bring a heavenly perspective to bear upon the problem of choice that they share with the audience. The gods, however, seem as undecided as the audience; their responses, which may be interpreted almost any way, suggest that Palamon and Arcite have, respectively, the attention, but not necessarily the support, of Venus and Mars. If the audience is encouraged to believe, with the knights, these responses to be auspicious, then the double partiality, equal and opposite, cancels the value of partiality. The gods' responses encourage the audience to make a choice but do not aid discrimination.

The final invocation in this masque-like scene, that of Emilia to Diana, once again urges the audience to consider which of the two knights is superior:

> Therefore, most modest queen,
> He of the two pretenders that best loves me
> And has the truest title in't, let him
> Take off my wheaten garland.
> (V.i.157–160)

Emilia's emphasis upon the criterion of love suggests that the follower of Venus holds the advantage, and likewise her belief that she will be "gathered" (V.i.170) bodes ill for the follower of Mars, the destroyer of harvests. But who does love Emilia the better? The terms of her comparison are provocative, but no conclusion can be made, since the evidence is insufficient. It cannot even be concluded retrospectively that events prove Palamon to have been her better lover since Diana never explicitly promises to favor the better lover; her signs are ambiguous but seem merely to promise that Emilia will be plucked. Events suggest that Arcite may have invoked the wrong god and Palamon the right one, but they do not assert any differences in quality that may help the audience to resolve the open contrast between the two knights. The resolution is attributed by Theseus to the gods, and thus the inability of humans to resolve such issues is underlined. In spite of Theseus' recognition of justice in his summing-up, however, the conclusion is unfair and unsatisfactory; as Richard Proudfoot observes, "we don't know why Arcite deserved punishment and can only see the divine solution to the human problem as inadequate."[18] To be thankful for "that which is" (V.iv.134–135) constitutes a significant admission that the faculty of choosing has been lost.

Bonduca does not at first suggest that there is anything complex about choosing between contrasted values. Indeed, not a little temerity is required to assert that the play suggests complexities of any kind. Parrott and Ball describe the play patronizingly as "not one that a modern mind can take at all seriously,"[19] and

Clifford Leech observes that it is "a simple affair of war" and that "there is an absence of complexity in the way our sympathy is directed."[20] Other critics have noted that *Bonduca* is constructed around contrasts. Eugene M. Waith describes four character contrasts in the play in which the contrast "is not between an honourable and a dishonourable person but between a right and a wrong way of attaining honour," although he appears to believe that the distinction between right and wrong is self-evident in spite of his slightly bemused observation, "At times victory seems less important than behaving as a noble warrior should. The emphasis is almost that of the courtesy book. . . ."[21] In a recent article Paul D. Green takes up the strong element of contrast in the play and shows how it informs the play's structure.[22] He reveals a welcome willingness to examine *Bonduca* in detail and provides a useful exposition of its apparent antithetical structure. He does establish that *Bonduca* depends on contrast but is not sufficiently aware, it seems to me, that the play is made dynamic by ambiguities that point to a fundamental parallelism beneath the superficial structure of contrast and that, consequently, make discrimination complex. Justification for such a claim is contained within the following argument, which takes Green's article as its starting-point.

Green suggests that the structure of *Bonduca*, which "shifts back and forth" between the two warring factions of Britain and Rome, symbolically "reinforces the basic differences in their values" (p. 305). According to him, certain "negative values are identified with Britain—for example, cowardice, fear, scorn, deceit, vindictiveness, and pride—whereas positive values, such as honor, courage, persistence, straightforward fighting, mercy, and self-confidence, are overwhelmingly linked with Rome" (p. 305). These distinctions, however, do not apply rigidly but cut across boundaries so that the contrast in character and attitudes "is found *within* the camps, not merely *between* them" (p. 309). The play does not present a "simplistic dichotomy of Roman honor versus British dishonor," but (in agreement with Waith) "in a more complex way, the contrast is between a right way and a wrong way of attaining honor. In other words, the Britons, who are not without their good qualities, nonetheless appear to fall short of *Roman* standards of honor, the chief measure of heroic worth throughout the play" (p. 308). The italics denote Green's awareness that not only the Britons but also the Romans in *Bonduca* do not necessarily live up to the touchstone of "Roman" honor, and, therefore, that the antithesis between Britain and Rome "is not wholly precise":

> the presence on the British side of masculine Caratach with his Roman principles undermines any such precision. And the fact that the most cowardly and treacherous character in the play is . . . the Roman corporal Judas . . . reinforces the impossibility of making an absolutely symmetrical contrast. In short, arbitrary labels may be assigned to values for the sake of convenience, but in reality the values cut across geographical and sexual boundaries.
>
> (p. 309)

If this statement implies Green's uneasiness about his earlier assertion of "basic differences" between the two sides, then it matches his explicit puzzlement over Fletcher's apparent sympathy with Rome at a time when Bonduca, or Boadicea, was, as he shows, "traditionally lauded in England as a national heroine" (p. 307).

It seems to me that Green's awareness of imprecisions and puzzles in *Bonduca* points him towards a realization, which he does not attain, of the play's structural ambiguities. For, while the broad canvas of *Bonduca*, as Green shows, is composed of sharp and obvious contrasts between a female Britain and male Rome that seem overall to encourage discrimination in favor of Rome, the detailed contrasts in the foreground offer so many ambiguities that the play suggests finally the enormous difficulties of discrimination. Neither side lives up to the touchstone of "Roman" honor, and the ability to live according to an ideal of honor itself seems to be questioned when the spokesman and apparent embodiment of the touchstone, Caratach, demonstrates, in Green's phrase, his "intellectual blindness" (p. 316). Green interprets the ending as confirmation of the Romanization of Caratach whose nobility is seen to be more "Roman" than "British" (pp. 308, 316), but it also confirms the interchangeability of the two sides. The earlier contrasts reveal that neither side is superior; both are culpable in similar ways, and both need to learn. Caratach's surrender—"*Rome* shall know / The man that makes her spring of glory grow" (V.iii.194–195)—is the beginning of that living synthesis foreshadowed earlier in the act by the identical qualities of Hengo's father and Penyus (V.i.70–73) and desired in the prophetic advice of Bonduca:

> If you will keep your Laws and Empire whole,
> Place in your Romane flesh a Britain soul.
> (IV.iv.152–153)

Indeed, the two sides have always been closer to each other than Green allows. Beneath the façade of an antithetical structure in *Bonduca* lie contrasts that are not absolute and self-evident but relative and forensic in that they invite examination. In the end it becomes clear that neither the Romans nor the Britons deserve outright condemnation or praise and that moral superiority cannot be judged unequivocally. Whereas in *The Two Noble Kinsmen* choice between contrasts is made impossible because the contrasts defy resolution, in *Bonduca* choice is made impossible because the apparent contrasts merge into ambivalencies and parallels. In the following pages I shall endeavor to show that the contrasts that Green finds to favor Rome are either ambivalent or balanced by contrasts that favor Britain, but first I shall try to reveal how Fletcher challenges the audience's capacity to judge.

The major basic difference between the two factions in *Bonduca* lies in their contrasting methods of presentation; Fletcher chooses to expose explicitly the Britons' shortcomings while similar Roman shortcomings go unremarked. The imperceptive member of the audience is therefore encouraged for a time to approve Roman conduct while joining in condemnation of the Britons. The apparent reversal of the audience's expectations of patriotic sentiments, however, which invites instinctive resistance and which encourages alertness to the play's implicit anti-Roman values, identifies Fletcher's concern to explore our ability to make judgments rather than to cater to distorting and imperceptive prejudgments.

It is significant that the play's opening scene dramatizes a corrective to simplistic jingoism and establishes the play's concern for balanced judgment and discretion, a key word in the play. The scorn for "These *Romane* Girls" (I.i.11) shown by the exultantly victorious Bonduca is firmly criticized by Catarach; such upbraidings, he argues, minimize the victory since there can be no honor in beating girls (I.i.34–38). He goes on to counter the distinction between Roman cowardice and the Britons' valor made by Bonduca with an account of Roman valor and the Britons' cowardice (I.i.56–124). Because the account is correcting Bonduca's magnification of the Britons (compare I.i.91), Caratach belittles them. Bonduca is chastened and repentant (I.i.145–149), and, after a further lecture by Caratach in which he voices his intense opposition to the invaders, she resolves that the Romans "shall have worthy Wars" (I.i.177).

Much has happened in this scene. Through Caratach's nobility and through Bonduca's humble acceptance of his advice and her maturing discretion, the Britons grow in stature. There is considerable backsliding later from this position due to the machinations of Bonduca's daughters, but for the moment the Britons have accepted honorable principles. In addition, although the scene may rely on contrast, the effect is ambiguous since there are two sets of opposing contrasts that tend overall to cancel out one another. The sequence of Bonduca's contrast of Roman cowardice and the Britons' valor and Caratach's contrast of Roman valor and the Britons' cowardice suggests that the two sides rank equally. This suggestion is later borne out when Swetonius is unobtrusively guilty of the same scorn for the enemy that Caratach schooled in Bonduca. Swetonius dismisses the Britons not as girls but as a mere fog:

> Do but blow
> Upon this Enemy, who, but that we want foes,
> Cannot deserve that name; and like a myst,
> A lazie fog, before your burning valours
> You'll finde him flie to nothing.
> (III.ii.75–79)

His scorn of the enemy is partly strategic, since he does not want his soldiers to know the enemy's full strength (II.iv.32–34), yet in this scene he is not addressing his soldiers but his officers, who are fully aware of their hazardous position. Unlike Henry V, who honorably exhorts his similarly outnumbered happy band of brothers, Swetonius chooses to scorn and insult the enemy. Caratach would not have been pleased, but Caratach continues to be tricked by these substandard Romans who are consistently but unobtrusively guilty of the dishonorable conduct for which Caratach reprimands his own side. He twice relieves the enemy because of a belief in honor that events show to be naive; he fights according to the rules of his idealized Rome, the Romans do not.

The common elements of hunger and its relief invite contrast of Caratach's generous feasting of the starving Romans with the Romans' vicious luring of the starving Hengo to his death. Caratach schools at length Nennius and Bonduca's daughters against taking advantage of the hunger of the captured Roman soldiers (II.iii.42–50). Once again the Britons are explicitly criticized for dishonorable conduct. Later, in a similar scene, Caratach prevents Bonduca's daughters from taking advantage of the enemy by means of a trick that he considers base and treacherous (III.v.53–86). The daughters had lured the officers Junius, Curius, and Decius, and their soldiers into a trap by means of Bonvica's deceitful offer to return Junius' love. In both instances Caratach frees the captives because he wants to win honorably (II.iii.43–45; III.v.63–69). The Britons are memorably reprimanded for their lapses, and our own judgment of their dishonor seems secure. After the battle the tables are turned, and it is now the Britons who are hungry, the Romans who have food. The hunger of Caratach and Hengo, fiercely lodged like "bear-whelps" (V.ii.115) on a steep rock, is used to advantage by the Romans; the lure of food brings Hengo down to where the cowardly Judas kills him. It is tellingly ironic that Hengo is killed by an arrow, a weapon that Caratach forbade Bonduca's daughter to use against the captive Romans (III.v.81–82). Although Judas seems to be the prime offender to honor here, his appropriate name—"if a little too obvious" as Green remarks (p. 309)—should not allow him to become the scapegoat for an action in which all the Romans are culpable. The obvious significance of Judas' name and of his red beard (II.iii.126) may seem designed to provide cover for the rest of the Romans, yet their camp contains many Judases. Earlier in the play, following the successful defense by Caratach and Hengo against Judas and his men, Judas and the Roman officers Decius, Demetrius, Curius, Junius, and Macer plan further measures against these Britons. Junius, perhaps anticipating the lack of honorable alternatives, charges Macer to use no foul play; Macer agrees, although his subordinate, Judas, expresses doubts about the feasibility of virtuous methods:

> *Junius.* But use no foul play, on your lives: that man
> That does him mischief by deceit, I'll kill him.
> *Macer.* He shall have fair play, he deserves it.
> *Judas.*   Heark ye,
> What should I do there then? You are brave Captains,
> Most valiant men; go up your selves; use vertue,
> See what will come on't: pray the Gentleman
> To come down, and be taken. Ye all know him,
> I think ye have felt him too: there ye shall finde him,
> His sword by his side, plums of a pound weight by him
> Will make your chops ake: you'll finde it a more labour
> To win him living, then climbing of a Crowes nest.
> *Decius.* Away, and compasse him; we shall come up
> I am sure within these two hours. Watch him close.

Macer. He shall flee thorow the air, if he escape us.
(V.ii.118–131)

The exchange is significant because when next we see Macer he is organizing foul play and ordering Judas to hang up the lure of food (V.iii.1). After killing Hengo, Judas is killed by Caratach and no recriminations against any Roman officer are made by Junius, who had vowed to punish foul play, or by anyone else. Swetonius, probably ignorant of the foul play that his officers have hypocritically countenanced, offers no apology to the grieving Caratach for Hengo's murder. Judas has expiated his sin; the Romans have submerged their sins in the satisfactions of victory.

The Romans too, it seems, require castigation from an honorable man such as Caratach, but then, like Caratach and the Britons, they would perhaps lose the war by it. Despite their protestations of honor, the Romans seek military advantage ruthlessly. Caratach is angered by the devious snare set for the Romans by Bonduca's daughters, but no one points out that Junius, Curius, and Decius are equally dishonorable in seeking devious victory, "the happiest vantage" (III.ii.43), by means of Bonvica's offer. Caratach saves the Roman prisoners from harm and torture, and he shows hospitality; in contrast Junius announces that he has tortured, off-stage and relatively unnoticed, the fellow sent by Bonvica to guide the Romans (III.ii.40). Junius' action smacks of policy and reveals his awareness of the harshness of war; Caratach's good manners are foolhardy. Caratach flamboyantly frees prisoners, whereas it is implied that the Romans take none alive. Although Nennius vows to defend the breach in Bonduca's stronghold until death (IV.iv.81–82), Decius' phrase implies that the Britons have not been killed fighting but have been massacred:

'Tis won, Sir, and the Britains
All put to th' sword.
(IV.iv.154–155)

Thus the structural antitheses that Green points out only suggest the existence of basic differences between the two sides, whereas in fact from the play's unremarked parallels and subtler contrasts no clear distinctions emerge. As our own discretion matures and causes us to delve beneath superficial judgments, we come to see that the Romans' apparent ethical superiority is a distortion of perception and that they triumph not because of their unpolluted virtue but because they are prepared quietly to seek advantage by any means,[23] while the Britons are hampered by Caratach's strident principle of honor, which, although admirable, proves disadvantageous in practice. Nearly all the contrasts between Britain and Rome that Green finds to favor Rome are ambiguous and invite the audience to be alert to the impossibility of making simple, evaluative contrasts. For example, contrasting imagery does not identify the contrasting morality of the warring factions as neatly as Green claims. He considers that images of noble and strong animals, lions, tigers, and eagles, are associated with the Romans while the Britons are compared less flatteringly with wolves, wasps, and buzzards (p. 306). It should be noted, however, that the spread of animal associations within both camps is very wide and not clearly divisive. To Green's list of noble animals used to describe the Romans may be added such ignoble associations as hogs (I.ii.73), dog-whelps (I.ii.96; V.ii.80), flesh-flies (I.ii.97), camels (I.ii.145), crabs (I.ii.148), adders (I.ii.166), pilchards (II.iii.52), goslings (II.ii.88), dormice (II.iv.86), squirrels (IV.ii.47), puppies (V.ii.79, 158), jackdaws (V.ii.86), dogs and rams (III.v.49). Fletcher seems to want to associate the Britons with native creatures such as foxes (I.i.101; I.ii.242; IV.ii.44), owls (I.i.105), hares and doves (III.v.149), and, like the Romans, with jackdaws (V.iii.120). Both the Briton Hengo (II.iii.65; IV.ii.74, 82; V.i.27; V.iii.113, 147) and the Roman Junius (II.ii.7; III.v.35, 39) are associated with chickens. Additionally, the Britons, like the Romans, are associated with strong and noble animals: Hengo is a lion's whelp (I.i.120), Caratach is a bull (IV.ii.46), Caratach and Hengo are bear-whelps (V.ii.115), while the Briton's army is a dragon (III.v.96).

Of course, the listing of images out of context can be misleading; interpretation depends on the context, on the speaker and his faction, and on his tone, which ranges in *Bonduca* from impassioned abuse to barracks-room banter. Additionally, the precise application of the image needs to be taken into account. Among the less flattering images used to describe the Britons listed by Green, only Caratach's image of buzzards, uttered at the defeat of his own fleeing soldiers, applies to the baseness of the Britons. The image of wasps is used to describe their numerical superiority, that of wolves to describe their hunger for victory, and neither image seems pejorative. Green mentions that the Romans—through their insignia—are associated with eagles (p. 306), but the image, which is spoken by Bonduca, is complex:

> We'll make our monuments in spite of fortune,
> In spight of all your Eagles wings: we'll work
> A pitch above ye; and from our height we'll stoop
> As fearlesse of your bloody Sears; and fortunate,
> As if we prey'd on heartlesse doves.
> (IV.iv.73–77)

Bonduca suggests that if the Romans are eagles, then the Britons are so much more powerful than eagles that they can treat the Romans as eagles treat doves; she proves her point when she prevents the Romans from capturing her. In a similarly relative image, Caratach resents the Roman attempts to make him and Hengo foxes; he changes the terms of the image by associating himself with the bull and by scorning the Romans as squirrels (IV.ii.44–47). His image is potent since Judas and his soldiers are seen to scamper squirrel-like from the belligerent Hengo and Caratach. In another image Penyus imagines the Britons to be vultures, but his image requires that the Romans correspond to "a few corrupted carcases" (II.i.26). In short, the animal imagery cannot be used to distinguish the moral values of Rome and Britain with any finality. On the contrary, the ambiguity of individual images and the variety of images applied to both sides suggest the similarity of Britain and Rome. Both sides are seen in terms of a variety of animals, strong and noble, fearful and base, cunning and cruel; the imagery denotes the beastly nature of the hunt for victory but does not clearly favor either protagonist.

Other imagery in the play seems incapable of supporting moral distinctions in the way that Green argues. The association of the Romans with the sun and fire and that of the Britons with fog and mist is not always as straightforward as in Swetonius' urgent battle cry quoted above (III.ii.75–79). Previously Penyus had devalued the image in recognition that the mists of Britain have greater potency than the noble sun of Rome:

> Honour got out of flint, and on their heads
> Whose vertues, like the Sun, exhal'd all valours,
> Must not be lost in mists and fogs of people.
> (II.i.39–41)

It is to Penyus that the other two sun images noted by Green are applied (p. 306); but Penyus is now dead, and the images fittingly describe a defeated and impotent sun in its "last eclipse" and "set for ever" (IV.iii.189, 210). Only the Briton Caratach describes Penyus as a star upon earth outshining heaven's (V.i.85). The Roman officer Macer sees Penyus in the same terms as Swetonius sees the enemy:

> Youth and fire,
> Like the fair breaking of a glorious day,
> Guilded their Falanx: when the angrie *Penyus*
> Stept like a stormy cloud 'twixt them and hopes.
> (II.iv.11–14)

Penyus himself pictures his disgrace in terms of cold, infectious mists (IV.iii.3–4). On the other hand, the Britons are not excluded from the imagery of light and fire. Junius' description of the attacking Britons as "wild-fire" seems to share the sense of fearsomeness present in Penyus' observation that their "gilt coats shine like Dragons scales" (III.v.117, 96) rather than the sense of ruinous rebelliousness applied earlier by Penyus to his own troops (II.i.82). Another image that springs to the mind of the watching Penyus seems to embody the impartiality suggested by the interchangeability of the rest of the images: "The Roman power shews like a little star / Hedg'd with a double halloa" (III.v.4–5). The image is not divisive but unifying; Britain, the "double halloa," and Rome, the "little Star," share one identity. Green seeks to find antithesis in other images—"The British hordes are like 'rank rushes' (I.ii.195), but the Roman phalanx is like a 'proud tree' (III.i.24)" (p. 306)—but in fact the images are not at the opposite ends of the scale of moral values. Petillius does not equate rank rushes with the Britons, but with their numerical superiority:

> In such a number, one would swear they grew,
> The hills are wooded with their partizans,
> And all the valleys over-grown with darts,
> As moors are with rank rushes.
> (I.ii.192–195)

In his imagery the Britons seem like trees on hillsides and rushes on moors, numberless as "autumnal leaves that strew the brooks / In Vallombrosa" (*Paradise Lost*, I.302–103). The suggestion of withering in Milton's simile is matched by one of festering in Fletcher's, but the implicit tone of moral baseness in "rank rushes" is tempered by the accompanying image of trees, which may be considered to signify nobility and strength. This seems to be Green's interpretation of "proud tree," an image that Nennius uses to describe the Roman phalanx, but it is doubtful whether Nennius wishes to convey any sense of the Romans' moral superiority:

> stick in each Roman heart
> A fear fit for confusion; blast their spirits,
> Dwell in 'em to destruction; thorow their Phalanx
> Strike, as thou strik'st a proud tree; shake their Bodies,
> Make their strengths totter, and their toplesse fortunes
> Unroot, and reel to ruine.
> (III.i.21–26)

It is immediately clear that Nennius has in mind a blasted, once proud tree whose overweening pride in its "toplesse fortunes" is directly responsible for its downfall. Nennius hopes for Swetonius' destruction, whereas in a related image Swetonius promises reconstruction; he sees himself as a "pine / Rent from Oeta by a sweeping tempest" that is refashioned into a mast and "defies / Those angry windes that split him" (I.ii.184–187). The one image is balanced by the other; that of Swetonius proves to be truer than that of Nennius, but neither denotes superiority.

Thus there seem to be ambivalent moral values contained in the play's imagery that do not support an antithetical structure. Should the lowliness of some of the images used to describe the Britons make them seem inferior to the Romans, one should recall some of the lowly images used to describe the hungry Romans, whom Hengo, for example, sees as empty scabbards and scarecrows (II.iii.61–63). Their emptiness seems to leave a visible mark, since throughout the play Judas is characterized as the personification of hunger or famine (compare II.iii.51, 85; IV.ii.50, 78). Green seems to have clinched his case for the antithetical structure of the play's imagery when he quotes Penyus' association of bravery with the Romans who have just put to flight the Britons, who are in turn associated with cowardice (p. 306): "these are true Romans, / And I a Britain coward, a base coward" (III.v.164–165). Penyus' associations have the full backing of events. Yet later in the play Judas' remark that Caratach "will come away with full conditions, / Bravely, and like a Britain" (V.ii.103–104) upsets the antithetical structure.[24] Although the remark lacks the compressed antithesis of Penyus', it is recalling the earlier scene in which the speaker was outbraved by the boy Hengo (IV.ii); Judas therefore provides the antithesis. Britons, like the Romans, are associated alike with cowardice and with bravery; they are parallel not antithetical to the Romans.

If the play's images do not offer clear aids to judging the protagonists, neither do the play's actions, some of which, as we have seen, are closely parallel on each side. Green compares the play's suicides and considers that of Penyus to be "quintessentially Roman" (p. 312) while those of Bonduca and her daughters are "somewhat tainted by circumstances" (p. 313). It seems to me, however, that there are flaws in Penyus' conduct and ennobling aspects to that of Bonduca and her daughters that make any evaluation by contrast problematic.

Penyus' quintessentially Roman suicide is flawed by his own sensationalization of his dishonor and by his reliance for guidance on Petillius, the honor of whose recommendations is modified by our awareness of his hope to gain promotion through Penyus' death. Penyus' repetitions (IV.iii.12, 19–25) wind up the frenzy in which he imagines himself the butt of popular scorn and ballads (IV.iii.13–15, 23), and he throws himself to the ground in flamboyant desperation. He shows little of that noble Roman resolve exhibited, for example, by Titinius in Shakespeare's *Julius Caesar* (V.iii), even when Penyus discloses his desire to die (IV.iii.97), since his desire does not accord with his actions. Petillius has to remind him of his faults and to taunt him to live with them—"dare ye know these ventures? . . . dare ye take it?" (IV.iii.122–123)—before Penyus is badgered into considering methods of suicide. Penyus seems to feel the need to justify his lack of immediate action ("I was only thinking") to Petillius:

> I am onely thinking now, Sir,
> (For I am resolved to go) of a most base death.
> (IV.iii.129–130)

His discussion of methods prolongs the inevitable Roman choice for which Petillius provides an unmistakable cue:

> *Petillius.* Die like a man.
> *Penyus.*   Why my sword then.|
> (IV.iii.141)

It is difficult not to perceive, in the insistent repetition of "your sword" in Petillius' response, sardonic relief that Penyus has finally followed his cue and unequivocal urging to get on with it:

> I, if your sword be sharp, Sir,
> There's nothing under heaven that's like your sword;
> Your Sword's a death indeed.
> (IV.iii.141–143)

As Penyus prepares to strike, he launches his suicide upon a sea of pathos. He wishes his death to be accompanied by a sympathetic earthquake affecting other men, and Petillius comforts him by pretending to feel "A kinde of trembling in me" (IV.iii.153–158). His vanity boosted, Penyus is coaxed into striking by a flurry of praise from Petillius:

> *Petillius.* The great and honoured Penyus—
> *Penyus.*   That again:
>   O how it heightens me! again, *Petillius.*
> *Petillius.* Most excellent Commander.
> *Penyus.*:   Those were mine,
>   Mine, onely mine.
> *Petillius.*:   They are still.
> *Penyus.*: Then to keep 'em
>   For ever falling more, have at ye, heavens.
>   (IV.iii.160–164)

Penyus' obsessive concern for his reputation and a good end is one aspect of his unappealing pride. Like Marlowe's Faustus, Penyus is motivated by pride that his fault seems beyond redemption: "There is no mercie in mankinde can reach me, / Nor is it fit it should; I have sinn'd beyond it" (IV.iii.81–82). The root cause of his dishonor lies in this earlier refusal to aid Swetonius. Although Penyus justifies his refusal in terms of the hopelessness of the situation, it is clear that his decision is determined by his pique at receiving a peremptory command from a man whom he regards as his junior:

> *Penyus.* I must come?
> *Macer.*   So the General commands, Sir.
> *Penyus.* I must bring up my Regiment?
> *Macer.*   Believe, Sir,
>   I bring no lye.
> *Penyus.* : But did he say, I must come?
> *Macer.* So delivered.
> *Penyus.* How long is't, *Regulus*, since I commanded
>   In *Britain* here?
> *Regulus*: About five yeers, great *Penyus.*
> *Penyus.* The General some five months. Are all my actions
> So poor, and lost, my services so barren,
> That I'm remembered in no nobler language
> But Must come up?
>   (II.i.1–10)

That it is Penyus' pride which has induced him to reject Swetonius' command is confirmed by several commentators. Penyus' conciliatory officer Drusus concedes his commander's "haughtinesse" (II.i.120–123), while in Swetonius' camp Petillius' wager that Penyus will refuse to come up is based on his knowledge of Penyus' confirmed nature: "Then keep thine old use *Penyus*, / Be stubborn and vain glorious, and I thank thee" (II.ii.98–99). Upon his reporting back to Swetonius, Macer clearly perceives that Penyus' decision stems from offended pride (II.iv.1–3) or, as Swetonius says, stubbornness (II.iv.20). It seems to me that Penyus' suicide is that of a still vainglorious man whose nobility is reduced in this scene, as it had been by his fit of pique earlier. Caratach is mistaken in this instance when he suggests that Roman glories make even pride a virtue (V.i.42–43).

Bonduca's pride, as Green notes (p. 305), is often referred to, especially by Swetonius (I.ii.249; III.v.175). He, however, seems to be referring to her pride formulaically and not from particular observation; anyone who dares to defy Rome, it is implied, would be deemed proud. In the opening scene, it may be recalled, we saw an exultantly scornful Bonduca who, nevertheless, accepts Caratach's schooling with humility:

> No more, I see my self: thou hast made me, Cousin,
> More then my fortunes durst; for they abus'd me,
> And wound me up so high, I swell'd with glory:
> Thy temperance has cur'd that Tympany,
> And given me health again, nay, more discretion.
> (I.i.145–149)

In contrast, Penyus never perceives the pride in himself.

Bonduca's preparation for suicide follows not loss of honor, as in the case of Penyus, but the total destruction of her power and hopes. She is left "desolate," her "haplesse children" defenseless against "Roman rape again and fury" (III.v.150–151). But when next we see her she is a commanding figure, fully resolved upon gaining victory through suicide, who towers above the Romans visually and figuratively:

> we'll work
> A pitch above ye; and from our height we'll stoop
> As fearlesse of your bloody Sears; and fortunate,
> As if we prey'd on heartlesse doves.
> (IV.iv.74–77)

Recalling and surpassing Penyus' pathetic yearning sixty lines earlier for a sympathetic earthquake, Bonduca's suicide is momentously accompanied by shakings of the earth. Bonduca revels in the Roman attempts to "shake the wall" (IV.iv.1), and Nennius continues her defiance:

> Shake the earth,
> Ye cannot shake our souls. Bring up your Rams,
> And with their armed heads, make the Fort totter,
> Ye do but rock us into death.
> (IV.iv.2–5)

Unlike Penyus' petty refusal to recognize a common tongue, "My Regiment's mine own. I must, my language" (II.i.20), Bonduca nobly rejects the Roman imperative:

> *Decius.*   Yeeld, Queen.
> *Bonduca.* I am unacquainted with that language, Roman.
> (IV.iv.8–9)

Unlike Penyus' uncertainty over methods of suicide, Bonduca unhesitatingly commands, "Bring up the swords, and poison" (IV.iv.85); the definite article denotes that the swords had already been selected and prepared. Whereas Penyus desires the appreciation of an absent world (IV.iii.158–164), Bonduca is surrounded by the world. Green calls her suicide "a sensational public spectacle" and implies that it is inferior to Penyus' "private affair of conscience" (p. 313), but in some ways Bonduca's final public defiance of Rome and her demonstration of the inability of Roman power to make her captive are acts of nobility superior to Penyus' huddled-up affair. Penyus kills himself pitifully because his career has foundered upon an error of judgment; Bonduca kills herself to defeat an insatiate enemy, and, in doing so, she fulfils Caratach's noble vow expressed in the first scene, which establishes the correct attitude to the invaders:

>   That hardy *Romane*
> That hopes to graft himself into my stock,
> Must first begin his kindred under ground,
> And be alli'd in ashes.
> (I.i.171–174)

Although the scene in its entirety has, as Green notes, less appealing features, Bonduca's suicide is designed to attract our respect and sympathy. She speaks like a good Protestant in rejecting the demands to "adore and fear" (IV.iv.14) the power of a Rome that is historically pre-papal but here emotionally papist:

> If *Rome* be earthly, why should any knee
> With bending adoration worship her?
> (IV.iv.15–16)

She holds out a vision of a pastoral Britain far fitter for reverence than the impiety and viciousness of Rome:

> Therefore 'tis fitter I should reverence
> The thatched houses where the Britains dwell
> In carelesse mirth, where the blest houshold gods
> See nought but chaste and simple puritie.
> (IV.iv.19–22)

Fostering the sympathy that she may have won from the Protestant British audience, she goes on to speak in fervent language of the integrity of the individual, of nobility based on worth and conduct, not on power and birth. Her rhyming couplets emphasize the universality of her sentiments:

> 'Tis not high power that makes a place divine,
> Nor that the men from gods derive their line.
> But sacred thoughts in holy bosoms stor'd,
> Make people noble, and the place ador'd.[25]
> (IV.iv.23-26)

Having taken the poison she enjoys so complete a "victory" over the "Poor vanquish'd Romanes" (IV.iv.150, 147) that she can feel pity for them and offer them counsel. The dying Queen's couplet of advice assumes a prophetic note of synthesis that claims defiantly to the last the superior role for Britain:

> If you will keep your Laws and Empire whole,
> Place in your Romane flesh a Britain soul.
> (IV.iv.152-153)

Bonduca does not disrupt, after all, the tradition of praise for Bonduca as a national heroine.

Our reactions to the entire scene, however, are confused by the death of Bonduca's younger daughter. The elder daughter conducts herself with Bonduca in a manner resembling the relationship of Hengo to Caratach; she is a chip off the same block and reinforces the noble defiance of her mother. Indeed, Bonduca asks her daughter to speak for her, knowing that her daughter's sentiments will echo her own and will provide a model for the younger sister (IV.iv.48-49). Petillius' admiration for her brave behavior, although his love-sickness for her is later ridiculed by his fellow officers, provides a commentary upon her actions clearly intended to support and direct the audience's response (IV.iv.61, 68, 119-121). Like her mother, she kills herself as she delivers a couplet of advice imbued with religious sentiments:

> Keep your mindes humble, your devotions high;
> So shall ye learn the noblest part, to die.
> (IV.iv.132-133)

However, the death of the younger daughter, Bonvica, does not imitate the attitude of noble defiance shown by Bonduca and her elder daughter. Green claims that because Bonvica is reluctant to die and because she "is practically forced to do so by the threats and curses of her mother and the blandishments of her older sister," her death "detracts substantially from the nobility of their deaths" (p. 313). But although Bonvica's death may detract from the rigidly Roman nobility of the suicides, it also contributes a sense of human weakness to the scene that can ennoble it. Bonvica's fear of death—like that of Cariola in *The Duchess of Malfi* which emphasizes through grim contrast the courageous submission of the Duchess (IV.ii)—is a humanizing touch that underscores the magnitude of all three women's actions and that reinforces their single-minded courage. Harold Child would seem to agree with this view of the scene when he suggests that her "dread of the suicide which honour compels her to commit" has "a wringing touch of Euripidean truth."[26] Her fearfulness surfaces early in the scene (IV.iv.29–30) and then remains submerged until she is confronted with the shock of seeing the swords and poison; death has materialized horribly. Bonvica is torn between the fear of death and her unwillingness to offend her mother whose insults, "ye whore," "A whore still" (IV.iv.86, 99), refer to Bonduca's associations of continued life with lust and of death with honor (IV.iv.31–42). The association is confirmed by Petillius' impulsive desire for the spirited elder daughter: "I would give an hundred pound now / But to lie with this womans behaviour" (IV.iv.120–121). The efforts of her elder sister to persuade Bonvica may commence with unappealing blandishments, but the sister's essential contrast of heavenly joys and earthly sorrows is finally telling. Bonvica is persuaded to kill herself by a reminder of the injustice and terrors of the world; in heaven "no Wars come, / Nor lustful slaves to ravish us" (IV.iv.111–112) as they had upon earth. Even the fear of death is minimized by the insupportability of living. Bonvica's repudiation of the world is also a repudiation of her mother's insults; her phrase "That steels me" (IV.iv.112) describes the firmness of her own decision to choose the path of honor that is followed by means of a physical strength matching her strong resolve. Her earlier natural reluctance makes the entire scene much more absorbing since it reveals in Bonvica, and implicitly also in her sister and in Bonduca, the humanizing realization of the enormity of their actions and of the difficulty of gaining through death freedom and honor. Bonvica presents a weak link in the chain that we watch with renewed intensity to see whether it will break; it does not.

Green argues that the nobility of the scene is further reduced by the use of swords and poison, since stabbing is associated with a masculine Roman death and since poison is scorned by Petillius (IV.iii.138–146) (p. 314). It seems to me, however, that because of the sword's association with masculine Rome and, above all, because of the strength and resolution required to stab oneself, the deaths of Bonduca's daughters are symbolically and visually highly heroic. Petillius' commentary on the elder daughter's nobility would seem to confirm this view. Petillius' scornful remarks to Penyus about the baseness of poisoning are embedded in the expediency of Penyus' suicide (Penyus presumably did not have poison to hand) and are forgotten as Bonduca lifts the "*great cup*" (IV.iv.85 SD), the size of which lends a ritualistic and ceremonious quality to the scene. Bonduca's death is characterized by her honorable defiance, which is acknowledged by Swetonius, "She was truely noble, and a Queen" (IV.iv.156). We react ambivalently to the elder daughter's slur on the suicides of Roman ladies, which Green points out. Her explanation that Lucrece died not for honor but from sexual disappointment—"*Tarquin* topt her well, / And mad she could not hold him, bled" (IV.iv.118–119)—probably does not rationalize "her own refusal at an earlier time to compensate by suicide for the dishonor of rape" as Green tentatively suggests (p. 314), but her reinterpretation of the story epitomizes her denigration of all things Roman and strives to establish herself as the new paragon, while at the same time implying something warped in her own sexuality. Green further suggests that in her comment that Roman ladies, like Portia, are "cowards, / Eat coals like compell'd Cats" (IV.iv.116–117), "she unwittingly reminds us of the 'compelled' death of her sister just moments before" (p. 314). Green's suggestion has validity only if the sister's death is caused by compulsion, and it seems to me that Bonvica, admittedly after some compulsion, accepts uncompelled the necessity of suicide, and she kills herself to escape compulsion. While the whole scene is shaped by the Roman attempts to compel the women to live, the women exploit their freedom to die unrestrained.

Surprisingly Caratach does not. I think it is fair to claim that the play intends us to be finally uncertain about any assessment of his character. There is little doubt that Caratach is a good man who cares lovingly for his little nephew and who refuses to take any unfair advantage over the Roman enemy. Although Caratach is certainly a brave fighter, events prove him a poor military thinker, and his "intellectual blindness in having freed Judas," to use Green's phrase (p. 316), is demonstrated by Judas' murder of Caratach's loved charge Hengo. Caratach's worship of honor, while an admirable ideal, seems misguided, since the world merely takes advantage of what becomes in practice a weakness; his faith in a Roman honor as pure as his own is, as we have seen, a delusion. Perhaps above all Caratach is not true to his ideals; in the play's first scene (I.i.171–174) he recognizes that he is engaged in a fight to the death with invaders who, he tells Hengo in one of the play's uninsistent but significant aids to balanced discrimination, are "ill men" excluded from heaven by their "violence, and strong oppression" (IV.ii.11–12), but at the end of the play Caratach surrenders alive to Swetonius knowing that he will be sent to Rome.

Such inconsistencies do not necessarily denote poor characterization or poor tragic writing[27] but recall the audience to the strategy of *Bonduca*. In saving the Romans' dishonorable murder of Hengo and the questionable honor of Caratach's surrender until the end of the play, Fletcher unmistakably and finally destroys any faith that we may still retain in the successful application of ideal standards of honor to practical situations. The destruction invites reconsideration of the play, and it becomes clear that the play has throughout been unobtrusively eroding the apparent antithetical structure supported by Caratach's praise of "Roman" honor and chastizement of the Britons' dishonor, which encourages the audience to imagine superficial contrasts between the two sides where there are deeply entrenched parallels. The Romans have always been less hampered than the Britons by nice points of honor, just as the Britons would have been had not Caratach intervened. At the end of the play, when the contrast based on honor is finally invalidated, the parallel interchangeability of Britain and Rome is suggested by Caratach's transfer. He alone does not seem to realize it but remains tragically unable to discriminate between his concept of "Roman" honor and the practice of the Romans in the play.

We sympathize with the moral purity of Caratach's ideal of honor, but we have also come to recognize the flaws in its application. "Roman" honor is theoretically admirable but foolhardy in practice; the Britons and Romans are equally prone to dishonorable actions, but practical success attends the side less hampered by theory.

Bonduca therefore traces the effects of honorable and dishonorable actions against a standard of ideal honor. In this respect it differs from *Troilus and Cressida* —in which Hector's self-defeating "vice of mercy" (V.iii.37)[28] invites comparison with Caratach's dangerous generosity—since Shakespeare's play systematically refuses to idealize, whereas *Bonduca* alludes to an ideal standard by which both sides have shortcomings. Assessment of the relative merits of the two sides in *Bonduca* is, however, both encouraged and hampered by the play. The ambiguous contrasts between a superficially honorable Rome, pragmatically adopting dishonorable methods, and a dishonorable Britain advancing admirable though self-defeating concepts, invite examination so that honor becomes the subject of a catechism, more serious and less one-sided than Falstaff's, which the audience is encouraged to answer. The contrast between Rome and Britain requires us to choose between them, but, unlike the contrast between, for example, Richard III and Richmond at Bosworth in which Shakespeare indicates our response, Fletcher is positively misleading. Britain and Rome move in parallel, and the audience feels for both sides attachment and detachment so that the implicit requirement to choose sides cannot be fulfilled. Such a requirement is mirrored by the explicit invitation to the gods to show favor in a scene which makes unavoidable the audience's need to choose.

The temple scene is central to the play's twin patterns of discrimination and ambiguity; the gods' responses are ambiguous, while the appeal to the gods to favor the Britons allows the audience the opportunity to play the gods, to decide whether the Britons deserve favor. The masque-like scene of solemnity, singing, music, and ritual actions such as the strewing of flowers (III.i.2 SD) contrasts tonally with the surrounding Roman scenes of drunken jocularity and preparation for battle; the third act begins with slow-moving ritual and ends with vigorous scenes of conflict. The temple scene represents a calm retreat that nurtures the reflection prompted by the Britons' addresses to the gods. The Britons' appeals for help to root out the pride of Rome elicit no response from the gods, but smoke begins to show when Bonvica laments her and her sister's dishonor. The value of this sign of comfort from the gods is reduced with Caratach's observation that no flame rises (III.i.53); the gods are seemingly sympathetic but noncommittal. Caratach's address that follows is slightly perverse in that he does not request favor but impartiality; he prays for a good clean fight and a fair result such as the divine Andate, "who hold'st the reins / Of furious Battels, and disordred War, / And proudly roll'st thy swarty chariot wheels / Over the heaps of wounds, and carcasses, / Sailing through seas of bloud" (III.i.59–63), might enjoy watching. Andate seems to approve, "It flames out" (III.i.77), but her sign of approval is soon extinguished, giving rise to uncertainty in Bonduca over the significance of the response. Caratach, however, is confident and is able to assure Bonduca of a favorable interpretation.

The scene is energized by the discrepancy between the note of confidence on which it ends—the last line is Bonduca's "Now I am confident" (III.i.86)—and the feeling of uncertainty in the audience. The audience may have hoped that the gods would help it to decide whether to support Britain, but in fact the gods seem to share the audience's predicament. The portents seem half-hearted and unsure; Andate seems to promise support not to the Britons but to "who does best" (III.i.71), a promise that suggests she will not influence events but merely reward the victor. Tiranes does not seem much moved by the wrongs done to the Britons by the Romans and offers some sympathy but no support. The difficulty experienced by the gods in choosing sides, even when the home side is pressing for favor, exactly mirrors the experience of the audience. The audience has a certain amount of patriotic sympathy for the Britons, but it also feels sympathy for the beleaguered Romans. By the start of Act Three we have witnessed the threats of torment uttered by the Britons to the captured Romans and also Caratach's magnanimity in releasing them. We have shown a good deal of appreciative interest in the comedy of Junius and Petillius, and of Judas. We have witnessed divisions in the Britons between Bonduca and Caratach, but we are beginning to feel that the Romans are imperfect, and we have seen Penyus' pride. Neither side seems worthy of wholehearted favor.

The rest of the play, as we have seen, offers no closed contrasts that justify our wholehearted support of either side. The play's façade of antithesis—between the two warring armies, between masculine and feminine principles, between honor and dishonor—seems to imply that judgment can be made and encourages a process of discrimination, but beneath this there lies a more substantial mass of detailed contrasts that cannot be closed and turned into antithetical aids to discrimination. They turn instead into ambiguous parallels. The apparent basic differences between Britain and Rome change upon meticulous inspection into aspects of their relatively similar natures.

Like Palamon and Arcite in *The Two Noble Kinsmen*, the factions of Britain and Rome in *Bonduca* are set in competition against each other, and a tantalizing requirement is made of the audience to discriminate between them. Both plays seem to suggest that discrimination is impossible because attempts to discriminate lead, in the case of *The Two Noble Kinsmen*, to a perception of distinctions whose relative merits cannot be adequately assessed, and, in the case of *Bonduca*, to a perception of the superficiality of distinctions.

NOTES

1. I accept the consensual view that *The Two Noble Kinsmen* is a collaborative work by Shakespeare and Fletcher. Paul Bertram's view (*Shakespeare and "The Two Noble Kinsmen"* [New Brunswick, N. J.: Rutgers University Press, 1965]) that Shakespeare is solely responsible seems untenable, and is scathingly attacked in Cyrus Hoy's review article (*Modern Philology*, 67 (1969), 83–88). The generally accepted division of authorship gives to Shakespeare the first and last acts with a little in between and to Fletcher the bulk of

the central acts and the sub-plot of the Gaoler's Daughter. For recent discussions see Cyrus Hoy, "The Shares of Fletcher and his Collaborators in the Beaumont and Fletcher Canon (VII)," *Studies in Bibliography*, 15 (1962), 71; and the editions by Clifford Leech, The Signet Classic Shakespeare (New York: New American Library, 1977, originally published 1963), p. xxiv; G. R. Proudfoot, Regents Renaissance Drama Series (London: Arnold, 1970), pp. xvi–xvii; N. W. Bawcutt, The New Penguin Shakespeare (Harmondsworth: Penguin Books, 1977), pp. 12–16. The present discussion of the play will not address problems of authorship but will attempt to examine the play as an integrated collaborative work whose effect in performance irons out the seams of collaboration.

2. N. W. Bawcutt, ed., *The Two Noble Kinsmen*, The New Penguin Shakespeare (Harmondsworth: Penguin Books, 1977), Introduction, p. 11.

3. Alfred Harbage, *Annals of English Drama, 975–1700*, revised by S. Schoenbaum (London: Methuen, 1964), p. 100.

4. William W. Appleton, *Beaumont and Fletcher: A Critical Study* (London: Allen and Unwin, 1956), pp. 56, 55. The appropriateness of the tribute is measured according to our estimation of Hengo. Frederick S. Boas felt that "[i]n the whole range of Elizabethan drama there is no more appealing figure of a child than this high-spirited, finely-tempered boy" (*An Introduction to Stuart Drama* [Oxford: Oxford University Press, 1946], p. 278), but, as Paul D. Green notes ("Theme and Structure in Fletcher's *Bonduca*," *Studies in English Literature*, 22 [1982], 305–316), Hengo has been "rather unfairly characterized as a 'quavering milksop'" by E. E. Stoll (p. 316).

5. References to *Bonduca* are taken from Cyrus Hoy's edition in *The Dramatic Works in the Beaumont and Fletcher Canon*, gen. ed. Fredson Bowers, IV (Cambridge: Cambridge University Press, 1979), 149–259.

6. Glynne Wickham, "*The Two Noble Kinsmen* or *A Midsummer Night's Dream Part II?*," *The Elizabethan Theatre* VII, ed. G. R. Hibbard (London and Basingstoke: The Macmillan Press Ltd., 1977), p. 196.

7. References to *The Two Noble Kinsmen* are taken from N. W. Bawcutt's edition, The New Penguin Shakespeare (Harmondsworth: Penguin Books, 1977).

8. Clifford Leech, *The John Fletcher Plays* (London: Chatto and Windus, 1962), p. 146. John P. Cutts, "Shakespeare's Song and Masque Hand in *The Two Noble Kinsmen*," *English Miscellany*, 18 (1967), 55–85, also quotes Leech whom he mistakenly believes to be suggesting that both episodes are by Fletcher (p. 83). Cutts considers that, unlike *The Two Noble Kinsmen*, the episode in *Bonduca* "has the merest *suggestion* of difficulties about it, with no indication of symbolic depth" (p. 83).

9. Philip Edwards, "On the Design of *The Two Noble Kinsmen*," *Review of English Literature*, 5 (1964), 103–104. Reprinted in Leech's edition.

10. Kenneth Muir, *Shakespeare as Collaborator* (London: Methuen, 1960), p. 127.

11. John P. Cutts, pp. 81–83.

12. Richard Proudfoot, "Shakespeare and the New Dramatists of the King's Men, 1606–1613," in *Later Shakespeare*, Stratford-upon-Avon Studies, 8, ed. John Russell Brown and Bernard Harris (London: Arnold, 1966), p. 256.

13 The dramatists shuffle Chaucer's order—Palamon, Emily, Arcite—with the possible intention of dissociating Arcite and Emilia.

14. *The Tempest*, The Arden Shakespeare, ed. Frank Kermode (London: Methuen, 1954).

15. M. C. Bradbrook, "Shakespeare and his Collaborators," in *Shakespeare 1971*, ed. Clifford Leech and J.M.R. Margeson (Toronto: University of Toronto Press, 1972), p. 31.

16. Kenneth Muir, p. 142.

17. Kenneth Muir implies that the conflict between this scene and Palamon's contrast "*with obvious sincerity*" (italics mine) of "his chaste conduct with that of libertines" (p. 134) shows the seams of the collaboration. Richard Proudfoot shares this view in his essay in which he finds that the play's several incoherences betray the incompatibility of Shakespeare and Fletcher. These explanations do not help to solve the problem of interpretation demanded in performance, and, since neither Shakespeare nor Fletcher was incompetent, it is a critical disservice to ignore the effects of deliberately provocative contrasts. M. C. Bradbrook suggests that the play's inconsistencies are designed to reflect the pleasing confusion of one of the play's sources, Beaumont's antimasque (p. 33). But, although there are imitations of masques in the play, it seems unlikely that confusion would without explicit guidance remind the audience of this masque.
18. Richard Proudfoot, p. 259.
19. Thomas M. Parrott and Robert H. Ball, *A Short View of Elizabethan Drama* (New York: Scribner's, 1943), p. 195.
20. Clifford Leech, *The John Fletcher Plays*, pp. 167, 164.
21. Eugene M. Waith, *Ideas of Greatness: Heroic Drama in England* (London: Routledge and Kegan Paul, 1971), pp. 153, 155.
22. Paul D. Green, "Theme and Structure in Fletcher's *Bonduca*," *Studies in English Literature*, 22 (1982), 305–316. References to this article are denoted in the text by page number.
23. This view contradicts that of Marco Mincoff, "Fletcher's Early Tragedies," *Renaissance Drama* 7, ed. S. Schoenbaum (Evanston, Ill.: Northwestern University Press, 1964), 70–94, who suggests that the Roman soldiers, although differentiated with artistry, all exemplify the same basic type and completely accept the artificial code of military glory (p. 86). They seem very pragmatic to me.
24. Judas' remark may perhaps be interpreted as a report of what Caratach swore, but in any case the rest of the speech demonstrates that even Judas perceives an association between bravery and at least this Briton.
25. James I would not have been offended since he would probably have felt that he possessed sacred thoughts in his holy bosom *as well* as claiming divine right.
26. Harold Child, "John Fletcher," *Essays and Reflections* (Cambridge: Cambridge University Press, 1948), p. 90.
27. As suggested by Harold Child, p. 90.
28. *Troilus and Cressida*, The Arden Shakespeare, ed. Kenneth Palmer (London: Methuen, 1982).

Competition for the King's Men?: Alleyn's Blackfriars Venture

S. P. CERASANO

When some unidentified Victorian forger altered material in the manuscript of Edward Alleyn's *Diary*, he concentrated his efforts on the years 1616 to 1618. Although his additions were minimal, his purpose was clearly to mislead subsequent readers into believing that there had been a strong personal connection between Alleyn and William Shakespeare; in fact, that Alleyn had purchased Shakespeare's share in the Blackfriars playhouse when the latter died.[1] Such a move on Alleyn's part would, of course, have been unprecedented. As a rule theater-owners were very territorial. Either a playhouse was owned by the company that performed in it, or if it was owned by non-players, the owners did not invest in more than one house at a time. Furthermore, proponents of the "rival companies" theory would find it unthinkable that a theater-manager of Alleyn's magnitude and entrepreneurial temperament, prone to expanding and controlling his business interests, would even have been allowed to buy into a competitor's playhouse.[2] As a consequence of this knowledge, then, we must discard any notion that there was a connection between Alleyn and Shakespeare's share in the Blackfriars playhouse. Alleyn bought a book of Shakespeare's sonnets when they were printed in 1609. No further association between the two men can be traced.[3]

The Blackfriars venture that Alleyn actually did pursue was distinct from the theater built by the Burbages in 1596. And owing perhaps to the fame of the Burbages' playhouse, scholars have paid Alleyn's little attention. We know that Alleyn's playhouse was located further south than the Burbages', closer to the Thames at Puddle Wharf, from which it took one of its names. (Alternately it was known as Porter's Hall.) The venture also seems to have been born of dire necessity, having been an attempt to find a house for the amalgamated Queen's Revels and Lady Elizabeth's companies when their lease in the Whitefriars ran out. Then, the company's managers—Philip Rosseter, Philip Kingman, Robert Jones, and Raphe Reeve—secured a royal patent stating that they possessed the "lycense and authoritie" to set up the Queen's Revels in a house to be built in the Blackfriars. Unfortunately when the house was only partially built, the inhabitants of the precinct complained to the Lord Mayor and aldermen that such an establishment would bring noise and violence to the neighborhood. Following a series of interchanges between the City and the Privy Council, construction was apparently halted. Philip Henslowe, who started financing the project shortly before his death in 1616, lost his money; as, presumably, did Alleyn, who had continued to support the project after his father-in-law's death. Their investments are thought to have totaled fifteen hundred pounds. Despite the steep expense and the numerous altercations that dogged the owners, however, few, if any, plays were performed on the premises. Those that may have been staged were performed in an unfinished building. What happened to the house and the property thereafter has been largely a matter of conjecture.[4]

As is the case with most theater properties, the affairs surrounding Porter's Hall are a more interesting tangle of persons and events than we might at first suspect; but it is necessary to reexamine the background of the enterprise if we are to understand what Alleyn was involved with when he made his investment in 1616. Therefore, it is my purpose in this article to reconsider the old history of Porter's Hall in the context of new documentary evidence, after which I would like to reconstruct the history of Alleyn's investment as it relates to the Burbages' earlier playhouse—to take up the hunch of the Victorian forger once again.

I

During Alleyn's lifetime, Porter's Hall was remembered as "Lady Saunders House" after Sir Thomas Saunders, its owner during the 1560s. For fifteen years (during the reigns of Henry VIII, Edward VI, and Elizabeth I), Saunders served as King's Remembrancer in the Exchequer. Although the means by which he came to own the property in the Blackfriars are unknown, gifts of leases from the Crown to its foremost servants were common. In London, property in the Blackfriars was frequently granted as a reward for service, as the estates of Sir Thomas Cawarden (the first Master of the Revels) and others will attest. Even if Saunder's house was not a gift of the Crown, his position and family background certainly furnished him with a living sufficient to purchase property in London and to maintain an estate in Charlwood, Surrey as well.[5]

In his will, written in 1563, Saunders made much of the "mansion house" in the Blackfriars, referring repeatedly to its value and finally bequeathing to his wife

> the vsage and lawfull occupacion of all my howsholdstuffe and Implementes of howsholde withe brasse pewter hangingces beddinges seelinges and other thinges nowe in my howse at the blacke friere in London whiche/ the same dame Alice holdeth for terme of her lyef with condission and assured truste she will make noe waste nor spoyle or eny other disorder thereof of the same howse garden and/ stalle or eny parte thereof.

Saunders was so protective of this property that he stipulated the terms of its ownership far beyond his death. Should Lady Alice decide to remarry she was bound to sign an agreement "to performe the premisses according to my true meaninge."[6] The estate in Charlwood was treated as second class by comparison, another indication that Saunder's well-furnished house was both sizable and expensive.

When Lady Saunders died, many years after her husband, the property was turned over to Sir Thomas's daughter as he had wished. From Saunders's daughter it passed to his grandson, Henry Goodyer, who married Margaret Daborne. It was Goodyer who sold the house to Robert Daborne, Sr., the father of the dramatist whose poverty is well documented in a set of letters to Henslowe in 1613. However, an indenture written in 1611 indicates that the lease was not transferred directly from the Saunders-Goodyer family to Daborne.

The property was previously "in the tenure or occupacion" of George Kingsmith (one of the justices of the Court of Common Pleas) and, more recently, of Sir Thomas Bodley.[7] There is, in addition, evidence that Sir John Portnarowe leased the property prior to 1600 for an indeterminate period of time.[8] Typically, the lease passed from aristocrat to aristocrat, a trend that is hardly surprising since property in the Blackfriars was generally in great demand by wealthy families who wanted a London home in an elite neighborhood. What is unusual, though, is that Robert Daborne, Sr., a haberdasher by trade, should have been able to acquire and maintain such a piece of property.

Documentary sources render a fairly telling picture of Daborne's financial situation. He was a member of the Haberdashers Company from 1577.[9] His family was of the middle caste, from Guildford, Surrey; but both he and his brother migrated north and established themselves in London. On 20 November 1578, Daborne was licensed to marry Susanna Treves (Travis),[10] whose brother Edmond became a key figure in the Blackfriars venture at a later date. The couple had four children: Robert the playwright, Thomas, Emme, and Margaret, who married Goodyer.[11] Without exception, each of the marriages in the Daborne family was but a small step up on the social ladder.

By the time Daborne, Sr. died in 1612, then a man about sixty years of age, he had been involved in at least two expensive merchant ventures. One well-documented affair concerned the *Vyolet*, a ship that he had financed in partnership with several other London merchants. Coming out of Spain the ship was seized and the financiers lost twenty-three hundred pounds "in sack and figs."[12] The second ship that Daborne helped to finance arrived safely in London, but the custody of its cargo became the basis for a significant lawsuit between Daborne and one James Woodcut.[13] These trading ventures, together with a suit involving Daborne and John Meerest,[14] suggest that Daborne maintained his living as a haberdasher until his death. Yet, like many of his contemporaries who became caught up in the prospect of foreign trade, he tended to rely upon outside investments, some of considerable size, in order to try to make his fortune.

Like many investors of the period, Daborne seems also to have made his fortune, and lost it, several times over. The Recognizances of Statutes Merchant (records of debt kept by the Lord Chamberlain) show Daborne to have been involved in a series of collections and debts. But, overall, the debts far exceed the payments. During the period from 1602 to 1608, perhaps his most active period financially, Daborne sometimes owed persons anywhere from forty to six hundred pounds.[15]

A group of indentures, drawn up over this same period of Daborne's career, point up similar tendencies. Daborne sold off many properties, in the city and elsewhere, while he seems to have acquired few. In 1593 he sold messuages in Aldenham, Hertfordshire for a hundred pounds[16]; in 1604 a messuage, a cottage, and a garden in Worplesdon, Surrey for thirty-six pounds[17]; in 1605, more messuages in Aldenham for a hundred pounds.[18] After a silence of three years Daborne again seems to have become desperate, this time selling off most of his London property. One piece, a messuage on Thames Street, he sold to a group of men including Sir Julius Caesar, then Master of the Rolls.[19] He disposed of two more tenements in 1609, both in the Blackfriars. The first group—one room with a chimney, a room with a bedchamber over it, and a "greate roome called the schoole and one litle yard"—went for a paltry £20 13s. 4d.[20] The second messuage was more substantial, bringing £104 3s. 4d.[21] Unfortunately, its exact location and composition are not described in any detail; so it is impossible to tell whether the sale proved a gain or a loss. What does seem clear is that Daborne was down to his last shillings and was sacrificing his holdings to pay off substantial debts.

The same fate almost befell thirty-odd messuages that Daborne held in the Blackfriars, including Lady Saunders's house. By 1604 he could not meet his yearly rent of fifty pounds; so he mortgaged his lease to his brother-in-law James Travis. Travis paid Sir Thomas Bodley, and Daborne managed to repay Travis, at least in part.[22] Then, in 1609, Daborne again became financially straitened; and this time he mortgaged the lease to one George Robines, whom he did repay fully. But his solvency was short-lived. The next year Daborne forfeited the lease to Bodley, who, not wishing to make a gain of Daborne's misfortune, made over the lease jointly to James and Edmond Travis. The Travises paid off all of Daborne's debts,[23] and then William Taylor (of Lincoln's Inn) and John Sherrington, two friends, gave bond in return for the fee simple (not the lease) of the Blackfriars houses to pay off any other debts Daborne had incurred.[24]

Daborne died in 1612 leaving his wife the remnants of what once had been a substantial estate. These included land in Aldenham, a lease on property in Surrey called Lyne Farm, and what was left of the property in the Blackfriars, including Lady Saunders's house. With the exception of Robert, Jr., each of Daborne's children received a share of the estate.[25] There is no obvious explanation provided for this omission; however, a lawsuit that erupted between the family members and Daborne, Jr. helps to clarify the elder Daborne's intentions.[26]

Simply put, Daborne, Jr. tried to hinder the sale of his father's properties, claiming to have an interest in the Blackfriars. His mother and several creditors to Daborne, Sr., including Goodyer, requested that the court of Chancery subpoena him and force him to agree to the sales. They stated that the elder Daborne's debts totaled a thousand pounds. This much has been noted in print before[27]; however, there is more information to be considered in this suit. Goodyer's part alone came to £264 13s. 4d.,[28] stemming from an agreement made on 11 October 1611 relating specifically to the Blackfriars property:

[for] all and eu*er*y theis mesuag*es* houses land*es* and ten*emen*t*es* whatsoever with all and singular ligh*tes* easemen*tes* yard*es* gardens backsid*es* ground*es* entries waies roomes p*ro*fitt*es* com*m*odities and app*ur*tenanc*es* whatsoever to the same or anie of them belonginge or in any wise app*ur*teyninge/ sometymes scituate lyinge and being within the/ libertie of Blackfriers london late in the tenure of occupac*i*on of George Kingesmith one of the Justic*es* of his ma^ties / Court of Common Pleas at Westm*inster* or his assignes and late in the tenure or occupac*i*on of Sir Thomas Bodley/ knight or of his assignes being to the nomber as they are now vsed of thirtie seue*r*all houses or ten*emen*t*es* or therabout*es* be they more or lesse And all other the land*es* ten*emen*t*es* and hereditamen*tes* whatsoever of hym the said Roberte Daborne/[29]

Of all the tenements, of course, Lady Saunders's residence could have been the piece that most appealed to Robert, Jr. There was already a playhouse functioning in the Blackfriars, and he may have seen potential for Porter's Hall to provide a second playing-space in the same area. Under these circumstances, it was almost predictable that Daborne, Jr. would fight for a piece of his father's estate, even though the family managed to side-step his pursuit by mortgaging the property later to Goodyer.

Given the alternatives the family could have adopted, this was probably the most sensible solution. Goodyer was, first of all, a member of the intimate family and, second, a young man of means with a solid background. (In 1601 he had borrowed a thousand pounds from Daborne, Sr., which he repaid in two years.[30]) Also, the Daborne family were not believers in sharing their inheritance with a prodigal son, and Goodyer evidently could be trusted to follow their lead. Among the depositions for their suit against Robert, Jr., both Daborne's wife and his son testified vigorously to Robert's bad character. Susanna Daborne stated that her husband wanted him to stay away from their tenants for fear that he would "disturbe" them. Thomas Daborne commented that the sole reason his father got so heavily in debt was Robert's unwise, excessive spending. According to Thomas, Robert repeatedly gulled his father out of money, which Robert wasted, without regard for anyone else in the family. The deponents in the case unanimously stated that Daborne, Sr. was in great debt to the Travises, even though no one was able to calculate a specific sum. Of all the deponents, though, Goodyer was certainly the most reasonable. He corroborated Susanna Daborne's testimony and took full responsibility for facilitating the sale of the lease. He thought, furthermore, that the Travises were blameless. After exculpating every member of the family, he could then urge, with a clear conscience, that really he should be first in line to handle the property in the future. He had, he reminded the court, been instrumental in the original sale to Daborne, Sr.[31] Apparently no decision was rendered in the case, at least no decision that pleased Daborne, Jr. In retaliation, he placed two counter-suits in Chancery, one against Taylor and Sherrington, the other against the Travises. Although the bills of complaint do not exist for these cases, the extant decisions give us some sense of the proceedings.

In the suit against Taylor and Sherrington judgment was given in favor of the defendants. On 1 June 1613 Daborne was ordered to pay the defendants' costs of 13s. 4d. "for want of a bill."[32] In the second dispute proceedings went further. Daborne claimed that his father owed his uncles three hundred pounds, owed Goodyer three hundred, and owed twenty-five to "one ffisher," but that the Travises refused to satisfy Goodyer and Fisher despite the fact that the Travises had already earned the whole of these debts, plus an additional seventy pounds, from the property. Daborne insisted furthermore that his father had signed over the lease on the Blackfriars to his uncles only for so long a time as it would take for him to make enough money to pay off his debts, after which it was to revert to Daborne, Sr. and his son.[33]

The suit took place in June 1613, and initially the Travises refused to answer the charges. When no answer was given by June 1614, a subpoena was issued. Still the Travises refused to come forth. In October another subpoena was issued.[34] Finally the Travises answered, but the case dragged on while witnesses were called. In June 1615—two years after the suit commenced—the court called for a full accounting of the debts owed by Daborne, Sr., along with a list of the Travises' gains on the lease.[35] Those records, if they were in fact delivered, have not survived; but we can verify £160 of the debt that the Travises claimed.[36] The last word in the case—on 25 January 1616—indicates that an order was issued and that the decision "remayneth wth m^r Phillips in m^r Totalls office." That the parties had come to some "consent" implies that arbitration had brought the suit to a conclusion to which all parties agreed.[37]

That conclusion, a complex one, was recorded in an indenture drawn up on 23 May 1616, which stated that, according to an agreement made on 3 April 1614, Goodyer, Susanna Daborne, and Robert Daborne, Jr. were turning the Blackfriars property over to Edmond Travis and Susan Candeler, his intended. The "property" included

> the possessions of Ser/ Thomas Saunders
> knight deceased scituate lyinge and beinge
> within the libertie of the Black ffryers
> London . . . being to the nomber as they
> are/ nowe or lately were vsed of thirtie
> seuerall houses or *tenementes*.[38]

In other words, since Taylor and Sherrington had paid off Daborne, Sr.'s debts and had made their share of the profits, the lease went back to the Daborne family and to Goodyer, who signed it over to Travis. It was under those conditions that Lady Saunders's house passed from the Dabornes to the Travises.

Surprisingly, given his character and his unfortunate luck in court, Robert, Jr. did not emerge from this flurry or lawsuits empty-handed. Somehow he managed to secure the lease to some messuages in Aldenham, and these he sold off to Philip

Henslowe for fifty pounds on 12 December 1615. What few assets he salvaged from his father's estate he liquidated to make a fast profit.[39] The reasons behind Daborne's panic reinforce that unfavorable impression one gets elsewhere of his character. During the family's property dispute, Thomas Daborne reported that Goodyer had previously been forced to file a writ of rebellion against Robert, Jr. and to instigate legal proceedings to retrieve money that Robert, Jr. owed his own father. Taylor and others interceded, managing to talk the parties into making agreements outside of court. Not long thereafter Robert was arrested by "mr Benion"—most likely William Benion the mercer who was associated with the Whitefriars playhouse. Daborne lied about his parentage and his age so as narrowly to escape prison.[40] If we believe the members of Daborne's family, he was motivated by cunning and artifice; although he could not gull Philip Henslowe who was then part-owner of the Fortune playhouse.

There is actually more reason to suspect that Henslowe used his distinct advantage over Daborne. As a shareholder in the Prince's-Palsgrave's Men, Henslowe kept the account books for the company. In so doing he also advanced funds to the playwrights who were hired to write material for the actors. In this capacity a series of letters, written between April 1613 and July 1614, have come down to us from Daborne to Henslowe. They testify to Daborne's growing poverty. In April 1613 he wrote that he was "put to a great extremity" by legal fees.[41] Less than a month later he pleaded to borrow twenty shillings more.[42] The following week he apologized to Henslowe for his "trubles," which "forced [him] to be trublesom"; he needed to collect nine pounds of the ten promised him.[43] The next week he protested that he had not been "idle" in his work; he would deliver the play "one Tuesday night," and he requested twenty shillings more to sustain him.[44] By August his "occasions pressed him" beyond reason. Despite his payment to Henslowe of half the benefits earned as a patentee of the Queen's Revels company, Daborne promised Henslowe still more money from the success of the play that he was still in the course of writing.[45] As the months passed Daborne's tone became increasingly woeful. He was having great difficulty keeping abreast of his expenses. In the meantime the patent on the Queen's Revels company, stipulating that the company would perform at the Whitefriars, had run out when the lease was terminated.[46] Daborne was far in debt with Henslowe, a burden he carried until 1616 when Henslowe, literally on his deathbed, returned several bonds for debts that Daborne owed, to Daborne's wife.[47]

II

The circumstances into which Alleyn stepped in 1616 were riddled with family strife and confusion. The Dabornes were at odds in court; the Henslowe family had broken out in legal disputes over Henslowe's will; and the Queen's Revels was waiting for the new playhouse to be built in the Blackfriars. In June 1615 two of the former patentees had secured a patent to set up their company in a house "within the Precinct of the Blacke ffryers neere Puddlewharfe . . . called by the name of the

Lady Saunders house or otherwise Porters Hall."[48] Except for Philip Rosseter, who was one of the King's musicians, none of the patentees for the Queen's Revels had been involved in the theater business before. Daborne, probably owing to his poverty, did not invest in the new Blackfriars venture; however, he and Henry Goodyer were the logical persons to have introduced Henslowe and Alleyn to Edmond Travis. Daborne's association with Henslowe had been primarily professional. But Goodyer was an acquaintance of Alleyn's older brother John[49] and was later instrumental in introducing Alleyn to John Donne's daughter, whom Alleyn married.[50] Therefore it is likely that Henslowe made his arrangements for the Blackfriars property by using his clout with a man who owed him a considerable amount of money. Alleyn, on the other hand, may have felt more amicably disposed, owing to his friendship with Goodyer. Whatever their personal feelings, the opportunity for Henslowe and Alleyn to open another business seems clearly to have been their sole provable motivation. In the course of events, however, they had personal and professional connections to take advantage of.

The properties surrounding Lady Saunders's house, as well as the mansion house, had been allowed to fall into considerable disrepair during the years that Daborne, Sr. owned them. And the Travises had not invested any money to keep them up. By the time Henslowe and Alleyn leased the properties, much renovation was required. From Alleyn's *Diary* it is evident that Henslowe made the initial investment of two hundred pounds. Alleyn followed up by paying out £1105 more to bring the buildings up to standard. What portion of this was spent on the playhouse cannot now be determined; but by 1623, Alleyn claimed to have spent fifteen hundred pounds on the property.[51] At any estimation his outlay was enormous. The annual rent of the building was only £160 per annum, and Travis had agreed to a fifty-year lease at that rate. Hence, it would seem, Travis was leasing disheveled property to Alleyn at a fairly low rate. In return Alleyn was responsible for any repairs necessary to refurbish the messuages.

Their agreement did not work out so neatly. In 1623, six years after the original lease was drawn up, Alleyn sued Edmond Travis in Chancery for failing to carry out his part of the contract. According to Alleyn, Travis was seized of "old decayed and ruined messuages" in the tenure of various persons in the Blackfriars. Travis made his agreement with Alleyn in the understanding that the required repairs would be costly. So, in addition to extending Alleyn a standard lease, he agreed further to levy a fine *surconcessit* on the premises, the purpose of which was to guarantee that any title of dower or jointure which Travis's wife might have would be void. Since Alleyn was planning to build a permanent business there, he wanted to be assured that Travis's wife could not interfere with the lease, should her husband pass away. By another obligation drawn up the same day Travis pledged that he would levy the fine before the second return of the following Easter term. Now, six years later, Travis had not levied the fine. Alleyn then urged a suit in Chancery because he could not gain relief at Common Law. This much of the situation has been noted in print by H. N.

Hillebrand in his study of the Blackfriars published in 1926.[52] But all this notwithstanding, there was much more to Alleyn's part in the affair.

As mentioned earlier, Henslowe contributed to the repair of the Blackfriars before his death. Renovation was already under way in April 1616 when he died, and Alleyn then apparently rushed the construction along. A letter from the Privy Council to the Lord Mayor (27 January 1617) states that the house is "allmost if not fully finished."[53] Because the carpenters would have had only one building season to get the structure in order, Alleyn must have laid out his first fifteen hundred pounds for the playhouse, perhaps in the hope that by the spring of 1617 the enterprise would be up and in operation.

Nevertheless, periodic complaints from the inhabitants of the area seem to have slowed progress on the theater. In August 1615, they petitioned the Lord Mayor to halt the building because of the "dailie annoyaunces" it would bring.[54] This position was seconded in a letter from Sir Edward Coke, whose opposition to the players was well established.[55] Throughout the proceedings the City was placed in an awkward position, between the affluent citizenry and the King's patent to Rosseter approving the site. There was no solution except to appeal to the Privy Council. What the Lord Mayor and aldermen received from the Privy Council on 26 September 1615 was a craftily worded order that forbade the continuation of construction on the playhouse on the grounds that the patent allowed for building outside of London, but not within it.[56]

Six months later Henslowe was dead; but Alleyn knew enough about local politics to realize that historically complaints on the part of the residents of the Blackfriars amounted to more noise than action. As early as the 1560s the inhabitants filed suit in Chancery against Sir Thomas Cawarden for defacing the local church and using it for the Queen's revels.[57] They complained around 1572 that one Henry Nailer had set up "three common bowlinge / Aleys on aley for a pleye commonly called nyne holes, and a place prouyded for a game called White and Black or for a diceing howse, or for both."[58] Finally, in November 1596, they again petitioned the Privy Council because Burbage was going to set up his playhouse in their vicinity.[59] In each case the complainants worried that entertainment was attended by "all manners of mischeefe," or sentiments to that effect. While it is tempting to see "Puritan" cant (Bentley's supposition) behind every complaint, it is just as legitimate to interpret the annoyance as the outcry of wealthy citizens who did not want their fashionable property devalued. Tax assessments from the early years of the reign of Edward VI indicate that the typical Blackfriars resident paying out anywhere between six and forty pounds per collection, with the average assessment having been well over ten pounds, and many over thirty. Sebastian Westcott, one of Blackfriars' more famous inhabitants, regularly paid out £16 16s.[60] In addition the area was the site of many prestigious happenings; for instance, the arrival of the French ambassador in 1571 was celebrated at the Blackfriars stairs.[61] Understandably, the residents were protective of their holdings, and playhouses drew crowds of people that resulted in "pestring and filling vp of the same Precinct . . . for that the same Precinct is allready growne very populous."[62]

Unhappily, Alleyn's attempts to get the theater built and operating backfired because although formerly the residents had failed to implement their opposition, this time the City stood firm. By 1616 the Corporation of London had issued an order that there were to be no more playhouses in the Blackfriars. Nevertheless Alleyn persisted, and for several years the City dogged him. As far along as September 1618 the City was still trying to pull the buildings down; Alleyn and his nephew urged their case "at Windesor" without success. On 10 August 1621, Alleyn again appeared in court, this time at Guildhall before the Court of Sewars "for y*e* Fryars."[63] Entries in Alleyn's *Diary* point out that he paid his rent to Travis for a time. Then he stopped abruptly when Travis failed to levy his fine. He tried his case initially at Common Law, but just as everything else surrounding Alleyn's venture had failed, so did his case.[64]

In retelling the Blackfriars story, Hillebrand went so far as to suggest that the suit came to nothing because he could not discover its consequences.[65] The outcome, for Alleyn, was not nearly as vague. Alleyn was absolutely successful in Chancery, as he always had been, perhaps because that court was so expensive to use or perhaps because the justices were used to dealing with persons of social standing. Alleyn drew up his bill on 18 June 1623. A week and a half later Travis responded with his answer.[66] By 13 October the decision had come down:

> It is herevpon ordered/ that both the s[ai]d p*ar*ties shall attend M*r* Jasper Hutton who is desired by/ this Cort to reconcile the s[ai]d differenc*es* by directing such a fine to be Levied as shall not impeach the said Jointure but shall s*er*ve onely to make/ good the s[ai]d Lease according to the purport thereof And if he cannot/ [end] the same but shall certify the defend*entes* or either of them . . . then this Cort will order for the plaintiffs releif as shalbee/ meete/[67]

The parties' "reconciliation" weighed in Alleyn's favor. By 22 February 1624 the Lord Chamberlain recorded that Edmond Travis, citizen and haberdasher of London, owed Edward Alleyn of Dulwich fifteen hundred pounds to be paid by the feast of the Annunciation.[68] Travis, though, was not solvent enough to pay off the debt. During the subsequent five years he had to borrow money from friends and relatives, to the sum of at least eight hundred pounds.[69] In his will, written in 1636, he mentioned tenements in St. Michael Cornhill and in the parish of Tottenham in Middlesex, but none of the property remained from his Blackfriars holdings.[70]

III

Although a reexamination of Alleyn's part in the Blackfriars venture does not answer all of the outstanding questions regarding the playhouse, it does help to resolve several important issues. One is simply the matter of ownership. From

Alleyn's expenditures, both his construction costs and the legal fees that he spent to protect the playhouse, it is evident that the major portion of the investment came from Alleyn, not Henslowe, as has been previously assumed.[71] That Alleyn was the active party explains why he repeatedly complained that the property was in a ruinous state when he took it over. Also we need to recognize that the rent of £160 was in no way "enormous."[72] After all, it included some thirty tenements. The major cost was for renovation, most of which Alleyn undertook in good faith that he could be assured of a reasonable return from the theater investment.

In light of the permission granted to Rosseter and the Queen's Revels to perform at Lady Saunders's house, Alleyn had no reason to anticipate the opposition that he encountered. It was not so much that "two houses in the precinct were too much,"[73] but that *any* playhouse in the precinct was objectionable. The residents had a tradition for complaining, one founded upon both "puritanical principles" and more mercenary concerns, such as the value of their property. There is no concrete evidence that the inhabitants of the Blackfriars were attempting to uphold "moral principles" alone.

Being a man of sound sense where business was concerned, Alleyn covered his bets as best he could. By 1615 the Fortune playhouse and the Bear Garden were both returning healthy profits; so it would appear that he felt ready to risk another major investment. Bentley writes that "Rosseter must have had influential backing if he intended to proceed in spite of the combined opposition of the Privy Council and the City corporation."[74] Indeed, Rosseter could scarcely have found more influential investors. The Henslowe-Alleyn partnership was one of the two most powerful in London's theater industry. The other was the Burbages', and since the first playhouse in the Blackfriars was owned by that syndicate, Rosseter had to take his plans elsewhere. Still it would be difficult to prove that Rosseter or Alleyn decided to locate their new playhouse in the Blackfriars either because they sought to compete with the first playhouse there or because they were inspired by the success of the Burbages' investment. If Chambers tells the story of the first Blackfriars correctly, it would seem that the theater was never an overwhelming success. After Henry Evans's financial collapse, it was the King's Men who brought success to the theater.[75] In a more general sense, in fact, financial success seems always to have had more to do with the company and its dramatists than with the location of a playhouse.

In the end, all that can be inferred from Alleyn's actions is that he calculated his risks, used his connections where he could, and provided the necessary funding when the time came. And when his venture was no longer lucrative he sold out, pressing to recover the whole of his original outlay. For him, the Blackfriars was quite clearly a business venture, and he meant—perhaps more dispassionately than scholars have thought previously—to make it pay off.

Lastly, it is no discovery to find that social connections were often important business connections, especially in the theater business; but it is interesting to note that Alleyn's only unsuccessful venture resulted partly from the Dabornes' ill fortune; that whatever personal clout had once assisted him in being able to complete the

Fortune in the face of local opposition was ineffectual in the case of the Blackfriars. There the Privy Council was willing to alter a royal patent on behalf of the citizens. But although the Council's motivations are unclear, Alleyn's are not. He wanted to possess his own playhouse in the Blackfriars, not a piece of Shakespeare's.

NOTES

1. The manuscript of Alleyn's *Diary* is at Dulwich College. George F. Warner has noted the modern additions in the notes to his transcription in the *Catalogue of Manuscripts and Muniments of Alleyn's College of God's Gift at Dulwich* (London: Spottiswoode, 1881), pp. 172ff. John Payne Collier, though a ready suspect for the forgery, printed some extracts of the diary in his *Memoirs of Edward Alleyn* (London: The Shakespeare Society, 1841), p. 106, but without the spurious material. Nevertheless, he suggested that Alleyn may well have bought a share from Shakespeare (p. 107).
2. See, for example, R. B. Sharpe, *The Real War of the Theatres* (London: Oxford University Press, 1935) and Alfred Harbage's *Shakespeare and the Rival Traditions* (New York: Macmillan, 1952).
3. Warner, *Catalogue*, MS II, 12.
4. The fullest description of the playhouse is that by Gerald Eades Bentley in *The Jacobean and Caroline Stage*, 7 vols. (Oxford: Clarendon Press, 1941-68), VI, 77-86 (hereafter *JCS*), from which I take my synopsis of the history of the theater.
5. W. H. Bryson, *The Equity Side of the Exchequer* (Cambridge: Cambridge University Press, 1975), p. 186.
6. PCC, Prob11/48, ff. 389r-391r (formerly 19 Crymes). These quotations are from 389r. Unless otherwise noted, all documentary sources are from the Public Record Office in London.
7. C24/351/77, C54/1921/44th part, and C54/2105/40th part.
8. REQ2/250/27.
9. Guildhall, MS 15857/1, f. 117v.
10. George J. Armytage, ed., *Allegations for Marriage Licenses Issued by the Bishop of London* (London: Harleian Society, 1887), I, 83.
11. Donald S. Lawless, "Robert Daborne, Senior," *Notes and Queries*, 222 (1977), 514.
12. Lawless, 515.
13. Lawless, 515.
14. C3/245/102.
15. LC4: 26/7, 26/8, 28/7, 196/91v, 196/161v, 196/235v, 196/245v. See also C54/1607/31st part and C54/1797/32nd part.
16. C54/1466/6th part.
17. C54/1787/22nd part.
18. C54/1808/10th part.
19. C66/1734/14th part.
20. C54/2049/32nd part.
21. C54/2045/28th part.
22. C24/372/11 and 409/54. One of Daborne's £50 debts is on record as C54/1921/44th part (1608).

23. C24/408/168 and 409/54.
24. C24/372/144.
25. PCC, Prob11/120, ff. 406^{r-v} (formerly 111 Fenner).
26. C2/JamesI/D2/3
27. See Lawless (note 11 above), Wayne H. Phelps, "The Early Life of Robert Daborne," *Philological Quarterly*, 59 (1980), 1-10, and Mark Eccles, "Brief Lives: Tudor and Stuart Authors," *Studies in Philology*, 79 (1982), 1-132. The section pertaining to Daborne covers pp. 28-36.
28. C2/JamesI/D2/3.
29. C54/2105/40th part.
30. LC4/194/422^r.
31. C24/408/168.
32. C33: 126/424^v and 126/721^r.
33. C33/127/23^r.
34. C33: 128/26^r and 128/90^v.
35. C33/130/1015^{r-v}.
36. LC4/26/8 (£80) and LC4/195/56^v (£80).
37. C33/131/545^r.
38. C54/2279/38th part.
39. C54/2229/31st part.
40. C24/408/168.
41. Walter W. Greg, ed., *Henslowe Papers* (London: A. H. Bullen, 1907), pp. 68-83 is a transcription of the letters between Daborne and Henslowe, now on deposit in the Wodehouse Library at Dulwich College. This quotation is from Greg, p. 68.
42. Greg, p. 69.
43. Greg, p. 69.
44. Greg, p. 70.
45. Greg, p. 71.
46. C66/1801/13th part.
47. See Jane Horton's deposition in C24/431/48, which describes the last hours before Henslowe's death.
48. C66/2075/20th part.
49. Warner, *Catalogue*, MS IV, no. 25 is an acquittance of a debt to Goodyer paid through John Alleyn (15 November 1590).
50. Warner, *Catalogue*, p. 50.
51. C2/James I/A1/16.
52. C2/James I/A1/16, noted previously by H. N. Hillebrand in "The Child Actors," Nos. 1-2 in Vol. 16 (1926) of *University of Illinois Studies in Language and Literature*, 237-248.
53. Bentley, *JCS*, VI, 84.
54. Bentley, *JCS*, VI, 80.
55. Bentley, *JCS*, VI, 81.
56. Bentley, *JCS*, VI, 83.
57. C1/1330/39.

58. SP46/16, ff. 41–45; this is from f. 41.
59. SP14/260, ff. 227–232.
60. E179: 144/87 and 145/174.
61. SP12/80, ff. 67ʳ–68ᵛ.
62. SP14/260 ff. 227ʳ⁻ᵛ.
63. Warner, *Catalogue*, pp. 173, 189. The records of the Sewars Commissions prior to the Great Fire have been destroyed.
64. I cannot locate any court records to confirm this.
65. Hillebrand, p. 247.
66. C2/James I/A1/16.
67. C33/145/21ᵛ (duplicated in C33/146/27ʳ).
68. LC4/200/114ᵛ.
69. LC4/200: 377ᵛ, 384ᵛ, and 460ᵛ.
70. PCC, Prob11/170, ff. 292ʳ–293ʳ (formerly 36 Pile).
71. Hillerbrand, p. 247, thought the reverse.
72. Hillebrand, p. 247.
73. Hillebrand, p. 244, an assumption also made by Chambers and Bentley.
74. Bentley, *JCS*, VI, 84.
75. E. K. Chambers, *The Elizabethan Stage*, 4 vols. (1923; rpt. Oxford: Clarendon Press, 1974), II, 508–509.

Lady Mary Wroth Describes a "Boy Actress"

MICHAEL SHAPIRO

Two significant but hitherto unnoticed metaphoric allusions to acting occur in *The Countess of Montgomery's Urania*, (1621), a long prose romance written by Lady Mary Wroth, the daughter of Robert Sidney of Penshurst and the niece of both Philip Sidney and the Countess of Pembroke. In these passages the author compares a deceitful woman to a boy actor impersonating a woman on stage. To the best of my knowledge, we have only one other piece of direct evidence of spectators' responses to the presentation of female characters on the English Renaissance stage. As I interpret Lady Mary's words, moreover, they challenge our current ideas about the nature of acting during the Jacobean period.

The first passage occurs in Book One of the printed portion of *The Urania*. A Queen, having pledged her love to one of her servants, has persuaded him to kill her husband, the King. When a delegation from one of the neighboring kingdoms arrives at her court to offer official condolences, she falls passionately in love with one of the captains. The more he resists her wooing, the more ardently this "chastlesse Queene" pursues him. Her first lover and "companion in mischiefe" learns of her attempts to seduce this stranger and spies on them when they are alone in her "Cabinet":

> there hee [her first lover] saw her with all passionate ardency, seeke, and sue for the strangers love; yet he [the stranger] vnmoueable, was no further wrought, then if he had seene a delicate play-boy acte a louing womans part, and knowing him a Boy, lik'd onely his action.[1]

The second passage occurs in the unpublished continuation of *The Urania*, a manuscript in the possession of the Newberry Library in Chicago. Here the author again compares a deceitful woman to a boy actor but does so in the course of an extended character description in the narrative voice. Unlike the previous passage, where the image of the boy actor is used to articulate the reaction of a man who is resisting a woman's seductive wiles, the metaphor here is a direct attempt on the author's part to present in vivid detail a villainess's guileful duplicity:

> A woeman dangerous in all kinde, flattering, and insinuating aboundantly, winning by matchless intising, and as soone cast of, but w^t hasard sufficient to the forsaken, or forsaker, her traines farr exceeding her love, and as full of faulshood as of vaine and endles expressions, being for her over acting fashion, more like a play boy dressed gaudely up to shew a fond loving woemans part, then a great Lady, soe

busy, so full of taulke, and in such a sett formallity, w^t so many framed lookes, fained smiles, and nods, w^t a deceiptfull downe cast looke, instead of purest modesty, and bashfulness, too rich Juells for her rotten Cabbinett to containe, som times a little (and that while painfull) silence as wishing, and with gestures, as longing to be moved to speake againe, and seeming soe loath, as supplications must bee as itt were made to heare her toungue once more ring chimes of faulse beeguilings, and intrapping charmes, witt being overwourne by her farr nicer, and more strange, and soe much the more prised, inchanting inventions, soe as her charming phansies, and her aluring daliings makes true witt a foole in such a scoole, and bace faulenes, and luxury the Jalours of her house, and unfortunate prisoners.[2]

As in the first passage, both the "play boy" and the villainous woman are skilled at creating the illusion of a model of femininity, an illusion completely contrary to the reality of their true natures.

Although both passages use the boy actor as a simile to denigrate a woman, neither condemns the player, his creation of a theatrical illusion, or his transvestism. Whereas puritan opponents of the stage regularly fulminate against actors for such transformations of social and sexual identity and are especially anxious about the kindling of erotic fantasies by the boy player/female character, Lady Mary uses the image of the actor without any moral bias against the theatrical transformation of actors' sexual identities.[3] Indeed her use of the image of the "play boy" bespeaks an esthetic sophistication that is consistent with her experience as a participant in court masques and, one presumes, as a spectator at performances given by professional players.

As a close friend of the Queen, Lady Mary Wroth took part in two Christmas masques that Anne had commissioned from Ben Jonson and Inigo Jones—*The Masque of Blackness* (performed 6 January 1605) and *The Masque of Beauty* (performed 10 January 1608). Professional troupes regularly performed at court as part of the extended Christmas revelry, so that Lady Mary Wroth would have had the opportunity to see twenty-one plays in 1604–05 and nineteen plays in 1607–08. It seems quite likely that she saw some if not all of them. The most active troupe in both of these seasons was the King's Men. Their contributions to the entertainments for 1604–05 (for which we have titles) include *Othello, The Merry Wives of Windsor, Measure for Measure, The Comedy of Errors, Henry V, Love's Labor's Lost,* and *Everyman In His Humor.* In the season of 1607–08 they performed sixteen of the nineteen plays offered at court. As an active member of the Jacobean court circle, Lady Mary was probably present at court for other Christmas seasons, as well as for the two in which she took part in masques, and consequently had abundant opportunities to see plays performed at court and perhaps in the London playhouses as well. Her "play boy," therefore, can be taken to reflect the performance practice of the leading professional troupes of London.[4]

The second passage suggests a rather broad style of playing, for both the deceitful female character and the boy actor must "*shew* a fond loving woemans part [rather] then a great Lady," that is, must represent an overly demonstrative type of woman rather than one whose demeanor is marked by aristocratic reserve. The woman's emotions, moreover, are feigned. The excessiveness and the falseness of her feelings are underscored by mention of her gaudy attire and "her over acting fashion," a phrase that suggests that both the woman and the boy player exaggerate their portrayal of a "fond loving woemans part."[5] The phrase "sett formallity" also connotes a studied artificiality, and the passage indeed catalogues what seem to be conventionalized ways—looks, smiles, nods, gestures—of representing this type of woman in life or on the stage.

The first passage omits such a detailed account of the "play boy's" repertory of tricks but perhaps implies them in the phrase "*all* passionate ardency." Far more significant is first the presence of the Queen's first lover as an audience whose presence theatricalizes the scene and second the introduction of the stranger, the captain, whom the queen tries to seduce and who is explicitly compared to a spectator watching a boy actor impersonate a woman. His reaction is twofold: he resists her charms and pleas for his love but, like an experienced theatergoer, admires "*onely* her action," that is, her technical expertise in pretending to be what she is not.

One wonders whether a similar amalgam of responses was possible if not common among theatergoers who admired boy actors for their ability to represent femininity and who might even be acutely sensitive to nuances of technique precisely *because* they were aware of the gender, if not also of the identity, of the male actor behind the female role. When Thomas Coryate saw actresses for the first time in Venice in 1608, he was astonished to see that they "performed it [played women, one presumes] with as good a grace, action, gesture, and whatsoever convenient for a Player, as ever I saw any masculine Actor,"[6] If, as S. L. Bethell has argued, most English Renaissance theatergoers could sustain a dual consciousness of actors and characters, they would have been particularly aware of the disparity between the boy player and the female role.[7] In other words, no matter how lifelike or realistic the impersonation of a woman, spectators not only understood themselves to be watching a boy actor but also were usually capable of appreciating his performance as a performance.

Such detachment did not seem to preclude emotional engagement in the dramatic illusion, an emotional response to a female character's plight. The balance between critical detachment and empathic engagement might vary among spectators and might change during the course of the play. Henry Jackson of Corpus Christi College, who saw the King's Men perform *Othello* at Oxford in September 1610, commends the company as a whole for acting decorously and aptly (*decorè, et apte agebant*) but singles out the boy who played Desdemona for "her" ability to evoke pathos in the murder scene:

> In quibus non solùm dicendo, sed etiam faciendo quaedam lachrymas movebant.— At verò Desdemona illa apud nos a marito occisa, quanquam optime semper causam

egit, interfecta tamen magis movebat; cum in lecto decumbens spectantium misericordiam ipso vultu imploraret.[8]

This particular spectator was responding both to the character's emotional situation and to the actor's skill in presenting that situation. The two seem to blend in his mind, as he uses the character's name and feminine grammatical forms but praises the actor's ability to evoke pathos for Desdemona by means of his facial expressions. The reaction of the Queen's servant-lover in the second passage quoted from *The Urania*, on the other hand, suggests a more disciplined form of dual consciousness or a type of spectator who could separate his awareness of the actor from his emotional responses to the mimetic illusion in order to observe and savor the performer's technical proficiency.

Lady Mary Wroth's two metaphoric allusions together might at first seem like persuasive evidence for the theory that acting on the English Renaissance stage was "formal." The second one suggests exaggerated mannerisms and itemizes conventionalized ways of representing model feminine behavior, while the first depicts a spectator capable of responding richly to both actor and character. "Formal" acting, it is argued, would have been recognized as stylized within the period itself. Adherents to this position argue that acting was stylized and probably systematized, and they place heavy emphasis on such analogous evidence as handbooks of gestures intended for orators. The rival theory of "natural" acting, on the other hand, argues that theatrical performances simply imitated life or created compellingly persuasive illusions of reality, and proponents of this view attach great significance to the testimony of spectators as to the verisimilitude of the performances that they witnessed.[9]

Although this debate has gone on for several decades, recent commentators have pointed out the limitations of the formal/natural dichotomy. One practical objection to the use of these terms concerns their elusive relativity of meaning. Styles in art change, and what to one age is natural is to a later age highly formal, the thesis of Erich Auerbach's *Mimesis*.[10] Indeed such changes of style occurred even within the seventy-odd years of the English Renaissance theater. At any given moment within this period, moreover, one could surely find practitioners of old-fashioned, mainstream, and avant-garde theatrical styles.

There are also important theoretical objections to the formal/natural dichotomy. To the extent that acting can be discussed by theatrical performers, taught to apprentices, and refined through discipline and training, it must have elements that can be codified and that may justify the term "formal." Nonetheless, spectators in virtually all periods from which we have accounts praise the actors they admire for the naturalness of their acting. Even in illusionistic theater, such testimonies may simply be a sign that intended effects were achieved, with no awareness of how those effects were created, or how the illusion of life presented was enlarged, intensified, and distorted. A great deal of acting that may seem natural from the audience's viewpoint may be formal from the actor's.

To complicate matters further, spectators use terms like *natural* or *true-to-life* with notorious imprecision. Sometimes such language seems to refer to the actor's apparent relaxed ease or absence of strain. In watching talented and skilful actors, we may get the impression, not of discipline or mastery of craft, but rather of relaxed grace, of effortless flow. As we say of such virtuoso performers—athletes and acrobats as well as actors—they make their achievements look so simple, so unlabored, that the cliché we reach for is frequently some variant of the word *natural*. The notion of "naturalness," however expressed, can also refer to the intensity of a performance or to its expressiveness or to its seamless welding together of discrete segments, rather than to its degree of verisimilitude.

Finally, Lady Mary Wroth's description of an onlooker's perception of a "boy actress" may help us to move beyond the stalemate of the formal/natural opposition. Her phrase—"knowing him a Boy, lik'd onely his Action"—crystallizes the principle of dual consciousness, a principle involved in virtually every theatrical impersonation, even when women play women, men play men, and boys play boys. When the disparity between actor and character is great, however, as in Lady Mary's simile, dual consciousness is closer to the surface of the audience's attention and hence more readily activated. Such obvious instances of disparity between actor and character as the boy-woman may, depending on other variables, either isolate the "boy actress" from other actor-characters or extend the spectators' dual consciousness to include the entire ensemble.

Whenever dual consciousness is activated, the distinction between "formal" and "natural" styles of acting becomes blurred. At such moments, spectators are encouraged to regard themselves as existing on the same plane of reality as the performers, as responding to the ways in which the latter inhabit and project their assigned roles. In some such situations, spectators may even adopt an insider's viewpoint—imagining themselves, as it were, more as participants in the behind-the-scenes world of the playhouse than as beholders of the world of the play—although the insider's viewpoint may in fact may be simply another, more subtly potent theatrical illusion.[11] Nevertheless, the insider's perspective, which is easily and quickly evoked (however short-lived) by any type of self-referentiality, renders the formal/natural dichotomy completely useless. If, as "participants," we are just as involved with how the material is being presented as we are with what is being represented, it hardly matters whether that material is rendered in a stylized or a naturalistic mode: either will seem artificial. And yet, as in great performances of operatic arias, that artificiality can be absorbing, compelling, and moving not only for the technical virtuosity that it demands but also for its power to encode human passions. In ideal situations, the performer's virtuosity and the character's passion become inseparably intertwined.

The two passages quoted from *The Urania* suggest that it was quite possible for spectators of the period to admire both the formal means and the natural effects involved in the presentation of a female character by a "play boy." While it is a truism, as Samuel Johnson observed, "that the spectators are always in their senses, and know . . . that the players are only players,"[12] we are sometimes blinded by our heritage of theatrical naturalism: the English Renaissance theater never required its spectators to pretend not to know what they always knew. Indeed some of the richest moments in the drama of the period result from just such interplay between the audience's perception of character and actor, its sense of mimetic illusion and theatrical reality, its awareness of representational effect and presentational means.

NOTES

1. Lady Mary Wroath [sic], *The Countesse of Mountgomeries Urania* (London, 1621), sig. I2.
2. Lady Mary Wroth, *The [first and] secound booke of the secound part of the Countess of Montgomery's Vrania*, manuscript in the Newberry Library, [Book I], f. 30 [2ᵛ]. I wish to thank Gwynne Kennedy for her help in transcribing this passage. I am also grateful to Ms. Kennedy and to Mary Lamb for informing me of these allusions in *The Urania* and for guiding me to them, as well as to the Newberry Library for granting me a Summer Fellowship in 1986.
3. On Puritan attacks on theatrical transvestism, see William B. Worthen, *The Idea of the Actor: Drama and the Ethics of Performance* (Princeton, N. J.: Princeton University Press, 1984), pp. 19-26. Worthen argues that the virulence of such attacks arises from the perception of transvestism as a form of "social and cosmic subversiveness" (p. 25). In replying to such attacks in *An Apology for Actors* (1608), Thomas Heywood argued that the audiences never forgot they were watching boy actors impersonate women and that they were even aware of particular performers: "To see our youths attired in the habit of women, who knowes not what their intents be? who cannot distinguish them by their names, assuredly knowing they are but to represent such a lady, at such a tyme appoynted?" Quoted in E. K. Chambers, *The Elizabethan Stage*, 4 vols. (Oxford: Clarendon Press, 1923), IV, 252.
4. Mary Susan Steele, *Plays & Masques at Court During the Reigns of Elizabeth, James and Charles* (Ithaca, N. Y.: Cornell University Press, 1926), pp. 139-144, 156-159. Compare the Court Calendar in E. K. Chambers, *The Elizabethan Stage*, IV, 119, 122-123, which lists sixteen plays for the season of 1607-08. Marchette Chute, *Ben Jonson of Westminster* (New York: Dutton, 1960), p. 141, using a shorter duration for the Christmas revels at court, counts fourteen plays. In any case, Lady Mary Wroth would surely have been at court on 27 December, 1604, to witness the masque in honor of the marriage of her cousin Philip Herbert to Susan Vere, who became the Countess of Montgomery, her close friend, whose name figures prominently in the title of *The Urania*. Similarly, Lady Mary was probably at court in the intervening years when friends and relatives were either honored by masques or took part in them. For possible connections between Lady Mary Wroth and other Jacobean court masques, see Margaret Anne Witten-Hannah, *Lady Mary Wroth's Urania: The Work and the Tradition*, Diss. University of Auckland, New Zealand, 1978, pp. 28, 188-192. For an account of the life of Lady Mary Wroth, with particular emphasis on her literary connections, see Josephine A. Roberts, "Introduction," *The Poems of Lady Mary Wroth* (Baton Rouge, La.: Louisiana State University Press, pp. 3-40.
5. This passage may contain one of the earliest usages of "overact" in the theatrical sense. *OED* quotes a line from Jonson's *Catiline* (1611)—"You over-act when you should under-doe" (II.iii.246)—but takes the word here to mean overdoing or going too far in an action. The earliest usage for which *OED* claims a theatrical meaning is from Massinger's

Believe As You List (1631)—"you disgrace your courtship / in overactinge it my lord" (V.i.2528-2529). See C. H. Herford, Percy and Evelyn Simpson, eds., *Ben Jonson*, 11 vols. (Oxford: Clarendon Press, 1925–52), V, 463, and C. J. Sisson, ed., *Believe As You List by Philip Massinger*, Malone Society Reprints (London: The Malone Society, 1927).

6. Thomas Coryate, *Coryate's Crudities* (London, 1611), p. 247. The preceding remarks are also worth quoting: "Here I observed certaine things that I never saw before. For I sawe women acte, a thing that I never saw before, *though I have heard that it hathe beene sometime used in London*" (italics mine). The underlined phrase is often omitted when the passage is quoted, as in Michael Jamieson, "Shakespeare's Celibate Stage," in *The Seventeenth-Century Stage*, ed. G. E. Bentley (Chicago, Ill.: University of Chicago Press, 1968), p. 76; and G. E. Bentley, *The Profession of Player in Shakespeare's Time, 1590-1642* (Princeton, N. J.: Princeton University Press, 1984), p. 114. If Coryate's information is accurate, English playhouse audiences may have seen actresses, probably when foreign troupes visited London, but the instances must have been extremely rare. When a French troupe appeared at Blackfriars in 1629, the presence of female performers evoked a strong negative reaction. See G. E. Bentley, *The Jacobean and Caroline Stage*, 7 vols. (Oxford: Clarendon Press, 1941–68), I, 25 and VI, 23. Chambers lists the recorded instances that Coryate may have heard of but concludes that "the exceptions . . . prove the rule" (I, 371n.). Might they not also have demonstrated the arbitrariness of the rule?

7. S. L. Bethell, "Shakespeare and the Actors," *Review of English Studies*, N. S. 1 (1950), 203. For a fuller discussion, see Bethell, *Shakespeare and the Popular Dramatic Tradition* (Durham, N. C.: Duke University Press, 1944), pp. 28–42. Compare Heywood, note 3 above. William E. Gruber, "The Actor in the Script: Affective Strategies in Shakespeare's *Antony and Cleopatra*," *Comparative Drama*, 19 (1985), 30–48, objects to the notion of a necessary tension between actor and role in Bethell's sense of "dual consciousness," arguing instead for a "lamination of actor with character" (p. 33). This formulation may be appropriate for other actor-character amalgams, where player and role are of the same gender, although Gruber sees the "boy actress" as "a formula through which masculinity is redefined and even reinvented" (p. 43). I would prefer to speak of *interplay* between character and actor, an expression that can include both Bethell's notion of tension or disparity and Gruber's idea of lamination, or both at once in whatever proportions. A similar type of dual consciousness was common at certain periods among audiences of the all-male Kabuki theater of Japan, according to Hirosue Tamotsu, "The Secret Ritual of the Place of Evil," in *Concerned Theatre Japan*, trans. David Goodman, 2:1–2 (1971), 14–21. Hirosue argues that the *onnagata*, that is, the actor who specialized in female roles, evoked erotic responses not only as both male actor and female character but also as the embodiment of a deeply desired "undifferentiated eroticism" (p. 17). Hirosue's explanation may also account for the extreme rhetoric of Puritan denunciations of transvestism on the English Renaissance stage (see above, note 3).

8. Quoted in Geoffrey Tillotson, "*Othello* and *The Alchemist* at Oxford in 1610," *TLS*, 20 July 1933, p. 494. Andrew Gurr, *The Shakespearean Stage, 1574-1642*, 2nd ed. (Cambridge: Cambridge University Press, 1980), p. 209, translates the passage as follows:

> not only by their speech but by their deeds they drew tears.—But indeed Desdemona, killed by her husband, although she always acted the matter very well, in her death moved us still more greatly; when lying in bed she implored the pity of those watching with her countenance alone.

The original Latin and a translation can also be found in Gamini Salgado, ed., *Eyewitnesses of Shakespeare* (New York: Harper and Row, 1975), p. 30.

9. See, for example, Worthen, *The Idea of the Actor*, pp. 13 and 235n. 7. For a brief summary of this debate and a list of recent work on the subject, see my "Annotated Bibliography on Original Staging in Elizabethan Plays," *Research Opportunities In Renaissance Drama*, 24 (1981), 32–33.
10. Erich Auerbach, *Mimesis: The Representation of Reality in Western Literature*, trans. Willard Trask (Princeton, N. J.: Princeton University Press, 1953).
11. See Raymond J. Pentzell, "Actor, *Maschera*, and Role: An Approach to Irony in Performance," *Comparative Drama*, 16 (1982), 201–226. Pentzell writes: "Indeed, once an audience perceives the actor as a *persona* distinct from his scripted character, there appears a dimension in which the actor will inevitably be taken as greater than his role no matter the role. . . . Once our willing pretense that the actor *is* the character is broken, empathy flows toward the necessarily more human *persona* of the actor as iron filings toward a magnet" (pp. 206–207). Bernard Beckerman, "Theatrical Perception," *Theatre Research International*, 4 (1979), 157–171, characterizes such a theatrical phenomonon as "opaque to the degree we are aware of its sensuous surface." Beckerman continues, "To the degree that we see through the phenomenal object to the fictional content, we can speak of the object's transparency. Both opacity and transparency are properties of the dramatic performance, though not equally present at all times [even in the same performance and for all spectators]" (p. 163).
12. Samuel Johnson, "Preface to Shakespeare" (1765), in *Johnson on Shakespeare*, ed. A. Sherbo, in *Works*, VII (New Haven, Conn.: Yale University Press, 1968), 77.

Alienation and Illusion: The Play-Within-a-Play on the Caroline Stage

CHARLOTTE SPIVACK

The effect of dramatic performance on the attitudes and emotions of spectators was a popular theme in the drama of the English Renaissance. The power of a stage production to move an audience to spontaneous and profound self-revelation was also a favorite argument among defenders of the popular drama against Puritan attacks on immorality in the plays. Thomas Heywood stresses the strictly moral effect of theatrical performance in his *An Apology for Actors*, where he cites many instances in which "we prove these exercises [plays] to have been the discoverers of many notorious murders long concealed from the eyes of the world," and he documents this claim with sensational details.[1] Hamlet's statement about the purpose of drama is similarly moral in its emphasis: "to hold, as 'twere, the mirror up to nature; to show virtue her own feature, scorn her own image, and the very age and body of the time his form and pressure" (III.ii.24–27).

Just as the whole play was capable of moving audiences to virtuous behavior, so the device of the play within a play was often used to move an onstage audience in the same direction.[2] Often the brief inset play functioned to expose the guilt feelings of the onstage spectators, even as Heywood claimed that the entire play could do with the large audience. This device is probably most familiar to modern audiences through Hamlet's play "The Murder of Gonzago," but there were many such interior plays in the Elizabethan period; some of them, like Hieronimo's bloody spectacle at the end of *The Spanish Tragedy*, were enacted to achieve revenge, and some, like Hamlet's, were intended to induce a confession of guilt.[3] Throughout the Elizabethan period the play-within-a-play remained primarily moral and didactic in function. During the 1580s and 1590s it continued to be a straightforward but theatrically effective device used to achieve justice (or at least a just revenge) or to point a moral.[4]

In the first two decades of the seventeenth century, the Jacobean playwrights moved somewhat beyond this conventional aim. The inset plays of the Jacobean period tend to explore the different levels of meaning implicit in the larger action of the whole play. The self-conscious theatricality of the drama during this time is manifested in the use of the interior play to produce "further realism through further illusion."[5] The old convention of moral purpose was not entirely abandoned but rather stretched to include thematic counterpoint. In Middleton's *Women Beware Women*, for example, the play-within-a-play is an elaborate wedding masque that not only brings about revenge but also serves to demonstrate, through the contrasting figures of Juno and Hymen, the difference between the genuine sacrament of marriage and the mere formality of the wedding ceremony. Similarly in *The Maid's Tragedy* the wedding masque, which represents the breaking loose of wild Boreas, hints at the subsequent release of restrained passions in the large play. Both masques comment on the reality of the outer play through symbolic action.

As the device of the play within a play continued on into the Caroline period, however, it underwent significant changes. Historians of the drama have largely overlooked the presence of these inset plays in stage pieces written after 1625, so that the change away from the conventionally didactic purpose and toward a new meaning has not been sufficiently realized.[6] To begin with, the Caroline dramatists used the interior play for psychological purposes. In keeping with the gradually increasing secularization of the seventeenth century, dramatists became less interested in seeking divine justice than in exploring human motivation. Furthermore they effectively, although probably unwittingly, undermined the established order of things by offering an alternative reality in the inner play.

It is in the drama of the 1620s and 1630s that the play within the play is first staged by a professional physician for a specifically medical purpose. It is here that the stage physician first tends the diseased mind as well as the ailing body. And it is here that the stage physician first discovers the therapeutic value of the amateur theatrical. Although the word "psychiatry" did not exist yet, the first "psychiatrists" on the English stage appear in the plays of Philip Massinger, John Ford, and Richard Brome. These "psychiatrists," who practice "the doctor's art"[7] on mental illness, discover a remedy for acute melancholy by adapting the old homiletic device for provoking confessions of guilt. In short, these doctors of the mind treat cases of severe depression with theatrical therapy.

By the time of the Caroline drama, then, although the venerable function of the internal play to expose the feelings of a guilty spectator still persists, the nature of that exposure begins to change in fundamental ways. Neither revenge nor exposure of guilt is the primary intention. Instead the emphasis shifts away from the moral impact of stage plays and toward their psychological effect. As the play-within-a-play explores the state of mind of the viewer, it shifts the focus from the deed as object to the doer as subject. Probing the inner tensions of the onstage viewer, revealing his inner conflicts, it becomes a means to cure mental aberrations, mainly melancholy. Of itself melancholy is no longer necessarily associated with guilt, and whether or not it is, the purpose of the interior play is to purge it.[8]

The sleepwalking scene in *Macbeth* provides us with a precise crux for indicating this new direction in the portrayal of guilt. As the physician in that play reflects upon Lady Macbeth's obsessive sleepwalking, he concludes that her perturbation is ultimately a moral problem, not a medical one. He feels that she needs a confessor rather than a doctor, since her ills are of the spirit and not of the flesh: "More needs she the divine than the physician" (V.i.78).[9] Macbeth responds, however, in terms of psychology rather than religion. Echoing his wife's vain hope of washing away the blood stains from her hands, he asks peremptorily:

> Canst thou not minister to a mind diseased,
> Pluck from the memory a rooted sorrow,
> Raze out the written troubles of the brain,
> And with some sweet oblivious antidote
> Cleanse the stuffed bosom of that perilous stuff
> Which weighs upon the heart?
> (V.iii.40–44)

And the unpersuaded Doctor replies, "Therein the patient / Must minister to himself" (V.iii.45–46). Macbeth's concern is not with repentance but with recovery, not with confession of guilt but with erasure of memory. Macbeth's reaction, which dismisses the need for moral absolution of genuine guilt in favor of a subjective relativism about mere feelings of guilt anticipates the evolving shift from homiletic to therapeutic purposes of drama. *Macbeth* is of course a Jacobean play, and Macbeth is a villain as he voices this morally unacceptable view.

Before exploring further significant changes in the Caroline play-within-a-play, I will pause for a look at two plays of Philip Massinger that illustrate the shift from homiletic to therapeutic, from moral to psychological. *The Roman Actor* (1626) contains three such plays within its larger framework, each designed to serve a somewhat different but essentially conventional purpose, but in contrast the interior play in *A Very Woman* (1634) serves a specifically psychological purpose.[10] The actor Paris, titular hero of the earlier play, fervently argues the superior exemplary value of stage plays over the "could precepts (perhaps seldome reade)" of the philosophers. Does any other moral instruction, he asks, "fire / The bloud, or swell the veines with emulation / To be both good, and great, equall to that / Which is presented on our Theatres?" (I.iii.80–83). The three interior plays represent different facets of this conviction.

The first use of the device, to teach a moral lesson, occurs in II.i where a play called "A Cure of Avarice" is presented. Its object is a rich miser whose conversion is expected to follow his perception of his own "deformity" in the person of an onstage covetous man, but the play fails as moral mirror. The intransigent miser admits "I am past cure" (II.i.436). A second interior play, in the third act, is intended to elicit an emotional response betraying guilt. This one is effective, for when the actor threatens in his role to hang himself, an onstage woman spectator cries out in passionate concern, thereby betraying her love for him. The third inset play is performed in the fourth act. The aim of this one is to bring about a real death under the guise of mere stage action. This play, close to Hieronimo's in its bloody purpose, also succeeds.

All three of these interior plays reveal an awareness of the subtle effects of histrionic action on the small, onstage audience that witnesses them. All three serve conventional purposes—moral reform, betrayal of guilt, and revenge. Furthermore all three are designed to achieve their purpose through the illusion of similitude. These plays all bear a microcosmic relationship to the play as a whole. Structurally all three represent the large play in miniature.

In Massinger's later play, *A Very Woman*, the play within a play is both introduced to serve a different purpose and structured in a way that does not reflect the play as a whole. In this play a physician stages a play for the specific purpose of effecting a psychological cure. The physician Paulo finds in drama a new remedy for his patient Cardanes, who has been suffering from feelings of morbidity. Cardanes' preoccupation with his own sense of guilt

> Hath rent his minde into so many pieces
> Of various imaginations, that
> Like the Celestial Bowe, this colour's now
> The object, then another, till all vanish.
> (IV.ii.5–8)

Guilt as a moral reality has thus dissipated into a psychological illusion subject to cure.

In appearance Cardanes is the conventional melancholy scholar, darkly clad and brooding, books in hand, a latter-day Hamlet. While he muses somberly on the wrongs that he has supposedly perpetrated against Don Antonio, Paulo appears to Cardanes in a series of disguises designed to evoke differing reactions from his patient. First Paulo appears as a Friar, with a tale of repentance. Although the tale is not a moral admonition as such, for Cardanes' guilt is in fact not real, nonetheless the presentation moves him close to despair, so that he tries to take his own life. The three spectators, silent audience to the proceedings, now step forth to disarm him. They leave, taking his weapons with them, and the doctor reappears, this time in the guise of a soldier. His eulogy to Honor moves Cardanes in a more positive direction so that he feels at peace with himself: "The discords of my soul / Are tun'd, and make a heavenly harmony" (IV.ii.158–159). But Paulo has one more disguise, that of a Philosopher, who appears to Cardanes accompanied by a good and an evil genius who sing a lyric in alternate stanzas. Unfortunately the text of the song does not survive. At any rate, the missing words complete the miraculous cure:

> Doctor, thou hast perfected a Bodies cure
> T'amaze the world; and almost cur'd a Mind
> Neer phrensie.
> (IV.ii.170–172)

By thus engaging his patient in a series of confrontations, with differing portrayals, the doctor has been able to relieve him of the illusion of guilt and of acute melancholia.

What is also significant here is the virtual substitution of theatricality for reality. The illusion of guilt has been vanquished by theatrical performance which is itself illusion, restoring a conviction of innocence that may well also prove illusory. The ability to act a role takes precedence over moral behavior. Playing with different levels of illusion in both inner and outer play casts a veil of theatricality over the lives of the offstage audience as well as those of the onstage viewers.

Paulo's play thus represents a dramaturgic innovation of a significant kind. It does not function as a mirror of the larger action in the play. It does not provide a microcosmic confirmation of the larger order of things but instead is a disjunctive action designed to serve an independent purpose. As a result, this kind of play within a play ultimately alienates the large audience from the play as a whole.[11] As long as the inner play reflects the meaning of the outer, then the outer play by implication reflects the meaning of the cosmic drama of creation. When the outcome of the whole play is subject to an improvised inner play staged by a physician more concerned with moodiness than morality, then the fate of the characters is divorced from the divinely ordered universe. The audience is forced to see itself as subject to theatrical definition. Identity is not fixed, and the feature of virtue and the image of scorn are matters of mere illusion. The age and body of the time are not formally established but susceptible to subjective representation.

In plays of John Ford and Richard Brome, as well as in the Massinger play, the old device of the play-within-a-play evolves into a new kind of theatrical performance, staged by a physician for a psychological purpose and designed to eliminate conventional distinctions among actor, audience, and playwright. This new version of the play within a play does not reflect the moral order implicit in the main action but rather is at odds with it, both contradicting and undermining it.

John Ford's play *The Lover's Melancholy* (1628) is centrally concerned with the power of stage performance to remedy mental strain.[12] The physician in this play is in effect a psychiatrist, for Corax, as a medical man, specializes in disorders of the mind. Obviously well-read in Robert Burton's popular and influential *Anatomy of Melancholy*, Corax deals with two patients, each suffering from a distinct kind of extreme melancholy.[13] One patient is an old man, Meleander, melancholy over the loss of his daughter, who disappeared years prior to the action of the play. The other is the young Prince Palador, who was the betrothed of the missing daughter, Eroclea. Palador's melancholy affliction has a depth beyond the merely amatory, however, for his is an intellectual as well as an emotional depression, bordering on the catatonic:

> sometimes speakes sence,
> But seldome mirth; will smile, but seldome laugh;
> Will lend an eare to businesse, deale in none;
> Gaze vpon Reuels, Anticke Fopperies,
> But is not mou'd.
>   (I.i.97–101)

For such a melancholic state, Corax has already prescribed exercise. When he notices Palador reading books for long periods of time rather than getting wholesome exercise, Corax reminds him of horse, hounds, and tennis balls. Corax realizes that the problem is primarily mental rather than physical, but he remains the medical man, aware of the inseparability of body and mind.

In the depths of his genuine concern over his two troublesome patients, the physician feels himself falling under the shadow of melancholy and laments his precious time spent in court:

> To waste my time thus Droane-like in the court,
> And lose so many houres as my studies
> Haue horded vp, . . .
> I need no Princes fauour; Princes need
> My Art.
>
> (III.i.1231–33, 1238–39)

But convinced as he is that his art can triumph even over those challenging and recalcitrant cases, he determines to achieve a cure for both men or leave the court forever.

Corax explains his elaborate plan for treatment. His therapy is based on theatrical presentation before the patient of a "trifle of mine owne braine" (III.iii.1558). The masque that he presents turns out to be a processional representation of six kinds of melancholy cited in Burton, that is, Lycanthropia, Hydrophobia, Dotage, Phrenitis, Hypochondria, and Wanton Melancholy or St. Vitus' Dance. The clothing worn by the performers suggests the nature of their ailments, but their brief speeches digress into irrelevant social satire. The masquer dressed in black rags and carrying a book, for example, looks like a figure of Dotage but his remarks about ambition are not specifically associated with the ailment.

At any rate Palador, shaken out of his lethargy by watching the masque, compliments Corax on the imaginative presentation but indicates an empty space on the printed plot. Corax explains that Love-Melancholy has been omitted from the performance because "'twas not in Art / To personate the shadow of that Fancy" (III.iii.1675–1676). He suggests that one of the other spectators, the youth Parthenophil, as an embodiment of genuine Love-Melancholy could not so "lymne his passions" as to act the part. Looking at the youth, Palador suddenly becomes distraught and dashes out of the room crying, "Hold!" At this moment Palador has become so personally involved that he is no longer a mere spectator. He is in effect the seventh masquer, playing the unassigned role of Love-Melancholy. Only later do both Palador and the theater audience learn that the "youth" is actually the missing Eroclea in disguise.

This complex and shifting play within a play poses disturbing questions. Who is spectator? Who is actor? The original masque, essentially irrelevant in content as it omits Love-Melancholy, does not cure but only distracts the patient. The ostensibly unstaged (actually staged by Corax) identification of an unrecognized figure with an unplayable role (according to Corax) unnerves the patient by thrusting him unwittingly into that very role that he has been in reality trying to escape. At this point both the onstage and the offstage audiences begin to lose the distinction between Corax's invention and Ford's plot.

As Corax attempts a diagnosis of Palador's violent response ("tis not a madnesse, but his sorrow's / Close griping griefe"), his clinical analysis is interrupted by the stormy arrival of his other patient, Meleander. This frenzied gentleman enters in a rage, wielding an ax. With his usual aplomb, Corax first calms him down by counter threats, then pretends to confide his own supposed sorrows to the old man. He identifies himself with Meleander by asserting that the cause of his own melancholy is his loss, long ago, of a beautiful daughter. In so doing he achieves a role reversal that proves psychologically effective. Touched by seeing his own perturbations thus projected by another individual, Meleander tries in his own way to offer consolation to Corax. Not surprisingly, such acting out of another's problems poses its dangers for the physician, who laments "some few houres more / Spent here, would turne me Apish, if not frantick" (IV.i.1951–52).

Corax has one more remaining bit of business, however, in order to finish his psychiatric commission. He must bring about the reunion of father and daughter. To accomplish this, he first resorts to more conventional medical means and prescribes a sedative cordial to ease the tensions of the melancholy old man. Then he turns to one more piece of theatrical therapy, sending three characters in succession to visit Meleander and present him with a series of honors. He is thereby made marshal and commander of the ports and learns the prince's wish to call him father. The purpose of these actions is to cheer him up so that he will be psychologically ready to accept the shock of his daughter's return. A fourth character then appears with one more gift, which is revealed as Eroclea herself. Does the reality of Eroclea imply the reality of Meleander's marshalship? There is no basis for judgment. Once more the offstage audience must remain confused as to which is real, which illusory. Unlike the inset plays of an earlier generation, neither this one nor the masque of melancholy emanates from a fixed center of meaning. The illusions as illusions affect the lives of onstage spectators, but the offstage audience is left adrift.

In this play Ford has subtly added one more dimension to the play-within-a-play formula. The actor representing Love-Melancholy is unable to personate a "shadow of that Fancy," we are told, yet his representation proves the most convincing part of the inner play, if he indeed is a part of it at all. Not only does Ford's inner play fail to confirm the universal order by analogy, but also it totally obliterates the line between inner and outer, illusion and reality. It lacks moral purpose altogether, its aim being strictly to modify melancholy. It is therapeutic, but it lacks contact with the substance of the outer play. The formal masque with its representations of all but Love-Melancholy is essentially irrelevant to Palador, and the honors presented to Meleander are fabrications (or so we assume). There is virtually no connection with the rest of the play until those final moments when, on the one hand, the young Prince so convincingly enacts the unactable, and, on the other, the old counselor is duped into receptivity. The inner play is but a game, but so is the play as a whole.

The play ends with multiple weddings and a festive celebration to be enjoyed by all. In such a harmonious conclusion the audience can only forget its momentary disorientation and sense of alienation from the compounded illusions and can even forgive the lapse into conventional medication on the part of this talented and imaginative physician who has been experimenting with as yet unrecorded techniques of theatrical therapy and at the same time revising the nature of the venerable stage convention of the inner play.

A decade after Ford's play, Richard Brome introduced another "psychiatrist" on the stage in his rollicking comedy of an upside-down world, *The Antipodes*. Brome's play, like Ford's, was influenced by Robert Burton's *Anatomy of Melancholy*, but Brome goes much further in developing the psychological themes and their attendant theatrical therapy. The play centers on the Joyless family, all of whom suffer symptoms of intense melancholy, brought about by different irrational obsessions. Worst of all is the son, Peregrine, "falling into madness" (I.ii.5). Only twenty-five, he has developed an obsession about travel, based on his extensive readings in travel literature, particularly the works of Mandeville:

> . . . he would whole days
> And nights (sometimes by stealth) be on such books
> As might convey his fancy round the world.
> (I.ii.38–40)

In a vain effort to prevent him from embarking on journeys to far-off places, his parents have forced him into a marriage, which now drives his sexually neglected wife nearly mad with frustration. The parents too have problems: Diana, the youthful stepmother, suffers abuse because of the fanciful suspicions about her fidelity on the part of her absurdly jealous husband, Joyless, whose suffering is beginning to show visibly—"some few yellow spots"—about the temples (I.ii.73). The confident and imaginative doctor cheerfully undertakes to cure the entire family. His aid will be the inventive Letoy who loves to stage amateur theatricals and who has a band of trained actors at his command.

Doctor Hughball presents his therapeutic master plan to Joyless, who reluctantly agrees to go along with it. The doctor aims to convince Peregrine that this would-be traveler is taking a real voyage to the Antipodes, on the other side of the world, where all behavior is the opposite of what one finds in England. Diana, who has never even attended a play much less taken a trip, is delighted by the prospect. The doctor and Letoy plan the psychological theatrical together. The doctor is to provide a "potion" (perhaps with the recipe inherited from Corax?) that will plummet Peregrine into a deep sleep as a transition to his imaginary voyage, from which he will awake already in the Antipodes. Letoy has prepared the actors for their part, with especial responsibility on the one actor who is good at ad-libbing:

> he makes such shifts extempore,
> (Knowing the purpose what he is to speak to)
> That he moves mirth in me 'bove all the rest.
> (II.i.17–19)

The skill in extemporaneity makes him an ideal participant in the complex internal play to follow, where spontaneity will be an important ingredient. Since Peregrine, like his stepmother, has never seen a play in his life, the opportunities are particularly promising.

The interior drama actually begins in the second act, when Peregrine, carried on a litter by two sailors, is informed of his arrival in the Antipodes. His memory of the journey hence is disturbingly vague,

> as if all had been
> Mere shadowy phantasms, or fantastic dreams.
> (II.iv.10–11)

Throughout the third act, a series of scenes demonstrates the Antipodean reversal of manners in this strange world, where poets go in silks and lawyers in rags, where wives rule husbands, and beggars bestow crowns on indigent courtiers. The focus here is on social satire, and the inverted society provides a delightful comment on contemporary London life. In the sixth scene, however, the attention shifts back to Peregrine, who suddenly plunges wildly into the performance. We are informed by a character named By-Play, who dashes in to complain of the "mad" young gentleman's behavior.

> He has got into our tiring house amongst us,
> And ta'en a strict survey of all our properties:
> Our statues and our images of gods, our planets and our constellations
> Our giants, monsters, furies, beasts, and bugbears,
> Our helmets, shields, and vizors, hairs, and beards,
> Our pasteboard marchpanes, and our wooden pies.
> (III.vi.3–8)

The role that Peregrine has suddenly assumed is a fascinating and significant one. Initiated into this strange world, so much the exact reverse of his own, he has projected himself into it and developed out of it a wish-fulfillment fantasy. His previous fantasizing about travel has now apparently turned into a concrete reality, and he exploits the dream come true by deciding to conquer this new world and establish himself as its ruler. The conquest requires an appropriate military-political coup, which is achieved with decidedly heroic flair. By-Play describes the action in vigorous language:

> Wonder he did
> A while it seem'd, but yet undaunted stood;

> When on the sudden, with thrice knightly force,
> And thrice, thrice puissant arm he snatcheth down
> The sword and shield that I play'd Bevis with,
> Rusheth amongst the foresaid properties,
> Kills monster after monster, takes the puppets
> Prisoners, knocks down the Cyclops, tumbles all
> Our jigambobs and trinkets to the wall.
> Spying at last the crown and royal robes
> I' th' upper wardrobe, next to which by chance
> The devil's vizors hung, and their flame-painted
> Skin coats, those he remov'd with greater fury,
> And (having cut the infernal ugly faces
> All into mammocks) with a reverend hand,
> He takes the imperial diadem and crowns
> Himself King of the Antipodes, and believes
> He has justly gain'd the kingdom by his conquest.
> (III.vi.14–31)

The dazzling theatrical props have in effect acted as a magic store for Peregrine, who has been propelled into this suggestive fantasy. As self-proclaimed ruler of this new reverse-style country, Peregrine enjoys the expansive new role with a series of judgments that somewhat recall the wise, common-sense decisions of Sancho Panza under similar circumstances. Peregrine proves a stern yet benevolent ruler, as he slowly but perceptibly slips from madness into, if not total sanity, at least a theatrical image of sanity.

As king he learns that he is to inherit a bride, the only daughter and heir of the late ruler. The supposed Princess who is presented to him is his disguised wife, Martha, still maddened by frustration, reluctantly agreeing to play the "ideal other" role in hopes of curing her husband. In his kingly role, Peregrine feels his manly nature stirring and approaches what is for him the new role of lover with unsuspected virility. The theatrical involvement is obviously bringing about a major transformation in Peregrine.

At this point Letoy, the theatrical manager in this elaborately staged cure, is confident enough of success to discuss with Joyless the therapeutic procedure in detail:

>   Observe the doctor's art.
> First, he has shifted your son's known disease
> Of madness into folly, and has wrought him
> As far short of a competent reason as
> He was of late beyond it; as a man
> Infected by some foul disease is drawn
> By physic into an anatomy,
> Before flesh fit for health can grow to rear him,
> So is a madman made a fool, before
> Art can take hold of him to wind him up
> Into his proper center, or the medium

>   From which he flew beyond himself.
>   (IV.xiii.3–14)

Since in the minds of Joyless and Diana the madness of melancholy and sexual impotence are one and the same disability, they are optimistic that the therapy that restored sanity will also establish and maintain sexual competence. It later becomes clear that Peregrine has proved his sexual prowess, for his wife Martha ecstatically anticipates "a few such nights more"(V.xii.29).

The play culminates in a ritual masque, in which the threats of Discord, Folly, Jealousy, Melancholy, and Madness are duly banished by Harmony, Mercury, Cupid, Bacchus, and Apollo. This enactment places Peregrine in the role of audience, in contrast to his play-acting in a psychological drama of his own dreams and wishes. Still a bit bewildered as to whether he sleeps or wakes, he is clearly recovered from his delusions and his melancholy. His father Joyless and his wife Martha have also recovered from their mental ailments. Like him, through role-playing in an unknown and fanciful universe they have expanded their notions of self and developed new selfhood. Reality and theatrical fantasy have not been in conflict, but the stage has served as an extension of life, through which acting flows into and merges with identity. The Peregrine who snatches the actors' stage props and wields power over an imaginary kingdom is no less real than the Peregrine who reads travel books.

The experience of catharsis through acting out fantasy is not enough, however, to provide a total cure. The Peregrine who conquers a pretend-kingdom has a new insight into his own individuality and is able to translate his new-found powers into real sexuality. But the catharsis achieved through this kind of theatrical performance is only the first step. The purgative effect is not an end in itself but prepares the way for building a new foundation. The new insights that produced this potential for action must in turn lead him further on the path toward individuation. Having played one role well, he must learn a larger role which will ultimately become the role of selfhood. Unlike the interior drama that produced sudden confessions from a guilty viewer, this drama does not bring about instant and total therapy but rather releases the potential for future, total therapy. Peregrine is neither morally purged of guilt nor psychologically cured. He is, as a result of his psychological involvement in theatrical performance, capable of being cured.

Furthermore, the techniques of therapy cast a wide net; along with the patient, the audience also experiences catharsis and subsequent insight. In *The Antipodes*, Brome cleverly manipulates the action so as to make the theater audience the real object of the satiric scenes in the fanciful Antipodean Community, and to the extent that the viewers recognize themselves, they gain psychological insight into their own feelings. Just as the Joyless family represents a sphere of actor-spectators around the drama of individuation focused on Peregrine, so the larger audience is in effect an extension of the family caught up in their own upside-down world of folly. The joyless ones of the large audience also experience the double catharsis of actor and spectator that provides new insights into their own unsuspected madness. The spectators have become in a sense silent partners in the theatrical experience. As a spectator of Brome's plays wrote when they were first produced: "In them we see ourselves."[14] But what is meant by "them"? Since Dr. Hughball's stage production is not a reflection of the large play but its polar opposite, with which play is the audience supposed to identify? Is it the neurotically melancholy world of the Joyless family or the satirically upside-down world of the Antipodean antic? Neither is a recognizable feature of virtue although both are images of scorn. In this play Brome has created such a total disjunction between inner and outer play that the audience is in effect equally alienated from both. Although it is true that the off-stage audience can *see* themselves in both, the issue of reality versus illusion is left unresolved. Theatrical representation has become a game, and the moral lesson offered by a stage play is simply the value of rewriting one's own part.

In *The Antipodes*, then, we witness the culmination of the long movement away from the use of the interior play as a primarily moral device. Throughout the sixteenth century the play-within-the-play reflected the salvationary emphasis of popular drama, which aimed ultimately to promote virtue and discourage vice. The value of play-viewing as a device to reveal guilt and inspire reform had been recognized in the medieval morality drama and later became a standard feature of Elizabethan revenge tragedy, where it often merged with the climax of the revenge plot. The interior play continued to be popular in the early seventeenth-century drama, where its purposes were still primarily moral although deepened philosophically to include speculation about levels of reality and shifts in identity. Throughout the Jacobean era, however, the inset play always assumes a microcosmic relationship to the larger play.

This gradual shift away from the moral function of interior plays to evoke confession, to purge the guilty conscience, and to restore justice was at the same time a movement toward a larger purpose. Psychological and therapeutic rather than moral and homiletic, the play-within-a-play took on a new structural relationship to the larger play. This new relationship had profound philosophical implications. Whereas previously the inset play was a mirror image of the large play, thereby confirming the ordered vision of that play, the Caroline inset play was disjunct from the whole. According to the established Christian-Platonic tradition of the Renaissance the stage play and the round theater in which it was performed both reflected the world created by the ultimate playwright, God.[15] To inject a play-within-a-play that does *not* occupy a small concentric circle within the larger circle of creation is to disturb the essential order of things. The spontaneous and autonomous interior play staged by an imaginative physician to alter the melancholy mood of a patient calls everything into doubt. The illusion of the larger play traditionally mirrors objective reality, but the illusion of the disjunctive inner play challenges that reality with another subjective illusion. Drama thus becomes a game, matching illusion with counter illusion.

The issue of identity as well as the nature of reality is affected by this new mode of theatricality. Although the Jacobean play within a play had experimented with the idea of disguised identity, characters returned to their defined roles at the end. As

Vindice learned in *The Revenger's Tragedy*, one may temporarily forget oneself and pretend to be someone else, but ultimately order is restored and one is held responsible for deeds performed in disguise. In the inset plays of Massinger, Ford, and Brome, however, there is no confirmed identity to return to. Individual identity may be recreated theatrically. Is Peregrine more or less himself after assuming a role in the make-believe Antipodean society? Since his initial melancholy role is itself the product of imaginative identification with the world of travel literature, his selfhood seems to lack both divine and social sanction and to depend rather on human esthetic endeavor.[16]

Peregrine's obsessions clearly fit the description of the baroque madman characterized by Michael Foucault in *The Order of Things* as "the man who is *alienated* in *analogy*. He is the disordered player of the Same and the Other. He takes things for what they are not, and people one for another; he cuts his friends and recognizes complete strangers; he thinks he is unmasking when, in fact, he is putting on a mask. He inverts all values and all proportions, because he is constantly under the impression that he is deciphering signs: for him, the crown makes the king."[17] The basis of the alienating analogy is, however, the play-within-a-play staged by Dr. Hughball. In the inverted world of this play, Peregine's mistaken perceptions subvert his former identity.

The effect of this perspective on the off-stages audience is inevitably alienating. Unlike the audience viewing *Hamlet* and feeling deeply satisfied by being in Hamlet's confidence and sharing his elation over the exposure of Claudius' guilt while observing the play, the audience watching *The Antipodes* has lost its moral anchor. Since Claudius *is* guilty, the inner circle of Hamlet's play reflects the outer circle of reality in the castle of Elsinore and by extension the world of Denmark. But by contrast in Brome's play the failure of the play-within-a-play to reflect by analogy the main play implies the failure of the entire system of analogy and resemblances in the Renaissance universe. As Michel Foucault also points out concerning the early seventeenth century, "The age of resemblance is drawing to a close. It is leaving nothing behind it but games. Games whose powers of enchantment grow out of the new kinship between resemblance and illusion; the chimeras of similitude loom up on all sides, but they are recognized as chimeras; it is the privileged age of *trompe l'oeil* painting, of the comic illusion, of the play that duplicates itself by representing another play, of the *quid pro quo*, of dreams and visions."[18] With resemblances suspect and similitude the occasion of error rather than a basis for knowledge, the relationship between the inner and outer play changes drastically. Until the end of the sixteenth century, the universe had been regarded as a web of resemblance and analogy, but in the seventeenth this vision was shattered and the old sanctity of the circle broken. The circular theater was no longer a precise microcosm, and the inset play was no longer a smaller concentric circle, reflecting the same ultimate reality. The inner play offered a disjunctive action in respect to the large outer play. As a result the theater audience could not categorically identify with the on-stage audience but instead had to choose between two equally alienating illusions.

Unfortunately *The Antipodes* was one of the last plays written and produced before the closing of the theaters in 1642. Although the English drama did not have the opportunity to develop this new kind of disjunctive dramaturgy, one might infer its potential from a French example, that is, Jean Rotrou's *Le Veritable Saint Genest* (1645). In this play about an actor who becomes converted through acting the role of a Christian martyr, Rotrou maintains a double perspective throughout the frame-play as well as the unusually long play-within-a-play. The inner play concerns the conversion of the martyr until the actor playing the role casts aside the script announcing his own conversion, thus literalizing his role. Not surprisingly his fellow actors are confused and at first simply compliment his convincing performance. As in the Brome play, the audience is alienated because the inner play does not reflect the large play but rather refutes it, substituting its own illusion as reality.

Although there are not many examples of the innovative Caroline play-within-a-play, those we find in the works of Massinger, Ford, and Brome are of considerable significance in the history of English drama. Both theatrically and philosophically they function in a different manner and for different purposes than the inner plays in Elizabethan and Jacobean drama. By no means a mere tag-end of a declining tradition, they inject new vitality into an old device, moving beyond the venerable homiletic tradition into a post-Renaissance mode of theatricality. It is perhaps ironic that the theatrical imaginations of Paulo, Corax, and Dr. Hughball were silenced by the Puritan closing of the theaters, but it is not really surprising, for their kind of illusion tended to undermine the established order. The histrionic role of the cavalier cause, on stage and off, was about to be upstaged by History.

NOTES

1. *An Apology for Actors* (London: Reprinted for the Shakespeare Society, 1841), p. 57.

2. The earliest study of the English play within a play was H. Schwab, *Das Schauspiel im Schauspiel zur Zeit Shakesperes* (Wien-Leipzig, 1896.) The pioneering study in English is F. S. Boas, "The Play Within a Play," *A Series of Papers on Shakespeare and the Theatre by Members of the Shakespeare Association* (London: Oxford University Press, 1927), pp. 134–156. Important recent studies are Leslie A. Fiedler, "The Defense of the Illusion and the Creation of Myth," *English Institute Essays*, 1948, ed. D. A. Robertson, Jr. (New York: Columbia University Press, 1949), pp. 79–94; Robert J. Nelson, *Play Within a Play: The Dramatist's Conception of His Art, Shakespeare to Anouilh* (New Haven, Conn.: Yale University Press, 1958), pp. 11–35; Arthur Brown, "The Play Within a Play: An Elizabethan Dramatic Device," *Essays and Studies* 13 (London: The English Association, 1960), pp. 36–48; Dieter Mehl, "Forms and Functions of the Play Within a Play," *Renaissance Drama* 8, ed. S. Schoenbaum (Evanston, Ill.: Northwestern University Press, 1965), 41–61. All of these studies are primarily concerned with the moral and didactic purposes of the interior plays.

3. Brown cites *The Spanish Tragedy* and *The Roman Actor* as examples of achieving revenge through the inner play and *Hamlet, The Roman Actor, The Jovial Crew* or *The Merry Beggars* as examples of discovering guilt.

4. Dieter Mehl concentrates on the differences between the Elizabethan and the Jacobean uses of the play-within-a-play. He finds that the early period focuses on the moral purpose of the interior play whereas the later period uses it to explore levels of reality. "In serious drama it often means a deep probing into the very nature of reality and the validity of certain moral positions" (p. 60). With the exception of a paragraph on *The Roman Actor* he does not refer to Caroline plays.

5. Brown, p. 48. Nelson also notes that Hamlet explores reality through illusion.

6. Nelson and Fiedler are both concerned with Shakespeare; as noted above Mehl includes only a brief comment on one Caroline play; Brown includes a paragraph on *The Jovial Crew* or *The Merry Beggars*. None of the studies of the play-within-a-play has discussed the three plays explored here; none, in fact, is concerned with the Caroline period of drama.

7. The phrase "doctor's art" appears in Richard Brome's *The Antipodes*. John Ford also refers to the skills of his doctor in *The Lover's Melancholy* as "art." The word "psychology", according to *OED*, was introduced into English in 1693 in a translation from the French of a study of Mankind, divided in two parts, Anatomy, or the body, and Psychology, or the soul. The word "psychiatry" did not come into use in English until the nineteenth century.

8. On the traditional correlation of guilt and melancholy see Robert Burton, *The Anatomy of Melancholy* (New York: Tudor Publishing Co., 1927), pp. 942–946. Burton's comprehensive study was the most complete and influential, but the subject of melancholy had been investigated earlier, as in Timothy Bright's *A Treatise of Melancholie, Containing the Causes Thereof, & Reasons of the Strange Effects It Worketh in Our Minds and Bodies with the Phisicke Cure, and Spirituall Consolation for Such as Have Thereto Adjoyned an Afflicted Conscience* (1586). Such works considered melancholy from both a physiological and a spiritual point of view, not having a concept of psychology as yet.

9. Citations are from the Signet edition of *Macbeth*, ed. Sylvan Barnet (New York, 1963).

10. Citations are from *The Plays and Poems of Philip Massinger*, ed. Philip Edwards and Colin Gibson, 5 vols. (Oxford: Clarendon Press, 1976).

11. On this point I take issue with Brown and Nelson who contend that the inner play, however at odds structurally with the frame play, tends to increase audience identification.

12. Citations are from *John Fordes Dramatische Werke*, in *Materialien zur Kunde des alteren Englische Dramas*, vol. 23, ed. W. Bang. Louvain: A. Uystpruyst, 1908, rpt. 1963. The play within a play is considered briefly in S. Blaine Ewing, *Burtonian Melancholy in the Plays of John Ford* (Princeton, N. J.: Princeton University Press, 1940), pp. 38–41. For a somewhat fuller treatment see Donald K. Anderson, *John Ford* (New York: Twayne Publishers, 1972), pp. 52–60. The chapter devoted to *The Lover's Melancholy* is appropriately called "Psychotherapy as Spectacle."

13. Theatrical therapy has become a standard technique in contemporary psychiatric treatment. For recent parallels to the techniques of Paulo, Corax, and Dr. Hughball see Ira Greenberg, *Psychodrama and Audience Attitude* (Beverly Hills, Calif.: Behavioral Studies Press, 1968). "Delusions and hallucinations are given flesh—and embodiments on the stage. . . . The ultimate resolution of deep mental conflicts requires an objective setting, the psychodramatic theatre" (p. 89).

14. All citations are from Richard Brome, *The Antipodes*, ed. Ann Haaker, Regents Renaissance Drama (Lincoln, Nebr.: University of Nebraska Press, 1966). The spectator's remark is quoted in the Introduction to the text.

15. Fiedler noted the analogy of the interior play to the "cosmic drama." For a history of the world-stage metaphor see Ernst Curtius, *European Literature and the Latin Middle Ages*,

trans. Willard Trask (New York: Pantheon, 1953); Charlotte Spivack, "The Elizabethan Theater: Circle and Center," *Centennial Review*, 13 (1969), 424–443.

16. It should be mentioned here that Stephen Greenblatt's *Renaissance Self-Fashioning: From More to Shakespeare* (Chicago, Ill.: University of Chicago Press, 1980) is also concerned with role-playing and identity, citing improvisation as "a central Renaissance mode of behavior," but his focus is on the sixteenth century, and he is not concerned with dramatic structures.
17. Michel Foucault, *The Order of Things* (New York: Random House, 1970), p. 49.
18. *Ibid.*, p. 51.

REVIEWS

Ben Jonson, Dramatist, by Anne Barton. Cambridge: Cambridge University Press, 1984. Pp. xiv + 370. Cloth $57.50; paper $18.95.

Reviewer: MICHAEL WARREN

The spare title of Anne Barton's book indicates the sharp focus that she maintains throughout, but it belies the depth and the amplitude of her work. Her concern is with Jonson as writer for the stage; although her presentation involves not just chronological development but historical contexts also, she directs her energies to detailed examination of the plays in terms of plot, characterization, stagecraft, and language, and to their interpretation. She founds all her exploration in a detailed knowledge of the documents of Jonson's life: the *Conversations with Drummond* are mined extensively and judiciously, the poems and masques (explicitly excluded as subjects from the book) are frequent objects of reference; his letters have their place too. Above all, she sees Jonson as a writer working in an urgent present who is nevertheless always concerned about the writers of the past—in the early part of his career the past of classical literature, in his later life the past of the great writers of the Elizabethan age. The book is informed constantly and unostentatiously by a sense of biography and history and is unashamedly old-fashioned in mode. The biographical inclination is evident in the book's title, which makes clear that it is about Jonson, not about a set of plays abstracted from their author or their origins. The history is present in the abiding sense of other writers and plays, of monarchs, of the court, and of social values. There is little attention given to large-scale socio-economic forces as determinants; rather, one is made aware of one particular individual's approach to his art during a period of social change. It is the diversity of that approach over almost forty years that is revealed most clearly: Jonson the restless experimenter, as complex in his artistic aims and achievements in the theater as he appears in the extraordinary details of his life. This excursion through Jonson's theatrical corpus leads the reader not only into an encounter with the curious idiosyncratic wealth of Jonson's work but also into frequent new thoughts about the works of other writers of his time; Barton's sense of the literary and theatrical context is rich, and she is generous in her investigations of relevant works of others. Moreover she maintains a wonderfully balanced stance towards her subject and his writing. Unlike so many books on Jonson this never presses the question of admiration or dislike of his personality. She reads the life and the plays with an imaginative sensitivity and understanding, recognizing peculiarity for what it is, not forcing irregularity into pattern, and not engaging in either censoriousness or apologia; it is clear at the end that she enjoys the experience of "Jonson" and admires the body of work, even as in the Preface she speaks of "Jonson's greatness as a writer of comedy" (p. xi), but the book is devoid of any sentimentalizing.

The Preface lays out the axes of thought: "His engagement with the classical world, although sometimes pedantic, was redeemingly romantic at heart. . . . Jonson's classicism was balanced, moreover, by a compensating attraction towards the irregular, the gothic, the contemporary and the strange. The rage for order which shapes his work is almost always met and, in a way, substantiated by an equally powerful impulse towards chaos and licence"(p. x). These propositions, not surprising in themselves, are worked out with appropriate judiciousness, tactful imagination, and great learning, but what stands out in the book are less customary considerations, and especially individual passages and studies. The first chapter contains an excellent discussion of the additions to *The Spanish Tragedy*. Barton sees no reason to doubt the attribution of the additions to Jonson; refuting others' objections by suggesting that one should not expect his additions to sound unmistakably like his own voice and that he would want his additions to be in harmony with the original rather than in conflict with it, she shows how the additions do nevertheless relate to Jonson's own work, specifically in their preoccupation with the father's psychological state at the loss of a child; the evidence from the poems on the deaths of his two children is adduced subtly, the additions interpreted shrewdly. I read the additions now with new respect and insight. But this passage has further importance for the way in which it connects with all the instances later of the relations of fathers and sons; and one is obliged to recall Jonson's own absent father, dead before Jonson's birth, and Jonson's troubled relation to the trade of his bricklayer stepfather.

Later in the book Barton draws attention to the role of the concept of trust in many of the plays. In discussing *Epicoene* she refers to a "duplicity, a lack of openness that seems habitual [that] informs the relations of Truewit, Clerimont and Dauphine throughout" and that she diagnoses as deriving "in part from an unfocused but omnipresent competitiveness, a need to keep other people, including friends, in their place"(p. 130); and she locates a similar aggression in the friendship of Quarlous and Winwife in *Bartholomew Fair*, something that goes beyond high-spiritedness, and that leads her to assert that "the humanity and tolerance of the lower classes is more in evidence in *Bartholomew Fair* than that of their betters" (p. 218). In that chapter on *Bartholomew Fair* she briefly introduces the idea of "trust"; in the next, on the *The Devil is an Ass*, she shows how it is fundamental to that play and then allows it to recur in her discussions of later plays, where she also adverts to the emphasis on "the coherence of the family as a social and personal unit"(p. 156). What she produces within the structure of a series of discrete chapters on individual plays is an elaborate web of connections; while the major concentration of each chapter is on the interpretation of a play (sometimes two), one becomes aware that, in the language in which she characterizes Jonson, Anne Barton is "a basically accumulative artist"(p. 219).

And this is particulary evident in what is probably the most exciting aspect of this book, its treatment of the later Jonson and the climate of Jacobean and Caroline nostalgia, beautifully delineated in a chapter entitled "Harking back to Elizabeth." There she brings together much that has been running through the book and recalls her own first chapter on "Jonson and the Elizabethans"; Jonson's relation to his Elizabethan past is shown to correspond closely to currents in the political and social climate of the day. But again there is a special value in the local insights within the general formulations. Barton shows in her study of *Bartholomew Fair* how Jonson begins his retreat from his obsession with the classics and turns to using the writings of Sidney and the Elizabethans as substitute points of reference; she illuminates his exploitation of materials from morality plays in the *The Devil is an Ass* and is strikingly acute in her demonstration of his imitation of Shakespearean form in *The New Inn*. If the chapter on nostalgia sums up much that has gone before, it also shows the peculiar way in which the wheel came full circle in Jonson's practice—from the rejection of Elizabethan modes to their acceptance. At the same time that circle is part of the book's elegantly unforced artistic design. Its power comes from a richness of texture that is established early, and constantly amplified; and from a wholeness of vision of the career. It is notable that that design can tolerate as a coda a last pair of chapters on *A Tale of a Tub* and *The Sad Shepherd*; in the former the case is well made for a late dating of the play, and in the latter she shows adeptly how *The Sad Shepherd*, "or something like it, was inevitable given the directions in which Jonson's mind had been moving during the 1630s" (p. 340).

While these threads that move through the book are all vital—I cannot pass over her exploration of the significance of names of characters—the book will probably be read a second time for its chapters on individual plays, and here I cannot deal with them all. Their value is somewhat unequal; all are energetic and vigorous studies, but the format entails that some commonplace things are said about the more popular works. No one writing a chapter on *The Alchemist* can avoid saying at some point that "The true alchemy of *The Alchemist* is linguistic" (p. 150), and Jonson's plays have never proved, and probably never will prove, a major fertile field for the battle of conflicting interpretations; deconstructionists have certainly found them of little attraction. However, that does not prevent Barton from producing, for instance, shifts of emphasis in the interpretation of *Epicoene* and *Bartholomew Fair* that make one reconsider one's customary stances.

At the same time, nevertheless, I found places of disagreement in matters of detail that led me to wonder whether even outside performance there is not room for more controversy over action, characterization, and general interpretation in these plays than is usual. For example, I have never regarded Dame Pliant's inability to "abide" Spaniards on account of the Armada, an event before her birth, as evidence of hysteria (p. 146) so much as of vacuousness; but then the production with which I was associated played her as a dumb blonde, also rendering the name Pliant in the context of Subtle's comment on the "erection of her figure" not as "drooping," as Barton reads it (p. 191), but as "supple, lithe" (as *OED* allows), thus giving her greater plausibility as the substitute whore for the elegant Don, as the object of rivalry between Face and Subtle, and as wife of Lovewit. Similarly, Barton suggests that at the end of this play, by contrast with the end of *Volpone*, "It is quite clear that in this master/servant relationship, Mosca [that is, Face] will never for an instant gain the upper hand" (p. 151); but such an interpretation is just one of many that are possible. Here it is not a matter of the indeterminacy of a dramatic text for performance, but rather an issue for judgment; I would argue that while Face has had to lose a great deal in order to survive, his defeat of Subtle and Dol and his manipulation of Lovewit suggest that he may yet control an unwitting Lovewit in the future. The vividness of Barton's readings makes them attractive, provocative, and persuasive; in this instance she provokes me to wonder whether we do not habitually treat the details of Jonson's plays with far less openness than those of Shakespeare.

I found myself, oddly enough, taking issue with her in a different way concerning *Catiline*. While the discussion is full of acute local perceptions, especially about the comic possibilities of the play and particularly in relation to Jonson's treatment of characters and their names, I am uncomfortable with her general formulation of her dissatisfaction with the play: "By refusing to make either Catiline or Cicero a focus of tragic attention, burlesquing Cethegus, handling Fulvia, Sempronia, and the other women in much the way he had the collegiate ladies in *Epicoene*, and generalizing the Chorus, Jonson consistently undercut and dissipated the tragic potential of his material. *Catiline* is something more than the icy neo-classical mistake it has often been thought to be. On the other hand, it reveals the extent to which Jonson, by 1611, was temperamentally committed to comedy" (p. 166). The generic antithesis rules too strongly here. At the risk of appearing to argue for the success or unity of *Catiline*, I would suggest that if Jonson's entitling it a "tragedy" and our experience of comic intrusion seem to create a problem, it might be resolved through the contemplation of some of Juvenal's satires with their blend of lofty vision, rhetorical grandeur, grotesque humor, and lurid details. Such a suggestion does not make the play a greater success, but it does perhaps provide an escape from the generic trap that Jonson's own prefatory letter baits with its language of "a legitimate Poeme" (although it is curious that the Quarto of 1611 does not bear the word *tragedy* on its title-page).

However, such cavils as these are small matters in any light, and especially in the light of the achievement of the chapters on the plays commonly termed (after Dryden) "dotages." In interpreting these works, siting them within the construction of a career, illuminating them with a sympathetic but never dazzled eye, Barton is excellent. In books on Jonson one usually reads the material on the plays after *Bartholomew Fair* with a dutiful forbearance, suspecting that a similar obligation to scholarly responsibility guided the author. Here the case could not be more different. Commenting aptly at one point that the author of the "Cary Morison Ode" of 1629 was hardly an artist of failing powers (p. 263), Barton reads these late plays as significant artistic adventures, attempts to find new forms to represent new visions. She is judicious in her positions; exploration and explanation are always ahead of enthusiasm. Only in the case of *The New Inn* does she propose a major reevaluation: "It is the first Jonson comedy in which the impact of the 1623 First Folio can be felt, brilliantly accommodated to Jonson's own interests and temperament. The result was a much misunderstood, but fine and haunting, play" (p. 284). The argument sent me back to the play again, and although I cannot be as excited about it as Barton is, I am persuaded by her interpretation of the action.

    This is a fine and haunting book. Its wealth of material, the richness of the detail, the cumulative power of its repetition of themes, all make it a work that obliges one to rethink one's attitudes both to individual plays and to the whole career. Even without consideration of the poems and the masques, Jonson and his plays seem more imposing and various than before.

The Subject of Tragedy: Identity & Difference in Renaissance Drama, by Catherine Belsey. London and New York: Methuen, 1985. Pp. xi + 253. $27.50.

Reviewer: PAUL GAUDET

    This book can be regarded as a sequel to and application of Catherine Belsey's *Critical Practice* (London and New York: Methuen, 1980). In her earlier work Belsey provides a critique of orthodox literary criticism, rejecting its assumptions of an autotelic text, a singular and author-ized meaning, and a reader's autonomy. She argues that meaning does not inhere in a text to be transmitted definitively or extracted perceptively. A new critical practice must recognize the social and historical determination of meaning (for the text *and* for the reader) and must allow for the circulation of meanings among text, ideology, and reader: "the work of criticism is to release possible meanings" (p. 144). The possibility of meanings is greatest in the *interrogative* text (her adaptation of Benveniste's distinction of three basic functions of discourse—*declarative*, *imperative*, and *interrogative*—in *Problems in General Linguistics* [Miami: University of Miami Press, 1971], p. 110). Belsey's subsequent explanation of what she understands an interrogative text to be constitutes a point of entry to her second book:

> The world represented in the interrogative text includes what Althusser calls 'an internal distance' from the ideology in which it is held, which permits the reader to construct from within the text a critique of this ideology. . . . In other words, the interrogative text refuses a single point of view, however complex and comprehensive, but brings points of view into unresolved collision or contradiction.
>   (*Critical Practice*, p. 92)

The Subject of Tragedy is about such collision and contradiction of discourses then and now.

Belsey acknowledges that the polemical and confrontational character of her study challenges and disturbs the conceptual stances on which traditional scholarship and criticism have been founded: "To propose an alternative to the humanist version of literary history is to offer a contribution to that rearrangement of our knowledge which signals the end of the reign of man" (p. 33). Her primary field of study is tragedy in English drama from 1576 to 1642, a period of transition—between the providential unity of the moralities and the affirmation of moral common sense of Restoration drama—in which "the stage brought into conjunction and indeed into collision the emblematic mode and an emergent illusionism. The effect was a form of drama capable at any moment of disrupting the unity of the spectator" (p. 26). Not only are instability, disruption, and conflict characteristic of dramatic and theatrical modes, but also they are symptomatic of social contest, of the plural and contradictory meanings ascribed to man and woman at this particular historical moment. Plays are the starting point; the project "is to identify a . . . discontinuity of meanings and knowledges, to chart in the drama of the sixteenth and seventeenth centuries the eventual construction of an order of subjectivity which is recognizably modern" (p. 4).

Belsey's resistance to notions of homogeneous culture and her corresponding insistence that reading practices should recognize historical difference are what inform her three three main objectives in this book: "to contribute to the construction of a history of the subject" (p. ix) in Rennaisance England; to identify and resist the asymmetry of gender meanings in our cultural and political traditions; and to bring together history and fiction. Her first aim is necessary because of absence. There is no history of the human subject because liberal humanism defines human nature in essentialist terms: man is unified, knowing, autonomous, and, above all, unchanging in his inherent qualities. Denying that man exists as an objective fact, Belsey sets out to trace the discursive processes that produced modern subjectivity and to destabilize the conservative analytical practices by which liberal humanism generates itself. A self-fulfilling cultural artifact, "the discursive hero of a specific class" (p. 14), liberal-humanist man emerged with the secularization of knowledge, the growth of mercantilist and imperialist interests, and the democratization of the state. By locating agency and meaning in a unified, independent subject (himself), man found a way of controlling his history, constructing his destiny, and legitimating both.

Belsey's exploration of discursive self-determination ranges over more than two centuries of English drama and refers to seventy-nine plays from *The Castle of Perseverance* to *The Fatal Friendship* (1698). For example, in discussing the evolution of the human subject, she argues that early and later morality plays place virtue and meaning outside the male protagonist, while dramatizing him as "a transitory configuration of fragments" (p. 17), confused, unaware, and lacking control over the states of his being. This decentering and discontinuity are reflected in the absence of the human figure in *Wisdom* (*ca.* 1460) and the use of multiple conferred (not chosen) names that indicate distinct modes of behavior for a single hero in *The World and the Child* (1500-22). Although later plays such as *The Spanish Tragedy* (ca. 1590) and *Doctor Faustus* (1592?) may produce the impression of interiority, primarily through soliloquy, they are characterized by the incompatibility of subject positions: the self possesses empirical knowledge of objects upon which he can act, but he still exists in a world where action and truth are validated from without and above. It is not until the Restoration that the human subject breaks free from the discursive instability of his dramatic predecessors: Jaffeir in *Venice Preserved* (1682) "is not represented as the battleground of conflicting cosmic forces, like Mankind, or of contradictory political imperatives, like the earlier revengers"; he is "the origin of his own actions" because his revenge is "motivated by individual psychological impulses" (p. 122). Liberal humanism, however, tends to rewrite the past in its own image. In its quest for an idea of personal identity that is single and stable, it exalts the self-assertion and isolation of Coriolanus, or Antony, or the Duchess of Malfi as integrity and heroic defiance, while tacitly suppressing alternative readings that link these characteristics with the Vice and define separation from the social as a transgression.

Belsey's rejection of any modeling and analysis of cultural history that is authoritarian and undifferentiated aligns her book with other recent studies. While she shares Stephen Greenblatt's conclusion that the human subject in the Renaissance was not autonomous, but was "the ideological product of the relations of power in a particular society" (*Renaissance Self-Fashioning* [Chicago: University of Chicago Press, 1980], p. 256), Belsey argues that the development of the masculine subject was, ironically, a reaction to the absolutist state, effectively shifting the emphasis from aristocratic control to bourgeois resistance. Jonathan Dollimore (*Radical Tragedy* [Chicago: University of Chicago Press, 1984], p. 155) asserts that essentialist humanism did not really emerge until the Enlightenment; Belsey's critique of anachronistic perspective moves its emergence back to the Restoration and contends that ideological production was a gradual process that cut across two centuries. By now readers of this review will know that Belsey's skirmish with liberal humanism is part of a larger struggle to connect "literature" with its predeterminate conditions, to decompartmentalize historical enquiry, and to de-neutralize or subjectify the professional study of cultural tradition that insists on pursuing an elusive source of ultimate meaning. This approach to fictional texts as a repository of the meanings that members of a social body understand and contest is Belsey's third objective; it is also her methodology to integrate dramatist, philosopher, and pamphleteer, court records and fictional characters, didactic tracts and sociological phenomena. A similar anti-disciplinary and anti-authoritarian emphasis can be found in two other books published in the same year: Jonathan Dollimore and Alan Sinfield, eds., *Political Shakespeare* (Ithaca: Cornell University Press, 1985) and John Drakakis, ed., *Alternative Shakespeares* (London and New York: Methuen, 1985).

What sets *The Subject of Tragedy* apart from these companion works is Belsey's foregrounding of gender and the collusive role of liberal humanism in the subordination of women. The resistance of political (male) subjects to tyranny, ultimately through revolution in the name of egalitarian rights, was an ironic process that led to an inequality of freedoms, to a less visible and more insidious form of entrapment for women in the displaced hierarchy of the family. The redefinition of the family is what installed women as dependent and inferior subjects by the late seventeenth century; the depoliticized, privatized, and sexualized discourse of humanism is what kept them there:

> Domestic relationships are defined as affective rather than political in a discourse which works to suppress recognition of the power relations which structure the family, and by this means liberalism opens a gap for the accommodation of an uncontested, because unidentified, patriarchy.
>
> (p. 199)

Belsey pursues this thesis by identifying some of the central inconsistencies and contradictions in Renaissance dramatic representations of women, as well as in the divorce controversy and the Puritan definition of marriage and the family as the cornerstone of order for church and commonwealth.

Belsey's paradigm is Alice Arden's crime of procuring and witnessing the murder of her husband in 1551. Belsey is intrigued that a not uncommon act of private violence elicited so many re-presentations and problematizations for at least eighty years after the event. Holinshed, for example, acknowledges the apparent irrelevance of this private matter for his larger project, yet goes on to detail the murder. This disproportionate interest cannot be accounted for because the crime's physical details, or circumstances, or moral dimensions were exceptionally terrifying but because of its subversive social and economic implications. The murder, a conscious and independent choice by a woman, constituted a threat to male supremacy at the beginning of a contest for the meaning of marriage and the institutional regulation of sexuality. In an often fascinating discussion, Belsey places the multiple efforts at redefinition in their preformal context and examines the manipulations and ambivalences of meaning that are the product of ideological collision. From these she infers a deep and widespread fear that women were disposed to recalcitrance and revolt—symbolically, that they were likely to murder their husbands.

Although the discussion of woman is grounded in Belsey's earlier conclusions about the emergence of the masculine subject, its information and alternative readings make this section the most intriguing one in the book. There is significant evidence for the legal inferiority of women. The murder of a spouse drew disparate punishments: men were hanged; women were burned for petty treason. The murder of a master by a servant was considered treason; but authorities disagreed whether a servant's murder of a mistress was treason or simply murder. Complaining speech was a punishable offence for women, but there was no corresponding crime for men. Similar inequities served to unfix the woman's position in the family, once the distinction between public and private, state and family, was instituted. The family hierarchy produced paradoxical situations for the woman, who was both authoritative mistress and subjected wife, aligned with the children in obedience owed to the master and yet aligned with the father as a mother to whom honor was due.

Belsey uses the incompatibility in the subject positions of women's speech to comment on a number of plays: she accounts for the discontinuities in Vittoria's four scenes in *The White Devil* (1612); she explores the inner contradictions of the absolutist definition of marriage as it is refracted in the several versions of the Griselda story; she draws attention to the conflicting definitions of marital relationships in *A Woman Killed with Kindness* (1603) and the irony that Anne Frankford's reinstatement in the family is contingent upon her death: "the stability of the family requires the subjugation of women to the point where they must be willing to efface themselves finally in order to preserve it" (p. 178). In contrast, Elizabeth Cary's *The Tragedy of Mariam* (1603–04?) dramatizes the problem of a woman's right to speak and formulates explicitly, even though it repudiates, such concepts as divorce initiated by women and equality of the sexes. The fact that Cary's play was a closet drama testifies to the general marginalization of women, whether through social expectations of silence or of acquiescent speech, through punishment as scolds for verbal transgression, or though the demonization of women who subvert the patriarchal meaning of femininity. For Belsey, it is no accident that witchcraft was made a statutory offence in 1542 and that executions peaked in the 1580s and 1590s when the divorce debate was also reaching a climax, and again from 1645 to 1647 "when women were claiming an unprecedented voice in the affairs of church and state" (p. 185). It is this partisan suppression of women in the name of objectivity, the exclusion of women from politics and political theory and analysis from the family, that Belsey has set out to expose in the drama of Renaissance England and in the history of its scholarly and critical reproduction.

Belsey's disclaimer that she is not writing "a social history of the period, but a (sketch-) map of a discursive field" (p. 4) is a clue to what is both stimulating and initially disappointing in her book. By avoiding a specificity that never gets beyond itself, she succeeds in providing an angular and provocative survey of more than two centuries. To do so in a book that is short in ratio to its task, however, Belsey risks generalizations that display gaps and inconsistencies comparable to those that she is examining. While she acknowledges that liberal humanism is changing, multiple, even contradictory, in its discourses and institutions (p. 7), her book enacts a monolithic conception. Similarly, there is a tendency to obscure more precise historical moments, to efface the very difference for which she argues. Her thesis identifies a period of change that moves through a late sixteenth-century crisis to a consolidation in the Restoration. Yet her method mingles quotations from the 1640s and 1690s to support observations about conditions in the sixteenth century; or it overrides the evidence of other sixteenth-century texts, which are not cited, to claim a distinctive status for seventeenth-century ideas and developments:

> Patriarchalism, which elicited some support in the sixteenth century, but gathered strength in the seventeenth, proposed an analogy between the obedience naturally

due to fathers of families and submission to the monarch in the interests of the people: 'As the father over one family, so the king, as father over many families, extends his care to preserve, feed, clothe, instruct and defend the whole commonwealth'.

(p. 99)

If one can infer from William Baldwin's *A Treatise of Moral Philosophy* (1548), which went through sixteen editions by 1600, the analogies of family/state and father/ruler were already commonplace before the seventeenth century. In the instance above, there is also a disparity between Belsey's introduction of the quotation from Robert Filmer's *Patriarcha* (written between 1635 and 1642, published in 1680) and what the passage actually addresses: Belsey is concerned with obedience and submission; Filmer focuses on a king's responsibilities as fatherly provider.

There are also occasions when Belsey's stance is less than interrogative, when her readings operate on singular or polarized assumptions. In her consideration of *The Castle of Perseverance*, she accepts as incontestable fact Richard Southern's view that the audience was included in the playing space, inside a round ditch (*The Medieval Theatre in the Round* (London: Faber & Faber, 1957), while omitting any reference to alternative explanations for the extant stage drawing that challenge Southern's reconstruction (for example, Natalie Crohn Schmidt, "Was There a Medieval Theatre in the Round?" in *Medieval English Drama*, ed. Jerome Taylor and Alan H. Nelson [Chicago and London: University of Chicago Press, 1972], pp. 292–315). Her assertion that Hamlet kills Claudius "in the light of an older knowledge, a submission to the divinity that shapes our ends" (p. 79) accepts a cliché that systematizes the play and flattens textual possibilities. Her observation that Shakespeare's comic heroines are the dramatic descendants of Lucres (of *Fulgens and Lucres*), "most notably Portia, who speaks with wisdom and authority to resolve the legal and moral dilemmas defined in *The Merchant of Venice*" (p. 195) completely ignores numerous recent readings that ironize Portia and problematize the play. At such moments, Belsey's method works against her theoretical principles.

Sometimes the book moves too quickly to realize its potential. After citing several legal complaints from husbands who feared murder by their wives, Belsey finds it surprising that in the corresponding period there were only two instances of women protesting a similar fear of their husbands (p. 136, n. 6). One possible interpretation is that, for women, intimidations were built into law. Later, without making the connection, Belsey refers to the judicial humiliation of women for speaking out of turn to protest against injury (pp. 181–182). Another instance of unexplored and unsubstantiated possibility is Belsey's claim that the drama of the period is less inhibited than propagandist texts (for example, James I's *Basilikon Doron* (1599) and Filmer's *Patriarcha*): "This is not because the dramatists were more radical (though they probably were . . .). It is primarily because narrative depends on the existence of obstacles, while propaganda depends on their elimination" (p. 100). When she turns her attention to the inscription of opposition in dramatic texts, she teasingly abandons another direction of enquiry: is there a comparable problematizing in non-dramatic fiction or were the dramatists really more radical?

I found myself repeatedly posing questions in reaction to Belsey's text and to what she does not say. Does interiority always have to be read as conforming to the liberal-humanist model of a single, stable, and unalterable self? Are there more flexible models of interiority that might allow us to see alternative notions of self in Renaissance drama? How does Belsey extricate herself from the discursive system that she interrogates? If recognition of cultural heritage and its processes of ideological formation is the pre-condition for change in the present, what needs to be transformed and what should be avoided? In specific terms, what revisionist models of society and scholarly investigation would she construct? But in retrospect I am inclined to see the dangling of questions and the gaps as deriving from divergent conceptions of what an academic book can be. Read as self-conscious polemic, *The Subject of Tragedy* is not a closed system that chokes dialogue but an extended "essay," a provocation that attempts to stimulate change by disturbing the environment of the reader. What it does not do at least points to what might be done (for example, more historical research in smaller socio-economic groups to refine our sense of difference, rather than reflexive indictments of "the patriarchal system"). It is left to each reader to engage the challenge and the undeveloped possibilities of this book. Those who automatically dismiss Belsey's work as fashionable humanist-bashing, or marginalize it as another eccentricity from the British new left/feminist axis, will simply prove her point that liberal humanism stigmatizes *fundamental* dissent as anti-social: "Resistance from within the social body is deviant or delinquent, legitimately ignored or penalized as the work of the enemy within" (p. 120).

Renaissance Tragedy and the Senecan Tradition: Anger's Privilege, by Gordon Braden. New Haven, Conn.: Yale University Press, 1985. Pp. xii + 260. $21.00.

Reviewer: MARION TROUSDALE

In a post-Saussurean world the received controversy as to whether or not Senecan plays decisively determined the shape of Renaissance drama could serve as a case study of an anachronistic view. G. K. Hunter put it succinctly in "Seneca and the Elizabethans: A Case-Study in 'Influence'," which appeared in *Shakespeare Survey* 20 in 1967 (pp. 17–26). "Once-upon-a-simple-time," Hunter noted at the beginning of that article, "while the modern languages were seeking to make their way as serious studies, the subject of "The Influence of Seneca on Elizabethan Tragedy" was quite self-evidently an example of what serious study could provide in modern literature. The scholar who set out to study an author ('B') learned that the scientific way of doing this was to discover, embedded in B, the echoes or reminiscences of an earlier author or work (which we may call 'A'). It was the business of the Ph.D. student, charged with the investigation of B, to discover his 'A'; then he could list the echoes and reminiscences, enlarge these into a discussion of 'influence'—and his dissertation was made." This was what John Cunliffe had done in 1893 in arguing for the importance of Seneca, *The Influence of Seneca on Elizabethan Tragedy* [London: Macmillan]. It was what Howard Baker did in turn in 1939 in *Induction to Tragedy* (Baton Rouge, La.: Louisiana State University Press), challenging Cunliffe's conclusions by finding Cunliffe's allegedly Senecan characteristics to be characteristic as well of the indigenous medieval *de casibus* tales.

We are left at this point in the controversy in a quantitative stalemate, with selective counting setting the score for each side. Gordon Braden short-circuits the alternating current by attempting to understand why the plays of an inferior Roman playwright might appeal to sixteenth-century readers. Any understanding of Senecan drama, he notes, depends upon "making explicable the workings and implications of furor as something other than an unaccountable upsurge of irrational savagery. Our perception of the value of first-century tragedy and epic, and of the intelligibility of their influence, depends on how much sense we can make of that central theme" (p. 28). He locates that appeal in the plays' privileging of anger and their encoding of a Stoic ethic. That furor he connects with the Greek *thymos*, the second part of the soul, in which pure ambition lies. This ambition in the Senecan context is deprived of its societal connections and becomes essentially a bid for power. The evil result of Medea's action "is neither denied nor regretted but welcomed and flaunted as the mark of success" (p. 47). The rhetoric that accompanies these heroes on stage is a rhetoric that creates, for Braden, a particular kind of selfhood. And it would seem to be this sense of selfhood, represented in part by the self-reflexive notions of Stoicism, that link such plays as *Oedipus* and *Hercules Furens* to *Tamburlaine* and *The Spanish Tragedy*. T. S. Eliot in "Shakespeare and the Stoicism of Seneca" (*Seneca, his Tenne Tragedies*, ed. T. Newton [New York: Knopf, 1927], p. ix), remarked: "Antony says, 'I am Antony still', and the Duchess [of Malfi] 'I am Duchess of Malfy still'; would either of them have said that unless Medea had said 'Medea superest'?" It is this essentially onimastic pointing, this space in which the individual as individual stands alone, that characterizes the Senecan hero for Braden and identifies the sensibility of Seneca with that of the sixteenth century. What Braden suggests is that the Senecan hero had about it a self-sufficiency that linked up with the sixteenth century's growing sense of individualism, flagged long ago by Burkhardt as the period's defining characteristic.

In this part of his argument Braden makes an interesting if problematic conceptual connection between the first century and the sixteenth, arguing that only a deep intellectual affinity can explain the later period's fascination with a writer who, from our own point of view, wrote plays that do not in any way measure up to the standards set by Sophocles or Euripides. Seneca's plays become, in Rosalie Colie's phrase, a set on life. The Elizabethans were attracted to Seneca, Braden's argument runs, because Seneca offered them a reading of human character that was already present in the ethos of the day. Literature, in this discussion of influence, is a way of reading life, and it is elements of a conceptual kind that link the sixteenth century with the first.

To see how problematic such questions of kind can be, one has only to compare Braden's reading of *The Spanish Tragedy* with Hunter's. Both use elements of kind to support the argument that they make; both arguments are persuasively presented so as to induce agreement; both, in short, seem judicious readings. If such is the case, one has to ask whether the idea of influence, let alone the idea of Senecan influence, can be regarded as an intellectually valid one. If two contradictory answers are possible and both are coherently argued, then the idea of kind itself, far from being evidential, must grow out of definitions that chameleon-like acquire the color of the context in which they occur. Hunter's discussion of Kyd appeared in Maynard Mack and George de Forest's *Poetic Traditions of the English Renaissance* (New Haven, Conn.: Yale University Press, 1982). *The Spanish Tragedy* he shows to be a play in which the medieval Christian heritage of a passive suffering Christ is overlaid with those other dramatically more viable characters on the medieval pageant wagons, the Herods and the Pilates, who, as Hunter notes, are dramatically more important and were recognized as such at the time. The actors of these Christian villains were paid more handsomely than the actor who played Christ. *The Spanish Tragedy* thus becomes generically placeable as "a martyr play without a tyrant," just as *Tamburlaine* would seem to be a tyrant play without a martyr. As Hunter remarks, "the religious martyr bears witness (martyria) to a truth that is only objectively valid for believers, only confirmed in the invisible world above. He can afford to be wholly passive in the compensating knowledge that God is active" (p. 93). Hieronimo is aware of the virtue of Christian patience. "Heaven will be revenged of every ill," he observes, after he claims vengeance to be his. "Then stay, Hieronimo, attend their will" (III.xii.1–5). But Hieronimo has too much of Herod in him to exhibit this kind of patience. God's vengeance, in Hunter's words, is too far away to be usable. Hieronimo rather plays the tyrant to his own despair.

The Spanish Tragedy for Braden, on the other hand, is the quintessential Senecan play. Having reviewed the strong statement against Senecan influence that Hunter had earlier made and noting that conscious and purposeful use of specific Senecan passages that he finds in *Bussy D'Ambois* to be "a somewhat exclusive affair," he observes that many of the general features that he has called Senecan can be found in the Herod of the Corpus Christi plays: "I am the greatest above degree / that is, or was, or ever shalbe," that Herod says; "the sonne yt dare not shine on me / and I byd him goe downe" (p. 179). Senecan influence can then be seen as "a development of or belated addition to this prior tradition." But he makes an additional point that "more than just the natural course of time separates later styles of declamatory violence from what the medieval stage has to offer" (p. 179). "Kyd brings England's unusually expansive version of Senecan selfhood into the crucial arena of revenge tragedy, where Renaissance drama forces that selfhood into its most intimate dealings with the lives around it" (p. 200). What Hunter sees as the development of two contradictory impulses within a continuing Christian tradition, Braden sees as a culture's response to a pagan mode of heroism.

Where then does this division of opinion leave us in our attempt to determine the nature of influence, and more particularly the nature of Senecan influence. One of Hunter's points in his earlier essay was that attributed influence, to be persuasive, has to be distinctive. It is not sufficient simply to find common characteristics if they are common to more than one kind. But Braden's discussion of Hunter's position shows that whether we attach Hieronimo to Seneca or to Herod we are looking at elements of kind. What is alike, as Braden suggests, is the medieval and the classical. If the Renaissance link with Seneca is a line that is made through kind, we are left, it would seem, in a muddle in which we still do not know how to account for the ways in which plays change in the middle of the sixteenth century. Seneca influences the native tradition because Seneca reflects the native tradition. How then in reflecting that tradition did Seneca effect its change?

No one can read Braden's discussion of Seneca without developing a new awareness and even a new respect for the long-winded and often tedious Roman playwright, and one almost has to agree with Braden that some kind of intellectual affinity is needed to explain the popularity across Europe of such an inferior dramatist.

At the same time the sixteenth century, as H. A. Mason pointed out long ago, often had bad taste in classical literature. And it seems obvious that Renaissance writers learned their craft from the writers whom they imitated in oblique and unpredictable ways. In a period in which imitation was consciously used as a mode of composition, influence is at once more diffuse and more pervasive than our conceptual tools are able to reveal. When I first wrote about imitation many years ago, I had become fascinated with a short treatise by Johann Sturm, published in a translation by Thomas Browne in 1570 as *A Ritch Storehouse or Treasurie for Nobilitye and Gentlemen* (*STC* 23408). Sturm instructs his students to keep three commonplace books as they read their way through the classical texts—one for things, one for words, and one for precepts of art. What particularly fascinated me at that time were the geometrical figures by means of which Sturm suggests that his students represent the ordering of the places they noted. It suggested to me a kind of atelier or even cook's kitchen with the trainees busily collecting all the supplies that they would need to have on hand in order to paint a useful portrait, assemble a tasty pie, write a Shakespearean play. At the best it seemed to suggest a highly developed professionalism, a kind of no-nonsense computer-approach to ancient texts, one designed to make it possible for apprentices in the shortest possible time to set up their own shops, create their own data banks. The model of sympathetic relation in this context seems less that of a son to his father, loyal but deviant, than that of an able car mechanic to a collection of spare parts. The model of Seneca was privileged but only for dismemberment, and what privilege does Seneca, when dismembered, retain? On the operating table, one might argue, especially when dismembered, all bodies look the same.

Such questions do not deny the possibility of influence, or even the possibility of its detection. When Hunter singles out the issue of distinction in kind, he is asking for the use of a part not commonly available in the shop. But in so doing he is noting not the nature of influence but the means of its proof. As with spare parts, so with Senecan and medieval characteristics it would seem to be those commonly available that are most likely to be in demand.

The exchange in Richard III's wooing of Anne requires that the words that echo between them be repeated so that the answer both uses and changes the sense of the language of the assault. To Anne's "He is in heaven," an accusation, Richard responds, "Let him thank me, that helped to send him thither," a use of the word heaven that draws upon the word's favorable sense in order to turn an act of murder into an act of deliverance. It is this verbal facility, a verbal facility characteristic of Seneca, that seems crucial to Braden. It seems crucial to me in other ways, for I think that the means by which Richard converts Anne's accusations into praises is symptomatic of the ways in which one author uses another, symptomatic of the existence in a verbal structure of semantic fields and of the ways in which we all draw upon those fields to make particular, individual use of the discursive conventions we hold in common. It is symptomatic of the ways in which we use something received to create something new, turning Saussure's *langue* into a commonly understood but still particular *parole*. Influence as we imagine it perhaps puts the emphasis in the wrong place. It is not the model in the sense of source that is decisive. It is the awareness of the maker who assembles his own particular collection of parts in order to make his own model. No one interested in Renaissance drama will want to miss reading this book, and no one who reads it will fail to learn from it. But there remains another book still to be written, one concerned not with kind as relation but with kind as difference. To imitate is to transform. If it is kind that attracted the Elizabethans to Seneca, then we must recognize the importance of Sturm's instructions, which anticipate the insights of Saussure. Sturm's manual on imitation marks out a paradigm of influence different from the one found here. To be similar is to be different. It is not to be the same.

Carnival and Theater: Plebeian Culture and the Structure of Authority in Renaissance England, by Michael D. Bristol. New York and London: Methuen, 1985. Pp. x + 237. $27.50.

Reviewer: THOMAS CARTELLI

For a work that is so far-reaching in its aims and so successful in realizing them, *Carnival and Theater* is a remarkably modest book. Eschewing entirely the self-promoting rhetoric and wilful obscurantism of much recent criticism, Michael Bristol has constructed a virtually seamless study of theater from the bottom up that should make a profound difference in the way that we read the works of Shakespeare and his contemporaries.

What most distinguishes Bristol's work from other recent attempts to bring contemporary literary theory to bear on Renaissance texts is his ability to join theory to practice and make the texts in question seem to speak for themselves in the series of illuminating applications that he provides. Bristol's success on this front is largely negotiated by his book's strong first movement where his theoretical perspective is presented with a conciseness that belies its scope and range of reference. Starting from the premise that theater is as much a "social institution" as it is "an art form," Bristol sets out to redefine the nature of the Elizabethan theater's relationship "to the social structure as a whole." Bristol finds the Elizabethan theater "situated quite ambiguously in relation to the established categories and fully legitimated functions of the formally constituted social order" (p. 8) and thus opposes himself to the idea that Elizabethan theater and society existed in a state of cultural unanimity characterized by mutually reinforcing values and assumptions. He considers the "old historicism" of E.M.W. Tillyard and Norman Rabkin's focus on "complementarity" and a "common understanding" equally committed to a "fundamentally reassuring and harmonious" view of "the social activity of theater" (p. 12), one that attempts to reconcile and thereby marginalize conflict and contradiction:

> Both Tillyard and Rabkin ignore the purposeful and limited character of traditions of everyday life and social observance that give rise to and are the precondition of any individual act of creativity. They also disregard one social group's expropriation of the forms created by another. Elizabethan drama was not created by and for 'Elizabethans' in general: both institutions and specific texts were created by well-defined communities with economic and political interests to advance, and with a great many internal conflicts about the form and purpose of their own art. Plays were performed in a variety of settings, sometimes with a homogeneous audience, sometimes in a more diversified and heterogeneous setting. And in any period a radically unbalanced view may take precedence over broader conceptions sanctioned by orthodoxy and consensus. All this suggests that historical reconstruction of 'the old works' must place struggle, social difference and cultural antagonism at the center of critical analysis, rather than consensus, harmony and accommodation.
> (p. 13)

Bristol's attempt here to displace "the reconciliatory strategy of conventional literary scholarship" (p. 13) with one that thrives on opposition will be familiar to anyone conversant with the interpretive procedures of most varieties of post-structuralist criticism. But in the pages that follow, he subjects some of the very same procedures to sustained scrutiny in setting out a critical agenda that is very much his own and that attempts to ground oppositional poetics in historically specific contexts.

Bristol specifically takes issue with the "revisionist strategies" of Stephen Greenblatt and Jonathan Dollimore in an otherwise sympathetic critique of their work. Consistent with his prevailing commitment to a broadly social approach to Renaissance cultural practices, Bristol considers Greenblatt's "tendency to confuse the wishful thinking of powerful people with an objective description of social reality" (p. 15) and Dollimore's "decision to make a case for a 'radical tragedy' by treating it primarily as a question of intellectual history" (p. 19) symptomatic of some of the same assumptions that prevail in "traditional scholarship" where "authority is divided or allocated between established power and the exceptional subject" (p. 19). In each instance, "the vitality, the continuity, the relative stability and abundance of popular culture" is either ignored or simply reestablished at the level of subplot (p. 19). It is at this point in his argument that Bristol openly declares his alliance with "the sociological poetics of Mikhail Bakhtin" and with Bakhtin's conception of Carnival which he proposes to elaborate in "a more detailed and circumstantial account of the relationship between popular culture, theater and dramatic literature in Elizabethan England" (pp. 19, 24).

One of Bristol's primary problems here is how to take "more literally" what in Bakhtin is a "system of images and transgressive rhetorical devices" and "to view Carnival as a concrete social reality in the context of early modern Europe" (p. 25). This is not a problem that Bristol completely resolves. In attempting to apply the findings and techniques of the *Annales* school of history to the contexts and conditions of Elizabethan England, Bristol sometimes implicitly asks that Carnival manifestations in early modern France be taken as indications of what transpired across the Channel. And his generally illuminating efforts to contrast or substantiate Bakhtin's theory of carnival with the insights and observations of Durkheim, Roger Caillois, and Victor Turner regarding the rituals and conventions of communal life occasionally return us to a level of abstraction that Bristol presumably seeks to avoid. Indeed, there are moments when Bristol addresses Carnival as if it were a self-generating phenomenon or the sum total of all its particular manifestations and thus susceptible to classification in terms of a set of definite, unchanging components and characteristics.

Bristol's problems are compounded by what he terms "the basic difficulty of access" (p. 44) to the presumably hidden life of popular culture within which Carnival thrived. He resolves this particular problem by observing that "the subordinate classes" of early modern Europe were not rendered "mute, unreadable and powerless" through subordination and by making a convincing case for the resilience and pervasiveness of their values and institutions:

Instead of an inference that popular culture cannot be observed anywhere, it seems more useful to assert that popular culture existed everywhere, though never in a 'pure' and uncontaminated form. The hypothesis of a dominant culture effectively secured from intrusions of the popular element and capable of administering the culture of the subordinate classes must be discarded in favor of a picture of a numerically small elite absolutely surrounded by a veritable demographic and cultural ocean of the 'inferior sort'. Popular culture is thus not hidden from view; virtually everything that survives is likely to contain some traces of its impact or to reveal a deflection from its enormous mass.

(pp. 45–46)

And he resolves some of his definitional difficulties when he comes to consider Carnival as "an idiom of social experimentation, in which utopian fantasies are performed and collective desires for a better life are expressed" (p. 52) and applies himself to a sustained study of "the texts of Carnival" that tells us more about what Carnival *does* in the domain of literary practice than what it *is* in the abstract. "These texts of Carnival," as Bristol writes, "situate themselves exactly at the frontier between elite and popular culture, the zone where reciprocal pressure, contamination, and the diversity of speech types and discursive genres is greatest" (p. 58). Although only roughly half of the texts in question are play-texts, Bristol's "carnivalized" readings of such works as Nashe's *Lenten Stuffe* reveal the extent to which all the texts of Carnival share the same "radical potentiality" that Bristol specifically associates with the "space" of the theater.

Bristol is especially successful at drawing revealing connections between "the late sixteenth-century polemic against the stage" and more modern attempts to marginalize the contribution of popular culture to Elizabethan play-texts (p. 113). Bristol sees the gradual institutionalization of the theater as a direct response to "a situation of maximum intellectual and affective openness, but minimum accountability" (p. 117) that obtained in the period prior to "the professionalization of writing for the stage" (1590–1610—p. 113). For example, he views Ben Jonson's advocacy "for this program of legitimation" as proceeding "from the same critique of popular culture, and from the same anxiety and resentment over the dispersion of authority in the intensified public life of the playhouses" that informed Phillip Stubbes's *Anatomie of Abuses* (p. 117). Jonson's "dramatic expulsion of the 'stage-keeper'" in his Induction to *Bartholomew Fair* "objectifies the displacement of a popular, improvisatory and extra-official participatory tradition by a legally sanctioned sequence of creation, transmission and 'purchase' of a finished literary product" (p. 119). One modern consequence of this achieved process of legitimation is how difficult it has become "to appreciate the priority of a heteroglot theater, its capacity to arouse genuine political anxiety, and its impact on social discipline and the structure of authority" (p. 123).

It is Bristol's ability to rearouse our own capacity to recover what has been lost in the process of the theater's appropriation by official culture that may in the end be the enduring achievement of this book. As the book proceeds, Bristol's arguments become so persuasive that the reader begins to appreciate the extent to which Bristol's methodology can be applied to Renaissance texts that have long been identified with the values of official culture. One of the more impressive acts of recovery that Bristol contributes in his series of applications involves bringing the conventionally marginalized Graveyard scene in *Hamlet* into dramatic focus as an unsettling representation of the organization of "secular authority" (pp. 188–193). That Bristol chooses to supplement his commentary on *Hamlet* with an equally adept discussion of Dekker's *The Wonderful Year*, a pamphlet with strong roots in popular culture, demonstrates the consistency of his broadly intertextual approach to Renaissance cultural practices. The only real disparity between theory and practice in *Carnival and Theater* is the authority that the book itself achieves in making so strong a case for Carnival as "a comprehensive 'art and science' of social and collective life" and for the Carnivalesque's "resistance to any tendency to absolutize authority" (p. 213).

Drama of a Nation: Public Theater in Renaissance England and Spain, by Walter Cohen. Ithaca, N. Y.: Cornell University Press, 1985. Pp. 416. $35.00.

Reviewer: JONATHAN DOLLIMORE

It is good to read a book with a substantial historical thesis, by an author with the intellectual integrity and confidence to state it clearly:

> The entire study pursues a single and simple hypothesis: that the absolutist state, by its inherent dynamism and contradictions, first fostered and then undermined the public theater. More precisely, the similarities between Spanish and English absolutism help account for the parallels between the two dramatic traditions, while the divergent courses of economic and religious development in England and Spain begin to explain the differences.
>
> (pp. 19–20)

There is no spurious complexity here, no obscurantism passing itself off as profundity. But if Cohen's language and argument are accessible, his perspective is by no means simplistic. He explores a process that is at once evolutionary and revolutionary, marked by contradiction and uneven development. His framework is eclectically Marxist, deriving from a spectrum of contemporary Marxist historiography and cultural theory.

On these grounds alone this book should be compulsory reading for those literary critics, humanist and otherwise, who legitimate their own political bad faith by castigating the allegedly reductive premises of that paradigm of political commitment, Marxism. This book is one of many which currently indicate that contemporary Marxist criticism has as complex and dynamic a relation to the writings of Marx as does contemporary psychoanalysis to Freud, or contemporary Christianity to the old and new testaments. Complexity and dynamism are usually allowed in the case of Christianity, sometimes in the case of psychoanalysis, rarely in the case of Marxism. Perhaps this distribution says something about differing abilities to challenge. (But once again we must allow for uneven development: in the United Kingdom at present the up-and-coming radical party is the Church of England.)

Cohen's book certainly challenges. Be warned: its even tones will disarm the unwary, and readers of quite different kinds may well find themselves assenting to arguments that undercut the premises of their own critical positions. It should be recommended to students with all the caution towards new thinking that the best literary critics have traditionally shown in such matters. Cohen's Marxism, avowed on the opening page—his historical project requires, he says, "a broad perspective, . . . [one] coherently available, in my opinion, only in the assumptions, theories, methods, and commitments of Marxism" (p. 9)—raises, I suppose, the specter of determinism; that is, the one-way determination of the superstructure by the material base. Cohen's study avoids this reduction, as indeed do the various marxisms on which his study draws.

Here is a rough summary of his position: although the public theater was primarily shaped by the structure of society, one cannot deduce the nature of the public theater simply from the salient historical movements of the age: "no significant area of social life can be reduced to a simple projection of other, more basic areas. . . . The theater was influenced by a multiplicity of forces, upon which it in turn reacted; . . . it had a history of its own, with its own logic and temporality" (p. 150). Even at the local, internal level "the theater's economic, social, political, and ideological heterogeneity precludes simple categorization" (p. 151). So an interpretation that seeks to avoid one-sidedness must confront the fact of the theater's social complexity; at the same time if it is to avoid mere description, it must attempt a theoretical synthesis.

But acknowledgment of the theater's own complexity and specificity does not then sanction the doleful convention of producing interminable close readings of texts. Alas, we live in an age too much concerned with the anatomy of the particular, be it text or individual psyche. We cannot believe this modern tendency to be healthy. On this we are with Sir Mungo MacCallum. There are some today who cannot address *Hamlet* in anything less than a (very long) chapter or, worse still, a whole book. Faced with this modern tendency, the fast-forward button is nothing less than a postmodern godsend, at least where the audio/visual magnetic tape is concerned. With practical criticism, however, we still have to rely on the traditional though rarely confessed strategies of speedreading or just not bothering.

Cohen's coverage of *Hamlet* requires neither. The play gets a couple of pages in Chapter Six and is mentioned elswhere in passing. Now that Francis Barker has demonstrated so astutely that "at the centre of Hamlet, in the interior of his mystery, there is, in short, nothing" (*The Tremulous Private Body: Essays on Subjection* [London: Methuen, 1984], p. 37), it should not be possible for anyone ever again to write a book about Hamlet or even *Hamlet*. The context in which Cohen's discussion of *Hamlet* occurs is fascinating: he relates the unique similarities between English and Spanish drama of the late sixteenth century and early seventeenth century to the simultaneous but independent fusion of popular and learned dramatic traditions in each country, a fusion that itself depended on the development of the absolutist state. The scope of his argument here is wide-ranging. Chapter Two, for example, not only addresses the theaters of Spain and England but also includes a comparative study of Eastern Europe, the western periphery, Italy, and France.

Cohen further contends that the theater is a contradictory but fundamentally artisanal institution; that in the late sixteenth century members of the bourgeoisie influenced the theater less as ideologues or politicians than as capitalists. He develops, and applies to the theater, some basic Marxist theories of labor, surplus labor, and modes of production (production as in "capitalist" rather than "theatrical"); his conclusion is in fact that the theater's mode of production was an "artisanally dominated, composite" one (p. 182). Here again we encounter the necessary complexity of Cohen's perspective. The public theaters constituted part of both the base and the superstructure, their function in one conflicting with their role in the other; aristocratic messages of plays could be, and were, subverted by their artisanal substructure or mode of production.

For a play like Marlowe's *Edward II* this approach is persuasive. The barons' opposition to Gaveston is seen in relation to the fact that, "throughout western Europe, royal centralization required the partial exclusion of the titular nobility from political power and its replacement by men of humbler station" more completely dependent upon monarchical good will (p. 232). So the hostility of the nobles towards Gaveston is more than "class condescension"; it is symptomatic of a "fundamental feudal attack on the formation of the absolutist state" (p. 233). One might add that it is indeed the cross-class rather than the homosexual nature of the Edward–Gaveston relationship that is so threatening. But, for various complex reasons, homosexuality has helped produce such alliances where they might not otherwise have existed, and it is this fact that helps explain why, in such cases, class antagonism is often displaced into or bound up with homophobic antagonism. If Marlowe's representation of homosexuality in *Edward II* is at all "enlightened," it is because he refuses that displacement.

Cohen's exploration of the relationship of the aristocacy to the theater is consistently revealing. He sees romantic comedy as rendering the successful adaptation of the nobility to social change, while satiric comedy dramatizes that class's failure to adapt; plays like Chapman's *The Widow's Tears* and Beaumont's *The Knight of the Burning Pestle* are rooted in a simultaneous aristocratic desire to exclude the citizen classes from the national polity and a fear that the opposite might actually be occurring—hence perhaps the frequently noticed moral instability of these plays.

In Spain the relative absence of a conflict between the modes of production reduced the ideological space for tragedy, and in contrast to England, the national history play continued long after the turn of the century. Even so, there occurred in Spain after 1600 a significant break with earlier serious drama:

> The Spanish equivalent to Shakespearean tragedy took the form of a symptomatic moral belt tightening, an aggressive effort to cope with the unfamiliar experience of defeat, an extreme reconsolidation of aristocratic ideology, a reassertion of the values that had accompanied earlier success, and hence a return to the past for a stylized and exaggerated code of honor.
>
> (pp. 311–312)

It is Spanish peasant drama that bears comparison with Shakespearean drama; the peasant plays offer a conflict between what is affirmed at the end (integration) and what is shown throughout (revolution). Cohen sees Lope de Vega's *Fuente Ovejuna* as a clear instance of this paradigm—the extreme toward which other peasant plays tend. Lower-class insurgency is powerfully and sympathetically represented, though finally that class is voluntarily reintegrated into monarchical rule. Likewise Shakespeare's tragedies portray violent upheaval ending either without a resolution or with a resolution that violates the logic of, and so is inadequate to, events. The illustrative case here is *King Lear*. Whereas the rebellion of Lope's peasants never reaches a full revolutionary consciousness or ideological rationale, Shakespeare's outcasts and lower-class characters articulate a thorough critique of hierarchy without discovering a political vehicle for their beliefs. The formal resolution in both the peasant plays and Shakespeare's is "the full dramatic realization of the inherent contradiction between artisanal base and absolutist superstructure in the public theater"(p. 322).

There are some things that Cohen does not explore in depth. I have in mind especially the interrelated issues of gender and desire. Of course Cohen does not ignore these, and I am not suggesting that they necessarily take priority over a class analysis. But I would like to see Cohen explore them further, and within the parameters established by this study, not least because the cultural formations of gender and desire may, like class formations, be given a materialist analysis. For example, several of the dramatists whom Cohen discusses articulate the powerful if confusing determinations upon gender and desire of urban and court existence, and of nascent capitalism. In certain plays we witness conflicts that are inextricably related to those between classes and within the individual psyche, though not of course coextensive with either.

Take the case of *Volpone*. Judicious as ever, Cohen remarks that "Volpone's and Mosca's commitment to wit, play, and the imagination can be overstated—Mosca, after all, proves in the end to be simply a young man on the make—[but] the tricksters' economic practices acquire at least a specious philosophical depth by recourse to a perverted classicism" (p. 294). This formulation seems, almost, to make the point while missing it. With Mosca and Volpone overstatement and excess are of their essence, an essence that, given its tendency to centrifugal disintegration rather than originating stasis, is no essence at all. Critics have of course noted the paradox: these two are degenerate yet vital. They are indeed perverted, though not necessarily in either the usual moral or the sexual sense of the term. (Actually though, thinking about it, one might also identify Volpone as a sadist and a fetishist; so perhaps the Freudian/sexual sense of the word *perverted* is appropriate.) But the history of the word *prior* to its use in the nineteenth century by the sexologists and then Freud, conveys something important about Mosca and Volpone and the social process that they articulate. It implies, for example, a deviation from a trajectory that not only halts progress towards an appropriate goal but also somehow goes against that goal. At the same time it refers to a deviation made possible by, and existing only because of, that goal. Yet this deviation is also an opposition to the goal that made it possible. Hence perhaps the slippage in the *OED* definition of perversion from "divergence" to "evil."

This kind of contradiction was generated in nascent as well as advanced capitalism. It figures in Jonson's plays, and also in Marlowe's, of which Cohen remarks: "the price of his radical inquiries was thus a form that risked incoherence and an ideology that bordered on nihilism" (p. 236). Marlowe's "radical inquiries" focused on contradictions that were, I think, more dynamic (and perverse) than Cohen allows.

We have learned recently of the way that power can create subversion in order to contain it and so perpetuate itself. But it is also true that these same strategies of social control can generate internal contradictions that become the site of resistance, the place where the subordinate contests the dominant. The trouble is, some pretty weird people turn up in such places, including, in the early seventeenth century, disaffected class fractions, melancholics, roaring girls, and malcontents.

The urban spaces that harbor such people are also the places where subcultures form. To be sure, these cultures are never independent of the dominant culture and its struggles, and the inner contradictions of the subcultures are one measure of just that fact. But they also become one place where alternative voices are heard—voices that are carried over into the theater and there offer certain kinds of oppositional commentary, including some that have fascinated critics: the comic and the carnivalesque, for example. One does not necessarily have to celebrate or sentimentalize these cultures and voices in order to understand that they disclose much about the very social processes that now occlude, now foreground, now demonize them. Most importantly perhaps, these people do not constitute a class, but what they say can constitute a kind of challenging political knowledge.

Stuart Hall and others have shown how Marx's and Engels's categories of class led them to classify the *lumpenproletariat* as at best irrelevant to historical struggle and at worst a dangerous hindrance. Cohen is neither punitive towards nor dismissive of those who do not align. But sometimes his generalizations and categories of classification are so broad or brief as to obscure the significance of subordinate voices and cultures that occur in the drama and that are socially significant even though they are not aligned with the larger class antagonisms. I thought this especially so in his discussion of satiric intrigue tragedy. It "specialized," he says, "in destruction" and was mainly reactionary even though "it helped remove the remaining ideological justifications of absolutism, to clear away the detritus of a disintegrating social system" (p. 370). Destruction, yes, but also, to risk anachronism, deconstruction; not just a demolition job but a turning of order against itself, a magnifying of contradictions within it to the extent that they prove internally stultifying; not just a negation but a demystification and delegitimation of ideological imperatives. Cohen cites Moretti as an advocate of the destructive view. But Moretti would also, I think, want to go further. He argues, after all, that Elizabethan and Jacobean tragedy constitute a spectacular exception to his general theory of literature itelf as a form of ideological legitimation—in effect, a form of containment (*Signs Taken for Wonders* [London: Verso, 1983]). It is a messy business to be sure. Attempts at delegitimation that are effective to any degree often produce violent reactions. In Althusser's formulation, repressive state apparatuses move in when ideological ones fail. But it is also at a certain level how history moves, and one that Cohen's large-scale overview of historical change can miss.

Other generalizations also say at once too much and too little:

> *Dr. Faustus* derives its power precisely from its dramatization of the conflict between Renaissance and Reformation. The resolution of the plot reveals that religion has more power than humanism. The ideological outcome, on the other hand, leaves something of a stalemate. Individualist aspiration, however attractive, leads to damnation. Protestant conventionality, by contrast, offers safety at the price of vitality. At once humanist tragedy and morality play, *Dr. Faustus* is in essence neither.
>
> (p. 378)

But if, as Cohen goes on to remark, "*Faustus* is at once the last important English morality play and one of the founding works of Elizabethan tragedy," the contradictions within it and the culture that produced it (and that it reproduced) must have been more dynamic than "the overwhelming sense of paralysis" that Cohen finds in the play would suggest (p. 378).

My sense of what Cohen might do additionally is mostly compatible with what he is already doing here so successfully. And I want to add—especially given the way some influential older (and not so old) critics have made it their task to police politically motivated criticism—some of Cohen's speculative generalizations are brave. He earns respect here as a writer *and* intellectual who takes speculative risks and remains undefensive in the process; he suggests, for example, that the utopian dimension of romance drama may help explain its relative depreciation in dramatic theory, adding:

Marxism has always wagered that in the long run human history would have, or at least could have, the structure of romance. Precisely in its utopianism, then, romance may offer a legitimate vision not of the prehistory lived in class society, but of that *authentic* history that may someday succeed it.

(p. 391; italics mine)

Cohen also quotes Jauss's comment to the effect that literature "'not only preserves actual experiences but also anticipates unrealized possibility'" and makes possible "'new desires, . . . and thereby opens paths to future experience'" (p. 346). Such future experience is inseparable from certain cultural differences and different kinds of knowledge, both of which may exist in partial, alarming and even *inauthentic* forms within existing history.

This is an important book. No one can fail to learn from it. I think it will be around for a long time.

Cumberland, Westmorland, and Gloucestershire, edited by Audrey Douglas and Peter Greenfield. *Records of Early English Drama*. Toronto: University of Toronto Press, 1986. Pp. xi + 547. $85.00.

Reviewer: CLIFFORD DAVIDSON

This volume in the Records of Early English Drama (REED) series includes the records of two northern counties, Cumberland and Westmorland, edited by Audrey Douglas, and of the West Country county of Gloucester (excluding Bristol, a separate county from 1373), edited by Peter Greenfield. These counties possess no major cities of the stature of, for example, Chester, York, or Coventry; hence this book differs considerably from previous REED volumes, which focused on municipalities where there were important theatrical texts or records. It is, however, a rewarding collection that does in fact help us to understand the drama of provincial and less well-known areas of the country prior to 1642.

The largest urban center to be covered in this volume is, of course, Gloucester, for which there was reported a miracle play on the topic of St. Nicholas staged by clerks in 1283–84 (p. 290). All that is known without question about this saint play is that those who performed it along with the boy bishop that year were given 26s. 8d. by the King, Edward I; nevertheless, this record, like other records from the medieval period that point out the popularity of the saint play, helps to illustrate the ubiquity of the genre. Greenfield speculates that the clerics could have been Augustinian canons from nearby Llanthony Priory, since *clericis* would not have been a term properly applied to Benedictine monks (p. 422). The play would almost certainly have been performed on the feast of St. Nicholas, as Greenfield notes, though we do not know enough about the Gloucester St. Nicholas play to suggest similarity to the extant medieval St. Nicholas plays, four of which appear (with musical notation) in the famous Fleury Playbook.

A little more than half a century after the Gloucester St. Nicholas play some other clerks presented a play (*ludum*) in the market place at Carlisle (pp. 63–64). This play was also a miracle play (*miraculum*). The date of the Carlyle production, in late June, coincides with the high season for such drama in the later Middle Ages. Presentation on the vigil of a major saint's day may further suggest that this drama too was devoted to the miracles (and perhaps martyrdom) of a saint. However, its outdoor production would most likely have distinguished the drama from the St. Nicholas play at Gloucester, where the play was probably staged indoors, perhaps in St. Peter's Abbey (p. 422).

After the Reformation Gloucester was the site of a production by visiting players of the *Cradle of Security*, a morality seen by R. Willis in his childhood (*ca.* 1570–79) and described late in his life in *Mount Tabor, or Private Exercises of a Penitent Sinner* (1639). The relevant passage from the latter work—a passage well known from the time when it was first noted by Malone—is presented here as an appendix. As Robert Potter has indicated, Willis's "recollection . . . emphasizes, not the crudeness, but the *impressiveness* of the play" (*The English Morality Play* [London: Routledge & Kegan Paul, 1975], p. 210). Willis's text, with the explanation that the *Cradle of Security* was a "Mayors play" designed to test the actors' skill and repertoire before they were given license to stage further dramas in the municipality, also corroborates the suggestion that the moralities were often plays presented to impress the authorities. As the previously published REED volumes demonstrate, there is little record of the actual playing of moralities. Interestingly, the *Cradle of Security* shares a conclusion with plays like Wager's *Enough is as Good as a Feast*, where the protagonist also ends badly—a conclusion that, because of its stern moral stance, may have been designed to counteract the anti-theatrical prejudice in an age of hostility to the stage and other kinds of entertainment. It is a hostility well documented in this volume.

For productions of medieval drama by local actors, however, Kendal in Westmorland would seem to have been more important than either Carlyle or Gloucester. Here a Corpus Christi play is recorded from the time of the incorporation of the municipality in 1575–76 (though the play was almost certainly much older) into the early years of the seventeenth century. While we have no text or description of the segments staged in this "play," in its own day it was famous enough, along with the local Kendal fair, to receive mention by Thomas Heywood in his *Apology for Actors* (1612). A play performed on a stationary stage rather than on wagons, it apparently was based on the Scriptures, and, if we can believe John Shaw's account of the old man who knew about "Salvation by Iesus" only through his memory of the Corpus Christi play of this town, it included the Crucifixion (p. 219). Its suppression, perhaps at a time when it was the last remaining Corpus Christi play in England, was probably due to what was perceived to be its Catholic content; John Weever insisted in 1631 that this play and others like it were "finally" put down "vpon good reasons" (*Ancient Funerall Monuments*, p. 405).

Like the previous REED volumes, this book attempts to be as inclusive as possible in the presentation of records, since plays merge into games and ceremonies that sometimes are noted in the documents by similar (and hence confusing) terminology. However, here as in the earlier REED volumes there has been a conscious attempt to avoid records that note liturgical practices, including those Holy Week and Easter ceremonies that are of immense interest to students of drama. It is nevertheless clear that liturgy, civic music, and drama have many points of contact and that it may be unwise and in fact impossible to separate one function from another. For example, the REED editor includes Cathedral Treasurers' Accounts dated 1633-34 that record the appearance of the waits at Gloucester Cathedral where they played "in the Quire" (p. 324). And a few years earlier the same accounts mention payment "To A poore Singingman at the intreaty of the Quiremen" (p. 322)—a singer whose principal job had unquestionably been liturgical rather than civic or theatrical, though he may have also been involved with both these other functions.

Unfortunately, therefore, records of the most important piece of property (if we may call it that) in the Holy Week and Easter ceremonies and music-dramas of the Middle Ages—that is, the Easter Sepulchre—are not included, though in describing his "principles of selection" Greenfield admits that he has observed notices documenting this item in churches in Minchinhampton and Gloucester (p. 273). It is not true in the case of Minchinhampton that the churchwardens' accounts of that parish record only "sepulchre watchings," since we know from John Bruce's transcriptions that there is also reference to sepulchre *making* in that municipality (*Archaeologia*, 35 [1853], 409-452). Fortunately the references to the Easter Sepulchre in Bruce's transcriptions of the accounts are reprinted in Pamela Sheingorn's *The Easter Sepulchre in England* (Kalamazoo, Mich.: Medieval Institute Publications, 1987), but the accounts, noting the Sepulchre in Gloucester, to the best of my knowlege, remain unpublished. The description of the Easter Sepulchre at St. Mary Redcliffe, Bristol (*EDAM Newsletter*, 5, No. 1 [Fall 1982], 10-12) provides convincing evidence for the need to give attention to other Sepulchres in this region and indeed elsewhere in England. Certainly records of Easter Sepulchres are at least as important as the references to football games on Shrove Tuesday at Carlisle.

The volume is meticulously edited, as one would expect in the instance of a REED publication. Two lapses may nevertheless be noted: (1) in the section for Gloucester Diocese, the visitation articles of Bishop John Hooper for 1551-52 are not included, though these are noted as mentioning "plays" in Ian Lancashire's *Dramatic Texts and Records of Britain: A Chronological Topography to 1558* [Toronto: University of Toronto Press, 1984], no. 687); (2) the author of *Bloody Mary* (1978) is Carolly (not Carolyn) Erickson (p. 423). But these are small blemishes in an otherwise exemplary volume.

Signifying Nothing: Truth's True Contents in Shakespeare's Text, by Malcolm Evans. Athens, Ga.: University of Georgia Press, 1986. Pp. x + 291. $25.00.

Reviewer: CHARLES H. FREY

This piece of frustrated fustian from the English educational far left adds little to by-now old accents of Terence Hawkes, Peter Widdowson, Derek Longhurst, Jonathan Dollimore, Terry Eagleton, Alan Sinfield, John Drakakis, and a host of brick-reducationists who would have Shakespeare and the culture that he comes from signify "nothing." Nothing but authoritarian oppression paradoxically controlling what should have been a Saussurean free play of signifiers. Nothing but politics invading our dreams. Nothing but freedom, spontaneity, and mystery denied. Evans testily tries for interminable pages to deconstruct the paradox, but he never can jettison, finally, his suspicion that Shakespeare, or, as he endlessly puts it, "the text" has a repressive Will of its own:

> the Shakespearean text itself re-presents writing as a 'dead letter' cut off from the 'spirit' or full presence of speech;
>
> (pp. 148–149)

> the text's refusal [*sic*] to allow dramatic representations, including 'characters', to be fixed, permanent, irrevocable;
>
> (p. 167)

> the text's own ideological raw materials;
>
> (p. 211)

> In the classic mode of carnival festivity, recapitulated in deconstruction, Shakespeare's text recovers the supplement from its secondary status, an act which confounds plenitude with heterogeneity;
>
> (p. 213)

> As ever the text is affirming nothing—yielding no more than a dream—and if its shadows offend, it can still hold up the disclaimer of being only a "Fairy toye", albeit one of considerable sophistication.
>
> (p. 223)

And so on. How strange it sounds, when one thinks about it, to provide all that animating force to a "text" that is forever said to be at once nonaffirming and at the same time filled with presentation, refusal, ideology, recovery, action, confoundment, offense, and sophistication. What Evans means, I think, is for the text not to affirm what others have said that it affirms but to affirm instead what he would have it affirm. Evans's book amounts to one long "Not you, but me!" Many books do this sort of thing, of course, but few so evasively as this one.

As an image of a properly despairing educator who could hardly bear to indoctrinate students in colonialist Honduras, one "Edward Harrison" is summoned up by Evans to expose the imperialist tendencies of *The Tempest* and of the establishment that has heralded its oppressive beauty and truth. This exposé dominates the first third of the book in successive chapters devoted to (1) Harrison's mission to arm Caliban against Prospero, (2) "*The Tempest*'s ideological 'unconscious'" (p. 49) as it incorporates "Christian communism" and radical utopianism, (3) the inadequacies of high academic readings of *The Tempest*.

For Evans's purposes, it is *almost* irrelevant that he feels constrained to admit (in a footnote): "The authenticity of the Harrison journal is in considerable doubt. I would ascribe to it here no more authority or truth than if it were, in fact, only a work of literary fiction" (p. 38). Evans never confronts the question of what may make one fiction more persuasive than another (or less persuasive than "non-fiction"), a question that might encourage him to reassess his dogmatic anti-empiricism. For, if Harrison's journal is a put-up job, a modern concoction by leftist academics to imagine forth the desirable guilt of British empire-builders, then Evans's readers would want to know that, and, I think, they should be informed. For our purposes, it does matter very much just what *order* of "fiction" we are dealing with, just as for our purposes it matters whether the holocaust really happened or not.

Evans argues that *Macbeth* as a play signifies nothing in the "paradoxically positive sense" of attacking the "unequivocal discourse of a metaphysically sanctioned absolutism" (p. 177), and he ascribes a similar function to a deconstructive *Hamlet*, "being as much 'about' its own linguistic and theatrical signifiers as anything else" (p. 130). In Evans's hands, "*As You Like It* begins to take on the character of the 'galaxy of signifiers' envisaged by Roland Barthes, where senses divide and multiply" (p. 154) and where images of gender and authority are undermined along with traditional "essentialist" interpretations (including, for Evans, most feminist ones).

Evans does admit, finally, to some impatience with the more extreme claims of deconstructionites that texts admit of illimitable and "unfounded" play (p. 209). Despite his insistence that Shakespeare's texts signify essentially nothing in themselves, Evans ends up castigating *A Midsummer Night's Dream* because "*the play* also suspends the contradiction between the patriarchal trade in young women carried out under auspices of the family and the spontaneous integrity of a unique and individual 'love', which Swift in 1723 could still describe as 'a ridiculous passion which hath no being but in plays and romances'" (p. 223, italics mine). And Evans attacks *King Lear* on similar grounds of avoiding true contradiction: "if traces of a popular utopianism are reproduced in the pleas of Lear and Gloucester for 'distribution', they are heavily policed by an Elizabethan discourse on Christian charity, which has less to do with turning the social order on its head than with confirming its inequalities by alleviating the symptoms that pose the greatest internal threat to the dominant religious ideology" (p. 230). So much for charity! Through these sorts of breezy Shakespeare-bashings, Evans in no way avoids the temptation he decries in others, the temptation to "interpret" by allegedly pointing to what is *really* out there, in the "text," in the "play."

One may heartily approve of Evans's politics, as I for the most part do (though I find his sociogrammatic structures, positing an elite that indoctrinates the masses, crude and outmoded, far superseded by the more complex and up-to-date paradigms of contested class identities outlined by Stallybrass, White, and others); still, one may feel compelled to question the value of Evans's book as a book to teach us about Shakespeare. It purports to be "an introduction aimed primarily at students" (p. 8), but it assumes a knowledge of semiotics, deconstruction, feminist criticism, marxist criticism, English social and political history, and pedagogical history far beyond the range of undergraduates and most graduate students. The book is written moreover in a fuzzy, sloppy, in-groupy, mixed-metaphoric style that thumbs its nose at careful thought:

> The most enhanced critical awareness in the text seem [*sic*] in fact to be those of the representatives of organized labour who recognize more enduring divisions of interest and relations of exploitation beneath the homogeneity of this construction of the nation and its culture.
> (p. 93)

> there is an inescapable undertow of negation, in which the hurly-burly of language which precedes the construction of these sealed hierarchical categories leaks back to interrupt the 'natural' quality their linguistic mode silently claims for itself.
> (p. 114)

> Like the 'nothing' of *Macbeth*, Hamlet's 'imperfect speaking' is, as Ophelia points out, 'naught', but its strategic hurly-burly points to the finite, fictive quality of all discursive constuctions [*sic*].
> (p. 127)

It is hard for me to see how Evans hopes to improve upon liberal interpretations of Shakespeare when he reduces the plays to dry exercises in communication theory: "So *Hamlet*, like *Macbeth*, addresses the *processes* by which the subjects and signs taken as read by a drama (and criticism) of plot, theme and character are constructed" (p. 137). Evans fools around for a while trying to imagine some use for the plays in enhancing critical awareness, but in the end he just trashes Shakespeare along with the culture he emerged from: "a play like *A Midsummer Night's Dream* could itself be seen as one of the backwaters of a tradition which values texts that point a continuing historical struggle for equality and democracy. . . . A future in which a developed 'critical awareness' can be achieved without the help of Shakespeare is no more intimidating than a present in which English graduates need know nothing of Winstanley and Coppe" (p. 262).

Ultimately, Evans's Macbethian attempt to behead authority (and to expose an idiot tale-teller's sound and fury) ends up privileging the neverland vision of 1640s Ranters and Levellers, of those who, having beheaded a real king, thought both his bodies might die. But the less mortal of the two bodies of Authority only puffs itself up in the face of fear and sneering. If Evans had filled his book less with what seem to me strained or cliché readings of the plays that aim only for headiness and more with feelingful, somatically tested, incorporative responses, he might have produced a body of commentary fit to feast with, or even on, Authority. For it seems to me still true that, even if Shakespeare and other Renaissance drama may be much misinterpreted by Authority, as much as it is by Evans-escent Malvolios, it nonetheless continues to provide for many appetites the equivalent nourishment not only of bread and circuses but also of cakes and ale.

Literature and the Discovery of Method in the English Renaissance, by Patrick Grant. Athens, Ga.: University of Georgia Press, 1985. Pp. ix + 188. $22.50.

Reviewer: SUZANNE GOSSETT

Recent studies of Renaissance literature have returned, in a modified form, to the familiar examination of the "history of ideas" as a background to literature. Often these books, based on French philosophy or semiotics, have an unfamiliar vocabulary, recasting old questions in a new guise. What used to be called a "world picture" is now likely to be called "ideology." The new historicism is much influenced by structuralism and cultural materialism and focuses on issues of power as constructed in and transmitted through literature. Provocative and often interesting to read, these works stimulate a rethinking of questions such as the place of literature in a culture or the relationship between the "subject" and the modes of production.

Yet there remains room for the more traditional forms of scholarship which provide the necessary underpinnings for, and controls on, the speculations of radical scholars. Background studies should inform us about which "meanings . . . were in circulation," permitting the "signifying practices" of literature (compare Catherine Belsey, *The Subject of Tragedy* [London: Methuen, 1985], p. 10). One example is Patrick Grant's new book, *Literature and the Discovery of Method in the English Renaissance*, a sequel to his earlier *Images and Ideas in Literature of the English*

Renaissance (London: Macmillan, 1978). Both books set literature in the context of intellectual history and concentrate on the seventeenth century, when the remains of a medieval world view yielded to that scientific understanding which we recognize as modern. The earlier book examined specifically "how some works of literature engaged problems posed about images by the new thinking about material nature" (p. 26). The new book is broader, since it deals with the general impact of the discovery of scientific method. In this work Grant remains concerned with the way in which poets investigate "the relationship between fictive images and truth" (p. ix), but now his attention goes into exploring how writers came to grips with the "double determinism" of Calvinism and of the world viewed as mechanical.

For Grant, the discovery of method means "a certain efficient organisation of knowledge, based on the assumption of responsibility for a mathematico-empirical investigation of nature, espousing a corpuscular theory of matter and, for practical purposes, depicting the universe in terms of geometrical configurations of mass in space." Most significantly, "the new method departed not only from the standard medieval model of the universe based on Ptolemy, but also from the metaphysical spirit which had informed and regulated it" (p. 11). Grant believes that Calvin's transcendent God removed metaphysics from the realm of the ordinary, thus leaving men in a world determined from "above" (by an absent God) and "below" (by mechanical forces) (p. 16). Since Grant declares himself (in opposition to the cultural materialists) as believing that "a fully poetic expression of faith cannot well endure a God who is not in and through the world, any more than it can endure the vision of an utterly materialised humanity" (p. 18), he has a personal stake in the analysis of these ideas.

Grant's announced purpose is twofold. He wants to set ideas in their context so that we may understand the force of their historical originality, and he wants to examine texts to see how "an idea is clothed in flesh and blood," remaining interesting even when technically outmoded (for example, we no longer believe in humors, but they stimulated important plays.) His interest in the "subjective life of ideas" justifies his turn to literature, both as evidence and examplar. In the philosophical upheaval of the rise of method, the poets, Grant believes, "resisted too complete an adherence to a mechanical view of the world" and "expressed something of the necessary interpenetrations between old-fashioned culture and new scientific theory." Since poets do not deal directly with the philosophical problems but submit beliefs "to the test of imagined experience," poetic symbols can express the difficulty of mediating between "the world poets experience and the God of their faith" (pp. 16–18).

Only certain writers were interested in these issues, and Grant chooses five examples: Thomas More, Ben Jonson, John Donne, Thomas Browne, and William Law. After establishing the nature of each writer's involvement with the new method, he looks at their writings for consequences of the new beliefs, "with special attention to two main issues . . . : first, literature's responsibility for monitoring the twin determinisms (of grace and mechanism) which the discovery of method carries at its heart; second, the discontinuity between metaphysical ideas and poetic symbols engendered by the new intellectual climate which accompanied the scientific revolution" (p. 18).

At this point the reader may well raise several questions. The choice of examples is not self-evident. These writers cover a period of more than two hundred years: William Law, writing in the eighteenth century, hardly shares Thomas More's Renaissance. Furthermore, the diversity of literature examined weakens the developmental, chronological reading that Grant offers. Although the question of method is raised in each chapter, Grant cannot contrast the effects of the new science in William Law's "rigorous masterpiece of Enlightenment spirituality" (p. 131) with those in Jonson's "humors" comedy. Similar material from different periods might have revealed more about the effects of the rise of method. For example, are the characters of Restoration drama different from those of Ben Jonson because they exist in an environment shaped and colored by the formation of the Royal Society? Grant's writers permit only indirect comparison, and the result is a book that—despite the Conclusion's attempt to suggest "a developing self-consciousness among [the] five authors with respect to the relationship of metaphysics to poetry" (p. 154)—seems to have been constructed arbitrarily from a host of possible examples.

Readers of this journal will be most interested in the chapter on Ben Jonson. Grant examines two plays, *Every Man In His Humor* (in its Folio redaction) and *Bartholomew Fair*, to show how Jonson's comedies "consider especially those areas of human behaviour where our actions appear as an uncertain amalgam of mechanical compulsion and free choice." In particular, the chapter argues, Jonson's characters are the products of a "traditional, humoral theory find[ing] itself richly and provocatively disturbed by procedures and assumptions growing directly from the discovery of method" (p. 51).

Grant contributes an historical foundation to the ongoing debate about the nature and significance of Ben Jonson's "humors." Traditional "humors" theory, he explains, was more metaphysical than mechanical. "Humors" were qualities, and for Galen "the primary qualities (hot and cold, dry and moist) have independent, objective existence" (p. 61). This theory was inevitably opposed by proponents of the new science, who believed only in measurable qualities of matter. Contemporary attacks on Galen, coupled with the progress made in anatomy, made control of temperament a source of disagreement. Under the Galenist principles, man is responsible for maintaining his own balance, and disease is viewed as a product of "moral indecorum." In the scientific view, disease becomes a "mechanical malfunction" (p. 57). The conflict is based on different views of the functional and metaphysical connections between body and spirit.

An admirer of Bacon, Jonson was fully aware of contemporary argument over the relation between body and soul. While Jonson could not accept a purely mechanical vision of man, his comedies, unlike his masques, maintained an essentially pessimistic vision of man's chances of conforming himself to virtuous action. Controlled by their impulses, Jonson's humorous, mechanical characters represent man viewed through the lens of modern method; their ability to correct themselves in response to traditional moral and philosophical imperatives is dubious.

The critical debate about the extent to which Jonson's characters are mechanical or determined is of long standing. Enck, for example, claims that "The humours figures . . . resemble marionettes, jerked this way or that by their irrational fantasies" (*Jonson and the Comic Truth*, [Madison: University of Wisconsin Press, 1957], p. 200). Barish and Levin both emphasize the determinism that lurks beneath the doctrine of "humors." On the other hand, James D. Redwine, following Lily Campbell, insists that Jonson's "humors" characters are conceived as "responsible free agents, not somapsychotic automatons" (*ELH*, 28 [1961], 319). Similarly Shenk emphasizes that habits are the foundation of moral character and that while "humors" "can and usually do constitute a part of the psychological flow, they are not its principal cause" (*Journal of Medieval and Renaissance Studies*, 8 [1978], 128).

In discussions of *Bartholomew Fair*, debates about determinism have centered on the puppets and the vapors. Critics disagree about the relation between vapors and "humors" and the extent to which these vapors are deterministic. Grant, usefully, refers Jonson's response to contemporary physiological theory. The vapors are spirits rising from the "humors" to affect the brain. Vapors and puppets—and the characters associated with each—are in opposition, but both are modes of departure from judgment. "Bad judgement . . . causes people to behave either like wooden dummies . . . or as creatures volatilised under the influence of spirits. . . . In both cases, departure from the ideal renders one subject to the body's determinism" (p. 68). Thus both the puppets and the vapors are figures for the body's mechanical operation. Grant reads the play's turning outward to the King as the only resolution possible for these opposites. As in a masque, the King alone can pass judgment, finding a "balance between puppets and vapours, between acquired knowledge and inherited temperament, between the body's inertness and the fluid operations of the spirits" (p. 74).

It is fair to ask how much this intellectual background assists in the appreciation of the works discussed. Grant's final comments on Jonson place the uncertainties of interpretation in a historical context, but they do not seriously modify previous readings of the plays. For him *Every Man In* reveals Jonson's awareness of "how obscurely *psyche* and *soma* interpenetrate" (p. 55), and the main concern of the play is to apply this to a definition of gentility. Yet the evidence Grant offers from the play itself is not illuminating, and the exact relation of social norms and "humors" is confusing.

In his conclusion about *Bartholomew Fair*, Grant returns to the concept of characters determined "from 'above' and from 'below'," but now these are the "twin determinisms of abstracting intellect and volatilised will" (p. 75); Calvinism seems to have been forgotten. (Grant says nothing about the symbolic significance of Grace or her name, which is discussed by many other critics and could have advanced his argument.) Such determinism posed problems for Jonson the humanist, who wished to believe that "virtue was to some degree teachable." Grant attributes the richness of

Jonson's exploration to his knowledge of current scientific trends and "the kinds of challenge extended by the new method to traditional morality" (p. 75). Yet almost all critics of *Bartholomew Fair* have had to come to grips with its insistent physicality and the implications this has for the reformation proposed at the conclusion. Grant has provided some background; questions of interpretation remain open.

The other chapters parallel the one on Jonson. Grant reads the ambiguous symbolism of the heart in Donne's *Anniversaries* as Donne's resistance to either sheer materialism or spiritual absolutes. The chapter on Thomas Browne, one of the most interesting in the book, demonstrates how Browne managed to be both an empirical scientist and an "old-fashioned" metaphysician, in contrast to his admirer Kenelm Digby (p. 104). Much of this chapter is devoted to a demonstration (tangential to the main argument but excellent) that a combination of the cross and circle is basic to the structure of *Religio Medici*.

One persistent subtheme which Grant never thoroughly develops concerns the implications of the new method for the poets' understanding of the relation between word and thing. Intermittently he notices that the rise of method was responsible for a split between signifier and signified. More felt the change in the new ideal of linguistic discourse based on humanist grammar; Jonson would have seen that the attack by Bacon and others on Galenic theory and "qualities" was "closely associated with scepticism concerning real, formal relationships between words and things" (p. 51). Even Thomas Browne recognized the insufficiency of language to describe reality adequately. Unfortunately Grant does not pursue this topic, so fundamental to modern linguistic analysis.

In the future Patrick Grant's book is more likely to be mined for its individual readings than read as a groundbreaking analysis of the effects of the rise of scientific method on literature. Nevertheless, we need such studies to remind us that literature is never divorced from the intellectual ferment of its own time. Political interpretations are more fashionable now than scientific ones, but for the seventeenth century changes on both fronts were critical. Grant's book is a good place to look for examples of the relation between science and literature.

Elizabethan Popular Theatre: Plays in Performance, by Michael Hattaway. Theatre Production Series. London: Routledge & Kegan Paul, 1982. Pp. xi + 234. Cloth $29.95; paper $12.95.

Reviewer: WILLIAM B. LONG

Michael Hattaway's *Elizabethan Popular Theatre: Plays in Performance* is a book of varying uses for different people. The first half essentially constitutes an updated and distilled re-presentation of E. K. Chambers's *Elizabethan Stage*. The Table of Contents of Part One, "The idea of Elizabethan theatre," reveals the scope of the undertaking: "1. Playhouses and stages: Seven playhouses; A drawing of the Swan; Halls and fairgrounds; The stage, the tiring-house, and the canopy; The furnishing of the stage; The auditorium. 2. Performances: City and Court; Audiences; Preparation and rehearsal; Scene building; Music and dancing; Dumb shows, set pieces, and jigs. 3. Players and playing: Playhouse economics; Acting styles; Plays and games; Boy players; Make-up and costumes; Clowns and tragedians, Shakespeare, Marlowe—and Brecht; Speaking the speech." To this are added fourteen pictures illustrating theater exteriors, stages, stagings, and actors—often reproduced but always welcome—and needed by many users of this volume. Reading through this list shows the immediate difference in approach from Chambers. Hattaway, of course, is not being encyclopedic; but more importantly, he is focusing the accumulated scraps of knowledge on the problems of placing functioning plays in their original venues to see what powers these released to make the plays work as theater pieces. Thus the first half of Hattaways's volume does not replace Chambers, but it is an excellent introduction for advanced undergraduates, beginning graduate students, or theater people seeking a grounding in the facts about and the usage of the Elizabethan theater. And it also can serve as a hundred-page refresher course for the more experienced sojourner in Elizabethan drama who has not read Chambers recently or who has not followed the increasingly voluminous and important scholarship in the last twenty-odd years.

There are a few problems. Occasionally Hattaway's perception is jarred: "the mere size of the stage demanded bold moves and large gestures" (p. 56); surely on a thirty by forty foot stage with the audience sitting and standing in such close proximity, such a grand style need not always have been in order. Or he forgets how cleverly and rapidly actors can change roles by very simple costuming changes such as the donning or doffing of a cloak: "The stage direction reads '*Enter a Devil*', presumably a player other than the one acting Mephostophilis who would not have had time to change in the seven lines between entrances" (p. 172). Particularly because the book is so free from typographical error (the only one I found is an unwanted "a" at the end of line 12 of p. 109), it is unfortunate that two unnecessary and ugly design features disfigure so many pages: prose extracts are not justified on the right margin, and only very rarely (pp. 51, 67, and 110) are there additional line spaces to set off extracts from commentary.

But it is the second half of the book that all persons interested in Elizabethan plays should find of great interest, for it is here that Hattaway puts his imagination into play with accumulated knowledge to show how Elizabethan plays worked in their theaters. This is not an exercise in literary criticism where plays regularly are discussed as if they were narrative poems. Hattaway is very well aware (as many [most?] of his readers will not be) that the plays as they exist on paper are but a fraction of their total realization—something analogous to the difference between a printed musical score and a fully staged live production of an opera.

> Inductions . . . remind us yet again of how the printed texts are records of only a part of Elizabethan plays. The effect of performances must have derived as much from music and spectacle as from the working out of plot and the creation of character. . . . The effect of these romances is cumulative as the dramatists and companies added episode to episode, mode to mode, re-enacting and celebrating scenic patterns derived from classical mythology, folk-tale, clownage, and the pageantry of Court and City, as well as mystery and miracle (saints') plays. These performances are not imitations of life but occasions for game and display by members of a company, and their structure is that of a musical suite.
>
> (pp. 131–132)

The difficulties modern actors often have in essaying Elizabethan roles usually stems from attempting a late twentieth-century approach to late sixteenth-century material, and Hattaway guides modern actors by explaining how the Elizabethans saw themselves. "Even when Elizabethans speak of what we might call 'identification' between spectator and player, they do this not in the context of situation and highly particularized characters but in terms of the player's art of distilling the actions proper to his part" (p. 78). Interpreting remarks about acting by Thomas Heywood (1608) and by James Shirley (1647), Hattaway notes that both

> feel tempted to imply an identity between the player and character and spectator and character respectively, both are equally insistent that the audience does not lose sight of the player's skill and thus of a distinction between the person represented and the person representing. Audiences were aware of two levels of action: that which was imitated and the spoken and physical gestures of imitation. Revivifying an old Platonic image, players commonly referred to themselves as 'shadows', insubstantial nothings compared with the 'matter' of their plays.
>
> (p. 79)

Interpreting with this background and from this perspective, Hattaway then imaginatively examines *The Spanish Tragedy, Mucedorus, Edward II, Doctor Faustus,* and *Titus Andronicus.*

For this reviewer, the main difficulty with this part of the book is that one could have wished that it were several times as long so that Hattaway could display what he has to say about more plays. Such, of course, is the purpose neither of this volume nor of the Theatre Production Series—nor is it necessary. What is of great value is Hattaway's methodology, and that is very well demonstrated. In the future, critics who discuss Elizabethan plays as if they had only tangential or even only accidental connections with the theater and theater people who act in and direct Elizabethan plays as if scholarship and criticism had provided them no tools to aid their grappling with the plays will have no excuses whatsoever.

To paraphrase Hattaway in his approach can be easily distorting and might appear over-simplifying; thus I have allowed more quotation than would be needed from a more conventional study. To follow Hattaway, the reader should have a good visual conception of the "Elizabethan" stage as outlined in Part One and then attempt to picture the happenings of the play under consideration. The more one does so, the more easily Hattaway's habit of mind can be assimilated; thus the reader is enabled to go forth and do likewise—and such is the purpose of this volume.

In regarding plays principally as narratives—usually as narrative poems unfortunately distorted and vulgarized for an audience who could not appreciate them properly, critics generally have neglected looking for structural elements that are indigenous to the dramatic form itself. Hattaway's dissections are always rewarding.

> If we approach the plays of Marlowe or Shakespeare's chronicle of Henry VI [as plays constructed of formal groupings and symmetrical tableaux] rather than looking in them for patterns of imagery or nice indications of 'character' we can see that they depend on scenes that follow one another with a strong architectonic rhythm, on moments that must have been realised by bold visual effects, formal groupings that tend towards tableaux, archetypal personages, frozen moments that would lodge in the spectators' minds.
> (p. 57)

. . .

> What emerges from this kind of analysis . . . is that plays of this sort moved from set piece, or from one gest or formal dramatic image, to another. There are important implications in that once we have realized [*sic*] that the set piece or formal group is a basic element of the Elizabethan play, we are in less danger of the moral reductivism that comes with a concentration on plot, on end-directed action, which deduces a play's meaning simply in moral terms from its resolution. Nor are we tempted to regard the dumb shows, songs, masques, etc., found in the plays as excrescences or 'insets' but rather we recognize them as evidence of the basic mode of Elizabethan drama.
> (p. 59)

While most teachers of Elizabethan drama generally are well aware of the basic features of the physical theaters, there has been little concentrated effort to unite this awareness with the understanding and interpretation of the plays written for them. Thus Thomas Kyd's importance usually is credited only as a writer of plays, not as a playwright—something that could be said by only reading *The Spanish Tragedy* and tracing its influence upon subsequent plays. But Hattaway is more basic; he looks into the ways the play is constructed: its crafting, its wrighting.

> Kyd was one of the first to learn how the physical arrangement of stage and tiring-house, the spatial relationship between players and spectators, made possible that combination of history and tragedy, the particular and the universal, that gives the popular drama of the Renaissance its distinctive resonances.
> (p. 102)

Hattaway is particularly good at trying to get his readers out of their present-day attitudes and expectations—showing them how and why Elizabethan plays are different and what to look for and how to appreciate these features:

> Like audiences at operas now who anticipate with pleasure favourite arias or pieces of spectacle, the Elizabethan did not see the play only through the eyes of the hero or assume that it was shaped about his consciousness. Rather it was for them a sequence of performed actions. Indeed Kyd may be said to have gained his effect by adding theatrical action to the long declamatory sequences developed by the academic dramatists and English Senecans; to have, in effect, created the 'scene' as the elemental dramatic unit. Without *The Spanish Tragedy* for a model, Shakespeare would not have written a play like *Richard III* in which so many scenes are based around a simple bold incident—or gest. . . . *The Spanish Tragedy*, then, is a Renaissance artefact, dependent for its effect on the bold architectural symmetry of its dramatic form and the statuesque massiveness of its characters.
> (p. 106)

Often a particularly insidious kind of anti-theatricalism has joined with the knowledge of the assumed wide popularity of Elizabethan drama to produce haughty critical dismissals of certain features of Elizabethan plays as being items merely thrown in to please the supposedly ignorant "groundlings." Hattaway's perception allows his readers to dispense with invented teleological explanations and to see the organic explanations in the various features of the plays.

> Kyd's use of specific dramatic emblems or speaking pictures . . . need[s] little comment but should not be dismissed as mere pandering to a vulgar taste for inexplicable dumb show and noise. [Such scenes] can serve as structural devices. . . . They have also a general effect, for these and many of the other scenes of the play are both artificial, and, for the Elizabethans, examples of the shows of their 'real' world. They have their origins in the pageantry of the court, the street dramas of executions, the illustrations to theological and moral tracts. They are images or icons that combine the everyday and the fictional, the real and the artificial, and which, by this combination, achieve their particular dramatic, eidetic effects. Only recently . . . have dramatic critics been able to react without condescension or embarrassment to the basic satisfaction this kind of popular show can provide. . . . These 'naive' images are the stuff of popular drama.
> (pp. 110–111)

Hattaway is careful not to imply that the staging of Elizabethan drama was static; the kinds of structures he discovers and their realizations on stage that he proposes offer an almost unlimited opportunity for using such insights in highly differing ways, as in these comments on *Faustus*.

> By depicting the practices of ceremonial magic—the magic of witches who employed demonic agents—Marlowe revealed the creative powers of ritual through all the spectacular devices the playhouses had to offer. The play is a great phantasmagoria of scenic properties, ceremonial and emblematic costumes, battle-games between powers of good and evil, action portrayed on the three levels of the stage, dances, music, Latin declamations, mirror scenes in which the portentous actions of the hero are travestied in the cross-talk and knockabout games of the playhouse clowns. The unlocalized and empty stage of the popular playhouses was as suited to the procession of shows as it was to narrative. The play moves from the

sardonic to the sublime, taps an important vein of folk culture as well as drawing on the high culture of theology. . . . Certainly the A text could like *Edward II* be performed on the simple stages available outside London: it does not stipulate an upper level from which the devils might preside over the conjuring of Mephostophilis and over Faustus' leave-taking of the Scholars, does not require a 'window' for the horned knight Benvolio, and omits the final scene in which the Scholars enter to find Faustus' scattered limbs—property limbs which a touring company may not have wanted to transport about.

(pp. 160, 161)

Hattaway often conjectures several ways in which scenes could be staged. Supposing that Henslowe's "sittie of Rome" property would be used for *Faustus*, Hattaway notes:

There is no way of telling whether this was a three-dimensional house, thrust out perhaps from the discovery space, or a painted cloth hung against the tiring-house façade and behind the papal throne, or even a structure that had stood on stage from the beginning of the play. The dialogue from ll. 51ff. indicates that Faustus wants to leave the stage to explore 'Rome' but that Mephostophilis entices him to watch the papal triumph, perhaps from the gallery. (Did they fly on to the stage together at the conclusion of the Chorus' speech?)

(p. 177)

Hattaway is agile and penetrating. The book is full of valuable observations about other plays and playwrights and is particularly sharp in pointing out how different playwrights—most notably Marlowe and Shakespeare—handle similar material. Again and again Hattaway shows what the Elizabethan stage could do to carry meaning and to bring the lines to life. His methods deserve the widest possible usage.

The New Inn, by Ben Jonson, edited by Michael Hattaway. The Revels Plays. Manchester: Manchester University Press, 1984. Pp. xii + 244. $46.00.

Reviewer: EJNER J. JENSEN

Unlike Dr. Johnson's lexicographers, textual editors are not harmless drudges; but few observers would classify editors among the more creative figures in academic life. They are more properly the servants than the masters of the texts that they bring to public attention, and even in the relatively independent functions of writing introductions and providing necessary information in notes, editors function best when they decline to thrust themselves forward, preferring an ancillary role to any show of learning or audacity of interpretation that might deflect attention from the text and its claims to interest or merit. Yet when an editor brings out a volume in a series so well established and distinguished as the Revels Plays, he does in a curious way invite a judgment not unlike what we impose on creative writers working within a well-defined genre. Like a sonneteer's, his efforts tend to be assessed in relation to those of others who have attempted the form, a form—if we can judge from earlier works in the series—neat and circumscribed but, in the best hands, capable of great variety and richness.

Michael Hattaway's edition of *The New Inn*, that problematic, embattled product of Ben Jonson's late years (perhaps his "dotage"), must necessarily, then, be graded according to high standards. Hattaway's management of the play's text, his annotations, and his Introduction are the three chief matters to be considered. The handling of additional material in the Appendices, while important, seems a bit apart from the main business here and can best be touched upon as a sort of addendum to my primary discussion. Textual matters occupy relatively little space (five and one-half pages) in the editor's thirty-eight page Introduction. *The New Inn*, unique among Jonson's plays in being published in octavo, is "a text that presents remarkably few problems" (p. 11). All editors of Jonson acknowledge obligations to the great labors of Herford and the Simpsons (*Ben Jonson*, 11 vols. [Oxford: Clarendon Press, 1925–52]), and Hattaway is no exception. To their table of press corrections to the text, he simply adds—in Appendix III—a list that enables a reader to see how the copies that he has collated (beyond those known to Herford and the Simpsons) would figure in their account.

But discussion of the text is one thing, its presentation another. Glaring errors appear in this volume. The first of these is at II.i.12, where the line, "Are still the first commodity they put off," ought to be the initial line on page 94 but appears instead as the last line on that page. The explanatory note regarding *put off* is correctly given as referring to line 12; so neither notes nor lineation is disrupted by the falling out of this line from its correct place. On the next page, at II.i.33, "now" is a misprint for *not*. More disturbing even than these errors is the confusion in IV.iv. Hattaway gives for lines 191–193 the following:

> A giant of the time, sure I will bear it
> Or out of the time, sure I will bear it
> Or cut of patience or necessity.

Herford and Simpson give the following for their lines 190–191:

> A Giant of the time, sure, I will bear it
> Or out of patience, or necessity!

How such an error crept into Hattaway's text is understandable but nevertheless a matter for regret. Beyond making nonsense of the immediate passage, it confuses the lineation of the rest of the scene and makes nonsense of the note to line 192: "*Or . . . or*] either . . . or." In the final act, the running head, "SC. IV," begins at page 193 and continues through page 201 even though V.v begins on page 196. Thus a note on line 33 of Jonson's "Ode to Himself" referring to V.v.5n. for a definition of *orts* requires more searching than one might suppose; and even when that note is located, it offers only a scrap of information where one might expect, at the least, a notice of Shakespeare's use of the word in *Troilus and Cressida*.

Nevertheless, the explanatory notes, like those in all editions in this series, are generally both full and helpful. It seems a bit curious, though, given Hattaway's emphasis on *The New Inn* as a theatre piece, that he does not use the notes more frequently to talk about possible stage business. Here again one finds some errors attributable to carelessness. A terse note on IV.iii.79 gives merely "preoccupation] bawdy" and refers the reader to "Arg. 102n." for further information; the correct citation should be Arg. 92n., where a reader does find a good deal of useful material. At I.i.31n., "sports of nature" is glossed as "Lat. *lusus naturae*," the Latin phrase followed by an extensive quotation in Latin from Thomas Moffett's *Insectorum sive Minimorum Animalium Theatrum*. Those with little Latin are put to hard shifts. It seems a mere show of learning, then, in an edition whose merits should include accessibility, for Hattaway to give such full documentation and not translate, but, I am told, it is Revels' editorial policy not to translate.

A few other problems appear in the handling of the notes. At III.ii.272n. *bona-roba* is glossed as "a showy wanton" and the reader referred to "*Pers*. 67n." and "*Alc*. II.vi.30n. (Revels)." But at IV.iii.22 the note, on the same word, directs the reader only to "*Pers*. 67"; in other words, the cross-referencing system has broken down. (Even without this breakdown, information about the term's use in *The Alchemist* is available easily only to those with ready access to the Revels edition of that play, although it is hardly surprising that Hattaway's edition should refer to another in the same series.) Finally, on this matter of notes, that on V.i.1 presents still another problem—seemingly endless deferral of reference. For *legacy*, the reader is referred to II.iv.16n. There the note, which might be expected to explain the Host's remark about Fly—"I had him when I came to take the inn here"—offers only a reference to "Arg. 118n." At the close of the "Argument" of the play on page 56, where line 118 appears, the note defines *portion* as "dowry" and refers the reader to E. A. Abbott, *A Shakespearian Grammar* (London, 1878) for help with "offers . . . with." A reader might be excused for not detecting the other note—separately numbered but also to line 118—on the previous page.

The third area of Hattaway's performance is the one in which he has the greatest freedom but also, arguably, the greatest disadvantages. His role as critic allows him to lead us into the play from new angles, to bring us to a new appreciation of the play's merits; yet he is dealing with a work that has enjoyed slight critical favor—primarily in the context of defensive maneuvering calculated to refute the view that *The New Inn* is properly to be considered a "dotage" of its author. On the whole, the Introduction is a winning plea for the merits of Jonson's play. Unwilling to judge *The*

New Inn as either "wholly a romance or wholly a parodic satire." Hattaway carves out a space for the play to assert itself as the product of a playwright more flexible about "generic purity" than he is often thought to be (p. 38). Moreover, Hattaway makes a strong plea for the play as worthy of performance. This is a bold notion when one recognizes that—apart from a 1903 production whose records have not been recovered by anyone interested in Jonson's plays on the stage—*The New Inn* has never had a stage production since its initial failure in 1629. But here Hattaway may be prescient or at least well-informed, since the Royal Shakespeare Company is currently (Fall, 1987) presenting the play at Stratford-upon-Avon. The Introduction, then, does its proper work and does it effectively, though it might be usefully supplemented by Anne Barton's discussion in *Ben Jonson, Dramatist* (Cambridge: Cambridge University Press, 1984), where the critical context is more meaningfully sketched in and where the case for a reassessment becomes more compelling.

Having glanced at the three areas outlined above, I find a few other matters that need attention. One is yet another explanatory note. At I.v.39n. Hattaway cites Dekker to good purpose in glossing the word *canting*. Later, in his note on II.v.42 ("A merry Greek, and cants in Latin comely"), he gives "cants] talks to elaborately; see I.v.39n." The preposition ("to") makes no sense, especially in light of the previous note. The designation of Appendix I, listed on the "Contents" page as "Ripostes and Replies to Jonson's 'Ode to Himself'," begins with "Repostes" on page 210. And—while this is hardly an error—I regretted that the editor's reserve about Jonson's naughty wordplay led him at II.i.51n. to gloss only bear—"sustain (a role) and expose (bawdy)"—in Lady Frampul's "I'll bear my part" and thus to miss a fine triple pun.

But it is on the chief business of an editor—his handling of the text, his judicious use of annotations, and his critical presentation of the work and the issues surrounding it—that Hattaway's labors should be judged. And if we think of this edition as representing a genre—the Revels Plays edition—it seems to have fallen short by a fair distance of the best work of its kind. Is it an act of unkindness to say that its price—nearly fifty dollars—also leads us to wish for something better?

Homo, Memento Finis: The Iconography of Just Judgment in Medieval Art and Drama. Early Drama, Art and Music Monograph Series, 6. Kalamazoo, Mich.: Medieval Institute Publications, 1985. Pp. xi + 219. 27 plates. Cloth $22.95; paper $13.95.

Reviewer: PETER W. TRAVIS

Perhaps because the six essays that constitute *Homo, Memento Finis* are all products of a National Endowment for the Humanities residential seminar, this volume is more than a miscellany. Rather, its essays read like chapters—each author alluding to the arguments of other essays, each employing similar styles and critical methods. Although the focus of the volume may be a bit wider than was originally intended, extending beyond the Last Judgment to the more general notion of "just judgment," the concerns of these essays are consistent and clear: to treat medieval drama, medieval art, and medieval religious texts not as influences upon one another but rather as kindred phenomena that reveal how medieval images were read textually and how medieval texts and plays were read imagistically. In light of this self-imposed charge, the volume is informative and successful.

The volume opens and closes with strong essays, the first exploring the earliest surviving medieval depictions of the Last Judgment and the last examining the radical transformation of these images in the English Renaissance. Pamela Sheingorn's "'For God Is Such a Doomsman': Origins and Development of the Theme of Last Judgment" offers a sensitive appreciation of the extraordinary difficulties that artists faced when they first attempted to render the eschaton into graphic images (as in a ninth-century Anglo-Saxon *Last Judgment* ivory) and into dramatic form (as in the twelfth-century *Sponsus* play). Since I take the volume's target readers to be medieval-drama scholars, Sheingorn's training in art history is especially instructive: her reading of a Romanesque tympanum, for example, in terms of its symmetries, hieratic orderings, triangular arrangements of forms, and organization in bands or registers serves as a caution to literary scholars who tend to see in the graphic arts only replications of scenes found inside the quite different spatial restraints of the stage. Houston Diehl's concluding essay "'To Put Us in Remembrance': The Protestant Transformation of Images of Judgment" book-ends nicely with Sheingorn's opening essay, as Diehl traces the revalorizing of medieval eschatological images into Reformation images which serve no longer as icons that contain divine truth within them but rather as man-made artifacts that merely evoke thoughts of the Last Judgment. In a sixteenth-century homiletic morality play, for example, St. Michael is replaced by the allegorical figure of Justice, who nevertheless holds St. Michael's most distinctive attribute, the sword, in his hand. And in such plays as Shakespeare's *Measure for Measure* and Webster's *The Devil's Law-Case*, scenes of secular judgment—with courtrooms, judges, and symmetrically balanced "good" and "bad" characters—are all informed by the mythic patterns and images of divine judgment but are so much a part of the natural, illusory world that they destabilize their moral prescriptions and thus undermine their audience's expectations.

Neither Ronald B. Herzman's "'Let Us Seek Him Also': Tropological Judgment in Twelfth-Century Art and Drama" nor Richard Emmerson's "'Nowe Ys Common This Daye': Enoch and Elias, Antichrist, and the Structure of the Chester Cycle" is concerned directly with the Last Judgment. Rather, Herzman explores the "presentness of judgment" (p. 84), the tropological bending of eschatological images into earlier stages of the Christian life in representative works of twelfth-century monastic culture: the sculptural program of the Church of St. Faith tympanum in Conques, a sermon of St. Bernard of Clairvaux, and the Benediktbeuren Christmas play. Emmerson, building upon his book *Antichrist in the Middle Ages: A Study of Medieval Apocalypticism, Art, and Literature* (Seattle, Wash.: University of Washington Press, 1981) examines the special role played by Enoch and Elias as Antichrist's opponents and as types of Christ—in illuminated Apocalypses, moralized Bibles, the *vitae Antichristi*, and the Chester Cycle.

David Bevington, director of the National Endowment for the Humanities seminar, is author and co-author of the volume's two remaining essays. In "'Man, Thinke on Thine Endinge Day': Stage Pictures of Just Judgment in *The Castle of Perseverance*," Bevington offers a thorough coverage of *Castle*'s costuming effects, stage properties, body gestures, spatial arrangements, and dramatic actions, almost all of which either derive from eschatological imagery or serve as concretized metaphors of the pilgrimage of man's life—such as the quenching of lust as a physical action requiring water, the prick of conscience and death's dart as stage properties, and man's spiritual nakedness reified by the physical unclothing of the figure of Mankind. In the volume's capstone essay, "'Alle This Was Token Domysday to Drede': Visual Signs of Last Judgment in the Corpus Christi Cycles and in Late Gothic Art," Bevington and Sheingorn focus upon the parallels between graphic and dramatic depictions of the Final Judgment—their non-illusionistic rendering of space, their exploitation of the semiotics of symmetry, their portraitures of human figures both personalized and generic. They are also careful to emphasize the differences between these two media: the Cycles, for example, preferred giving artistic expression to the Acts of Mercy in contrast to the arts' depiction of the Psychostasis, the final weighing of souls.

Accompanying these six essays are twenty-seven carefully chosen plates, ranging from a fourth-century sarcophagus lid to a seventeenth-century Protestant emblem of "doome-eternal." As reproductions, three of these plates are inadequate: the Conques Last Judgment scene is dark, its figures minuscule (No. 2); details in the Rogier van der Weyden altarpiece can be made out only with difficulty (No. 15); the eschatological scene in the background of Jan Sadeler's *Mankind before the Last Judgment* is too blanched out to be identified as such (No. 25).

Homo, Memento Finis appeared six years after the completion of Bevington's National Endowment for the Humanities seminar, and the results of this long gestation period are both positive and negative. Written by six scholars, each of whom has contributed important work in related areas, these essays are of a piece—consistently sound, intelligently researched, carefully complementary. The volume will serve as a reliable and informative source for years to come. There is nevertheless a stolid and settled sameness to the essays, which is perhaps not surprising when a communal effort has spanned such a length of time. Still, *Homo, Memento Finis* is the most accomplished critical collection yet to be published in the Early Drama, Art and Music series.

The Drama of Dissent: The Radical Poetics of Nonconformity, 1380-1590, by Ritchie L. Kendall. Chapel Hill and London: University of North Carolina Press, 1986. Pp. ix + 286. $30.00.

Reviewer: ARTHUR F. KINNEY

The concern with *dissent* in Ritchie Kendall's title for this remarkably original, informed, and informing study, is with religious nonconformity, not political rebellion; his concern is to evaluate the countermovement to orthodox religious thought in England in selected writers from the Lollards to Martin Marprelate (and looking forward, at the end, to the work of John Milton) in order to determine both a kind of counter "literary" tradition and their consistent use of theatrical metaphor. "It has been the principal contention of this investigation," he sums near the close,

> that much of nonconformist writing is, in the deepest sense of the word, dramatic—and, more often than not, self–dramatizing. Each of the works studied . . . documents the invention of identity in a theater of the soul: the elect personality's struggle to enact its ideal self and secure its legitimate spiritual inheritance. The experience culminates in the sense of calm that comes from the acceptance of one's saintly role on a divine stage. What transforms this rite of self–awareness from a private ceremony of complacency into a public celebration of the mystical unity of Christ's body is the nonconformist insistence that the triumph of the individual is the triumph of the community.
>
> (p. 204).

Implicit in such an argument, of course, is the work of Ernst Curtius, who first explored the topos of all the world as a stage in his pioneering study of the Latin traditions in the Middle Ages as well as the work of G. W. Owst and others who have traced pulpit imagery for us, including that of the theater; and there is a curious blending—even a sleight of hand—at the end when the customary medieval traditions such as the dialogue between body and soul—again implicity—become quietly appropriated to the central line of argument. But this study is also deeply informed by the affective stylistics first put forward, and later worked out and defined, by Stanley Fish, and by certain strategies of discourse analysis now so attractive, so that an enriched and detailed study of rhetorical tactics allows Kendall to focus on phrases and maneuvers that have been unrecognized before. What results is always thought-provoking and often provocative.

We have long been accustomed to what Kendall lists as "the doctrinal, disputational, pastoral, and literary documents" of the nonconformists; what links them here, however, is that they are seen as "the products of an inherently theatrical imagination" (p. 8). In fact, "the Puritan with both malice and mischief contrived to hoist the theater with its own petard"; "the radical reformer reveals himself not as a single-minded enemy of the drama but as its troubled lover" (p. 8). It is an arresting observation. "Although the reformers tended to excoriate representational drama, they nonetheless labored tirelessly to transform their own world of letters into a theater of the soul" (p. 8). Such an employment of metaphor was not, he argues, an accidental or unconscious one, but a deliberate attempt to overcome the opposition by undermining it. Thus—and here is his crucial step—"The poetics [sic] of radical dissent are steeped in ambivalent theatricality" (p. 8).

The examination begins with such Lollardian texts as *The Lanterne of Li3t* (pp. 25 ff.) where the author takes on the role-playing that can link him with Old Testament authority (that is, he practices Aristotelian *ethos* by choosing Scriptural models for his *imitatio*). He also refashions events as imitations of Christ's life, either by modeling himself after Christ in experience or conduct or by invoking the ideas and stances found in the later Pauline writings. The style, both plain and contentious, also has biblical exemplars. For the Lollards, "All species of Christian belief are combative by nature" (p. 41), a view that leads naturally enough to the kind of inherent disputation or the explicit disputatious attitude that from the birth of drama had also been inherent in theater. And like the early Greek tragedies or the contemporary medieval mystery plays, these Lollard writings are based in developing opposition—at first to the monks, later to orthodox faith, and, by the time of Marprelate, to the Elizabethan Settlement. The inherent playlet, from *Exodus* to *Doctor Faustus*, was reflected by the early nonconformists: "The dynamics of [their] exorcism were most pronounced and, therefore, perhaps most effective when the opponent closely resembled the Lollard. The proof of the principle is the special animosity that the Lollard reserved for the friar. Had the mendicant orders not existed, the Lollard would have had to invent them. As they did exist, they constituted the perfect dark mirror of the Lollard mind, a nemesis whose failings enacted the most terrible of Lollard nightmares"(p. 42). The religious orders provide the Lollards continuing opposition and cause but also force their ambivalence. "The practice of equivocation, evident in both the studied vagaries of nonconformist responses and the exasperation of fulminating examiners, begins early and lasts long. Although examinates undoubtedly resorted to such tactics to evade the consequences of their heresies and goad their tormentors, the prevalence of equivocal response is testimony to an instinct for the limits of knowledge as well as a bent for self-preservation or sadistic delight" (p. 46). In this they could not lose: "By summoning the Lollards into their courts and eventually burning them at the stake, the bishops provided the reformers with their own recurrent drama of redemptive sacrifice" (p. 57). At such moments, it is perhaps difficult to unwind the threads of straightforward narrative, dramatic situation, nonconformist position, and rhetorical ploy in this argument, just as behind it classical rhetoric and poetic and the history and practice of orthodox preaching and scriptural exegesis become interwoven with nonconformist polemic. But in one sense this difficulty does not matter, for Kendall's purpose—and one at which he succeeds admirably—is to highlight the manipulative verbal ploys of the dissenters in the late Middle Ages and early Renaissance to show not simply their theatrical imagination, which they shared with others, but the imaginative and creative writing that became their own—and that we have tended to overlook. Their work, then, was verbally richer than has been acknowledged. The *Examination* of William Thorpe, for example, uses a literary structure of accretive development employing flashbacks to *create*, through the devices of fiction, an apparently autobiographical account (p. 63). And here too is the sleight of hand: "Thorpe's own autobiographical saint's life, its theatricality displaced from the stage to the soul and finally to the text, is an example of this Christian art" (p. 67). So too *Pierce the Ploughman's Crede* (pp. 73–80).

And there is also John Bale, who actually turned to the drama to forward the cause of nonconformity. For him, "the Catholic regressively sought shelter in a world of ceremonial play, ignoring the more laborious worship God now demanded"; he therefore depicted them as "always gamesters" addicted to "the pursuit of play" where "they exult in impersonation, disguise, and deception. Success for them is measured in finely turned jests and well-executed jokes," and "Their language exhibits the same gamesome spirit" (p. 97). This "self–intoxicating elegance of rhetorical flowers" (p. 99) was answered, in Bale, by the plain-speaking that we have long associated with the Puritan movement; but Kendall finds Bale's writing "not so much plain as it is crude and brutal" (p. 99). His "abrasive speech" (p. 100) is meant to "peel away the centuries of corrupted theology beneath which the gospel's truth lay buried" (p. 100); yet to do so causes an oppositional rhetoric which here is likened to nonconformist dramatic technique that goes back to Thorpe and forward to Marprelate. Bale thus transforms Christian history from fall and redemption—something Christian—to "purity, decline, and renewal" (p. 101)—something more conventionally dramatic, theatrical, and Puritan. His plays constantly align, on the one hand, verisimilitude with the vices (and the orthodox and Catholic traditions) and, on the other, conceptual disputations with conversion and with corrective Puritan belief and practice. So in *Johan Baptystes preachynge*, "The rational appreciation of John's arguments—pursued through an earnest process of logical inquiry and authenticated by the gift of understanding—replaces the mystery play formula of ceremonial mimicry" (p. 112). The point is an extremely fine one, for Kendall goes on to show (pp. 114–115) how Bale's drama is also essentially *figural* (although he does not use this term); "it was the historian's duty to underscore the congruence between the sacred and the profane, the events of the Bible being the sole glass through which the meaning of secular history might be read" (pp. 114–115). By contrast, "*King Johan* is an exercise in theological disputation" in which "its author was anxious to ensure that his pronouncements would carry authority" (p. 115) so that his conceptualized response is grounded not in idea but in allegory. Building on Lollard techniques of dramatic disputation, "The godly, John had suggested" in Bale's play, "speak words powdered with the wisdom of biblical citations; Sedition's are seasoned instead with gross obscenities, witty wordplay, and nonsensical alliteration" (p. 117). King Johan himself, moreover, "More than any of [Bales's] other protagonists . . . resembles the isolated heroes of Lollard tradition: scorned, abused, and examined for their heretical beliefs. Like Thorpe, he learns to see his life as a reenactment of Christianity's primal drama—the trial and execution of the son of God for his challenge to the corrupted institutions of contemporary religion" (p. 120). But like the literary artist of the Lollard tradition, Bale sees John's "sainthood" proved "by his enshrinement in a text—the purified chronicles of England—rather than in the gaudy confines of an earthly tomb" (p. 121).

Throughout, Kendall's study is one of uncustomary elegance matched with a precise and refined sensibility to language and to rhetorical positioning. But its finest contribution is to our understanding of Martin Marprelate. Happily, the vexed and vexing problem of authorship is quickly dismissed for the larger and more substantial issues of meaning and significance. For Kendall, Martin is the most sophisticated of the nonconformist writers, the most aware of the instability and slipperiness of language, and the most imaginative and inventive in finding ways to rein in merriment with seriousness and to play out seriousness with high jinks. Indeed, Martin's own fluid stance not only complicated his persona but also caused his argumentation to be immensely difficult to handle: little wonder the replies to his works were so serious and (consequently) so ineffectual; no wonder his identity was sought hard by officials; no wonder he became a *cause célèbre*. It is Kendall's contention—and why not?—that all of Martin's family, including Martin, Sr. and Martin, Jr., were quite possibly Martin himself, this switch in names simply an extension of his basic deployment of language.

> What emerges from Marprelate's racy tales of ill-speaking and ill-living Anglicans is a portrait of a verbal universe folded in upon itself, its life- and truth-giving links to the common speech of man and the inspired word of God utterly severed. The bishops and their supporters are the heirs of Jack Upland's lawless friars, John Bale's repressed monks, and William Turner's compromising priests; they are the aimless wanderers in the nonconformist vision of human history, condemned to expend their spirits in idle play rather than fruitful work. In the end, they can only

understand each other and then imperfectly. Martin's assaults on the anarchy of Bishops' English no doubt eased the strictures his conscience had placed on his own use of a language given more to 'merry mirth' than 'honest communication.' Just as Bale had closeted the demons of play into the subplot of the Vices, thereby liberating himself to pursue his own lawful play, so Martin drew a circle about his prelatical gamesters in order to sanction his own holy gaming.

(pp. 193–194)

Martin moves into "the narrow confines of syllogistic propositions" (p. 196) and then outward again to a network of puns on John Whitgift, Archbishop of Canterbury, as "John of Cant." and T. C. as both Thomas Cartwright, one of the authors of the Puritan *Admonition to the Parliament* of 1578, and Thomas Cooper, his pamphleteering opponent who had first modestly and inadvertently used those initials himself. Kendall says, with striking pregnancy, "Martin and his sons are the true heirs of Tyndale; they are men who combine wisdom with the martyr's thirst for spiritual warfare"(p. 203). His pamphlets, under whatever name with whatever authorship, thus "are nonconformist dramas" with *fictional personae* "in which the trial of truth is a kangaroo court and the act of self-discovery is in fact a self-serving sleight of hand" (p. 204). In making his own *persona*, rather than dropping autobiographical clues, Martin, like his predecessors, constantly links nonconformity with martyrdom, thus appropriating the most powerful autobiographical position of all for himself. What results is the drama of the soul (the earlier dialogue of the soul enacted) that marks for Kendall the drama of dissent throughout its history in nonconformism.

In a brief epilogue, Kendall suggestively shows how his approach might also be developed in reviewing (or re-viewing) Milton's art from the early *Comus* (a masque, after all) through the two epics to *Samson Agonistes* (another drama). Indeed, the Lady's triumph in *A Maske at Ludlowe*, as it was properly called—

> Thou art not fit to hear thyself convinc't;
> Yet should I try, the uncontrolled worth
> Of this pure cause would kindle my rapt spirits
> To such a flame of sacred vehemence,
> That dumb things would be mov'd to sympathize,
> And the brute Earth would lend her nerves, and shake,
> Till all thy magic structures rear'd so high,
> Were shatter'd into heaps o'er thy false head—

"bears all the earmarks of a nonconformist victory" (p. 214). There is the later subsequent admission that the Lady was later saved not by her belief but by the intervention of God's grace, but that is not part of Kendall's argument here, just as it is not part of the nonconformist drama of dissent. The admission is revealing: this drama seems also to have been peculiarly myopic and backward-looking even as it learned to play and appropriate verbal strategies of the opposition. The real value of Kendall's study is that in so adroitly revealing the range and variety of the nonconformist imagination he also points to its inconsistencies and its decidedly severe restrictions.

Humanist Poetics: Thought, Rhetoric, and Fiction in Sixteenth-Century England, by Arthur F. Kinney. Amherst, Mass.: University of Massachusetts Press, 1986. Pp. xvi + 529. $35.00.

Reviewer: PHILIP ROLLINSON

This comprehensive, well-written study traces the evolution of Tudor prose fiction through exemplary writers from Thomas More to Thomas Nashe in the context of classical and continental Renaissance influences. The progress goes from optimistic humanism at the beginning of the sixteenth century, enthusiastically believing in the educability and perfectibility of man through fictional imitation, to pessimistic skepticism at the end of the Elizabethan age. Cicero and especially Seneca (Letter 65) are the chief of a multitude of classical influences discussed. Erasmus' *Praise of Folly*, Castiglione's *Courtier*, *The Pleasaunt Historie of Lazarillo de Tormes*, and Montaigne's *Essaies* are the principal continental influences discussed in this evolution from beginning to end and new beginning in "*L'infinito universo et Mondi*: The Development of a Posthumanist Poetics" (the concluding chapter). The exemplary English writers reviewed in successive chapters are More, Gascoigne, Lyly, Greene, Sidney, Nashe, and Lodge.

Professor Kinney has read carefully, thoughtfully, and much, and this literary history of Tudor prose fiction in the sixteenth century is both informative and perceptive. It is not, however, the last or complete word on the subject (nor is it intended to be). For one thing, in his emphasis on Seneca, Cicero, and other moral and rhetorical sources (including Aristotle's *Rhetoric*), Kinney fails to discuss the tremendous influence of Aristotle's *Poetics* (which is rarely even mentioned) on Elizabethan prose fiction. This lack is painfully evident in the analyses of Greene's *Pandosto* and Lodge's *Rosalynde*, which have so obviously been made to conform to Aristotelian prescriptions about the structuring of poetic imitations. In general the enormous influence of drama and dramatic theory on sixteenth-century prose fiction is largely ignored or viewed from other perspectives (except in occasional rhetorical slips, as, for example, the frequent reference to interior monologues as "soliloquies").

Kinney's use of the terms "humanism" and "humanist" is also somewhat limited. Although he does discuss two very important humanist, that is, Renaissance Latin, works, Erasmus' *Encomium Moriae* and More's *Utopia*, he means these terms to refer to sixteenth-century prose fiction written in English and the writers of the English works that he discusses. Very few other works of continental or British humanism are mentioned (it would have been interesting to put Barclay, for example, beside Sidney and Nashe). Everything, however, cannot be done at the same time, and this study is already of considerable length. It admirably demonstrates how immersed English prose writers of the sixteenth century were in the classics and in continental letters.

Roman Satirists in Seventeenth-Century England, by William Kupersmith. Lincoln, Nebr. and London: University of Nebraska Press, 1985. Pp. xii + 189. $19.95.

Reviewer: KATHARINE EISAMAN MAUS

This book discusses the translations of Juvenal, Horace, and Persius in the seventeenth century, beginning with Jonson's adaptations in *Sejanus* and *Poetaster*, working through the century to "Dryden and his Myrmidons." It gives some attention to the work of every seventeenth-century translator: Barten Holyday, Robert Stapleton, William Barksted, and Thomas Creech, for example, as well as better-known contemporaries like Chapman and Vaughan. In the Preface Kupersmith writes:

> My original object was to investigate the background to Alexander Pope's *Imitations of Horace* and Samuel Johnson's *London* and *The Vanity of Human Wishes*, and to find out how Roman satire was read by Englishmen in the Restoration and early eighteenth centuries. . . . But in the process of writing this book my focus narrowed to concentrate on the methods used by translators into verse.
>
> (p. ix)

In its final form the book concentrates heavily on issues of poetic technique: on the choice and management of verse form, on the finding of "cultural equivalents" for words and practices that have no precise English corollaries, on the various attempts to approximate the tone of the Latin originals.

After a few introductory remarks, each chapter proceeds in the same fashion. A quotation from Horace or Juvenal is followed by a translation, as literal as possible, into English prose. Then Kupersmith comments briefly on the passage, pointing out particular felicities and explaining obscurities. There follows the seventeenth-century English translation of the passage under discussion. Then Kupersmith provides a little more commentary. Then there is another quotation in Latin, and so on. Passages quoted in English and Latin take up well over a third of this short book. Since many of the writers that Kupersmith discusses are not ones his readers will have in their memories or even in their libraries, the necessity for extensive quotation is obvious. The real problem is that although Kupersmith's remarks are usually sensible and sometimes illuminating, he just does not have enough to say.

Why not? In narrowing his focus, Kupersmith has defined his topic practically out of existence. His book lacks any strong governing conception. He writes in the Introduction that he has tried to avoid "generalizations and theoretical statements about what a good translation might be," but the result is not, as he hopes, "a way of discussing and evaluating seventeenth-century English adaptations that would be empirical" (pp. xi–xii). For in practice he relies upon apparently unexamined assumptions, based upon his appreciation for Pope and Johnson, about what the Romans are doing and how an English writer ought to respond to them. Predictably, the earlier writers suffer. Ben Jonson, for instance, is at his best when he "anticipates the neoclassicists" (p. 6) or when he abandons his usual practice and "takes a detour that leads, in a sense, into the eighteenth century" (p. 14); most of the rest of the time he is "frigid" and "primitive." Teleology has its uses in literary history, and I do not find Kupersmith's evolutionary rhetoric necessarily inappropriate, but he does need to describe and defend his method with some self-consciousness and conviction. In fact his assumptions not only remain tacit but seem to be positively disclaimed at times, as when he notes that his material fails to show "a clear line of development culminating in the Dryden translation of 1692" (p. 87).

Kupersmith's methodological reticence is merely one sympton of his apparent discomfort with generalizations of any sort. He gives his readers a series of observations upon particular lines and cruxes but no context in which such observations could be meaningfully integrated. To provide such a context, he would have had to enlarge the scope of his investigation, to discuss at least briefly the literary, social, and intellectual milieu in which the translations were produced. Do changes in the laws pertaining to literary endeavors—particularly the censorship laws—conduce to the development of the imitation as a form? Does seventeenth-century speculation about the origins and nature of language affect attitudes toward the process of translation? Do the cavalier poets' graceful and ideologically tendentious conflations of Roman and English culture in their original verse suggest political motives for the translation of Latin texts in the turbulent mid-century? These are, of course, large questions, but that is no reason to avoid them. Kupersmith is a lively writer, scornful of pedants and "literary-critical bores" (p. 9), eager to enliven Latin satire and Restoration literary politics by drawing modern parallels. The racy irreverence of some of the writers that he studies seems to have rubbed off on his prose. On topical allusions in Horace and Juvenal, for example, he writes that "many of the identifications in the scholia in the margins of manuscripts . . . are probably wild guesses by late classical grammarians who had nothing better to do while waiting for the Goths to arrive and get on with their sacking and looting" (pp. 147–148). Unfortunately these flashes of wit do not compensate for the intellectual thinness of the performance. His book may alert scholars to some of the more obscure seventeenth-century translators, but there is far better work on the neoclassicism of the major writers by Jonas Barish, Richard Peterson, Annabel Patterson, Jonathan Post, Earl Miner, and others.

Christopher Marlowe: Poet for the Stage, by Clifford Leech, edited by Anne Lancashire. New York: AMS Press, 1986. Pp. ix + 250. $39.50.

Reviewer: R. A. FOAKES

This posthumous study of Marlowe appears ten years after the author's death and has been edited by Anne Lancashire as an act of homage to a distinguished critic and scholar. As I was reading it I began to wonder whether Clifford Leech would have changed much had he been able to take into account recent work on Marlowe, such as Robert Weimann's discussion in *Shakespeare and the Popular Tradition in the Theatre* (trans. Robert Schwartz [Baltimore, Md.: Johns Hopkins University Press 1978]), or the chapter on *Doctor Faustus* and *Edward II* in Michael Hattaway's *Elizabethan Popular Theatre* (London: Routledge, 1982), or the Revels edition of *Tamburlaine* (ed. J. S. Cunningham [Manchester: Manchester University Press, 1981]), commissioned by him. I believe the answer is "no," and not merely because he would not have wanted to make significant alterations to an argument that was forged out of a lifetime spent in the study of Elizabethan and Jacobean drama; I think he would have felt, rightly, that the book has sufficient independence and strength to stand as it is and complement other available accounts of the dramatist. There is an authority and weightiness in the writing that makes this lucid, comprehensive study of Marlowe a book that will, I suspect, be much quarried by students of the drama.

At the same time, its historical conditioning and limitations are now perhaps more evident than they would have been in the author's lifetime. His argument depends upon a radical revision of the traditionally accepted chronology of Marlowe's plays, a chronology popularized by T. S. Eliot's essay (1919), which assumed that the dramatist developed from simple, and simplistic, bombast in the early *Tamburlaine*, to the intensity of high tragedy in *Doctor Faustus*, and towards a maturer style, hesitating on the edge of caricature, in *The Jew of Malta* and *Dido* (*Selected Essays* [London: Faber, 1932], pp. 119-125). Leech's dissatisfaction with this conception of Marlowe's peotic development arose in large part from his acute response to the plays as texts for performance, and he was among the first to recognize the complexity of *Tamburlaine*. He saw that comedy is "woven into the fabric of the first scene of Act

I" (p. 61) in the mockery of Mycetes; he also saw that Tamburlaine himself is not presented simply as in a "tragic glass" (Prologue, line 8) but courts absurdity at times, as in the killing of his son Calyphas: "A great figure who is impelled to this act of butchery is over the brink of absurdity" (p. 63). So Marlowe did not begin with huff-stuff tragedy and develop later a tone to suit farce; Leech noticed how comedy runs through all of Marlowe's work and so felt that he had to come to terms with the problem of "Marlowe's Humor," to cite the title of an essay that he published in 1963 (*Essays on Shakespeare and the Elizabethan Drama in Honor of Hardin Craig* [Columbia, Mo.: University of Missouri Press, 1962], pp. 69–81.

He rooted his explanation for Marlowe's use of comedy in the traditions that lay behind his work, notably the moral play with its dominant figure of the comic Vice. If Marlowe deliberately incorporated comic material, he "had warrant in the moral plays" (p. 61), and a chapter is given over to the question "*Faustus:* A Moral Play?" in an effort to show that Mephistopholis is "though not so named, a manifest Vice" (p. 107) in a play that both displays and questions by finally subverting the shape of the traditional morality. At the same time, if Marlowe was consciously using comic elements to undermine Mycetes and to create ambivalence and irony in his presentation of Tamburlaine, the traditional idea of Marlowe's development ceases to make much sense. So Leech proposed a radically revised chronology of the plays. The dating of them after *Tamburlaine* remains largely speculative, and he did not need to discount documentary evidence in boldly rearranging the plays in relation to "the measure of coherence" (p. 23) thereby given to Marlowe's writing. After *Dido* (1586), he groups *Tamburlaine* and *Doctor Faustus* as "cosmic tragedies" (p. 23), written in the years 1588–90, and believes these were followed by *Edward II*, *The Massacre at Paris*, and *The Jew of Malta* in 1590–92. This scheme preserves the concept of a dramatist developing, but in a different way, from "cosmic tragedies, showing their heroes at odds with the universe," to plays like *Edward II*, which are "noticeably silent or casual about the cosmos and show man alone determined on, and successful in, his fellows' destruction. If there is a simple logic in the matter, we might say that Marlowe proceeded from cosmic tragedy to social drama" (p. 20).

So Leech replaces a traditional view of Marlowe's "development" by a different one, dependent on a chronology that will not seem plausible to everyone. The strength of his conception of Marlowe, confirmed in recent critical studies of the plays, is that the dramatist is seen as a powerful artist who from the beginning of his career was consciously controlling and manipulating his material and his audience. It is appropriate that Leech's book culminates in a chapter on "The Acting of Marlowe and Shakespeare," in which Marlowe's use of formal rhetoric and set speeches is seen as making special demands on the actor, who must be eloquent and detached and yet must also somehow (the "how" is not made clear) generate sympathy: "Marlowe's character is a construct that belongs to the drama alone. . . . The actor cannot simply 'identify'; he must deliberately compose his portrait along the lines that the play's words and actions and scene demonstrate" (p. 208). Well, yes, as in Ben

Jonson's plays, the actor has to give himself and project, and cannot slide into the part, as is possible in many Shakespearean roles.

It might be argued that there is a greater absorption into the part in, say, the roles of Edward II and Faustus than in that of Tamburlaine, a greater internalization in characters conceived as contained within the context of the action, rather than providing theatrical display for the audience; and such a view might suggest a different chronology and a way of getting off the hook of concepts like "development" and "coherence," which require Leech to think of *Doctor Faustus* as an early play. His welcome emphasis on the problems of acting Marlowe's plays raises questions about his chronology, and it seems in other ways to set him somewhat at odds with himself, in fact, for while he acknowledges that the "dominating effect" of *The Jew of Malta* is comic, he wants all the same to find in it "a sense of the tragic" (pp. 173-174). It is as if after all he cannot reconcile himself to a conception of Marlowe as developing from plays of a mainly tragic tone to writing plays that refuse to be tragic. If he is right to find a Bradleyan sense of tragic waste in *Doctor Faustus* and to argue that the tragic hero "confronts the cosmos, while the merely comic figure confronts only society" (p. 163), then it seems inconsistent of him to find a "tragic note" in *Edward II*, a play that, as he says, "merely focuses attention on certain aspects of the human scene" (pp. 143-144).

Leech is to some extent trapped in his need to claim coherence in Marlowe's development and cannot find a way of dealing fully with the simultaneous awareness of heroism and absurdity that he was among the first to highlight in the plays. Others, like Eugene Waith and Judith Weil, have confronted this issue, which is one source of the continuing fascination that Marlowe generates. Leech puts his finger on such problems and amply shows why Marlowe is a great dramatist; whatever its final limitations, his commentary on the plays and poems is full of acute perceptions and sound good sense, and the book will be valued for these qualities. Anne Lancashire's labor of love in preparing it for the press should not go unnoticed; it is a pity that her work, completed in 1980, has taken so long to reach publication.

The City Staged: Jacobean Comedy, 1603-1613, by Theodore B. Leinwand. Madison, Wis.: University of Wisconsin Press, 1986. Pp. viii + 230. $25.00.

Reviewer: CAROL LEVENTEN

Theodore Leinwand focuses on those city comedies performed from 1603 to 1613 that are explicitly concerned with status groups and that "render critically" one or more types—citizen-merchants, gentleman-gallants, and women—"caught up in the urban social economy" (p. 9). His concern is not with social roles *per se* but with the reciprocal relationship between the staging of social conflicts and the "extratheatrical reality" informing that staging—a relationship that he describes as mutually constituting (p. 3). Analyzing city comedy's plotting and characterization in terms of contemporary Londoners' perceptions of the changing city and its populace, he finds that stage performance "both parodies and refracts" social roles played out in the streets and brings them into sharp relief (p. 10). The stereotypical characters of city comedy are presented as such, he argues, so that audiences may come to see typecasting for what it is and understand its limitations; thus, the exaggerated "types" of city comedy (never conceived of as realistic) suggest discrepancies between stereotypical roles and actuality, and the plays challenge audiences' prejudices: because a "spectator comes to see a stage gallant as a stage merchant can never see him . . . he awakens to the tyranny of stereotyping" (p. 7).

Leinwand's approach is neither author- nor play-centered; instead, he offers separate chapters on each category of typecasting—merchant-citizens, gallants, and women (wives, whores, widows, virgins)—as they are presented in the plays; each category, in turn, is introduced by an examination of extratheatrical attitudes (that is, in contemporary pamphlet literature and conduct books). Accordingly, a given play is typically discussed in several sections of the book (compare Alexander Leggatt's approach in *Citizen Comedy in the Age of Shakespeare* [Toronto: University of Toronto Press, 1973]). This scheme, while not without merit, does present difficulties in view of Leinwand's controlling vision, which stresses the *interaction* (or self-canceling collision?) between stereotype and stereotype: we never see that interaction and must flip from chapter to chapter if we seek to synthesize his discoveries about the workings of typecasting in any one of the plays discussed (for example, the three *Ho* plays, *Michaelmas Term* and *A Chaste Maid*, *I* and *II Honest Whore*, *The Knight of the Burning Pestle*, *The Roaring Girl*, *Epicoene*, and *The Alchemist*). As a result, generalizations tend to be repeated from chapter to chapter rather than cumulatively developed, and carefully nuanced arguments are not built. This is unfortunate, because Leinwand's discussion of individual plays is far from reductionist. His analysis of contemporary debate about changing social roles is sensitive to its inconclusive, often contradictory nature, and he frequently reminds us of the ways in which city comedy signals its awareness of those contradictions. An integrative concluding chapter would have helped greatly.

With the merchant-citizen, "a man with an identifiable economic role" but "an uncertain 'social place' " (p. 22) as well as with gallants and women, Leinwand does locate authorial differences. Although virtually all merchants are cast in predetermined social roles, Dekker and Webster disrupt anticipated alliances in their two *Ho* plays and present "blurred social configurations" that require the audience to "rethink conventional stereotypes" (p. 47), he says, while Middleton typically presents overdetermined characters that out-stereotype the stereotypes and hence "permit" audiences to question convenient assumptions. In *Michaelmas Term*, for example, Leinwand says that the exaggerated social roles in the play world are different enough from extratheatrical presentations to allow us to conclude that Middleton is parodic: he believes that Middleton satirizes the *convention* of the merchant in Quomodo, not the merchant himself. But, Leinwand suggests, such satire can cut two ways: at the same time that Middleton reveals the crudeness of "antibourgeois formulations," his parodic caricatures reinforce them on another level.

The bulk of Leinwand's analysis of gentleman-gallants focuses on the representation of self/role distinctions (the "relation between an enacted role and a central self" [p. 114]) as it explores contemporary efforts, onstage and off, to redefine a class in flux. An extremely interesting discussion of Lovewit and Truewit supports Leinwand's judgment that Jonson is unique among the playwrights of city comedy in truly questioning the premises of the prevailing social structure. Characteristically, however, while the genre deflates the pretensions of the gallant as much as it does those of the citizen, it nevertheless stages the former as "a man with an essential social identity, a core self that underlies a set of theatrical personae," in contrast to its staging of the merchant-citizen as a "master pretender" trapped in and by his role (p. 90). Leinwand believes, then, that city comedy (Jonson's excepted) reveals an underlying acceptance of and confidence in the social system that it stages, a belief that he pursues in two very different ways. On the one hand, Leinwand hypothesizes that these plays, in locating a secure self in the gentleman, the sponsor of prevailing ideologies, do not simply privilege the gallant over the merchant but extend the same possibility to the latter: they suggest "(perhaps only tacitly) that equivalent selves must be found for the merchant-citizen and for women" (p. 91). On the other hand, Leinwand also asserts that the playwrights were reluctant to alienate the social class that supported and protected the theaters, that their privileging of the gallant is self-interested, and that they do ultimately treat the two groups very differently: the gallant has a self as well as a role, the merchant does not.

At this point it becomes apparent that Leinwand seems reluctant to acknowledge both the implicit contradictions of his readings and the direction in which they appear to be taking him. He is actually proposing, almost offhandedly, that city comedy is grounded in a conservative class-bias that legitimates privilege, and that the net effect of its caricature of social stereotypes is not, after all, to "permit" or "require" audiences to question their accuracy and adequacy (his stated thesis) but ultimately to *contain* the impulse to caricature.

His detailed analysis of women's roles (to which he devotes about a third of the book) is similarly equivocal: city comedy exaggerates the extratheatrical typecasting of wives, whores, widows, and "chaste maids" both to criticize and to perpetuate such compartmentalization. Leinwand reiterates the familiar observation that self-sufficient, intelligent female characters are often the "structural hinge," the center of action, yet the stage women who succeed in breaking free from compartmentalized roles and who can appear to be monstrous—or simply human—are ultimately undermined or contained: just as Moll in *The Roaring Girl* is both fantasy and monster, a character who achieves autonomy at the expense of her "real self," the wives in a play like *Westward Ho*, who use their "native wit" to reinforce their own integrity rather than to humiliate rivals (as gallants do), are ultimately brought to heel, and their plot is reduced to "a good story . . . one more merry tale of women's resourcefulness" (p. 153). The self-fashioning, self-assertive woman of city comedy is "a possibility held out to the audience," but "her eventual containment is a measure . . . of the prevailing masculine ideology" (p. 154), Leinwand concludes: "what looks liberal is in fact rather conservative" (p. 159).

That assertion, and the route by which it is reached, indicate some of the strengths and limitations of this book. Certainly the chapters on women and gallants, despite their occasional truisms, lay the groundwork for a more searching critique of city comedy, since Leinwand's embedded argument centers on containment, on issues of patriarchy and class. The tentative judgments that he makes, almost in passing, within individual chapters need to be argued rather than asserted, and their implications need to be addressed. But Leinwand seems to want it both ways: city comedy awakens its audience to the distortions and inadequacies of compartmentalized roles, expands possibilities; city comedy reinforces compartmentalization and defers to the concerns of a defended, conservative patriarchy. What are we to make of a Middleton who simultaneously perpetuates and exposes the crudeness of antibourgeois clichés? Of a Dekker and Webster whose *Westward Ho*, in similarly mocking citizens and gallants, seems to offer a basis for mutual solidarity but actually perpetuates class animosity and mutual distrust? To put it bluntly, Leinwand waffles. It may well be possible to identify bipolar pulls in the genre—to formulate a thesis that more adequately accounts for and integrates the contradictory claims in this book—but *The City Staged* does not do so. Its more provocative sections certainly suggest directions that future studies might profitably pursue.

Part of the problem inheres in methodology and conceptual framework. Leinwand's explicit thesis—that city comedy "permits" or "requires" audiences to perceive (and then reject) the "tyranny of stereotyping" that pervades extratheatrical role-playing—raises problematical questions about intentionality and/or performance issues that need to be addressed but are not. If one's central argument turns on the possibilities of a Jacobean audience's response, one needs to face up squarely to the limitations of contemporary evidence. Leinwand refers, for example, to the "expectation" of *Eastward Ho*'s authors "that the Blackfriars audience would have been alert to the ways a play might parody its own assumptions" (p. 64), yet the "expectation" is simply deduced from the text. Unaccountably, the single documented instance of contemporary reception that he does cite—the audience's failure to appreciate the demonstrably parodic achievement of Francis Beaumont's *The Knight of the Burning Pestle*—undermines rather than supports Leinwand's claims: "This 'unfortunate child' of a play was 'exposed to the wild world, who for want of judgement, *or not understanding the privy mark of irony about it* . . . utterly rejected it' " (p. 65; italics mine).

Moreover, because his effort to recontextualize city comedy focuses on issues of cultural production and reception and hence links Leinwand, willingly or not, to the new historicism, it raises questions about his point of departure. Comparatively little work has been done on city comedy as a genre, and while Leinwand very clearly articulates his differences from earlier studies by Leggatt and Brian Gibbons, he does not convey a mastery of the large body of recent work on Renaissance drama that is equally relevant to his topic. It is not necessary in the 'eighties to justify at length the introduction of "extratheatrical" evidence in a study of theatrical probing of gender and class issues; it *is* necessary to indicate just how one's own study diverges from other revisionist inquiries. The way in which Leinwand sets up straw figures but fails to contextualize his own critical framework makes his work appear dated or naive. For example, he repeatedly invokes, only to dismiss, Alfred Harbage's view that public and private theaters were significantly different yet oddly perpetuates it in his own chapter divisions. At the same time, he freely employs the term "self-fashioning" while referring obliquely and only once to Stephen Greenblatt (omitted from the index) as "one biographer of Sir Walter Ralegh" (p. 87). Similarly, his discussion of patriarchal containment of women and the illusory freedom obtained by disguise has important affinities with parts of Peter B. Erickson's *Patriarchal Structures in Shakespeare's Drama* (Berkeley, Calif: University of California Press, 1985), yet Leinwand treats city comedy as if it existed in a theatrical vacuum, allowing that audiences would remember the previous decade's disguised heroines of Shakespearean comedy but dismissing them as irrelevant to the women of the genre under consideration. If city comedy and romantic comedy do indeed explore gender issues in markedly different ways, this study does not begin to locate or to account for those differences, and it superficially identifies as differences what may actually be telling similarities.

Uneven and frequently frustrating, *The City Staged* strikes me as a draft—an often intriguing, potentially important, but incomplete draft in need of substantial clarification—rather than a finished study. It is unfortunate that Leinwand's editors did not encourage him to resolve its difficulties before publication. The jacket describes it as an "energetic" study; but it is the reader who will need considerable energy to distinguish its merits from a blurred and shifting focus, a lack of cohesion and integration, and a conceptual framework and method inadequate to the task at hand.

Changing Landscapes: Anti-Pastoral Sentiment in the English Renaissance, by Peter Lindenbaum. Athens Ga.: University of Georgia Press, 1986. Pp. xii + 234. $27.50.

Reviewer: THEODORE B. LEINWAND

Anti-pastoral sentiment, writes Peter Lindenbaum, is a "contentious" stance, assumed in opposition to "a cast of mind that either seeks an easy, carefree existence anywhere in our present world or indulges overmuch in dreams of better times and better places" (p. 17). Anti-pastoralists speak in unison for the active life and against relaxation. Indeed, Sidney, Shakespeare, and Milton were willing to ignore pastoral's "contemplative ideal," to substitute for it an identification of pastoral with escapism, if this would help them to make their case for engagement with the complex, confusing here and now.

In two chapters on Sidney, Lindenbaum sets out to minimize the often remarked differences between the *Old Arcadia* and the *New*. He argues that both works have as their animus an anti-pastoral bias: Arcadia is not a setting with true recreative potential; it does not offer inner peace; it is in fact no different from any other setting. Sidney's princes, in both versions, are fallible men. They are not entirely up to the model of active virtue presented by Euarchus or to the model of patience set by Pamela. But neither does Sidney's pessimistic anti-pastoralism imply that any one of us, whether within or without Arcadia, can easily master the "doing and suffering" that nobility and virtue demand. Lindenbaum points to "providential intercession" (the duke is not dead) in the *Old Arcadia* and to Pamela's faith and patience in the *New Arcadia* as evidence of Sidney's insistence on human limitation and frailty. Lindenbaum's Sidney is resigned to "constant struggle" and he is "distrust[ful] of ideal natural settings" (p. 73). He is tolerant of human failings, he is broadly ethical, and he is not without humor. However, he is unable to reconcile public duties with private desires, and he has no doubt about our need for vigilance in "a world we must, in the end, use the explicitly Christian term of 'fallen' to describe" (p. 90).

Lindenbaum's own humanist rhetoric, as well as his account of Sidney's humanism, entails some rather free-floating ethical precepts. One wonders just how particular Lindenbaum takes Sidney's criticism of the late sixteenth-century nobility to be. Does Lindenbaum see in the *Old Arcadia* and the *New* a lesson for Elizabethan courtiers in general, or for the Sidney circle, or is this something of a self-critique? Unlike a number of recent readers—David Norbrook and Annabel Patterson among them—Lindenbaum is not interested in grounding Sidney's ethics in contemporary politics. Even more to the point, Lindenbaum's procedure seems at odds with his account of Sidney's own intention. The poet is said to intend "actual and historical . . . settings" (p. 78) in his *New Arcadia* (not Virgilian landscapes of the mind—or so Lindenbaum reads Virgil), and one might well expect equally actual and historical matter. But Lindenbaum's ahistorical and unparticularized humanism is all too like Basilius' recourse to pastoral retreat. In one footnote, Lindenbaum contrasts his approach to pastoral with that of Stephen Greenblatt, Richard McCoy, and Louis Montrose, noting that he looks at "pastoral more as a literary convention than as a social form . . . focus[ing] upon the more general ethical and ideological biases of . . . pastoral writers" rather than upon "political motives" (p. 225 n.3). What makes Lindenbaum's emphasis odd is less the value of a humanist approach in itself than the way such an emphasis seems to run counter to Lindenbaum's seemingly favorable account of Sidney's intention. Sidney's anti-pastoral sentiment entails an insistence on politics in Arcadia as well as outside Arcadia: it too is "a land that must be governed" (p. 79). But Lindenbaum's own reading of the two works detaches itself from the Elizabethan "constant struggle" with which he argues Sidney believes his reader must engage. Lindenbaum's reading of Sidney's anti-pastoral Arcadia is analogous to the melancholic pastoral of Sannazaro that Lindenbaum tells us Sidney objects to. The "pressing activity of day-to-day living" that anti-pastoral sentiment deems inescapable, the form and pressure of Sidney's very age, these are Sidney's but not Lindenbaum's concerns.

Lindenbaum's discussion of Shakespeare's anti-pastoralism turns on his argument that Shakespeare "sought to undermine romanticizing pastoralism" (p. 109). The plays would have us accept the corrosive effect of time, and they ask that we reckon responsibly with adult sexuality. *As You Like It* and *The Winter's Tale* are thus structured as debates: Rosalind's realism and engagement versus Jacques's escapism, his final retreat; Hermione and Perdita's acceptance of time and the flesh versus Leontes/Polixenes' nostalgic, pre-sexual (or anti-sexual) sentimentalism. This is certainly accurate, though mention of Murray Schwartz's brilliant work on *The Winter's Tale* ought to have been made somewhere on pages 116-118. But perhaps Lindenbaum, unlike Shakespeare, argues too decidedly for what he deems "realistic," not escapist. Corin, Silvius and Phebe, William and Audrey "help Shakespeare establish a realistic picture of pastoral life" (p. 101); Time, in *The Winter's Tale*, "asserts the play's ultimate realistic bias" (p. 111); Bohemia is the "actual countryside" (p. 119); and Bohemia offers a "picture of life in a realistically perceived pastoral setting" (p. 127). We need only note that princess Perdita is an ever so *un*realistic "pastoral figure" to recognize that Shakespeare also seeks to undermine romanticizing *realism*. Realistic Hermione's confidence, wit, and warmth (p. 116) are no match for Leontes' very real power because anti-pastoral sentiment in Shakespearean drama can be as inadequate as its rather easily faulted opposite.

In the last section of *Changing Landscapes*, Lindenbaum turns to *Paradise Lost* and argues that Milton's anti-pastoral sentiment informs his account of Adam and Eve in Eden. Lindenbaum writes persuasively that Milton's is "a particularly uncontemplative Paradise" (p. 149), that the poem calls for "an active Edenic life" (p. 144). The two cogent discussions of physical labor and love-making in Eden permit Lindenbaum to apply his thesis to *Paradise Lost*, arguing that life in Eden is at least as complex and demanding as life after the fall. Some of the broadly ethical and even political issues that motivate anti-pastoral sentiment in Sidney and Shakespeare seem to drop out of the chapter on Milton. However, this same chapter includes two very fine close readings—one of Belial's speech in Book Two, and the other of Raphael's conversation with Adam, particularly the latter's confession of the difficulty that he experiences when dealing with Eve.

Changing Landscapes makes a compelling, if not entirely new case for our need to acknowledge the civic humanist in Sidney, Shakespeare, and Milton. Each is committed to the active life, and each expresses a profound distrust of retreat—whether for escape or for contemplation. Lindenbaum argues (briefly) that such sentiments spring from anti-monasticism and from versions of Protestantism in late sixteenth-century and early seventeenth-century England. (In one truly memorable line, we read that "anti-pastoralism can be said to constitute another, a literary, closing of the monasteries"—p. 186.) He does not, however, particularize just what sort of praxis the anti-pastoral sentiments of an Elizabethan or Jacobean courtier might encourage. To speak of the active life in itself as a positive ideal is to stop short of regarding the precise activity to which an aristocrat might commit himself. Certainly Sidney and Shakespeare's active aristocrats are cautious—not quite as ready to "join with . . . fellowmen and insist on . . . common humanity" (p. 190) as humanist rhetoric suggests they would be. Milton presents a different case, but again one wants at least to consider the sorts of activity in which a seventeenth-century Englishman faced with "a difficult Eden" might engage. Perhaps consideration of the politics of English anti-pastoral sentiment could follow upon the consideration of its ethics that Lindenbaum manages so well in this volume. Or perhaps the two ought not to stand apart.

The Court Masque, edited by David Lindley. The Revels Plays Companion Library. Manchester: Manchester University Press, 1984. Pp. 196 + 12 of illustrations. Cloth $25.00; paper $15.00.

Reviewer: CATHERINE M. SHAW

This is the first volume in a series whose General Editors, E.A.J. Honigmann, J. R. Mulryne, and R. L. Smallwood, describe in the Preface as a Companion Library to the Revels Plays designed "to provide students of the Elizabethan and Jacobean drama with a fuller sense of its background and context" (p. vii). In his Introduction, however, David Lindley adds that a further purpose for this specific volume is "to take issue" with the indifference of scholars toward the court masque. That there has been, he says, only "a thin trickle of significant scholarly studies" is evidence that the masque has been "largely neglected or lightly dismissed" (p. 1). Surely this statement is out of date. It is true that an archaic view of the masque lasted well into the twentieth century. When, in 1941, Herford and the Simpsons published Volume VII of their monumental *Ben Jonson* (Oxford: Clarendon Press), which includes the first critical editions of all of Jonson's masques, a sub-title, "Embellishing a Triviality," in the *Times Literary Supplement* review (15 November 1941) certainly shows lingering critical bias. However, of the four hundred and sixteen entries in David Bergeron's checklist *Twentieth-Century Criticism of English Masques, Pageants and Entertainments 1558-1642* (San Antonio, Tex.: Trinity University Press, 1972), over three hundred appeared in the thirty years between 1941 and 1971, Bergeron's *terminus ad quem*. And the Select Bibliography that Lindley provides and the notes following each of the ten essays also show that there has been no abatement during the 1972-84 period in which scholarly and theoretical approaches to the masque and its literary and historical environment have shown the same broadening of critical horizons as has been accorded other forms of Renaissance theater.

The best essays in this volume give evidence of this breadth of interest. For his stimulating contribution, "The reformation of the masque," David Norbrook draws upon Renaissance critical commentary within and without specific literary works and the excellent work of modern "revisionist" historians and places the confrontational aspects of courtly entertainments within the "complex interactions" (p. 95) of Stuart England. His argument dispels any remaining notions that masques were little more than servile flattery and any idea that their age was one of monolithic religious-political-esthetic polarizations. John Creaser's essay, "'The Present aid of this occasion': the setting of *Comus*," complements Norbrook's. The word *setting* is to be taken in its broadest sense. It first means the physical aspects of actual performance, which, he argues convincingly, were appropriate to viceregal ceremony. Also, however, and more importantly, Creaser's essay deals with how Milton dealt with the challenges of the familial, social, religious, and political "setting" in which Milton found himself when he accepted the commission from the Earl of Bridgewater.

Sara Pearl chooses as her subject the Jonson masques written between 1620 and 1625 and relates them to *The Staple of News*, which returned Jonson to the public stage after a ten-year hiatus. Pearl not only sets the works against the changing political and religious tensions in the court but also draws upon public anxieties raised when in 1620 translations of the Dutch news-sheets were regularly printed. "For the first time," she says, "ordinary people were able to discuss, assess and interpret national and international political events for themselves" (p. 61). Discussing the five masques in order and relating them directly to *The Staple of News*, Pearl shows how the masques reveal in mirror images, distorted or otherwise, Jonson's attitudes to the political and religious situations and the manner in which through them he was led to a different satiric mode.

David Lindley's own essay, "Music, masque, and meaning in *The Tempest*," although it deals specifically with only one play and its music, adds much to the important and larger subject of masque elements in drama and the ambivalences in audience response to them both in the age of Jacobean discontent and, by extension, in "all time." The diversity of music in *The Tempest*, he says, "exploits and explores the tensions" within the play that question whether a brave new world has been achieved (or can be achieved) in the theater or without (p. 47). "Not only," he shows, "are the characters on stage pushed hither and thither by Prospero's music, but it works its end upon our senses also, with an undeniable insinuation" (p. 58). In "Dryden's *Albion and Albanius*: the Apotheosis of Charles II" Paul Hammond carries our interest in masque into the post-Commonwealth era and discusses the way in which Dryden recast elements of the pre-war masque into different dramatic relationships. The result, he shows, "has an altered, more polemical, relationship with its audience" (p. 170).

John Peacock challenges the idea that the Italian impact on Inigo Jones tells the whole story of the development of the eclectic art of this remarkable man. Peacock argues convincingly that even before the arrival of Henrietta Maria in England, Jones's work showed distinctly French affinities and that in his designs of the 1630s there is "a new richness of content and stylistic development which show further signs of French influence" (p. 155). He provides the reader with superb illustrations and descriptions by which to compare Jones's designs with those of Italian artists working in France whose craft had already been mediated by the impact of the French Renaissance and with those of such distinguished and original French artists as René Boyvin and Jacques Callot.

The other essays, though not without interest, are less challenging because they are more narrow or uncertain in their argument. John Pitcher, for example, gives a close textual analysis of Samuel Daniel's masque, *Tethys Festival*, within which he particularizes specifically the allusiveness and elusiveness of its "numbers and modes (or figures)" (p. 40). In "'Death proves them all but toyes': Nashe's unidealising show," Elizabeth Cook chooses a modern play as her frame of reference, and thus her essay seems oddly out of focus in a volume supposedly meant to provide fuller "background and context" for Elizabethan and Jacobean drama. Nashe's complex juxtapositions between the unreal world of the allegorical figures and the real world represented by Will Summer—between masque and mockery—shows *Summer's Last Will and Testament* to be an early example of the kind of generic confrontation that became an established practice of later Tudor and Stuart masque-writers and of dramatists who used masque for ironic effect. Will Summer himself is Nashe's ironic pointer. He is at once Henry VIII's dead jester, interrupting and nagging the performers and insulting both the matter and the style of their show, and also allegorically he is the dying season. Through him, as G. R. Hibbard has pointed out, "the death of summer in Croyden, in the year 1592, took on a special significance and acquired an unwonted depth and poignancy from the proximity of the plague-ridden city. To Nashe and [thus] for those for whom he wrote life itself appeared as brief holiday from the terror of death" (*Thomas Nashe: a Critical Introduction* [Cambridge, Mass.: Harvard University Press, 1962], p. 90.).

Helen Cooper suggests that the simple staging of medieval drama and the complex sets for masque both integrated playing-space and audience. Players and spectators, she says, come to inhabit the same world, and therefore "location" comes to have significant meaning. The same, she says, is not true for regular Renaissance drama. Counter to much modern criticism, this position argues against any audience distancing in the former or direct involvement in the latter. There seems to be an inconsistency in Jennifer Chibnall's essay on Caroline masque form. She encourages a return to considering masque as a literary object even though she says that the "Caroline masques [are] . . . the least amenable to being read as literature" (p. 78). She then discusses various masques that she sees as reflecting the uncertainties and social realities of the age.

In all, then, although *The Court Masque* offers a wide variety of consistently well-written essays, the number that provide genuinely new insights or encourage a broader perspective in critical approach to an art form central to understanding the interlocked complexities of its age is somewhat disappointing.

The World at Play in Boccaccio's *Decameron*, by Giuseppe Mazzotta. Princeton, N. J.: Princeton University Press, 1986. Pp. xvi + 280. $32.50.

Reviewer: MICHAEL D. BRISTOL

The title of Giuseppe Mazzotta's book *The World at Play in Boccaccio's "Decameron"* conveys only a partial sense of the author's project. Play, game, the consolations of leisure and of imagination as enjoyed by Bocaccio's *brigata* are certainly central concerns of this essay, and especially the complex play of self-conscious artistry in the structure of the *Decameron* both at the level of individual tales and at the level of strategic organization and tactical positioning of tales within the work as a whole. However, play is situated within a larger and more complicated dialectic that seems to have been crucially important for the entire culture of the late medieval and early modern periods, namely the dialectic of *serio-ludere*, the paradoxical mingling and interconnection of jest and earnest. Mazzotta's book is a substantial and useful contribution to a large and rapidly growing body of scholarship that interprets a wide variety of cultural forms in the light of the serio-comic. The strength of this contribution lies in its combination of traditional scholarly erudition and a discrete elaboration of current issues in literary theory. Boccaccio and the text of the *Decameron* are consistently positioned at the center of Mazzotta's domain of inquiry, and although his discussion of the material is clearly informed by contemporary theoretical discourse, those concerns are treated as subordinate or tangential to the illumination of the literary material itself.

The topos of *serio-ludere* has been investigated and traced by Ernst Curtius, in *European Literature and the Latin Middle Ages* (trans. Willard Trask [Princeton, N. J.: Princeton University Press, 1953]), where, interestingly and revealingly the discussion of this cognitive strategy is allocated to several lengthy excursuses appended to the text. Curtius shows that the mode of serio-comic writing was important throughout the Middle Ages, and not just for literature, for achieving the function of *ridendo dicere verum*. It is not entirely clear either in his discussion of jest and earnest, or in the subsequent discussion of "kitchen humor" what exactly might be funny about the truth or how it could be treated as a laughing matter. One possible answer to this is provided in Rosalie Colie's *Paradoxia Epidemica, The Renaissance Tradition of Paradox*, (Princeton, N. J.: Princeton University Press, 1966), which demonstrates that paradox and even radical self-contradiction have been seen not as mere figures of speech but in fact as fundamental structural features of truth or at least of the understanding that the *logos* must always exceed and thus cancel every determinate verbal formation, including even paradox. A second possible approach to the dialectic of *ridendo dicere verum* is the one suggested by Mikhail Bakhtin in *Rabelais and His World* (trans. Hélène Iswolsky [Bloomington, Ind.: Indiana University Press, 1984]).

> In the Renaissance, laughter in its most radical, universal, and at the same time gay form emerged from the depths of folk culture; it emerged but once in the course of history, over a period of some fifty or sixty years (in various countries and at various times) and entered with its popular (vulgar) language the sphere of great literature and high ideology. It appeared to play an essential role in the creation of such masterpieces of world literature as Boccaccio's *Decameron*, the novels of Rabelais and Cervantes, Shakespeare's dramas and comedies, and others. The walls between official and nonofficial literature were inevitably to crumble, especially because in the most important ideological sectors these walls also served to separate languages—Latin from the vernacular.
>
> (p. 172)

Bakhtin's view is that the serio-comic is best explained in light of contingent social differences and the articulation of those differences in the diversity of speech types characteristic of every concrete socio-cultural reality. This formulation is related to the privileging of "reported speech" with its parodic double intention, a formulation that would seem to have some decisive pertinence for a text such as the *Decameron*.

Mazzotta clearly follows the first of these two lines of investigation, avoiding the radical interpretations of Bakhtin in favor of a more strictly literary and "philosophical" treatment of the serio-comic. This strategy does have certain advantages, as the following paragraphs will show. However, the decision to set aside the analytical and historical categories suggested by Bakhtin is consequential and in some sense decisive for the working out of this project. Boccaccio's writing does seem to be engaged with popular culture in the sense Bakhtin describes. Mazzotta chooses to focus attention on the learned and philosophical contexts of the *Decameron*, more or less excluding any sustained consideration of material culture and of the popular element in Boccaccio's social milieu. This choice may be justified, but Mazzotta never argues the case, preferring instead a take-it-or-leave-it presentation of what he regards as the appropriate context and methodology for understanding the *Decameron*.

The methodology adopted for this study is a version of the rich philological scholarship practiced by an earlier generation of scholars, mostly of European origins, of whom the best known are Leo Spitzer, Ernst Kantorowicz, Erich Auerbach, and of course, Curtius. The strength of this method is in a range and depth of learning that generates a very high density of citation and cross-reference in classical and patristic sources. And it is a method that permits larger issues of cultural and of socio-political organization to be addressed. By using this method Mazzotta is able to situate the *Decameron* within an extensive intertext that relates the central topic of play or esthetics to an array of non-literary discursive codes such as medicine, law, commerce, theology, together with both learned and vernacular understanding of sexuality and gender difference. In each chapter of *The World at Play*, we are shown a variation on Boccaccio's central dialectical strategy, which is to position the playfulness, *anomie*, or untruth of literary fiction over against an opposing nomological discourse so as to reveal a fictitious and lawless center at the heart of every truth-claim. Revelation of the heartless and meretricious character of lawful "knowledge" paradoxically redeems the "virtue" of storytelling. Mazzotta shows that the governing distinction between *fiction* and *knowledge* is to a considerable degree gender-coded. In Boccaccio, however, the orthodox and invidious contrast between the "effeminacy" of play and the "manly virtue" of true knowledge is overturned or canceled by the complicated narrative interaction among the various stories and storytellers.

The pivotal chapter in *The World at Play in Boccaccio's "Decameron"* is entitled "Plague and Play," and it is here, in his analysis of the frame narrative, that Mazzotta presents the dialectical pattern that controls the structure of Boccaccio's text. Plague is, of course, both the englobing reality of the garden where the *brigata* retreats to tell its stories and as well the dystopic "elsewhere" of the harmonious *locus amoenus*. Boccaccio situates plague within a larger cosmic and providential scheme, but plague itself is the mode of radical disorder and the dissolution of categories. The symptoms of plague signify both the abolition of signification and the fundamental helplessness of any institutional knowledge such as medical science. Plague is thus an image of a radical and terrifying *anomie*, a sovereign power of undifferentiation that has the force of an irresistible law. Play, usually understood as the frivolous denial of the real and the serious aspects of human life, becomes in such a context a kind of law unto itself. The retreat of the *brigata* into the privileged space of entertainment, pleasure, and imaginative harmony is far more than mere escape, since the company accept the "rules of the game" as binding within that space. The lawfulness of play stands as the dialectical antithesis to the random destructiveness of plague. A complicated opposition is thus established between the sovereign and irresistible truth of undifference represented by plague and the precarious and fragile "untruth" of a storytelling game that recreates difference and reestablishes human purpose at the level of the narrative impulse. Boccaccio complicates the situation, however, by hinting at a kind of complicity between the two terms. Plague and play both objectify, though in different ways, an irresistible tendency towards *anomie* concealed within the guise of a binding imperative. Mazzotta's argument is that this complicated dialectic is a powerful cognitive instrument that Boccaccio uses to carry out an encyclopedic critique of his own intellectual and social milieu.

Within the dialectical pattern set forth in the discussion of plague and play, Mazzotta explores several different areas of discursive practice elaborated in the *Decameron*. In his discussion of "The Marginality of Literature" Mazzotta distinguishes Boccaccio's project from Dante's magisterial "exegesis of the *Logos*." The *Decameron* raises the more troubling question of the meaning of literature in a world of history (plague) from which the *Logos* is absent. In such a world, desire, fantasy, and even a perverse will to deception continually obstruct the possibility of stable meanings. The "literary" and "mimetic" character of desire invest the realm of value, which is of course radically deranged by excess of imagination.

> the marketplace, the privileged realm of values because there properties are traded, is also the locus where the crisis of exchange occurs on account of the fantasies of power, imaginary self-constructs, private interest, passions, and unbridled desires which converge in and lie under all deals merchants strike.
>
> (p. 78)

The effeminate world of storytelling—even when it is little more than mere gossip—"seems both to mock and imitate the world of men's business with its production of real wealth and lure of real adventures" (p. 79).

An even more interesting variation on this pattern is presented in the discussion of "Allegory and the Pornographic Imagination," and in the three subsequent chapters on sexuality in both its pathetic and its farcical manifestations. Allegory, on an orthodox reading, is that mode of knowing that takes the desiring soul beyond the contingent and sometimes seductive surface towards a view of "naked truth." Pornography, on this view, responds to a perverse fascination with pleasing but meretricious appearance. But, Mazzotta argues, "Pornography is an allegory, for like allegory it needs a cover. . . . in the present figuration of pornography, morality is the chaff hiding the erotic fruit" (p. 119). Mazzotta concedes that this perverse view is exactly opposite to what Boccaccio sanctions in other contexts, but Mazzotta nevertheless maintains that the hidden complicity between allegory and pornography is essential to the literary *and* to the moral structure of the *Decameron*. This would seem to point to a kind of "lewdness" in the moralizing allegorist's desire for truth, especially naked truth. Such "lewdness" would be as deeply incompatible with anything that might be called "love" as the most callous fantasy of the pornographer. But even love is finally a mode of duplicity, a force that is alternately harmoniously binding (eros) and violently divisive (desire as mimesis).

Mazzotta's account of the pathos of storytelling in the *Decameron* has a distinctly post-modern feel throughout. The argument is conducted through multiple close readings of individual tales, readings that gradually accumulate an overpowering sense of dispersal and of *mise-en-abîme*. The art of the *Decameron*, he argues, is not a mode of irony, since irony is "an intellectual weapon that establishes the hierarchy of the mind over the body" (p. 261). Instead, Boccaccio's art is to be understood as the art of laughter, which entails the full acknowledgment and acceptance of fatuity in human affairs. Play thus emerges as a positive virtue and indeed as the necessary antithesis to the classical and patristic ideal of *gravitas*. On Mazzotta's reading, Boccaccio is an important precursor of the Italian Humanists and especially of their ideal of *civile conversazione*. Boccaccio is "anti-systematic . . . his sense that there are no unvarying rules or fixed moral absolutes leads him to elaborate *an art of the possible* . . . a universe of relative, multiple perspectives and reversible metaphors" (p. 261). By extension, then, Boccaccio anticipates certain latter-day Humanists, and in particular those literary "pragmatists" whose aims have been articulated by Richard Rorty. In this outlook *civility* and *conversation* are exalted above partisan stands and philosophical systems, and politics is viewed as, proverbially, the "art of the possible." The book thus hints at a powerful continuity, a kind of *longue durée* within Humanism. It is Mazzotta's sympathy with that tradition that accounts, I think, both for the deployment of a traditional philological methodology and for the preference for a certain contemporary theoretical vocabulary. It also accounts for the relative neglect of any detailed account of material culture or of the popular element in those Florentine neighborhoods that Boccaccio *and* his characters frequented. Within the limits of this ideological orientation, however, this is a coherent and persuasively argued account of Boccaccio's position within a serio-comic tradition that scholarship is no longer able or willing to marginalize. It should engage the attention of anyone interested in the human seriousness of play and in the construction of social reality in the domain of the imaginary.

Literary Theory/Renaissance Texts, edited by Patricia Parker and David Quint. Baltimore, Md.: Johns Hopkins University Press, 1986. Pp. vii + 399. Cloth $30.00; paper $12.95.

Reviewer: PETER ERICKSON

The title *Literary Theory/Renaissance Texts*, with its sharp juxtaposition of theory and text, appears to parallel that of another recent volume co-edited by Patricia

Parker—*Shakespeare and the Question of Theory* (London: Methuen, 1985). But the force of the two volumes is quite different. The emphasis on questioning theory in the earlier volume (see my review in *Shakespeare Quarterly*, 37 [1986], 516–520) is greatly decreased in this new collection; where *Shakespeare and the Question of Theory* relishes the ferment arising from the interplay and clash among multiple theories, here not only does deconstruction dominate but the primary effect is the assimilation of a moderate version of deconstructive technique into an ongoing tradition of Renaissance studies. In his Introduction, David Quint notes how the contributors' "engagement with contemporary theory" includes "resistance to its most radical conclusions and consequences": "The present essays steer a middle course between the univocal text and triumphalist canon on the one hand and the dispersion of both text and canon on the other" (p. 15). The nicely detailed but cautious essay by Patricia Parker exemplifies what this "middle course" means in practice. The essay ends:

> It may be that what leads us historically from the forms of dilation and delay in the Renaissance to those more recent texts that inform Derrida's invocation of a limitless "diff*e*rance" is an exclusively post-Renaissance questioning of those very limiting structures . . . . But it may also be that both a simple Derridean reading of Renaissance texts and a rigorous opposition to it run in their potential onesidedness the risk of missing the contradictory presence in the Renaissance of both strains at once, the structure and what eludes or exceeds it, and hence of what might be most fascinating of all to theory.
>
> (pp. 205–206)

This is a cogent formulation of a crucial theoretical issue, but it strikes a happy medium in the negative sense that it is so tentatively and inconclusively put: the sustained theoretical exploration that could provide a firmer position is missing.

The two essays that stand out as the most theoretically rigorous and challenging contributions are those by Stephen Greenblatt and Louis Adrian Montrose. (For a full item-by-item survey, consult Miranda Johnson Haddad's review in *Shakespeare Quarterly*, 38 [1987], 371–375.) Their impact is increased because of the authors' close connection as the two foremost practitioners of "new historicism"; a force field and dialogue are in effect created. New historicism has never been a completely uniform approach. Montrose's review (*Criticism*, 23 [1981], 349–359) of *Renaissance Self-Fashioning*, the founding document of new historicism, outlines the disagreements with Greenblatt that Montrose develops in his essay here five years later. Nonetheless, the shift from book review to essay makes these differences more public and more urgent. My goal will be to sketch the differences between the two versions of new historicism represented by Greenblatt and Montrose and to account for their increasing prominence. I wish to declare at the outset my feeling that Greenblatt and Montrose are not only preeminent new historicists but also among the best critics of their generation; I intend my close scrutiny of their essays as testimony to the power of their respective achievements and to their central importance to the future development of Renaissance studies.

The contrast between Greenblatt and Montrose is especially pronounced here because Greenblatt's essay shows him at his most provocative and prescriptive and thus highlights with particular clarity the direction of his iconoclastic impulse. The specific purpose of his essay is to decenter psychoanalytic interpretation by depriving it of its claim to primacy. The central argument is that the historical gap between Freudian psychoanalysis and the "prepsychoanalytic fashioning of the proprietary rights of selfhood" in the Renaissance (p. 223) is so great as to disrupt any sense of smooth continuity between the two and hence any direct, straightforward application of the former to the latter. This barrier cannot be dissolved because, though psychoanalysis has distant origins in the Renaissance, it can come fully into being only by canceling Renaissance modes of thought; the result is to keep psychoanalysis perpetually at one remove and to reduce its status as an analytic perspective on the Renaissance to what Greenblatt calls "belatedness":

> If psychoanalysis was, in effect, made possible by (among other things) the legal and literary proceedings of the sixteenth and seventeenth centuries, then its interpretive practice is not irrelevant to those proceedings, nor is it exactly an anachronism. But psychoanalytic interpretation is causally belated, even as it is causally linked. . . . I do not propose that we abandon the attempts at psychologically deep readings of Renaissance texts; rather, in the company of literary criticism and history, psychoanalysis can redeem its belatedness only when it historicizes its own procedures.
>
> (p. 221)

This conciliatory gesture of refusing to exclude "psychologically deep readings" is in part disingenuous, for allowing psychoanalysis to "historicize its procedures" is tantamount to forcing it not only to concede its own diminished explanatory power but also to accept the priority of new historicism.

In Greenblatt's new historicist stance, the critic speaks for the past against the present, defending the past against the conventions and orthodoxies of modern belief-systems. Greenblatt makes this defense into an aggressive offense by turning the tables and using the past to challenge and revise the present. Modern assumptions are inadeqate not only to the past but to the present as well; thus psychoanalysis is called into question even in its own historic home territory when Greenblatt insists on "a disconcerting recognition: that our identity may not originate in (or be guaranteed by) the fixity, the certainty, of our own body" (p. 218). For Greenblatt, this move against contemporary preconceptions is essential preparation for the proper relation between past and present; only when both past and present have been freed from the certainty of fixed patterns can the encounter between them occur:

> The power of the story of Martin Guerre, as Natalie Davis helps us understand, lies not in an absolute otherness that compels us to suspend all our values in the face of

an entirely different system of consciousness, but rather in the intimations of an obscure link between those distant events and the way we are now.

(p. 217)

The encounter—the "intimations of an obscure link between those distant events and the way we are now"—consists of a simultaneous apprehension of points of contact and points of difference. With this moment of historicized existential awareness, we reach the heart of Greenblatt's vision. The critic's function is to bear witness to such moments, and it extends no further.

The question arises whether this understanding of history adequately addresses the issue of belatedness that Greenblatt deploys against psychoanalytic criticism. The problem is not peculiar to psychoanalysis since all modern interpretation, including new historicism, is belated. Even in Greenblatt's version of "*histories*—multiple, complex, refractory stories" (p. 217), history is a selective reconstruction that is shaped in part by the critic's contemporary preoccupations. Greenblatt's allusion to this process is so oblique that it constitutes an avoidance:

> But if we reject both the totalizing of a universal mythology and the radical particularizing of relativism, what are we left with? We are left with a network of lived and narrated stories, practices, strategies, representations, fantasies, negotiations, and exchanges that, along with the surviving aural, tactile, and visual traces, fashion our experience of the past, of others, and of ourselves.
>
> (p. 218)

The crucial word "fashion" occurs, but its operation obscures our agency in organizing this rich material, making our historical self-fashioning appear the product of a history that, however subtle, has an unqualified objective force. In this regard, the essay by Montrose stands in sharp contrast with its opening emphasis on "a recognition of the agency of criticism in constructing and delimiting its object of study, and of the historical positioning of the critic vis-à-vis that object" (p. 305). Comparable attention to the critic's agency is missing in Greenblatt where the shaping power of the critic is presented as the historical facts of the matter rather than reflexively as his chosen perspective.

I think a psychological approach has more to contribute to critical self-awareness than Greenblatt acknowledges. Even if the bearing of psychoanalysis on Renaissance culture is tangential and even if in our own time psychoanalysis is not a self-evident truth but a cultural construct, a fiction, it still has application to the contemporary critic. When Greenblatt opposes a self-contained, self-validating Freudian system, I agree. But I want to go on to note the striking affinity between Freud and Greenblatt in their delight in (and need for) story-telling and to suggest that, like Freud's, Greenblatt's narrative mode should be seen in part as a psychological dynamic, an emotional configuration, that can give us access to the relations with authority that are being narrated. Greenblatt's own power and authority as narrator are tacitly implicated in the stories of Renaissance authority he re-narrates. The most important questions that Greenblatt does not ask, however, are less psychoanalytic than political.

Both Greenblatt and Montrose would agree, as the latter puts it, that "the critic exists in history" (p. 305), but this does not mean the same thing for each critic. The history of our own period, from within which we write and whose tensions are in one way or another expressed in our work, involves politics. Yet, while Greenblatt's writing is remarkable for its inclusion of the self—its often moving allusion to his own role, his own contingency—this self-reference is not political. If, hypothetically, the reader asks Greenblatt what the political implications of his argument are, where he stands politically, the tacit response is to reformulate the question, change to a metapolitical topic, and stress the problematic contingency of any ground on which one might wish securely to stand. But this apolitical stance has a political by-product since Greenblatt's representations of Renaissance texts frequently either actively accommodate or are passively congenial to conservative, traditionalist critics. For example, Greenblatt's position on *The Faerie Queene* (pp. 223–224) demonstrates that new historicism is less completely new than it appears and that new and old historicism meld at a major point.

It is this dilemma regarding the silence about politics within new historicism that has now come to the fore in Montrose's work: his project is to reinstate politics in new historicism. The timing and urgency of this project are partly accounted for by external pressure. Its initial phase of novelty over, new historicism now has its own visible history and is thus subject to the outside assessment exemplified by Jean Howard's incisive survey *(English Literary Renaissance*, 16 [1986], 13–43). Howard sees a danger that, "Ironically, the 'new history' may well turn out to be a backlash phenomenon: a flight from theory or simply a program for producing more 'new readings' . . ." (p. 19). The aspect of theory I am most concerned with here is the concept of ideology, a concept that of all the new historicists only Montrose has fully explored (p. 306). Countering a new historicist tendency to see history as the positive term and to dismiss ideology as the negative term, Montrose rejects this dichotomy and convincingly develops a combined historical and ideological analysis in which both terms carry equal weight.

One of Montrose's distinguishing marks among new historicists is his use of approaches that Greenblatt would consider "belated." Although it is difficult to gauge the precise extent of Montrose's commitment to Marxist and feminist perspectives, they give his criticism a political edge missing in Greenblatt's. The Marxist element appears in Montrose's use of the East German critic Robert Weimann as a counterpoint to Foucault's essay "What is an Author?" (p. 319) and in his use of the British Marxist Raymond Williams to correct Greenblatt's "insufficient allowance for the mediatory individual and collective agency of the prince's subjects . . ." (p. 331). The feminist element appears in Montrose's critique of Greenblatt's work on Spenser: "To write as a male reader, identifying unselfconsciously with Guyon's position, with Guyon's gaze, leads to a misrecognition of the gender-specific character of the self-fashioning process . . ." (p. 329; Greenblatt's recent essay "Fiction and Friction" [in *Reconstructing Individualism*, ed. Thomas G. Heller *et al.* (Stanford, Calif.: Stanford University Press, 1986)] represents a first attempt to treat gender as a central topic, but it is too early to tell how this effort will be integrated into Greenblatt's work as a whole).

Montrose's image of Renaissance culture is different from Greenblatt's because its political dynamic is more complicated and places greater stress on conflict. Montrose opposes "Greenblatt's characterization of Spenser's relationship to political authority" as "an unequivocal inscription of the dominant ideology" (p. 320), his "suggestion of an absolute and totalistic structure of royal power, cynically and successfully recuperating every contestatory gesture" (p. 330). As I have noted in my review of *Political Shakespeare* (edited by Jonathan Dollimore and Alan Sinfield [Ithaca, N. Y.: Cornell University Press, 1985] in *Shakespeare Quarterly*, 37 [1986], 251–255), Greenblatt's emphasis on the containing power of authority is particularly strong in his essay on "Invisible Bullets: Renaissance Authority and its Subversion," and this tendency is echoed here in Greenblatt's delineation of Hobbes's concept of authority (p. 222) in which, having rejected psychoanalysis as "a totalizing vision" (p. 217), Greenblatt seems caught up in his own totalizing substitute.

Montrose's alternative explores the artist's potential "refashioning of the queen as the author's subject" in an art conceived as "an interplay between submission and resistance to the project of royal celebration":

> By "resistance" I do not mean to suggest any concerted program of sedition, of political opposition or subversion. Rather, it is a matter of the text registering the felt but perhaps not consciously articulated contradiction between Spenser's exalted self-representation as an Author and his subjection to the authority of an other....
> (p. 323)

The scope of the keyword *to contest* hinges on the delicate, densely packed phrase "felt but perhaps not consciously articulated." The lack of a comprehensive overview of *The Faerie Queene* means that Montrose's terms are not fully explicated and tested. We cannot assess Spenser's treatment of Belphoebe (pp. 323–329), for example, without a larger context putting Belphoebe in relation to Britomart; Montrose's discussion of Britomart, Radigund, and Artegall (in his essay "'Shaping Fantasies': Figurations of Gender and Power in Elizabethan Culture" on *A Midsummer Night's Dream* in *Representations*, 2 [1983], 61–94; 76–79) is necessary to complete the analysis. In the present essay however, the range of meanings covered by the artist's contestatory power is narrow, presented largely in negative verbs that underline the defensive nature of gestures toward mastery. There is a disproportion between the concept of the artist's reciprocity and the modesty of the concrete evidence for it, as though after setting out to disagree, Montrose in the end comes very close to confirming Greenblatt's analysis. John Harrington's power "to articulate a frustrated desire for mastery over the sovereign mother/mistress" (p. 326) is a minimal power indeed, and Montrose fails to revise a writer whom Greenblatt has made very much his own (*Renaissance Self-Fashioning* [Chicago, Ill.: University of Chicago Press, 1980], pp. 168–169).

I believe that Montrose deserves full credit for his courage in extending his definition of the "critic in history" to include explicit reference to his own political stance. Yet I find Montrose's image of impotence—"a nagging sense of professional, institutional, and political impotence" (p. 332)—shocking, far more shocking than Greenblatt's image of contingency. I also find it difficult to avoid a sense of correspondence between Montrose's image of the beleaguered Elizabethan subject and his construct of the impotent academic. (My comments on Montrose's essay here have subsequently been rendered largely out-of-date by his brilliant, powerful revision and extension of this material in his presentation at the "Redrawing the Boundaries" session at the 1987 Modern Language Association Convention.)

Two particular points in Montrose's contemporary political vision strike me as unnecessarily limiting. First, Montrose defends the humanities by means of a programmatic antitechnological attitude that implies a replay of the Snow-Leavis two-cultures debate. Montrose appears to countenance in his politics a lack of sophistication that he would not tolerate in his scholarship when he too easily reverts to a Leavis-like position, as though the career of Raymond Williams had never happened. Similarly, David Quint's foreshortened history, with its clichéd invocation of "mass communications" and "faceless, technocratic society" against which "romantic" "refuge" is presented as the only alternative (p. 6), omits Raymond Williams's decisive break with Leavis's antipathy toward mass media and Williams's successful effort, starting thirty years ago with *Culture and Society, 1780–1950* (London: Chatto & Windus, 1958) to find a more complex alternative to the dual pro/con options. Specifically with regard to technology, I think of Williams's work on television and, more recently, on the new information technology in the section on "Culture and Technology" in *The Year 2000* (New York: Pantheon Books, 1983): there is no simple hostility to technology here. Or, to shift to an American context, it is as though Montrose were content to adopt as an adequate politics the simplified pastoralism described by Leo Marx (in *Ideology and Classic American Literature*, ed. Sacvan Bercovitch and Myra Jehlen [Cambridge: Cambridge University Press, 1986]), despite Montrose's brilliantly complicated understanding of Renaissance pastoral.

Second, Montrose restricts his political view to the narrowly framed arena of the university—to "the possibilities for limited and localized agency within the regime of power and knowledge that at once sustains and constrains us" (p. 333). This formulation seems to me to pass from modesty as healthy realism over to modesty as ingrained, self-fulfilling pessimism; I think it is possible to be more ambitious without succumbing to incurable optimism. Cultural heritage plays a significant role in the formation of political consciousness and social action, and critics are in a position to interpret, revise, and change, not merely to transmit, the tradition. I disagree with the conservative inflection that David Quint gives to this process when he describes it as "remotivat[ing] the idea of the humanist canon" (p. 16). We shall certainly underestimate our potential if we treat Renaissance studies as a self-contained field and portray ourselves exclusively as Renaissance specialists; for we then cut ourselves off from the larger perspective of the culture as a whole, a perspective that we need if the Renaissance critic is fully to exist in a history that includes the present. Change does not depend entirely on our revaluations of Renaissance texts; the cultural tradition is changing under our feet because of new developments in black and women's literature in our own historical period, to which we must be alive.

Montrose acknowledges that his "disagreements with [Greenblatt's] admirable book arise within the scope of a shared project" (p. 339). This common project may extract a price if Montrose's more active skepticism can only make explicit what may be implicit in Greenblatt's scholarly neutrality: namely, a dispirited political vision. This convergence raises the question—by no means definitively answered yet—to what extent politics can be included within the established new-historicist purview and whether or not there are strict limits to change from within this purview.

The Idea of the City in the Age of Shakespeare, by Gail Kern Paster. Athens, Ga.: University of Georgia Press, 1985. Pp. xii + 249. $24.00.

Reviewer: NANCY ELIZABETH HODGE

Acknowledging the tradition of city/country dualism illustrated in Maynard Mack's *The Garden and the City: Retirement and Politics in the Later Poetry of Pope, 1731-43* (Toronto: University of Toronto Press, 1969), Raymond Williams's *The Country and The City* (New York, N. Y.: Oxford University Press, 1973), and Northrop Frye's *The Anatomy of Criticism* (Princeton, N. J.: Princeton University Press, 1957) and *The Stubborn Structure: Essays on Criticism and Society* (Ithaca, N. Y.: Cornell University Press, 1970), Gail Paster considers a different tradition: that of the city as a literary construct containing its own antitype. She cites Burton Pike's *The Image of the City in Modern Literature* (Princeton, N. J.: Princeton University Press, 1981) as the most recent of a number of studies confronting this mixed response to the city. Drawing on the works of Shakespeare, Jonson, and Middleton, she explores their representations of this dialectical formulation, which, she argues, finds repeated expression in Renaissance English dramatic literature. Urban literature, she contends, incorporates and demonstrates the paradox of the city as "ideal community" and "predatory trap" (p. 3), a site capable of (and often defined by) concurrent and combative expressions of individual development and social commitment juxtaposed against filth, transience, crowds, and clamor.

At the beginning of her study of the evolution of the city's dual identity, Paster cites Renaissance theorist George Puttenham's reference to Amphion, the music of whose harp encouraged and accompanied the creation of cities. However, in *The City of God*, Augustine recalls the fratricide of the archetypal founder of the city, Cain, Amphion's antitype. Augustine concludes that the city embodies the division of human nature, of good and evil, the "essential dialectic" explicit in its "bipolar image" (p. 11), the antithesis between the actual and the ideal city, between Rome, "the negative pole of the . . . dialectic" (p. 12), and Jerusalem, the city of God. In the Book of Revelation, John of Patmos provides the most vivid and violent polarity: that between Jerusalem, celestially arrayed bride, and Rome, magnificently adorned whore.

For classical authors, Rome's mythic strength and enormous historical power dwarf the efforts of panegyrists praising it. Drawing from the works of the Renaissance authors Petrarch, Remigio de Girolami, Flavio Biondo, and Leone Battista Alberti, Paster presents the struggles of these Italian humanists as they grapple with the significance of Rome in ruins—"an evocative symbol of the instability of fortune . . . [yet] tangible proof of the former glory of the city and thus a symbol of human potential" (p. 22). But this qualified adulation coexists with knowledge of Renaissance Rome's decline and the concomitant claims of Venice and Florence to have superseded it as world city. These claims result at least in part from the incorporation of classical form into Italian urban planning—as seen in the works of Bruni, Brunneleschi, Alberti, Leonardo, Palladio, and Vasari. Striving for proportion not only fulfills practical requirements but also fosters civic order, and, as in the work of Filarete, creates synthesis rather than antithesis between city and countryside. Yet while Renaissance theorists resurrect the city as "ideal form of social organization" (p. 30), Paster reminds us of the urban centers described in More's *Utopia*, where city and countryside, while wholly at peace with each other, remain segmented, where regularity of life enfeebles rather than encourages freedom.

Paster then turns to the possibilities of the city as revealed by Horace, Juvenal, and Plautus, whose works reflect the dichotomy of response that Paster attributes to writers of the English Renaissance. Horace examines the perils to individual integrity endemic to city life; only a withdrawal from urban ambition to the values of agrarian life allows those whom the city honors to accept those honors, cognizant of their evanescence. Isolation is not an end, however. Horace registers awareness that from his personal retreat, the farm at Tivoli, he views the whole of Rome, a panorama reinforcing his debt to the city, which he represents as an intelligent, humane power and the donor of the farm itself. Juvenal's satires, like those of Horace, reject Roman life, but "the personal bitterness into which [he] occasionally lapses suggests that he rejects Rome because Rome has already rejected him" (p. 44). Outrages of the urban present obliterate a virtuous agrarian past. Endless competition in vice and for patronage reveal that the personal detachment Horace applauds has within two centuries disappeared into coarse self-interest. Juvenal's verses reflect the change that he sees from a society in which the poet might inspire correction to one in which he can only vent spleen; "one survives, finally, despite, not because of, Rome" (p. 50). Plautus, inhabitant of the rigidly moralistic Rome that Juvenal can only long for, develops characters in urban Greek settings. Representative of the saturnalian impulse, his works set the status quo on its ear, picturing an amoral society with no familial affection and very little emotional involvement in the promised erotic activity that will insure the perpetuation of the city; "the psychic penalties of Roman life stand revealed" (p. 34).

Centered in classical Rome, the first Renaissance dramatic texts that Paster considers are *Titus Andronicus*, *Coriolanus*, and *Julius Caesar*. Each chronicles the politics of the city destroying a hero at the moment when "he most completely embodies the ethos of the city" (p. 59). In *Titus Andronicus* the "lacerating self-division" (p. 66) of Rome is expressed through the conflict of warring families, with the "chief exemplar for the stern Roman code . . . [becoming] its chief victim" (p. 76). In *Coriolanus*, Paster contends, the issue is "class," a term that many scholars now choose to discard in favor of "stratum" or "status." Paster emphasizes that both *Titus* and *Coriolanus* depict a Rome requiring citizen self-sacrifice. The city allows little space for an "ethical icon" like Titus or a giant warrior like Coriolanus. Tracing architectural imagery, Paster stresses the inevitable competition between the monumentality of Rome and the monumentality of the individual. It is the body of the city that must prevail. Again, in *Julius Caesar*, a patrician order finds itself dwarfed by a heroic individual. In this play, pervaded by lesser individuals' niggling preoccupation with the attributes or positions of others, we witness a city that resists yet continually courts its own dissolution. All three of these works reflect a devouring civic order, whether incipiently "cannibalistic" (p. 76) or enacting some hierarchy of predator and prey in which Rome, to perpetuate itself, must consume "the heroes it nurtures and immortalizes" (p. 90).

Paster then moves to what she considers the essentially satiric mode of *Timon of Athens*, *Sejanus*, and *Catiline*. In each play, she concludes, further unavoidable decline awaits, however difficult to imagine. The city in these works combines the forces of Amphion and Cain, creativity and fratricide. Following the banquetting that reveals the materialism of a society consumed by "destructive interdependence," Timon retreats to the cave, a "presocial site" fit for the misanthropy that appears the logical consequence of the "chronic failure of the human community" Timon experiences (p. 108). In *Titus Andronicus*, as in *Timon*, "the tragedy of the hero is the tragedy of his city because ongoing civic process requires the destruction of the very men in whom the city is most fully reflected" (p. 123). In *Sejanus* we see the title character as representative of Rome, a "paradigmatic sycophant . . . in a play that dramatizes social decline by sexual parody of self-denying service to the state . . ." (p. 114). Again, in *Catiline*, ironic analogies between ambition and sexual power enrich the illustration of the absurd pomposity of Cicero and Catiline, two equally ambitious individuals. Jonson's "dramatization of Rome insists . . . on the disparity between the great idea of commonwealth and the flawed ability of even its best citizens, who are capable of articulating its ideals but incapable finally of preserving them" (p. 122).

Particularly valuable is the chapter dealing with Jonson's masques and Middleton's civic pageants. Paster points out the resonances between these works and those of Italian Renaissance humanist architects: all are intended to represent "an ideal image for the actual communities where [their creators] lived and worked" (pp. 124-125). In the masques and pageants the image of the "city starved by cannibal feasting on its heroes" is "replaced by the sublimated self-gratification of official homage, the community feeding on its idealized reflection" (p. 125). With masque and antimasque, a dialectic becomes explicit: "hierarchy, regularity, [and] harmony" are subjected "to time, to sense, and especially to the physical world of obdurate things" (p. 131). The masque celebrates the court and its members as timeless entities at civilization's center; the antimasque ridicules upward mobility while celebrating those who organize the functions of the sublunary world. Yet the pageants naturally focus on the city. Those writers who secured pageant commissions (often in celebration of a Royal Entry or the Lord Mayor's installation) manage to accord London signal importance because of the "power and protection" that it offers the King (p. 140). In Jonson's masques, fame is accorded to those celebrated simply because they belong to the court. In Middleton's pageants, while London's growing mercantile power fuels the concept of "imperial destiny centered in London" (p. 147), wealth is subservient to bounty, to works. Service and responsibility are glorified in occasional forthright challenge to the aristocratic notion that great men, through pedigree, grace, and favor, are born great or have greatness thrust upon them. The pageants stress that the Mayors enjoy the privilege and challenge of achieving greatness "to glorify the city for whom such labors are undertaken, to make the city's sense of self as satisfying as the court's" (p. 149).

Paster next addresses a selection of city comedies by Jonson and Middleton, including *Every Man in His Humor, Every Man Out of His Humor, The Alchemist, Epicoene, Bartholomew Fair, Volpone, Michaelmas Term, A Chaste Maid in Cheapside, A Mad World, My Masters, The Devil is An Ass, A Trick to Catch the Old One*, and *Your Five Gallants*. These plays reveal a contrasting evaluation of the city: a vision of "urban society in the sway of natural law as predatory appetite" (p. 152). They decipher the emotional and material chaos that follows the abrogation of customary bonds of community. The grasping, clawing, and consuming that characterize the actions of Jonson's plays convey an "ironic fellowship" of predatoriness (p. 157). In Jonson's works, as in Juvenal's, disgust fuses with fascination at the reciprocal feeding and confusion inherent in human connections. Jonson shows a city that, for its own survival, requires the sacrifice of essentially willing victims, hopeful supplicants at the altar of possible promotion. For Middleton even more than Jonson, the city rests upon unknown networks of familial, sexual, and financial obligation, all further complicated by individual isolation, sexual perversion, and gluttony. And immigrants to London in *Michaelmas Term* are as eager as their city brothers and sisters to grasp and gain. All end by being gulled, yet aspirations continue to be limited only by the resourcefulness of the individual's imagination. Paster refers to the apparent "class" warfare (p. 174) embodied in these plots, a conflict between citizens and gentry scrabbling for place and possessions, continually feeding a city that itself has become "a version of the Renaissance overreacher, unwilling to let anyone or anything go" (p. 177).

Paster last analyzes Shakespeare's city comedies, as she terms *A Comedy of Errors*, *The Merchant of Venice*, and *Measure for Measure*. Though not set in London, each play fulfills her criteria for city comedy because it presents a comic crisis for a character that "interlocks with the crisis of an entire social order" (p. 178). In these works Shakespeare explores the tensions between civic and individual identity, exacerbated by a situation in which, by either following or disregarding a "monstrous law," the city undermines itself (p. 179). In *Comedy of Errors*, Paster notes the ambiguities inherent in attempting to understand private life apart from civic life. Here Paster makes her case with facility; at least in Ephesus, communal and public life cannot be divided from the private. The fragility of both facets of life is all too easily threatened by fraternal rivalry, metamorphosis, and betrayal. The city itself becomes, as in Jonson, the theater within which characters struggle to achieve a recognizable form; at the same time the city remains "an essential agent and object of change in that experience" (p. 186). In *Merchant of Venice*, Paster notes the Venetian ethos that requires a Shylock for the continued generosity of an Antonio: "malevolence and generosity are precisely interdependent" (p. 196). However, she too easily accords Antonio an awareness of "self defined apart from fortune and men's eyes" (p. 182). It is difficult to credit such a reading in a play that seems so dependent on personal estimation in men's (and women's) eyes. Antonio's struggle seems an effort not so much to divorce the self from the public as to insure that the public accords him the position and repute that he desires. Nor does Paster clarify the interdependence of the Venice/Belmont sites. What does Belmont represent? Venetian antitype? ironic city? pastoral retreat? In a study of the idea of the city, the reader expects this conundrum to be addressed more explicitly. In the Vienna of *Measure for Measure*, we see a city inhabited not by community but by a collection of selves. Paster explores the natures of Isabella, the Duke, and Angelo all of whom suffer from some degree of "narcissistic self-regard" (p. 208). The Duke, whose withdrawal threatens the social order of Vienna, orchestrates a test of virtue and a confrontation; ultimately he stages the image of a working community. The individual narcissism at work in this Vienna, however, causes us to question who among these players is capable of true community.

Paster concludes that "the city is not simply a dominant setting of English Renaissance drama. In classical tragedy and city comedy, as we have seen, it is the subject" (p. 220). Not all readers will be willing to go so far. Yet Paster ably demonstrates the presence in these works of a near-Augustinian doubleness (Cain and Amphion, Rome and Jerusalem, whore and bride) at work in her city subjects, and she successfully argues for awareness of the "predatory destruction or near-destruction of the individuals [whom the city's] mythic aspirations have nurtured" (p. 220). With an admirable balance of erudition and wit, Paster's intelligent readings (particularly those of the classical tragedies, the masques and pageants, and the city comedies of Jonson and Middleton) develop individual perceptions that are in many instances fresh and compelling. In addition to the book's obvious appeal for those who wish to explore these plays from a new perspective, Paster's study will be of interest to those who wish to elicit political agendas for these playwrights, those who wish to explore the Renaissance English consciousness of great continental cities (Venice, Florence), and those who investigate pastoralism and its opposite. Examination of the evolution of these plays from source materials may also provide a logical addition to the work done here. Paster has located and progressed a good distance down an intriguing avenue.

In a work free from most printing errors, one problem should be noted. In the text itself, footnote numbers for Chapter Seven run straight through, from 1–52. In the endnotes, however, number 16 is omitted so that the numbers run 1–15, 17–53. The reader must jump down one entry from 16–52 for the appropriate information.

The Doctrine of Election and the Emergence of Elizabethan Tragedy, by Martha Tuck Rozett. Princeton, N. J.: Princeton University Press, 1984. Pp. ix + 329. $32.50.

Reviewer: LOIS POTTER

While there may be many reasons why no other European country produced anything like the English tragic drama of the Renaissance, it has always seemed likely that one of these must be the particular nature of the English Reformation. Martha Rozett's book examines one aspect of its history, the controversy over the doctrine of predestination that is usually called Calvinist (though in fact it has a much longer history), and considers its relation to the development of tragedy. She has a simple and cogent thesis: the doctrine of election implies a clear-cut division between saved and damned, "us" and "other"; tragedy implies an awareness in the spectators that the "other" is also "us." Yet the latter attitude is also implicit in the former. What interests her is the movement between them.

Noting that the audiences for plays and for sermons must have been largely the same, Rozett compares the language of drama with Protestant pulpit oratory. She establishes the existence of a twofold response to the doctrine of election on the part of preachers: on the one hand reassuring a doubtful congregation as to its chances of salvation; on the other, warning it against presumption. Her most interesting perception is that dramatic characters themselves frequently illustrate the difficulty of achieving a balance between the two states. Many of them *do* presume. Marlowe's protagonists in particular often proclaim their "elect" status, as when Tamburlaine calls himself the Scourge of God. Faustus is a particularly disturbing figure because his attempts at "resolution" parody the assurance of the elect while his despair represents the opposite danger; moreover, his fate seems to contradict that belief in the constant availability of divine grace in which the audience, as congregation, would have been taught to believe. In *Edward II* the second part of the play takes a new direction by assimilating Mortimer and Edward to the stereotypes of an older drama, the dual-protagonist play with its contrast between Worldly Man and Heavenly Man. This interpretation makes more sense than usual out of the apparently out-of-character piety shown by Edward in the later scenes. A similar pairing (between Richard and Richmond) is found in the last act of *Richard III*, but *Richard II*, although it seems based on a similar contrast, complicates it: Richard's self-awareness and piety are incomplete; Bolingbroke's isolation is potentially tragic. The book ends with a short discussion of *Macbeth*, the most complete example of the self-conscious transformation of a protagonist into "other."

Professor Rozett deliberately limits her scope to the relation between doctrine and drama, taking little account of theatrical or political factors. However, she does suggest, following David Bevington's *From "Mankind" to Marlowe* (Cambridge, Mass.: Harvard University Press, 1962), that the practice of doubling parts in the morality play accustomed the audience to having opposed responses to the same actor, if not the same character. But she says surprisingly little about the cycle drama, which probably had even more influence on the playwrights of the 1580s and 1590s. It is probably not true that, as she argues, the dominant popular form was the morality—we have only the evidence of what got printed, and the works most likely to get printed were those that could be used for government propaganda. Anyone who has seen the York Mystery Cycle will recall the extraordinary sensation produced by the Last Judgment scene, as characters from all ages of history mill around on the stage and then, at God's command, are driven into groups on the right and left. Yet much of this sense is due to something that the original performances would have lacked: continuity of impersonation by a large cast throughout the cycle. When the saved and damned were seen for the first time only in the Doomsday play and when roles like Judas and Pilate were shared by a number of actors, they would obviously have had less capacity to involve the emotions of their audience. It is possible that the rise of a professional theater is the most significant factor in the development of the tragic protagonist.

It might have been useful to consider also the way in which the dramatists themselves guard against presumption. After the triumphantly unrepentant final speech of Aaron in *Titus Andronicus*, Shakespeare never again gave a villain the last word; Richard III dies in silence, Iago refuses to speak; Macbeth (though the stage directions are confusing) certainly goes offstage fighting and is perhaps killed there; even the repentant Edmund is carried off to die. The reason may be that the dramatist was aware of a dilemma: a repentant death was unbelievable (and, usually, theatrically unsatisfying); a reprobate one was unedifying. Or perhaps the principles of identification and "otherness" did not operate quite as straightforwardly as Professor Rozett suggests: a defiantly unrepentant villain might have encouraged some degree of audience identification or at least admiration (as such figures surely do later in Webster). To pass judgment, in any case, argues presumption on the part of the other characters and so, ultimately, of the author. "So bad a death argues a monstrous life," comments Warwick when Cardinal Beaufort dies without making a sign to show that he is thinking "on heaven's bliss," but the saintly Henry replies, "Forbear to judge, for we are sinners all" (*2 Henry VI*, III.iii).

Professor Rozett shows some interesting parallels between the techniques of sermons and those of plays, and her analysis of individual works (such as *Gorboduc* and *Titus Andronicus*) shows a capacity for careful discrimination that counteracts that somewhat strait-jacketing nature of her topic. But many of her assumptions are outdated or, at least, need more questioning than they are given here. She treats the movement from didacticism to tragedy as a consistently upward one, culminating in plays that involve the audience in the sufferings of a guilty protagonist—in other words, *Faustus* and Shakespeare's major tragedies, especially *Macbeth*. There is no attempt to deal with tragedies contemporary with *Macbeth*, such as those of Jonson and Fulke Greville, which fall outside this pattern of Darwinian evolution. It is a pity that Alan Sinfield's *Literature in Protestant England* (Totawa, N. J.: Barnes & Noble, 1983) came out too late for Rozett to sharpen her own theoretical assumptions against it. Sinfield's view is that Renaissance literature reflects a tension between Calvinist and Humanist views, and that Reformation theology, by polarizing Christian attitudes, encouraged scepticism. Thus, he claims, the ending of *Faustus* calls the doctrine of predestination itself into doubt, since "when we see Faustus panic-stricken in his last hour we think again about the God who has ordained it" (p. 119). Rozett, on the contrary, assumes an instinct to identify with the protagonist that leaves no room for the kind of questioning that Sinfield describes. It is clear that these two scholars are envisaging two different plays—a Brechtian one and an Aristotelian one. Yet both use the concepts "we" and "the audience" in much the same way, approaching the text as a reader, yet describing the reactions of a hypothetical audience. How far, I wonder, does "the audience feels" ever mean anything except "I feel"?

The book contains a few errors. In *The Castle of Perseverance*, Covetousness does not conquer Mankind in battle but wins him over more insidiously, late in life. The ghost in *The Spanish Tragedy* is Don Andrea, not Andreas. It is Northumberland, not Bolingbroke, who refers to the "tediousness and process" of their journey toward Berkeley Castle. A number of quotations are cited from secondary sources, and references (for example, to *Basilikon Doron* on p. 56) are not always complete.

Play-Texts in Old Spelling: Papers from the Glendon Conference, edited by G. B. Shand with Raymond C. Shady. New York: AMS Press, 1984. Pp. ix + 161. $34.50.

Reviewer: PHILIP R. RIDER

The Glendon College, York University conference on "The Preparation of Old Spelling Renaissance Play-Texts in English" was held in Toronto on 12-13 April 1978. In an informal talk to the conferees, Skip Shand, one of the conveners, explained that he had recently become one of the editors of a complete old-spelling edition of Thomas Middleton; he decided, therefore, that it would be a good idea to assemble a group of old-spelling editors and find out how such an edition should be done. *Play-Texts in Old Spelling* prints the twelve papers written for the conference. As Shand and Raymond C. Shady write in their Introduction, "We aimed at a how-to conference rather than a why-to, assuming that the well-worn debate between the merits of old spelling and modern spelling could be set aside while old-spelling editors talked specifically about old-spelling editions" (p. 2).

Shand's opening remarks appropriately set the informal and casual tone of much of the conference, but the "why-to" question was not to be so easily dismissed; in various and subtle ways it insinuated itself into the conference until, by the third and final session, it could no longer be denied. Time and again questions were raised about who reads an old-spelling edition, whether the expense of printing full historical collations was justifiable, and what, exactly, is the intended function of an old-spelling edition. The subservience of how-to to why-to was becoming more and more obvious. It culminated in Philip Edwards's assertion that "'If it were to do again, I would never do an old-spelling *Massinger*. . . . I lost my faith'" (p. 6). Of Edwards's statement Shand and Shady comment that "a roomful of old-spellers went into a brief but dizzy tailspin" (p. 6). It is no exaggeration to say that the conference ended in a somewhat gloomy atmosphere. The question of the worth of compositor studies, how many commentary notes to provide, and whether the physical restrictions of kerned letters may have an effect on spelling simply refused to displace some of the larger issues involved in the production of old-spelling editions.

The papers collected in *Play-Texts in Old Spelling* do not fully reflect the tone of the conference because they were, of course, written before the conference. The editors' Introduction summarizes the discussions that took place at each of the sessions and takes note of the kinds of questions and issues raised by the conference.

The opening address of the conference was delivered by S. Schoenbaum and is reprinted here under the title "Old-Spelling Editions: The State of the Art." It is clearly an introductory talk, casual in tone and historical in content. Schoenbaum surveys the state of some of the major old-spelling editions, including those of Beaumont and Fletcher, Chapman, and Massinger, and comments at some length on the Herford and Simpson *Ben Jonson,* which at that time was gradually going out of print and being replaced by the abridged paperback edition. As a quick survey of the important issues and projects in twentieth-century editing, Schoenbaum's essay is exemplary. He outlines the current state of the Variorum Shakespeare and the nearly mythical old-spelling Shakespeare. There is little in Schoenbaum's remarks that will startle the reader, but it is a graciously written overview.

Robert Kean Turner's "Accidental Evils" argues for "logic, consistency, elegance, and sensitivity" in an editor's treatment of accidentals (p. 28). Using the Oxford *Massinger* for his examples, Turner points out that editors are often erratic and inconsistent in their emendation (or lack thereof) of accidentals. He points, for example, to *The Unnatural Combat,* II.iii.75, which reads in its corrected state, "To mourn a brothers losse (however wicked)." The editors, believing the parentheses to be authorial, accept this reading over that of the uncorrected state ("To mourne a brothers losse however wicked,"). Turner thinks it is "thoughtless," however, to include *mourn* when *mourne* is an authorial spelling and when it seems reasonable to assume that the compositor dropped the *e* to make space for the parentheses.

Turner feels that accidentals should be altered if in their original form they interfere with the reader's understanding. The emendation of accidentals is not necessarily the "correction" of accidentals, however, and editors must be wary of illogical, inconsistent, and excessive emendation that may result in a distortion of authorial practice.

The longest and most detailed essay in *Play-Texts in Old Spelling* is Paul Werstine's "The Editorial Usefulness of Printing House and Compositor Studies," which sets out to show "with some fresh examples that editors can benefit from researching the printing houses and compositors who produced the texts they edit" (p. 35). Specifically, Werstine demonstrates that a study of the printer William White and of his compositors who set the First Quarto (Q1) *Love's Labour's Lost* shows the Quarto to be a reprint.

Werstine's paper itself has an interesting publication history. Originally delivered at the Toronto conference, it was revised for publication in *Analytical & Enumerative Bibliography* [*AEB*], 2 (1978), 153-165. Shortly thereafter, two more articles on the same subject appeared: George R. Price, "The Printing of *Love's Labour's Lost* (1598)," *Papers of the Bibliographical Society of America,* 72 (1978), 405–434, and Manfred Draudt, "Printer's Copy for the Quarto of *Love's Labour's Lost* (1598)," *The Library,* Sixth Series, 3 (1981), 119–131. Each of these disagreed with Werstine and with each other about the printer's copy used for *LLL* Q1 and about the number of compositors and their shares.

The version of Werstine's paper as published in *AEB* is reprinted in *Play-Texts in Old Spelling,* but to it is appended an "Afterword" that is three times the length of the original essay and that refutes Price and Draudt. By its length and its detail, the Afterword is a bit of a distraction from the other offerings in this collection, but it does seem to prove Werstine's point and, taken with the original essay and those by Price and Draudt, demonstrates both the complexity and the value of compositor study. Indeed, the disagreement over the interpretation of the data illustrates some of the problems raised by the conference.

Barry Gaines, in "Textual Apparatus—Rationale and Audience," raises the important question about who is interested in the bulky and expensive apparatus—particularly the historical collation and the list of emendations of accidentals—that accompanies critical editions. He writes, "Does it come as any surprise when I assure you that no one is really interested in reconstructing the copy-text from the apparatus which accompanies a critical edition?" (p. 68). And, "Of what value is it to know that in the first scene of *1 Henry IV*, the name *Douglas* is first italicized in Q3, *Jacke* in Q8, *Yedward* in F3, *Peto* in the Dering MS., and all the others in Q5? If there is significance in this welter, it must be made clear by the editor in the textual introduction. It cannot be distilled from the [list of emendations of accidentals] by even an interested reader" (p. 69).

Gaines does not contest the worthiness of the editor's doing full collations, making critical choices among variant readings, and emending accidentals according to some rational principle. Rather, he argues that these "worksheets" need not constitute the bulk of a printed edition (p. 69). For the great majority of readers, the added cost of printing such notes is not justified by their worth. Gaines says that the textual introduction is a much more valuable part of the apparatus because it is here that the editor can elucidate to the reader the value of the collations and emendations: "Here is our opportunity to display the results of our labors. Here are hypotheses and conclusions instead of worksheets. Here the editor can produce stylish prose instead of endless lists" (p. 70).

Henry D. Janzen's "Preparing A Diplomatic Edition: Heywood's *The Escapes of Jupiter*" is perhaps the least substantial of the papers, but it is interesting none the less. Janzen simply explains how he went about preparing his Malone Society edition of the play. The article will be especially enlightening to beginning editors, and particularly to those with little experience in working with manuscripts, because the author points out some of the difficult problems that he had to face.

The most entertaining and enlightening of the Toronto presentations was Randall McLeod's, here reprinted under the Hitchcockian title "Spellbound" from its appearance in *Renaissance and Reformation*, New Series 3, 1 (1979), 50–65. McLeod's thesis is that an editor needs to distinguish between old spelling and "old typesetting"; that is, what the modern editor sees as variant spelling may instead be arrangements of pieces of type that have nothing to do with spelling but which were chosen for their physical characteristics.

The most common instance of this situation can be seen in the problem caused by kerning. At the Toronto meeting McLeod used large wooden letters to demonstrate kerning; in *Play-Texts in Old Spelling* he photo-reproduces many examples of individual words and lines from old texts, one of which will suffice here to demonstrate his point. In *Eastward Hoe* Q1 the name "Quicksilver" is always spelled "Quicksiluer" (with a long s) when it is set in roman. In italic, however, it appears as *Quicksiluer*, *Quick siluer*, *Quickesiluer*, *Quick-siluer*, *Quicksiluer* (with short *s*), or *Quicke-sil-* (with the last syllable carried over to the next line) (p. 86). These may be spelling variants, but the italic *k* is a kerned letter and its kern does not set properly next to the kern of long *s* without bending or breaking one of them. The addition of an *e*, a short dash, or an en-space between *k* and *s* allows for much easier setting.

The evidence of kerning, as well as the evidence of letters set as ligatures, is almost entirely lost in the modern typesetting of old-spelling editions. This is unfortunate because such evidence is probably more meaningful than has commonly been recognized.

Although Philip Edwards does not specifically disagree with McLeod, he does object to the recent stress on "the bewildering technology . . . chiefly concerned with investigating the material methods of transmitting texts," which he says has often barred "the best minds" from involving themselves in critical editing (p. 97). In "The Function of Commentary" Edwards suggests that no matter how textually and technically correct an edition may be, if it has no commentary it is no edition at all. He writes that "an editor has to make sense of his text" and that he must "justify what he has established, and that includes sharing his understanding of the text with his readers" (p. 99). Nothing in Edwards's essay is revolutionary, but it is solid, sound advice, both theoretical and practical, about the preparation of commentary notes to accompany an edition.

One of the uses for commentary is to clear up confusing or contradictory stage business. Edwards points out that a modern reader may be confused about what is happening on stage at a particular point: "is a certain character on or off the stage? Surely, says the reader, he can't be on stage while this is going on, yet I can't find any exit for him. Is there a note about this? Is the text sound?" (p. 100). David Bevington makes a similar argument in "Editorial Indications of Stage Business in Old-Spelling Editions." Bevington argues that the editor has several obligations with respect to stage directions.

First, the editor is obligated to add bracketed stage directions at any point where the reader is in danger of being confused. This does not mean he or she is to clutter the text unnecessarily with detailed commentary on every action of every actor or with "speculative or interpretative" directions (p. 110). It does mean, however, that the editor must realize that he or she is editing a text meant for performance and that stage business must be kept in mind.

Secondly, the editor must carefully reexamine the stage directions added by earlier (particularly nineteenth-century) editors. A number of these were superfluous, some were misleading to the reader, and frequently they were written without a clear sense of the physical stage.

As Bevington wants clearer stage directions, Richard Morton wants greater use of annotation to explain old spellings. In "How Many Revengers in *The Revengers Tragedy*? Archaic Spelling and the Modern Annotator," Morton pleads for increased use of spelling glosses by editors of both modern- and old-spelling editions. Although the degreee of annotation needed is determined in part by the intended audience, some uses to which it might be put include: explaining archaic spellings, resolving doublets (*lie/lye*), providing evidence "of authorial or compositional habit" (p. 118), distinguishing between apparent substantive variants, providing linguistic information, and interpreting dialect.

Reavley Gair, in "In Search of 'the mustie fopperies of antiquity'," also argues for more explanation, in this case in the commentary notes. Where Edwards wrote that "an editor should be very reticent in telling his reader how to react to his text as against helping him to understand what is going on" (p. 101), Gair says that an editor should not, and indeed cannot, write neutral commentary. Rather, the editor should provide sufficiently extensive commentary so that the reader understands not just the words of the play but is also given guidance in its meaning. The editor's explanation, for example, of the political-intellectual-religious milieu of the play need not be confined to the introduction but should be continued through appropriate critical-historical commentary notes.

Gair's essay is perhaps the least well developed of all those in the collection. It raises, implicitly, a number of questions without resolving them. What material is appropriate for the commentary notes and what for a historical introduction? How discursive can an explanation be and still be called a "note"? And once again, as it had throughout the conference, the spectre of audience appears in the background. What is the audience for a critical old-spelling edition? If the primary audience is other scholars, they will not (presumably) require extensive annotation. The student reader will (presumably) require more annotation, but how much and of what kind? Gair says that the "average reader" who is unlikely to see the play performed is most likely to need interpretative annotation; but will this reader ever even read the play? And at what point does reading the annotation become a distraction from reading the text?

Then in "Excessive Annotation, or Piling Pelion on Parnassus," S. P. Zitner argues that much commentary is unnecessary and distracting. Taking a sample page from the New Arden *Othello*, Zitner shows that of the nine notes on the page, only three are genuinely useful while two others may be helpful; all of them, however, suffer from excess, particularly in citing parallel illustrative passages and in making obscure critical observations. "However helpful," Zitner writes, "annotation can be a distraction for the student, a nuisance for the printer, and for the publisher a fiscal menace" (p. 135).

One of the causes of excessive annotation is "institutionalization"—we learned to annotate in graduate school in order to show off what we knew, to prove that we had done all the necessary background work in the related fields. And since we had all this knowledge, and since it was not likely to be tested for or asked for in any other way, and since we hated to "waste" it, it got dumped into the commentary notes in a welter of parallel passages, cross-references, refutations of readings, rehearsals of scholarly disagreements over individual points, negative findings ("I looked everywhere for this, but just couldn't find it"), and assorted speculations. Zitner calls this "the lore of the profession," and suggests "that an attempt should be made . . .

to clear annotations of all merely 'institutional' observations, and . . . that many of the items in the first drafts of annotations (especially when these convey 'background' information), ought to be scrutinized with a view to possible inclusion in the introduction or to separate publication" (p. 139).

The final essay in this volume is "Old-Spelling Editions: The State of the Business in 1978," by Jon Stallworthy. From his position as former Deputy Publisher of the Clarendon Press, Stallworthy is able to speak knowledgeably on the practical aspects of publishing. Most of the article is devoted to advice to editors and authors on how to choose a prospective publisher and how to deal with the publisher on matters far removed from the concerns that the scholar had as he or she did research. He treats, briefly, such problems as how to convince a press to publish one's edition, whether to work with a literary agent, how to handle royalties, the economies of "hot metal" printing as opposed to lithography, and the difficulties–for editor, reader, and publisher—of multi-volume editions.

The experienced scholar will learn little from Stallworthy, who says that he has taken as his model Clifford Leech's essay "On Editing One's First Play" (*Studies in Bibliography*, 23 [1970], 61–70). For the beginner, however, Stallworthy provides an overview of a part of the scholarly publishing world that the typical academic researcher is unlikely to see.

Curiously, Stallworthy concludes his contribution by reprinting a brief essay by Robert Halsband entitled "Dust Jackets to the Rescue" (*Scholarly Publishing* [Oct. 1977], 54–56). This is a lightweight piece about how Halsband handled the problem of providing complimentary copies of his book to all of the people who expected to receive them. (He gave dust jackets instead.) Now Halsband's story has a certain undeniable charm to it, and surely most readers will find it enjoyable, but its relation to Stallworthy's essay is only tangential and its appearance here smacks of a space-filling technique.

With Schoenbaum's talk on the state of the art opening the volume, it is appropriate that the subject of the state of the business should close it. The position of these two essays reminds one of the conflict between art and business that underlay much of the discussion at the conference. Questions in which this conflict was central were raised again and again in one form or another. Can (should) a scholar commit him- or herself to the great expense of time and effort required to produce a state-of-the-art edition if the state of the business requires the cost of such an edition to be prohibitive for the buyer? Can (should) a young scholar make the investment of time required for an editorial project if his or her tenure committee demands more rapid and more numerous publications? Should an editor aim for a modernized text without a burdensome apparatus in exchange for more eager acceptance by a publisher? And if he or she does produce a modern-spelling edition, has he or she been unfaithful to his or her "art"?

The questions of who reads a critical old-spelling edition and whether such an edition is even feasible is today's economy are not easily answered; I think that no one who attended the Toronto conference expected to find the answers there, and certainly they are not provided in *Play-Texts in Old Spelling*. On the other hand, these are important questions and they are questions that are not likely to go away in the near future. And that brings me to a recommendation about the audience for *Play-Texts in Old Spelling*.

Although anyone interested in the creation and production of critical texts will find this book interesting, I think it should be required reading for anyone just beginning a career as a scholarly editor. Shand and Shady write in their Introduction: "For better or for worse, there is a staggering amount of information and knowledge required for an editor to prepare old-spelling play-texts for publication" (p. 3). The great value of *Play-Texts in Old Spelling* is that it provides, through example and explanation, an excellent overview of the kinds of "information and knowledge" required. A new editor may not be aware that compositor studies, emendations of accidentals, commentary notes, and author's royalties are all a part of the complicated process of bringing a newly edited text before the public. As one sits in a great library patiently trying to transcribe the crabbed handwriting of a seventeenth-century scribe, it may be difficult to realize that at some time later, perhaps years later, a decision will have to be made about whether this edition should be typeset or printed by photo-offset. And, at the other end of the process, when one's publisher suggests dropping the long tables recording the historical collation in order to keep the published price down, it can be difficult to remember exactly why that time-destroying, eye-straining collation is so important. And all along the way, from the time one first decides he or she is going to edit a particular text until the moment he or she places the author's copy of the published book on his or her shelf, there are hard decision to make. *Play-Texts in Old Spelling* does not make the decisions, but it does make the reader aware of many of the kinds of decisions that will be needed and it provides examples of how some of those decisions have been made by other editors.

Marlowe and the Politics of Elizabethan Theatre, by Simon Shepherd. New York: St. Martin's Press, 1986. Pp. xix + 231. $27.50.

Reviewer: HARRY KEYISHIAN

Simon Shepherd's cultural-materialist study seeks to do much more than influence our view of Marlowe: it aims in general to challenge traditional notions about authorship and texts and about the relationship of texts to their cultural/ideological contexts. It exhibits the strengths and weaknesses of the movement to which it belongs: on the one hand, a vigorous commitment, grounded in post-structuralist and Marxist historical analysis, to promoting a critical and pedagogical revolution in literary and cultural studies; on the other hand, the uncritical privileging of a specific ideology and the deployment, in its service, of a sectarian and opportunistic critical methodology designed to advance its political program.

The book sets to its work even before it is opened: Craig Dodd's cover design turns the de Witt sketch of the Swan into a cultural-materialist cartoon. For the word *proscenium* under the royal couple at center stage, he substitutes "ideology"; the spectator's entrance (*ingressus*) is called "subjectivity," the tiring house "pleasure," the middle gallery "power," and the upper gallery "class."

The relabeling, providing an alternative way of "reading" social relationships in the theater, is in line with one of Shepherd's main aims, which is not to substitute definitively "true" labels for "false" but to suggest that labeling in general is an ideological activity motivated by the social aims of the labeler and hence never capable of describing absolute or ahistorical "truth." Shepherd wishes to identify a *social* meaning in Marlowe's play-texts by invoking societal/ideological contexts through which they may be most usefully understood by readers (critics, students, teachers) interested in changing contemporary society. As he puts it, the Marlowe texts "could be said to take a number of the ideological truths of the Elizabethan theatre and reveal them to be discourses, and to show those discourses spoken within power relations" (p. 210). And because they *could be said to*, he elects to speak of them as if that is indeed what they do; and he encourages others to discuss and teach them in the same manner.

Shepherd's methodology allows him to fall back on such limp formulations as saying that a given scene "could be said" (p. 15) to contest a given viewpoint or that one play "potentially represented" (p. 30) a social institution and another "could be seen as an ironic investigation" (p. 67) of a given topic. Perhaps they could, but (just as easily) they also could not, and the reader is likely to feel stranded at times in a foggy critical climate.

But Shepherd's are, of course, familiar cultural-materialist purposes: compare Terry Eagleton's call for criticism that "explore[s] how the signifying systems of a 'literary' text produce certain ideological effects" (*Literary Theory: An Introduction* [Oxford: Blackwell, 1983], p. 212); Jonathan Dollimore's reference to analysis that "concentrates on the formative power of social and ideological structures" (*Political Shakespeare*, ed. Jonathan Dollimore and Alan Sinfield [Ithaca, N. Y.: Cornell University Press, 1985], p. 3); and Catherine Belsey's expressed wish not merely to reveal how play-texts signify but to "put them to work for substantial political purposes which replace the mysterious aesthetic and moral pleasures of nineteenth-century criticism" (*The Subject of Tragedy* [New York: Methuen, 1985], p. 10).

The reader is warned, then, not to look for traditional analyses of play-texts here. With considerable rearranging, cutting, and pasting, one might find in Shepherd's pages a number of "readings" of Marlowe's plays, but to do so would undercut what Shepherd is trying to accomplish in stressing the provisional rather than "fixed and true" (p. xviii) nature of all readings. Shepherd is anxious for us not to think "that the meanings that can be found by me now can be found always, irrespective of material or historical situation" or that they were "intended by authors." Rather, he relies on the notion that "the text can generate meanings despite its proclaimed project" and "permits in its structure my reading" (pp. 48–49). To put this another way, Shepherd (as I read him) thinks that while a text can veto certain readings, it otherwise is open to all manner of critical manipulation that a critic can devise.

Author's intentions are not a factor in this approach. Indeed, even to refer to the texts as "Marlowe's plays" suggests that the playwright had a proprietorship in them that Shepherd would deny. (He identifies them, rather, for convenience, as the "Marlowe texts.") In addition, traditional "readings" emphasize an artistic unity in texts that Shepherd feels is not there—considering the manner in which theatrical texts were (allegedly) shaped in rehearsal and collaboration—and not even desirable, since successful artistic closure hampers the all-important work of transforming political consciousness.

Shepherd's approach divides literary/critical phenomena into categories of Good Things and Bad Things, somewhat in the manner parodied years ago in Sellar and Yeatman's *1066 and All That*, but with a Brechtian twist. For example, the fact that audiences take pleasure in Barabas's fooling of Lodowick in *The Jew of Malta* is characterized as a Bad Thing, because it hides the real power-relations that exist between the parties ("The comic pleasure is treacherous" [p. 174]). On the other hand, when a scene fails as comedy—for example, when Barabas unamusingly disguises himself as a musician to spy on his foes—that is a Good Thing because it "withholds the expressiveness of tragedy and the pleasure of comedy and consequently makes a critical distance from which to view both racial role-playing and performance itself" (p. 176).

Shepherd's principle seems to be that the playwright who succeeds in entertaining, amusing, engaging, or moving an audience is deluding it; but a playwright who "fails" at these things is doing something of value by cultivating the audience's skepticism about prevailing values and thereby putting it in mind of the ways that art contains and expresses ideology. Thus alerted, the audience (or the critic or student) is likelier to be induced to take political action against the dominant ideology of capitalist liberal humanism (a *very* Bad Thing).

Other *Bad* Things include "author-centered approaches" (p. xviii); "the critical predisposition toward unity and decorum" (p. 55); characters whose language achieves "full expressivity" (pp. 16, 108); "psychological realism" (p. 110) and "the portrayal of the unitary subject" (p. 81); plays and theatrical modes that create a "truth-effect which would give authority to examples of necessary obedience" (p. 51) and thereby cause an audience to lose "its distancing awareness of show and [take] pleasure only in the illusion of fully expressive persons that is constructed by later Renaissance drama" (p. 109). Also, patriarchy, criticism "based on wonky ideas about homosexuality" (p. 198), and "the politics of that institution known as Eng. Lit." (p. xix). (On this last point, compare Eagleton's declaration that "Departments of literature in higher education . . . are part of the ideological apparatus of the modern capitalist state" [*Literary Theory*, p. 200]).

Other Good Things: a play-text that deconstructs ideology, that "works actively on its audience, bringing ideas to their notice, situating them ideologically, making problems of concepts that might usually have been taken for natural or commonsensical" (p. xvi); critical positions that are "socialist and anti-patriarchal" (p. xviii) and that produce "a properly political understanding of . . . artworks" (p. ix); metadramatic knowledge (p. 53); the "critical spectator" (p. 83); readings that are openly "provisional" (p. 92); "mixed form" (p. 71), "montage" (p. 55), ironic juxtaposition, and scenic displays that undercut verbal assertions (pp. 23–24); the practice of "problematising theatrical pleasure" (p. 208); Machiavelli's denial of natural law (p. 86); dramatic texts (like Marlowe's) that "construct an awareness of the values they embody, if not a resistance to them" (p. xv). Also, Stephen Greenblatt and Jonathan Dollimore, because they "examine the relationship of drama and ideology in a way that produces a properly political understanding of the artworks" that they discuss (p. ix).

Although Shepherd's book is often lively and amusing, it does sound, at least to me, as if he envisions a glumly propagandistic theatrical and critical universe, in which the transformation of political consciousness is the only countenanced activity. But of course other cultural-materialist critics have also emphasized the ways prevailing critical practice works ideologically to uphold the dominant culture and have proposed ways of reading and teaching Shakespeare's texts (in Alan Sinfield's words) "differently—drawing attention to their historical insertion, their political implications, and the activity of criticism in reproducing them" (*Political Shakepeare*, p. 137).

For his part, Shepherd is particularly concerned with the relationship between Elizabethan theater (as a social institution) and the rest of Elizabethan society. Admitting that it is hard to assert that any particular text is "radical" or to know "if any or all of the audience saw it that way," Shepherd does feel it possible to discuss "how the plays address their audience, how they ideologically place the viewer, so that something might be inferred about the position from which audiences make judgements of a playtext" (p. xv). Noting that plays can both affirm prevailing values and encourage critical inspection of them, Shepherd defines the politics of Elizabethan theater as "the relationship between dominant ideologies and the questioning/affirming strategies of the individual text" (pp. xvii-xviii). (Here too he follows the general approach, endorsed by Terry Eagleton, of reestablishing the study of rhetoric as a central mode of analysis.)

In expressing his hostility to "realist" conventions and liberal-humanist views about selfhood and identity, Shepherd stresses what he deems the harmful social effects of Shakespeare's dramatic practices—his eloquence, his skilled dramatic structure, and his realistic characterization, all of which reinforced the dominant political ideology by practicing what Margot Heinemann calls the "politics of empathy" (in *Political Shakespeare*, p. 214).

Shepherd views the late 1580s and early 1590s, by contrast, as a golden age for the interrogation of language, institutions, and power structures. Marlowe "showed" that speech was not a transparent guide to the inner person but, rather, that it could and often did disguise true power-relations and the role of force in political life. For example, Shepherd suggests that by juxtaposing the bleeding corpses on stage at the end of *I Tamburlaine* with the scarlet robes put on by the protagonist's victorious generals, the Marlowe text subverts the verbal promise of peace with which the play concludes (pp. 23-24).

Reactionary Shakespeare, on the other hand, treats language as a mirror of the soul and thereby disguises what Marlowe had exposed. This is why Shakespeare has his present status among us, Shepherd feels: Shakespeare deceives us by presenting characters and situations that seem real in language that seems natural. Speaking of the treatment of Cade in *2 Henry VI*, Shepherd writes: "here as elsewhere Shakespeare's early texts reinvest the written with an aura that his contemporaries often demolished (no wonder academics love his work!), and also attack the common people (no wonder academics, etc. . . .)" (p. 33).

Having deplored Shakespeare's influence on dramatic language, Shepherd next attacks his influence on dramatic form. Shepherd wants to give readers the wherewithal to "counter and question the critical predisposition towards unity and decorum" (p. 55) that Shakespeare forwarded. Specifically, Shepherd asserts that early playwrights used ironic juxtaposition ("montage") as a means of exposing and criticizing the dominant ideology of Elizabethan politics. In reaction, the Elizabethan power-structure encouraged the development of dramatic form because it feared that "disordered work played to a large audience might open the gaps for 'crooked subjects', and fail to create the truth-effect which would give authority to examples of necessary obedience" (p. 51). Likewise, modern-day editors who try to produce unified, coherent literary texts are thereby "undervaluing . . . performance work" (p. 71).

Shepherd maintains that before unity became the dominant literary ideal, plays exhibited "sharp contrasts of rhyme, blank verse, prose," and so forth, contrasts that "constituted [the audience] as critical spectator" (p. 83) and motivated critical reading/viewing/listening. To support his argument Shepherd relies a good deal on the fact that "theatre audiences shouted back at the stage" and that they "were seen as 'seditious', not as ripe for civilising but as deliberate opponents to order" (p. 9). What we have thought of as artistic development, therefore, is the power structure's way of lulling those critical sensibilities that earlier theater practices had sharpened.

Shakespeare's retrograde influence is also traced in his effect on characterization: he fostered psychological realism and thereby disguised the fact that "definition of the individual was an ideological battleground" (p. 84) in his day. The fact that in our time only "unitary" characterization is accepted as realistic and that "realism is valued as more serious than non-realism" (p. 81) is seen as sinister; it reveals the ideology of dominant critical thinking. Lines that might have "encouraged critical listening . . . cease to have their former provocative metadramatic function" (p. 82).

Dramatic characters become "non-problematic" and "depoliticised" (p. 83); audiences are rendered passive. Shakespeare contributed to this development in *Titus*, Shepherd says, "and it is not necessarily a healthy one, though it goes down a bomb at A level and Stratford" (p. 83).

When he examines dramatic texts, Shepherd seeks for the ways that they hide or expose the social/economic/political realities of Elizabethan society. That the Roman state oppresses Titus Andronicus and that Lavinia is brutally silenced are, for Shepherd, reflections of repressive Elizabethan policies—the closing down of printing presses in the late 1580s for example. But by making Titus' speech "expressive and sincere" and his inner person "knowable" (p. 84), Shakespeare disguises the ways that personhood is defined and the individual constructed in society. In *Doctor Faustus*, on the other hand, "comic language and action play on the idea of a constructed man"; such stylistic elements as the play's "sharp changes in tone, the writtenness of the alliteration, the absence of inner debate . . . unsettle our view of the speaker as a fixed unitary subject" p. 95). (Again, Shakespeare does a Bad Thing, Marlowe a Good.)

Although Shepherd argues his points with a considerable degree of learning and vigor, his assumptions and methology too often seem arbitrary, if not downright specious. For one thing, it seems implausible that Marlowe's audiences found the theatrical conventions of their time too crude to credit, since it has always been possible to induce "truth-effects" in naive audiences by means that more sophisticated viewers would find transparently conventional and manipulative. Marlowe's theatrical means were certainly adequate to induce a "truth-effect"—as adequate, say, as the means effectively used by writers of nineteenth-century melodramas, or makers of silent films in the early twentieth century, to enthrall their audiences. It is far likelier that later audiences, with experience enough to appreciate the point of metatheatrical usages, would respond the way that Shepherd says audiences of the 1590s responded.

Shepherd does somewhat better in commenting on the ways that artistic practices (and the ideology they embodied) shaped social attitudes. He observes that dominant Elizabethan ideology (reflected in Hooker) assumed reason and morality to be inbred, derived from natural law: it defined the "wrong" individual as one in whom private desire blocked reason; it conceived rebellion, like envy and greed, as a fault in the individual; it encouraged the idea that virtue dictated behaving in conformity with the interests of the community. But plays that proclaim conformity as a virtue, and thereby reinforce the idea of a "common cause," impede the audience from seeing the state as a "contestable grouping of interests," an "inegalitarian hierarchy" (p. 85); they encourage identification with and sacrifice on behalf of the state. Shepherd proposes an approach to *Doctor Faustus*, via definitions of the individual offered by Hooker, Machiavelli, and the Puritans, that shows the text undoing those assumptions of the dominant culture.

Clearly, however, Shepherd does not intend his "readings" of Marlowe's plays to be set up against other interpretations. Rather, he plays off the texts to influence and reorient the critical practices of his readers. As well, he characterizes and evaluates playwrights on the basis of the political impact of their artistic practices. Marlowe does a Good Thing in effectively exploring Machiavellianism in *The Jew of Malta* through the character of Ferneze and in presenting Faustus as a "constructed" individual responsive to ideological address.

In the second half of his book Shepherd focuses on specific character-types (messengers, prophets, scholars, Turks, fathers, women) who help him make the case for the political value of pre-Shakespearean dramatic traditions and "chuck out the window the belief that Elizabethan drama was simply a clumsy stage in theatre's growing up toward psychological realism" (p. 110). On these topics—and such others as the relationship of fathers and sons, of the stage-foreigner and the entertainer, of the cultural influence of Puritanism, among others—Shepherd can be intriguing, challenging, and informative, and his book can be read with profit by readers interested in Elizabethan political and social life and its rhetorical structures.

In my view, however, Shepherd's mobilization of critical resources in the immediate service of political commentary ultimately serves to discredit his work. Shepherd is open about the matter: he comments, "there are limits to the readings I would countenance and, as with everybody else, these readings are set by my own political values and commitments—in my case I work from a position which is socialist and anti-patriarchial" (p. xviii). In applying this methodology Shepherd is apparently following Eagleton's view that "any method or theory which will contribute to the strategic goal of human emancipation, the production of 'better people' through the socialist transformation of society, is acceptable" (*Literary Theory*, p. 211).

But this surely will not do; it invites intellectual opportunism that anyone can exploit. It is one thing to recognize and identify the ideological, culture-bound bases of literature and criticism: that is valuable work to which both Marxist analysis and post-structuralist theory can contribute. It is quite another to treat texts as conveniences, blank (or nearly blank) slates on which either a dominant or an insurgent critical practice can inscribe what it chooses, to suit its political purposes.

It disturbs me, for example, that Shepherd would surely need to reverse his privileging hierarchy were he to be writing in a socialist state about socialist art that prizes "truth-effects" and artistic closure as much as bourgeois art does and that wants, as little, to have its discourse revealed as ideology. That he admits as much when he says he might write differently of these materials in a different "material or historical situation" (p. 48) does not improve matters, in my view. Further, Shepherd's methodology seems fatally subjective, since other cultural-materialist critics (like Dollimore in *Radical Tragedy* [Chicago, Ill.: University of Chicago Press, 1984]) have managed to find subversion inscribed even in some of Shakespeare's texts.

Further, in joining the pack that today privileges critical over artistic practice, Shepherd advances what seems to me a particularly dreary cause. While it is good to be rid of the naive assumption that artworks have "autonomy" and ahistorical meaning, it is supremely ungrateful and a repudiation of human experience to deny their special transforming qualities, the elements that have made them beloved, enriching, and liberating for countless generations, whether under feudalism, capitalism, or socialism. (Here, of course, I reveal my own critical assumptions and biases in valuing what I perceive to be the long-range aesthetic and moral liberation forwarded by art more highly than I do its short-term potential to advance political movements.)

But even more, I find myself distressed by the pegadogical program offered by Shepherd, *et al.*, under which (as I read their recommendations) students would be taught to believe that they have no greater obligation to a text than to construe it in a manner that supports their (or their teacher's) ideological preferences. I do not know much about the students whom Shepherd and the other cultural materialists teach. I know my own, though—American students, not of the first or even second rank, at a large university with a reputation for pragmatic mass education—and I feel tremendously the need to get them to read responsibly and rigorously, to get them to open their minds to transforming texts and attend carefully to the function of words and ideas in a world morally debilitated by a massive and systematic contempt for "meaning," however that worried word must be construed these days. We ought not to waste the opportunity we have as teachers to help students see more clearly, sagely, and subtly by encouraging them to follow fundamentally flawed critical practices, no matter how "progressive" the end.

Dramatic Design in the Chester Cycle, by Peter W. Travis. Chicago, Ill.: University of Chicago Press, 1982. Pp. xvi + 310. $20.00.

Reviewer: J.A.B. SOMERSET

The student of the Chester Cycle is blessed with an *embarras de richesse* of scholarship remarkable in its scope and authority: to mention W. W. Greg, F. M. Salter, L. M. Clopper, R. M. Lumiansky and David Mills is to remind us that Chester's besetting puzzles of texts, forms of presentation, dates, and theatrical history are being answered with satisfactory hypotheses or solutions. It is clearly time for a thorough and concentrated account of the artistry and design of the Chester Cycle, and the present volume has largely succeeded in providing this.

In the meantime other scholarship has continued to appear: Lumiansky and Mills's *The Chester Mystery Cycle: Essays and Documents* (Chapel Hill: University of North Carolina Press, 1983) and Clopper's extensive review of it in the pages of this annual ("The Chester Cycle: Review Article," II [1985], 283–291) appeared too late for Travis. These later contributions support some of Travis's suggestions and might lead him to reconsider others. On the question of authorship Travis recognizes that Chester is "a composite of pageants constructed in quite different ways" (p. 31), and he detects layers of revision in some pageants (p. 56); as he proceeds, however, the idea of "the Chester dramatist, an intellectual playwright" (p. 169) increasingly appears. Lumiansky and Mills toy with the same idea, employing "playwright(s)" to suggest it; Clopper agrees, as well, that one playwright "went through the cycle at one point adding, adapting, and altering to make it a coherent whole" (p. 284). Lumiansky and Mills also conclude that the manuscripts of Chester are copies of an Exemplar full of alternative versions, insertions, and cancellations; they term it a "cycle of cycles" and propose that their edited cycle is "a convenient abstraction" that was never produced in its present form (Ch. 1). This editorial hypothesis lends theoretical authority to Travis's decision to treat as "accretions" (and disregard) certain passages in the Early English Text Society text; these "accretions" (p. 69), however, are better considered as alternative possibilities. On the whole these later investigations confirm Travis's conviction that the Chester Cycle, for all its textual and historical puzzles, deserves to be studied as an artistic whole.

The foregoing matters are addressed in the second chapter; in the first Travis sets the Cycle in the context of medieval celebrations of Corpus Christi—surprisingly, in that Chester achieved its greatest scope (and current form) as a Whitsun cycle; at Corpus Christi (before 1505) it was largely a Passion play, performed in "place and scaffold" manner. Why not, then, consider the celebration of the Feast of Pentecost? Travis's use of the phrase "the Corpus Christi play" (with its suggestion that there was a single form of play proper to that feast) echoes Kolve (*The Play Called Corpus Christi* [Stanford, Calif.: Stanford University Press, 1966]) and is increasingly questioned now not only on Chester's evidence but also because of the wide variety of saint plays, Passion plays, folk dramas, Creed plays, miracle plays, and what have you that were produced to honor that feast across England and Europe. The impulse to honor the sacrament and increase popular devotion took a remarkable number of dramatic forms. Travis suggests that the Chester Cycle was designed with three defining functions: it was to be a dramatic *summa* of the primary tenets of Christianity, a dramatic interpretation of the history of salvation, and a model for the spiritual education of every Christian. Within this framework, Travis outlines his intent to probe how the plays control dramatic illusion, the ways they define the audience, how they manipulate dramatic and historical time, the sense they define of the audiences' role as believers, and their manner of interpreting the meanings of the actions they dramatize. The first of these, discussed in the opening chapter, is left rather tentative because the terminology used, "dramatic illusion," remains undefined except by synonym with "a world of artistic illusion" and in opposition to "nonillusionistic game" (an idea originating with Kolve). The Chester Cycle, more than any other, appeals to its auditors to believe in the veracity of its actions, as Travis argues, but its appeal is to the truths of Christian history as seen through representational mimetic action.

Chapter Three and those that follow present the heart of Travis's book, a "careful study, part by part, of the . . . Chester . . . cycle." (p. 69). Paginae I–V are explored with regard to how the Cycle interprets Old Testament time, carefully avoiding anachronism except in carefully controlled circumstances such as the Abraham and Isaac pageant ("an example of typological drama at its best" [p. 83]). In suggesting here how the dramatist has "harmonized typology and 'realistic' mimetic action" (p. 83), Travis makes us wish for fuller discussion of the dramatic impact of that "realistic" action; the experience of seeing the play in the cycle at Toronto impressed me rather with the clash between the typology (Abraham as God, Isaac as Christ) and the stage image (Abraham as suffering father, Isaac as initially uncomprehending son). The theatrical dimension is one that this study, in general, could explore more fully. In Chapter Four we explore the comic transition achieved in the Nativity Group—a progress towards the identification of the community with the Saviour that one may see both within the group as a whole, and in its individual episodes (for example, the shepherds, whose "spiritual procession . . . objectifies an inner process of growth" [p. 728]). Chapter Five accounts for the ministry plays' sparse dramaturgy by, importantly, pointing out that they depend heavily upon St. John's Gospel, adopt a conservative dramatic style, and concentrate upon Christ's divinity rather than his humanity; these are aspects of conscious artistic decision. Here Travis uncovers theological reasons for a dramaturgy that others have found unexciting (contrasting it with other cycles); the account is a convincing one. Stress on Christ's divine aspects is also appropriate, one might note, in a cycle to be performed at Pentecost.

Travis's discussion of the ritualized treatment of the Passion exemplifies a tendency in his treatment to assume a dramatic effect rather than demonstrate how it came about. The action of Christ's tormentors' stretching Him on the cross, we read, is "mercifully brief (unlike the staging of this action in the other cycles) [but] the brutality of their actions and the pathetic sight of their victim were *clearly intended* to evoke a profoundly agonized response from the audience" (p. 185; italics mine). The looked-for comparison with other plays is not made; the account rather assumes that the spectacle of Christ on the cross would arouse profound emotions, much as do the services on Good Friday, without showing the dramatic means that produce this effect despite the merciful brevity of the staging. In a number of other places the opinions of other critics about the dramatic effectiveness of particular passages are addressed, but not satisfactorily answered; for example, Travis writes of Pagina XXII: "criticized by one scholar as having been 'rapidly conceived and executed,' this relatively brief pageant (340 lines) is in my judgment an unusual success, for it transforms the tenor of the cycle entirely . . ." (p. 229). But a few lines later the play is described as "totally undramatic" (p. 230); one wonders about the writer's criteria of success.

With the consideration of the Resurrection group, we come near the heart of the cycle's structure, for Travis suggests that study of this group brings us "to requesting a definition of the major dramatic designs of the entire cycle" (p. 193). He finds this definition in the pattern of doubt reinforced into faith, seen most clearly in Thomas but elsewhere as well. Beyond this pattern, Travis suggests that during the Whitsun shift of the plays a "credal design" was incorporated into them, culminating in the creation of their creed by the twelve Apostles at Pentecost. (Here, particularly, more attention might have been given to the feast which the Cycle, in its present form, was designed and enlarged to honor.) The argument is subtle, as are the traces of the credal design, and too lengthy to go into here; the structure, Travis concludes, was likely not discerned by many except the most discerning of the audience. Travis has amassed a great deal of persuasive evidence, which will need to be carefully considered by those who, used to delicate subtlety in the plays of Shakespeare, have tended to deny it in those of his predecessors. Equally subtle in argument is a final chapter that focuses on the sham ministry of Anti-christ, which, Travis admits, may be seen just as "fun and games" but may be "concerned with the purpose and end of art" (p. 241). He admits that he is interpreting Chester's esthetic "from a quite limited part of single pageant" (p. 239); therein lies a danger, for it seems reasonable that a matter so important would be addressed at many points in the cycle. The discussion also needs to be linked to the account, mentioned earlier, of the type of dramatic illusion that the plays are designed to induce.

In sum, there is much food for thought in the pages of this book, while one may not agree with all the arguments it contains, or may feel that in some places the evidence is pressed a little too far. A tendency to allow hypothesis to harden into fact is discernible in places as well; for example, on page 49 a "suspicion" becomes a "judgment" within two lines. A more rigorous proof-reading should have removed a few puzzling errors: for example, "IV and MS H of V" [IV and V of MS H] (p. 57); "judge judged" [judged] (p. 121); "structure" [structured] (p. 210). But the blemishes are insignificant when weighed against the book's scope, wealth of detail, and many thoughtful insights. It is to be welcomed for its attempt to encompass and explain not just this or that *part* of the Chester cycle, but rather the underlying ideas that give the Chester pageants coherence as a work of art.

Devon, edited by John M. Wasson. Records of Early English Drama. Toronto: University of Toronto Press, 1986. Pp. lxxvi + 623. $108.00.

Reviewer: WILLIAM TYDEMAN

Despite the intrinsic interest of what is being explored, the impressive resources that exist to back individual effort in the field, and the consciousness of being engaged in labor of lasting value, the volume editor employed on the Records of Early English Drama (REED) project is not automatically a scholar to be envied. After sifting through the entire gamut of relevant archival materials (and as the REED operation extends its domains, the net needs to be cast over a far wider range of potential sources), the diligent investigator may still be left at the end of a marathon survey contemplating usable items drawn from only a restricted number of centers that offer, moreover, records either so fragmentary in nature or so fitful in occurrence that it becomes dangerous to seek to base on them any conclusions of unchallengeable validity. The ultimate reward may be feelings of frustration however illogical, and as one reaches the close of Professor Wasson's lucid but diffident introduction to the present work, it becomes hard to resist the reiterated impressions of understandable wariness that it conveys:

> Ironically, the closer a researcher comes to 'completeness' in a project such as this, the more apprehensive that person becomes that the mass of records collected will still not give a true picture of entertainment in the county. . . . We can only be aware that what is extant is one scene from a larger play and be very cautious about making generalizations. . . . In some ways more disturbing than [the] great gaps in the extant records is the knowledge that the records that do exist can be very misleading. Scribes in any age tend to make note of the unusual rather than the commonplace. . . . a researcher feels not only that the extant records are a small sample upon which to base generalizations but also that even those records we do have are not telling the whole truth. . . .
>
> (pp. xxvii–xxviii)

Not that Professor Wasson has any reason to apologize for inadequacy in his efforts or even for paucity of his findings in themselves. This is by no means a slim volume, as befits an English county whose importance and status were far more highly regarded in pre-industrial Britain than they are (by all but Devonians) today. *Devon* contains over three hundred pages of actual textual entries relating to entertainment meticulously transcribed and edited, supported by over one hundred pages of translations to assist those whose command of medieval Latin is indifferent or non-existent, a few pages of miscellaneous notes, and a substantial and stimulating listing of visiting companies in the county, far more extensive than that made available in the comparable Norwich volume. Latin and English glossaries and a helpfully arranged index assist in swelling the book to proportions ample enough to justify the high price that it is evidently necessary to charge. Why then does the reader, apparently in common with the editor himself, come to suspect after lengthy perusal that a long and exhausting trawl has dredged up a rather unrewarding haul?

One explanation undoubtedly lies in the fact that this volume represents a new departure in the REED annals, and one to which we shall have to learn to adjust as the series goes marching on. All the volumes previously issued in this magisterial set have stemmed from major medieval civic centres—York, Chester, Coventry, Newcastle, and Norwich. With this assemblage of gleanings from Devon, REED makes its first foray into the shires. Hence, instead of a consolidated collection of documentary evidence relating to dramatic activities within a single coherent urban milieu, we here confront a more heterogeneous body of material, in which such civic centers as Exeter and Plymouth certainly feature strongly, but without possessing the same richness and concentration of dramatic interest that Chester, Coventry, and York records supply so plentifully. Readers anticipating a strong rural flavor to this volume are also likely to be disappointed: theatrical and analogous pastimes no doubt took place amid the tors and coombs of this delightful county, but little of it seems to have left behind documented traces in the archives, so that while our knowledge of performances in towns and cities is supplemented, even enhanced, by *Devon*, Professor Wasson is unable to reveal very much about more pastoral recreations. Perhaps this will be the pattern that all the "county" collections will follow as they emerge from the University of Toronto Press as year succeeds to year.

In addition, the Devon editor has had more than his fair share of lacunae and dead ends to cope with, which one rather fears may prove to be the case for those tackling other English shires, let alone the remoter regions of the British Isles. Much depends, of course, on just how many records one expects to have survived into the present, but it is a saddening reflection that of the ten modern municipal boroughs in the county, the records of all but five are missing, and those of Totnes are sadly deficient in the kinds of information sought for. Of the 430 urban and rural parishes whose records were checked, no more than precisely ten per cent could provide appropriate material, even if Professor Wasson bravely accepts this as a statistically valid sample, particularly as it covers a good cross section of the county's variegated parish communities. Certainly, sixty per cent of these fragmentary churchwardens' accounts do include evidence of drama and other related entertainments, but to offset this bounty, household and monastic accounts were discovered to be almost non-existent, only one entry in the entire volume being extracted from material of monastic origin, Devon's ten abbeys, two collegiate churches and numerous priories (other than Cowick) yielding nothing.

On the other hand, one might expect such borough records as survive to provide (other than at Totnes) rich pickings: Barnstaple, for example, as an important port, market town and wool center, has an excellent set of accounts examined at the end of the last century by J. O. Halliwell-Phillips, but of these only those of the receivers have relevance to REED, and while these are particularly full and detailed for the years 1461–82, the custom of recording gratuities awarded to entertainers seems to have become inconsistent after the latter date, so that the chance of building up a total picture for the town's expenditure in this sphere is lost. (At certain places the civic authorities may simply have discontinued making such payments, under the influence of a strictly puritan idealism.) Dartmouth, too, with the "almost bewildering variety of its medieval and Renaissance records" whets the antiquarian appetite, but in fact only fifty individual items of relevance have been discovered and reproduced, drawn from a mere handful of twenty different sources (p. xiv).

As one might anticipate, it is therefore Exeter and Plymouth that provide the bulk of the entries collected here, but in the case of both centers, there is less that is of importance and appeal to be found amid the documents under scrutiny than one might hope. Exeter, with one of the largest and most nearly complete collections of civic records in the country outside London, can also offer its cathedral and diocesan archives, "almost overwhelming in their number and variety," and thus could not fail to supply some first-rate items. Yet as far as diocesan records go, outside of entries in the registers of medieval bishops, most notably those of the redoubtable John de Grandisson, whose injunctions to his clergy have long constituted a familiar element in histories of medieval drama, there are "disappointingly few references to early drama" (p. xvi). Wasson concludes that Exeter was not a cathedral church whose chapter cared a great deal for religious dramatics, or if clerics did stage ceremonies or plays of the liturgical type there, either they were not recorded, or the records of such events have perished.

Similarly, with the city itself, although it is clear enough that Exeter sponsored one of the earliest Corpus Christi cycle presentations known to us (an entry in the Mayor's Court Roll for June 1414 speaks of the annual performance as a happening "ab antiqua Consuetudine" [p. 82]), it is equally clear that the references are not sustained, even if in the 1480s and '90s isolated entries seem to indicate that the Corpus Christi Guild of local Skinners was maintaining the tradition with a single play. But as to the size and scope of the original enterprise, the allocation of episodes to guilds, the detailed lists of expenses that so enliven our understanding of similar presentations elsewhere, Exeter's archives, copious as they are, are silent. From Plymouth, too, we learn that some kind of a performance once graced Corpus Christi Day, but the records do not assist us in reconstructing exactly what went on: the documents can tell us little more than that there was a Corpus Christi guild in charge of proceedings and that the Tailors' guild was expected to build and maintain a pageant for the annual procession. More revealing are the references to other civic entertainments, including visits by travelling performers whose presence, however, seems to have been discouraged in the town towards the end of the 1590s.

Indeed, it is where they record fitfully but frequently the visits of touring troupes that the Devon materials most happily illuminate the study of early drama in the British Isles. One receives the impression that however much clerks failed to record by way of local amateur drama, a far higher proportion of professional visitations was set down, at least on such occasions as payment was made out of municipal funds.

From this evidence, the editor is quite legitimately able to highlight the fact that the county, despite its distance from major centers of population, received what might appear to be a remarkable number of visits from touring groups, not just in the late sixteenth and early seventeenth centuries, but from about 1400 onwards. Appearances by these companies—listed here under the names of over two hundred known or putative patrons and over twenty locations of origin including London and Ireland—offer us a vivid picture of performers on the move from the opening years of the fifteenth century, descending on the towns and villages of the West Country, importing the newer forms of entertainment into communities where an annual Robin Hood ceremonial was perhaps the sole dramatic fare on offer until the tourists' groups became a feature of the leisure scene, and at a far earlier date than was once appreciated. The evidence for touring enterprises in one rural English county is perhaps the most valuable feature of the entire work.

The format of the REED volumes has been planned so carefully that it perhaps smacks of uncharitableness to demand further refinements, but if the editorial team could be persuaded to supply running titles akin to those for the text pages for those pages devoted to the translations, it would certainly make the task of finding specific entries far speedier. Of the translations themselves, it is worth observing that while they strive for as literal a rendering as possible "in order to help the reader understand what the documents say" (p. 315), there does seem to be some inconsistency involved in the procedures that are followed. On some occasions the translation is made so literal as to sound like a school pupil's stilted efforts to cope with a sight passage; thus an entry on page 3 extracted from the Penitential of Bartholomew of Exeter quoting St. Augustine on actors is translated on page 317:

> Why does he who gives to actors, he who gives to prostitutes, give? Why don't those people give to (ordinary) human beings? All the same, they (the givers) are not there taking care for the character of God's activity, but the wickedness of human activity.

Yet this dogged—not to say doggerel—insistence is not matched by any reluctance to change the Latin word-order in the English renderings: the sole document from Tavistock, for instance, printed on pages 278–279 and translated on page 434, while admittedly a mass of subordinate phrases, is quite unnecessarily readjusted to make smooth modern prose, so that an utter novice would receive a false notion of which bits of the Latin referred to which bits of the English. Fortunately, REED material is probably never likely to become the study of many people who lack at least the rudiments of Latinity.

Reviewing a single volume of REED in isolation is apt to make a reviewer appear guilty of ingratitude; of course, some volumes are bound to contain richer and more piquant fare than others, and this is an inevitable corollary of the entire ambitious project. What matters is that at long last the relevant materials are being actively, systematically, and intensively examined. The final impact of the operation now in train will be capable of comprehensive assessment only when the last volume appears on the shelves of libraries and bookshops, and scholars can begin to compile that near-definitive account of early dramatic performance in Britain that has always been seen as one of the editorial board's most cherished goals. It is heartening to know that the recent severe cutback in funding for the project is being energetically countered with every weapon at the organization's disposal, and it is devoutly to be wished that private enterprise will step in, if other sources of support bow out. The quality and interest of Professor Wasson's researches should serve to impress on all those at work in the field of the traditional humanities what a tragedy for the world of international scholarship it will be if funds dry up completely before the whole of Britain has been scoured for evidence of dramatic activity with the same selfless persistence as is demonstrated here.

Women and the English Renaissance: Literature and the Nature of Womankind, 1540–1620, by Linda Woodbridge. Urbana and Chicago: University of Illinois Press, 1984. Pp. 364. Cloth $21.95; paper $10.95.

Reviewer: ELIZABETH H. HAGEMAN

In this brilliant book Linda Woodbridge takes on, as she says in her Exordium, a "gargantuan" task (p. 1)—the study of the relationships between Renaissance debates about woman's nature and other literary genres, both dramatic and nondramatic. Woodbridge's argument is appropriately complex and multi-faceted, for while she is aware that Renaissance literature is informed by a real ambivalence toward women, she takes pains to emphasize the significance of literary conventions in Renaissance writing and to remind her readers not to assume a simple relationship between literary portrayals of women and authors' (or audiences') ideas about them. Moving from 1540 (the publication date of Sir Thomas Elyot's *Defense of Good Women*) to 1620 (the date of *Hic Mulier*, an essay attacking women who wear men's clothing, and *Haec-Vir*, which criticizes foppish men), Woodbridge chronicles the history of Renaissance treatments of women in literature. She is utterly accurate when she says that her reader must be "prepared for a dizzying sense of topsy-turviness" (p. 7), because so much of what she proposes runs counter to received commonplaces about the period. Woodbridge argues that some "misogynistic attacks on women were responses to defenses of women and not the other way around, that the purpose of attacks and defenses was (from at least one perspective) the same, that Renaissance attacks on women are more congenial to modern feminism than are Renaissance defenses of women" (pp. 7–8). Because the relationship between literature and life is so complicated, some will be startled to read "that literary misogynists are intended as tools in the defense of women, that hostility toward the opposite sex was recognized as a step toward normal sexual maturity, that Shakespeare's transvestite heroines reveal his essential conservatism about sex roles, that Renaissance literature dramatizes the serious consequences of jest, that . . . the Renaissance typically characterized womankind in general as weak and timid while portraying individual women as sturdy and aggressive" (p. 8). So much of what Woodbridge says is so startling that the reader does have to work hard to take it all in. And the whole enterprise is made even more dizzying by Woodbridge's own witty, paradoxical style.

In the opening chapter of the study, Woodbridge defines a genre that she calls the "formal controversy": works that "argue a thesis about Women, with the help of logic and rhetoric" (p. 13). After a full analysis of stock *topoi* of the controversy—satiric antifeminist *personae*; lists of exemplary women like Eve, Lucretia, Cleopatra, and Penelope presented to prove or disprove the worth or worthlessness of all women; and appeals to authorities like Aristotle or Solomon, for example—she traces the influence of the controversy on other literary work, including the drama, of the period. She notes the moralizing tendency of prose tales about women, and she comments on the litigious assertions about womankind heard on the Renaissance stage. She cites a number of late sixteenth-century plays—among them John Phillip's *Comedy of Patient and Meek Grissil*, Thomas Garter's *Most Virtuous and Godly Susanna*, and the anonymous *Godly Queen Hester*—whose stories are based on the same exemplary tales that the controversialists used, but she admits that they could have been learned from sources other than the controversy itself. The most important influence of the controversy is on the the development, in the drama, of an hitherto ignored character type whom Woodbridge names "the stage misogynist" and whom she treats in her last two chapters.

"In his pure form," Woodbridge writes, the stage misogynist "is a kind of humours character, whose governing trait is a testy disregard for the female sex" (p. 275) and whose literary ancestors include "the Renaissance version of the Cynic Diogenes" (p. 276), the *persona* of the grumbling detractor of women in the formal controversy, the Vice figure of the secular morality plays on the Tudor stage, and "the soldier who returns to find his martial masculinity inappropriate in a civilian world where women's tastes and values prevailed" (pp. 278–279). He embodies, as she says, "almost allegorically, the Renaissance controversy about women" (p. 276). Often, as with Sextus in Thomas Heywood's *Rape of Lucrece* or Ilford in George Wilkins's *The Miseries of Enforced Marriage*, he actually participates in debate about women; other times his presence simply evokes the debate in the audience's mind by introducing one side of the issue. Many mysogynists' views are discredited by their illogical generalizations from one negative example. Largely as a result of that error, the plays in which the stage misogynists appear "are almost ritual vindications of Woman, wherein the misogynist performs an antimasque function, embodying the discordant and disruptive elements of reality which must be banished before a woman can achieve wholeness, happiness, human respect" (p. 290). The many examples of stage misogynists Woodbridge cites (Enobarbus, Iago, Benedick, Troilus, Bosola, and a host of others) verify her assertion that the character type is in fact an important presence on the Renaissance stage—and that the stage misogynist rarely if ever speaks for the playwright or his play. Instead, Woodbridge convincingly argues, the stage misogynist is part and parcel of a new, almost feminist attitude to be found on the Jacobean stage of the second decade of the seventeenth century. In her final chapter, then, Woodbridge treats *Swetnam the Woman-hater Arraigned by Women* (1618), whose subplot's major figure is a dramatized version of Joseph Swetnam, author of the mysognyistic *Araignment of Lewde, idle, froward, and unconstant women: Or the vanitie of them, choose you whether* of 1615. Her lively account of the play will lead many readers scurrying for a copy, as will her provocative assertion that it could possibly have been written by Webster.

One of the many strengths of the book derives from Woodbridge's subtle ability to distinguish between what some writers call text and subtext—and then to suggest possible relationships between them. One of her avowed goals is the demonstration of the "role of literary convention" in written works of the Renaissance in order to "retard the wholesale appropriation of literary materials as documents in the history of popular attitude; by showing how certain recurrent literary structures and character types seem to reflect the real world, I hope to remind the strictest aesthetician that there is some connection, however sublimated or oblique, between female literary figures and women of flesh and blood" (p. 7). One of the most interesting portions of her book, then, is the section in which she observes that the "unprecedented misogyny" (p. 249) in the English drama of the first decade of the seventeenth century was followed by a "new image of women" beginning about 1610—and claims that the new image responds to the demands of a new generation of female theatergoers: "In creating a gallery of assertive female characters, the drama, one cannot help suspecting, was holding the mirror up to nature" (p. 263). That statement is based, let me add, on more than a suspicion, for Woodbridge outlines interesting (if not conclusive) evidence that in the second decade of the seventeenth century London women *were* claiming and achieving new freedoms.

Buttressing Woodbridge's claim that most writers involved in the formal controversy were more concerned to show their literary skill than to discuss the true nature of womankind is the fact that two of them—Edward Gosynhyll and C. Pyrrye—wrote arguments on both sides of the issue, as did the playwright Nathan Field when in 1609–10 he presented *A Woman Is a Weathercock* and its "recantation," *Amends for Ladies* of 1610–11, and Thomas Middleton when his *Women Beware Women* and *More Dissemblers Besides Women* were bound together in the edition of 1657. This is not to say that Woodbridge wants us to believe that the works in the formal controversy are not to be taken seriously as documents in the social history of the period; her point is that both defenses (which insisted that women *are* chaste, silent, and obedient, rather than asserting that women should not be judged on artificial, foolish standards) and attacks on womankind served "to enforce a certain mode of behavior" (p. 134). Moreover, Woodbridge claims that "the formal controversy prevented serious questioning by creating the illusion of real debate. Whatever its literary merits, as feminism the debate was a sham" (p. 134).

While I am delighted to note Woodbridge's emphasis on the literary aspects of the formal controversy, I do think, however, that she goes too far in asserting that it flourished in an age when everyone—women included—believed that woman is "the weaker vessel." Only briefly does she allow a point that she indicated in an excellent article about marriage treatises that she published some years ago under the name L. T. Fitz: "'What Says the Married Woman?': Marriage Theory and Feminism in the English Renaissance," *Mosaic*, 13 (1979), 1–22. It seems to me that the Renaissance insistence that women should be "housebound, nurturing, chaste, modest, and silent" should indeed be read through a "'no smoke without fire' interpretation" (Woodbridge, p. 135). If Renaissance men (and a few women) are writing about women's behavior, we know that the issue was grating on their collective nerves. Games, even literary ones, play out topics that matter, as Woodbridge's own comic tone in this book often demonstrates.

Woodbridge quite rightly insists on analyzing the works by female participants in the formal controversy with the same literary techniques that she applies to their male counterparts. Believing that the men's statements were insincere and knowing that *sincerity* and *emotion* are code words used by literary critics to trivialize writing by women, Woodbridge almost has to assert that Jane Anger, Rachel Speght, Esther Sowername, and Constantia Munda entered the debate for purely literary reasons. Would it not be possible to say that the women used their rhetorical skills to argue causes that they cared about—and that the men whose rhetoric debases women are betraying heartfelt and sincere (if sometimes subliminal) disdain for womankind? True as it is that the women only seldom moved far beyond the conceptual constraints imposed by the male culture that surrounded them, as Woodbridge herself sees and as other scholars have demonstrated, many women who wrote during the Renaissance did share if not feminist, then protofeminist feelings. Since none of the writers under consideration here meant to be a twentieth-century feminist, it seems a trifle unfair to call their protest writing a "sham." Woodbridge's comments on female friendship might well have included an analysis of Aemelia Lanier's "To Cokeham" in her *Salve Deus Rex Judaeorum* (1611); Woodbridge's brilliant section on the idealization of womanhood in sonnet sequences could have been enlarged by an awareness of Lady Mary Wroth's *Pamphilia to Amphilanthus* (published in 1621); and her brief allusions to Elizabeth Cary's *Mariam* (published in 1613 but probably written in 1602-04) would have been more interesting if Woodbridge had commented on the fact that the play had a female author. My guess is that a detailed consideration of *Mariam* would have led Woodbridge to refine her belief that (except for the more brazen women of the 1610s) Renaissance women cowtowed to Renaissance men.

These complaints to the contrary, however, I must return to my original assertion that Woodbridge's book is very good indeed. The range of materials that she cites is quite astonishing (her bibliography of primary sources is ten pages long), and each chapter offers new and important comments on Renaissance literature. The section on women in sonnet sequences by Renaissance men is (even without mention of Lady Mary Wroth) particularly insightful, and the comments on female characters as gossipy irritants to male characters is a nice counter to those readers who have continued to think that the Renaissance was a happy interlude in the history of women. And as Woodbridge stresses in her Peroratio, the vitality and excellence of some female characters on the Renaissance stage are due not to a Renaissance belief that women are men's equal but to individual playwrights whose "hearts were very impressed with (and often quite fond of) exuberant English Woman exactly as they found her. Though they write of Grissills for their peace, in the Rosalinds their pleasure lies" (p. 327).

The Knight of the Burning Pestle, by Francis Beaumont, edited by Sheldon P. Zitner. The Revels Plays. Manchester: Manchester University Press, Pp. x + 190. £50.00.

Reviewer: MICHAEL HATTAWAY

This is the first major scholarly edition since 1908 of one of the most popular plays of the English Renaissance, and it will add weight to the series to which it belongs. The very popularity of such a text, however, creates problems for its editor, who is bound to feel that he can do little more than synthesize the efforts of previous scholars who have written about the play or published it in series that are less ambitious than the Revels. *The Knight of the Burning Pestle* offers no major textual problems. The First Quarto is the only authoritative text, and according to Zitner, it derives from author's fair copy "unrefined by use in the theatre" (p. 1). He endorses the results of Cyrus Hoy's authorship tests (which attribute the play wholly to Beaumont) without, however, giving any account of their substance. He does reproduce, though, the evidence that Hoy used to work out the stints of the two compositors who worked on the text. Like other recent editors, he is confident that the publisher's epistle offers sufficient evidence for him to conclude that the play "was written and first performed at the Second Blackfriars Theatre by its children's company in 1607" (p. 10). (Although it offers no further information in this area, it is surprising that the title-page of the First Quarto is not reproduced or transcribed as is usual in this series.)

Sheldon Zitner's account of the children's company that performed the play stresses associations of the group with ritual seasonal festivity, and he gives some account of the carnivalesque elements that might be expected in a performance. However, the bulk of the critical introduction is devoted to the literary aspects of dramatic traditions that the editor feels inform the play. *Eastward Ho* and *The Isle of Gulls* are, Professor Zitner considers, the play's important antecedents, and he places *The Knight* into the wider contexts of prodigal play, romantic comedy, and play of citizen adventure.

The editor spends much space on character studies, without perhaps linking these to his account of performance styles that would create in the audience what S. L. Bethell termed "multiple consciousness" (*Shakespeare and Popular Dramatic Tradition* [London: King and Staples, 1944]). The particular demands upon the players, called upon both to attend to the inset play, "The London Merchant," and to mediate between this and the audience, make it difficult to consider "characters" as having the kind of consistency or personality that we find even in other texts from what is scarcely an age of dramatic realism. In other words it might have been useful to reverse the order of the Introduction and describe the play's performance mode before turning to its content. Zitner rejects the reductive and deterministic accounts of earlier writers on the play who attempted to explain its nature (and early failure) by linking it to the supposed tastes of an audience defined by class. It is, he argues, "better described as a delighted sharing of popular taste than as a moral or intellectual rejection of it, or as a class-conscious satire of the popular audience" (p. 31) and he supports his reading by stressing its capacity to arouse delight, which he describes by using Freud's distinction between innocent and tendentious wit. On other occasions, however, he feels compelled to rescue the play from divertissement and establish it as a criticism of life. So, on the Citizen and his Wife: "What emerges from this is not mere silliness, but glimpses of the creativity and unexploitative concern of people whose familial roles were apparently more absorbing than similar roles today, and the humanity of a workplace where economic roles had not yet dwindled to those of a master and hand" (p. 33).

Appendices reproduce a Commonwealth droll based on the Barbaroso episode as well as a Prologue spoken, probably by Nell Gwyn, at a Restoration revival. This adaptation stands as a testimony to the delicacy of Beaumont's talent as the play seems murdered by Augustan categories of lampoon, burlesque, and farce that appear therein. Further appendices describe the traditions and textual problems of the play's "interludes" and reproduce the music that survives for the snatches of song in the play. (Somewhat perversely the excerpts reprinted offer words other than those Merrythought actually sings.)

The commentary, perhaps inevitably, draws heavily upon those of previous editors (my own included), although there is a good proportion of innovative and sagacious notes. The stage history notes performances in 1635, 1662, 1665–67, 1682, 1898 and then samples amateur and student productions this century. We also learn that in 1919 Noel Coward played Rafe in Birmingham with what he himself described as "a stubborn Mayfair distinction which threw the whole thing out of key" (p. 45). What a contrast with a production in French at Bourges in 1971 that "emphasised (or perhaps created) the anger attending the capitulation by 'The London Merchant' troupe to the will of George and Nell, the submission of Art to the Bourgeoisie" (p. 46).

CORRESPONDENCE

Correspondence

from JONATHAN DOLLIMORE

Dear Editor,

It has been brought to my attention that Charles R. Forker is seriously misleading in his review of *Political Shakespeare* (*Medieval and Renaissance Drama in England*, III [1986], 310–315). He writes, "Dollimore . . . writes on *Measure for Measure*, drawing chicly upon Bakhtin, to argue that the background of sexual licentiousness in the play . . . amounts to the 'anarchic, ludic, carnivalesque' subversion 'of a repressive official ideology of order' in Vienna" (p. 313).

In fact, I cite this interpretation of the play and this use of Bakhtin only and precisely in order to repudiate them (p. 73). Further, the interpretation I then propose owes nothing to Bakhtin, and is probably incompatible with his work (for which, incidentally, I have considerable admiration).

I've no interest in arguing issues of principle with Mr. Forker but would request that you correct this misrepresentation, in the interest of reviewing and scholarly standards if nothing else.

Sincerely,

Dr. Jonathan Dollimore

Correspondence

from J. R. MULRYNE

Dear Editor,

There are reasons to be grateful for Thomas L. Berger's review of Brian Parker's edition of *Volpone* (*Medieval & Renaissance Drama in England*, III [1986], 338–343). Berger's is in no sense a routine notice based on slight study; it is the outcome of immensely thorough labor, and everyone with an interest in Jacobean theater owes him gratitude for the seriousness with which he has undertaken the reviewer's normally thankless task. The next reissue of *Volpone* will be improved as a result of his industry. As a general editor of the series, I am also grateful for the high expectation that Berger rightly entertains of Revels editions and for the praise that he lavishes on this one. His commendation of Parker's outstanding Introduction and of his "rich and full" commentary, the product of Parker's "vast reading," entirely agrees with my own estimate of the edition's high quality and with the opinion of those who have reviewed it elsewhere.

Berger devotes the first page of his five-page review to praise. The other four he gives to itemized objections to points of textual detail. It is true that item-by-item discussion may be necessary in reviewing editions of texts, but a reviewer has a duty to discriminate between significant error and instances that are minor or trivial. Berger has failed in this duty and has moreover supposed error or omission where none has taken place. The accumulation of instances that Berger cites gives the misleading impression of editorial neglect on Parker's behalf. Privately, Parker has replied to Berger's list of instances one by one. Here it will be more appropriate to summarize Berger's objections and to bring out the underlying assumptions that serve to place many of them beside the point and render others directly mistaken.

Berger has caught in the text of *Volpone* ten errors that have substantive or semi-substantive implications. All represent slips of proof-reading. The most serious are "dispersed" for "dispensed", "best" for "beast", "piercing" for "piecing", "Nor" for "Ne", "an" for "my" and the omission of "and", "now", and "the". Ten errors of this kind, even in a text as lengthy and complex as *Volpone*, may be thought too many. Apology and an undertaking to correct would be in order. But six times Berger calls these slips "emendations" and complains that they are unannotated, even when it is perfectly plain (from the appearance of the correct reading when the text is cited in the commentary, for example) that a deliberate change of reading is not intended.

This represents unfair practice and is characteristic of the stance of conscious denigration that Berger adopts.

Berger raises a series of objections to hyphenation in Parker's text. As Berger knows, the silent modernization of spelling is Revels practice. Objection therefore to Parker's silent omission of a hyphen in Jonson represents objection to series policy, not to Parker's editing. Contrariwise, when Parker *introduces* a hyphen not in Jonson, Berger complains on the grounds that "my copy of Webster's does not hyphenate the word" (bed-rid). I should be surprised if his copy of Webster's hyphenates "scarlet cloth" or "too tender" or "my Lord," locutions where Berger objects to Parker's failure to hyphenate, in two cases calling the practice "emendation" and complaining about the absence of collation. In essence, Berger is asking for the sort of collation that Revels editions do not provide and complaining when Parker has not provided it. One might make similar points about Berger's criticism of Parker's treatment of italics.

Berger makes heavy weather out of Parker's decision to place the play's Head Title where the Quarto (Q) places it (after the Dramatis Personae, Argument, and Prologue), rather than where the Folio (F) places it (before Argument and Prologue). Revels editors regard the placing of the Head Title as a matter of typography or format and therefore as one that does not require commentary or collation notes. The antagonistic bias of Berger's reviewing becomes evident in his use of this matter of the Head Title as his instance for Parker's alleged violation of the (correct and reasonable) principle that "requires the editor to justify, if only cursorily, his rejection of F in favor of Q readings in cases where F makes sense" (p. 340). Parker has consistently done so. Aside from the Head Title, Berger finds only one slip, when Parker inadvertently gives Q's "FINE MADA. WOULD-BEE" preference over F's "FINE MADAME WOULD-BEE" in the list of Dramatis Personae. This *is* a slip, but one which has no significance whatsoever, so far as the text's "readings," ordinarily understood, are concerned. Berger's only other complaint lies in Parker's arrangement of the Dramatis Personae in a manner that follows two earlier Revels editions rather than F. Again this is a matter of format. Parker indicates the F arrangement in his collation notes but does not justify (as a Revels editor is not required to do) his departure from it. Berger in other words accuses Parker of editorial neglect of an important principle but offers in support of his case only irrelevant matters of typography and format.

Berger has identified a number of "errors" in Parker's textual notes. One or two of these are themselves errors on Berger's part. For example, he has misunderstood the Revels convention "61.1", meaning "the first line of the stage direction following line sixty-one." He also asks Parker for more than is required when he complains that the variant F speech-headings "ATO.1" and "ATO.3" are not collated; Revels practice, as the General Editors' Preface makes plain, is that "speech headings are silently made consistent." When Berger complains that Parker has deleted a speech-heading from one note, he overlooks the fact that the collation is here concerned solely with line-division and that the speech prefix, being extra-metrical, is properly excluded. There are a few other instances where Berger's complaints are misconceived, either in asking for details that a Revels editor does not give or failing to understand the conventions adopted in Revels collation notes. Yet Berger *has* spotted errors, almost all minor, and we are grateful to have them pointed out. His reporting verges on the mischievous, however, when he complains that collation notes should not be part of the commentary notes on page 159; what has actually happened is that a machining error at the printer's has placed a rule above, instead of below, these collation notes. His concluding question to Parker, affecting as it does to misunderstand a perfectly plain sentence relating to Jonson's biography, can only at best be regarded as pedantry.

Perhaps the most unsatisfactory aspect of Berger's review comes at the outset of the pages of adverse criticism after the applause. Berger describes Parker's work on copies of Q and F in such a way as to give the impression that Parker has been neglectful, even that he has misled the reader over the extent of the editorial study that he has undertaken. In fact, Parker spells out (footnote 7 to page 53 of the Introduction) the twenty-one copies of Q that he collated in detail, as well as naming the further six copies that he did not collate. Parker is also quite specific about his work on copies of the Folio, of which (as Berger notes) seventeen were collated in detail, and a further twenty-three were checked against these fully collated copies. The labor of collating seventeen Folio copies of a long, densely written play such as *Volpone*, especially when that comes on top of a detailed collation of twenty-one Quarto copies, can probably only be appreciated by those who have undertaken similar efforts on an equally difficult play. Such people are few in number. It would have been more generous and fair-minded of Berger to note the massive labors that Parker has accomplished (even while regretting, if he wished, that they are incomplete) rather than to complain with characteristic overemphasis: "Another ten copies [of F] remain uncollated, uncompared, unexamined, unchecked." Mere hostility turns to active misrepresentation when Berger infers, wrongly, from his own observation of F, that Parker may have missed a further state of the outer forme of sheet M. He attempts to give the implied inattention on Parker's part some credibility by noticing two turned letters in the (modern printer's) setting of the Introduction to the Revels edition. The fact of the matter is that Parker's scrupulous textual scholarship has revealed, as no previous editor's has done, the inadequacy of Herford and Simpson's bibliographical analysis, and this has led him to a different evaluation of Q and F. Berger fails to note this important contribution to scholarship.

To turn briefly, now, to matters of more general interest. Berger's attack on the Revels *Volpone* may represent no more than a failure of the reviewer's duty to be objective. But it may also proceed from an inexplicit hostility to the kind of edition that the Revels plays represent. Few would deny the massive contribution that the series has made to the study of Elizabethan and Jacobean theater, first under Clifford Leech, and then under David Hoeniger. The present general editors (Ernst Honigmann, Eugene Waith, David Bevington, and I) hope to continue and extend this contribution.

More thorough than other modernized editions, the Revels series addresses itself to students of the theater of the period, whether these are to be found in universities, contributing to the amateur or professional stage, or outside these categories. Such a readership entails editorial decisions about how a text is presented, how it is introduced, and what kinds of explanatory apparatus are offered. The first decision is modernization itself. It was a melancholy conclusion of some of the members of the Glendon Conference that the answer to Stanley Wells's question "Who wants to read old-spelling editions except old-spelling editors?" was "almost no one" (See *Play-Texts in Old Spelling* [New York: AMS Press, 1984], p. 5). If that conclusion is too extreme, the old-spelling editors gathered at Glendon certainly disposed of the notion that an old-spelling text, however scrupulously edited, can reach the platonic ideal of "being" the author's original. Even setting aside Randall McLeod's brilliantly clever discussion of the interaction of old typesetting and old spelling (pp. 81–96), the practical problems of reaching back to an author's ur-text are insuperable. The well-worn argument that only an old-spelling, old-punctuation presentation "fits" an old text not only begs questions but in the light of modern analyses of the act of reading is lacking in theoretical rigor.

Every edition of a period play (a modern play, too) represents a recreation, both in its textual presentation and in its commentary (for the commentary implicitly guides the reader's reading). A possible conclusion of this line of thought is a kind of solipsism, reasoning that we can each only be our own editors; and in a particular sense this is true. But if we are to publish editions, that is, if we are to share our editing, we have to accept that we are engaged in an act of reading out of which our readers' readings will come. The notion of an autonomous "text" is a miasma. Another conclusion to the same line of reasoning is that as editors we should—or may—wholly remake, indeed rewrite, the plays we edit, in the image of our own knowledge and sensibility. We can no doubt reject this option also, on the grounds of practicality and of the probable artistic results, even if not of logic. Of course, in whatever we do, we need to be in scholarly terms exact; and this is where Berger's review, in noting errors, is helpful. But the modernizing editor has the advantage of being conscious that he *is* recreating his play, addressing his endeavors as aptly as he can to a conceivable body of readers. He is not pursuing an unattainable—and I think philosophically inert—conception.

Perhaps the notion of giving access to the play is theoretically imprecise, for the play as an independent, unperceived entity does not exist. But the notion is sufficiently practical to guide Revels editors in deciding what kinds of information to give or withhold. Thus Revels editors do not always comment on typography or format, these being no more than the incidental features of a now irrelevant "text." Nor do they identify turned letters or variously presented speech prefixes. They collate as many copies of their originals as is consistent with practicality. Because early copies are sometimes very numerous, the editor has to exercise his judgment in favor of completing his edition, rather than pursuing every last copy and leaving his editorial task unfinished. He has also to bear in mind, and live within, financial constraints: microfilm will not do for certain collation tasks, and travel to every library owning an original may be prohibitively expensive. He will always tell his reader what he has done. The Revels editor does not offer an historical collation. In the light of the general philosophy of the series, it would be absurd to try to exhume the skeletons of previous editions; if these bones live they live only in the context of the entire earlier edition. Revels editors aspire to the "chaste, beautiful and slim" commentary of Philip Edwards's Glendon remark (p. 4), but they also bear in mind the still unravished purity of some of their readers' ignorance of the Elizabethan period.

It would be my own view that in so far as the book trade and universities can support us, editors of Elizabethan plays may quite properly accept a pluralist editorial economy, bringing out both old-spelling and modern-spelling editions. Both species should be aware of the limitations of what they are doing. It does none of us any good to offer prejudiced reviewing of the kind of edition that we dislike. If my own preference, in times of shortage of resources, goes to the modernized text, it is because, to offer a final Glendon quotation, "Our work *applies* . . . when it's in modern spelling, when we can really share our own love for the plays with each other, with actors and students" (Anne Lancashire's remark, p. 6). It is a not ignoble ideal, and a theoretically defensible one.

J. R. Mulryne

Index

(Included are the names of persons and the titles of Medieval and Renaissance plays.)

A Larum for London, 86 n.15
Abbott, E. A., 254
Aberle, David F., 45 n.8
Aggeler, Geoffrey, 92, 104 n.7
Agrippina, 15, 49 n.28
Alberti, Leon Battista Degli, 290
Alice Pierce, 88 n.32
Alleyn, Edward, 56, 57, 58, 60, 61, 62 n.3; 65, 75, 76, 83, 88 n.41; 173–186
Alleyn, John, 180, 185 n.49
Allington, Sir Giles, 49 n.29
Alphonsus, Emperor of Germany, 67
Althusser, Louis, 236
Anderson, Donald K., 209 n.12
Anne of Denmark, Queen, 143, 188
Anger, Jane, 321
Appleton, William, 143, 170 n.4
Aquinas, St. Thomas, 35
Archer, Edward, 64, 68, 70
Arden, Alice, 220
Arden of Feversham, 74
Aristophanes, 15
Aristotle, 263, 296, 319
Armstrong, W. A., 139 n.10
Armytage, George J., 184 n.10
Arthur, Prince of Wales, 27, 29
Ascham, Roger, 13
Asconius, 15, 46 n.9
Ashton, Robert, 138 n.3; 139 n.7
Asply, William, 82
Astington, John, 141 n.31
Aubrey, John, 25
Auerbach, Erich, 190, 194 n.10, 280
Augustine, St., 290

Bacon, Francis, 245, 247
Baker, Howard, 224
Bakere, Jane A., 8, 10 n.15; 11 nn.27, 28
Bakhtin, Mikhail, 2, 9, 10 n.11; 11 n.29; 229, 279, 280, 327
Baldwin, William, 222
Bale, John, 260
    John Baptist's Preaching in the Wilderness, 260–261
    King John, 261
Ball, R. H., 152, 171 n.19
Bandello, Matteo, 14, 44 n.3

Bang, W., 209 n.12
Barclay, Alexander, 264
Barish, Jonas A., 246, 266
Barkan, Leonard, 45 n.5
Barker, Francis, 233
Barksted, William, 264
Barnes, Barnabe, 14
    The Devil's Charter, 28–29, 86 n.15
Barnes, Roger, 75
Barnet, Sylvan, 209 n.9
Bartholomew of Exeter, 317
Barton, Anne, 213–217, 255
Basile, Giovanni Battista, 14, 44 n.3
Bawcutt, N. W., 50 n.40; 170 nn.1, 2, 7
Baylie, Simon, *The Wizard*, 62 n.3
Beaumont, Francis, 14, 123, 133, 134, 135, 171 n.17; 297
    The Knight of the Burning Pestle, 233, 269, 271, 322–324
    and John Fletcher, *Cupid's Revenge*, 45 n.5, 123, 125, 128, 129, 130, 131, 134, 135, 137, 138, 141 n.31
    A King and No King, 17, 18, 33, 41, 42, 43, 66, 139–140 n.14
    The Maid's Tragedy, 66, 123, 127, 128, 129, 130, 131, 132, 134, 135, 196
    Philaster, 66, 139–140 n.14; 141 n.31
    and John Fletcher and Philip Massinger, *Thierry and Theodoret*, 123, 137, 138
Beckerman, Bernard, 194 n.11
Beeston, Christopher, 54, 88 n.41
Bell, Henry, 75
Bell, James Harle, 46 n.8
Belsey, Catherine, 217–223, 243, 304
Belt, T., 54
Benediktbeuren Christmas Play, 257
Benion, William, 179
Bennett, Paul E., 85 n.7
Bentley, G. E., 67, 87 nn. 27, 28; 140 n.21; 181, 183, 184 n.4; 185 nn. 53–56; 186 nn.73, 74; 193 n.6
Beneviste, Emile, 217
Benwell, Gwen, 9 nn.5, 6, 7; 10 n.12
Bercovitch, Sacvan, 288

335

Berger, Thomas L., 329–333
Bergeron, David, 48 n.17; 276
Bernard of Clairvaux, St., 257
Berry, Herbert, 88 n.30
Bertram, Paul, 169 n.1
Bethell, S. L., 189, 193 n.7; 323
Bevington, David M., 44 n.1; 257, 258, 295, 300, 332
Biondo, Flavio, 290
Birde, William, 73
Black Joan, 88 n.32
Blayney, Peter, 79, 89 n.43
Blount, Charles, Lord Mountjoy, 25
Boas, F. S., 170 n.4; 208 n.2
Boccaccio, 278–282
Bodley, Sir Thomas, 175, 176
Bohannan, Paul, 45 n.8
Boklund, Gunnar, 44 n.3
Boleyn, Anne, Queen, 28
Boleyn, George, Viscount Rochford, 28
Boleyn, Mary, 28
Borgia, Cesare, 29
Borgia, Lucrezia, 29
Borgia, Rodrigo, Pope Alexander VI, 29
Born, Hanspeter, 88 n.36
Boswell, James, the Younger, 62 n.3; 89 n.49
Bowers, F. T., 87 n.16; 92, 93, 104 nn.5, 6; 140 n.24; 170 n.5
Boyvin, Rene, 277
Bradbrook, M. C., 150, 170 n.15; 171 n.17
Braden, Gordon, 92, 93, 104 nn.11, 12; 105 n.22; 223–227
Bradley, A. C., 268
Bradley, Henry, 58
Branholt, 88 n.32
Brecht, Bertolt, 296, 305
Briggs, John Channing, 109, 110, 120 nn.3, 5
Bright, Timothy, 209 n.8
Bristol, Michael D., 228–231
Brome, Richard, 14, 196
    The Antipodes, 202–206, 207, 208, 209 nn.7, 13
    The Jovial Crew, 208 n.3; 209 nn.6, 13
    The Lovesick Court, 33, 35, 36, 37, 38, 39, 40, 43, 47 n.12; 50 nn.42, 43
Bronescombe, Bishop, 1
Brooke, Nicholas, 120 n.7
Broude, Ronald, 105 n.20
Brown, Arthur, 208 nn.2, 3; 209 nn.4, 6, 11

Brown, John Russell, 170 n.12
Browne, John, Sr., 64
Browne, Robert, 80
Browne, Thomas, 226, 244, 247
Bruce, John, 239
Bruni, Leonardo, 290
Brunneleschi, Filippo, 290
Bryan, George, 54, 76
Bryson, W. H., 184 n.5
Buc, Sir George, 136
Bueler, Lois E., 45 n.5; 47 n.12; 47–48 n.15; 50 n.43
Burbage, Cuthbert, 68
Burbage, James, 55, 57, 58, 60, 173, 174, 181, 183
Burbage, Richard, 54, 56, 58, 60, 68, 88 n.37; 173, 174, 183
Burbon, 88 n.32
Burby, Cuthbert, 65, 68, 71, 72, 73, 74, 78, 83, 84, 87 n.18
Burkhardt, Jacob, 224
Burn, Richard, 48 n.24
Burre, Walter, 78, 83
Burton, Robert, 25, 48 n.22; 199, 200, 202, 209 n.8
Bushell, Thomas, 73
Butler, Martin, 140 n.22

Caesar, Julius, 16, 123
Caesar, Sir Julius, 176
Caillois, Roger, 229
Cairncross, A. S., 88 n.39
Caligula, 15, 46 n.9
Callot, Jacques, 277
Calvin, Jean, 244
Cambyses, 15, 47 n.9
Campbell, Lily B., 246
Campbell, William, 49 n.26
Candeler, Susan, 178, 180
Candido, Joseph, 45 n.4
Cannon, Charles Dale, 86–87 n.15
Capell, Edward, 68, 87 n.19
Carlell, Lodowick, 14, 18
Carr or Ker, Robert, Earl of Somerset, 143
Carter, John Stewart, 49 n.32
Cartwright, Thomas, 262
Cartwright, William, 62 n.3
Cary, Earnest, 47 n.9
Cary, Elizabeth, *The Tragedy of Mariam*, 221, 321
Cassius, Dio, 15–16, 47 n.9
Castiglione, Baldassare, 263
The Castle of Perseverance, 218, 222, 257, 296

Catherine of Aragon, Queen, 27, 28, 29, 30
Catiline, 15, 46 n.9
Catullus, 15
Cavendish, Margaret, 14
Cawarden, Sir Thomas, 174, 181
Cecil, Lady Dorothy, Countess of Exeter, 29
Cecil, William, First Lord Burghley, 93
Cenci, Count, 29
Cerasano, S. P., 61
Chamberlain, John, 29, 138 n.3
Chambers, E. K., 55, 57, 58, 59, 61, 62 nn.2, 4; 63, 68, 69, 86 n.12; 88 n.35; 89 nn.42, 45; 140 nn.21, 23; 183, 186 nn.73, 75; 192 nn.3, 4; 193 n.6; 248
Chapman, George, 14, 47 n.9; 107–121, 264, 297
    The Blind Beggar of Alexandria, 65, 73
    Bussy d'Ambois, 107–121, 225
    The Conspiracy and Tragedy of Charles, Duke of Byron, 45 n.5
    A Humorous Day's Mirth, 65, 73, 83
    The Widow's Tears, 233
    and Ben Jonson and John Marston, *Eastward Ho*, 134, 269, 271, 299–300, 323
Chapman, George ?, John Fletcher, Philip Massinger, and ? Ben Jonson, *Rollo, Duke of Normandy*, 123, 129, 134, 135
Charles I, 48 n.17; 49 n.29; 133
Chaucer, Geoffrey, 145, 148, 170 n.13
Chester Cycle, 7, 8, 257, 310–313
Chettle, Henry, 14
    Hoffman, 70, 87 n.28
    The Life of Cardinal Wolsey, 83
    and ? Robert Greene, *John of Bordeaux*, 56–57, 89 n.48
    and Anthony Munday, *The Death of Robert, Earl of Huntingdon*, 65
    The Downfall of Robert, Earl of Huntingdon, 65
    and Thomas Dekker and William Haughton, *Patient Grissil*, 65, 73
Chetwinde, Philip, 65, 68, 85 n.4
Chibnall, Jennifer, 278
Child, Harold, 166, 171 nn.26, 27
Chilton, P. A., 50 n.39
Chrimes, S. B., 49 n.26
Chute, Marchette, 192 n.4
Cicero, 15, 46 n.9; 263

Cicero, Quintus, 15, 46 n.9
Cinthio, Giambattista Giraldi, 14, 44 n.3
    Orbecche, 44 n.3
Clark, A. C., 46 n.9
Clarke, W. K. Lowther, 48 n.24
Claudius, 15, 46 n.9; 49 n.28
Cleopatra, 15, 16
Clodia, 15, 46 n.9
Clodius, Publius, 15, 46 n.9
Clopper, L. M., 310, 311
Cloth Breeches and Velvet Hose, 80
Clyomon and Clamydes, 72
Cohen, Walter, 231–237
Coke, Sir Edward, 181
Coleridge, S. T., 133, 140 n.19
Colie, Rosalie, 225, 279
Collier, John Payne, 68, 184 n.1
Condell, Henry, 54, 64, 66, 69, 76, 77
1 Contention of York and Lancaster, 76
Cook, Ann Jennalie, 93, 105 n.14; 133, 140 n.22
Cook, Elizabeth, 277
Cooke, Alexander, 54
Cooper, Helen, 278
Cooper, Thomas, 262
Cornish Ordinalia, 1–11
Coryate, Thomas, 189, 193 n.6
Cotton, William, 64, 67
Coward, Noel, 323
Cowell, John, 125, 126, 129
Cowly, R., 54
The Cradle (or Castle) of Security, 238
Cranmer, Thomas, Archbishop of Canterbury, 28
Creaser, John, 276
Creede, Thomas, 74, 82, 83, 89 n.46
Creech, Thomas, 264
Croce, Benedetto, 44 n.3
Croston, W., and Man, ?, *Aeneas and Queen Dido*, 88 n.40
Cunison, Ian, 105 n.24
Cunliffe, John W., 47 n.9; 105 n.23; 224
Cunningham, J. S., 266
Curtius, Ernst, 209 n.15; 258, 279, 280
Cutts, John P., 148, 170 nn.8, 11

Daborne, Emma, 175, 176
Daborne, Margaret, 175
Daborne, Margaret II, 175, 176
Daborne, Robert, Jr., 175, 176, 177, 178, 179, 180, 183, 185 nn.27, 41
Daborne, Robert, Sr., 175, 176, 177, 178, 179, 180, 183, 184 n.22
Daborne, Thomas, 175, 176, 177, 179
Daniel, Samuel, *Tethys Festival*, 277

Dante, 29, 281
Danter, John, 82, 83
Dasent, J. R., 86 n.9
Davenport, Arnold, 47 n.9
Davis, Natalie Zemon, 48 n.16
Day, John, *The Isle of Gulls*, 134, 323
de Forest, George, 225
de Girolami, Remigio, 290
de Witt, Johannes, 304
Dekker, Thomas, 14, 231, 255
   II Honest Whore, 269
   Old Fortunatus, 65, 73
   The Shoemakers' Holiday, 65
   and ? John Marston, *Satiromastix*, 86 n.15
   and Thomas Middleton, *I Honest Whore*, 269
   The Roaring Girl, 269, 270
   and John Webster, *Northward Ho*, 269
   Westward Ho, 269, 271
   and Henry Chettle and William Haughton, *Patient Grissil*, 65, 73
Devereux Rich, Penelope, 25
Devereux, Robert, Second Earl of Essex, 25, 107, 108, 109, 110, 112, 116, 119
Dick, Oliver Lawson, 48 n.23
Diehl, Huston, 256
Digby, Kenelm, 247
Dido and Aeneas, 88 n.32
Dodd, Craig, 304
Dodson, Daniel, 22, 48 n.20
Dollimore, Jonathan, 115, 121 n.8; 219, 229, 240, 287, 304, 306, 309
Dominik, Mark, 87 n.29
Domitian, 15, 46 n.9
Donaldson, Ian, 139 n.8
Donne, John, 180, 244, 247
Douglas, Audrey, 237–240
Downton, Thomas, 76
Drakakis, John, 219, 240
Draudt, Manfred, 298
Dryden, John, 216, 277
Dudley, Robert, Earl of Leicester, 93
Duke, John, 54
Durkheim, Emile, 229

Eagleton, Terry, 240, 304, 305, 306, 309
Eccles, Mark, 185 n.27
Edward I, 237
Edward III, 63, 68, 69, 70, 71, 72, 74, 87 n.18; 88 n.33
Edward VI, 28, 174, 181

Edwards, Philip, 101, 106 n.30; 147, 170 n.9; 209 n.10; 297, 300, 301, 333
Eliot, T. S., 47 n.9; 224, 266
Elizabeth of York, Queen, 28, 48 n.26
Elizabeth I, 28, 72, 93, 123, 125, 139 n.5; 174
Elizabeth, Electress Palatine and Queen of Bohemia, 48 n.17; 136, 139 n.7; 143
Elyot, Sir Thomas, 318
Emmerson, Richard, 257
Enck, John J., 246
Engels, Friedrich, 235
Erasmus, 263
Erickson, Carolly, 240
Erickson, Peter B., 272
Euripides, 15
Evans, Henry, 183
Evans, Malcolm, 240–243
Ewing, S. Blaine, 209 n.12

The Fair Maid of Bristow, 86 n.14
"the famous historye of Iohn of Gaunte sonne to Kynge Edward the Third wth his Conquest of Spaine and marriage of his Twoo daughters to the King[es] of Castile and Portugale," 81
The Famous Victories of Henry V, 67, 72, 76, 82
Fiedler, Leslie A., 208 n.2; 209 nn.6, 15
Field, Nathan, *Amends for Ladies*, 320
   A Woman is a Weathercock, 320
Filarete (*alias* Antonio Averlino), 290
Filmer, Robert, 222
Finkelpearl, Philip J., 100, 104 n.3; 133, 140 n. 19; 141 n.30
Fish, Stanley, 259
Fisher, ?, 178
"Five Plays in One," 58, 59
Fleay, F. G., 53, 58, 59, 60, 61, 62 n.6; 63, 68, 75, 77, 87 nn.15, 22
Fletcher, John, 14, 123–141, 297
   Bonduca, 143–171
   The Chances, 70
   Demetrius and Enanthe or The Humorous Lieutenant, 123, 128, 131, 132
   The Faithful Shepherdess, 128, 129
   The Loyal Subject, 123, 129, 131
   Monsieur Thomas, 40, 45 n.5
   The Tragedy of Valentinian, 123, 129, 130, 134, 136

Index

A Wife for a Month, 123, 127, 128, 132
The Woman's Prize, or The Tamer Tam'd, 89 n.48
Women Pleased, 18
and Francis Beaumont, *Cupid's Revenge*, 45 n.5; 123, 125, 128, 129, 130, 131, 134, 135, 137, 138, 141 n.31
A King and No King, 17, 18, 33, 41, 42, 43, 66, 139–140 n.14
The Maid's Tragedy, 66, 123, 127, 128, 129, 130, 131, 132, 134, 135, 196
Philaster, 66, 139–140 n.14; 141 n.31
and Philip Massinger, *The Custom of the Country*, 123, 127
The Double Marriage, 123, 129, 130, 134, 136
The Prophetess, 123, 137–138
Sir John van Olden Barnavelt, 136
and William Shakespeare, *Two Noble Kinsmen*, 36, 66, 69, 143–171
and Francis Beaumont and Philip Massinger, *Thierry and Theodoret*, 123, 137, 138
and Philip Massinger and ? George Chapman and ? Ben Jonson, *Rollo, Duke of Normandy*, 123, 129, 134, 135
Florio, John, 35, 50 n.41
Flugel, J. C., 28, 49 n.31
Foakes, R. A., 85 n.6
Ford, John, 14, 196
The Broken Heart, 24–25, 40
The Fancies Chaste and Noble, 45 n.5
The Lover's Melancholy, 199–202, 207, 208, 209 nn.7, 13
'Tis Pity She's a Whore, 17–18, 23–24, 25, 33, 34, 35, 41, 42, 43, 49 n.29
Forker, Charles, 327
Forman, Simon, 69
Foucault, Michel, 207, 210 nn. 17, 18; 286
"Four Plays in One," 59, 60
Francesca da Rimini, 29
Francis I, of France, 33
Frederick V, Elector Palatine and King of Bohemia, 136, 139 n.7; 143
The French Doctor, 72
Freud, Sigmund, 14, 45 n.7; 46 n.8; 232, 235, 285, 323

Friar Bacon and Friar Bungay, 56, 76, 81, 89 n.48
Froude, J. A., 105 n.18
Frye, Northrop, 289
Frye, Roland Mushat, 30, 49 n.29
Fulgentius, 16, 47 n.9
Furness, Horace Howard, 49 n.27

Gaines, Barry, 299
Gair, Reavley, 301
Galen, 245
Gardner, R., 46 n.9
Garter, Thomas, *The Most Virtuous and Godly Susanna*, 319
Gascoigne, George, 14, 263
and Francis Kinwelmershe, *Jocasta*, 15, 45 n.5; 47 n.9
Gauer, Denis, 14, 45 n.6
Gaunt, John of, Duke of Lancaster, 26
Geckle, George, 106 n.31
Gehman, Henry Snyder, 50 n.38
Gibbons, Brian, 272
Gibson, Colin, 209 n.10
Girard, René, 46 n.8; 101, 106 nn.29, 32
"Godfrey of Bulloigne with the Conquest of Ierusalem," 82, 89 n.48
2 Godfrey of Bulloigne, 89 n.48
Godley, A. D., 47 n.9
Godly Queen Hester, 319
Goffe, Thomas?, *The Careless Shepherdess*, 68
Goldberg, Jonathan, 139 n.7
Golding, Arthur, 16, 47 n.11
Goodale, Tho., 54
Goodman, David, 193 n.7
Goodyer, Henry, 175, 176, 177, 178, 179, 180, 185 n.49
Gosynhyll, Edward, 320
Gough, Robert, 54
Grandisson, John de, Bishop of Exeter, 316
Grant, Patrick, 243–247
Graves, Robert, 18, 47 nn.10, 14
Green, M. A. E., 105 n.19
Green, Paul D., 153, 154, 156, 157, 158, 159, 160, 161, 163, 164, 165, 166, 167, 170 n.4; 171 n.22
Greenberg, Ira, 209 n.13
Greenblatt, Stephen, 210 n.16; 219, 229, 272, 274, 283, 284, 285, 286, 287, 288, 289, 306
Greene, Robert, 14, 263
James IV, 82, 84
Orlando Furioso, 56

and Thomas Lodge, *A Looking-Glass for London and England*, 17, 74, 81, 82
Greene, Robert?, *George a Greene*, 65, 74, 76
1 Selimus, 76
and Henry Chettle, *John of Bordeaux*, 56–57, 89 n.48
Greenfield, Peter, 237–240
Greg, W. W., 53, 54, 55, 56, 57, 58, 59, 60, 61, 62 nn.2, 3; 63, 77, 78, 81, 85 nn.1, 2; 86 n.8; 87 n.28; 88 n.32; 185 nn. 41, 42–45; 310
Gregory, Patrick, 46 n.8; 106 n.29
Greville, Curtis, 66
Greville, Fulke, 296
Gruber, William E., 193 n.6
Gurr, Andrew, 193 n.8
Gwyn, Nell, 323
"gyve a man luck & throw him into the Sea," 89 n.42

Haaker, Ann, 209 n.14
Haddad, Miranda Johnson, 283
Hall, Stuart, 235
Hallett, Charles, 92, 104 nn.8, 9
Hallett, Elaine, 92, 104 nn.8, 9
Halliwell-Phillips, J. O., 315
Halsband, Robert, 302
Hamlet, 77
Hammond, Paul, 277
Hanmer, Sir Thomas, 26, 49 n.27
Harbage, Alfred, 45 n.5; 138 n.1; 170 n.3; 184 n.2; 272
Hardicanute, 88 n.32
Harding, Samuel, 14
Hargrave, Francis, 105 n.16
Harrington, John, 287
Harmer, L. C., 50 n.41
Harris, Bernard, 170 n.12
Harris, Charles, 48 n.24
Harris, Markham, 1, 5, 7, 9 nn.1, 7; 10 nn.13, 14, 17; 11 n.23
"Harrison," "Edward," 241
Harvey, Gabriel, 56, 58, 59
Hastings, Henry, Third Earl of Huntingdon, 94
Hathaway, Richard, 89 n.45
Hattaway, Michael, 247, 252–255, 266
Haughton, William, 14
and Henry Chettle and Thomas Dekker, *Patient Grissil*, 65, 73
Hawkes, Terence, 240
Heinemann, Margot, 140 nn.20, 23, 29
Heller, Thomas G., 287
Heminges, John, 64, 66, 69, 76, 77

Henderson, Mary Isobel, 46 n.9
Henslowe, Francis, 71
Henslowe, Philip, 57, 59, 60, 61, 65, 66, 67, 69, 70, 71, 72, 74, 75, 76, 77, 78, 79, 82, 83, 85 n.6; 86 nn.8, 15; 87 nn.25, 26; 88 nn.31, 32; 173, 174, 175, 178–179, 180, 181, 183, 185 nn.41, 47; 252
Henrietta Maria, Queen, 277
Henry V, 79
Henry V, 83, 89 n.48
"Henry VI," 61, 77
Henry VII, 28, 48 n.26; 49 n.26
Henry VIII, 27, 28, 29, 30, 174
Henry, Prince of Wales, 48 n.17; 108, 109, 124, 143
Herbert, Sir Henry, 136
Herbert, Mary, Countess of Pembroke, 187
Herbert, Philip, Fourth Earl of Pembroke, 25, 192 n.4
Herford, C. H., 193 n.5; 253, 276, 298, 331
Herzman, Ronald B., 257
Herodotus, 15, 47 n.9
Hester and Ahasuerus, 77
Heywood, Jasper, 14
Heywood, Thomas, 192 n.3; 193 n.7; 195, 238, 249
Edward IV, 70
The Four Prentices, 89 n.48
The Rape of Lucrece, 319
A Woman Killed with Kindness, 221
and William Rowley, *Fortune by Land and Sea*, 20
Hibbard, G. R., 170 n.6; 277
Hieronimo, 70, 79, 87 n.28
Hillebrand, H. N., 180–181, 182, 185 n.52; 186 nn.65, 71–73
Hirschig, G. A., 47 n.9
Hobbes, Thomas, 287
Hoeniger, David, 332
Holinshed, Raphael, 220
Holland, John, 54, 56
Holyday, Barten, 264
Homer, 107, 109, 118, 319
Honigmann, E. A. J., 275, 332
Hooker, Richard, 308
Hooper, John, Bishop of Gloucester, 239
Horace, 264, 265, 290
Horne, P. R., 44 n.3; 47 n.9
Horton, Jane, 185 n.47
Howard, Catherine, Queen, 28
Howard, Jean, 286
Howard-Hill, T. H., 140 n.28

Howell, T. B., 49 n.29
Hoy, Cyrus, 138 n.1; 140 n.15; 169–170 n.1; 170 n.5; 322
Hughes, Thomas, 14
   The Misfortunes of Arthur, 13, 45 n.5
Hunter, G. K., 104 n.1; 105 n.23; 223, 224, 225, 226, 227
Hyginus, 16

Ide, Richard, 107, 109, 110, 115, 117, 119, 120 nn.1, 4, 6; 121 nn.9, 10
Ingram, William, 71, 88 n.31
Islip, Adam, 81
Iswolsky, Helene, 279

Jack Straw, 81, 82
Jackson, Henry, 189
Jackson, Holbrook, 48 n.22
Jackson, John, 46 n.9
Jackson, MacD. P., 88 n.33
James I, 48 n.17; 72, 123, 124, 125, 126, 127, 128, 129, 132, 133, 134, 136, 137, 138 nn.2, 3, 4; 139 n.7; 141 n.30; 143, 171 n.25; 222
James V, of Scotland, 28
Jamieson, Michael, 193 n.6
Janzen, Henry D., 299
Jaszi, Oscar, 139 n.10
Jauss, Hans Robert, 237
Jehlen, Myra, 288
Jenner, Henry, 2, 9 nn.8, 9
John, King, 123
Johnson, Robert Carl, 47 n.9
Johnson, Samuel, 191, 194 n.12; 252, 265
Jones, Inigo, 188, 277
Jones, Richard, 65, 73
Jones, Robert, 173
Jones, W. H. S., 50 n.44
Jones, William, 64, 65, 67, 75, 78
Jonson, Ben, 14, 66, 213–217, 230, 235, 244, 245, 247, 254, 265, 267–268, 276, 289, 292, 294, 296
   The Alchemist, 66, 86 n.11; 215, 216, 254, 269, 270, 292
   Bartholomew Fair, 214, 215, 216, 230, 245, 246, 247, 292
   The Case is Altered, 18, 45 n.5
   Catiline, 15, 45 n.5; 66, 192 n.5; 216, 291
   The Devil Is an Ass, 214, 215, 292
   Epicoene, or the Silent Woman, 20, 214, 215, 269, 270, 292
   Every Man in His Humor, 66, 76, 78, 81, 83, 84, 188, 245, 246, 292
   Every Man Out of His Humor, 66, 83, 86 n.10; 292
   The Gypsies Metamorphosed, 136
   The Masque of Beauty, 188
   The Masque of Blackness, 188
   Mortimer, His Fall, 78
   The New Inn, 215, 216, 252–255
   Poetaster, 264
   Richard Crookback, 83, 89 n.48
   The Sad Shepherd, 215
   Sejanus, 66, 127, 264, 291
   The Staple of News, 276
   A Tale of a Tub, 215
   Volpone, 20, 66, 215–216, 234–235, 292, 329–333
   and George Chapman and John Marston, *Eastward Ho*, 134, 269, 271, 299–300, 323
Jonson, Ben ?, and John Fletcher and Philip Massinger and ? George Chapman, *Rollo, Duke of Normandy*, 123, 129, 134, 135
Julia, 15
Jung, Carl Gustav, 43
Juvenal, 15, 47 n.9; 216, 264, 265, 290, 291, 292

Kantorowicz, Ernst, 280
Kaufmann, R. J., 42, 51 n.50
Kempe, Will, 65, 76
Kendall, Ritchie L., 258–262
Kennedy, Gwynne, 192 n.2
Kennedy, Judith M., 45 n.3; 47 n.14; 50 n.45
Kermode, Frank, 170 n.14
King Leir, 81, 89 n.42
Kingman, Philip, 173
Kingsmith, George, 175
Kinney, Arthur, 263–264
Kinwelmershe, Francis, and George Gascoigne, *Jocasta*, 15, 45 n.5; 47 n.9
Kirkman, Francis, 68, 70, 85 n.4
Kirschbaum, Leo, 65
A Knack to Know a Knave, 65, 85 n.7
A Knack to Know an Honest Man, 73, 87 n.18
Kolve, V. A., 311
Korn, Francis, 46 n.8
Kupersmith, William, 264–266
Kyd, Thomas, *The Spanish Tragedy*, 73, 76, 79, 81, 195, 208 n.3; 214, 219, 224, 225, 226, 249, 250, 296

Lake, Anne, Lady Roos, 29, 49 n.32
Lake, Sir Arthur, 29
Lamb, Mary, 192 n.2
Lancashire, Anne, 266–268, 333
Lancashire, Ian, 239
Langley, Francis, 71, 88 n.31
Lanier, Aemelia, 321
Law, William, 244, 245
Lawless, Donald S., 184 nn.11, 12, 13; 185 n.27
Leavis, F. R., 288
Leech, Clifford, 140 nn.15, 26; 144, 153, 170 nn.1, 8, 9, 15, 20; 266–268, 302, 332
Leggatt, Alexander, 269, 272
Leinwand, Theodore B., 268–272
Lemon, Robert, 105 n.16
Leonardo da Vinci, 290
Levin, Harry, 246
Levin, Richard, 105 n.13
Levi-Strauss, Claude, 46 n.8; 48 n.15
Lewis, John D., 139 n.10
Ley, William, 68, 70, 85 n.4
Like Unto Like, 88 n.32
Lindenbaum, Peter, 273–275
Lindenberger, Herbert, 139 n.9
Lindley, David, 275–278
Ling, Nicholas, 73, 86 n.14
Lodge, Thomas, 14, 263
  and Robert Greene, *A Looking Glass for London and England*, 17, 74, 81, 82
The London Prodigal, 69, 86 n.15
Long Meg of Westminster, 72
Longhurst, Derek, 240
Longsworth, Robert, 1, 7, 9 nn.2, 3, 4; 11 nn.24, 25
Look About You, 89 n.48
Lorkin, Thomas, 69
Lucrece, 127, 129
Lumiansky, R. M., 310, 311
"the lyfe and deathe of Heliogabilus," 82, 83
Lyly, John, 14, 263
  Mother Bombie, 18
Lyly, John ?, *The Maid's Metamorphosis*, 89 n.42

MacCallum, Sir Mungo, 232
Machiavelli, Niccolo, 306, 308
Mack, Maynard, 225, 289
Madison, Kenneth G., 49 n.26
Mahomet, 72
Malatesta da Verrucchio, 29
Malatesta, Giovanni (*alias* Gianciotto), 29
Malatesta, Paolo, 29

Malone, Edmond, 61, 62 n.3; 65, 84, 238
Malory, Sir Thomas, 13
Man, ?, and W. Croston, *Aeneas and Queen Dido*, 88 n.40
Mandeville, Sir John, 202
Manfredi, Muzio, 16, 47 n.9
Margeson, J. M. R., 170 n.15
Marguerite of Navarre, 14, 31, 32, 33, 34, 35, 36, 37, 38, 39, 40, 44 n.3
Marlowe, Christopher, 14, 68, 73, 74, 75, 77, 78, 235, 252, 266–268, 303–310
  Doctor Faustus, 65, 72, 73, 77, 162, 219, 249, 251, 252, 259, 266, 267, 268, 295, 296, 308, 309
  Edward II, 63, 70, 75, 77, 78, 233, 249, 266, 267, 268, 295
  The Jew of Malta, 72, 73, 76, 77, 83, 89 nn.42, 48; 266, 267, 268, 305, 309
  The Massacre at Paris, 72, 73, 76, 77, 267
  1 Tamburlaine, 72, 73, 76, 77, 78, 83, 84, 224, 225, 266, 267, 268, 295, 307
  2 Tamburlaine, 72, 73, 76, 77, 78, 83, 84, 224, 225, 266, 267, 268, 295
  and Thomas Nashe, *Dido, Queen of Carthage*, 88 n.40; 266, 267
Marprelate, Martin, 258, 259, 260, 261, 262
Marston, John, 14, 15, 47 n.9; 66
  Antonia and Mellida, 97
  Antonio's Revenge, 91–106
  The Fawn, 133
  The Malcontent, 45 n.5; 66, 79, 89 n.42; 133
  and George Chapman and Ben Jonson, *Eastward Ho*, 134, 269, 271, 299–300, 323
Marston, John ?, and Thomas Dekker, *Satiromastix*, 86 n.15
Marx, Karl, 232, 235
Marx, Leo, 288
Mary of Guise, 28
Mary, Queen of Scots, 93
Mason, H. A., 226
Mason, John, 14
Massinger, Philip, 14, 196, 297
  Believe as You List, 136, 141 n.29; 192–193 n.5
  The Bondman, 45 n.5
  The Guardian, 18

The Roman Actor, 70, 197, 198, 207, 208, 208 n.3; 209 n.4
The Unnatural Combat, 298
A Very Woman, 197, 198–199, 207, 208
and John Fletcher, *The Custom of the Country*, 123, 127
The Double Marriage, 123, 129, 130, 134, 136
The Prophetess, 123, 137–138
Sir John van Olden Barnavelt, 136
and Francis Beaumont and John Fletcher, *Thierry and Theodoret*, 123, 137, 138
and John Fletcher and ? George Chapman and ? Ben Jonson, *Rollo, Duke of Normandy*, 123, 129, 134, 135
Mauss, Marcel, 105 n.24
Maxwell, Baldwin, 85 n.5
Mazlish, Bruce, 49 n.31
Mazzotta, Giuseppe, 278–282
McClure, N. E., 49 n.32
McCoy, Richard, 274
McIlwain, Charles Howard, 124, 126, 138 n.2
McLeod, Randall, 299, 300, 332
McMillin, Scott, 88 n.37
Medici, Alessandro de, 29, 49 n.32
Medici, Lorenzino de, 29
Medvedev, P. N., 10 n.11
Medwall, Henry, *Fulgens and Lucres*, 222
Mehl, Dieter, 208 n.2; 209 nn.4, 6
Menander, 15
The Merry Devil of Edmonton, 66, 70
Middleton, Thomas, 14, 45 n.8; 271, 289, 292, 294, 297
A Chaste Maid of Cheapside, 20, 269, 292
The Family of Love, 20
A Mad World, My Masters, 292
Michaelmas Term, 269, 270, 292
More Dissemblers Besides Women, 320
No Wit, No Help Like A Woman's, 18
The Phoenix, 133
A Trick to Catch the Old One, 20, 70, 87 n.28; 292
Women Beware Women, 21–23, 25, 127, 195, 320
Your Five Gallants, 292
and Thomas Dekker, *1 Honest Whore*, 269
The Roaring Girl, 269, 270

and William Rowley, *The Changeling*, 33
Millington, Thomas, 73
Mills, David, 310, 311
Milton, John, 13, 41, 160, 258, 262, 273, 274, 275, 276
Comus, 262
Mincoff, Marco, 140 n.26; 171 n.23
Miner, Earl, 266
Moffett, Thomas, 254
Montague, Walter, 14
Montaigne, Michel de, 35, 263
Montemayor, Jorge de, 14, 18, 40, 45 n.3
Montrose, Louis Adrian, 274, 283, 284, 285, 286, 287, 288, 289
More, Sir Thomas, 244, 245, 247, 263, 290
Moretti, Franco, 133, 140 n.18; 236
Morton, Richard, 300
Mucedorus, 70, 72, 86 n.15; 249
Muir, Kenneth, 148, 150, 170 nn.10, 16; 171 n.17
Mulryne, J. R., 48 n.19; 275
Munda, Constantia, 321
Munday, Anthony, *John a Kent and John a Cumber*, 89 n.48
and Henry Chettle, *The Death of Robert, Earl of Huntingdon*, 65
The Downfall of Robert, Earl of Huntingdon, 65

N-Town Cycle, 7
Nailer, Henry, 181
Nance, R. Morton, 10 nn.13, 14, 18
Napier, Henry Edward, 49 n.32
Nashe, Thomas, 56, 58, 59, 230, 263, 264
Summer's Last Will and Testament, 277
and Christopher Marlowe, *Dido, Queen of Carthage*, 88 n.40, 266, 267
Neale, J. E., 105 nn.21, 25
Needham, Rodney, 46 n.8
Nelson, Alan H., 222
Nelson, Robert J., 208 n.2; 209 nn.5, 6, 11
Nero, 15, 46 n.9; 49 n.28; 124, 125
Nevill, Lady Anne, 48 n.25
Nevill, Richard, First Earl of Salisbury, 48 n.25
Newton, Thomas, 14, 47 n.9
Niccolo III, Marquess of Ferrara, 29
Nicoll, Allardyce, 120 n.2
Norbrook, David, 273, 276
Norris, Edwin, 5, 9 n.1; 10 n.13
North, Sir Thomas, 47 n.9

Norton, Thomas, and Thomas Sackville, *Gorboduc*, 123–124, 133, 296
Nungezer, Edwin, 54, 86 n.13

Octavia, 15
Oglander, Sir John, 138 n.4
Oliver, H. J., 87 n.25
Ornstein, Robert, 104 n.2
Ovid, 16, 17, 47 n.10
Owst, G. W., 259

Palladio, Andrea, 290
Pallant, Ro., 54
Palmer, Kenneth, 139 n.6; 171 n.28
Parker, Brian, 329–333
Parker, Matthew, Archbishop of Canterbury, 26
Parker, Patricia, 282–289
Parr, Catherine, Queen, 28
Parrott, T. M., 152, 171 n.19
Parthenius, 16
Paster, Gail Kern, 289–294
'a pastorall plesant Comedie of Robin Hood and little Iohn,' 81
Patterson, Annabel, 136, 141 n.29; 266, 273
Paul, Cedar, 89 n.49
Paul, Eden, 89 n.49
Pausanias, 40
Pavier, Thomas, 74, 81, 82, 86 n.14
Payne, John, 44 n.3
Peacock, John, 277
Pearl, Sara, 276
Peele, George, 14
    The Arraignment of Paris, 70, 87 n.28
    David and Bethsabe, 30, 81, 84
    Edward I, 45 n.5; 81
    The Old Wives Tale, 72
Pentzell, Raymond J., 194 n.11
Penzer, N. M., 44 n.3
Persius, 264
Peterson, Richard, 266
Petrarch, 290
Phelps, Wayne H., 185 n.27
Philip II, of Spain, 136
Phillip, John, 14
    Patient and Meek Grissil, 319
Phillips, Mr., 54
Phillips, Augustine, 66, 76, 88 n.41
Pike, Burton, 289
Pinciss, G. M., 89 n.46
Pitcher, John, 277
Plato, 15, 40, 46 n.9
Plautus, 15, 290, 291
Plutarch, 15, 47 n.9

Pope, Mr., 54
Pope, Alexander, 265
Pope, Thomas, 76
Porter, Henry, *Two Angry Women of Abingdon*, 65, 73
Portnarowe, Sir John, 175
Post, Jonathan, 266
Potter, Robert, 238
Prawdin, Michael, 89 n.49
Preston, Thomas, 14
    Cambyses, 15, 47 n.9
Price, George R., 298
Prosser, Eleanor, 93, 104 n.4
Proudfoot, Richard, 148, 152, 170 nn.1, 12; 171 nn.17, 18
Prouty, Charles T., 50 n.35
Puckering, Sir Thomas, 69
Puttenham, George, 127, 128, 139 n.9; 290
Pyrrye, C., 320

Quinn, Esther Casier, 10 n.16
Quint, David, 282–289

Rabkin, Norman, 228
Ramsey, G. G., 47 n.9
Randolph, Thomas, 14
    The Jealous Lovers, 18
The Ranger's Comedy, 76
Rankins, William, 89 n.45
Raysor, Thomas M., 140 n.19
Redwine, James D., 246
Reeve, Raphe, 173
Reibetanz, John, 139 n.11
Rice, George P., 139 n.5
Rich, Baron, 25
Richard II, 123
Richard, Duke of York, 48 n.25
Richard III, 29, 48 n.25; 79
Rickert, R. T., 85 n.6
Rickey, Mary Ellen, 50 n.36
Roberts, James, 86 n.14
Roberts, Josephine A., 192 n.4
Robertson, D. A., Jr., 208 n.2
Robin Hood and Little John, 84
Robines, George, 176
Robinson, Forrest G., 139 n.9
Roderick, 88 n.32
Rogers, Richard, 68, 70, 85 n.4
Rolfe, J. C., 46 n.9
Roper, Derek, 47 n.13; 51 n.49
Rorty, Richard, 282
Rose, H. J., 47 n.9
Rosenblatt, Jason P., 49 nn.28, 30
Ross, Charles, 48 nn.25, 26
Rosseter, Philip, 173, 180, 181, 183

Rotrou, Jean, *Le Veritable Saint Genest*, 208
Rouse, W. H. D., 47 n.11
Rowley, Samuel, 73
Rowley, William, 70, 87 n.29
   The Birth of Merlin, 70
   and Thomas Heywood, *Fortune by Land and Sea*, 20
   and Thomas Middleton, *The Changeling*, 33
Rozett, Martha Tuck, 294–296
Rutter, Joseph, 14

S., W., *Locrine*, 65, 85 n.4
   The Puritan, 64, 65, 70, 87 n.28
Sackville, Thomas, and Thomas Norton, *Gorboduc*, 123–124, 133, 296
Sadeler, Jan, 257
Salgado, Gamini, 193 n.8
Salingar, L. G., 44 n.3
Salter, F. M., 310
Sannazaro, Jacopo, 274
Saunders, Lady Alice, 174, 175
Saunders, Sir Thomas, 174
Sausurre, Ferdinand de, 227
Scarisbrick, J. J., 49 n.33
Schmidt, Nancy Crohn, 222
Schoenbaum, S., 45 n.5; 138 n.1; 170 n.3; 171 n.23; 208 n.2; 297, 298, 302
Schore, George Robin, 48 n.23
Schwab, H., 208 n.2
Schwartz, Murray, 274
Schwartz, Robert, 266
Sebastian, King of Portugal, 136
The Second Maiden's Tragedy, 127
Sellar, W. C., 305
Seneca, 14, 15, 47 n.9; 92, 93, 97, 115, 223–227, 263
2 Seven Deadly Sins, 53–62
Seymour, Sir Edward, 28
Seymour, Jane, Queen, 28
Seymour, Sir Thomas, 28
Shady, Raymond C., 297–303
Shakespeare, William, 16, 18, 43–44, 55, 60, 63, 64, 65, 66, 68, 69, 70, 74, 77, 78, 79, 84, 85 nn.4, 5; 86 n.15; 87 nn. 19, 25, 29; 88 n.33; 127, 129, 143, 173, 184, 184 n.1; 209 n.6; 226, 228, 240–243, 252, 272, 273, 274, 275, 289, 306, 307, 313
   All's Well That Ends Well, 14, 33, 69
   Antony and Cleopatra, 69, 219, 320
   As You Like It, 20, 69, 81, 241, 274
   The Comedy of Errors, 14, 45 n.4; 69, 188, 293
   Coriolanus, 69, 219, 291
   Cymbeline, 69
   Hamlet, 13, 14, 26–27, 28, 45 n.4; 49 n.28; 66, 69, 86 n.14; 101, 136, 195, 207, 208 n.3; 209 n.5; 222, 231, 232, 233, 241
   1 Henry IV, 69, 79, 83, 87 nn.18, 24
   2 Henry IV, 66, 69, 82, 83, 84
   Henry V, 27, 66, 69, 81, 83, 89 n.48; 158, 188
   1-3 Henry VI, 69, 76
   1 Henry VI, 61, 88 n.36
   2 Henry VI, 77, 296, 307
   3 Henry VI, 77
   Henry VIII, 14, 30, 69
   John, 69
   Julius Caesar, 69, 87 n.24; 161, 291
   King Lear, 14, 20, 45 n.4; 66, 69, 86 n.14; 89 n.44; 234, 241–242, 295
   Love's Labor's Lost, 69, 188, 298
   Macbeth, 69, 127, 136, 196–197, 241, 295, 296
   Measure for Measure, 14, 33, 44 n.3; 45 n.4; 69, 87 n.24; 134, 188, 256, 293
   The Merchant of Venice, 66, 69, 83, 89 n.48; 222, 293
   The Merry Wives of Windsor, 66, 69, 83, 188
   A Midsummer Night's Dream, 66, 69, 241
   Much Ado About Nothing, 66, 69, 81, 82, 84, 320
   Othello, 42, 44 n.3; 66, 69, 188, 189–190, 295, 320
   Pericles, 14, 35, 45 n.4; 69, 86 n.15; 89 n.44
   Richard II, 66, 69, 78, 79, 295, 296
   Richard III, 14, 26, 45 n.4; 48 n.25; 66, 69, 77, 79, 83, 88 n.39; 89 n.48; 97, 127, 168, 227, 295
   Romeo and Juliet, 66, 69, 77, 88 n.39
   The Taming of the Shrew, 20, 69, 76, 89 n.48

The Tempest, 69, 87 n.24; 149, 241, 277
Timon of Athens, 69, 291
Titus Andronicus, 65, 66, 69, 76, 85 n.7; 86 n.8; 249, 291, 295, 296, 308
Troilus and Cressida, 66, 69, 83, 86 n.14; 126, 168, 254, 320
Twelfth Night, 36, 37, 38, 69
Two Gentlemen of Verona, 69, 76
The Winter's Tale, 14, 69, 87 n.24; 274
and John Fletcher, *Two Noble Kinsmen*, 36, 66, 69, 143–171
Shand, G. B., 297–303
Sharpe, R. B., 68, 184 n.2
Shaw, John, 238
Sheingorn, Pamela, 239, 256, 257
Shepherd, Simon, 303–310
Shenk, Robert, 247
Sherbo, A., 194 n.12
Sherman, Stuart P., 49 n.29
Sherrington, John, 176, 177, 178
Shirley, James, 14, 249
    The Coronation, 18, 45 n.5
    The Court Secret, 18, 45 n.5
    The Gentleman of Venice, 18–19, 45 n.5
    The Opportunity, 18, 45 n.5
    The Traitor, 29
Shore, Jane, 127
Shorey, Paul, 46 n.9
Shullenberger, William, 51 n.47
Sibly, John, 105 n.21
Sidney Herbert, Mary, Countess of Pembroke, 25
Sidney, Sir Philip, 25, 127, 134, 139 n.9; 187, 215, 263, 264, 273, 274, 275
Sidney, Sir Robert, 187
The Siege of London, 72
Simpson, Evelyn, 193 n.5; 253, 276, 298, 331
Simpson, Percy, 193 n.5; 253, 276, 298, 331
Sincler, John, 54, 77
Sinfield, Alan, 219, 240, 287, 296, 304, 306
1 Sir John Oldcastle, 65, 70, 73, 79, 83, 87 n.26
2 Sir John Oldcastle, 83
Sisson, Charles J., 89 n.44; 140 n.29; 193 n.5
Sly, Will, 54, 77
Smallwood, R. L., 275

Snodham, Thomas, 64
Snow, C. P., 288
Sophocles, 15
Southern, Richard, 222
Sowername, Esther, 321
Speght, Rachel, 321
Spencer, T. J. B., 48 n.21
The Spencers, 78
Spenser, Edmund, 13, 286, 287
Spitzer, Leo, 280
Spivack, Charlotte, 210 n.15
Sponsus, 256
Stallworthy, Jon, 302
Stallybrass, Peter, 242
Stanley, Ferdinando, Fifth Earl of Derby, 93
Stapleton, Robert, 264
Stark Flattery, 88 n.32
Steele, Mary Susan, 192 n.4
Steevens, George, 62 n.3
Stein, Robert, 43, 51 n.51
Stevens, Martin, 11 nn.21, 26
Stoll, E. E., 170 n.4
Stone, Lawrence, 19, 20, 48 nn.16, 17; 94, 105 n.20
Stubbes, Phillip, 230
Sturm, Johann, 226, 227
Strachey, James, 45 n.7
Stroup, Thomas B., 50 n.36
Suckling, Sir John, 14
    Aglaura, 47 n.12
Suetonius, 15, 46 n.9
Swetnam the Woman-hater Arraigned by Women, 320
Swift, Jonathan, 241
Swynford, Catherine, Duchess of Lancaster, 26

Tacitus, 15, 46 n.9
1, 2 Tamar Cham, 72, 76, 83
Tamerlane, 89 nn.48, 49
The Taming of A Shrew, 67, 76, 77
Tamotsu, Hirosue, 193 n.7
Tarlton, Richard, 55, 56, 57, 58, 59, 60, 61, 67
The Tartarian Cripple, Emperor of Constantinople, 64, 78, 80, 83, 84, 89 n.48
Taverner, Richard, 47 n.9
Taylor, Jerome, 222
Taylor, Mark, 45 n.4
Taylor, William, 176, 177, 178, 179
Tennyson, Alfred, Lord, 117
Terence, 15
Thomas Lord Cromwell, 63, 64, 65, 66, 67, 70, 79, 83

Index

Thomas of Woodstock or *The First Part of the Reign of Richard the Second*, 89 n.48
Thornberry, Richard, 72
Thorpe, William, 260, 261
"Three Plays in One," 58, 59
Tilley, Morris Palmer, 49 n.27
Tillotson, Geoffrey, 193 n.8
Tillyard, E. M. W., 228
Tooley, Nicholas, 54
Touchet, Mervyn, Second Earl of Castlehaven, 49 n.29
Tourneur, Cyril, 14
Tourneur, Cyril ?, *The Atheist's Tragedy*, 47 n.12; 50 n.37
  The Revenger's Tragedy, 29, 33, 86 n.15; 207
Trask, Willard, 194 n.10; 210 n.15; 279
Travis (Treves), Edmond, 175, 176, 177, 178, 180, 181
Travis (Treves), James, 176, 177, 178, 180
Travis, Peter W., 310–313
Travis (Treves) Daborne, Susanna, 175, 177, 178
Troilus and Cressida, 83
The Troublesome Reign of King John, 70, 87 n.26
The True Tragedy of Richard, Duke of York, 67, 76
The True Tragedy of Richard III, 76
Trundell, John, 86 n.14
Turner, Robert K., Jr., 47 n.12; 139 n.12; 140 nn.14, 25; 298
Turner, Victor, 229
Twemlow, J. A., 48 n.26
Tyndale, William, 101, 106 n.30

Vasari, Giorgio, 290
Vaughan, Henry, 264
Vega, Lope de, *Fuente Ovejuna*, 234
Vere, Susan, Countess of Montgomery, 192 n.4
Villiers, George, First Duke of Buckingham, 136
Vincent, Thomas, 54
Virgil, 273
von Sturmer, John Richard, 46 n.8

Wager, W., *Enough Is as Good as a Feast*, 238
Waith, Eugene, 105 n.22; 153, 171 n.21; 268, 332
Wakefield Cycle, 7
Wallace, C. W., 62 n.4
Waller, A. R., 139 n.13; 140 n.16

Warner, George F., 184 nn.1, 3; 185 nn.49, 50; 186 n.63
A Warning for Fair Women, 86–87 n.15
Wasson, John M., 314–318
Waugh, Arthur, 9 n.5
Webster, John, 14, 296, 320
  The Devil's Law-Case, 256
  The Duchess of Malfi, 20, 21, 28, 29, 33, 40, 44 n.3; 127, 166, 219, 320
  The White Devil, 20, 21, 35, 127, 221,
  and Thomas Dekker, *Northward Ho*, 269
  Westward Ho, 269, 271
Weever, John, 239
Weil, Judith, 268
Weimann, Robert, 266, 286
Wells, Stanley, 332
Wentersdorf, Karl P., 72, 88 nn.33, 37
Werstine, Paul, 298
Westcott, Sebastian, 181
Whigham, Frank, 21, 48 n.18
White, Allon, 242
White, Edward, 73, 74, 81, 82
White, William, 298
Whitbread, Leslie George, 47 n.9
Whitgift, John, Archbishop of Canterbury, 262
Wickham, Glynne, 143, 170 n.6
Widdowson, Peter, 240
Wilkins, George, *The Miseries of Enforced Marriage*, 20, 86 n.15; 319
William I, Prince of Orange, 93
Williams, Raymond, 286, 288, 289
Willis, R., 238
Willson, David H., 138 n.4
Wilson, F. P., 62 n.5
Wilson, Robert, 14
Winwood, Sir Ralph, 138 n.3
Wisdom, 218
Wise, Andrew, 82, 87 n.18
Witten-Hannah, Margaret Anne, 192 n.4
Woodbridge, Linda, 318–322
Woodcut, James, 175
The World and the Child, 219
Worthen, William B., 192 n.3; 194 n.9
Wright, William Aldis, 44 n.2
Wroth, Lady Mary, 187–194, 321, 322

Yeatman, R. J., 305
Yong, Bartholomew, 45 n.3
York Cycle, 7, 295
A Yorkshire Tragedy, 69, 86 n.15

Zitner, Sheldon P., 301, 322–324

Contents of Previous Volumes

Volume I (1984)

Professional Actors in the Middle Ages and Early Renaissance
　JOHN WASSON

The Saint's Legend as Mimesis: Gallican Liturgy and Mediterranean Culture
　E. CATHERINE DUNN

Henry VIII's Entertainment for the Queen of Scots, 1516: A New Revels Account and Cornish's Play
　W. R. STREITBERGER

Corrida of Blood in *The Spanish Tragedy*: Kyd's Use of Revenge as National Destiny
　FRANK R. ARDOLINO

The Contemporary Perception of Marlowe's Tamburlaine
　RICHARD LEVIN

The Royal Ruse: Malcontentedness in John Marston's *The Malcontent*
　ROBERT B. BENNETT

Marston, Calvinism, and Satire
　SCOTT COLLEY

Machiavelli, Policy, and *The Devil's Charter*
　JACQUELINE E. M. LATHAM

Heroic Passion in the Early Tragicomedies of Beaumont and Fletcher
　ROBERT Y. TURNER

Epicoene: A Comic Hell for a Comic Sinner
　MICHAEL FLACHMANN

"An Acceptable Violence": Sexual Contest in Jonson's *Epicoene*
　BARBARA C. MILLARD

Exploiting the Tradition: The Elizabethan Revenger as Chapman's "Complete Man"
　RICHARD S. IDE

Art within *The Second Maiden's Tragedy*
　DAVID M. BERGERON

"Spectacles fashioned with such perspective art": A Phenomenological Reading of Webster's *The White Devil*
　RUPIN W. DESAI

"Disaster with My So Many Joys": Structure and Perspective in Massinger and Dekker's *The Virgin Martyr*
 LARRY S. CHAMPION

The Globe Bewitched and *El Hombre Fiel*
 HERBERT BERRY

Dekker Observed: Review Article
 DORIS ADLER

Printing History and Provenance in Two Revels Plays: Review Article
 PAUL WERSTINE

REVIEWS

Muriel St. Clare Byrne, ed. *The Lisle Letters*
 WILLIAM B. LONG

Douglas Duncan. *Ben Jonson and the Lucianic Tradition*
 ROLF SOELLNER

Charles A. Hallett and Elaine S. Hallett. *The Revenger's Madness: A Study of Revenge Tragedy Motifs*
 HARRY KEYISHIAN

Jacqueline Pearson. *Tragedy and Tragicomedy in the Plays of John Webster*
 CHARLES R. FORKER

Volume II (1985)

Local Drama and Playing Places at Shrewsbury: New Findings from the Borough Records
 J.A.B. SOMERSET

Cosmic Characters and Human Form: Dramatic Interaction and Conflict in the Chester Cycle "Fall of Lucifer"
 NORMA KROLL

Seven Actors in Search of a Biographer
 JACKSON CAMPBELL BOSWELL

Man's House as His Castle in *Arden of Feversham*
 LENA COWEN ORLIN

"A bed / for woodstock": A Warning for the Unwary
 WILLIAM B. LONG

Descent Machinery in the Playhouse
    JOHN H. ASTINGTON

Chapman's *Caesar and Pompey* and the Fortunes of Prince Henry
    ROLF SOELLNER

Three Plays in One: Shakespeare and *Philaster*
    LEE BLISS

Jonson's Alchemists, Epicures, and Puritans
    ROBERT M. SCHULER

The Playhouse as an Investment, 1607-1614; Thomas Woodford and Whitefriars
    WILLIAM INGRAM

The "Business" of Shareholding, the Fortune Playhouses, and Francis Grace's Will
    S. P. CERASANO

The Prison-House of the Canon: Allegorical Form and Posterity in Ben Jonson's *The Staple of News*
    DOUGLAS M. LANIER

Three Charges against Sixteenth- and Seventeenth-Century Playwrights: Libel, Bawdy, and Blasphemy
    DAVID McPHERSON

The Chester Cycle: Review Article
    LAWRENCE M. CLOPPER

REVIEWS

Leonard Barkan, ed. *Renaissance Drama*, New Series, IX
    ROBERT E. BURKHART

Lee Bliss. *The World's Perspective: John Webster and the Jacobean Drama*
    CHARLES R. FORKER

Fredson T. Bowers, ed. *The Dramatic Works in the Beaumont and Fletcher Canon*, Volume 5
    WILLIAM PROCTOR WILLIAMS

Ann Jennalie Cook. *The Privileged Playgoers of Shakespeare's London, 1576-1642*
    STEPHEN BOOTH

Irene G. Dash. *Wooing, Wedding, and Power: Women in Shakespeare's Plays*
  ELAINE UPTON PUGH

Jonathan Dollimore. *Radical Tragedy: Religion, Ideology, and Power in the Drama of Shakespeare and His Contemporaries*
  HARRY KEYISHIAN

Coburn Freer. *The Poetics of Jacobean Drama*
  PAUL BERTRAM

Stephen Greenblatt. *Renaissance Self-Fashioning: From More to Shakespeare*
  ALAN SINFIELD

R. Chris Hassel, Jr. *Renaissance Drama & the English Church Year*
  ALICE-LYLE SCOUFOS

William B. Hunter, Jr. *Milton's "Comus": Family Piece*
  PHILIP B. ROLLINSON

Alexander Leggatt. *Ben Jonson: His Vision and His Art*
  SCOTT COLLEY

Lois Potter, gen. ed. *The Revels History of Drama in English*, Volume IV, 1613-1660
  CATHERINE M. SHAW

Hugh M. Richmond. *Puritans and Libertines: Anglo-French Literary Relations in the Reformation*
  WILLIAM EDINGER

Gary Taylor and Michael Warren, eds. *The Division of the Kingdoms: Shakespeare's Two Versions of "King Lear"*
  GEORGE WALTON WILLIAMS

Volume III (1986)

Robin Hood and the Churchwardens in Yeovil
  JAMES D. STOKES

Kyd's Ordered Spectacle: "Behold . . . / What 'tis to be subject to destiny"
  RICHARD C. KOHLER

Marlowe's Mixed Messages: A Model for Shakespeare?
  CAROL LEVENTEN DUANE

"The Historie of King Edward the Fourth": A Chronicle Play on the Coventry Pageant Wagons
    STEPHEN K. WRIGHT

Heywood as Moralist in *A Woman Killed with Kindness*
    FREDERICK KIEFER

"Lend me your dwarf": Romance in *Volpone*
    DAVID M. BERGERON

"Jeered by Confederacy": Group Aggression in Jonson's Comedies
    HELEN OSTOVICH

"Then thus I turne my language to you": The Transformation of Theatrical Language in *Philaster*
    NICHOLAS F. RADEL

Snakes in *Catiline*
    CLIFFORD J. RONAN

"On ye walls": The Staging of *Hengist, King of Kent*, V.ii
    LESLIE THOMSON

A New Way to Pay Old Debts and The Country-House Poetic Tradition
    ALBERT H. TRICOMI

Some New Perspectives on the Spanish Setting of *The Changeling* and Its Source
    DALE B. J. RANDALL

The Broken Heart: An Allegorical Reading
    MARIE L. KESSEL

Popular vs. Scholarly Editions of Renaissance Letters: Review Article
    SUSAN ZIMMERMAN

Renaissance Plays and Their Contexts: Review Article
    CLIFFORD DAVIDSON

John Payne Collier's Reputation: Review Article
    G. P. JONES

Shakespeare's Elusive Globe: Review Article
    S. P. CERASANO

History of a Tradition: Review Article
    IAN LANCASHIRE

REVIEWS

Judith Anderson. *Biographical Truth: The Representation of Historical Persons in Tudor-Stuart Writing*
    SCOTT COLLEY

Johannes H. Birringer. *Marlowe's "Dr Faustus" and "Tamburlaine": Theological and Theatrical Perspectives*
    DAVID KAULA

Martin Butler. *Theatre and Crisis: 1632-1642*
    DOUGLAS HOWARD

Larry S. Champion. *Thomas Dekker and the Traditions of English Drama*
    HARRY KEYISHIAN

Clifford Davidson. *From Creation to Doom: The York Cycle of Mystery Plays*
    ALEXANDRA F. JOHNSTON

Alan C. Dessen. *Elizabethan Stage Conventions and Modern Interpreters*
    D. F. ROWAN

Jonathan Dollimore and Alan Sinfield, eds. *Political Shakespeare: New Essays in Cultural Materialism*
    CHARLES R. FORKER

Richard Dutton. *Ben Jonson: To the First Folio*
    DOUGLAS M. LANIER

Reavley Gair. *The Children of Paul's: The Story of a Theatre Company, 1553-1608*
    WILLIAM B. LONG

Jonathan Goldberg. *James I and the Politics of Literature: Jonson, Shakespeare, Donne, and their Contemporaries*
    ALEXANDER LEGGATT

J. C. Gray, ed. *Mirror up to Shakespeare: Essays in Honour of G. R. Hibbard*
    JEANNE ADDISON ROBERTS

Stephen Greenblatt, ed. *The Power of Forms in the English Renaissance*
    GAIL KERN PASTER

Katherine Eisaman Maus. *Ben Jonson and the Roman Frame of Mind*
   WILLIAM BLISSETT

Peter Meredith and John E. Tailby, eds. *The Staging of Religious Drama in Europe in the Later Middle Ages: Texts and Documents in English Translation*
   STEVEN URKOWITZ

Paula Neuss, ed. *Aspects of Early English Drama*
   JOHN WASSON

R. B. Parker, ed. *Volpone or The Fox*, by Ben Jonson
   THOMAS L. BERGER

Sara Jayne Steen, ed. *The English Moore; or The Mock-Marriage*, by Richard Brome
   HENRY D. JANZEN

John Gordon Sweeney, III. *Jonson and the Psychology of the Public Theater*
   RUSS MCDONALD

Ronald W. Vince. *Renaissance Theatre: A Historiographical Handbook*
   STUART M. KURLAND